IN THE CHILDREN'S E

Unaccompanied Children in
American-Occupied Germany, 1945–1952

Among the hundreds of thousands of displaced persons in Germany at the end of the Second World War were approximately 40,000 unaccompanied children. These children, of every age and nationality, were without parents or legal guardians and many were without clear identities. This situation posed serious practical, legal, ethical, and political problems for the agencies responsible for their care.

In the Children's Best Interests delves deeply into the records of the United Nations Relief and Rehabilitation Administration (UNRRA) and the International Refugee Organization (IRO) revealing the heated battles that erupted among the various entities (military, governments, and NGOs) responsible for their care and disposition. The bitter debates focused on such issues as whether a child could be adopted, what to do with illegitimate and abandoned children, and who could assume the role of guardian. The inconclusive nationality of these children meant they became pawns in the battle between East and West during the Cold War. Lynne Taylor's exploration and insight into the debates around national identity and the privilege of citizenship challenges our understanding of nationality in the postwar period.

(German and European Studies)

LYNNE TAYLOR is an associate professor in the Department of History at the University of Waterloo.

GERMAN AND EUROPEAN STUDIES

General Editor: Jennifer J. Jenkins

LYNNE TAYLOR

In the Children's Best Interests

Unaccompanied Children
in American-Occupied
Germany, 1945–1952

UNIVERSITY OF TORONTO PRESS
Toronto Buffalo London

© University of Toronto Press 2017
Toronto Buffalo London
www.utorontopress.com

ISBN 978-1-4875-0235-5 (cloth)
ISBN 978-1-4875-2194-3 (paper)

(German and European Studies)

Library and Archives Canada Cataloguing in Publication

Taylor, Lynne, 1958–, author
In the children's best interests : unaccompanied children in
American-Occupied Germany, 1945–1952 / Lynne Taylor.

(German and European studies ; 27)
Includes bibliographical references and index.
ISBN 978-1-4875-0235-5 (cloth)   ISBN 978-1-4875-2194-3 (paper)

1. United Nations Relief and Rehabilitation Administration.
2. International Refugee Organization. 3. World War, 1939–1945 –
Children – Germany (West). 4. World War, 1939–1945 – Refugees –
Germany (West). 5. Abandoned children – Germany (West) – History –
20th century. 6. Adoption – Germany (West) – History – 20th century.
7. Child care – Germany (West) – History – 20th century. 8. Germany –
History – 1945–1955. I. Title. II. Series: German and European studies ; 27

D810.C4T39 2017   940.53'161   C2017-904304-8

This book has been published with the help of a grant from the Federation
for the Humanities and Social Sciences, through the Awards to Scholarly
Publications Program, using funds provided by the Social Sciences and
Humanities Research Council of Canada.

University of Toronto Press acknowledges the financial assistance to its
publishing program of the Canada Council for the Arts and the Ontario
Arts Council, an agency of the Government of Ontario.

Canada Council   Conseil des Arts
for the Arts   du Canada

ONTARIO ARTS COUNCIL
CONSEIL DES ARTS DE L'ONTARIO
an Ontario government agency
un organisme du gouvernement de l'Ontario

Funded by the   Financé par le
Government   gouvernement
of Canada   du Canada

Contents

Acknowledgments

This has been a project long in the making, and it has received support from myriad sources. I would like to take this opportunity to acknowledge the financial support of both the Social Sciences and Humanities Research Council of Canada and the Remarque Institute of New York University. I would like to also acknowledge my indebtedness to Pamela Quanrud, Eric Wenberg, Barbara Lutz, and James Bourdaghs for allowing me to impose on their hospitality too often while working in the archives. I would like to thank Kirrily Freeman, Tracey White, and Megan Koreman for their invaluable feedback on the manuscript. And finally, but definitely not least, I want to thank David for his unceasing support on this journey. He has lived this story as much as I have, and his belief in the project has been unwavering. By way of some small compensation, I dedicate this book to him.

IN THE CHILDREN'S BEST INTERESTS

Unaccompanied Children in
American-Occupied Germany, 1945–1952

Introduction

In the immediate aftermath of the Second World War, the European continent faced a humanitarian crisis of enormous proportions. Tens of millions of people had been driven from their homes during the war by the Nazi regime, as forced labourers, as grist for the system of extermination and concentration camps, by the events of war itself, or by the war's devastation, especially in its final months, as the eastern part of the continent was liberated from the Germans by the USSR. Millions of these people ended up in the various occupation zones of Germany, with the largest concentration in the US Zone of Occupation, including tens of thousands of what were called "unaccompanied children."

The story of child victims of war or disaster is one that never fails to make headlines, drawing attention to a crisis in a way nothing else does. It is no accident that almost every appeal for disaster relief donations shows a photograph of a young child, eyes staring soulfully into the camera. The image of the lost, abandoned, or dead child embodies all the pathos of the disaster or crisis, and tugs at the heart-strings of all but the most cold-hearted. This has been especially true since the early twentieth century, when children became recognized as a separate and bona fide category of victims of war and disaster requiring special consideration and care, as made clear in the burgeoning body of literature that has been produced in the past two decades on children and war.

Interest has also been growing in the refugee phenomenon more generally, and the plight of people displaced by war or other disasters. Although both natural and manmade disasters have a history eons old, the Western world's response to the care of the victims of those disasters changed dramatically in the twentieth century. Prior to the First World War, responses were individual or private, in the form of charitable or voluntary agencies. With the mass displacements resulting from both the Russian Revolution of 1917 and the Great War, for the first time in the West, an international response was organized by the League of Nations when it appointed Fridtjof Nansen as High Commissioner for Refugees. For a variety of reasons, the High Commissioner was not as successful as had been hoped, but the office did set an expectation and a pattern for an international, state-supported response to refugee crises. The pressures created by the sheer volume of humanity on the move during the period of the First World War required it, as did the growing state security regimes with their concomitant requirements for controls over both an individual state's citizens and over the movement of refugees, especially those displaced from their country of residence and/or nationality into another nation state. With the advent of the Second World War, all national governments involved recognized that this war would also generate a refugee crisis of unprecedented proportions, and one that would require an international, state-driven response. This ultimately led to the creation of the United Nations Relief and Rehabilitation Administration (UNRRA) in 1943, with forty-four signatories.

UNRRA's mandate was an impressive one and global in scope, with missions throughout Europe, as well as in Asia. Although originally conceived of as a short-lived organization whose primary purpose was to provide immediate material relief to the expected floods of refugees (termed "victims of war" in its constitution) in any area under the control of any of the United Nations (the signatories), a secondary part of UNRRA's mandate was to provide rehabilitation for those victims, as requested by a member government. Exactly what was meant by the term "rehabilitation" was never made clear, perhaps because the expectation was that these refugees would return home as quickly as possible, which would explain the emphasis on short-term relief and the initially short lifespan of the Administration. In a number of its missions, material relief was indeed UNRRA's sole task, but in Germany, for one, its task (and that of its successor organization, the International Refugee Organization, or the IRO) soon expanded in unanticipated ways. This was because in many parts of the world, including Germany, the refugee crisis, or more accurately, the displaced persons crisis (the term for those refugees for whom UNRRA and the IRO were mandated to care) did not, in fact, get resolved quickly. While millions returned to their homes in the summer months of 1945 – most willingly, many not – when the dust settled after the mass movements, there were still some six hundred thousand to seven hundred thousand displaced persons in

Germany either unable or unwilling to return to their homelands. The last displaced persons camp in Germany did not close until 1957 – this was the Lignen displaced persons camp in the British Zone, while in the US Zone the last camp closed in 1952.

This book focuses on the story of that remnant population of displaced persons in the US Zone of Germany, and one subset of it in particular: the group called "unaccompanied children." The challenges for the various agencies and agents responsible for the care and ultimate disposition of unaccompanied children revealed both the very real limits of this effort at interstate cooperation in humanitarian relief and the inconsistencies in the treatment of displaced persons. This is not just a story of the Cold War, although that is one aspect of it, but a story of a battle over children seen as national property, and one that reveals starkly the degree of confusion surrounding the notion of "nationality."

Unaccompanied children were children who had been separated from their families or orphaned by the events of the Second World War. Minors without legal guardians, these children ranged in age from babes in arms to teenagers; they were of every nationality, and at the end of the summer of 1945, they numbered between thirty thousand and forty thousand in the US Zone. They had either been brought to Germany during the war as forced labourers, children of forced labourers, or stock for the Nazis' plan to rebuild the master race, or they had been born in Germany to forced labourers. These children posed special challenges for the international agencies made responsible for their care, as well as for the American occupation authorities, not least because, in many cases, the identities, even the nationalities, of these children were unknown, which put their legal status into jeopardy and made their appropriate disposition unclear. Because of the difficulties in definitively determining the nationality of many of these children, they became a focus of sometimes fierce international debate over their fate, with the emerging West German state being determined to keep the children it deemed to be German and various other national governments just as determined to reclaim and bring home "their" children. Caught in the middle, and as deeply involved in an always fraught debate over what was in the children's best interests, UNRRA (to mid-1947) and then the IRO, on the one hand, and the American occupation authorities, on the other, fought constantly over what was an appropriate solution for what became an increasingly intractable problem. Lacking legal guardians, it was unclear who could or should determine what was in these children's "best interests," let alone what exactly constituted their "best interests" in the first place. Should these children be left where they were or removed and either repatriated or resettled? How were these children best protected? Who would decide? These were extremely contentious questions – and they lay at the root of a multivalent debate over the fate of these unaccompanied children that raged for seven years.

Crucial was the need to determine if not a child's identity, then at least its nationality. This proved as difficult an exercise as determining a child's identity, in part because of the lack of convincing evidence of its nationality. It was further complicated by the way in which the concept of "nationality" was used, or misused, at the time by those parties responsible for managing the children's ultimate disposition. At the heart of the debate over the future of these unaccompanied children was a clash between a definition of nationality based on citizenship (insisted upon by the upper levels of administration at UNRRA, as well as the military authorities, who provided direction to UNRRA) and a definition of nationality based on ethnic identity (used by the displaced persons population). As so astutely pointed out by Liah Greenfeld, by the late nineteenth century, there existed two types of national identity: one whose basis of membership was "civic," that is, identical with citizenship, and one that was "ethnic," based on a set of attributes or commonalities from which was constructed a particular ethnic identity.[1] These two types of nationality were not always mutually exclusive, but they were also seldom synonymous. In the mid-twentieth century, the distinction was not well understood, and the result was considerable confusion around the question of national identities, with serious consequences for many displaced persons, and especially for the unaccompanied children.

"Nationality" was also used as a political weapon at this time to advance the domestic and international agendas of the various states and agencies involved in settling the displaced persons question. The searing experiences of the chaotic period after the First World War, when new nations were carved out of the European landscape wholesale, as well as the vicious racism of the Nazis, had served to reinforce a deep ethnic self-awareness among the various populations of Europe, especially among Eastern Europeans. Thus, the concept of "nationality" was very much in a state of flux in the late 1940s. The immediate postwar period was a time of tremendous fluidity in many ways. At the risk of overstating the case, the Second World War had caused a fundamental rupture with the pre-war era on many levels, and the notion of national identity was one such rupture. With the enshrinement of the Wilsonian concept of national self-determination in the peace treaties that followed the First World War, a Pandora's box had been opened. The Second World War and its immediate aftermath saw the mobilization of national identity and national self-determination for a variety of purposes and political motives that had little to do with the more abstract intellectual debate over what constituted a nationality, but happily borrowed from it.

This sense of ethnicity was carried forward into the immediate postwar period and informed the way in which the displaced persons identified themselves. Moreover, various national governments (especially the Eastern European governments) resorted to both civic (citizenship) and ethnic national identities as suited their purposes, mobilizing both as a means of homogenizing their populations and of eliminating from their ranks those considered threats to national stability. The various international agencies trying to deal with the displaced persons crisis in Germany, for their part, failed to understand the distinction between nationality and ethnicity, or its ramifications, which left them unprepared for the raging debate that erupted around the determination of nationality, one that became particularly heated in discussions of the fate of unaccompanied children.

We see in that debate over what constituted a nationality, and over which nationalities would be recognized, a clash between a legalistic definition of nationality in terms of citizenship and a more abstract definition of nationality as something broader, determined by ethnic and cultural boundaries. At this time of great uncertainty, groups fought to take advantage of this postwar caesura to carve out for themselves a new identity and a new space in the postwar world and, in so doing, establish the legitimacy of their claimed nationality. In the fight over the identity and the fate of unaccompanied children, the confusion and the conflict over national identity, as well as the manner in which it was manipulated, was made clear. The consequences for the children were profound.[2]

There are several bodies of literature with which this book intersects: the literature on the American occupation, which largely focuses on US-German relations and the reconstruction of West Germany; the literature on displaced persons, which has focused on the postwar experience from the displaced persons' perspective and is largely organized by specific ethnicity and dominated by studies of the Jewish, Polish, Lithuanian, and Russian experiences; the literature on children and war, which has mainly centred on wartime experiences and the story of the Jewish child survivors; and the literature on the international non-governmental agencies established to deal with the postwar refugee and displaced persons crisis. This book fits contextually into the burgeoning literature on refugee populations more generally, including the question of postwar German refugees or expellees.

Recently, as interest has grown in the immediate postwar period, there has been an explosion of literature, as well as a flurry of often-annual conferences, on both the postwar refugee question in Europe, and especially in Germany (which includes the displaced persons, but lumps them in with all the other refugees on the move in the late 1940s) and on the displaced persons question in particular. There were a few key studies done in the 1950s of the displaced persons specifically and the postwar refugees more generally, but since then, the subject has received little attention until quite recently. Those earlier studies focused on the mass population displacements of the immediate postwar period, displaced persons and other postwar refugees combined, and included works by E.M. Kulischer, *Europe on the Move: War and Population Changes 1914–47*; J.B. Schechtman, *European Population Transfers, 1939–1945*; and Malcolm Proudfoot, *European Refugees, 1939–1952: A Study in Forced Population Movement.*[3] Michael Marrus's monograph, *The Unwanted: European Refugees in the Twentieth Century,*[4] attempted to build on this – "to look at the many different kinds of refugees and dislocated people in the same context" – in a way that Jessica Reinisch also called for in her introduction to the collection of essays she and Elizabeth White edited, entitled *The Disentanglement of Populations: Migration, Expulsion and Displacement in Post-war Europe, 1944–9.*[5]

Ironically, unlike most history which has been written initially from a top-down perspective, be it beginning with the story of government and government decision-making and its consequences – classic political history – and then only afterwards from a bottom-up perspective that explores the impact of those decisions on the ordinary person, the literature on the displaced persons crisis in Germany began with the story of the displaced persons, written from the perspective of the displaced persons. Much of the literature has also been ethnicity or group specific. Thus, there is a limited body of literature that focuses on each of the experiences of Polish, Ukrainian, Baltic, and Soviet displaced persons, often with a focus on the challenges faced by the diaspora upon resettlement outside of their birth nation.[6] There is also a voluminous literature on the postwar experiences of the Jewish displaced persons or survivors.[7] These literatures seldom speak to one another and instead focus on the challenges faced by each specific group within the context of both the displaced persons camps, but especially within the emerging postwar and Cold War context; the impact upon their own particular nationalities or ethnicities and their drive to assert those identities; and the challenges the displaced persons faced in rebuilding their lives. In each case, and especially in the case of those works dealing with the Jewish displaced persons, the exploration of the displaced persons experience is rich (see Atina Grossman's 2007 work, *Jews, Germans, and Allies: Close Encounters in Occupied Germany* as an example of this[8]), but nonetheless this particular genre of displaced persons studies has largely evolved into a set of historiographical silos.

In the past decade, there has been a shift away from these silos towards a more encompassing understanding of the displaced persons experience and of the very concept of "displaced person." Mark Wyman's *DP: Europe's Displaced Persons, 1945–1951* and Wolfgang Jacobmeyer's *Heimatlosen Ausländer: Die Displaced Persons in Westdeutschland, 1945–1951* anticipated this shift in focus.[9] It is perhaps Daniel Cohen's 2012 work, *In War's Wake: Europe's Displaced Persons in the Postwar Order*, that sets the tone for this most recent refocusing, with his exploration of the creation of a new identity, that of "displaced person," forced upon these refugees by dint of the bureaucratic structure that provided aid and assistance based on eligibility, and which was only partially determined by one's nationality.[10] Anna Holian, in her book, *Between National Socialism and Soviet Communism: Displaced Persons in Postwar Germany*,[11] compares how displaced persons of various ethnic identities understood themselves, categorized themselves, constructed narratives to explain their situation, and how they organized politically to protect and pursue their own interests in postwar Germany. Adam Seipp's 2013 work, *Strangers in the Wild Place: Refugees, Americans, and a German Town, 1945–1952*,[12] takes this a step further by comparing the experiences of not just categories of displaced persons, but also those experiences with that of German refugees expelled from Eastern Europe after the war's end. These are just examples of the ways in which scholars have attempted recently to nuance the story of the displaced persons experience, by looking at it from the perspective of the category of "displaced person," in the first instance, and to think more comparatively about those experiences. In these studies, too, the authors have recognized the complicated relationship between the displaced persons, the occupation authorities, and occasionally the German authorities and German populations (native and refugee).

This book also draws upon and augments another body of literature, that which looks at the postwar American occupation in Germany. If not "official" histories, these works are largely studies of the military government, and fall into the category of military and administrative histories, explaining the nature of the various iterations of the occupation governments, their priorities, and their structure. While useful, they fail to devote much space to policy as implemented by the occupation forces, and even less to the challenges of dealing with the displaced persons (the numerically much larger German refugee population occupied much more of the occupiers' time and energies).[13]

The third body of literature is a slim one. This literature addresses the history of UNRRA and the IRO – the organizations themselves, their operations, and their work in the field in Europe. There are several books on UNRRA, for example, *Outcast Europe: Refugees and Relief Workers in an Era of Total War, 1936–48*, by Sharif Gemie et al. and *Armies of Peace: Canada and the UNRRA Years*, by Susan Armstrong-Reid and David Murray.[14] However, these focus on UNRRA's relief work and, in the case of *Armies of Peace*, the politics surrounding its creation; they do not explore child search specifically, nor the internecine politics surrounding UNRRA's operations on the ground in Germany, and none of them stretch the story into the IRO period (1947–52), even though the displaced persons camps continued to operate until 1952. There are, in addition, two official histories: one of UNRRA by George Woodbridge, *UNRRA: The History of the United Nations Relief and Rehabilitation Administration* (1950), and one of the IRO, by Louise Holborn, *The International Refugee Organization: A Specialized Agency of the United Nations – Its History and Work, 1946–1952* (1956).[15]

A fourth body of literature, which is voluminous, deals with the tragic story of children in war. It is not surprising that the story of child victims of war draws considerable attention, and the history of children during the Second World War especially has spawned a large library of works. Most of these have focused on the period of the war itself, and on children's wartime displacement and victimization, with the exception of a subset that addresses the Jewish child survivors of the war and the Holocaust.[16] A few venture into the postwar period, most notably Tara Zahra's 2011 book, *The Lost Children: Reconstructing Europe's Families after World War II*.[17] It is the work with which this book most closely intersects. Pan-European in scope, and stretching from 1914 to 1950, *The*

Lost Children explores the history of child welfare practices in Europe in the period before the Second World War (accounting for the first three of the six chapters) and in France and Czechoslovakia in the period after the war. Zahra also explores the clash between those child welfare practices and the postwar emphasis on the rights of a nation to get "its" children back, the latter of which ultimately is privileged, she argues, over the rights of the child. Her focus is largely on the evolution of child welfare practices in the context of war and upheaval – how it came to be understood that the worst threat to children was to be separated from their family and, by extension, their nation, as this would cause the children severe and irreparable psychological harm. Thus, in the aftermath of the Second World War, the focus of relief work directed at children was not just to meet their immediate material or physical needs, but to reunite families in order to best address the children's psychological needs. Zahra points to the 1948 United Nations Universal Declaration of Rights as evidence of the pervasiveness of this belief, which enshrined the family as "the natural and fundamental group unit of society."[18] For the states to which these children "belonged," however, these children represented a "lost human patrimony" and the nation's recovery.[19] Many states, then, strived to reclaim these children, whether or not it meant the children would be reunited with their families (although Zahra notes that they were not necessarily interested in reclaiming *all* their children, only those deemed assimilable). She concludes, first, that children became "a precious spoil of war," a form of social capital, which is a key observation.[20] Second, Zahra argues that in the battle between children's needs and rights fought for by the humanitarian agencies on the ground, on the one hand, and the nation states fighting to claim their children, on the other, generally national interests won out at the expense of children's rights.

Zahra makes two important points: (1) children had become "spoils of war" and, (2) in the end, and despite protestations that the children's best interests were paramount, national interests trumped the children's interests. She argues that even the welfare workers concerned with dealing with the children participated in this privileging out of a belief in the paramountcy of family and national culture and identity in ensuring a child's health, both mental and physical. But Zahra has missed a key factor in the calculations of the welfare workers when determining what was "best" for unaccompanied children, namely, the need for a legal identity based in citizenship, which would ensure that the children would have someone to protect them and advocate for them and which would guarantee them the ability to participate fully in society and the economy upon reaching adulthood. This required full citizenship somewhere. Each child needed an unambiguous and recognized legal identity in the form of citizenship in some country in order to be able to survive in the twentieth-century world. This became a driving concern by 1949. In the end, citizenship could and often did trump ethnicity as a source of "national identity" for the purposes of the children's ultimate fate.

Chapter One

UNRRA Gets Started

The United Nations Relief and Rehabilitation Administration (UNRRA) was born of a number of mutually reinforcing concerns, all of which coalesced to drive the creation of an agency that would address the immediate needs of a postwar Europe. Those concerns were the experience of the immediate aftermath of the First World War, a push to create a United Nations organization, and a British-led drive to amass foodstuffs in anticipation of the eventual liberation of Europe. The traumatic upheaval that had followed the First World War, the first time that people in such numbers had been displaced by war, civil war, and ethnic cleansing, creating a refugee crisis of unprecedented proportions, had been a sobering lesson. Almost as soon as the Second World War began and Great Britain made clear that it was going to continue to fight, people started to plan for the war's end and what was confidently, if dauntingly, anticipated to be a refugee crisis numbering in the millions. As early as October 1939, US President Franklin D. Roosevelt was predicting that "when this ghastly war ends, there may be not one million but ten million or twenty million men, women and children belonging to many races" who would be refugees.[1] Others, such as Sir Herbert Emerson, High Commissioner for Refugees of the impotent League of Nations since that January, shared a similar, foreboding belief.[2] All recognized the implications of what would be a humanitarian crisis on a massive scale that would require an international response if complete anarchy were to be avoided. Organizing and mobilizing that international response, however, was going to prove a serious challenge.

The context in which UNRRA came into being included the drive to found the United Nations Organization. Ironically, UNRRA was part of the response to the failure of the League of Nations, created after the First

World War to oversee the peace, guarantee the new borders in Europe, and ensure collective security by "respect[ing] and preserv[ing] against external aggression the territorial integrity and the existing political independence of all members of the League."[3] Although the League had proven largely impotent in the face of the overwhelming challenges of the 1930s, the desire for an international body that could truly ensure collective security had not waned. Roosevelt was a tireless advocate for the creation of what would become the United Nations, an organization to be modelled on the League, but modified to address what were perceived to be the League's fatal weaknesses. In the summer of 1941, Roosevelt was discussing the need for such an organization with the British Prime Minister, Sir Winston Churchill, and its basic principles were articulated in the Atlantic Charter, issued that August. In January 1942, less than a month after the United States entered the Second World War, Roosevelt, Churchill, and representatives of the Soviet Union and China as well as of twenty-two other nations signed what came to be known as the United Nations Declaration – this was the first official use of the term "United Nations." By 1943, the US State Department had written an initial draft charter for this new international body, and by the end of 1943, both the Senate and the House of Representatives had passed resolutions in favour of its foundation.[4]

The need for an organization to deal specifically with the anticipated flood of refugees in the postwar period was clear to all. The experience after the First World War had proven that. By 1926, there had been an estimated 9.5 million refugees in Europe, at least three million of whom had been forcibly expelled from their homes and countries. In partial response to this humanitarian crisis, parts of which were being only fitfully addressed by various non-governmental organizations, the Council of the League had asked Fridtjof Nansen to serve as High Commissioner for Refugees. When originally established, the High Commission for Refugees was intended to deal with the only serious refugee problem of that moment, namely, refugees from revolutionary Russia. However, the High Commission soon found itself the object of appeals for assistance from a group newly created by the extensive redrawing of borders after the war and national exercises of ethnic cleansing, as a result of which whole segments of various nations' populations suddenly found their citizenship voided. These were the stateless: people who had lost their citizenship either due to shifting borders or government actions. Without citizenship, these refugees were without a legal identity and so not permitted to cross international borders, and thus unable to either repatriate or resettle. They included the Russian emi-grés, but many others as well. The lack of identification papers soon became a source of serious international friction. The High Commission for Refugees, whose mandate was restricted to coordinating the efforts of private agencies who were to fund and carry out the actual work, and which was itself always considered a temporary agency, was limited in what it could accomplish. One of its most significant accomplishments was the establishment of the Nansen passport, an identity card issued by the League of Nations to stateless refugees and honoured by fifty-two national governments; this passport was the first refugee travel document, and the Nansen International Office for Refugees won the 1938 Nobel Peace Prize for its efforts to establish it.[5] By the 1930s, with the growing flood of refugees, primarily Jews, created by the new Nazi regime in Germany, the League found itself overwhelmed.

In spite of its failure, the League of Nations set an important prec-edent in a number of ways. First, all were now aware that there would be a refugee crisis at the war's end on a scale hitherto unseen. Second, the High Commission for Refugees (like the League of Nations for the UN) provided a model for UNRRA, both in terms of what worked and what did not. Included in that was the very important, if prosaic, accomplishment of devising procedures for registering, documenting, and certifying people as refugees, and thus creating a particular pop-ulation with an identity that was recognizable, identifiable, and thus quantifiable. This gave them an official, legitimate identity. If nothing else, it made them visible. And third, Nansen helped to foster a political will among governments to address the refugee question on an interna-tional level. He made national governments, and especially the major powers, aware of the question's existence, as well as persuading them to recognize the issue of refugees as something that they should not ignore, both for pragmatic security and moral reasons.[6]

Initial Planning

When war finally erupted with Nazi Germany, part of the context was an international commitment to international cooperation. Also, part of it was recognition of the inevitable complexity and chaos of the coming postwar period, including the probability of a huge refugee problem. The international response was a disjointed one. In the first instance, Great Britain and the various governments in exile realized that, when the war finally ended, the impending need for relief would be enormous. They pledged to amass enormous reserves of foodstuffs for the relief of the peoples of Europe at the war's end, initially independently, but soon as part of a coordinated effort led by the British government.

At the same time, the US government had begun to make its own plans for postwar relief. The Department of State established a committee to make recommendations on postwar policy to the President, and its subcommittees closely monitored the activities of the new Requirements Bureau. The State Department also began to draft a proposal for an international relief agency. This would prove the preliminary plan for UNRRA. Following the invasion of North Africa in November 1942, pressure mounted. Negotiations continued apace with the Soviet Union, Great Britain, and China (this relief agency would be truly global in scale) for the establishment of a new relief agency, and Roosevelt appointed Herbert H. Lehman director of the Office of Foreign Relief and Rehabilitation, in charge of managing the American response. The implication was that Lehman was his preferred choice for director of any future relief organization, and indeed, Lehman was heavily involved in drafting the foundational agreement for UNRRA.[7] Finally, after lengthy negotiations between both the four core nations and an additional forty Allied and associated governments, the text of the agreement establishing UNRRA was formally adopted on 9 November 1943.

At the same time as UNRRA's establishment, and complicating matters, the Intergovernmental Committee on Refugees (IGCR) was resurrected. The IGCR had been the result of the 1938 Evian Conference, called by the President of the United States. At the time, Roosevelt had invited representatives of approximately thirty governments to discuss the enormous refugee crisis that had resulted from the Austrian Anschluss and the increasingly harsh anti-Semitic legislation being enacted in Germany. The conference established a permanent international refugee organization, the IGCR, with two main purposes: (1) to bring order to the mass exodus from Germany and Austria and (2) to negotiate the resettlement of these refugees in potential recipient countries.[8] For the first years of its existence, this organization floundered, underfunded and lacking the support of its member governments, including the United States. In 1943, in response to considerable public pressure to act following the revelations of the mass extermination of the Jewish people in Europe, the British and American governments revived the IGCR and extended its remit to all refugees "who, as a result

of events in Europe, have had to leave, or may have to leave, their countries of residence because of danger to their lives or liberties on account
of their race, religion or political beliefs" – this was a significant expansion of the IGCR's mandate.[9] Its task was meant to be complementary
to that of UNRRA. Simply put, UNRRA was constrained strictly to the
maintenance, care, and repatriation of displaced persons in the postwar
period, with the ultimate goal of assisting all to return home, while the
IGCR was charged with the responsibility of assisting those displaced
persons who, for various reasons, did not wish to repatriate.[10]

As well, plans were being laid for governing Germany after the war.
In the end, the decision was made to divide Germany into occupation
zones, each to be governed by one of the major Allies, until Germany's
ultimate fate could be determined. Initially it was a tripartite plan, with
a zone each for Great Britain, the United States, and the Soviet Union.
At the Yalta Conference in February 1945, the French were given a
fourth zone, carved out of the US and British zones. All four zones were
governed by the Allied Control Council (later known as the Allied Control Authority), comprised of the four commanders of the Allied forces.
The purpose of the Allied Control Council was to ensure consistency in
policy across the zones, but any decision made by the Control Council
had to be unanimous before it could be enacted. If the members could
not reach agreement on a particular issue, the commanders were free to
enact policy within their own zones as they saw fit.

Running largely in parallel to these international diplomatic efforts,
the various military authorities were developing plans for the invasion
of the European continent. At the Casablanca Conference in January
1943, the United States and Great Britain agreed to combine efforts in
the eventual invasion and to create a Combined Chiefs of Staff to manage and coordinate the two countries' war efforts at the highest level.
Although it took until December 1943 before the Supreme Commander,
Allied Expeditionary Force (SCAEF) was named – General Dwight
D. Eisenhower – the development of the joint command had begun
soon after Casablanca, in order to ensure efficiency and avoid conflict
between the two military machines. Eisenhower's Supreme Headquarters, Allied Expeditionary Force (SHAEF) was formally established in
London, England, in January 1944. SHAEF consisted of several divisions: G-2 responsible for intelligence; G-3 for planning and operations; G-5 for civil affairs and military government (initially the two
were not differentiated); G-6 for publicity and psychological warfare;
as well as special staff divisions. From the start, then, there were three

parallel structures created to deal with the expected humanitarian crisis: UNRRA, the IGCR, and SHAEF's G-5 division, all operating in the context of four different occupation zones, under different military governments, ostensibly coordinating their governance through the aegis of the Control Council.

The chief concern of G-5, the military division directly responsible for the anticipated refugee crisis, was the potential impact of the humanitarian crisis on military operations, as the various militaries confidently expected to be still fighting the war in the midst of massive population shifts. Mindful of the need for civilian relief, the militaries recognized the urgent need for a civil administrative structure for territory still under military control post-liberation. It was also considered crucial that the military retain control over the refugees during the liberation period, to ensure that the civilian refugees did not impede the progress of their forces. To use General Eisenhower's words, G-5's purpose, "although humanitarian in results, was 'to help us win the war.'"[11] In the first instance, care of the displaced civilian population would be a military responsibility, at least until the military operations were completed. It would be some months before UNRRA's operations would start in the liberated territories.

UNRRA's Marginalization

There were several reasons why mobilizing the United Nations Relief and Rehabilitation Administration was not considered a viable alternative to mobilizing G-5, at least from the perspective of SHAEF. First, leery of being trapped into working with a multinational civilian agency over which it would have little control, SHAEF was reluctant to enter into any kind of formal agreement with UNRRA.[12] Second, SHAEF could not conclude an agreement with UNRRA until UNRRA had received the express consent to operate in the liberated territories from all national authorities concerned – initially, France, the Netherlands, Luxembourg, Yugoslavia, and Norway. UNRRA had to negotiate these agreements with each national government, not SHAEF. Given the short time frame, it was considered unlikely that UNRRA would be able to negotiate the necessary agreements in time, and SHAEF felt it needed to plan an alternative solution to the problem.

Another factor limiting the scope of UNRRA's potential contribution was that, at this point, its constitution restricted it to "any area under the control of any of the United Nations," which turned out to be problematic. Strictly speaking, this appeared to exclude UNRRA from operating in Germany and the territories of any of Germany's former allies. In fact, as early as June 1944, the chiefs of staff had raised the matter with respect to any potential UNRRA activity in France. Given that UNRRA was not authorized to operate in "ex-enemy" territory, this was interpreted to include France, which had been occupied by Germany since 1940.[13] When this oversight was realized, Resolution 57, passed at the Second Council Session of UNRRA, held in September 1944, authorized the organization to carry out operations in enemy or ex-enemy areas, but only for "such a time and for such purposes as may be agreed upon between the military command, the established control authority or duly recognized administration of the area on the one hand and the Administration on the other and subject to such control as the military command or the established control authority may find necessary."[14] This amendment allowed UNRRA to operate in Germany, but only with the agreement of the authorities in control of the country. However, in the absence of a formal agreement with the Supreme Commander of the Allied Expeditionary Force, the military refused to (and technically could not) call on UNRRA.[15]

The lack of an agreement was, in part, due to a technicality and, in part, a turf war. No one could agree on who should sign an agreement with UNRRA for operations in Germany: Should it be the Allied Control Council or SHAEF? SHAEF was not going to last for long. Once the military phase of liberation was completed, the plan was to dismantle SHAEF and replace it with a military government. Any agreement signed with SHAEF, then, would only be effective for the duration of SHAEF's existence and would not necessarily transfer to the successor military government. From the perspective of the Control Council, responsible for coordinating governance of the four occupation zones after liberation, it feared having its hands tied by any arrangements made by SHAEF, so the preference was for the Control Council to extend the invitation. However, the Control Council required unanimity among its four members – Great Britain, the United States, France, and the Soviet Union – and the Soviet Union refused to sign the proposed memorandum. In the end, UNRRA was going to have to negotiate with SHAEF, but the delay further sidelined the Administration at a critical juncture.[16]

Working from the basic principle that the refugees could not be allowed to impinge on military operations, SHAEF crafted its refugee plan. Its objectives were straightforward, and it was clear that SHAEF believed the refugee issue would be a short-term problem only. The displaced persons were to be repatriated as quickly as possible. In the interim, provision was to be made for their well-being and measures were to be taken to ensure the prevention of epidemics. The machinery put in place to do these three things was to be international in nature, and "place maximum responsibility and control in the hands of Allied national authorities at the earliest practicable date," with the caveat that the Supreme Commander of the Allied Expeditionary Force would retain de facto supreme responsibility and authority at all times and in all areas to the full extent required by the military situation. As the military advanced into enemy territory, the Civil Affairs Division of G-5 SHAEF would establish a military government in its wake. With regard to refugees and displaced persons, its responsibilities would include the following: supervising indigenous authorities in establishing processing centres; supervising the administration of the centres; supervising the indigenous authorities in the control of refugees; and calling forward SHAEF displaced persons specialists and national liaison officers as necessary. These national liaison officers would be accredited by the various Allied national governments and assigned to SHAEF. It would be these liaison officers who would assist the new military government in supervising and controlling their nationals in processing centres and in the geographical area of responsibility of the formation to which they were attached, not UNRRA. The liaison officers also were to assist in the following: identification, registration, classification, and disposition of their nationals; procuring repatriation clearance from their governments for their nationals; issuing repatriation visas; reporting on numbers of their nationals in formation areas; communicating with their nationals; and recommending plans for their repatriation.

All of these were responsibilities that UNRRA had assumed it would be assigned. Instead, UNRRA would only operate in the military and liberated areas upon the request and with the permission of the SCAEF and the Allied national authorities, respectively, and only in an advisory or observer role: "to observe and assist in the execution of plans for dealing with refugees and displaced persons," in the words of the Plan, not "implement," a critical distinction.[17] The IGCR would continue in its responsibility for those apparently few displaced persons obliged to leave their homes for reasons of race, religion, or political belief and who could not or would not repatriate; it would help them find new places to settle, with UNRRA caring for them in the interim.[18] National liaison officers would perform the tasks UNRRA had believed were to be its own.

These liaison officers had already begun to appear on the ground well before SHAEF had enshrined their role. Discussions about their deployment had begun as early as May 1944. Poland was among the first to request permission to send representatives to France to collect its nationals, and SHAEF was intrigued by the idea. The US 21st Army Group also had proposed using Allied liaison officers to deal with displaced nationals. If these liaison officers were accredited to the Supreme Commander and attached to SHAEF military formations operationally, it was thought they would be more easily controlled than UNRRA – a seemingly attractive and simple solution.[19]

With this in mind, SHAEF signed agreements with a number of countries establishing the terms for the deployment of national liaison officers and military missions. Not only were they to control and limit the movement of their nationals in the case of standstill instructions from SHAEF (e.g., displaced persons were supposed to remain where they were until informed otherwise), these national liaison officers would provide care for their national displaced persons, including medical supervision, to prevent epidemics. They would register all displaced persons, including Allied and enemy nationals, as well as persons of doubtful, dual, or no nationality using a standard procedure dictated by and forms provided by SHAEF. These records would serve as the individual displaced person's basic personal record. The national missions would also establish processing centres for returning displaced persons in their home countries to facilitate the movement of their national displaced persons into, through, and out of their territory. And they would turn over to SHAEF any and all enemy displaced persons upon demand.[20] In one neat move, SHAEF had effectively sidelined UNRRA by allocating many of its supposed responsibilities to the new liaison officers. By mid-September 1944, SHAEF and the Army Groups were requesting Polish, Dutch, Russian, and other liaison officers be brought forward, as there was a desperate need for assistance.[21] Arrangements were also being made for the organized repatriation of French, Luxembourgeois, Belgian, and Dutch displaced persons. As long as their movement did not impede military operations, SHAEF was pleased to move out these displaced persons, with the one caveat that they had to move directly to their countries of origin.[22]

In a move that further undermined the potential involvement of UNRRA, the national liaison officers' status vis-à-vis SHAEF was regularized in early November 1944. These civilians were to be given a non-combatant status similar to that of war correspondents and civilian technicians attached to the American and British forces. They would wear officers' uniforms, but without badges of rank. Instead, they would have a patch on their left sleeve reading "Repatriation Official." They would also carry certificates of identity as non-combatants.[23] By late November, the 6th Army was requesting twenty-four liaison officers (seven French, two Belgian, two Czechoslovakian, two Yugoslavian, four Russian, four Polish, two Italian, and one Greek). SHAEF Mission France also requested permission to bring forward an additional fourteen French liaison officers, and there was a further request for another ten Polish officers and one Greek officer.[24]

In spite of being marginalized in this manner, UNRRA attempted to prepare for the field. Herbert Lehman, now director general of UNRRA, was keen that the Administration be ready to act if and when the opportunity arose. In August 1944, Lehman warned Fred Hoehler, the director of UNRRA's Displaced Persons Division and the man who would be managing what was anticipated to be one of the most important functions of UNRRA, to prepare to have teams called forward. While Lehman admitted it was still unclear "just what relation UNRRA will have with regard to the arrangements for the assembly of displaced persons into centers and for the organization or administration of border stations," he felt it very likely that UNRRA would quickly require substantial numbers of personnel. It was crucial, he cautioned, "to be ready to cooperate in every way with the military authorities and with governments." As Lehman explained, he preferred Hoehler to have too many people, rather than too few, and they had to be ready to move on the instant.[25] UNRRA's reputation and success would hinge on its ability to respond quickly and effectively.

Others within the Administration were more hesitant, and the discussion raged about what tasks UNRRA should and should not take on given its limited resources. Personnel remained quite limited, in spite of Lehman's urging, and there was still no field operations structure established, let alone staffed. UNRRA's coffers were also not overflowing. The director of the DP Division was one of the hesitant, wary of overstretching his resources, his conversations with the military not instilling any great confidence in him. While he was cautiously optimistic about the military's general attitude towards UNRRA, which he thought was favourable, Hoehler was less optimistic about the role that the military envisioned for UNRRA. His expectation was that

at no time in Germany will we [UNRRA] be operating entirely on our own. In the first instance we will be working as individual agents of SHAEF, taking over specific tasks within the general program for displaced persons as they are assigned to us by SHAEF Displaced Persons Executive (DPX). These tasks would provide only administrative coordination and specific services, and would not – repeat NOT – include supply and transportation. In the second phase, as agents of the military authorities *under* the Allied Control Commission [Hoehler's emphasis], we would continue to act for a short period. In the third phase, the ACC would delegate full authority to UNRRA to work on its behalf with the Allied Government Representatives who are in Germany to serve their Nationals, to provide the coordination of services for all displaced persons, in the administration of regional offices and the actual administration of assembly centres. This would before long become a total UNRRA operation in Germany – always, of course, working with the Allied Control Commission, which would be the only governmental authority within Germany.[26]

Hoehler's suspicion was that, aside from G-5's Displaced Persons Branch, SHAEF was largely indifferent to UNRRA. In the interim, he proposed restricting UNRRA's role to administrative and advisory support and its primary role "to [expediting] the exodus of residents of these centers to their own homes or other place of resettlement."[27] Hoehler remained convinced that UNRRA would not be able to field more personnel than this, and his mounting fear was that SHAEF may suddenly call on UNRRA's Displaced Persons Division to provide hundreds of teams instantly to deal with what he well understood (far better than the military forces) was a massive refugee crisis in the making.[28]

What changed from SHAEF's perspective was that the liaison officers became problematic. If the expectation was that most displaced persons would be returned home quickly, then the national liaison officers made sense, or they should have. Problems were developing, however, that quickly made this solution less attractive to SHAEF. Originally, the liaison officers were supposed to be drawn from military personnel, but the various national authorities involved were having trouble coming up with enough military personnel for the job, and so they turned to civilians. SHAEF reluctantly approved this, but it did raise concern about the possible calibre of the officers. The concern proved prescient, as the Allied governments still had considerable difficulty coming up with qualified liaison officers. SHAEF had already fielded six French, four Czech, two Belgian, and nine Dutch, and was planning to send out a further fifty French, fifteen Belgian, twelve Czech, sixteen Dutch, and twenty Polish liaison officers by late April, but it was not enough. The Army Groups were pressing for still more. The request for additional

Russian liaison officers was especially difficult. SHAEF could come up with twenty-five, but none spoke English. In the end, SHAEF warned the Army Groups that they would have to go to the US Army High Command for Europe, or ETOUSA (European Theater of Operations, United States Army), for translators if they could not manage with the liaison officers they had.[29]

Second, the handling of displaced persons was starting to slip out of SHAEF's control. The various national authorities – the French and the Soviets especially – regarded their liaison officers as independent agents. France proposed establishing its own repatriation agency in Germany to handle the repatriation of both French displaced persons and prisoners of war, one that would operate independently of SHAEF; this would have set a dangerous precedent. If France were allowed to do this, then every one of the Allies would have to be allowed to do the same. The opinion at SHAEF was that this would be a very bad thing for several reasons. Such a body would be ineffective, in the first place, as it would not control the means for carrying out its task of finding, collecting, and moving its nationals – especially not transportation which, of necessity, the military controlled. Thus, these agencies would be at best, ineffective and at worst, a nuisance. There was also the fear that these agencies would "tend to do a great deal of 'free wheeling,' to the embarrassment of [SHAEF]." The conclusion was that such agencies would be a disaster and that SHAEF Headquarters "must act as coordinator and cannot permit any of the Allied countries to operate independently." While it was appreciated that the various national authorities had to remain informed and should be consulted on matters of national policy, control over the displaced persons had to rest with SHAEF.[30] Yet SHAEF did not have the resources to deal with the displaced persons situation, either in the liberated territories or in Germany – or rather, did not wish to devote the resources to this problem. UNRRA was viewed, suddenly, as a viable alternative.

Finally, the liaison officers were proving incapable of maintaining order among the displaced persons population. Few in SHAEF, even at the upper levels, had more than a vague understanding of the internecine national tensions, even implacable hatreds that laced through the displaced persons population. By way of an example, it was only in April 1945 that the military in the field became aware that there were two very different and very hostile factions in Yugoslavia – the Royalists and the pro-Tito Communists. The 21st Army Group, who reported the presence of the factions, explained that its solution had been to separate the two groups into different displaced persons camps, but this would inevitably mean that one group would be without a national representative. SHAEF's response was not terribly helpful: "The Provisional Yugoslav Government, recognized both by the US and British Governments, was established as a result of an agreement between King Peter, through his Ministers, and Marshal Tito. Officially therefore there are no separate Royalist and Tito factions, since both owe allegiance to the official Government." Thus separate camps were not necessary. SHAEF's position was that the liaison officers accredited to SHAEF were representatives of the Tito government and they represented all Yugoslavians; however, pending instructions from the US and British governments, the dissident ringleaders should be transferred to another camp.[31] While SHAEF's position was technically correct, and the diplomatic implications of recognizing the two factions to the point of allowing them their own camps were explosive, the instructions did little to alleviate the already poisonous tensions in the streets and barracks of the camps.

Things were no less complicated with the Poles. Both the Provisional Government in Warsaw and the Polish government in exile were petitioning SHAEF regarding the disposition of the Polish displaced persons. On 1 May 1945, Commandant Aleksander Bekier, the secretary to the Polish Delegation, and a Dr Jedryahowski demanded an immediate meeting with Brigadier Salisbury-Jones of the Displaced Persons Branch of G-5 SHAEF. As Salisbury-Jones was not available, they agreed to meet with Lieutenant Colonel V.R. Paravicini, chief Allied liaison officer for the Displaced Persons Branch. It was a delicate meeting for Paravicini, as these men were official representatives of the Polish Lublin government, which had not yet been recognized by SHAEF (the anti-Communist Polish government in exile was still considered the legitimate government of Poland at this point). Jedryahowski explained that he was there to repatriate the Polish prisoners in Buchenwald and Dachau, including what he believed to be three hundred children. Paravicini prevaricated, arguing that the identification and repatriation of displaced persons of all nationalities was a subject of careful study by SHAEF already and that there were enough accredited liaison officers in the field that the care and repatriation of these people would not be an issue. Jedryahowski argued that, because of the horrific condition of these people's circumstances, it would be simple humanitarianism to repatriate them as quickly as possible and that all they wanted was to get back to Poland as quickly as possible, something only the Provisional Government could make happen.[32]

At the same time, the Polish ambassador in Washington, DC, for the London-based Polish government in exile approached the combined chiefs of staff. He expressed concern that SHAEF seemed to be operating under the assumption that all the Polish displaced persons would want to repatriate, evidenced in the fact that SHAEF was concentrating them east of the Rhine. The ambassador feared that these Poles might be put in the same camps as Soviet citizens, which might "lead to regrettable incidents and disorder." He also feared that, if repatriation was delayed several months and these people remained idle for an indefinite period of time, it would be both hard on their morale and a strain on Allied supply lines. Surely, he argued, it would be better to allow a large number of them to move west of the Rhine where they could take up productive work and, in that way, contribute to the common Allied cause. And he proposed Colonel Jan Kaczmarek, as the head liaison officer for the Polish government in exile, to act as the resident expert on all matters Polish in Germany.[33] Another representative of the Polish government in exile, meanwhile, had also brought pressure to bear on the British prime minister over the issue of the repatriation of Polish displaced persons.[34] SHAEF prevaricated again.

In late April 1945, Lieutenant Colonel Fuller, acting chief of the Displaced Persons Branch of the Prisoners of War and Displaced Persons Division of SHAEF, together with a Captain Neiman did a tour of the 12th Army Group's Communication Zone and reported back on the state of affairs. It was not good. They were greatly disturbed by the actions of Russian officers in the field, who, in several instances, had arrived at displaced persons camps and announced that they had come to take over its internal administration, without prior knowledge or orders from either SHAEF or 12th Army Group. In addition, these officers were a menace on the roads, as they generally drove high-speed sedans and reportedly drove in excess of 80 mph, "causing a growing mortality among dogs and chickens."[35]

Liaison officers were turning out to be a less-than-optimal way of dealing with the displaced persons crisis. Using national liaison officers meant that the politics of the homeland got in the way of the displaced persons' care and that care became instantly politicized, a complication SHAEF had not anticipated. Nor did the military have any control over the liaison officers, who acted with complete independence and disregard for the military's needs, concerns, or orders. In addition, SHAEF was being swamped with all manner of queries from the Soviet Union, Yugoslavia, Poland, and other countries, all demanding a greater voice in the policies being enacted regarding the care of their nationals and permission to send missions into Germany to seek out their nationals. Mobilizing UNRRA was becoming an increasingly attractive option.

There had always been some within SHAEF who had promoted this. Their argument had been that the refugee problem was basically an international one by dint of the numerous nationalities involved, so ultimately the problem went beyond the strict scope of either SHAEF or the subsequent military government in Germany. Moreover, the personnel in SHAEF and the coming military government who were charged initially with dealing with displaced persons had other, more permanent functions to perform and "cannot therefore conveniently carry such responsibility indefinitely." For this reason, it always had been clear to at least some that UNRRA should "in due course be invited to assume responsibility for Allied Displaced Persons in occupied Germany at a time and under conditions to be determined by the Governments of Britain, the United States and the USSR."[36] This position was shared by the combined chiefs of staff, who had been always very much in favour of involving UNRRA to the fullest extent possible and as quickly as possible.[37] It had been SHAEF that had chosen to restrict UNRRA's presence.[38] By late 1944, given the enormous numbers of displaced persons under SHAEF care – estimated to be over three million in the three western SHAEF-controlled zones of Germany (1,494,000 Western Europeans, including 877,000 French; and 2,191,000 Eastern Europeans, including 840,000 Soviet and 681,000 Polish displaced persons) – and given the problems with the liaison officers, SHAEF was forced to revise its plans for the management of the displaced persons.

The revisions were encapsulated in SHAEF's Administrative Memorandum No. 39, Displaced Persons and Refugees in Germany, released 18 November 1944, which became the foundational document for future policy regarding displaced persons and their care. SHAEF continued to retain ultimate administrative authority over displaced persons and refugees during what was termed the "military period." Once the armies had advanced beyond an area, responsibility remained a military one, but in the hands of the newly established military government or the national authorities, once re-established. The military district commanders were responsible for the location, care, and control of United Nations displaced persons, and were authorized to move them to assembly centres if necessary (defined as camps or "accommodation areas" under direct military control). The military district commanders were to free from confinement any United Nations nationals or nationals of neutral countries who had been interned or otherwise held under restraint by the German authorities due to race, religion, or activities in favour of the United Nations and put them under Allied military control or restriction, as appropriate. The commanders were to safeguard the health and welfare of the United Nations displaced persons (and not allow them to disperse until they were taken care of), including the protection of their property and rights. They were to register the displaced persons and arrange for their repatriation. They were also to supervise the German authorities who were required to provide all necessary material aid for the United Nations displaced persons, including care, shelter, maintenance, and medical attention.

UNRRA remained able to operate in Germany only on the invitation of the Supreme Commander of the Allied Expeditionary Force (SCAEF). It was not authorized to care for or repatriate any ex-enemy or enemy displaced persons or refugees found in Germany, with the exception of the stateless or those persons persecuted for race, religion, or activities in favour of the United Nations. Administrative Memorandum No. 39 defined "Displaced Persons" as "civilians outside the national boundaries of their country by reason of war, who are desirous but unable to return home or find homes without aid; who are to be returned to enemy or ex-enemy territory." United Nations displaced persons were defined as "displaced nationals of the United and associated Nations." And stateless persons were defined as "persons who have been 'denationalized' or whose country of origin cannot be determined, or who cannot establish their right to the nationality claimed." In addition, UNRRA would supply the personnel needed to take over in whole or in part the administration and management of assembly centres for United Nations displaced persons, if desired by the military commanders. UNRRA was also required to provide its own specialists, such as medical and welfare officers, as needed, and its own administrative personnel. Such personnel would wear a prescribed uniform and would be provided with identification marking them as non-combatants accompanying the armed forces.

Thus, UNRRA personnel would operate under military control – and sufferance – and the military chain of command would be used for their direction. The IGCR, incidentally, would continue to be responsible for the resettlement of persons "obliged to leave their homes for reasons of race, religion or political belief and [who] cannot or do not desire to be returned to their homes." UNRRA would provide the displaced persons with temporary care, for a period of time agreed upon with the IGCR, at which point the IGCR would assume responsibility for those not yet repatriated or resettled.

Administrative Memorandum No. 39 also formalized (and restricted) the use of Allied liaison officers. As in the case of UNRRA personnel, these liaison officers would be called forward by SHAEF as they were required. Formal representatives of their various national governments, they would be accredited to SHAEF, attached to the headquarters concerned, and subject to military command and control. Liaison officers would be permitted to act upon instructions from their own governments but only as were consistent with the requirements of the military authorities. Their tasks would be the following: to assist in the identification and repatriation of their nationals, to issue repatriation visas, to assist in the preparation of statistical reports of displaced persons, and to assist in controlling their nationals. This included managing health and welfare programs, as well as communications with their nationals, assisting in coordinating transportation arrangements for repatriation, and in security checks of their nationals.[39] Now, rather than being the persons responsible for making these various activities happen, national liaison officers were merely to "assist."

Finally, Administrative Memorandum No. 39 ordered the establishment of assembly centres for the displaced persons, where they would be provided with shelter, food, clothing, and medical care. Border control stations would be created, and all movement in and out of Germany was to be strictly controlled by the Allied military authorities. United Nations displaced persons who arrived at the frontiers without proper documentation, after being examined by counter-intelligence personnel, would be processed at the border control station and directed to the nearest assembly centre.[40] This was the clearest articulation of the division of responsibility yet.

After months of confusion and turf wars, an agreement was signed on 25 November 1944 between General Dwight D. Eisenhower (SCAEF) and UNRRA's Director General Herbert H. Lehman regularizing relations between SHAEF and UNRRA. This agreement arranged for UNRRA to assume, in the post-military period, "those responsibilities with which it may be charged and to insure a continuous uniformity of policy in the military and post-military periods." UNRRA's task would be to assist in the "maintenance of health, welfare, registration, administration and movement of the nationals of such states and of other Allied countries displaced in enemy or ex-enemy territories." The agreement confirmed that UNRRA would operate under the control and authority of the SCAEF.[41] SHAEF would remain firmly in control of the displaced persons situation, while drawing upon UNRRA and the national liaison officers when needed. As SHAEF explained in a memo to the field, military commanders remained "wholly responsible" for assembly centres for United Nations displaced persons.[42]

Thus, the military's solution was to use UNRRA but curtail its freedom of operation, making it responsible to and dependent upon the military. UNRRA would become a part of the Allied military machine, with its staff attached to the military at all levels, operating only upon the military's express invitation. Its activities were restricted to the health, welfare, registration, and administration of United Nations displaced persons only. Prisoners of war, enemy nationals, and ex-enemy nationals were not within its purview. Beyond this, UNRRA's exact responsibilities were not clearly defined. Simply put, UNRRA's task was to assist the military. By November 1944 it was clear that, while UNRRA *might* play some role in Europe, it would be a subordinate and supporting role, at the behest and whim of the military authorities.

UNRRA's Mobilization

The "Agreement to Regularize the Relations between the SCAEF and UNRRA" was signed none too soon, as the military units in the field were being overwhelmed by the sheer number of displaced persons. The field commanders quickly began calling for UNRRA teams to be brought forward to take over the care of displaced persons.[43] In December 1944, SHAEF suddenly requested two hundred UNRRA assembly centre teams, as well as additional UNRRA personnel for liaison work at SHAEF. SHAEF was willing to allow the teams to be phased in, but they wanted them all in the field by April 1945. That amounted to the mobilization of twenty-five teams every two weeks, beginning 1 January 1945, ramping up to fifty teams on 15 March and 1 April. Furthermore, SHAEF warned, should Germany collapse before April, the mobilization would have to speed up.[44] By February, SHAEF was warning UNRRA to expect a request for a further three hundred teams to be brought forward in June and July 1945.[45] Fred Hoehler's nightmare was coming true.

As Hoehler had predicted, this posed a serious challenge for UNRRA's Displaced Persons Division. First, these teams required a different kind of person from those who had been recruited to date. Up to late 1944, UNRRA had been recruiting administrators and high-level operatives – as regional directors and for senior administrative posts. These people expected to be given what Hoehler characterized as "a responsible position." Few were interested in fieldwork. UNRRA would have to recruit a different kind of person, one who would be willing to do the grunt work in the field, and approximately a thousand of them were needed quickly.[46] Just ramping up such a mammoth recruitment program was going to take time and money, neither of which was in great supply.

UNRRA had neither the personnel to meet SHAEF's demand nor the organization in place to manage its new, amplified role on the continent. Nor were its liaison operations with SHAEF working well.[47] By late February, the European Regional Office, responsible for managing UNRRA's European operations, was thoroughly confused as to how many teams were being called forward or when (the first sign of a pattern of miscommunication that would become distressingly common over the entire life of the Administration) – whether it was 450 or 750 teams that were requested, and at what pace they were to be phased in. Whatever the number, it was a considerable and very sudden jump from the original plan for two hundred teams by April 1945, and UNRRA's pace of recruitment could not match this sudden surge. SHAEF clarified that it was a total of 750 teams that were needed (the 200 teams requested on 2 December 1944; an additional 250 teams requested on 3 February; and, in the same February letter, notice of a possible request for an additional 300 teams in June and July 1945) and warned UNRRA that personnel departing from the United States should be fully clothed and equipped for field duty with standard items and personal equipment "commensurate with army officers, except firearms."[48] Based on the ideal team composition as outlined in UNRRA's *Welfare Guide*, which required thirteen personnel per team, this would have amounted to a total of 9,750 new recruits. By 5 May 1945, UNRRA had recruited a total of only 2,734 personnel (enough to staff the initial 200 teams) and had put 119 teams in the field.[49]

By late March 1945, SHAEF was getting increasingly impatient with the apparent disorganization of UNRRA and with its pace of recruiting. The first eight teams, composed of ten to twelve personnel each, had only just been dispatched to UNRRA's staging area in Granville, France – almost three months after the date the first teams were due.[50] SHAEF sent repeated requests to UNRRA for status updates on meeting its target of 2,600 personnel (the number needed to staff the first 200 teams).[51]

The European Regional Office finally reported that they had recruited a total of 1,202 persons to date, or 46 per cent of the total required for the first group of two hundred teams, but that they expected to have the full complement by 15 April 1945. This meant, however, that the soonest that the last of the two hundred teams would be on the continent would be 1 June 1945. The delay, UNRRA pointed out, was not its fault, but largely due to the difficulties UNRRA had encountered in getting adequate supplies of clothing, equipment, and transport for its people. This was, after all, UNRRA made clear, the responsibility (and, by inference, the fault) of the US War Department.[52]

Although American UNRRA personnel had been issued uniforms and clothing, they had not received any of the necessary mechanical or personal equipment – not even mess kits or bedding – in spite of being promised this equipment in Administrative Memorandum No. 39.[53] So far, the War Department had outfitted only the first two hundred teams, with no arrangements made for supplying the remaining teams, nor was it clear whether any supplies at all would be forthcoming for the non-American UNRRA personnel.[54] Not only did the UNRRA personnel require personal equipment, they also needed their own transportation. Without it, the teams could not even get to Germany from their staging post in France (Granville), let alone assist with the displaced persons once there. The military suggested that UNRRA could be given captured and reconditioned German vehicles. This was not an optimal solution, as the diversity of types of vehicles and the lack of spare parts meant that they would place a considerable strain on military repair depots and seriously compromise UNRRA's operations; it was, however, the best the War Department could, or would, do.[55]

SHAEF may have been frustrated with UNRRA's slow pace, but UNRRA was as least as frustrated with SHAEF's inability to live up to its side of the bargain. On 31 March 1945, Hugh Jackson, UNRRA's deputy director general for regional liaison, wrote Lieutenant General W.B. Smith, chief of staff at SHAEF, explaining that, while UNRRA was, in principle, willing to do all that it could to assist the military in its task, certain conditions had to be met before UNRRA would commit more than two hundred teams to the field. Until he was certain that the additional teams would get the clothing, equipment, and transport they would need, Jackson refused to commit to recruiting more personnel. In addition, he needed more staging room on the continent. Granville was too small and inadequate a staging centre to accommodate the number of personnel that the military demanded, so Jackson requested that another centre, which could house a thousand, be found for UNRRA. Without these commitments from the War Department, Jackson argued, "the Administration would be undertaking responsibilities which would have no chance of fulfillment."[56]

SHAEF was not sympathetic to UNRRA's complaints. The military had inspected Granville and concluded that it was adequate to UNRRA's purpose, so UNRRA would have to stay put until a location closer to the German border came available.[57] The military finally did agree to give priority to outfitting an additional 250 teams, although reluctantly, acerbically noting that it was "at the expense of equipment badly needed for Line of Communication Troops." In late March, SHAEF sent in a request for supplies for 550 UNRRA teams (13 persons each, 20 per cent of whom would be American). These were the teams due to be brought forward between 15 April and the end of July. The American personnel would be provided with basic personal equipment stateside, but the rest needed to be supplied and they were expected to number approximately 6,000. Thus, the requisition list included 6,000 complete sets of battle dress and individual field equipment, on the same scale as issued to American personnel for field duty, 3,300 two-man tents, 550 cooking utensil sets, 1,650 jerry-cans for water, 1,100 stretchers, 550 medical panniers, 550 medical haversacks, 2,200 hurricane lamps, 1,100 galvanized pails, 1,100 shovels, and 550 typewriters.[58]

Transportation was a more difficult matter. The War Department was finally persuaded to make a bulk allocation and to release a variety of reconditioned vehicles from the US Ministry of Supply. The reliability of the vehicles under field conditions was considered doubtful, but it was the best the War Department would do.[59] UNRRA would be responsible for spare parts. Given the competition for equipment and facilities between the fighting forces, hospitals, returning prisoners of war, manpower reinforcements, and the need for rest areas for troops exhausted by the long battle, this was all that could be allocated. As SHAEF's chief of staff, Lieutenant General Smith, explained, "I fully recognize that UNRRA is unable to obtain in the open market most of its necessities for this purpose, but I am equally convinced that energetic and determined management by the Administrators will produce quite satisfactory results."[60] Although G-5 finally promised in May 1945 the delivery of seven hundred trucks, the premise remained that one would have to make do and think creatively.[61]

The challenges in the field facing both the military units already in place and the new UNRRA teams being recruited were daunting, even if they had been adequately equipped, which they were not. Millions of refugees were on the move, in the midst of the last months of the military campaign and in spite of instructions to stay put until otherwise ordered. With or without SHAEF's or UNRRA's assistance, the vast majority of refugees had returned home by late June 1945. By 8 June, for example, G-5 was reporting that Czech displaced persons were being repatriated at a rate of 4,000 a day, with a total of 10,000 so far repatriated. As well, large numbers of Czechoslovakians had been moved southward into the 21st and 12th Army Group areas (which bordered Czechoslovakia), in anticipation of eventual repatriation.[62] By 26 June, some 1,453,000 Western Europeans had arrived in France, including approximately 1,390,000 French – practically all the French displaced persons who had been in Germany, according to the French government.[63] Most of these displaced persons had not waited for SHAEF, but instead, had self-repatriated. At least this was a problem that had largely resolved itself, to the relief and satisfaction of SHAEF. The repatriation of Eastern Europeans was not so easily accomplished (a story beyond the parameters of this study), but still, the Americans estimated that the total number of Soviet citizens repatriated as of 26 June was 1,569,131, with another 735,675 still to be moved out.[64] By mid-July, Brigadier General S.R. Mickelsen of SHAEF's Prisoners of War and Displaced Persons Division reported that some 4,000,000 displaced persons, Soviet and non-Soviet, had been repatriated (east and west), with 2,000,000 remaining.[65]

The exact count will never be known because of the chaos of the time, the drive to just get people back to their homes no matter what, and the extensive self-repatriation. Assuming that Mickelsen's numbers from 30 June are reliable, and they probably are as reliable as any, there had been an estimated 5,851,601 displaced persons in total in the SHAEF Zone – which excluded the Soviet-occupied territory – among them over 2,000,000 Russians and almost 1,300,000 French. By the end of July, Mickelsen reported to General Lucius Clay, now deputy military governor, that with the repatriation phase almost completed, there remained only approximately 500,000 displaced persons in Allied-controlled territory. Over 5,000,000 displaced persons had been moved out in a matter of just over two months – an astounding feat.

From the outset, it had been a task that had threatened to overwhelm the Allied forces and their resources. The process of repatriation had been a messy, chaotic, upsetting, sometimes violent one, and decidedly all-consuming. Throughout, the Allies' focus had been squarely on the challenges of getting these millions of people home before the winter set in. This focus meant that a significant subset of the displaced persons population was largely ignored, namely, those who could not or would not return home. These men, women, and children had been unceremoniously dumped into assembly centres cobbled out of army barracks, schools, warehouses, and even stables, until they could be dealt with later.

UNRRA's role to date had been quite circumscribed. Because the number of UNRRA teams actually in the field was insufficient, and those teams not up to strength, the US Army units tended to do the work themselves rather than turn it over to UNRRA, even though individual UNRRA personnel were generally regarded quite favourably by the G-5 staff elements in the US Army.[66] In a late July report of a tour of UNRRA's operations, Joseph P. Harris reported that the Army officers with whom he had spoken "generally praised the work which had been done by the DP teams, saying that they had been of great assistance and that some of the teams had done unusually fine work," but that, in spite of the praise, "it would be generally true to say that they have not functioned effectively." Harris offered several reasons for this. The UNRRA teams appeared to lack effective leadership, both in the field, where many team directors seemed underqualified or inadequately trained for their jobs and, as a result, incapable of planning and administering camp operations effectively. This deficiency was compounded by a lack of direction from either district or zonal headquarters, both because of those headquarters' lack of organization and because conditions in the field made regular communications difficult. In most cases, the UNRRA teams were badly understaffed. In some instances, a single UNRRA officer had been left to manage a camp of several thousand, an untenable situation. No camp being managed by UNRRA was adequately staffed, forcing the spontaneous recruitment of displaced persons as interpreters, drivers, cooks, and secretaries, a solution that seemed to work well at least for the moment, although it did contribute to a sense of UNRRA operating in crisis mode. In those cases where the UNRRA teams were assisting the Army rather than running a camp themselves, the relationship was a difficult and tense one – the UNRRA-Army relationship had not been well delineated – resulting in ineffective management of the camp. Conditions in the camps varied enormously. In some centres, the teams found themselves focused on the "bare essentials of their task, ensuring adequate feeding arrangements, helping to improve accommodation and the cleanliness and sanitation of the centre, etc." In other centres, where the conditions were better, the teams could begin their welfare function and, among other things, establish schools for children, organize cultural and recreational events and activities, and assist displaced persons in finding their relatives and friends. The fluidity of the displaced persons population, which meant that assembly centres came and went as the need arose and disappeared, combined with the fluidity of the military administrative structure, by necessity forced the teams to be flexible and mobile, responding quickly to changing circumstances; however, this mitigated against effective camp management and made UNRRA look reactive and slipshod. Finally, of course, the ongoing shortages of basic materials, transport, and supplies (of every kind, ranging from typewriters and paper to rubber stamps and inkpads) also made it difficult to function effectively.[67]

As the dust settled by mid-summer 1945, there dawned a growing realization that, while the displaced persons problem was considerably reduced, the objective of returning all of the displaced persons home by the winter had not and, more importantly, would not be met. Millions had been successfully repatriated, but hundreds of thousands still remained. As the mass repatriation drives of the summer months wound down, attention now shifted to the dilemma of the remnant. Decisions had to be made as to how these remaining displaced persons were going to be cared for, and how their final disposition would be arrived at.

Those decisions were shaped by several factors. From the start, the military authorities and the Allied Control Council had assumed that all the displaced persons would return home. They still confidently expected that would be the case, even for the recalcitrant sitting in the assembly centres in August 1945. This remnant continued to be considered a short-term problem, and this consideration shaped the way in which the military administrations approached the issue in the autumn of 1945. At the same time, the Allies' primary focus had shifted elsewhere, to bigger issues – the flood of German refugees arriving daily from Eastern Europe, the drive to get the European economy and governments functioning again, and not least, the growing tension with the Soviet Union. In the grand scheme of things, five hundred thousand displaced persons did not figure prominently, and handing responsibility for them over to UNRRA would ultimately seem an easy and simple solution.

The mobilization of UNRRA was not going to be straightforward, however. First, SHAEF had been, by this time, wound down. The Allies' plans had always been to establish tripartite control over Germany (then quadripartite, after the addition of the French Zone of Occupation) on an interim basis, once the military phase of the operations was over and Germany had either surrendered or been defeated. With the termination of hostilities, SHAEF was to be dissolved and replaced with a jointly run military government for the whole of Germany, managed through the vehicle of the Allied Control Council. The Control Council would be made up of the commanders of the four major Allied armies, each of whom would be responsible for the administration of their own zone. In the US Zone, that administrative responsibility was going to be shared by the United States Forces, European Theater (USFET) and the Office of Military Government, United States (OMGUS). USFET constituted the remaining tactical forces left on the ground in Germany after demobilization and redeployment began and was led by the army commanders. Its primary responsibilities were to offer security and support to OMGUS, the military government, while retaining responsibility for the care and disposition of the displaced persons, among other matters. OMGUS, which was intended to be a civilian operation eventually (although in practice it remained populated with ex-military personnel for many of the crucial years and always reported to the US War Department), was responsible for the governing of the zone, re-establishing democracy and the German economy, and liaising with the German authorities as they were re-established.[68]

This replacement of SHAEF created a technical problem for UNRRA's nascent operations in Germany, as the agreement that constituted its invitation to function there had been with SHAEF, and SHAEF no longer existed. Thus, UNRRA had lost its authorization. Again, it was unclear who could or should sign a replacement agreement, and it took several months of discussion to determine a solution. The first alternative considered was to have the Allied Control Council sign an agreement for Germany as a whole, but that was again contingent upon all four members agreeing to UNRRA's deployment in their respective zones. When, in April 1945, the Soviet Union made it clear it was not going to allow UNRRA into its Zone (but did not object to its mobilization in other zones), the British and American members of the Control Council agreed that zonal agreements similar to the SHAEF-UNRRA Agreement, but uniform across the British, US, and French zones, would be the answer.[69] By this point in time, the American military was keen to turn over responsibility for the administration of the remaining displaced persons centres in the US Zone to UNRRA as soon as UNRRA was in a position to assume that responsibility, with UNRRA personnel replacing military personnel in the camps, beginning with the lower ranks, to enable it to draw down its commitment of military personnel as it demobilized its troops.[70]

The details were ironed out by late June. On 22 June 1945, G-5 issued a statement outlining what it believed would be the relationship between UNRRA and the military after the termination of SHAEF's combined command – and it represented a sea change in attitude. The desire was for UNRRA to assume "maximum responsibility for displaced persons operations in the US/UK/French zones of occupation," with the crucial caveat that ultimate authority over UNRRA operations would rest with the US, British, and French Zone commanders. The Combined Displaced Persons Executive of the Allied Control Council continued to exist, but it would not develop new policy. Instead, control over the displaced persons policy had devolved to the zonal level. The hope was that the final transition of responsibility to UNRRA would happen by 1 October at the latest.

UNRRA's responsibilities expanded enormously as a result. The organization was now going to administer and operate the assembly centres and transit camps, beginning on or about 15 August. It would be responsible for arranging the transit and reception of repatriating displaced persons in the receiving countries (although the military would continue to be responsible for the necessary transport and facilities). UNRRA would also be responsible for the operation of a registration service and a tracing bureau for the purpose of locating and reuniting displaced persons, and for supervising United Nations voluntary societies and other international agencies operating in Germany and dealing with displaced persons.[71] By 21 July, UNRRA's deputy director general, Edward Rhatigan, had arrived with a nucleus of staff to set up UNRRA Central Headquarters for Germany, and USFET was pleased to report to the War Department that discussions and planning for the turnover to UNRRA were "proceeding satisfactorily."[72] By late July, in spite of no formal agreement between USFET and UNRRA having been signed yet, the two had agreed that UNRRA would assume full responsibility for the displaced persons operations by 1 October.[73] As explained in a memo issued to the field commanders, they had agreed to extend the SHAEF-UNRRA Agreement until a new one was concluded (it would finally be signed only in February 1946).[74]

The actual transfer did not go smoothly, as logistical problems had continued to hamper efforts to ramp up UNRRA's operations. UNRRA continued to have difficulty finding good people on such short notice. While UNRRA had been able to field more teams (with 332 assembly centre teams in the field by mid-July, totalling 2,656 personnel, as well as a further 754 personnel in reserve at Granville, and 157 UNRRA staff integrated into the military staffs at various levels), they were not the numbers SHAEF had expected. Second was the perennial problem of the lack of an adequate supply of clothing, equipment, and transportation. The vehicle situation had now improved somewhat, in that they had vehicles (if still too few), but these were reconditioned and prone to requiring extensive maintenance due to the punishing conditions in the field.[75]

UNRRA also suffered from a grievous lack of a coherent organizational structure at the upper levels of the European operation. It was not until 1 July 1945 that one could speak of any such structure at all, when Vernon Kennedy was appointed acting director for the US Zone. With the establishment of a Zone Headquarters, some regularity was brought to the relationship, but UNRRA's operations at the zonal level and below continued to be hampered by these offices' inability to secure the needed staff. Those shortages, although gradually alleviated by November 1945, continued to compromise operations.

The situation was aggravated by the demobilization of the military forces in the US Zone that autumn. Now that the war in Europe was over, the troops either were being sent to the Pacific Theatre or, with its end in September, back to the United States. As military personnel was reduced, UNRRA personnel was increasingly expected to pick up the slack, both inside and outside the camps, even before UNRRA had an agreement in place and well before the official 1 October transfer date. Alex Squadrilli, deputy district director for UNRRA's Western Military District in the US Zone, vented his and others' frustration when he complained to Alvin Guyler, UNRRA's director for the US Zone and his immediate superior. UNRRA personnel were expected to step in "even now as they have done in the first phase of this operation: without adequate understanding and support from UNRRA higher headquarters; without the benefits of necessary stenographic and clerical assistance; without the moral support of clearly-defined instructions on policy and, in many instances, without even the elemental provision of a proper uniform, overcoat, shoes, or cap for their personal dress." Squadrilli's office was doing everything possible to give them support, but without even the most basic elementary tools. Moreover, being the office closest to the field, Squadrilli's people were getting the brunt of complaints of the organization's shortcomings that made "the position of many of our people in the field well nigh intolerable." The disillusionment, disappointments, and difficulties in the field were deeply demoralizing for the field personnel.

Squadrilli argued that the combination of a civilian organization operating in conjunction with a military one was "doomed to tremendous difficulties from the start, by the very nature of the combination." The military's lack of respect for and distrust of civilians undermined the cooperative effort. Even if the organization's prestige had reached down to the lower military levels, which it had not, and even if there had been adequate respect and confidence, it would still be a difficult situation. Add to this the weaknesses and failures of UNRRA and "one cannot hope ever to see the satisfaction and pride of a successful well-run operation with high morale and desirable results." UNRRA Zone Headquarters seemed increasingly distant and out of touch with the very immediate and desperate needs of the field and with little sense of the very real physical conditions in which the field personnel operated. There was a deep need for a sharp dose of reality higher up the chain of command.[76] Squadrilli was also frustrated that the military at the lower level seemed not to recognize its obligations to support UNRRA. In mid-October, every Military Government detachment was reminded that "it must serve UNRRA field personnel, whether or not they have actual attachment orders. Documents signed by the District Director or Field Supervisor certifying that the individual is an employee of UNRRA is sufficient to warrant service by Military Government." Nonetheless, too often, the detachments were denying UNRRA personnel the basic services they were due – including access to fuel and supplies, transportation, and accommodations – making the lives of UNRRA personnel difficult and their task impossible.[77] By November 1945, this had been corrected to some degree. UNRRA had now established a functioning administrative structure and a working relationship with the military.[78] It had not, however, been an auspicious beginning.

Chapter Two

Unaccompanied Children

In the chaos of those summer months of 1945, little attention was paid to the plight of a particular subset of the displaced persons population, a group that would become known as unaccompanied children: children either orphaned or separated from their parents and siblings by the events of war. Theirs was a particularly wrenching story. Ranging in age from infants to teenagers mature beyond their years, these displaced persons would pose a special challenge to all who were responsible for their care. Legally minors, the children were without guardians to care for them. As minors, these children did not have the right to make decisions for themselves about their future, nor was there anyone obvious who could assume that responsibility. This basic legal dilemma would shape their lives and would largely shape policy regarding their care and disposition, or more seriously, derail efforts to articulate policy regarding their care and disposition. The situation was complicated enough for those unaccompanied children whose identity and nationality were known, but for those whose identity, and especially whose nationality, was uncertain or unknown (and sometimes, unknowable), determining their ultimate fate was a matter of extended and heated legal and political debate and dissension. In a world in which an individual's place, and legal status, was increasingly determined by one's nationality, the inability to ascertain a child's nationality proved almost paralyzing. The fight that erupted over these children and their disposition, although they only numbered in the tens of thousands, would prove to be a long and nasty one, as the various agencies involved in their care and disposition argued over what was in the best interests of these children. The fate of the unaccompanied children was as tied up in the competing agendas and priorities of these various agencies, as it was in the emerging Cold War.

Planning

Both the Supreme Headquarters, Allied Expeditionary Force (SHAEF) and the United Nations Relief and Rehabilitation Administration (UNRRA) had recognized from the beginning of their separate planning processes that children generally were going to require special handling. Both had recognized that there would be two categories of children: accompanied (those children who were travelling with legal guardians) and unaccompanied. SHAEF was more sanguine than UNRRA about their care, anticipating as it did that the displaced persons population would disperse in a matter of months, including the children. Nonetheless, SHAEF acknowledged that unaccompanied children whose nationality could be verified still would need to be protected until such time as they could be turned over to their respective governments or reunited with their parents. For those children SHAEF anticipated being responsible for their care until they were reunited with their parents or, in the case of the unidentified and untraced remnant, turned over to UNRRA for care and to the Intergovernmental Committee on Refugees (IGCR) for disposition. Until that time, SHAEF directed from the outset, the children were not to be adopted or placed in permanent homes, nor were they to be allowed to accompany adults to points outside Germany, whether those adults were United Nations nationals or otherwise. Instead, the Military Government detachments caring for the children were to maintain and protect them in assembly centres or another appropriate place until they received further instructions from SHAEF Headquarters.[1]

UNRRA's Child Welfare Division[2] had given the issue rather more attention during its planning exercises, given both its proclivities and because it estimated the population of children, accompanied or not, would be both a larger one than SHAEF perhaps believed (initial UNRRA estimates ranged from a million downward to 300,000[3]) and a longer-lasting one.[4] The unaccompanied children in particular were a subject of considerable discussion in the planning undertaken by the Child Welfare Division in 1944. The speculation as to how these children might have ended up in Germany, separated from their families, ranged widely. The older ones, it was thought, might have been deported to

Germany as forced labourers. Many of the younger children might have been put in the care of others because their parents were in danger with the authorities for reasons of race, religion, or political affiliations. Some of the older children, it was believed, were deported from Poland, Belgium, and Luxembourg to Germany. It was also expected that unaccompanied children would be found ("uncovered" was the term used) who were born of unions between United Nations nationals and enemy nationals, and that many of these would be children who were unwanted, uncared for, and very likely abandoned by both parents.[5]

UNRRA recognized that few of these children, whether accompanied or unaccompanied, would be repatriated immediately, so they would require care for the interim. At its most elemental, UNRRA would be responsible for their most basic needs: food, shelter, and clothing. The assumption was that the children would also require much in the way of special counselling services. They were expected to exhibit serious behavioural problems as a result of having "little behind them in the way of normal family or home life or of steady reassuring experience in an environment where they feel safe and wanted" – problems such as delinquency, improper socialization, difficulties adjusting to postwar society, emotional issues, and physical developmental difficulties. The objective was to ensure that the period of care at an UNRRA assembly centre be a "constructive experience and ... every opportunity for expediting restoration of normal growth and development ... fully utilized."[6]

Note that UNRRA, from the start, was assuming responsibility for both the children's physical and psychological care. This was based on the assumption that the adult displaced persons population would be dealing with serious socialization and psychological problems of its own and so would be in no condition to care for its children. Care for the children had to take into consideration the lack of a stable larger community.[7] However, this did not mean the removal of children from their families. UNRRA was determined that family units, when they existed, were to be preserved, unless the child's circumstances in that unit were dire. Support for accompanied children would be provided through and to the family unit. Unaccompanied children, however, would require special facilities where they could be gathered together, registered, housed, and provided counselling as needed, while their families were traced.[8]

UNRRA's ultimate objective was to reunite the unaccompanied children with their families at the earliest possible moment. If that proved impossible, then it would return the children to their respective national governments as soon as circumstances permitted. As made clear in the training material created in 1944 for the Welfare Division's welfare workers, "No effort is too great to ensure that every child has the opportunity of being restored to his own people and country, and that no child is determined to be stateless or left dependent in enemy territory, whose nationality can possibly be determined and repatriation effected."[9]

From the beginning, it was understood that restoring a child to its family in the chaos that would be the immediate postwar period would be a challenging task. Martha Branscombe, initially chief of the Child Welfare Section of UNRRA Central Headquarters, in Washington, DC, and then of the European Regional Office in London, quickly came to that conclusion in late 1944 while developing protocols for the identification and registration of children, as well as for locating the parents or relatives of unaccompanied children. Branscombe, for one, believed that it was a very real possibility that, in the cases of many of these children, there would be little or no documentation, and so their identities would be unknown and information about their families, nationality, and status scant.

Children accompanied by an unrelated adult would be in a particularly precarious legal position, she worried. After all, if the adult decided he or she wanted to keep the child, there was little that could be done to prevent it, unless some alternate form of guardianship was established. Branscombe wanted some body established that would protect the child's right to be reunited with its parents and its parents' rights to the return of their child. Without this, it was unclear exactly who had the authority to make decisions for an unaccompanied child in UNRRA's care. Interestingly, Branscombe did not actually want UNRRA to be that body (she did not think it was a good idea, given UNRRA's temporary nature), but did insist that someone had to.[10]

Nationality was recognized from the start as a crucial question in the context of the ultimate disposition of the displaced persons children. The nationality of accompanied children, those in the care of at least one close relative, was considered to be straightforward. The various national governments' laws accommodated the various combinations and permutations possible in this situation. However, the issue of determining the nationality of unaccompanied children was more challenging, although the degree of complexity was not recognized this early on. Ultimately, nationality lay at the heart of the question of what do with those children who had been separated from their families, either permanently (as orphans) or temporarily (having been separated from them by the war). As legal minors and thus not permitted to take legal responsibility for themselves – in spite of having survived the war on their own – nationality would determine the care and "disposition" of unaccompanied children (to use the term of the moment). Thus, the key questions were: How were these children's nationalities to be determined? Who was to make the final ruling on that nationality? Who was to act as their legal guardian (which was also a function of nationality)? And how would those children whose nationality could not be determined be handled? Not many in authority were terribly concerned, yet – but a few, like Martha Branscombe, were becoming so.

In March 1945, the Welfare Division released its *Welfare Guide: Services to United Nations Nationals Displaced on Germany*, UNRRA's most comprehensive statement of its planning and policies to date. The *Welfare Guide* included a special section (Section D) devoted to Children's Services, which outlined a comprehensive process for the registration of each child that came into the Welfare Division's care, for this would be crucial to the process of tracing relatives.[11] The *Welfare Guide* also reaffirmed what the Welfare Division understood its responsibilities to be regarding unaccompanied children: to reunite each child with its family if at all possible or to return the child to its homeland, in the event that its family could not be located. This would, of course, require the determination of the child's nationality or, at a minimum, its citizenship – not necessarily the same thing.

The matter of unaccompanied children was becoming increasingly urgent as the Allies moved into Germany. On 11 April 1945, the Displaced Persons Branch of G-5 SHAEF released a statement that large numbers of children were being uncovered, and it estimated that there could be over ten thousand unaccompanied children among the displaced persons population in Germany. Branscombe immediately wrote to Sir George Reid, the director of UNRRA's Welfare Division, urging him to take steps to ensure that child welfare specialists were assigned to all schemes dealing with the care and protection of such children, and that Aleta Brownlee be attached to the UNRRA field headquarters staff as principal child welfare specialist. Brownlee was a woman with considerable competence in the field, Branscombe explained, and would be invaluable.[12] She also suggested that a child welfare specialist be attached to each Army Group, in addition to the area welfare officer already assigned. Finally, Branscombe pushed for the creation of a corps of child welfare workers who would be ready for immediate assignment to assembly centres or other points where children were being cared for.[13]

Events, however, threatened to eclipse Branscombe's and the Welfare Division's plans. The care of unaccompanied children had quickly become complicated as the military moved into Germany. SHAEF's policy regarding their care was abandoned in the anarchy of the moment. Instead, the children got caught up in SHAEF's drive to resolve the displaced persons problem quickly and the devolution of handling the displaced persons to the forces in the field. Disturbing rumours circulated about movements of children being arranged by the military forces in the field without consulting any branch of UNRRA, and in direct contravention of SHAEF's own directives. For example, on 14 July 1945, United States Forces, European Theater (USFET) requested authority from SHAEF to move approximately 140 Polish teenagers to Rome from the US Zone, 3rd Army Area. These boys had been taken prisoner by the Germans after the Warsaw Uprising of 1944. USFET had heard that the Poles had established the equivalent of a high school in Rome, and it was thought this would allow the youths to continue their education. There was a quick response back, indicating that no one at SHAEF knew of such a school and that the matter was under investigation by Polish authorities in Rome. Meanwhile, the boys should stay put.[14] On 20 July, 3rd Army G-5 requested clearance from USFET to transfer fifteen hundred schoolchildren from Mittenwald to Recklinghausen in Germany where, they were told by the local Red Cross workers, the local Military Government detachment was willing to take them in.[15] On 13 July, G-5 at USFET Headquarters got a request from the Netherlands that thirty Dutch children en route to Switzerland from Theresienstadt concentration camp in Czechoslovakia be allowed to remain in Switzerland temporarily for health reasons.[16] USFET Headquarters also received a request from the Belgian government for permission to send three Belgian officers into Germany to search for a group of seven hundred Belgian children who had been on holiday in southern Germany prior to the outbreak of the war, and to arrange their repatriation, if found.[17] The ad hoc solutions proposed reflected SHAEF's attitude towards the displaced persons in general, namely, that all the displaced persons were going to return home immediately, including the children, and a lack of apparent alternatives, as UNRRA had not yet been mobilized. The result was that UNRRA's Child Welfare Division was being eclipsed by events, as control over the disposition of these children slipped from its grasp.

Temporary Care Programs

Contributing to UNRRA's marginalization was the quick emergence of an initially more attractive alternative to its mobilization: a number of temporary care programs outside of Germany that became available that summer. These would have the double benefit, from the perspective of SHAEF, of getting the children the care they needed, while removing them from Germany and therefore from the military's care and expense. Indeed, in June 1945, contrary to its earlier instructions, SHAEF had ordered that all unaccompanied children under the age of seventeen be evacuated from Germany and given temporary asylum in Allied or neutral countries. The Displaced Persons Division of UNRRA, surprisingly, had concurred. Sending the children for care outside of Germany would "drain off" children from the camps in Germany, reducing UNRRA's responsibilities and expenses. Furthermore, as it would be the IGCR that would ultimately determine the children's final disposition after the programs ended, the scheme would establish definitively that the IGCR was functioning, for it had been largely uninvolved and ignored to date. As UNRRA had no facilities for the children's care, the Displaced Persons Division thought it an excellent solution to move them out of Germany.[18]

As early as February 1945, Mr Langrod of UNRRA's Displaced Persons Division, had proposed just such a scheme. This opportunity, he suggested, could be used "for building up and fortifying the young bodies, and for re-adjusting what has not been corrupted by the enemy beyond any hope of remedy." This could not be done in Germany, "where the atmosphere would be unhealthy and detrimental," nor in the liberated countries, which were preoccupied with their own problems. Instead, Langrod proposed gathering up the unaccompanied children and, once they were identified, moving them "to countries most suitable for their asylum, where they should stay until their situation (economical [sic], legal, domestic) is clarified" – such as Switzerland, Turkey, Great Britain, Ireland, Sweden, and overseas countries untouched by the war. There, he anticipated, they could be placed in private homes for six to twelve months, to build their strength and to "adjust," at which point, presumably, the IGCR would determine their ultimate disposition.[19]

This idea gained traction within the Displaced Persons Division, but the Child Welfare Division was left out of the conversation, although the rumours flew. In a meeting on 13 April 1945, those rumours were confirmed when Branscombe and her colleague, Anne Wood, were told that representatives from the Displaced Persons Division and the Health Division were going to Sweden to discuss the possibility of temporary care for unaccompanied children. Shocked, Branscombe and Wood protested that these staffs were not competent in the field of child welfare and that the Child Welfare Division must be involved in any such discussions.[20] It did not bode well for either the Child Welfare Division or the Welfare Division, as they were being neatly sidelined.

There were actually three proposals from private welfare agencies being considered by SHAEF. The Oeuvre de Secours d'Enfants, a Jewish welfare agency associated with the American Joint Distribution Committee operating in France, was coordinating with the French government to bring Jewish stateless children from Buchenwald to France. This plan was far enough advanced that it had been brought to the SHAEF Mission in France for approval. The American Joint Distribution Committee was also working on a plan to move the Jewish children of the Belsen camp in the British Occupation Zone to England. While this scheme was not as advanced as the Oeuvre de Secours d'Enfants scheme, pressure was mounting to approve it quickly. Finally, Don Suisse pour les victimes de la guerre, a Swiss voluntary agency, had approached SHAEF about the possibility of using Switzerland as a temporary refuge for children from the concentration camps.

Benjamin Youngdahl, of the Displaced Persons Branch at SHAEF, as well as a few others at SHAEF, did not share the military authorities' general enthusiasm for these programs. They were disturbed by both the rapid pace at which these schemes were taking shape and by the fact that it was private welfare agencies organizing them. Youngdahl echoed Branscombe's concerns about the children's rights. Before the children were moved anywhere, he argued, the basic facts of their condition had to be ascertained, including their nationality and their identity. As he noted, "In a period of 'fluidity' many things might happen which ought to be avoided," and he feared that things were moving so quickly that serious mistakes would be made that would fatally compromise the children's futures. In a message to Sir George Reid, he intimated that SHAEF Headquarters was not yet wedded to these schemes, but that UNRRA had to decide immediately whether it wished to assume responsibility for the disposition of these children.

The alternatives were two. If immediate removal seemed the best solution, then UNRRA could agree to act as the overall planning agency and assume basic responsibility for the children until the IGCR could assume it. If immediate removal did not seem like the best solution, then UNRRA needed to draft its policies and alternative plans as quickly as possible and coordinate them with the appropriate agencies. While only three groups of children were currently involved, there was no telling how many more unaccompanied children would be uncovered or schemes hatched. The onus was on UNRRA to clarify its position and policies quickly.[21] The implication was that, if UNRRA did not act soon, it would be left out of the equation.

With this and some pressure exerted by the Welfare Division in Washington, the director general of UNRRA, Herbert Lehman, instructed the European Regional Office that it was essential that UNRRA assume responsibility for any such projects, and in order to ensure that such movements were in the children's best interests, child welfare specialists be assigned immediately to work with the military in determining the disposition and care of these children. No child was to be removed from Germany until its status and a proposed plan of care for it had been established. Lehman identified four staff already in Europe who could be assigned to this task immediately (Eileen Blackey, Joan Kain, Dorothy Pearse, and Olive Biggar), and he was prepared to appoint a Headquarters person to take overall responsibility, if necessary.[22]

The response from the Displaced Persons Division was terse, explaining that "qualified child welfare staff" would be used in these programs and that the suitability of the persons suggested by him would be "borne in mind," but that having a Headquarters person assume responsibility would not be necessary.[23] As the director of the Welfare Division at UNRRA Headquarters, Mary Craig McGeachy reported, in frustration, "I cannot say that the Displaced Persons Division has shown much understanding of their [the Welfare Division in both Washington and the European Regional Office] view. But we are courting justifiable criticism if for lack of creating the proper facilities out of the pool of child care officers which have already been recruited by the Welfare Division, we allow 'unaccompanied' children to be taken over by voluntary societies without proper arrangements for supervision."[24] Relations remained frosty between UNRRA's Welfare and Displaced Persons divisions.

In spite of being locked out of the planning, the Welfare Division did all it could to prepare for dealing with the problem of unaccompanied children, including investigating the potential legal problems, establishing procedural guidelines, recruiting the necessary child welfare officers, and consulting with various national governments, who were all keen to have the Welfare Division's help in finding their lost children. The Displaced Persons Division, however, resolutely refused to allow them into the field. As a result, the Military Government detachments in charge of the camps were increasingly turning to private voluntary agencies to make decisions about the children "on the spot." As McGeachy explained to Lehman, "If this situation continues without UNRRA taking any steps to exert its responsibility, problems for hundreds of children will be created, for which UNRRA will later be held responsible."[25]

The Welfare Division continued to push hard to take on the role proposed by Youngdahl and assume responsibility for the temporary care of all unaccompanied children, arguing that SHAEF would eventually ask UNRRA to do so anyway.[26] The Displaced Persons Division, however, continued to believe that the temporary care programs were a good solution.[27] While UNRRA dithered, plans for the children's moves went ahead, without UNRRA's input. By early June, the French government and SHAEF had approved the admission of a thousand children to France, under the auspices of the American Joint Distribution Committee and with the assistance of the Oeuvre de Secours d'Enfants. The plans for Switzerland were moving apace, and a new plan for the movement of another thousand unaccompanied children, as part of a larger move of ten thousand displaced persons, to Sweden was finalized.[28]

By this time, even the Displaced Persons Division was becoming alarmed, not because of the nature of the temporary care plans, but by UNRRA's exclusion from the planning. In mid-June, Fred Hoehler, the director of the Displaced Persons Division at UNRRA Headquarters in Washington, contacted Tom Scott, his counterpart at the European Regional Office, spurred by an article in an American newspaper about a group of 250 Jewish children who had been removed from Germany and taken to France. According to the article, instead of being handed over to the sponsoring Jewish society in Paris as planned, a French government official had insisted on assuming responsibility for them. When the Red Cross and UNRRA workers escorting the children tried to intervene, the French government official ignored them. He argued that "the children were in France now" and would be cared for by the French government. When the UNRRA workers protested, he responded, "UNRRA is to have nothing to do with the children once they enter France." According to the journalist, these children were to be turned over to the Non-Sectarian Committee of Social Organizations of the Resistance, with no thought given to their Jewish heritage and faith. As Hoehler wrote, "According to the article, this will happen over and over again, because of the competition for population among the various governments. Children, it stated, would be a commodity, grabbed off by everyone, without particular concern for the child and his welfare," a prospect that, belatedly, filled him with alarm.[29]

Hoehler was also increasingly concerned by the growing influence of the private voluntary agencies in Germany. UNRRA was supposed to approve all agreements signed between SHAEF and the voluntary agencies and to supervise those agencies, but this seemed to be increasingly a nominal role. If he had to approve these agreements, which he felt he was obliged to do, Hoehler would at least have liked to have some knowledge of the organizations, their personnel, and their services so he could do so intelligently. His division was also being swamped with queries about its "location index." As people began to search for their relatives and friends, they were turning to UNRRA's Displaced Persons Division for assistance. This had caught Hoehler flat-footed, not even knowing if UNRRA was establishing any kind of tracing service.[30] UNRRA was quickly losing ground in the battle to control the care of displaced persons.

Pressure was mounting from all sides for UNRRA to assume responsibility immediately for the unaccompanied children. Martha Biehle, the American resident representative at the IGCR, wrote Hoehler in alarm, clarifying that the IGCR was not only not the instigator of any of the plans, but was completely uninvolved in the Swedish and British plans. The IGCR had been asked to assume legal responsibility for the ultimate resettlement of the children in the Swiss and French cases, but she was adamant that it could carry no financial responsibility. The implication was that responsibility might very well come back to haunt UNRRA, all the more galling as UNRRA had no say in how the money was spent.[31]

Grace Aves, of UNRRA's Welfare Division, expressed her concerns to her superior, Director George Reid, that allowing these temporary care plans to go ahead without UNRRA's involvement would set a very bad precedent. UNRRA's role in and responsibility for making plans for these children had to be sorted out with SHAEF Headquarters immediately, before damage was done. Conrad Van Hyning, of UNRRA's Welfare Division in Washington, also raised the matter with Michail

Menshikov, UNRRA's deputy director general, Bureau of Areas, reiterating the Welfare Division's concerns.[32]

The pressure was not coming from just within UNRRA or the IGCR. There was growing public interest in the plight of European children and in UNRRA's apparent failure to properly care for them. In June 1945, a committee of the US National Commission on Children in Wartime[33] was invited by the American government to review UNRRA's operations vis-à-vis these children. It consulted widely across UNRRA (the Welfare, Health, Displaced Persons, and Food divisions), as well as with the United Nations Interim Commission on Food and Agriculture, and the US president's War Relief Control Board. In the end, the National Commission expressed its confidence in UNRRA's approach to the complex problems facing it, but took the opportunity to remind all that the basic international agreements that had established UNRRA expressly required that all foreign relief programs operating in a given country had to be run with the agreement and cooperation of UNRRA. More specifically, it stated that all measures relating to the care of displaced children should be taken under the direction of UNRRA with the advice of qualified child health and social workers and in accordance with policies laid down by such authorities. Priority should be given to the children's identification so that they could be reunited with their families as quickly as possible, and policies should be developed immediately by the highest military authorities and UNRRA regarding what services UNRRA could provide the children in territories under military control.[34]

The review brought the issue even further into the public eye and elicited a flurry of inquiries from the media regarding UNRRA's child welfare activities and especially about the needs and problems of displaced children. UNRRA's current practices were not standing up well to external scrutiny.[35] Nor were they standing up to internal scrutiny. Fred Hoehler himself was subjected to some pointed questions from Merrill Rogers, chief of UNRRA's Writers Section, who wanted to know whether "the conflicts of jurisdiction and administration of repatriation" had been resolved – an allusion to the turf war between the Displaced Persons and Welfare divisions. Hoehler obfuscated, arguing there were no conflicts of jurisdiction, but that the situation was complicated.[36]

The scrutiny went beyond just the public relations staff in UNRRA. By this time, the General Council of UNRRA was also concerned, and its Standing Technical Committee of Welfare struck a Working Committee on Children to do its own review of existing policies and operations relating to the welfare of children. The Working Committee's frustrations with the state of affairs were several. First, the reporting from the field in Germany was abysmal, so poor that it was not even clear how many child welfare specialists were available or deployed. Second, while policies and procedures for caring for unaccompanied children ostensibly had been worked out jointly by the European Regional Office and SHAEF's G-5 Division, it was not clear whether they were being implemented. The Working Committee reiterated the Welfare Division's position that UNRRA had an obligation to provide welfare services for victims of war, which especially included children. Key was to conclude an agreement with SHAEF that would clarify UNRRA's role and allow it to assume responsibility for the children's temporary care.[37]

Faced with a looming public relations fiasco, and the realization that the temporary care programs were not adequately protecting the children's interests (he seems to have been quite shaken by what happened in France), as well as serious censure from the highest levels within his own organization, Fred Hoehler admitted defeat. On 26 June, he suggested to Commander Jackson, deputy director general of UNRRA, that UNRRA assume responsibility for unaccompanied children.[38] By early July, UNRRA had taken control of the four temporary care projects under development. Initially, UNRRA was content to make use of the programs, as they offered a short-term solution to a difficult situation. At this point, UNRRA had few child welfare staff on the ground in Germany, and the facilities at their disposal were quite rudimentary. These programs still appeared to be a good alternative, as long as they were brought under UNRRA's management.

Of the four temporary care programs under consideration, the Swiss program was the most advanced. The Swiss terms were simple, if rather restrictive. Don Suisse pour les victimes de la guerre, with assistance from the Swiss Red Cross, was willing to grant temporary asylum to a maximum of two thousand children, preferably under the age of twelve, drawn from among those "most urgently in need of rehabilitative services." (The Swiss did not want adolescents because they felt they did not have enough suitable staff to deal with them.) They would take children from any country, race, and religion for a maximum of six months, although Don Suisse was willing to extend the time period in exceptional circumstances. Don Suisse preferred unaccompanied children, but agreed to consider both children accompanied by parents and those whose parents granted permission for them to go to Switzerland. It was also agreed that the entire plan for the children's care and resettlement would be subject to the supervision and approval of UNRRA and that UNRRA would remain responsible for the children's final disposition.[39]

The first group of 81 boys arrived in Switzerland from Buchenwald, which was located in the British Zone (these programs were not necessarily specific to a particular occupation zone) on 25 June; a second transport of 110 arrived on 27 June, with other transports following quickly. The first group's arrival went relatively smoothly, but the second shocked the Swiss, as the boys were mostly over sixteen years old. At least 48 were over seventeen years of age, and the ages of 79 were, in the words of the Swiss, "doubtful."[40] Relations between Don Suisse and UNRRA swiftly deteriorated from that point on. Don Suisse accused the UNRRA personnel at the originating camp of falsifying the documents of many children in order to hide their age and of sending children too ill to be taken care of in the program and instead requiring hospitalization. Of the young men from the transports, 190 were put into detention in Bad-Gurnigel, where they were placed under the care of the Swiss military. Once their quarantine period was over, UNRRA was informed, all those born before 1 July 1928 were going to be turned over to the police for repatriation to the German border, where they would be dumped unceremoniously. Don Suisse rather drily suggested that UNRRA might want to make preparations for meeting the youths there.[41]

C.H. Alspach, the displaced persons representative in Geneva for UNRRA and the initial respondent to Don Suisse, was as unimpressed with the Swiss. Rather cavalierly, Alspach dismissed their protests over the children's age, arguing that it would be impossible to find that many truly unaccompanied children who were under the age of twelve, and that many such came with older siblings, from whom they could not be separated.[42] He, in turn, protested that the Jewish children in detention were being refused the opportunity to practise their religion, as well as access to Swiss Jewish agencies, and he demanded that this change.[43] Alspach found it alarming that it was the Swiss federal police who controlled the children's handling in Switzerland, not Don Suisse.[44]

The UNRRA field workers who had been involved in the transport, for their part, bristled at the Swiss criticism of their work. Hansi Pollak, who had been the one most closely involved in the operation, was furious at Don Suisse's condemnation. She pointed out that it was Don Suisse's representative, Sister Kasser, who had done the selection and screening of the children, and it was she who had selected the 304 children for the train. There had been considerable urgency to get the transport out, as the Russians were scheduled to occupy the area within five days, and a train (which was not easy to arrange given the shortage of rolling stock) had come available, although Sister Kasser had seemed oblivious to the urgency. When more children showed up for the transport than expected, her solution had been to rescreen all the children individually before allowing them on the train, further delaying the transport. When Pollak and the other UNRRA workers had offered to help, she had refused their assistance.[45] For her part, Dr Marianne Flügge-Oeri of Don Suisse was annoyed by Alspach's flippant dismissal of their concerns and unsympathetic to Pollak's indignation.[46]

After a month of brittle negotiations, two UNRRA representatives, Dr R.L. Coigny and Grace Aves, met with the Swiss authorities and representatives of Don Suisse (Mr Olgiati and Dr Lindt), among others, in late August 1945 to repair relations. It was agreed at the meeting that "after apologies on both sides ... the best thing was to forget the deplorable incidents which had arisen in the past." When Don Suisse asked UNRRA whether it would remove those in police custody from Switzerland, Coigny replied that UNRRA would do so if that is what the Swiss government wanted, but as these youths were going to Palestine soon, he asked whether it would be possible to leave them in Switzerland until then. The police finally agreed to allow these youths "to stay exceptionally for convalescence purposes," but made it clear that future transports had to strictly observe the terms of the initial agreement. As a result, Coigny and Aves left Switzerland optimistic that relations had been repaired and the way paved for more transfers.[47] Indeed, Don Suisse confirmed that it was willing to take the remaining 1,650 children, but in accordance with the conditions of the original 4 June agreement, the children had to be twelve years of age or younger and with a well-defined nationality; they would only be allowed to stay in Switzerland for a total of six months; and Don Suisse was to be informed at least twelve days before the convoy's arrival of the number, age, sex, and state of health of all children on the transport.[48]

Then things got messy. When Don Suisse's representatives arrived in Munich on 30 October to escort the next transport of children to Switzerland, they refused to take them, complaining that they did not meet the requirements that had been set by Don Suisse. So the escorts returned to Switzerland without the children, to the dismay of UNRRA's people. Colonel Charles Schottland, assistant director of relief services for UNRRA Germany, spent the next two weeks trying to sort out what had gone wrong. As best he understood it, the selected children had been cleared by Don Suisse, and the escorts' objections were just wrong. Schottland complained that their unjustified refusal had caused considerable inconvenience and unnecessary expense, and he pushed Don Suisse to sort things out with the escorts at their end. When they had done so, they were to let him know, so that the fiasco would not be repeated yet again.[49] Schottland was unaware that Don Suisse meanwhile had been pushing the European Regional Office for a written guarantee that, once the six months were up, UNRRA would remove the children from Switzerland. Apparently the project's success hinged upon receipt of this promise. On the eve of the children's departure for Switzerland, Conrad Van Hyning had decided that the European Regional Office could neither honour the original agreement nor give the guarantee. When he discovered this, Schottland fired off a desperate memo to Hyning begging him to reconsider, as it would jeopardize what was, he thought, in spite of everything, an "unusual opportunity for good rehabilitative care that these children will not get in Germany."[50]

While Schottland was trying to salvage the transport, reports started to come back from Switzerland that things were not going as well there as hoped. The Swiss seemed unprepared for the children when they arrived and conditions were not what UNRRA had been led to expect. Uniformly, the Swiss were dismayed to find that the children were in better physical condition than expected. They were, in the words of one UNRRA worker, evidently "too healthy, too fat"; apparently, they had been expecting emaciated escapees from the camps. Furthermore, the Swiss refused to recognize the very real emotional needs of the children, as well as the need for both psychological rehabilitation and vocational training. Instead, they were fixated solely on wanting to help "more needy children," that is, those with physical deficiencies. The Swiss did not abuse the children, but they did not know what to do with them. The priest responsible for the older children was particularly flummoxed and inept in dealing with his charges.

It was also unclear just exactly who was supposed to be caring for the children. Various Jewish organizations in Switzerland had lobbied Don Suisse for guardianship of the Jewish children, to which Don Suisse had agreed. However, the resulting organization created by the Jewish community, called Hilfe und Aufbau, soon disintegrated in the face of divisions within the Jewish community. This meant that the care of the children was being shared by the Jewish community, Don Suisse, and the Red Cross. Increasingly, the feeling among UNRRA's welfare people was that they could do a better job of caring for the children in the children's centres in Germany that they were establishing than in the Swiss facilities. It was also becoming increasingly clear to the field officers that those in UNRRA's Washington office and the European Regional Office who were planning these moves were giving little thought either to the children's very special needs, or to the close relationships with social workers, teachers, and fellow children formed in the children's centres in Germany and now being sundered, and even less to what would happen to the children after they arrived in Switzerland. In short, it did not appear that Switzerland was any great improvement.[51]

At the same time, a temporary care program in England was taking shape. Since May 1945, the American Joint Distribution Committee had been working to bring Jewish unaccompanied children to England for care. The children in the Belsen concentration camp in particular were a priority, given the horrific conditions in which they had been found.[52] Initially, the government of Great Britain had agreed to allow a maximum of a thousand children aged up to fourteen years into Britain.[53] By September, the program had been narrowed somewhat. The children were required to have been in a concentration camp and be under the age of sixteen by the time they arrived in England. They had to have, or to believe they had, relatives in England, the United States, Western Europe, or Palestine, or be complete orphans. They would be allowed to stay in England for a maximum of two years before being required to move to another country, unless they could be reunited with family in England. No child with mental challenges or active tuberculosis was eligible for the program. The plan was to bring 150 to England from the British Zone in three moves: on 15 October, 29 October, and 12 November 1945.[54]

The first transport from Belsen finally happened on 30 October, although it almost did not occur. By late October, considerable opposition to the move had mobilized. The official objection of the Zionists in Belsen itself was that, given the British attitude towards the Jews and Palestine, they did not trust the British to care for the children properly. The president of the Jewish Relief Committee (one of the camp committees) stated flatly that he "denied that the British Military Authorities had the moral right to determine whether unaccompanied children of displaced persons might go, and that the remaining Jewish children in Europe belonged to the Jewish people." There was some sense among the UNRRA workers that it was also because they feared that, once in

England, the children would be absorbed into English homes and never get to Palestine. There was increasing pressure from outside the camp, too, from the Central Committee of Liberated Jews in Bavaria in particular, who insisted that none of their group should be resettled until Palestine was opened to all Jews wishing to go there. The anger and discord ran deep throughout the camps and, in at least one instance, had resulted in violence and the destruction of important records. While the 15 October movement did happen (on October 30, however), it was unclear whether either of the remaining two moves would.[55]

By this time, UNRRA's staff had become increasingly disenchanted with the idea of temporary care abroad, either in England or Switzerland. Besides the frustrations already discussed, they were having difficulty coming up with enough children who met the stringent conditions imposed by the various recipient countries.[56] Second, although some children had been found who might qualify, many of the children were resistant to the plan, as too, were the staff in the assembly centres and children's centres. These children had established relationships with the social workers, as well as with the teachers and the other children at the centres in which they had been housed in Germany, which was something not to destroy without significant cause. The age requirement often meant breaking up groups that had been together for a long time and were very close. There was also concern about the quality of care and food the children were receiving in Switzerland, a country rumoured to be suffering food shortages. At least in Germany, the children were displaced persons and thus received special consideration in the distribution of food. (At this time, displaced persons were granted generous rations, greater than those allotted to the Germans.) No one had a good sense of what the living conditions would be like in the host countries, nor of the quality of the care (although Gwen Chesters, an UNRRA child welfare specialist, had recently visited Switzerland and was pleased by what she saw), nor of the adequacy of the staff, both in numbers and calibre.[57]

Finally, the growing role of liaison officers was making it increasingly difficult to find children for these temporary care programs. The increasing power of the liaison officers, gratis SHAEF, meant that no child could be put into a temporary care program without the approval of their respective national liaison officer. This added yet another layer of complexity to the process, by adding another layer of review. It also complicated the selection of children for the programs, as certain liaison officers forbade the movement of their children outside of Germany – the Soviet liaison officers, in particular. Yugoslavia was especially fussy about which of "its" children it would let go abroad, insisting on its right to review each case individually before granting approval.[58]

The Polish situation was particularly complicated. The Communist regime in Warsaw, by now recognized diplomatically as the legitimate government of Poland, objected to the programs, especially the British one, and was slow to give UNRRA any direction at all. In October, Warsaw finally announced that, while it would allow Jewish Polish children to go to England, it would not allow non-Jewish Polish children to do so. Although it was not concerned with what happened to the Jewish children, Warsaw was determined to keep non-Jewish Polish children out of the hands of the London Poles (the remnants of the wartime and anti-Communist Polish government in exile), and if they were allowed to go to England, there was a very real possibility that they would never return to Poland. On the other hand, Warsaw was willing to allow Polish children, Jewish or not, to go to Switzerland for a short time, as long as it was involved in the development of their long-term plans.[59]

The situation had become too complicated, for too little obvious benefit to the children. As of 28 November 1945, the temporary care programs were cancelled, other than the one movement of seven hundred children already scheduled to go to the United Kingdom. The European Regional Office had decided that it needed to revisit the whole matter of temporary care abroad and to reassess "UNRRA's total responsibility for unaccompanied children and what policies were needed in order to fulfil it," finally acknowledging the importance of "proper safeguards in the selection of children, guardianship, and continuing responsibility for their care" – concerns that had been voiced repeatedly in the field, but until now, ignored. Until this was sorted out, no children were to leave Germany for either temporary or permanent care.[60]

The temporary care programs proved a failure in terms of finding a solution to the children's care; however, they did at least establish the legitimacy of child welfare and end the turf war between the Displaced Persons and Welfare divisions. In addition, the importance of access to the expertise of the Child Welfare Division had been recognized. Ten welfare officers were now in the field, operating in a supervisory capacity at an area level, three of whom had "outstanding experience in the field of child welfare." In anticipation of assuming full responsibility for the displaced persons operations in Germany on 1 October 1945, UNRRA's operations in Germany were being fleshed out and the people being brought forward to run the German operations recognized the importance of child welfare matters.[61] At the same time, child welfare personnel became increasingly interested in child search.

Child Search – Trial

Initially, in spite of all the planning, and with the exception of the temporary care programs, little attention had been paid to unaccompanied children. Since UNRRA's mobilization in July 1945, the energies of both SHAEF and UNRRA had been focused on setting up camps and assembly centres for the entire displaced persons population and meeting the most basic needs of this constantly changing and shifting population, as well as on the repatriation of the millions of displaced persons. Due to the constant turnover in camp populations and the "resultant pressure of work," there had been little effort made even to register the displaced persons in any kind of an organized fashion. Thus, no one had any idea how many displaced persons there were, let alone how many children there were in the camps, accompanied or not. The exact composition of the displaced persons population was only vaguely understood, based on impressions, not precise data. Nor had much thought been given to how unaccompanied children might be located and identified as such.[62]

The initial assumption had been that all children, like all displaced persons, would gravitate to the camps and assembly centres, so the focus of attention was on the camp populations, with only a foggy sense of those displaced persons who continued to live outside of the centres and camps – the "free-living," as they would soon come to be called. Little effort was made to search out displaced persons, either adult or child. In practice, the UNRRA child welfare workers largely relied upon unaccompanied children being brought to their attention. Under the pressures of the summer and the staff shortages, those children who were so identified were indeed largely part of the camp populations. The first hint that this might be insufficient came with a conversation between Françoise Dissard of the French Mission of Repatriation in Germany and Marjorie Bradford of UNRRA's Welfare Division. Bradford had met Dissard once before, in Paris. This time, Dissard had just returned from a tour of the area under the control of the First French Army in Germany, and she thought Bradford might be interested in what she had discovered in Stuttgart (which was not technically in the French Zone of control, although it was near the border).

The commanding officer in Stuttgart had asked Dissard to make enquiries about children of United Nations nationality in the area. She had visited all the Burgermeisters in the villages surrounding the city and, based on information they had provided, uncovered some two hundred United Nations children in a period of two weeks. Unexpectedly, they were found in private German homes or German nurseries, mostly in groups of four to ten – the children of mothers who had been foreign workers in Germany. These women had left their children with these families and nurseries in the hope that their children would get better care than they would in the labour camps and that, in this way, their children would avoid the bombing in the bigger cities. The mothers often had paid for the children's care out of their own meagre wages. The arrangement apparently had had the approval of the German authorities, as there were records kept, and there had been no attempt to destroy the children's identities. While the records were not necessarily complete, there was enough information to get a name and nationality for most of the children. Disturbingly, these children had been effectively abandoned. Many of the mothers either had died, been moved away during the war, fled Germany in the war's aftermath, or been repatriated in the mass movements in the summer of 1945. In most cases, payments for the children's care had ended with German defeat.

Dissard believed that, given the food shortages and the precarious position of these now abandoned children, it behooved UNRRA to locate and take control of them quickly. The French had moved the children she had uncovered into a special children's centre set up by the French Red Cross. What Dissard wanted to know from Bradford was whether UNRRA had plans to make a similar, more sustained search or whether she should be mobilizing voluntary agencies to continue the hunt. Second, as she was also starting to get queries from mothers who had returned to France and were now seeking their children, Dissard wondered what kind of mechanism UNRRA was putting in place to reunite families. Bradford was very intrigued by Dissard's findings, reassuring her that UNRRA was very interested in leading such searches and was setting up a location index. In fact, neither was happening yet, as no one had considered the possibility of United Nations children being cared for by German families. Bradford immediately wrote to the UNRRA liaison officer at SHAEF, a Mr Edmison, to find out if such searches were happening elsewhere and, if so, how far along they were. If not, Bradford was keen to use Dissard's discoveries in Stuttgart to prod the military into conducting similar searches elsewhere, at least on a test basis, to determine if the phenomenon was widespread.[63]

By August 1945, enough evidence of young children of United Nations nationality in German homes and institutions had accumulated to convince the American military. Plans were put in place for a systematic search for both adults and children in German communities, homes, nurseries, institutions, and hospitals. Burgermeisters were required to compile lists of all displaced persons living outside displaced persons centres, and all displaced persons were instructed to register with their local Burgermeister.[64] In addition, the plan in the US Zone was to canvass all institutions and agencies caring for children, focusing on child welfare agencies such as the Jugendamt (Youth Welfare Office), foster home placement agencies, kindergartens, and nurseries, as well as churches and schools. If that did not appear to uncover all the children, then the search would be continued through a widespread publicity program and a house-by-house census. Each child would be screened immediately by child welfare workers and all information pertaining to its identity, history, and nationality would be recorded, as well as an initial assessment of the calibre of care being received. Based on that assessment, the worker would determine whether the child would remain in situ, be removed to one of the two children's centres newly opened in the Zone, or participate in a temporary care program (these were still operational at this point).[65]

The UNRRA teams in the field moved quickly. By mid-August, almost half of the teams had reported back, and they had uncovered 912 unaccompanied children under the age of sixteen. The teams' excitement and optimism was palpable. In Feldafing, the American Joint Distribution Committee team had investigated 250 reported cases, and determined that 142 were actually children under sixteen and unaccompanied. In Weilheim, a group of 48 children from an organized "Hitler group" had been found; most of them were Hungarian, although 16 or 17 of them claimed to be Czech. As well, a number of Jewish Hungarian children had been reported to the welfare office, including possibly a number of unaccompanied children. In Landsberg, of the 209 children originally reported, more than 150 were thought to be ex-enemy Hungarians (thus not eligible for UNRRA assistance), but they could be repatriated to their homeland along with a large group of adults.

Once the rumour spread that children up to the age of sixteen were being registered with child welfare services (this was the age of majority set in the *Welfare Guide* issued in March 1945[66]), the Landsberg centre found itself swamped with 310 youths. In reality, many were over the cut-off age, some even as old as twenty-one, but their rush to register was a reflection of their determination to get UNRRA's help. The majority of the unaccompanied children in this centre appeared to be Polish Jews, with a few Hungarian Jews and non-Jewish Poles as well, many of whom believed they had absolutely no family left. In Regensburg, a total of 427 children were reported, including a group of 61 Polish boys, aged ten to fifteen, who were being cared for as a boy scout troop in a tent camp outside of the city centre – considered by Mrs Pick, the welfare worker doing the search in Regensburg, to be an unorthodox but ultimately acceptable form of short-term care. As well, Mrs Pick had uncovered 13 Polish and Ukrainian infants in a small children's home (Kinderheim) in Arrach, aged three to eighteen months, and suffering from malnourishment. It was, she reported, unclear whether all would survive, although a welfare worker and a medical doctor were going to assess the children, and provide emergency food supplies or remove the children as their condition indicated. In another children's home, this one in Windberg, Mrs Pick uncovered 26 girls, aged twelve to fourteen, most of whom were believed to be Yugoslavian. These were not all she had found. She uncovered a further 64 Polish children in Bergsdorf; 33 Yugoslavian children in Gergweis; 40 more in the area around Vilshoven; and 57 boys in Engertsham. In total, only 19 of the 427 were in displaced persons centres and only 3 were with displaced persons families outside of the centres. The rest were in German institutions and homes.

At Hohenfels, the child welfare team uncovered 12 unaccompanied children, all Polish. A further 134 Yugoslavian children had been discovered in Neumarkt, although they had returned to Yugoslavia already, as part of a larger transport (disturbingly, the Yugoslavian liaison officer had not been consulted before their departure). Furthermore, increasingly, the teams were uncovering Polish Jewish children who had entered Germany after the war's end, to avoid the wave of anti-Semitism sweeping Poland. Three groups of youths had arrived in one week, without clothing or possessions, the first numbering 69, the second numbering 50. Reportedly, they had been in concentration camps during the war and had returned home with the war's end but were on the move again, fleeing Poland to avoid the violence.[67]

These initial results were fruitful, if alarming. It is doubtful that anyone had anticipated the scale of the problem. Mrs Pick's experience in the Regensburg area was an especially revealing one, if a shock, her success an indication of what might be accomplished but also of the possible size of the problem. In her case, the initial estimate was that there were 101 unaccompanied children of United Nations nationality in the area. Mrs Pick had instead uncovered a total of 427, and this just in German institutions – she had not had the time to investigate any private homes. Given her results, it seemed that a child search operation was both necessary and could become much larger than initially anticipated.

Apparently these results convinced the American military of both the need to find these children and for a more systematic approach to the search, so that they could be either reunited with their families or repatriated. By the end of August 1945, UNRRA and the newly established Office of Military Government, United States (OMGUS) had devised a plan for a more coherent search. The target was unaccompanied children of "Displaced Persons definition" who might be in German homes, hospitals, nurseries, or other children's institutions. OMGUS Headquarters directed local Military Government detachments to instruct their welfare officers to assist UNRRA in its execution. Burgermeisters were directed to submit lists to the Military Government of all German homes, orphanages, nurseries, and hospitals where such children were known to be living and to supply lists of all children of United Nations nationality known to be living in their district, with a deadline. When that information was secured, selected welfare staff would investigate each child. Both a DP2 card (the standard registration card) and a two-part supplementary record form, consisting of a face sheet (a form used to collect the interviewee's biographical information, as well as a chronological narrative record of their life history), would be completed for each child. One copy of the DP2 card would be submitted to the newly created Tracing Bureau, a part of the Displaced Persons Branch of the Combined Displaced Persons Executive, US Army, to facilitate tracing (the term given to the process of identifying an individual displaced person and locating family members). Every effort was to be made to obtain information about the child from all available sources – e.g., parents, relatives, those caring for the child, officials – bearing in mind that it might not be possible to identify the child immediately. All information would be recorded in duplicate, with one copy kept at the District Office and one sent to the Combined Displaced Persons Executive. The investigation would also include an assessment of the child's current living situation in order to determine whether it should be removed or not.[68]

There was a degree of scepticism among UNRRA's welfare workers about the reliability of any returns from the mayors. Some German officials and institutions had proven cooperative, especially Dr Bamberger, head of the Jugendamt in Munich, but others had represented United Nations children as German, either out of fear or distrust, or perhaps even to ensure their jobs. Some families with United Nations children had proven equally uncooperative, either out of affection for the children, or because the children represented a source of labour.[69] The expectation was that UNRRA would have to do some random samples, and where there was a significant difference between UNRRA's results and a Burgermeister's report, investigate further.[70]

While they awaited the survey's results, the test searches continued. Maria Liebeskind, an UNRRA welfare worker, visited twenty-one institutions and kindergartens in the Munich area, as well interviewed a number of children living outside of the assembly centres, uncovering a total of twenty-six children, as well as six others from a list provided by the chief of police in Heidelberg. (His list had had thirty-seven names on it, but most had either repatriated, moved on, or been reunited with their families – not an uncommon situation.)

Liebeskind's findings uncovered complexities to the children's histories that UNRRA had not anticipated. For example, two French children were located in the Heim Jugendland in Schlierbach, their mother in a hospital in "Elsas [sic]" with tuberculosis. The children had been brought to Germany and put in the home by the Nationalsozialistische Volkswohlfahrt (NSV, a Nazi social welfare organization). There were, apparently, four other siblings in Germany – a nine-year-old brother and an eight-year-old sister, both of them with a German family of an unknown address, as well as two older siblings aged twelve, their location also unknown. A Polish child, Alicja Rogoszinskaja, aged fourteen, was found living with a Polish woman, Mrs B. (as she was described in the report), who was not a relative but had found Alicja in a transit camp in Poland, separated from her parents. Mrs B had taken care of the girl since, and their relationship seemed a very caring one. Mrs B had two children of her own, but considered Alicja her third child, and stated that she intended to take Alicja with her when she returned to Poland where she hoped she might be able to find the child's mother, or at least so she claimed.

In all, Liebeskind had found eleven children in institutions whose mothers were living outside the institution, but were still in contact with their children. She also found four children whose mothers had abandoned them and whose institution had been unable to trace the mothers. These stories raised some important questions that had not yet been considered. The question in these cases was whether the mother should be consulted before making plans for the child, particularly on the question of repatriation. Especially, was UNRRA obliged to trace the missing mothers, and if the mothers could not be found, what was to be done with the children? And what should be done with the two Russian children (one aged two-and-a-half years and the other, six months), whose mother had died in hospital from a gunshot wound? As Olive Biggar, a district welfare officer, astutely pointed out when she passed on Liebeskind's memo to her supervisor, Eileen Blackey, the more fundamental question was how much case service could UNRRA provide to the individuals in this group.[71] Sorting out their stories, tracing family members, and providing the kind of careful individual care these children needed was going to be extremely labour intensive and time-consuming.[72]

Biggar's point was well taken and discussed extensively at the district level. The conclusion was that UNRRA had no right to "undertake investigation or planning for unaccompanied children unless we are prepared to provide the case service work necessary." Yet, these children could not be ignored. It was agreed that UNRRA would not get involved in the care of children who were in their mothers' care and whose care was adequate; however, if the mothers requested assistance, that assistance should be forthcoming. In cases of abandonment or orphans, the children were considered decidedly UNRRA's responsibility. That said, for very practical reasons (primarily a lack of adequate housing and supplies), the conclusion was that a child should not necessarily be removed immediately from a German institution unless the circumstances were unfavourable, instead waiting until concrete plans for the child had been finalized. Fatefully, it was also decided at this point that, given the lack of a legal guardian, the appropriate liaison officer would act as a substitute; the national liaison officers would have the final say about any determination made regarding the nationality of an unaccompanied child.[73]

With these decisions, UNRRA committed itself to providing the necessary casework; it could see no acceptable alternative. Unbeknownst to UNRRA at the time, the decision to give liaison officers the final voice in a child's fate would become a serious obstacle for child search and child care in the successful re-establishment of certain subsets of unaccompanied children. These decisions would ultimately drag UNRRA into a morass of policy issues that it had largely been able to skirt up to this point, as well as into conflict with the Military Government.

Chapter Three

Child Search Launched

By the autumn of 1945, the United Nations Relief and Rehabilitation Administration (UNRRA) had committed itself to the search for unaccompanied children, despite the misgivings of some. No one anticipated the scale that the undertaking would ultimately encompass, nor the amount of resources it would require. Nor did anyone anticipate the deep hostility that it would engender. Child search would become a flashpoint, enflaming relations between UNRRA, the Office of Military Government, United States (OMGUS), and various national governments, on the one hand, and UNRRA and the German population and nascent government, on the other. Nor did anyone anticipate the complexities of the issues surrounding this small subsection of the displaced persons population.

Child Search – Germanization Discovered

Initially, it behooved UNRRA to get a more concrete sense of how large a population these unaccompanied children might constitute and what would be the most appropriate approach to locating them. A small number of child search officers fanned out across the US Zone, investigating German institutions and following up on leads and rumours as they came in. District 2 Welfare Officer Olive Biggar launched three test screenings, in Mannheim, Wiesbaden, and Ludwigsburg, where a number of unaccompanied children were found. Other teams in Marburg, Ulm, and the Heidelberg area were also running searches.[1] Jean Troniak alone, another UNRRA child search worker, soon uncovered over 135 unaccompanied children.[2] The officers' approach was a bit haphazard, but the findings were a salutary lesson on just how complex and entangled the children's stories were. A few examples suffice to demonstrate both the tortured routes taken by the children and the challenges both of trying to identify them and of determining the best solution for them.

A group of twenty-two Yugoslavian boys, aged eleven to seventeen, uncovered by Susan Pettiss, yet another child search officer, at a displaced persons camp in Berchtesgaden demonstrates the complexity of the situation. These boys had all been removed from their homes by the Nazi occupation forces in Yugoslavia. Some knew they had lost their parents; others did not know if theirs were alive or dead. All had first been brought to a collecting camp in Osjek, Yugoslavia, and from there sent to Dresden via Vienna and Linz. Some had stayed in Dresden; others had gone to Neuhausen, near the Czechoslovakian border, where they had been used as forced labour cleaning up rubble, or on farms or in munitions factories. Some of the older ones had worked in the regular army, transporting food and ammunition. When the war ended, not wanting to be caught in the Russian zone, they had drifted westward, through a collecting camp at Eer and then on to Nuremberg. From there, they went through the displaced persons camps at Ansbach and Reichenhall before arriving at Berchtesgaden. At Reichenhall, a former officer of the Yugoslavian forces had made himself the boys' tutor and leader, and he was teaching them to read and write. None of the boys wanted to return to Yugoslavia, or at least not at that moment. For some it was a matter of having no family or home to which they could return. Others wanted to get training in a profession first. All were hostile to the new Communist regime in Yugoslavia.[3]

Pettiss contacted the Yugoslavian liaison officer to tell him of the boys, and he agreed to grant them all visas and to work out arrangements to repatriate them. However, he made it clear that under no circumstances would the boys be forced to return to Yugoslavia if they were not willing to go. Pettiss returned in late October to speak to the boys again and discovered that they opposed any attempt to plan their repatriation. They feared the uncertainties in Yugoslavia, especially "in respect to the political set-up." Pettiss suspected that the teacher, who admitted to being a Royalist, was turning the boys against repatriation, although he insisted that he was not trying to influence them.[4] Unsurprisingly, when the Yugoslavian liaison officer visited the boys on 14 November, accompanied by Pettiss, he was met with considerable opposition and open defiance from the boys, who refused to return to Yugoslavia. According to Pettiss, "It became obvious that the children were being propagandized by their professor and a woman who was helping to care for them." The decision was to remove the children to a "neutral" environment, probably Kloster Indersdorf (an UNRRA children's centre), but that would have to wait until another group of Yugoslavian children already there were moved on.[5]

These boys' story was not so unusual. On 20 October, Susan Pettiss found a group of fifty-four children in a German children's home in Kaufbeuren who had been evacuated from Klosterbruck near Oppeln in Silesia on 21 January 1945. The nun in charge of the group explained that they had no documents or identity papers because they had had to leave so quickly, and that they were part of a larger group of approximately three hundred children taken on trucks by the German military. Apparently the children had been divided into five groups and scattered to different parts of Czechoslovakia, Silesia, and Germany. The route followed by this particular group was from Klosterbruck to Kaufbeuren via Neisse, Jagerndorf, Zeigenhals, and Altheide. The Kaufbeuren children were German, Polish, and Czechoslovakian, although the nun was unable to say exactly how many were of which nationality. Language was no help, as the children all spoke only German, although some recalled Polish being spoken in the home. The nun only admitted to five of the children being unaccompanied, all Czechoslovakian. She also mentioned another group of approximately thirty-four Silesian children located in Schongau, living in the Kloster under the care of two nuns. When Pettiss visited Schongau, she found the same situation – no identity papers, no documents, no addresses for the parents, and questions about the children's nationality. The nuns admitted to two Czechoslovakian children and one Polish child, but as Susan Pettiss put it in her report, "How many half Polish or half Czech children are still there? Nobody knows, except the nuns maybe who want to keep their children." She was very sceptical that these nuns really knew nothing of the children's parentage, having cared for them for years.[6]

On 8 November, another group of sixteen children, this time Czechoslovakian, were discovered living in a house in Bad Reichenhall with a Czech teacher. They were part of a larger group of one hundred who had been evacuated during the war. This group had set out on foot with their teacher as the Russians approached and finally made it to Bad Reichenhall. The conditions were so poor there, it was decided that, once they were registered, they would be moved to the Indersdorf children's centre, space permitting.[7]

By January 1946, UNRRA child search workers had uncovered a total of sixty-six hundred children, forty-nine hundred in the US Zone alone.[8] This had been accomplished with little assistance from either the American occupation authorities or the German mayors, in spite of the census exercise, and using admittedly improvised methodology. In the US Zone, the return rate on the census had been a measly 20 per cent. In those areas for which lists had been compiled and where UNRRA workers had been able to follow up, extensive inconsistencies had been uncovered and very few truly unaccompanied children located.[9] Whether the mayors were wilfully not cooperating or, given the destruction of their cities, simply overwhelmed with competing demands on their time and very limited resources and so unable to comply, this was not the route to go.

The consensus was that a more coordinated, effective, and efficient search for children in private homes and in German institutions was needed. This push became that much more urgent after information was received from two sources, the Polish Red Cross and the UNRRA child search officer, Jean Troniak, which suggested that the scope of the problem might be even larger than previously thought, and which helped to explain the presence of so many children who were United Nations nationals in German homes and institutions.

This information confirmed what numerous national liaison officers had been telling the child welfare specialists at UNRRA since November, namely, that a large number of their children were missing and hidden in German homes – through adoption or otherwise. These were children who had been brought to Germany during the Nazi period, often by the Nationalsozialistische Volkswohlfahrt (NSV, or National Socialist People's Welfare organization), initially placed in German children's homes to Germanize them, and then adopted into German families.[10] In fact, the program was much more than this, but the Poles could not know that.

This Germanization program actually had been administered by the Lebensborn organization, a branch of the SS, and was one result of a broader SS eugenics policy initially intended to encourage racially pure SS couples to have more children and to address the decline in the German birth rate since the First World War. These racially pure children ultimately were intended to be part of the rebuilding of the Aryan master race and of the colonization of the eastern reaches of the expanded Nazi realm. Lebensborn was established by the SS to assist in that project by providing welfare assistance to SS families having a large number of racially valuable children and to offer maternity and child care facilities to expectant mothers, married or not, if they could prove the racial purity of their expected children.

Lebensborn was unsuccessful in encouraging a noticeable increase in the birth rate, even among members of the SS, so with the advent of war, its mandate was expanded to include the capture of racially valuable children – children conceived as a result of fraternization between German troops and foreign women in occupied territory and children of racially valuable parents in the occupied territories. These latter children largely came from Eastern and Southeastern Europe and, in many cases, were taken from their parents by force. Others were orphans, having lost their parents to the war with and occupation by Germany. While the Lebensborn organization administered the program, it often turned to other SS agencies, such as the NSV, to assist it in this process.[11] Lebensborn had been a secretive organization and few understood either its mission or its reach. The Polish explanation of the program was only a garbled version of its actual history, but that was shocking enough.

The UNRRA child welfare officers had been completely unaware of it and were flabbergasted to hear that such a program had existed. Nonetheless, the Polish government was adamant both that it had happened and that Poland had lost thousands of children this way, especially from the Polish province of Silesia. The Polish government became increasingly insistent that UNRRA begin a proper search for its kidnapped children and that they be repatriated immediately upon recovery. As J. Makowiecka, a Polish Red Cross inspector for maternal and children's welfare and repatriation, explained to Eileen Blackey, an UNRRA child welfare specialist, the Nazis had intended to completely Germanize Silesia. Part of this effort involved removing Silesian children from their homes and placing them in German institutions and private homes in order to make them "forget their language and religion and be brought up like German children." Makowiecka was clearly distressed that these children still remained in these conditions and argued that they needed to be removed from this environment as quickly as possible. To leave them in German homes would constitute "a danger from the national point of view and still in the largest humanity scale [sic]."[12]

The Polish Red Cross organization had compiled a list of the names of children who had been taken and Makowiecka offered to assist in their location and repatriation.[13] Makowiecka claimed, in fact, to have already uncovered twenty-five children near Munich whose parents had been located in Poland, part of a larger group of sixty-six children, the remainder of whose parents were still being traced (and so were not ready to move back to Poland yet). In addition, there were another seventeen children in the British Zone who she believed were Germanized Poles.[14] That Makowiecka had been conducting her own search was further impetus for a more sustained and vigorous effort from UNRRA; the voluntary agencies were threatening, still, to eclipse UNRRA at its own game. Moreover, it was not just a Polish concern. The chief Yugoslavian liaison officer estimated that there were between twenty-five hundred and three thousand Yugoslavian children in Germany.[15]

At the same time, Jean Troniak and his Child Search Team 566 also had uncovered evidence of the Germanization program. In the process of surveying German children's institutions in the Regensburg area, Troniak's team had discovered a group of children in a barracks located on the edge of the village of Kallmünz, approximately twenty kilometres north of Regensburg.[16] Five nuns ran this improvised camp, with a Sister Serafina as its director. The nuns proved to be openly hostile to the UNRRA team's efforts to register the children and singularly uncooperative. When the UNRRA team initially arrived, before any of them had had a chance to say anything, Sister Serafina had announced that all the children were German and that they would not give up any of them. There were no records for the children, other than a handwritten list of names and birth dates. As the team started interviewing the children, however, it became increasingly certain to the interviewers that many of them were not German. As evidence, they pointed to the names of two of the eight babies, Xenia and Sonia, who they considered decidedly non-German. Other evidence suggested to the team that some of the other babies might be Russian, Czech, or Hungarian. When they interviewed the older children, they concluded that at least one should be assumed to be Serbian, given that he knew some Serbian words and that he stated his grandparents lived in Yugoslavia. Many of the children appeared to be Polish: their parents had Polish names; the children knew the Polish language; and many of them, when they began to relax with the interviewers, told stories of being taken from their homes by the NSV. Initially, when interviewed, the team reported the children insisted on speaking German, but eventually words in Serbian or Polish would come out. When they were encouraged to speak that language, the children's fluency often improved instantly. As one boy, Rudolf, said, "If your father was German and your mother was Polish, the NSV took you away from them and made you speak only

German. I heard sometimes when you had spoken nothing but German all day long, they would give you candy." The other boys agreed that this was NSV policy.

The discovery of these boys seemed to confirm the existence of the Germanization program and energized the child welfare workers, at the same time as horrifying them. These were boys who appeared to have been kidnapped and stripped of their nationality. The evidence, such as it was, seemed to demonstrate that, at least in the minds of the investigators. In hindsight, the evidence was slight and unreliable – the supposed nationality of the child's name, the presence of non-German words in a child's vocabulary, interviews with the staff who were caring for the children, interviews with young children whose memories were hazy at best. It was thin ground upon which to build a case, although this was not recognized at the moment. Nor did the team realize the very complicated nature of the ethnic make-up of the population of Silesia, where Poles, Germans, Czechs, and others had intermingled for centuries. Inter-ethnic marriage was not uncommon, and so it would not have been unusual for people from this region to have some knowledge of the different languages. If these children came from Polish Silesia (which no one, not even the nuns, was disputing), all that was certain was that they had had Polish citizenship at one point. It did not necessarily mean they were of Polish ethnicity. However, it also did not mean they were necessarily of German ethnicity. Neither, in fact, was obvious – something not realized by the team, in its excitement.

The second revelation for the team was the circuitous route taken by the children. When Troniak pieced together their route, it was a spider's web. Apparently, he reported, all of the older boys had passed through a home in Klosterbruck, as had some boys uncovered at another home in Neuhaus am Inn. However, others had passed through NSV homes in Grottkau and Neustadt, each of which might have had as many as four hundred children in them, according to the children. There had been five different transports that ended in Kallmünz: forty-seven boys who came from Neustadt via Pilsen, Czechoslovakia; thirty children aged two to fourteen, who came from the Marienstift children's home in Peicherwitz in Silesia (near Breslau) with Sisters Serafina, Hidelika, and Sofia; eighteen children aged two to fourteen from an NSV home in Liegnitz, Silesia; twenty children from a maternity home in Liegnitz; and another twenty from another NSV home, also in Liegnitz. Klosterbruck had been used for children "whose parents in part still spoke both languages," as the Silesians explained it, suggesting that a

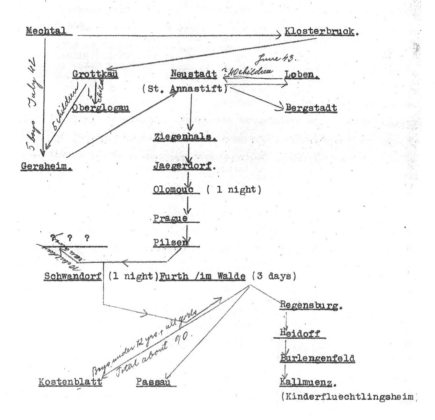

Figure 3.1. Transport Route 2, by Jean Troniak, Child Registration Memo No. 3, 8 March 1946 (PAG 4/3.0.11.3.3:14, I 3.1, Checking of Institutions).

child who went through that institution was not German, but there for the purpose of Germanization, or so argued the team.

As Troniak and his team traced the web of children's transports out of Silesia and Czechoslovakia and into Germany, it grew more and more complicated; see Troniak's schematic (Figure 3.1) for a graphic depiction of the circuitous routes taken, and the divergence and convergence of the transports. Aside from Klosterbruck, other key collection points appeared to be Liegnitz in Silesia and Franzenbad in Czechoslovakia. As other staff from these homes were interviewed, they revealed that there were children of forced labourers from the east among the infants in particular, Russians, Poles, and Ukrainians primarily, at least a thousand of them. As they continued their investigation, Troniak's team grew convinced that these children had been a part, but only a small part, of a well-organized and complex program of transports of children, few of whom appeared to be actually German. The implications were staggering. As they wrote in their report, "All our investigations have centered on only a very small part of Silesia. What has happened to the children's homes in other parts? How much information could we get about the whole Germanisation program by questioning everybody from Silesia who had any connection with the children's homes we now have in our records?" Tracking the Germanization scheme seemed one way of tracking down the lost children.[17]

Based on the information Troniak's team had been compiling over the course of February 1946, there were forty-five children's institutions in Poland and Upper Silesia that had been involved in the Germanization program, and it appeared that over 3,000 children from those institutions had ended up in Germany.[18] By the end of February, they had interviewed 363 children, with another 255 to go, scattered over sixteen different locations around and in Regensburg. The team believed there were in total approximately 1,000 children in the immediate area, based on the evidence it had gathered. Disturbingly, the nationality of the majority of the children was unclear. By the month's end, the scale of the search program was becoming more obvious: 4,843 unaccompanied children had been uncovered in the US Zone, 3,463 of them Jewish, and a full quarter of all of these children had come from Poland.[19]

The prevailing sentiment of many people in UNRRA was perhaps best expressed by Team 556 in its late February report: "If we allow these Germanized children – the cream of Poland, Czechoslovakia and other lands, to remain in Germany and grow up as German children, the Nazis will have accomplished one of their aims. It is imperative that we not allow them this victory. And quite apart from this consideration is the humanitarian aspect, the reuniting of families separated by the war. Either consideration alone is sufficient to justify the whole program of tracing, registering, and restoring these children to their homes."[20]

Child Search – Commitment

By early 1946, UNRRA had firmly committed itself to the search for unaccompanied children. However, it was clear that the Child Welfare Division and its new Child Search Branch were going to have to rethink their strategy, as their existing approach was inefficient and their limited resources, overwhelmed. The numbers of children being uncovered had far exceeded anyone's expectations and the one children's centre, Kloster Indersdorf, was swamped. Indersdorf had, by mid-August 1945, twenty-six children in residence (most under the age of two years), with another thirty to fifty children expected in a matter of days. Not only was it short on space, but it was also short on staff to deal with the enormous caseload. The displaced persons camps at Feldafing and Regensburg had established separate facilities for unaccompanied children in response to the dire need, and a receiving centre had just been opened in Straubing that provided short-term accommodation, but this was still not enough. More facilities were needed immediately. Moreover, the numbers uncovered also suggested that there were many more unaccompanied children to be found, threatening to overwhelm the few child welfare and search officers in the field. More staff was essential.

Based on the assumption that there were many more children to locate outside of the displaced persons assembly centres and camps, it was also clear that the Child Welfare Division and its Child Search Branch would have to rethink their search strategy. Relying upon the mayors to identify United Nations children in their communities' midst had proven a fruitless exercise. On the other hand, visiting German institutions and child-caring agencies, such as the Jugendamt (Youth Welfare Office), Caritas Verband, the Catholic Innere Mission, and the Lutheran Innere Mission, had proven quite successful. Finally, to date, UNRRA had had little opportunity to delve into governmental records, such as police registration lists, identity certificates, birth registrations, adoption records, school records, and food ration records. This, it was thought, could also be quite useful.[21] A more sustained and efficient search protocol was needed.

In late February 1946, UNRRA Central Headquarters released its new "Plan for Location and Documentation of United Nations Children in German Institutions and Families," outlining the new approach to be used in all three western zones for accelerating and expanding the search for unaccompanied children. This plan built on what seemed the most successful procedure – that of Jean Troniak's team. It would mean visiting every German children's institution and interviewing any and all children who might be non-German, as well as the staff of the institutions, and following up leads uncovered from those interviews, wherever they led. The records of both the Nazi regime and of the national governments that had lost children had to be thoroughly mined for names and leads. The plan emphasized the need to collect as much information about each child as possible and, when the documentation was complete, it was to be forwarded to the newly established Child Tracing Section of UNRRA's new Central Tracing Bureau so it could begin tracking down (or "tracing," to use the vernacular of the operation) the child's family.

When a child's file was deemed to be as complete as it could be, the case would be referred to the appropriate national liaison officer for a final determination as to whether the child was of their nationality or not. If the child's nationality was clearly established as a result, the child was to be removed to an UNRRA installation pending repatriation, in order to allow such children to "become re-oriented in their own language and culture before returning home." This would also facilitate repatriation, by amassing the children at collection points so that the necessary transports could be more easily implemented. However, if there was still any doubt, the child was to remain where it was living until a decision could be made about its status, unless the care it was receiving was inadequate.[22] This was going to be a mammoth undertaking – labour intensive and time consuming, as the child search officers sifted through the population in Germany and the records of Europe, looking for clues. It would also, ultimately, put the child search operations on a collision course with the American occupation authorities, with the German population and the Landesjugendamt (Land Youth Welfare Office), and with many of the governments whose children were the target of the search operations, especially those who would form the emerging Communist bloc. Both the February plan for locating and registering unaccompanied United Nations children in Germany and the mobilization of the two teams that UNRRA requested permission to establish in the US Zone, were quickly approved by the Military Government.[23] Both teams were up and running by the end of March, although not in full complement.[24]

Simultaneously, the Military Government launched its own version of a search – a rather disturbing vote of non-confidence in UNRRA and its plans, and perhaps reflecting a desire to resolve this issue quickly and with the dedication of a minimum of resources. Demonstrating a stronger faith in the power of such instructions than UNRRA had, on 25 March 1946, OMGUS issued a directive to the Länder Offices of Military Government, instructing them to direct the appropriate German authorities to provide a list within sixty days of the number of living United Nations orphaned, abandoned, or unaccompanied children now residing in the US Zone and who had entered the Zone after 1 October 1938 and who were under sixteen years of age as of 1 January 1946. The list was to include each child's name, address, place and date of birth; the languages spoken by the child; the parents' nationality, address, names, and languages spoken; information about the child's separation from its parents; the health of the child; and the child's present living conditions.[25]

This was, in fact, the third call for a population survey to be made by German authorities, although the first focused solely on unaccompanied children.[26] For the third time, the mayors failed to comply. Of the 163 Stadt and Landkreise (municipal and district administrative units) in Bavaria, 69 failed to report at all (although the child search teams had independently located 660 unaccompanied children in those same 69 districts). Thirty-eight Stadt and Landkreise in Wuerttemberg Baden did submit information, identifying 276 unaccompanied children of non-German nationality among their residents. The child search teams, however, had already processed 3,000 children from that same region, casting serious doubt on the reliability of the surveys.[27] Too often, what information was received from the German authorities proved incomplete and seriously inaccurate, listing children who were not unaccompanied, German children, children whose names had changed from the lists provided, and names of children who could not be located.[28] If nothing else, the results confirmed the justice of UNRRA's decision to launch it own search exercise.

By March, the UNRRA search in the US Zone for unaccompanied children outside of the assembly centres was well underway, under the direction of Eileen Davidson, the new UNRRA child welfare officer in the US Zone.[29] Troniak's team continued to look for children in the Passau area, in which there appeared to be at least twenty, and very probably more children. The second team fanned out across the zone.[30] By March, UNRRA Central Headquarters in Germany had compiled enough evidence, although fragmentary, to become convinced that the NSV indeed had been at the heart of a Nazi program to import children for Germanization purposes by the hundreds, and probably thousands.

Alarmingly, it was finding it difficult to convince OMGUS of the significance and possible scale of the NSV's operations.[31] In fact, OMGUS's interest in child search was beginning to wane, its focus beginning to shift to other, more fundamental tasks, such as the reconstruction of the German economy and government.

In spite of the Military Government's disinterest, UNRRA's child welfare people continued to dig, asking the War Crimes Branch of the US Army for assistance (which it agreed to provide[32]); delving into the records of German welfare agencies, as well as educational and religious institutions; interviewing children and staff responsible for the children;[33] and working with the Polish Red Cross (which had been designated by the Polish government as officially responsible for the repatriation, reception, and after-care of unaccompanied Polish children), among other voluntary agencies, to collect information from the countries that had lost children in this way.

By May, the UNRRA workers' excitement was clear. The Polish Ministry of Education had agreed to use its records to assist UNRRA. Cornelia Heise, a child welfare officer, was reporting that they had "amassed a great many details about the sources from which children came into Germany, particularly from the Silesian area, [including] the names of dozens of institutions and ... names of persons involved in the transportation and a body of reports about the medical experiments and Germanisation procedures." The people in the Child Search Branch pushed for permission to go to Poland to pursue the investigation from the Polish side, but with little success. Meanwhile, they were trying to compile as much information as they could.[34] And they were uncovering more and more children.

In early May, for example, UNRRA Team 567 reported having interviewed 156 Jewish children and 133 non-Jewish children, including Yugoslavian Volksdeutsche from the Banat.[35] Among these were 21 children found at Kloster Dietramszell (a convent). This particular case highlights yet another complication for the child welfare workers, as a number of the children being uncovered were discovered to be of United Nations citizenship (most commonly Polish, Czechoslovakian, and Yugoslavian), but German ethnicity (i.e., Volksdeutsche). UNRRA's responsibility to these children was unclear.

Of the 21 children at Dietramszell, 19 were thought to be Polish nationals and the remaining 2 were considered to be Czechoslovakian, and in both cases, also of German descent (Volksdeutsche). The children apparently had been brought to the convent as part of a larger group of 44 children removed from a Munich orphanage by a priest who had been upset by the horrid conditions in which they were living. In total, there had been approximately 250 children in the original orphanage, of German, Hungarian, Polish, and Czechoslovakian nationalities. All the children had been taken over by a Catholic welfare organization and parcelled out to various Klosters, including Dietramszell, and to one private home in Pollach, as well as to a few farmers in Beutelsbach. All of these children were potentially of concern to UNRRA, but this meant both tracking them down and determining their nationality.[36] The same team's director reported separately that his group had interviewed a total of 102 children in April in a number of institutions in and around Bad Tölz and Wolfratshausen, and many of them were Yugoslavian, Polish, or Czechoslovak, and likely Volksdeutsche.[37]

As news spread that UNRRA was seeking out unaccompanied displaced persons children, Germans began to report children in their care on their own volition, both private individuals and German institutions. Their reason for doing so was simple. In many cases, these individuals and institutions had been receiving payment for the child's support while in their care and those payments had ceased, the person making the payments having disappeared. It cost money to care for a child, and these caregivers requested that either UNRRA start paying for the child's care or remove the child from the institution or home. This was, for many, a difficult decision. One such child was Bernard Roby, who had been brought to UNRRA's attention by a Mrs Ilse Muller, who was living in Fleck and caring for him. Bernard was born on 8 December 1943 to a French mother, Louise Roby, who had been brought to Munich forcibly, where she had worked in a munitions factory. Not wishing to remain in a forced labourers' camp with an infant son, Louise Roby came to Mrs Muller in January 1944 to work as a housekeeper. In July 1944, the three of them moved to Fleck. On 1 November 1945, Mrs Roby left for France, leaving the child with Mrs Muller with assurances that she would be back in three weeks to collect him. Mrs Muller had heard nothing from Mrs Roby since, and with six children of her own and a husband in the hospital, she could no longer take care of Bernard. She had written to UNRRA in the hope that they could trace the mother or perhaps get the child into a French foster home. She was not keen to give him up because she was fond of the child, but she knew that the mother was, too, and she could not continue to care for the child.[38]

In other cases, it was out of concern for the children's welfare, such as the group of thirty "cripple children" (due to complications from tuberculosis in most cases), aged two to fifteen years, in the Crippled Children's Hospital in Volkmarsen and reported by Father Bolten of the Catholic Church in Arolsen. Eighteen of the children were Polish. They, too, had come from Silesia with Polish nuns, fleeing the Russian advance. In this case, Father Bolten was not trying to divest himself of the children, but seeking medical supplies, blankets, and bed linen.[39]

The Jugendamt offices, as the chief source of care and support for all German children without a family, were especially keen to remove from their care any non-German children who UNRRA would be willing to take in. Thus, the Frankfurt Jugendamt informed UNRRA of a group of forty Jewish children, who apparently had been placed in a number of children's homes in Germany in 1943 and 1944 by Caritas Verband, a German Catholic welfare association.[40] In another instance, the Marburg Jugendamt informed UNRRA of two illegitimate children who had been under German institutional care since birth. In both cases, the mothers were Polish. In both cases, the fathers had been paying their support, but since the war's end, had stopped doing so. In one case, the natural father was known to be German; in the other, the natural father was Dutch. As the mothers were both Polish and the children illegitimate, the Jugendamt argued, this made the children Polish by law and so "the costs for the child ought therefore to be paid by the UNRRA or the child must be brought in a home fitted up for the Poles."[41]

By 31 December 1946, there were 6,526 unaccompanied children identified as such in the US Zone: 5,036 were registered as Jewish, 405 as Polish, 159 as Yugoslavian, and 532 children were identified as "others and undetermined." In addition, by that date, 914 unaccompanied children had been repatriated (most to Poland), 166 reunited with relatives, and 131 had emigrated (most to the United States).[42] However, there was a growing fear that many more children remained to be uncovered, a fear heightened by UNRRA's termination date (then set for mid-1947) being only months away. A January 1947 report by the Landesjugendamt of Bavaria, now finally operational, inadvertently suggested as much. At that point, this Landesjugendamt had 33,014 children in foster homes, with an additional 159,419 under guardianship of some form; 8,334 in various institutions, sanitoria, and hospitals; and 1,824 expellees, refugees, and foundlings. Although the Landesjugendamt reported that, by its count, it had only 198 non-German children in its care, UNRRA was less convinced. Seeming to confirm their darkest suspicions, UNRRA child search officers were still occasionally stumbling across large groups of potentially Allied children, such as a group of 4,000 unaccompanied children uncovered by the team in Forchheim in October 1946, 50 per cent of whom were suspected to be Allied.[43]

It was a race against time to uncover, identify, and repatriate or resettle as many of the still hidden children as possible, before UNRRA's operations came to an end. The decision was made to focus the teams' energies where they were most likely to have the greatest return on the investment of their time – the institutions – especially given that the number of personnel was shrinking rapidly. With the Administration's closure looming on the near horizon, staffing was being reduced and individuals were beginning to look for alternate employment.

It was still believed important to locate and trace children in German foster families (and the welfare workers continued to do so, as well as seek resolutions for those children already uncovered), but all concerned recognized that removing children from these particular environments was "a very delicate job and [would] require their most skilled workers and [most significantly] a considerable investment of time in each case." Better to focus on the institutions, it was concluded, where such complications were minimized. Expectations were also that the review of German institutions could be completed as early as January 1947, well within the timeline for UNRRA's operations, another advantage.[44] Searches of homes would continue, but institutions would be the focus.

Plans were drawn up to facilitate this last push.[45] The Child Search Branch and the Child Tracing Section were consolidated into one operation and tracing functions were decentralized to the level of the zones within the new structure.[46] The care program, especially in the children's centres, was strengthened at the same time. Cornelia Heise was made head of both sections, the new Child Search and Tracing Section and the Child Care Section. The number of personnel was also reduced to fifty, the argument being that the resources could be more efficiently allocated now.[47] This proved especially frustrating for Heise, who found it extremely difficult to maintain the pace of the search in the face of such significant cuts – approximately 25 per cent at a time when they were also assuming the work of the Tracing and Documents Branch. She fought hard to keep her most experienced personnel, but it was difficult. Working conditions continued to be a problem: there was a constant shortage of transportation and especially of fuel for the few vehicles they did have, as well as of adequate accommodations (when the office was relocated to Wiesbaden, most of the staff ended up sharing rooms), messing and supplies (problems that were never corrected).[48] All this was at a time when the volume of records that had to be processed meant that additional, not fewer, personnel and equipment were urgently required, including, for example, typists, clerks, typewriters, tables, chairs, and filing cabinets. There were still, as of early May 1947, lists of approximately twenty-five thousand names to be checked and carded; thousands of birth certificates to be filed; as well as all the records and documents of the child search officers to be sorted and filed.[49] To make matters worse, in the process of restructuring, personality conflicts flared, as some senior personnel refused to adapt to the new structure or to accept supervision from certain individuals. The clashes threatened to undermine the child search program's last efforts utterly and to destroy the already undermined morale.[50]

Individual cases continued to be followed up as they came to the attention of the Child Search Branch. In one instance, Eileen Blackey referred two children from the Kreszentia Home to the Polish Red Cross for investigation. These two children apparently had undergone intensive Germanization in Poland, were evacuated as the Red Army swept through that country, and eventually ended up in the Kreszentia Home.[51]

Mary Meylan, an UNRRA child welfare consultant in District 5, was sent to Austria to follow up on other outstanding cases. Apparently there were several children, thought to be Yugoslavian, who had parents or relatives in Austria with whom she was able to make contact, as well as several cases of children of doubtful nationality, for whom she was seeking identifying documentation. As was not unusual, she was working sometimes from incredibly sparse information. In one instance, a brother and sister only knew that they had stayed in a women's cloister for a year, near a little lake, not far from Innsbruck by train. Meylan hoped that, if she could just locate the cloister, it might be possible to get additional information about the children that might get them a step closer to their parents.[52]

In February 1947, Charlotte Babinski uncovered yet another children's home, this time in Oberlauringen, with 35 children from Upper Silesia who appeared to have come from an NSV home in Pless.[53] All the teams were working flat out to try to find as many children as possible. UNRRA Team 1071 registered 283 children between mid-February and mid-March 1947 (out of a total of 389 checked).[54] On the other hand, as late as mid-February, District 1's Children's Registration Team 1048 had only been able to cover forty-eight of the ninety-nine Landkreise (counties) in its district.[55] It was an uphill battle, and the pace was necessarily slow given the lack of information, transport, and staff.

Increasing numbers of youths were wandering into UNRRA district offices, both from other zones and shifting between districts within the US Zone, looking for opportunities to either repatriate or emigrate to Palestine or the United States.[56] These young men and women, in all likelihood, were driven to register by the news that UNRRA would soon be shutting down. Still others, even after all this time, were being discovered in the regular assembly centres. These included children who had been registered under the names of their informal foster parents – in effect, spontaneously and unofficially adopted – and whose foster parents had come to realize belatedly that they could not continue to care for them (or no longer wished to do so) and now sought to turn them over to UNRRA. In one assembly centre, twenty-five children, identified as Polish Ukrainian, were found in just such circumstances, and all of them had been in the care of one woman.[57]

Even while the individual cases were being pursued, most effort was focused on Czechoslovakian and Polish children, as both countries' Ministries of Social Welfare seemed keen to assist UNRRA. The hope was that this support could be leveraged in some way to compensate for the diminishing UNRRA personnel. In mid-January, Eileen Blackey and Cornelia Heise toured Czechoslovakia, meeting with representatives from the Czechoslovakian National Tracing Bureau, the Child Welfare Branch of the Ministry of Social Welfare, the ministries of Foreign Affairs and the Interior, and the UNRRA Mission in Czechoslovakia. Paul Edwards, now UNRRA's director for the US Zone, followed up with his own visit to Czechoslovakia, where he met with the Ministry of Social Welfare and pressed for a swift investigation of the outstanding cases.[58]

The Czechoslovakian government agreed to do what it could, in spite of its own personnel shortages, if it meant it would get its children back.[59] This was especially good news, as the child search team based in Munich (District 5) had uncovered a number of "new clues in regard to children who may be of Czechoslovak origin," during the investigation of German institutions in the previous two months. A number of children uncovered had come via a typically circuitous route: evacuated from the Stupava Children's Home near Bratislava in early April 1945, arriving in Passau on 11 April, from where they immediately moved to Waldkirchen, then Neu-Ötting, and finally to the Kreszentia Home in Alt-Ötting. More Czechoslovakian children had been identified in

Districts 1 and 3 as well, and their processing was also underway. The hope was the Czechoslovakians would be able to identify these children, in anticipation of a transport in early March 1947, scant months before UNRRA's closure.[60] Time was short.

There was also considerable hope that a number of the Polish cases might finally be resolved. In January 1947, Eileen Blackey received news that the Polish social welfare authorities had found a cache of five thousand individual files of children put into the Germanization program, with full identifying information, including photographs and what were described as "typical Nazi evaluative comments."[61] A frisson of hope swept the child search officers – that this new trove of information might rejuvenate investigations that had come to a standstill and allow cases to be closed. At the same time, the Polish government proposed sending three more staff to join the Polish Red Cross in Germany to assist in child search and care, who UNRRA was pleased to accept, pending approval from the Military Government.[62] Two finally arrived in mid-March, Roman Hrabar and Wiktor Pietruszka, with broad powers on matters pertaining to the location of children.

The additional Polish staff members brought with them not the five thousand records uncovered in Lodz (those remained in Poland), but voluminous materials regarding Nazi practices and organizations, a master list of children whose records were available in Poland, and sample records of individual children. The master list consisted of seven thousand to eight thousand names, complete with ages, places of birth, parents' names, and last addresses. The sample records were amazingly fulsome, sometimes even containing photographs, the German and matching Polish names, and notes on the child's evaluation for Germanization purposes. The files that remained in Poland consisted of six thousand cards with generally minimal information (these had been transcribed to the master list), but which indicated in most instances that the children were of Polish nationality, and also a thousand records of children placed in foster families. In most instances, these, too, indicated that the child was Polish, and this was also recorded on the master list. In addition, there were fifteen hundred face sheets or summary outlines prepared by the Social Welfare Office in Poland, compiling information from case records, some of which contained as many as a hundred pieces of correspondence. These records sometimes gave the German, as well as Polish name of the child, and often indicated the child's destination in Germany. (Later, to the considerable disappointment of both the child search workers and the Polish officials, after more careful scrutiny, it would become clear that records containing both the child's Polish and German names were the exception rather than the rule.)[63] This latest store of information was both exhilarating and, perversely, frustrating, coming at the late date that it did. With mere months left for searching, to have evidence of thousands of unaccompanied children who had not yet been located was deeply distressing for the child search and welfare officers.

Chapter Four

Legal Complications

It was not just a matter of too many children to be screened, too little information, and too little time. As more and more unaccompanied children were uncovered, some special subgroups emerged that required special consideration. They were not numerous, but these children raised serious, knotty welfare and legal issues, the answers to which were not immediately evident but, UNRRA's welfare workers believed, could not be ignored. These particular children consumed considerable resources as UNRRA personnel wrestled with their cases. Aside from the kidnapped children, there was a small group of army mascots – boys who typically had been informally adopted by American military units and, in a sense, treated as the unit's pet or good luck charm. Generally spoiled by the troops, these boys (and they were all boys) found adapting to postwar realities difficult, and they posed a particularly difficult challenge for UNRRA's child welfare workers. These workers were also faced with questions about how to handle illegitimate children, whether of American military personnel (especially challenging were the Mischlinge, or children of black American soldiers and DP mothers), of displaced persons parentage, or of mixed German/displaced persons parentage. The number of children abandoned or neglected was also surprising and distressing, and UNRRA's policies regarding their care and legal status were unclear. More generally, because all unaccompanied children were legally minors and therefore not permitted to take responsibility for themselves, and because they were not going home any time soon, the question of who was to act as legal guardian became crucial. This also begged the question of at what age a child was considered an adult and, not necessarily the same thing, at what age a child should have the right to participate in decisions being made about its future. Finally, and tied to the question of guardianship, there was the question of whether an unaccompanied child could be adopted and, if so, at what point? Who would have to approve such an adoption in order for it to be considered legal, not just in Germany, but in whatever country the child would ultimately settle? To answer these questions was critical. Otherwise, no unaccompanied child could be settled permanently with his or her rights protected. The answers were not self-evident, let alone forthcoming. This left UNRRA's Child Welfare Division and Child Search Branch in an extremely difficult situation.

Mascots

Army mascots had been identified as a potential problem very early, but with the demobilization of the American forces beginning in the autumn of 1945, the problem became that much more urgent. As the American troops had moved through and then settled in Germany, a number of boys attached themselves to the units as unofficial mascots, with the soldiers' acquiescence, even encouragement. As early as July 1945, Eileen Davidson, an UNRRA child welfare specialist, was repeatedly urging UNRRA's director for the US Zone, J.H. Whiting, to notify the US military that UNRRA was willing to take on these children and to ask that instructions be issued to that effect, requiring all army personnel to report such children (who were under age 18) to their local Military Government detachment.[1] Yet, in spite of a July military instruction expressly forbidding the practice of keeping these mascots, it continued, the soldiers taking pity on the boys.

As mascots, the boys enjoyed an especially privileged lifestyle. Such was the case of Michael Goldberg, who came to UNRRA's attention in early January 1946. Goldberg, a sixteen-year-old Polish Jew and survivor of the Dachau concentration camp, had been taken under the wing of Staff Sergeant Patton of the Military Government detachment in Munich, having been "adopted" by the 45th Division in May 1945, when Dachau was liberated. Patton, the messing officer, had taken responsibility for Goldberg. The boy was living with him, although not working for him. In fact, in the words of the investigating officer, "Sgt Patton seemed to have the attitude that since the boy had had such a harsh break in life, he should now get every possible advantage. As a consequence the boy has been given a Mercedes-Benz car and chauffeur and has been free to do what he likes all day. At night he accompanies the American soldiers for his recreation," although Patton insisted that he did not drink with the men.[2]

Pierre Ponthier was another such mascot. By all reports, he was "a difficult boy to handle" because he appeared to have a drinking problem (he had been found intoxicated one evening while in the company of some American soldiers). He wore GI clothes and seemed to be "wandering at will." A military officer, Captain Tippett, had brought the boy to UNRRA facilities in Pasing, having forbidden Pierre to visit any of the enlisted men's clubs or to come near the post.[3] Yet another boy, Bobby (last name unknown), was apparently employed in some manner by someone he called his captain (Bobby was kitted out in an Army uniform, complete with a few decorations), but it was never clear what exactly this employment entailed, or whether it was just a means of escaping the routine at the children's centre where he was registered. Bobby spoke of working in the mess or in the motor pool and talked admiringly of a seventeen-year-old Dutch Jewish boy working there.[4]

The soldiers had promised many of the boys that they would take them back to the United States when they were demobilized, which they categorically could not do. Sometimes, as with Pierre Ponthier, an officer might realize the damage being done and attempt to turn the boy over to UNRRA for care, generally with disastrous consequences. In other instances, as with Michael Goldberg, the officer involved tried to help the boy adjust, however ineffectively. In Michael's case, when Patton received news that his unit was returning stateside in February 1946, he finally approached UNRRA. Realizing that Michael "would be left in a lurch," Patton proposed that the boy continue to live with the troops until their departure, but attend classes at the Indersdorf children's centre, with a chauffeur taking him back and forth from the base each day.[5] More often, the boys stayed with the units right until the moment of embarkation, when they were abruptly abandoned, sometimes literally at dockside. As demobilization accelerated, more and more of these boys were being abandoned by the troops, at which point they turned up at the gates of the children's camps, either on their own volition or escorted by military personnel, without warning.

By the spring and summer of 1946, their numbers had grown. That January the 508th Parachute Regiment stationed at Heddernheim near Frankfurt reported three mascots they wished to turn over to UNRRA: a sixteen-year-old Italian boy, a fourteen-year-old Latvian boy, and a thirteen-year-old Russian. They had been with the outfit for months, but the new commanding officer had decided that the troops could no longer keep them.[6] Virginia Poste, a child welfare specialist in UNRRA District 2 interviewed a further four such boys in May and June. Another UNRRA child care officer, Charlotte Babinski, registered six boys who had attached themselves to army units in and around Deggendorf. Several more were uncovered in Berlin.[7] The American port commander in Antwerp, Belgium, an embarkation point for American troops, finally losing patience with having to deal with the mascots, ordered their removal from the city by 5 June. He estimated there could be as many as a dozen involved.[8]

The alternatives for the boys were limited. In a few cases, the troops' departure was far enough in the future, and the boys were close enough to their eighteenth birthday, that they could be left safely with the army units, the hope being that they would reach technical adulthood before being abandoned, and so would no longer be eligible for child welfare services at the moment of crisis. Some of the mascots, whose national identity was clear, and who were willing, were turned over to their national liaison officers for repatriation. The remainder faced entering the children's centres, generally Indersdorf. It was not an appealing prospect, either for the centres' staff or the boys. Having been "showered with so many luxuries of life," the staff was extremely sceptical of the boys' ability or, indeed, willingness to settle into what was going to be a far more restricted and less lavish lifestyle. The boys, for their part, were often deeply disillusioned by their erstwhile friends who had abandoned them so summarily. Like Michael Goldberg, who was crushed when it became clear to him that his army buddies "could not (and probably did not want to) take him to America at this point," these boys were often bitter and resentful.[9]

Making the situation worse was that UNRRA typically did not find out about these boys until literally the moment of a unit's departure for the United States. In spite of the instruction issued the previous summer, the American military typically was still not reporting mascots to UNRRA until the last moment. This meant that the young men were being dumped on UNRRA's doorstep abruptly, which did not allow any planning to help them bridge the gap between "the exaggerated attention they received while living in the military units and the modest place they must assume in other living arrangements."[10] The boys were uniformly

> unprepared for the jolt they experience by removal from the army units, where they have been the center of attention, to a place where they are but

one of a group. It leaves them confused, resistant to any restrain [*sic*] and routine, and usually looking for an opportunity to get back to the Army ... Many of them, having learned a bit of English, describe themselves as United States citizens. Others rely heavily on vague promises that they will be taken to Amerika [*sic*] or adopted ... Some of their army sponsors are far-sighted enough to initiate correspondence to locate the boys' families or relatives but in most instances the youngsters are left, when the army moves out, with no beginning made toward a permanent solution for them.[11]

From the perspective of the UNRRA child welfare workers, the looming threat of redeployment, the lack of any kind of continuity in supervision or training for the future, the lack of any effort to teach the youngsters the fundamental values they needed, the education missed during the period of the war, as well as the way in which the mascot experience made the boys restless and inclined to rebellion and delinquency meant that life as a mascot was not a good thing. However, as Marion Hutton, acting director of UNRRA Team 182, so astutely put it, when the boys faced a choice between the routine and constraints of the children's centre and the glamour and freedom of a mascot's life, "What we [UNRRA] consider well-seasoned reasoning is to the boy frustrating dribble."[12] The mascot's life was simply too glamorous.

The boys also proved quite disruptive, undermining the morale, as well as morals, in the children's centres and creating considerable problems. It proved almost impossible to establish any kind of rapport with the boys, which made it very difficult to get accurate information from them. They were, instead, inclined to "romance about themselves, and their experiences." For their part, when the boys became too frustrated, they simply walked out of the centre and disappeared into the general population, typically after only a few days. One boy stole another's identity before disappearing; some took other, younger boys with them when they left. Equally frustrating, most claimed to be American-born, having been well coached by the GIs, making it difficult to determine their true identity, which not uncommonly turned out to be German. However, this was not typically confirmed until after they had been in the centres and had "wasted a great deal of [the] Welfare Officers' time as well as been [a] bad influence on the other children." As a result, the centres were increasingly reluctant to admit the mascots to their facilities, and there were mounting calls for some other arrangement to be made for this especially troublesome category of unaccompanied children.[13] The growing sentiment was that these boys needed a sense of "belonging to a group within which they [could] respect themselves," and that the children's centres were not it.[14]

The mascots became a particular issue in Bremen, which was emerging as a major embarkation point for transports going to North America. Bremen grew to be a focal point for mascots, while lacking any facilities for dealing with them, nor was it clear that UNRRA would be able to establish any such facilities given the security requirements in the enclave.[15]

The military police in Bremerhaven, the actual port, reported that they were arresting approximately ten boys daily by late March 1947. That June the Military Government in Wiesbaden, where Bremen was located, estimated that there were between fifteen and thirty mascots in the immediate community.[16] Finally, in May, a "boys' hotel" was established in Bremen for the mascots, although it proved to be no more than a temporary solution and inadequate.[17] Late that September the YMCA established a school for former GI mascots in Wartenberg, Bavaria – a small gesture that did little to address the needs of this tiny, but problematic subset of the unaccompanied children population.[18]

Illegitimacy and Abandonment

Of special concern were the numerous illegitimate children being uncovered. Some were the illegitimate children of displaced persons mothers and American soldiers – a small group numerically, but one with the potential to pose a serious problem in terms of the disposition of the cases. From the beginning, United States Force, European Theater (USFET) had washed its hands of this problem. In a memo issued in early March 1946, USFET Headquarters declared that no individual in the military service would be required or asked to admit paternity. If an individual did so voluntarily and expressly stated that he was willing to provide financial or other assistance to the woman involved, his commanding officers and other branches of the Army would assist him in "effecting those desires," where appropriate. However, in the absence of an admission of paternity, or of a judicial order or decree of paternity issued by a court of law in Germany or in the United States, USFET refused to take any action other than to pass along the complaint to the soldier's commanding officer, who was then charged with bringing it to the attention of the purported father. The memo also stated explicitly that no member of the military service who had been redeployed would be returned to Germany against his will to answer a complaint in a paternity or support case, nor would the American military forces countenance any American military personnel being "processed" in a foreign jurisdiction. If the military personnel had been discharged or released from active duty before the letter of complaint was received, the complainant was to be informed that any communications she wished passed on to the purported father would be forwarded by the War Department, but a soldier's discharge or release from service would not be delayed because of any pending complaint.[19]

Children of black GIs posed a unique challenge. The number of cases was again, in 1946, small – perhaps several dozen. While there were also many such children born to German mothers, UNRRA's attention was focused on those born to displaced persons mothers and the impact of their interracial make-up on their ultimate settlement. As an illegitimate child of a white mother and a black father, the concern was that the child would not be accepted in either the United States or in the mother's home country, which was often Poland, the most common nationality among the mothers.[20] Indeed, some argued that the prejudices in the United States were well known and severe enough that it might be better for such children to go to Poland, where they might be considered merely "curiosities."[21] Initially, the Polish government seemed willing to consider taking in these children and had recognized them as Polish nationals, although from the beginning, it was concerned about the children's future in Poland, as there were no blacks in that country and for that reason, they would be very "conspicuous." The preference of the Polish government seemed to be for an alternative solution to be found, and the Polish liaison officer had willingly approved the removal of two such children to the United States under the auspices of the US Committee for the Care of European Children.[22] By the year's end, however, the Polish position had hardened – that it was better not to repatriate these children to Poland, where they would face great difficulty in being accepted.[23] This raised the basic question: if the child was a Polish national (deriving its nationality from its mother due to its illegitimacy) but could not go to Poland (or if it was not in its best interests to go to Poland), where should the child go? And what was to happen to the child if its mother wanted to repatriate to her homeland?

This was only a subset of a bigger problem, namely, the large number of illegitimate children being uncovered. Many had been born during the war years to forced labourers, concentration camp survivors, and others, and either left with German families by their mothers or taken from their mothers forcibly. Still others were infants, born after the war. Pregnancies among single mothers had climbed among the displaced persons population after the war. In one Polish camp alone, Wild-flecken, it was estimated that there were some five hundred women with illegitimate children in early 1947.

The implications of this were twofold. Although these women were willing to consider repatriation in principle, they would not return to their homeland with an illegitimate child. The social stigma would have been insurmountable (something the men at UNRRA Headquarters in Germany initially did not understand). Thus, illegitimate children were a serious impediment to the repatriation of a number of adult displaced persons. The result was that many of these women, like Bernard Roby's mother, were swift to abandon their children, creating yet another humanitarian problem for UNRRA, to whom responsibility for these children fell.[24]

In still other cases, the mothers were found to be incapable of care, as in the instance of Maria U. It had initially appeared that she had abandoned her eleven-year-old son, Janusz, in the camp at the Infantry Kaserne in Augsburg. As it turned out, she had been arrested upon discharge from the Augsburg hospital and taken to Munich for treatment for a venereal disease, and she had not been given a chance to return to the camp to sort out her affairs before being admitted. She had been absent for two months by the time the child welfare workers became aware of the boy's situation. In this instance, Maria U. seemed genuinely interested in and concerned about her son, as he was the only one of her four children to have survived the war. However, in the words of the child welfare officer, "She does not ... appear to be very responsible and spoke at times incoherently and almost irrationally. She appears a little ashamed of her conduct which led to her present illness but tries to justify herself by saying that she lived with the same man for 11 months although she admits she knew he had a wife and 2 children in Roumania. He has apparently left her and gone back presumably to his family." According to the UNRRA worker at the camp, Maria U. had never done a particularly good job of caring for Janusz, who had been crippled in an air raid and so, in the opinion of the worker, needed special care and training. (The ultimate recommendation, then, was to give Maria a chance to demonstrate that she could care for the boy upon her release from the hospital, but otherwise the boy should be admitted to a children's institution.)[25]

This was not an uncommon concern; neglect was an ongoing issue. In June 1946, Ellen Trigg, an UNRRA child welfare specialist for District 1, reported that her team continued "to be forced to accept tiny infants neglected by unmarried mothers. Three of these infants accepted had been so rejected and neglected that they died soon after they came under our care." Arrangements were made subsequently to admit such infants to the displaced persons hospital for as long as the medical staff thought the children needed their "very specialized medical attention."[26] The growing suspicion was that this at least partly explained the high infant mortality rate in the camps – infanticide being one possible solution for the distraught mothers.[27] There had been, in fact, some "conspicuous cases in which mothers have attempted to kill their children, have given them away promiscuously, or have abandoned them because they could not face return to their home countries with the child."[28] In yet another typical case, a young woman had given birth to a boy as a result of a brutal rape, and she did not wish to keep the child, arguing that she was too "immature and delicate" and would not be able to give him as good a future as UNRRA would be able to arrange.[29] Finally, unaccompanied children were being turned over to UNRRA by displaced persons families who had taken in these children, effectively informally adopting them by registering them as their children when entering the assembly centres. However, as repatriation and resettlement opportunities arose, the families no longer wanted responsibility for children who were not theirs, and so only now turned them over to UNRRA.[30]

Some welfare workers, especially those trained in social welfare practices, had become adept at handling the problem expeditiously and effectively, identifying situations that might lead to abandonment and acting pre-emptively, working with the mother to persuade her to keep the child, or at a minimum, to ensure that the child's records were complete and that the child did not disappear if abandoned. But many of the less trained personnel were floundering. It meant that often little was known about many of these abandoned children, in spite of most being born in displaced persons hospitals, making it impossible to confirm that they were truly abandoned, rendering their status unclear and UNRRA's responsibilities and authority ambiguous. Other abandoned children had been in the camps for months or even years, bouncing between displaced persons families, before UNRRA found out about their existence, making tracing the child's birth family, or even determining the child's nationality almost impossible.[31]

Convinced that "many of these mothers have fundamentally rejected their children and cannot be induced to remain with them," the workers had come to the conclusion that they needed a way of formalizing the mothers' rejection of their parental responsibility, so that they could then find some kind of resolution for their children – perhaps some kind of a legal release form that would work as formal recognition of a mother's abdication of her parental responsibilities, while not compromising the child's legal rights.[32] Ultimately, this option was abandoned. The legal experts considered it nearly impossible to draft a consent form that would be both legally binding and acceptable to the many countries involved. This was, always, a major obstacle to a legal solution for the children. Any legal decision made had to be constructed in such a way as to be acceptable under the statutes of the occupation forces, German law, and the laws of the homeland, a near-impossible task. Instead, it was recommended that, in each case, the appropriate national liaison officer be consulted as to the legal requirements of the particular child's particular country – a non-solution, as this addressed only one component of the potential conflict and did not address the issue of those children whose nationality was either unknown or unrepresented.[33] Those in the field pressed those further up the administrative chain of command for some clarification of how to handle this situation, but with little effect.[34]

Age of Majority

The question of at what age a child would be considered to have reached adulthood was yet another left unanswered.[35] It remained, however, an important one, for it both determined the pool of potential cases for UNRRA's Child Search Branch and had very concrete implications for those youths who may or may not have found themselves able to access the special services made available to children. It also seriously complicated decisions about repatriation and resettlement, for age of majority determined which teenagers' cases required the approval of a liaison officer.

In the first months of operations, the proposed age of majority ranged from fourteen to eighteen, creating considerable confusion. By the autumn of 1945, in the US Zone, SHAEF was using age sixteen as its upper limit. Initially, during the planning stages in 1944 and early 1945, UNRRA had considered using fourteen as the age of majority – a recognition of the children's forced maturity – but there was concern that this would have compromised the adolescents' care. The scientific literature of the time dealing with teenagers and their problems argued that there

was substantial evidence that this group would face even more serious problems of adjustment and resettlement than the younger children
and would desperately need special expert assistance. To let them be
absorbed into the wider pool of adult displaced persons (which is what
would have happened with an age of majority set so low) would be to
deny them that help.[36] Thus, the age of majority set in UNRRA's *Welfare
Guide* issued in March 1945 set the cut-off age for eligibility for child
welfare services at sixteen.[37]

In the end, age eighteen increasingly became the technical norm
throughout the UNRRA period, with even UNRRA ultimately advocat-
ing that age, the logic being that it was "the age at which most young
persons are likely to be reasonably self-directing and want to plan for
themselves."[38] It also reflected the preferences of those national governments that expressed one. The governments of Poland, Yugoslavia, and
Czechoslovakia made it clear that they believed the age of "individual
choice" was eighteen and no younger. The two agencies authorized in
1946 to arrange for the resettlement of unaccompanied children – the
Jewish Agency for Palestine and the US Committee for the Care of European Children – both also used age eighteen as their upper limit.[39] As
well, the American Military Government officially used eighteen as the
age of majority. In its directive of July 1946, in which USFET outlined
the parameters of its responsibility for unaccompanied children and
the procedures for their location, care, and disposition, children were
defined to be those under the age of eighteen. In May 1946, a directive
sent by USFET Headquarters to the field detailing the protocol for dealing with the children's repatriation and resettlement also used this age.
This was confirmed officially a year later in Military Government Regulation Title 20, issued by the Office of Military Government, United
States (OMGUS), which outlined what it understood to be extant policy
as of 1 June 1947.[40]

The policy was often violated in practice, however. Eighteen remained
the official age of majority and the age to which the Eastern European
governments insistently clung; however, this rule was often flouted.
Some agencies sponsoring resettlement projects were using fifteen as
a cut-off age, rejecting older children (i.e., aged 16–18).[41] Washington
and the Military Government had effectively recognized this in practice, if not in their official directives, by allowing persons aged sixteen
and older to apply for visas for emigration to the United States.[42] In the
various censuses required of the Burgermeisters, who were instructed
to differentiate children from adult United Nations nationals in their

districts when conducting the censuses, the age given for children varied between eighteen, sixteen, and fifteen.[43] OMGUS used sixteen as its upper age limit, as in the proposed Allied Control Authority's directive on determining the nationality of unaccompanied children,[44] even while allowing children as young as fourteen to decide whether they wanted to repatriate or resettle.[45] In a 1947 screening exercise, the American Military Government was removing children as young as fifteen from the camps if deemed ineligible for assistance.[46] Finally, in practice, it was not unknown for child welfare workers to allow unaccompanied children as young as twelve effectively to decide their own fates, by refusing to repatriate any over that age, as "most children [were] adults by experience and hardship and ... capable of knowing their own minds at an earlier age."[47]

As a consequence, over the course of 1946 and into 1947, child welfare workers were increasingly reluctant to force youths aged between fourteen and eighteen to repatriate against their will, whatever the insistent demands of their national governments, and were convinced that the American Military Government was as reluctant.[48] UNRRA pushed to have it recognized officially that many teenagers under the age of eighteen, while still requiring special, age-specific care, were also mature beyond their years and were quite capable of making a decision for themselves regarding resettlement or repatriation. These youths had fended for themselves during the war years, and to deny them a voice now would be to try to shove them back into a role, namely, that of an immature child, that was manifestly ill-suited and would only serve to antagonize them. The suggestion was that sixteen be used as the minimum age at which an individual could have the right to choose repatriation or resettlement.[49] Even this compromise was never embraced, and by March 1947, UNRRA was caught in a difficult situation. National governments continued to insist that all children of their nationality under the age of eighteen had to be repatriated. There was a growing number of cases, however, in which repatriation did not seem the best solution for a child. Nevertheless, UNRRA felt obliged to obtain permission for any alternative solutions from the national governments or liaison officers involved for all under eighteen, as the liaison officers had become de facto guardians of unaccompanied children whose nationality was determined. This almost inevitably meant resolution was considerably delayed, as the liaison officers and/or national governments typically took an inordinately long time to respond to specific queries, if they responded at all.[50] UNRRA was hamstrung and the

children trapped – or at least until they turned eighteen, gained adulthood, and could then decide their future for themselves.[51]

Adoption

Yet another issue that created difficulties was that of whether unaccompanied children could be adopted, either by fellow nationals or others.
In May 1945, SHAEF had directed that "under no circumstances should
children be adopted or placed in permanent homes," a recognition of
the fluidity of the situation in the war's immediate aftermath and the
danger of children disappearing into the masses on the move before
there was a chance of reuniting them with their families. When SHAEF
ceased operations, this instruction remained in effect. This, however,
had not prevented children from being informally adopted by displaced
persons families, who simply declared the children as theirs when first
registering with UNRRA. In the chaos of the summer and autumn of
1945, and with no documentation with which to double-check the information, UNRRA officials were in no position to challenge the claims. It
was also not unknown for displaced persons families to spontaneously
adopt unaccompanied children after entering the camps. This was easily done, given the chaotic conditions and lax security of the UNRRA
camp offices where the registration documentation was kept. In a camp
of several thousand, administered by an UNRRA team of perhaps a
dozen officers, the displaced persons simply had to get access to the
child's DP2 identity card, tear it up, and fill out another, declaring the
child a member of their family.[52] It was also not unusual for an unmarried mother to give up her baby to a married couple, either displaced or
German. Often this was done with the connivance of the liaison officers
and welfare workers, who thought this was an effective solution – the
child now, instantly, had a family to care for it. Two examples can serve
to demonstrate the nature of these ad hoc arrangements.

Helene Rokita, approximately two years old and a Polish Catholic,
had been abandoned, apparently thrown out a window by her mother.
All that anyone knew of the mother was that she was probably unmarried; she had completely disappeared. A Polish Catholic couple had
taken Helene in; they were in their mid-thirties and had no children
of their own, although they had been married a number of years. The
husband claimed to be an engineer, and the couple had been taking
quite good care of Helene. They made it clear that they wanted to adopt
her. When the child welfare officer dealing with the case warned them

that the birth mother might some day be found, they offered to act as foster parents instead, until either that happened or it was determined that the mother would not be found. Meanwhile, after ensuring they planned to repatriate, a representative of the Polish Red Cross gave the couple temporary guardianship until they could return to Poland with Helene, at which point they could discuss their future plans.

Second was the case of a two-year-old Catholic boy, Tadeus Motowsky. Both his parents were believed to be dead – the mother certainly – and he had been turned over to UNRRA Team 175. Two Polish women, a mother and daughter, had become very attached to the boy and had taken him into their home, with the team's permission. They now wanted to adopt the child. In this case, the district child welfare officer refused, arguing that the mother and daughter did not constitute a "normal" family. Instead, the officer wanted the child sent to Kloster Indersdorf for repatriation and confirmation of the father's death.[53]

In fact, at least in the case of illegitimate children being voluntarily given up by their mothers, some welfare workers had semi-formalized the procedure. In these instances, after investigating the mother's reasons for abandoning her child and evaluating the prospective adoptive family, the case typically was reviewed by the camp's national committee of the nationality involved, the welfare officer, and the appropriate liaison officer. If all approved of the plan, the mother was asked to sign a release form, which was turned over to the adoptive parents, along with a birth certificate. This was not intended to serve as a formal adoption (it could not), but rather a formalization of a foster care arrangement. The expectation was that the child's adoption would be legalized in the adoptive parents' native country upon their repatriation. These documents were intended to facilitate that legalization. Inevitably, it meant that unaccompanied children were leaving Germany with their new families.[54]

The whole process was disturbingly ad hoc, and several national governments were growing increasingly uncomfortable with the practice. Informal working agreements had been struck with various repatriation representatives, most crucially those from Poland, Yugoslavia, and Czechoslovakia, clarifying what they would and would not consider for their nationals. In those instances in which adult nationals wanted to adopt a child of their own nationality, they were informed that they should wait until after repatriation to effect the adoption, as adoptions completed in Germany would not be recognized in the home country. According to these agreements, adults who did not wish to repatriate were forbidden to adopt orphan children of their nationality (the children were to be repatriated). Finally, unaccompanied children of a determined nationality could not be adopted by individuals of another nationality.[55] These were, however, only informal arrangements, and while OMGUS had not objected to them, it had also not formally sanctioned them.

These arrangements did not address the mounting pressure from another direction that came in the form of a flood of applications from both outside and inside Germany to adopt. UNRRA regularly received offers to adopt from North America, as well as from across Western Europe and from within Germany, from both American military and civilian personnel, as well as from displaced persons and Germans. Many such offers were coming from the United States, the result of the effective press coverage of the child search operations. UNRRA consistently and resolutely resisted the option, informing applicants with what was tantamount to a form letter, that no adoptions of displaced children in Germany were being authorized by either OMGUS or the national governments concerned. As was explained to the supplicants, this was "to safeguard the children who, although alone in Germany, may have parents or relatives in their home countries. It is intended that no children will be made available for adoption until everything possible has been done to determine that they are [truly] orphans and that they do not have a country to which they can be returned."[56]

Making the situation even more complicated was a growing trend by late 1946 on the part of potential adopters to use the German courts, which were functioning once again, to arrange adoptions, sidestepping the occupation authorities and UNRRA in so doing. The courts' justification in taking on these cases was that under Military Government Proclamation No. 2, German law remained valid unless it was explicitly annulled by the occupying authorities – which had not happened with regard to German adoption law.[57] Disturbingly, at least from the perspective of some at UNRRA, given the serious life-altering consequences for the children, OMGUS generally seemed to take a rather nonchalant attitude towards this practice, its philosophy being "the more persons we get out of Germany, whether children or not, the better."[58] In fact, by November 1946, USFET was also beginning to bow to popular pressure and pronounced itself open to the idea of American personnel adopting European children, "so long as all concerned are completely informed as to immigration laws and other attendant problems." As for US military personnel, they should be allowed to adopt as long as they "can obtain indication from an American Consul that an immigration visa to the US will be issued to the child." However, USFET still refused to formally declare a policy until the matter had been fully examined. All queries received were told that no adoptions were permitted yet, but were then redirected to the US Committee for the Care of European Children as the one possible source of children available for adoption.[59] Thus, at the end of 1946, the initial policy established by SHAEF, that no United Nations child could be adopted in Germany, still held technically. The reality was much less clear-cut.

By mid-1946, many in the upper echelons of UNRRA felt a formal military directive reasserting the SHAEF policy and its principles was crucial, for several reasons.[60] First, tracing relatives was proving to be a slower, more time-consuming task than initially anticipated, and UNRRA's predilection was to ensure that enough time was allowed to ensure that the tracing efforts were not going to bring results before deciding on a child's fate. The goal always remained the reunification of an unaccompanied child with its family or near relatives if at all possible. The fear was that if a child were adopted into a family and removed from Germany, only to discover later that members of its birth family were still alive and looking for it, reunification would be impossible. Not only would subsequent tracing of the child be very difficult, as UNRRA did not keep track of children after their situation had been resolved, unwinding the web of legal entanglements in order to reunite the child with its birth family across national boundaries would be practically impossible.

Second, USFET's Legal Division was quite concerned about the complicated web of laws that surrounded the adoption of a foreign national in Germany. Every country had different laws on the subject of adoption – laws that generally clashed with the German laws. Reconciling them was going to be enormously difficult, if not impossible. But, the Legal Division argued, "in order to ensure the validity of the adoption, particularly if the child is to be removed from Germany to another country ... both the adoption laws of Germany and that of the country of which the adopter is a national [must] be fully complied with."[61] If adoption were to be permitted, the legal counsel for both USFET and UNRRA strongly urged it include a clear, well-considered procedure that recognized the desires and adoption laws of the national governments of these children – which generally forbade the adoption of their children by people of other nationalities, with the exception of Jewish children, and insisted on the children's repatriation, with the sole exception of children with no immediate family in their homeland, but with close relatives elsewhere in the world who were willing to take in the children.[62] The risk, otherwise, was that the adoption would not be considered valid in the destination country, putting the child in an extremely precarious legal position.[63]

There was also the serious problem of trying to evaluate, at a distance, the social and economic conditions of the adoptive family and the difficulty of arranging for a probationary period of supervision by some appropriate agency – the normal assessment procedure before adoption was approved in the United States at the time.[64] UNRRA insisted that, just as in the case of adoptions happening under what might be considered more normal circumstances (read: circumstances in the United States) and as was the standard practice (at least in America), home visits, which would allow a careful assessment of the suitability of the adoptive parents and their home, were crucial. Without them, the (American-trained) welfare workers could not in all good conscience determine whether the adoption was in a child's best interests and whether the child would be properly cared for. UNRRA did not even have sufficient staff to do effective home assessments in Germany, in those instances where prospective adoptive parents were located in the country. (These would have been of little use anyway, given that these domestic arrangements were temporary in most cases and so a dubious measure of what the domestic circumstances would be like in the United States.) It manifestly could not do home visits in other countries. Thus, before any adoption could be recommended, the only solution seemed to be to refer the case to "recognized child welfare agencies in those countries for investigation," not a particularly practical alternative.[65]

In addition, there was the very real problem of visas. In the case of Americans (either civilian or military personnel in Germany or queries from the continental United States) wanting to adopt children, adoption did not guarantee the child's entry into the United States, as adoption did not grant the child American citizenship. The child remained an alien, and required the appropriate visa document to enter the United States, issued by an American consular officer. Adoption did not confer any special status or prioritization to the child, who would be required to apply for a visa from the available quota – and the quotas allotted to to most Central and Eastern European countries were heavily oversubscribed. The application process was also a very cumbersome and time-consuming one, with multiple layers of approval (including the UNRRA District Child Welfare Division, national liaison officers, USFET, and the American consular authorities) to be navigated. Entry visas were difficult to get, and adoptive families faced the daunting prospect of a separation of months, even years, before being able to bring the child to the United States, a warning repeatedly issued by OMGUS and USFET, with little apparent effect on the flood of inquiries.[66]

At least on this matter, UNRRA and the American occupation authorities were in accord. None were willing to encourage adoption. UNRRA was against encouraging adoption for the following reasons: it did not wish to become a child placement agency; it was not authorized to deal with adoptions (the 1945 SHAEF directive was still extant); its first obligation was to reunite the child with its birth family in the first instance and to repatriate the child in the second; and it did not think it was possible to safeguard the child's best interests under the circumstances. The American authorities were equally reluctant to support adoption because of the long delays and lack of assurance that the child would receive a US visa. The approach taken, then, was to refer potential adoptive parents to the US Committee for the Care of European Children, the only agency with the authority to deal with this issue, and to warn potential adopters of the pitfalls ahead.[67]

It was not a solution, as things continued to deteriorate. Not only were the German courts continuing to rule on adoptions without notifying either the Military Government, USFET, or UNRRA, but individuals were becoming increasingly bold in their efforts to obtain children. One particularly egregious example was the Billy Rose project announced in the 23 March 1947 edition of the *Stars and Stripes*. The *New York Times* was quoted as reporting that Billy Rose and his wife, Eleanor Holm, were planning to go to Europe within the month to select twenty-five European orphans, aged four to six years, who they intended to adopt and raise on a large estate at Mount Kisco, New York.[68] Adoption remained a fraught and unresolved issue.

Guardianship

Underpinning all of these legal questions was a more fundamental one: guardianship. Unaccompanied children were legal minors, legally unable to make decisions for themselves concerning their care or fate. Someone had to assume that responsibility. Martha Branscombe,[69] initially chief of the Child Welfare Section of UNRRA Central Headquarters in Washington and then of the European Regional Office in London, was the first to raise questions about the legal status of unaccompanied children in a query to Sir George Reid, director of the Welfare Division, in October 1944. Who, she asked, would be legally responsible for the unaccompanied children pending their repatriation (it was expected this might take some months to make happen) and based on what legal procedures? In Germany, where martial law would be imposed, it was unclear what laws would pertain or if they would adequately protect these children. Would UNRRA be appointed guardian ad litem or given legal custody of the child?[70] If that were the case, would the welfare officer act as UNRRA's agent in these cases?[71] The answers were not obvious, either to Branscombe or to Reid.[72] They were, however, critical. Children accompanied by an unrelated adult were in a particularly precarious legal position. Unless some alternate form of guardianship was established, if the adult decided he or she wanted to keep the child, there was little that could be done to prevent that adult from doing so. Once a child's nationality was established, then that responsibility could transfer to the appropriate governmental authority, but someone had to assume responsibility for those children whose nationality had not yet been determined or whose nationality was undeterminable. It also had to be made clear exactly who had the authority to make decisions for an unaccompanied child in UNRRA's care (which could not be the unrelated putative guardian): Could an adult who purported to be the child's parent remove the child from the centre and under what circumstances? Who could authorize medical care? Who could authorize placing the child in foster care? Branscombe wanted some authority established that would "protect the child's rights to return to his own people and similarly to safeguard the right of the parents to have their child restored to them." If not UNRRA (and Branscombe advised against this option, because of the Administration's temporary nature), then who?[73]

Initially, not all agreed with Branscombe that the situation was as potentially complex or worrisome as she painted it to be, or that the children's rights were in jeopardy. Eyre Carter of UNRRA's Legal Division was one such person who disagreed. Whether the children's nationalities were determined or not, he argued, UNRRA's responsibility was one of maintenance only, which did not require legal guardianship or custody. Children whose nationality could be determined were the responsibility of the appropriate national authorities. Those whose nationality could not be determined were the responsibility of the Intergovernmental Committee on Refugees.[74] In Carter's estimation, none of these children would be in UNRRA's care long enough for guardianship to be an issue, given that all would be going home soon (the assumption of the moment, i.e., 1944).[75]

Branscombe disagreed vehemently. She insisted that, while there was no question that UNRRA would provide maintenance for displaced unaccompanied children, this was not effective protection of the children and their rights. Although Branscombe agreed that UNRRA itself could not assume legal guardianship or custody, it behooved the organization to clarify the question and work out with the appropriate authorities an adequate arrangement to ensure the care and protection of these children for the transition period, that is, before their repatriation or before turning them over to the Intergovernmental Committee on Refugees, when they were under UNRRA's care.[76] Someone, she argued, had to take legal responsibility for these children during that time or they would be left quite vulnerable.

As tensions mounted in the first months between the Displaced Persons Division and the Child Welfare Division over this question – Branscombe's assistant found evidence that the Displaced Persons Division had been meeting separately with UNRRA's legal counsel to discuss the issue of the legal status of unaccompanied children[77] – the Welfare Division at Central Headquarters in Washington became equally concerned. Apparently unbeknownst to either Branscombe or the Displaced Persons Division, Central Headquarters had already been examining these questions and was annoyed by the duplication of effort. More importantly, Headquarters rejected as specious the Displaced Persons Division's claim that these matters were not a matter for the Welfare Division. These questions were welfare issues of the highest importance, and ones in which the Welfare Division maintained it had to be involved fully.[78]

UNRRA Central Headquarters was as disturbed as its Welfare Division by the Displaced Persons Division's proposal to allow unaccompanied children to remain with unrelated adults. The Displaced Persons Division had argued that, if a child was being well taken care of by friends or distant relatives, and if efforts to trace the child's parents proved ultimately futile, it "would be wrong to break down the relationship with the friends that brought the child to the Assembly Centre, when another permanent relationship will [just] have to be set up later on." Better to place the child with a family temporarily and, even if those adults were repatriated, to permit the child to leave with those adults, with UNRRA making arrangements with either the national government involved or a voluntary agency acting on UNRRA's behalf while the child was temporarily placed in the new country. The logic was that it was "in the child's best interests not to break up a relationship with an adult until the child's ultimate destiny has been settled."[79]

Central Headquarters was withering in its critique of the Displaced Persons Division's proposal. It would be impossible to manage such an arrangement for even a child whose nationality was known – requiring, as it would, the approval and involvement of the child's national government, that government's child protection authorities, and the receiving country's government. Coordinating this from the field in Germany in the midst of the chaos of the invasion and liberation, while ensuring adequate protection of the child's status and rights pending further efforts to trace relatives, would be impossible. For children whose nationality was unknown or who were stateless, to allow them to leave Germany in such a fashion would compromise their rights fundamentally. After all, it might take considerable time to trace a child's family, and if the child meanwhile had moved to another country other than the one in which a family member was finally located, "the possibilities of the child's being returned to his own people and country may be made impossible by legal complications" created by moving the child across national borders. There was also the very real concern that the unrelated adults' affection for the child might not survive repatriation and re-establishment in their homeland, which would leave the child stranded in a foreign country with no rights, no benefits, and no advocate. The Welfare Division's strong belief was that welfare policy could not be divorced from legal matters and repatriation arrangements, and that both divisions had to be involved in the formulation of policy, especially regarding the unaccompanied children.[80] Nor, as Branscombe scathingly pointed out (as explained earlier), did SHAEF's policy allow children of undetermined nationality to be adopted, placed in permanent homes, or to accompany adults to points outside Germany, whether those adults were United Nations nationals or not, as it would remove the children from the jurisdiction of the responsible authorities – i.e., the military – which violated SHAEF's established policy.[81] Finally, under no circumstances did SHAEF's policy allow children to be placed with unrelated adults, even temporarily.[82]

This was yet another policy exercised in the breach. The temporary care programs of the summer and autumn of 1945 were perhaps the most egregious violation of this. While the SHAEF memoranda might have seemed to suggest that SHAEF had assumed the role of guardian, in fact, the language only obliged the American military authorities – SHAEF, and then USFET – to provide maintenance and care. No directive was ever issued clarifying who legally would act as guardian. As a result, the governments of the various nations involved considered themselves to be the guardians of all unaccompanied children of their nationality in Germany, and that the occupying authorities held "quasi-parental" responsibility only for those children whose nationality was unknown or undetermined.[83] In practice the national liaison officers assumed the role of legal guardian for those unaccompanied children determined to be of their nationality. The final decision on a child's future – be it repatriation, resettlement, or adoption – fell to these liaison officers.

This solved the problem for those unaccompanied children whose nationality could be determined, at least from a technical standpoint. However, there were various subsets of unaccompanied children who were left without legal guardians, and therefore no one to protect their interests. Those children whose nationality was impossible to determine or who were deemed stateless, few as they were in number, were left without any representation – no one who could legally make long-term plans for them – not resettlement, not repatriation, not adoption.[84]

Another subset of unaccompanied children for whom liaison officers were not a solution were those whose nationality was known, but whose countries had not been recognized diplomatically and so did not have liaison officers in Germany. Such were the Baltic republics: Estonia, Latvia, and Lithuania. The issue of the Baltic children, as they were often referred to, became increasingly intractable. The Baltic republics occupied a diplomatic "no-man's-land." Absorbed into the Soviet Union in 1940 after their military invasion by that country, the Soviet Union argued that the citizens of the Baltic republics were now Soviet citizens. However, that absorption had not been recognized diplomatically by either the United Nations or the United States. At the same time, they were also no longer recognized internationally as independent states. This meant that, while the US Military Government allowed Estonians, Latvians, and Lithuanians to refuse to accept the Soviet liaison officers as their own, it also refused to consider accrediting liaison officers from the Baltic republics. This left the Balts without a liaison officer to speak for them in the US Zone and put them in a peculiar position: not stateless, as their nationality was acknowledged and recognized, but without a voice. For unaccompanied Baltic children, this was especially problematic. No Baltic liaison officer meant no legal guardian, as the occupying authorities refused to allow Soviet liaison officers to even comment on decisions made about these children.[85] The Soviet Union, on the other hand, insisted loudly and continually that its liaison officers spoke for the Baltic displaced persons, including the children – a patently unacceptable alternative for most Baltic displaced persons. The consequence of this for the children, who universally refused to repatriate voluntarily and who UNRRA refused to repatriate forcibly (no matter what demands the Soviet liaison officers made), was that UNRRA had no one to approve plans for the final disposition of unaccompanied Baltic children and so could not resolve any of these cases. The children were caught in the camps. It was particularly frustrating, as opportunities were starting to open up for emigration to the United States through the aegis of the US Committee for the Care of European Children, which had stepped up its operations in Germany by the autumn of 1946.

Given the pressure being brought to bear on UNRRA by mid-1946 to clear the displaced persons camps, including the children's centres, the situation became increasingly untenable. In October 1946, the European Regional Office instructed the field that where UNRRA Resolution 92 required "consultation with representatives of Governments, such consultation in cases involving displaced persons of Latvian, Lithuanian or Estonian origin should be carried on with the accredited representative of the USSR." This was a controversial move, as it contravened the policy of the occupying authorities, who recognized the Soviet liaison officers' authority only over those Baltic displaced persons who wished to repatriate and forbade consultation with those liaison officers on general Baltic displaced persons questions. Perhaps the objective was to force the Military Government's hand. The impact of the instruction from the European Regional Office to implement Resolution 92 was to create considerable consternation in the field, as it directly conflicted with zonal policy as determined by the Military Government, without changing the situation. The field personnel continued to refuse to refer any cases to the Soviet liaison officers, unless the child (or its parents, if they had been located in the homeland) specifically requested repatriation. The instruction was soon withdrawn and the issue remained unresolved,[86] and the well-entrenched practice that had evolved remained – because the guardianship question had never been settled. Any decisions as to a child's nationality or final disposition continued to require a national liaison officer's approval. If there was no national liaison officer, either because the child's nationality was unknown or because of political reasons, then it remained unclear who could make that final decision, and the decision was postponed.

What is striking in this review of key legal challenges facing the child welfare workers is the deep reluctance of the Military Government and USFET to tackle them. The reasons were myriad and will be explored in more detail later, but are worth identifying here. The small numbers of such children meant they could and did slip off the list of priorities. The Military Government's attention had, by 1946, shifted away from the displaced persons population in general, and the unaccompanied children especially, to the twofold issue of helping Germany cope with the influx of German expellees from Eastern European countries and the need to revive the German economy and institutions. In addition, their reluctance was a reflection of a growing frustration with a population (the displaced persons) who, from the occupiers' perspective, should have been dispersed already. As the Cold War hardened into place, the unaccompanied children – most of whom were from Eastern European countries – became pawns in the battle taking shape between the United States and the Soviet Union, with UNRRA and the children caught in the middle, one more weapon in the battle. Finally, the matter got pushed aside further by the need to deal with yet another refugee issue taking shape: the growing flood of infiltrees entering Germany from Eastern Europe, Jewish for the most part.

It was becoming increasingly clear that the question of the determination of an unaccompanied child's nationality was crucial to the resolution of the child's fate. It was also becoming clear by late 1946 that the determination of nationality for certain children, on which other legal questions often hinged, had no easy answer. Yet, without a nationality, an unaccompanied child had no clear future.

Chapter Five

The Infiltrees

Resolution of the displaced persons question more generally, as well as the special issue of unaccompanied children, was hampered by the influx of yet another group of claimants on the resources of the United Nations Relief and Rehabilitation Administration (UNRRA) and of the Military Government, one that threatened to overwhelm operations in the US Zone. This group had not figured in anyone's calculations in early 1945, but had become yet another complication by the end of that year and a crisis by the middle of the next. This group became known as "infiltrees," or more bureaucratically, "post-hostilities refugees." These were not displaced persons, strictly speaking, although some had been such at one point. These were people pouring into the Western occupation zones of Germany after the Second World War had ended, and the vast majority of them were Jewish. They came for a variety of reasons: to escape postwar persecution in Eastern Europe (which was especially the case for many of the Jewish infiltrees), to avoid political persecution at the hands of the new Communist regimes, or in search of opportunities for a better life elsewhere. The infiltree movement did not become a flood until the late autumn of 1945, although a trickle of Jewish refugees already had been moving towards Palestine since that January. UNRRA knew about the movement, as it had been asked informally by Britain to consider caring for these refugees, even though they did not technically meet the criteria of displaced persons (not having been displaced by the war, but only leaving their homes after the war's end). UNRRA Germany had reluctantly agreed, pending agreement on the part of both the American government and UNRRA Headquarters – reluctantly, because according to contemporary estimates there were some sixteen thousand Romanian Jews and two thousand Polish Jews in Czechoslovakia poised to enter Germany, and given the devastation in Hungary, a further twenty thousand Hungarian Jews might soon follow. Such an influx would be overwhelming.[1] Among the infiltrees were numerous unaccompanied children.

The Context

In late August 1945, UNRRA Team 501 in Berlin reported that "daily at our DP Centre numbers of refugees from Poland, Esthonia [sic], Lithuania etc. come seeking food and shelter and transport through the Russian Zone of Germany to either British or American Occupation Zones." The stories they told the team's director, G.J. Taylor, about conditions in their countries led him to conclude that "there is likely to continue to be a movement from these countries."[2] UNRRA child welfare specialist for the US Zone, Cornelia Heise, reported:

> For instance a woman in Feldafing center went to Poland, brought back a four year old child which had been left with a farm family, and came back to Feldafing. Others come to Feldafing and Landsberg directly from Poland to search for members of the family, having learned of the Jewish centers here. One child appeared, whose parents had been recently shot in Poland. 15 year old Eliaz Feferkorn, Polish Jewish, has been in seven different concentration camps in Poland and Germany during a period of 2 1/2 years. He was then liberated in Poland and one week ago came to one of the centers. 15 year old Mozes Gilman, Polish, lived in the Ghetto in Poland from 1940 to 1944. He spent one year in two different concentration camps, then came to Landsberg D.P. camp. He set out on his own to find his family, though all of them were last known to be in concentration camps. After a 3 day futile search in Poland he came back to the center at Feldafing ... [Finally a] new group [of children] has come to light, those who never left Poland, but had been living in woods as partisans, and experienced almost greater hardships than the children in the concentration camps.[3]

The numbers began to escalate in earnest in October, arriving primarily in Berlin and Bavaria. The infiltrees included adults and children and both Jews and non-Jews who had been in Germany, had repatriated, but now were returning to Germany (often with their families who had been left behind in Poland during the war). There were also Jews and non-Jews who were leaving their homelands for the first time, seeking to avoid the apparently rampant postwar persecutions there. Still others were leaving in search of better economic opportunities. Comprising a significant portion of this movement, the Jewish infiltrees were being moved out in a highly organized fashion by the American Joint Distribution Committee.[4] They followed well-defined routes – through Prague or Budapest to Vienna, Salzburg, and then to Munich – along which they received well-organized care. It was a deliberate plan on the organizers' part to force the question of the fate of Jews in Palestine, their ultimate destination.[5] When the infiltrees finally reached Germany, they quickly overwhelmed the assembly centres and camps. As their numbers grew, the UNRRA teams running the various displaced persons centres sought advice as to whether these people should be admitted to the camps, as did the district administration of UNRRA, because technically these people fell outside of UNRRA's mandate.[6]

Initially, the United States Forces, European Theater (USFET) declared that Military Government Law No. 161 governed the situation – non-Jewish United Nations displaced persons who had willingly repatriated in the past and had returned to the US Zone would not be granted the "status or treatment of UN displaced persons." Jews who had recently infiltrated from Poland would be temporarily cared for in segregated installations, separate from United Nations displaced persons camps or in Jewish centres for persecutees. There, they would receive care until a decision was made regarding their disposition.[7]

Although Military Government Law No. 161 was implemented, few on the ground were impressed by the consequences. The steady stream of infiltrees was beginning to overwhelm the communities where they landed, aggravating already marked shortages of shelter and food, and raising questions about public safety, with large numbers of people "wandering around with no place to sleep or eat."[8] Informally, the field had been told that "no camp director should turn away those looking for shelter," but the reality was that the camps simply did not have the space for the additional people. The problem was becoming critical.[9] When American military detachments were approached for help with housing, they refused, arguing that there were neither enough buildings nor supplies to make more camps possible. Instead, UNRRA personnel were instructed to refuse the returnees admittance to the existing centres, as they had been ordered to do, although the military personnel also refused to put this in writing. The UNRRA teams found themselves in an increasingly impossible position: "This situation [is creating] an extremely difficult situation and at times intolerable conditions of work for the UNRRA teams whose direct job it is to take care of the well-being of the displaced persons and it is impossible for a relief organization, such as UNRRA is, to refuse assistance and support to those who seem to be entitled to this relief and support. On the other hand, being under military orders, it is impossible for the teams not to comply with such orders."[10] For some, the horror was unbearable. The picture painted in a letter to friends back home in New York City by Sidney Flatow, a member of the UNRRA team at Camp Zeilsheim, one of the Jewish camps near Frankfurt, was heart-rending and reflected the belief on the part of many UNRRA workers faced with this newest wave of misery that, while these people may not be displaced persons technically, they fell under the United Nations mandate for displaced persons care "within the spirit of any proper definition." They were "truly here [in Germany] as a fundamentally direct result of the war."[11] Flatow wrote in his letter:

The greatest and most pressing problem since coming here is the eternal problem of the wandering Jews. The Jews fleeing the current terror in Poland arriving here, ill, in tatters, exhausted, cold and starving, they find there [sic] way here against the greatest odds. Many fall by the wayside. Children hidden these many years in the woods, survivors of the German terror, they knock on our doors here. The camp is jammed, in many instances people are sleeping three and four in a bed. After weeks on the road, braving the cold, footsore, weary, they arrive here only to be refused admission. This unpleasant heartrending task of turning them away is mine. Yet, how can I do it? It is a terrible thing to have gone on and on buoyed up by the hope of being accepted by UNRRA, living only for the moment when they can rest their numb and weary bodies and then at the end of the long quest to be turned away. Now, having nowhere to go, eternally unwanted, standing in front of my door, bemoaning their fate, refusing to budge, shouting that they rather would die than go on another step. I am however, under a direct order from the military not to register another person and yet no provision is being made to provide for another camp. The military feel that they have done enough for the Jews. Judge Rifkind is moving heaven and earth to get another camp opened to accommodate these persons who are in extremis, but I am face to face with the actual problem in terms of living people. They shout at me "Where are we to go?" And I cannot answer. I have been on the verge of throwing up the sponge a few times as I'm just about done in, but that will accomplish nothing. What can I tell the people whose very existence depends on the answer. They look to the UNRRA as the only possibility of continuing to live. Pregnant women, women with babes in arms, crippled former partisans and soldiers, unaccompanied children (a 7 year old lad stood outside my window gnawing on a raw cabbage like some little animal, after four years in the woods), the lame, the sick, the halt and the blind, the world's dispossessed knock at my door and tear at the walls of my heart. Yesterday, a woman fought her way into my office, sat down on the floor and nursed her child. She said nothing, just sat there staring at us in mute terror finally imploring me to take her and the child in and register them. After three weeks on the road her husband had died of the flu, she couldn't go another step and bemoaned the fact that she had not perished in the crematorium with her sisters ... On my own responsibility, I registered the two days' accumulation of over three hundred persons.[12]

These newest refugees were not only a humanitarian crisis, they also represented a serious political crisis. UNRRA director for the US Zone, A.R. Guyler, best articulated the challenge that these new refugees posed, when he wrote on 12 October 1945: "This may very well develop into a problem of considerable dimensions and is rendered particularly difficult by its close connection with the entire maze of questions relating to sovereignty, citizenship and statelessness in the east of Europe."[13] The politics did not take long to erupt. In December, the British closed their zone to any further infiltrees coming in through Berlin, and USFET refused to allow any infiltrees coming through Berlin into the US Zone. The British concern was that the ultimate objective of the infiltrees was Palestine to which Britain was not willing to grant them entrance. This very quickly created tremendous pressure in Berlin, where the number of infiltrees reached 6,300 by 5 January 1946, overwhelming the sectors' resources.[14] Reaching quadripartite consensus about the fate of these people had proven impossible, other than a declaration by the Directorate of Prisoners of War and Displaced Persons of the Allied Control Authority that it did not consider these refugees to fall within its area of responsibility. Thus, each sector was dealing with the infiltrees as they saw fit, while the Directorate requested direction from the Allied Control Authority (the quadripartite council ostensibly coordinating policy across all four occupation zones) as to what should be done with these people, and to what extent further illegal entry into the sectors could be prevented.[15] The Soviet solution was to move their share of the infiltrees into the Soviet Occupation Zone of Germany, reducing the number of registered infiltrees in Berlin to 2,782.[16] The French and American sectors, however, remained swamped.

The infiltration of Jews from Poland into Bavaria had reached such a critical level and resulted in such overcrowding by early November 1945 that General Truscott, 3rd Army, was finally given permission to establish special centres for them. Like UNRRA, Truscott took the position that he would not "stand by and permit people who need help to go unaided." This was a controversial position within the ranks of the army, with others arguing that the United States should not be taking sole responsibility for these people as doing so would open Germany to a flood of potentially hundreds of thousands of Eastern Europeans. The problem was that it was not just Polish Jews who were fleeing – a number that might have been manageable, as estimates of the total number of Jews in Poland were between fifty thousand and eighty thousand – but also Hungarian and Romanian Jews (who were thought to number in the hundreds of thousands), as well as many, many non-Jews.[17]

In the face of this onslaught, USFET modified its position and agreed to deem those infiltrees who could be considered persecutees to be eligible for UNRRA aid. However, it insisted that those infiltrees who were not persecutees would not receive assistance, whether they had been considered displaced persons at an earlier point (e.g., prior to their repatriation) or not.[18] The effect was to restrict access to aid largely to Jewish infiltrees. UNRRA was put in charge of the new camps that would be established to accommodate them.

This was a controversial decision, even within UNRRA's ranks. Sir Humfrey Gale, personal representative of UNRRA's director general and head of the European Regional Office, objected to the restriction to solely Jewish infiltrees as inhumane and likely to actively discourage displaced persons still in Germany from repatriating, as they would be reluctant to return home if there was no turning back should it not work out. The uncertainty of what awaited them would, thought Gale, make many reluctant to consider such an irreversible decision. UNRRA's Washington Headquarters agreed with Gale, that this would be an extremely difficult measure to implement, for both administrative and humanitarian reasons.[19] The European Regional Office issued an instruction to the field, formally endorsing what had become the practice in the camps – no displaced persons would lose their right to UNRRA assistance because of an unsuccessful attempt at repatriation, so anyone returning to Germany after repatriation would continue to be eligible for UNRRA care. As for those "falling within the categories known to have been the object of Nazi persecution or discriminatory legislation (for example Jews)," they would be assumed to have been displaced from their homes during the war, and therefore to be displaced persons. These people would also be eligible for UNRRA care in Germany, "irrespective of the date they left their country of previous residence."[20] Thus, UNRRA took it upon itself to extend coverage to include non-Jewish infiltrees.

These extensions (both USFET's to aid the Jewish infiltrees and UNRRA's to aid all infiltrees) were controversial moves, as they antagonized both the British and a number of Eastern European governments, including the Soviet Union. The British maintained there was no basis in UNRRA's resolutions to provide aid to post-hostilities refugees, either non-Jewish or Jewish. Instead, they argued, the originating countries should be asking UNRRA for supplies to care for their post-hostilities refugees *within their own boundaries*.[21] The British were quite intransigent on this issue, and would remain so, with significant consequences for the US Zone. For their part, the Eastern European governments did not take kindly to UNRRA providing succour to refugees fleeing their regimes, individuals who they dismissed as malcontents. Unsurprisingly, it remained impossible to get quadripartite agreement on how to deal with the post-hostilities refugees.[22] As was the case in Berlin, this meant that policy would be set at the zonal level and, therefore in the US Zone, by the American Military Government – which meant that the US Zone would continue to be a safe haven for these particular persecutees.[23] All incoming Jews were to be considered persecutees and victims of discriminatory Nazi legislation by virtue of their being Jewish, and so they were not required to present any evidence to prove their eligibility. Non-Jews, on the other hand, were required to provide evidence of persecution, such as concentration camp numbers; with proof of persecution, however, they, too, would receive assistance.[24] In the British Zone, they would all continue to be denied care.

By January 1946, the number of infiltrees in the US Zone of Germany was estimated to be between twenty thousand and twenty-five thousand individuals, with still more on the way.[25] On 18 February, J.B. Krane, of UNRRA's Reports and Analysis Branch, wrote that he could reliably report that approximately four thousand Jewish infiltrees were known to have entered Bavaria in the previous forty days, an average of a hundred daily. In the previous two weeks, an average of four hundred persons from Hungary and Romania had been processed through the UNRRA transit centre for Jewish infiltrees in Munich. Krane was certain that this was not all of them, but that many had slipped in unnoticed.[26] By May, UNRRA District 5 was reporting that the infiltrees arriving in Munich were numbering six hundred to seven hundred weekly. Furthermore, based on information from various sources, as well as from the infiltrees themselves, it appeared that there were, poised on the borders of Poland, "huge numbers of infiltrees … waiting to come into the American Zone."[27] The new UNRRA director for the US Zone, J.H. Whiting, warned his staff in May 1946 that they could be facing a possible influx of eighty-five thousand additional infiltrees, on top of those already received.[28] By June, the Army officially reported an average of three thousand to four thousand infiltrees weekly through the checkpoints, but it was clear that many more were coming in else-where; according to an internal report of the Military Government, the estimated actual rate of influx was now up to ten thousand monthly.[29]

Infiltree Children

Among these infiltrees were groups of unaccompanied Jewish chil-dren, generally over the age of twelve (old enough to be self-sufficient in the eyes of the welfare workers), although some were as young as two years. The groups were considerable in size, ranging from fifty to five hundred individuals, chaperoned by unrelated adults, and arriv-ing at the gates of the displaced persons camps unannounced. Between 16 December 1945 and 8 January 1946, at least eighteen such groups arrived in the US Zone. The cover story given in most instances was that these children had been gathered up by the International Red Cross in Hungary and placed in children's homes there under the leadership of Jewish adults. As the food situation was becoming critical in Hungary and Czechoslovakia, these children were, so it was explained, moving through to Switzerland. In fact, once they had arrived in Germany and been admitted to the children's centres, inevitably the adult leaders who had accompanied them requested that the children be allowed to continue on to Palestine, not Switzerland. It also turned out that, while most of the children were unaccompanied, a number of them still had parents or relatives in Hungary, Czechoslovakia, or Poland – although the leaders generally had some kind of documentation from these par-ents giving their children permission to go to Palestine.[30] Rumours sug-gested that this exodus was just the beginning of what might become a flood, including one that an estimated forty thousand more children were soon to move into Germany.[31] While there were non-Jewish infil-trees in this movement, this was becoming primarily a Jewish matter, especially among the unaccompanied children.

The American military was not coping well with this issue. In October 1945 USFET had authorized UNRRA to provide "reasonable care" to infiltrees pending the determination of a definitive policy on the matter, and in April 1946, Third Army Headquarters had reaffirmed this by instructing its division commanders to hold open surplus accommodations for a thousand infiltrees and to prepare for an additional eight thousand to ten thousand within the next sixty days, but neither the Office of Military Government, United States (OMGUS) nor USFET had yet clarified the status of these people.[32] And, in spite of instructions from USFET Headquarters, the commanders in the field were resistant to making these accommodations. One division commander had informed the UNRRA district director verbally that "he will accept no infiltrees into his area, and will provide no more space." At least one military brigade had taken matters into its own hands and directed the UNRRA teams in District 1 to refuse admission to all infiltrees with the exception of Jews, persecutees, unaccompanied children, and those who needed to be admitted because they were sick or for other humane reasons. The director of UNRRA District 2, R.C. Raymond, was convinced that the Military Government had "adopted an ostrich-like policy," no matter what it said publicly. Although it had declared it would accommodate a thousand people weekly, in practice it had "practically denied that the people are there and has kept repeating that they will stop coming." This patently had not happened, although the Army seemed to be under the impression that, if they refused to establish a much-needed transit centre in Frankfurt (something the District had been requesting for months), it would "somehow put a stop to the influx." The only thing that was preventing a full-blown humanitarian crisis, in Raymond's opinion, was the extraordinary effort of the UNRRA personnel on the ground in securing the supplies needed.[33] A.C. Dunn, the director for District 3, headquartered in Regensburg, was finding the lower echelons of the Military Government there just as uncooperative, giving priority to the needs of German expellees over those of the displaced persons (at this point, thousands of ethnic Germans were being summarily expelled from various Eastern European countries and transported to Germany without warning or planning).[34] By mid-September, the US Zone had absorbed a total of 43,326 infiltrees, and the total displaced persons population in the US Zone had risen by mid-August to 418,720, in spite of the Military Government's wilful denial.[35]

The general impression of the Military Government was that the Jewish infiltrees were destabilizing the region, both in numbers, having doubled the number of Jewish displaced persons in the Zone according to one estimate, and in their failure to integrate into the community. While the Military Government considered German Jews to have reintegrated effectively – finding housing, work, receiving adequate rations, and enjoying the fruits of what was considered to be an opportunistic and superficial "pro-Semitism" – they maintained that the Eastern Jews did not fit in well, nor did they try to. These Jews hated the Germans fiercely, were not at all interested in the reconstruction of Germany, and did not want to work with Germans. The feeling was returned: with the arrival of these refugees, the Military Government pointed out, the area had experienced "a marked revival of anti-Semitism." It also firmly believed that these Jews were inclined to participate in the black market and other criminal activities. The picture being painted of the infiltrees was not a flattering one, and it reflected the growing impatience of the lower echelons of the Military Government with displaced persons in general, and this subsection of the displaced persons population in particular, which it dismissed as largely made up of a criminal element.[36] The Military Government also resented the increased pressures infiltrees put on already overcrowded facilities and the mounting cost they represented, especially when it was clear that the infiltrees were not at all interested in being "absorbed into the German community but wish[ed] to emigrate to lands of their own selection."[37]

One immediate consequence of the Military Government's reluctance to assist UNRRA with the infiltrees was a serious shortage of housing. By the summer months of 1946, the situation was becoming dire.[38] Infiltrees were forced to remain at collection centres that had been designed for a two- or three-day stay at the most, not as permanent habitation, and not just in Berlin. These accommodations were grossly inadequate and badly overcrowded. At one point in June, Funk Infiltree Centre had eighteen hundred persons in it, while its official capacity had been set at five hundred. By the end of that month, the number of inhabitants had only dropped to twelve hundred. Disturbingly, but not unexpectedly, given the horrid conditions in the makeshift camps, hundreds upon hundreds of the new arrivals "packed up their belongings and departed privately, with no authorization.[39] UNRRA and the Military Government had lost control.

On 22 June 1946, the Third US Army finally issued a directive, pledging to provide accommodation for four thousand infiltrees a week.

Jewish refugees were to be admitted at any of six points of entry at the border of the US Zone in organized, pre-planned movements: one on the Austrian border, where the railroad between Salzburg and Munich crossed, and five along the Czech-US Zone border (Hof, Selb, Tirschen-reuth, Furth-im-Wald, and Pocking). This directive enshrined much of what had become practice. All Jewish infiltrees were to be cared for in Jewish centres with the same standards of food, shelter, and care as currently available in established Jewish displaced persons assembly centres.[40] Those displaced persons who crossed national frontiers after the end of hostilities (which date was ultimately set at 1 August 1945[41]) were only eligible for care if, prior to crossing the national frontiers, they "were obliged to leave their country or place of origin or former residence, or were deported therefrom by action of the enemy because of race, religion or activities in favour of the United Nations." This had the impact of limiting eligibility to persecutees. There were two caveats to the directive, the same as those first imposed. In the case of victims of discriminatory Nazi legislation, such as Jews, "no concrete evidence need be demanded in order to prove eligibility." In the case of others claiming to fall within the definition of persecutee, they were required to produce concrete evidence of discrimination, such as concentration camp numbers. Any infiltrees who did not meet these requirements were to be reported to the Military Government for removal from UNRRA care.[42] The efforts to corral the infiltrees were for naught. They continued to cross into the US Zone wherever they wished, rather than at the six official crossings, and many continued to arrive unannounced, either individually or in large transports of sometimes hundreds, over-whelming reception centres and camps that were neither ready to receive them nor capable of absorbing them.[43]

As a result, many of the Jewish infiltrees ended up establishing them-selves outside of the displaced persons camps, joining the thousands of Jews, both the long-established and the recently arrived, who lived in increasingly self-contained independent communities, including kib-butzim. Many of these kibbutzim had even set up their own farms, with the objective of rehabilitating their people both culturally and vocation-ally. A product of the Zionist movement, their explicit goal was to build a Jewish national identity, one that ultimately would be rooted in Pal-estine, and to create a just communal society based on the principles of social cooperation; equality among all members, including giving equal value to all types of work; "self-labour" (in that members of the kibbut-zim tended to the needs of the community and its economy themselves, rather than relying on others to perform those tasks); and direct democracy. In these villages, the group lived and worked together and jointly owned all property.[44] Children were to be raised by the collective in communal housing, separate from their parents.[45] These were fiercely independent, autonomous communities, intended to be self-sufficient, with the explicit political goal of forcing the creation of an independent Jewish state.

These kibbutzim had emerged with little or no help from UNRRA. Always UNRRA had provided a certain degree of support, but only informally, ranging from food and clothing to the provision of just medical services or Red Cross packages. With the expansion of the free-living option (i.e., living outside of the camps) and the kibbutzim, however, UNRRA was being increasingly inundated with requests for much more significant levels of support in the form of schools, workshops, and recreation facilities, in addition to food and other supplies. UNRRA welfare workers were sympathetic, as these communities offered opportunities for constructive rehabilitation that were impossible to provide in a camp environment and denying them aid would be to penalize their inhabitants for showing initiative "and for taking a positive view toward their lives." Nevertheless, UNRRA was not set up to deal with these kinds of novel arrangements.[46]

UNRRA camps, even the new infiltree centres UNRRA had been ordered to open, were unable to cope. These centres were understaffed, quickly overwhelmed, and plagued by intense political battles between various Jewish factions, especially over the future of the unaccompanied children.[47] And while the Army had been instructed to provide accommodations, in the field, it remained largely indifferent, if not actually hostile. Major Flannery, a field operations officer in UNRRA District 3 Headquarters, noted:

On the ground, displaced persons and UNRRA are just one of a multitude of problems facing the Army. Therefore, the Army delegates this responsibility, as much as possible ... Much can be said about how much of this lack of response can be laid at the door of the individual's attitude in the Army toward displaced persons and UNRRA; and much can be said for the Army's lack of competent personnel, re-deployment, other responsibilities, etc., but the fact remains that in order for UNRRA to function, in many instances, UNRRA must take the initiative ... Movements, to a large degree, the local tactical units handle fairly well and it is the only phase of this operation that ... is solely within their power to handle, without the

source being Military Government. The two greatest needs of this operation are accommodations and supplies, without which it cannot succeed.
Yet, these two basic necessities must be obtained from Military Government sources and Military Government has not the slightest interest – with
very few exceptions – in UNRRA or displaced persons. Their interest and
responsibility is the antithesis of displaced persons – refugees [German
expellees] … yet, we are utterly dependent upon them in the final analysis
for all physical assets necessary to our operational efficiency.[48]

The situation worsened further that summer, when both the British
and French zones refused to admit any more infiltrees. The decision
of the British military was especially crucial, as the French Zone had
a much smaller displaced persons population as a whole. The commander-in-chief of the British Zone ordered that any displaced person
who had been repatriated once and later returned was to be treated as a
refugee and not as a displaced person. Second, he directed that no further displaced persons were to be registered after 1 July 1946.[49] In addition, after that date, the British would refuse displaced persons status to
all displaced persons in their Zone who were living outside of assembly
centres, with the exception of unaccompanied United Nations children
and children of displaced persons mothers.[50] The impact was to deflect
all infiltrees to the US Zone, increasing the flood streaming across its
borders. Over the course of July, the number of Jews in the US Zone rose
by thirteen thousand, the largest infiltration to date. While efforts were
made to better regulate what was now a steady inflow, both the military detachments and the UNRRA teams were still repeatedly caught
by surprise – an anticipated movement of five hundred would turn out
to be a thousand, for example. Unofficial movements also continued,
in spite of the shortage of transportation and UNRRA's best efforts to
stave them off. Small groups appeared almost daily, unannounced and
unanticipated. Individuals showed up at camp gates, weeks after first
arriving in the Zone.

This new influx of infiltrees exacerbated the overcrowding. Estimates
placed the saturation point at some time in mid-September 1946, given
the rate of inflow, although that point had already been reached in
some regions by late July. As a result, displaced persons continued to
be housed in substandard facilities, including tents. In the Cham and
Landshut areas, there were not even plates, bowls, or eating utensils
available – tin cans were used instead. Both UNRRA staff and displaced
persons organizations were furious, but they could do little given that

the Army considered this housing adequate. Ironically, however, when those in the military personnel were confronted physically with the infiltrees, their attitude changed dramatically. District 3 Director Dunn explained, "As so often happens, when actually confronted with the misery of people, officers and men felt as keenly as we do their lack of facilities," finally realizing that displaced persons could not be "handled like troops, that there were babies involved, and sick people, and Kosher [dietary] considerations." The problem threatened to become truly serious as winter drew closer, for there was no expectation that the infiltrees would be moved out before the foul weather set in. The US Army continued to reject suggestions that Germans should be removed from selected communities, arguing that it would "disrupt German industry and economy."[51]

By August, USFET warned UNRRA to expect sixty thousand more infiltrees before the end of October and an additional forty thousand between October and July 1947. In view of the coming winter, this made the issue of accommodations critical. Current facilities were completely inadequate for an intrusion of a hundred thousand infiltrees, as well as the forty thousand free-living displaced persons (displaced persons already in Germany but living outside of the camps) who were expected to seek admission to the centres over the next five months. Many of the accommodations were not winterized and so would have to be abandoned for the winter months; others, facilities vacated by the army and turned over to UNRRA, were completely unsatisfactory, having been stripped of light fixtures, plumbing, window fixtures, etc., and requiring months of work to make them livable. Aggravating the situation, in many areas, the local Military Government units refused to allocate UNRRA more facilities with the express purpose of keeping displaced persons and infiltrees out of their communities. It was particularly galling that the displaced persons were being shunted into facilities that were clearly substandard and well below the living standards of the Germans. Whiting warned the Third Army that if something was not done about the situation, UNRRA could "no longer accept responsibility for a situation as uncontrolled as the one now presented."[52]

In among these tens of thousands of infiltrees were large numbers of unaccompanied infiltree children, who were proving just as vexatious a problem for the Child Search Branch and the Child Welfare Division as the adult infiltree population was for UNRRA more generally. Although adults and families had been arriving in the US Zone (as well as the other zones) since July and August 1945, including a trickle of unaccompanied children, a major wave of unaccompanied Jewish children began to arrive that December and continued through January and February the next year, with most of these children coming from and through Hungary. In both waves of infiltrees (the first between December 1945 and January 1946 and the second between June and August 1946), they arrived without notice and without any indication of how many were coming, which left UNRRA's child welfare people operating in the dark. In many instances, Headquarters only heard about the children after they had arrived and inserted themselves in the camps. This meant a complete absence of any planning for them at anything above the field level. At the field level, it was a mad scramble.

The steady stream was unnerving. The first transport to arrive at the Deutsches Museum in Munich (a transit camp meant for short stays only where displaced persons were registered, sorted, and then moved on to more permanent shelter), appeared on 16 December 1945 – a group of 120 unaccompanied Polish, Hungarian, and Czechoslovakian Jewish children from Hungary under the care of Dr Osterweil, a Hungarian Jewish doctor. Another group arrived a week later – another 120 children, via Salzburg, and under the care of Dr Czinner Tibor and his wife. On 27 December, a third group of 123 children aged six to fourteen arrived, accompanied by 26 adults aged eighteen to twenty-three. In the first week of January, yet another group of 50 arrived, followed by three more groups before 13 January, numbering 309 children in all. Although the numbers were very fluid, UNRRA Team 165 reported that it had, within its region, 1,995 such Jewish infiltree children by late January 1946. In the midst of considerable confusion, UNRRA's child welfare people were able to open a children's centre at Struth on 7 January to accommodate them, soon followed by a second centre at Lindenfels, near the Jewish camp of Lampertheim.[53]

The children's stories were harrowing. The first arrivals were in very poor health – malnourished and commonly arriving with nothing but the clothes on their backs.[54] Olive Biggar, a district welfare officer, had pulled together a sampling of their stories for Cornelia Heise, UNRRA's child welfare specialist: Leizer Cheykin, aged nine, had been with his parents in the Rubozewicz Ghetto. By his account, the family fled the ghetto when the Germans started shooting, and hid with a farmer for nine months, where one sister died of a heart attack. His mother and another sister were caught and immediately shot, at which point Leizer was hidden in the woods by a family friend who was a partisan and then brought to the Zeilsheim camp in Germany by this friend in October

1945 so he could go to school. In another case, Ferdinand and Henryk Ferderber, aged ten and six, had stayed with their governess in a Polish village; their parents had died in 1942. They remained there until liberated by the Russians, at which point they were brought to Zeilsheim by a Palestinian soldier of the Jewish Brigade. Benjamin Kabina, aged fifteen, had escaped from the train that was taking his whole family to Treblinka in 1942. He worked for the partisans and was wounded twice, the second time, just one day before liberation. After two months in hospital, the Russians sent him to a naval school in Sverdlowsk, where he stayed for three months. He then returned to Poland, "but left because of the persecution of the Jews." He arrived in Zeilsheim with a friend in November 1945. Abraham Milemski, aged sixteen, had been sent to the Radogosrcz concentration camp in Lodz in 1939. After a few months, he was unfit for work, so was returned to the ghetto where his family lived. On 12 November 1942, he saw his mother and father beaten to death. He and his two sisters were then taken to Auschwitz, where the sisters were murdered on the day they arrived. At Auschwitz, Abraham was beaten with a thick rubber strap. Following liberation, he was taken to an English hospital. Upon his release, he returned to Lodz to look for relatives but did not find anyone, so he came to Zeilsheim, hoping to go to school.[55]

In the second wave (beginning June 1946), unaccompanied children largely arrived as part of kibbutzim, chaperoned by a number of adult and teenaged leaders, and primarily to District 5, centred on Munich.[56] Hundreds were pouring across the border daily, beginning in August, and rumours reported that an additional twenty thousand were poised on the Czechoslovakian border, ready to enter the US Zone that month.[57] By late autumn, the flood had abated, but the numbers remained a guess. This was, in part, because the infiltree population was very mobile, even in Germany, shifting in and out of, and between, the temporary tent cities set up by the Army to accommodate them. It was also in part because the tent cities remained under military not UNRRA administration, and the Army would not provide UNRRA with a head count. This meant that UNRRA did not have a good grasp of how many infiltrees there were, let alone the number of children or what was happening to them. Its best estimate was that there were a total of twenty thousand Jewish infiltree children in the Zone, approximately six thousand of them unaccompanied. Thirty-five hundred were in children's centres, with plans in place by early October to make space for an additional thousand. All unaccompanied infiltree children were supposed to be moved directly to the children's centre at Rosenheim for processing (in operation by mid-September), but the Army was shipping them out hither and yon, to camps that were not equipped to handle them. This was adding to the already considerable confusion, and the child search people had turned to the Jewish Agency for Palestine in the hope that it might have representatives in the tent cities who could notify UNRRA if and when a transfer of this nature was happening, as the Army did not see fit to keep UNRRA informed.[58]

The most immediate task was to locate adequate installations to house the children – not an easy task given the severe crowding in the existing centres and the Army's reluctance to open new space.[59] However, by October, UNRRA had opened six more permanent children's centres for Jewish children. By December, the children's housing crisis had been averted: a large reception centre was operating in Rosenheim with a capacity of a thousand; there were ten centres spread over the four districts (with four of them located in District 5, the district that had received the bulk of the infiltrees), with a total capacity of thirty-five hundred; and some children had been placed in the International Children's centres at Prien and Aglasterhausen. Rosenheim was not really satisfactory, as it was intended as only a transit centre and so too cramped to be truly adequate as a more permanent residence – but at least it was an improvement over tents. Rosenheim had the added benefit of giving UNRRA a place in which to house the children temporarily while they were being assessed and more permanent and suitable plans devised – giving UNRRA a much-needed opportunity to plan.

Importantly, the decision was made to leave the children grouped in their kibbutzim in the new children's centres, rather than "interrupting the pattern of organization which had given the children the greatest security during this intermediary period."[60] Although it flew in the face of social welfare practice as UNRRA understood it, this made sense as their stay in Germany initially was expected to be short and that the children (and all the infiltrees for that matter) would be moving to Palestine very quickly. Indeed, the Jewish Agency for Palestine had reassured UNRRA repeatedly, throughout the spring and into the summer, that receipt of immigration certificates for admission to Palestine was imminent and that unaccompanied Jewish infiltree children would be given priority in their distribution once received. The Jewish Agency for Palestine had been selected to act as liaison officer for the Jewish displaced persons, and so it had been given responsibility for managing the certificates.[61] UNRRA had concluded that its role should be to provide care for the children while they were in the zone and to encourage the Jewish leaders "toward the soundest future for these unaccompanied children," so that the "best interests of these children is protected in so far as is possible" – a rather more "hands-off" approach to these children's care than was the norm. While in the zone, the kibbutzim would continue to provide primary care for their charges.[62] The expectation was that UNRRA would have to do little other than provide food and shelter, and certainly no long-term planning, as the children would not be in Germany long enough to warrant it.

The immigration certificates were supposed to be issued by the British government to admit Jews to Palestine, which was a British Mandate at the time. However, the British steadfastly continued to oppose opening Palestine to the European Jews, in spite of mounting international pressure, and especially pressure from the United States, which had begun in late 1945 and only increased over the course of 1946. Thus, through 1946, the British refused to issue any certificates, only finally releasing them in March 1947 and then, only in the British Zone; the British also resolutely refused to consider infiltrees into their zone as displaced persons, and so they were denied UNRRA care there more generally, as well as access to the certificates.[63] This meant that, rather than quickly flowing through and out of the US Zone, the infiltrees remained in it, crowded into inadequate and cramped makeshift camps. By January 1947, the influx had slowed to a trickle, and the numbers were much what they had been in October: approximately twenty-five thousand children among a total Jewish population in the US Zone numbering some 140,000. Of those twenty-five thousand children, some six thousand were unaccompanied, and almost twenty-five hundred of them were infiltrees. As the infiltrees backed up in the camps, the concern shifted from managing the influx to the now predictable problems of inadequate housing and shortages of the basic necessities, ranging from winter clothing and shoes to light bulbs, household furniture, linens, and recreational materials.[64] And as the child welfare workers realized that the children were not leaving any time soon and as they became more familiar with both the children and the kibbutzim, their concerns grew.

One immediate task was to register the children.[65] At a minimum, UNRRA needed an accurate head count of all unaccompanied Jewish children under the age of eighteen and their full registration. This would allow UNRRA to plan the services required, now that the children were going to be in their care for some time, including education, medical care, recreation and welfare services, and tracing. Registration would also allow a child to take advantage of all "opportunities for care" that might become available, be it Palestine, Great Britain, or the United States (for those with relatives in either country) – especially since the Palestinian option did not seem to be as certain as first professed by the Jewish Agency for Palestine.[66]

Efforts to register the children, however, were initially, very effectively stymied by the kibbutzim leadership (known as the madrichim), who saw little need to cooperate with UNRRA and were determined to maintain control over the children. As reported by one of the registration teams, "The majority of these people think only of emigration to Palestine and feel they should be moved at once regardless of restrictions, quotas and other formalities concerning the movement of a group of people in an orderly and systematic way. They regard everything that is not a direct effort to get them to Palestine as unnecessary."[67] Thus, the madrichim refused to cooperate in the registration exercise. If pressed too hard, their response was to move the children without warning to another centre or location, rather than submit.[68] District 2 Director Raymond explained in his June 1946 report:

> One morning last week, we had a trainload of 200 unaccompanied Jewish children arrive in Frankfurt. The Joint Distribution Committee was able to find temporary care for them, but before we could make any plans for moving them into camps, a Representative of the Central Committee [the Central Committee for Liberated Jews – the official representative body for displaced Jews in the US Zone] had dispersed 90 to Lampertheim, 70 to Zeilsheim etc. The children arrived at these camps at odd hours without warning. I believe that you can readily see what problems this creates, and it does not need to be pointed out that the Central Committee is working entirely on its own without relation to UNRRA.[69]

Persuading the leaders to cooperate was a slow process, and only happened when it was made clear to them that, without registration, they would never receive clearances from USFET to remove the children to Palestine.[70] Complicating the process of winning over the Jewish leadership were the considerable differences of opinion within the Jewish infiltree community itself over objectives, approaches, and politics, and especially over the handling of the unaccompanied children. Indeed, there were "so many groups interested in the Jewish children and making controling [*sic*] decisions that it [was] difficult for child welfare to take its place." They ranged from extreme orthodox to secular in nature, making it difficult to coordinate policy and programs across the groups (there were at least six dominant kibbutzim: Hashomar Hazair, Dror, Noar Zioni, Nochum, Aguda, and Mizrochi[71]). This was all rather frustrating for the child welfare workers, who increasingly felt they should be participating more closely in the care and planning for the children, but who either did not understand or were not sympathetic to the Zionists' efforts to force the opening of Palestine to Jewish immigration, or the role the children might play in that effort.[72]

By September, it was clear that something had to be done to coordinate efforts between the myriad of Jewish voluntary agencies working in the Zone – in addition to the Jewish Agency for Palestine and the American Joint Distribution Committee, the Central Committee for Liberated Jews in Bavaria, the Jewish Relief Unit, and the Vaad Hatzala were present – as well as to facilitate dealings with the various kibbutzim. At this point that Susan Pettiss was appointed child welfare officer for Jewish children. Her task was to develop and establish a program for the children's care in coordination with the various Jewish agencies involved.[73] By late 1946, a child care committee was struck, made up of representatives from several Jewish agencies – including the Jewish Agency for Palestine, the American Joint Distribution Committee, and the Central Committee for Liberated Jews in Bavaria – and it was given the task of planning for all Jewish children in the Zone, both accompanied and unaccompanied, infiltree or not.[74]

The child care committee's focus included moving the remaining children in Rosenheim into permanent children's centres (where they could receive better care and would be in better facilities), the establishment of mental hygiene (to use the then-current term to refer to psychiatric and psychological support) and educational programs for the children, and training for the madrichim.[75] The calibre of the madrichim was one of the child welfare workers' major concerns by this point. It was apparent that few were trained in child welfare or education, and UNRRA was becoming very concerned about the calibre of the madrichim in terms of their skills and knowledge. "Often young, inexperienced, and going through a rehabilitative period of their own after their war experiences," the child welfare workers feared that the madrichim were not in a position emotionally or in terms of training to help their younger charges make the enormous adjustments necessary in order to be able to move forward in their lives. As an example, Pettis offered the story of one of the madrichim, a sixteen-year-old girl who was, in her words, "extremely alert and vivacious." Nonetheless, the girl

> had been forced to hold her mother in her arms while the Germans shot her. She saw her father hung by the Germans. She was thrown into a ditch with many half-dead Jewish people and later taken to a concentration camp. She managed to escape and lived in the woods with the partisans in Russia. She fought with them and has received the Red Star decoration and several other citations for valor and courage. She had completely lost track of her only relative, a brother, when she was called to Minsk to be awarded her medal. She was one of a group who were participating in the celebration. The individuals were called up alphabetically and directly after her name was called another person with the same name was called and it turned out to be her brother.[76]

Pettiss feared that such a girl, at sixteen, was in no position to help others make the adjustments that she herself was still making. This might have been less an issue if the children had moved onto Palestine quickly, where they could receive more professional assistance, but now that they were trapped in Germany, the madrichim's lack of training in child welfare was becoming a serious issue. Fortunately, it was an issue that all the Jewish agencies and the kibbutzim recognized as a valid one.

The first training course was held for twenty madrichim at Rosenheim in November, and it was enormously successful. After that, the training was expanded, drawing in workers from the various voluntary agencies. The educational plans were as successful, with a standardized school curriculum for the whole zone in place by mid-May 1947, a standard pay scale and classification for teachers, and arrangements made for the printing and distribution of books and educational material. Negotiations for the removal of children from substandard centres to better accommodations also continued over the winter and spring months. Generally, the child care committee proved an effective vehicle for coordinating resources, preventing the duplication of effort, and allowing UNRRA to leverage the personnel available through the agencies while still maintaining some degree of control over at least the voluntary agencies' activities.[77] It also had the effect of gaining UNRRA more influence over the care of the children, as well as providing a vehicle for navigating the rocky shoals that were Jewish infiltree politics.

Of as much concern for the child welfare workers was the politicization of the children's plight and future. It appeared to some that "the movement of these children and the extent to which they are clearly being used for political purposes seems to eclipse completely any thought of the best interests of the individual child, a situation in which the exercise of the Child Welfare function as understood by UNRRA is difficult to carry on."[78] As the child welfare workers began the process of documenting the children, this became increasingly apparent and increasingly disturbing.

Equally disturbing was the discovery that while, in many instances, this group of infiltree children were technically unaccompanied upon arrival in Germany in that they were present in Germany without a legal guardian, in fact, their families were known and so they were not, truly unaccompanied, i.e. without a guardian. In a number of instances, it actually had been their parents who had initiated their move. The parents' logic had been simple: if the children were sent to Germany as part of a kibbutz, this would get them out of Poland more quickly, as the kibbutzim were given priority in the transports, and the children would get better care along the way. The parents planned to follow along later. In other cases, evidence was emerging that some parents had not agreed to their children's removal. This became evident when a memo from the Hungarian Red Cross was erroneously sent to UNRRA in the US Zone in Austria, expressing concern about some of the Hungarian Jewish children recently sent to Germany. The Hungarian Red Cross explained that it was receiving a growing number of queries from parents, asking that their children be returned home rather than sent on to Palestine, raising the possibility that some had left home without their parents' consent or even, perhaps, knowledge.[79] Ellen Trigg, a child welfare officer in District 1, reported that at the Ulm camps sixty-four infiltree children had been located by their parents in a single week.[80] As children were interviewed, it became apparent that still others had been coerced into going to Palestine. Those not interested in going to Palestine often faced intense peer pressure from those determined to go to Palestine. In at least one instance, that pressure was so unbearable that a boy had run away.[81]

Harry Liebster of UNRRA Team 567 was one of the first to encounter this particular situation when conducting interviews in UNRRA Camp Föhrenwald, in Wolfratshausen. When interviewed privately, some of the youths made it clear that they did not want to go to Palestine, because they would have to work as farm labourers, rather than at the trades they had already acquired.[82] While debriefing two kibbutzim groups at the Struth Children's Centre, Liebster's team discovered that some of the children had relatives in the United States and England. In some cases, the relatives were actually their parents who were demanding that their children join them there, rather than go to Palestine, as the children ostensibly wanted to do. Eileen Davidson, child welfare officer in District 1, drily noted, "This problem is still being worked out."[83] It became increasingly imperative in the minds of the child welfare staff that no children should be allowed to go to Palestine without first being registered and traced, and ensuring that they did not have parents.[84] If the children had parents in Germany, it was proposed, they should be reunited with them.

Both of these objectives clashed with those of at least some of the Jewish agencies and certainly with the kibbutzim. The Jewish Agency for Palestine, for one, had serious reservations about the wisdom of such reunions. Their fear was that, if the children were reunited with family members, it would lessen their chances to get into Palestine. As the Jewish organization responsible for allocating the certificates for entrance to Palestine, the Jewish Agency for Palestine had established a system of prioritization with top priority given to orphaned or unaccompanied children. Families with children were ranked seventh, almost the lowest priority, on the assumption that family units had a better chance of "leading a normal existence if left behind, or in any circumstances, because of the strength gained from their unity." Any unaccompanied child removed from its kibbutz and united with its relatives, even if they were not the child's parents and even if the removal were to be just for the waiting period (i.e., temporary), would lose its priority placement.

Others argued that to reunite these children with their parents, now living in displaced persons camps in Germany, would undermine the hard work that had been put into creating installations that were "providing the children with a reasonably wholesome life of study, planned recreation, free time, punctual meals, and so forth, in a relatively ordered, calm and secure atmosphere." If a child was reunited with its parents, the child would be removed from the children's centres and sent to a regular displaced persons camp, and generally these camps were quite overcrowded and less able to meet the child's specialized needs. In many instances, the family had to share one room, and often with another family besides. This meant that the children lived and slept in one room with a number of adults of both sexes, not a salubrious arrangement, and one in which conflict between school and "the street" and home and "the street" was aggravated, surrounded as the children would be by unemployment, the black market, and other corrupting influences. By staying together in the children's centres, they had an opportunity for vocational training and "a cultured life," as well as better supplies and food, which they would not get in a regular camp. In fact, many parents had expressly requested that their children be admitted to the children's centres, because they themselves were unable to care for them in the regular camps. These children would also stand a better chance of being accepted by the new resettlement programs (e.g., to Canada, the United States, and Australia) if they were unaccompanied.

As Cornelia Heise pointed out, however, this effectively complete separation of a child from its parents flew in the face of "the general thinking in child welfare ... that the family is one of the most important values in the children's life, and that everything should be done to keep families together and strengthen the tie between parents and children." It left many of the child welfare workers deeply uncomfortable. On the other hand, the child welfare workers were also concerned that any benefits gained from placing the child with its relatives for a short period of time would be outweighed by the impact of the subsequent break with the family group. Thus, UNRRA's decision was that children should be reunited with their parents, but that they should not be released to other relatives. This was also because it was difficult to prove the latter relationship: there was the real danger that the relative, who may or may not actually be related to the child, might be claiming the child simply to better her or his chances at emigration. This was a concern raised by Leo Schwarz, director of the American Joint Distribution Committee in the US Zone. It made more sense to encourage relatives to visit the children in the centres, but not to allow their removal – thus preserving the children's status, but also recognizing the importance of family to the children's psychological well-being. The cases then would be investigated on an individual basis to determine what would be in any particular child's best interests.[85] This acknowledged the children's ambiguous legal status – as United Nations children, they were now wards of the US Army and the relevant government concerned, which meant that the relatives had no rights or responsibilities regarding the children; nor did UNRRA, for that matter.[86]

This did not resolve the matter. Well into the period of the International Refugee Organization (IRO), the madrichim fought the tracing efforts and blocked communications between parents and children. Although the American Joint Distribution Committee attempted to assist UNRRA in maintaining family connections, itself less dedicated to the drive to get the children to Palestine at all costs, this proved an impossible task. In many cases, by the time tracing officers had tracked down the children's relatives, sometimes in other countries, the children had already moved to Palestine illegally. As soon as news that parents had requested their children's return reached the camps, the children "disappeared." In those all-too-common instances when the madrichim refused to give up a child, the case was to referred to the Jewish Agency for Palestine for resolution.[87]

In the transition period from UNRRA to the IRO, March to June 1947, some twenty-four hundred Jewish children disappeared in this way, with the quiet acquiescence of the child care staff.[88] The pattern was the same always. The entire population of a children's centre would leave quietly en masse, without notice and generally at night. They typically headed for Marseille, from where they would take a ship to Palestine. Such was the case at the Lindenfels Children's Centre. On 13 September 1948, UNRRA child care workers were informed that the entire population of the centre (212 people, including 100 unaccompanied children) had been evacuated the previous night, with the exception of twenty-nine individuals, largely youths. The kibbutz leader and even the camp administrator had been part of the exodus. Passing through Marseille, they were reported to have taken a ship to Genoa and then on to Tel Aviv. Other Jewish children's centres cleared in the same manner. In each case, the IRO was not informed until after the fact.[89] By July 1947, enough Jewish children had left Germany that the IRO was able to close four Jewish children's centres and begin to plan for the closure of Deggendorf, a particularly substandard institution. By August, the number of centres remaining open was four. By September 1948, the situation had largely resolved itself, with little assistance from the IRO, other than to not interfere.[90]

This particular subgroup of unaccompanied children had posed additional challenges for the child welfare workers, adding to the complexity of the legal, political, and ethical questions revolving around the disposition of the children they found under their care. In every instance, infiltree or not, Jewish or non-Jewish, the child search and welfare workers fell back on the principle of determining each child's case history as fully as possible before allowing any decisions to be made about the child's future. In each instance, the principle of reuniting a child with its parents or immediate family was considered the paramount and ideal solution to a child's future. It was in this instance, however, difficult to properly enforce. Other agendas clashed with the principle of reuniting a child with its parents, including those of the Zionist organizations determined to move these children to Palestine, and of the American Military Government which was becoming reluctant to commit the resources necessary to ensure the children were "properly" cared for and settled.

Chapter Six

Obstacle: The Landesjugendamt

By late 1946, child search had become quite complex. Not only were there many more unaccompanied children than anticipated and even more believed still to be uncovered, but also the children's files were becoming increasingly complicated, as the simple cases had been resolved already. It was proving difficult to find satisfactory resolutions for particular subgroups of unaccompanied children, in part because it was proving impossible to determine their identities definitively and in part because the occupation authorities, both zonal and the quadripartite Allied Control Commission, refused to make the policy decisions necessary to make resolution of their status possible. The influx of infiltrees almost derailed the child search and welfare process, overwhelming the already straitened resources of the Child Welfare Division, especially as the largest wave arrived at a time when the United Nations Relief and Rehabilitation Administration (UNRRA) was under considerable pressure to wind down its operations. The legal complications and the demands of the infiltree population were both serious obstacles to a successful conclusion to UNRRA's child search project.

By late 1946, too, other obstacles had taken shape that threatened to shut down the child search operations completely. With only a small window of opportunity remaining as UNRRA's deadline for closure of its operations loomed on the near horizon, the American occupation authorities – especially the Office of Military Government (OMGUS) – and the re-emerging German authorities, as well as the German population all became increasingly hostile to the search for unaccompanied United Nations children. By early 1947, German intransigence over the removal of children identified as United Nations nationals by UNRRA, but considered German by the Landesjugendamt (Land Youth Welfare Office), had escalated into a well-effected war against their removal from German homes and institutions, with the wholehearted support of OMGUS. By early 1947, elements within OMGUS were actively working to terminate the child search operations.

UNRRA was initially established with a very short lifespan. Originally, UNRRA was to end operations on or before 1 July 1946. Just at the moment when UNRRA was supposed to be shutting down, the child search teams were uncovering more and more unaccompanied children. It took a last-minute reprieve in the form of Council Resolution 92, passed in March 1946, to extend UNRRA's life for an additional six months, to 31 December 1946 (admittedly, not as a result of the state of child search operations particularly, but because the larger displaced persons question had not been resolved in time). Although the extension was granted, it was done with pointed criticism of UNRRA's work to date. UNRRA's General Council took its European operations to task for not having successfully resolved the displaced persons question and instructed the Administration to first and foremost encourage repatriation, as well as remove all "handicaps," such as the antirepatriation propaganda circulating in the camps, that were blocking prompt repatriation. It was to immediately register and inventory all displaced persons, their skills, and previous employment experience (a reflection of what most interested prospective recipient nations about the displaced persons, namely, their employability) and sort the displaced persons into those who wished to repatriate and those who did not. For those displaced persons who refused to repatriate, UNRRA was directed to find an alternative solution for them, including the possibility of resettlement (marking an important expansion in the options available to UNRRA). The message was clear: the camps were to be emptied.[1]

The Child Search Branch and the Child Welfare Division remained determined to uncover the hidden children; however, there was also a second drive that conflicted with the child search mission, but that was very real: "to liquidate the Displaced Persons problem as speedily as possible." It was decreed that it was "the responsibility and duty of every UNRRA employee to do all within his power to aid the repatriation of displaced persons to their homelands, having in mind of course that force may not be used."[2] The reprieve added pressure to the child search program in the form of a very tight deadline. Any unaccompanied children had to be uncovered, identified, and their fate resolved before UNRRA terminated its operations by the year's end. UNRRA's mandate ultimately would be extended for one additional six-month period, but that was not known at this time; the decision was not made until August 1946 to extend the deadline to 30 June 1947 and then only because it was unclear as to when UNRRA's successor organization, the International Refugee Organization (IRO), would be operational. This did nothing, of course, to reduce the instability undermining UNRRA's operations generally, and child search specifically, and it did very little to resolve the ongoing challenges. The short-term, last-minute nature of the reprieves exacerbated an already tense situation, contributing to a pervasive sense of uncertainty about the search program and the fate of the children, as well as undermining UNRRA's legitimacy more generally, as it became increasingly a spent force.

One further obstacle compounded the situation and threatened to bring child search to a grinding halt even before UNRRA closed its doors, namely, the hostility of the German population, the Jugendamt offices, and OMGUS – and their increasingly strong objections to child search.

The Landesjugendamt and the Vexacious Matter of Removal

The situation was made more complicated by the growing intransigence of the German authorities and institutions, especially the Landesjugendamt and its branches, as well as the German population, to the removal of children from their institutions and homes. From the beginning, UNRRA had worked on the principle that any unaccompanied non-German child living in a German institution or with a German foster family, and whose nationality was clearly established and confirmed by the appropriate liaison officer, would be removed from that institution or family and moved to an UNRRA facility in anticipation of the child's reunion with its family or repatriation. Any child being subjected to abuse or suffering from inadequate care, and who was suspected of being non-German, would also be removed to UNRRA care. Otherwise, the child was to be left in situ until a decision could be made regarding its status, either repatriation or resettlement.[3]

The practice that had evolved for removal was straightforward: the UNRRA officer would identify a child for possible removal, get confirmation of the child's nationality from the putative liaison officer (who, in acknowledging the child as being of that nationality, was then assuming responsibility for the child), and request the local military detachment to actually physically remove the child. The military detachment's participation was considered crucial for several reasons. First, the actual physical removal of a child from a home could be quite a traumatic, even violent event, especially if the caregivers objected. A military police presence helped in that situation, as a single UNRRA welfare worker (normally a woman) on her own, or even in a pair, would be incapable of enforcing a removal. Second, the American military detachment's presence at the moment of removal gave the Military Government's imprimatur on the exercise, reinforced UNRRA's authority, and legitimated the removal, even if it did not justify it in the eyes of the Germans. This process was working well as late as March 1946, although the child welfare workers increasingly demanded "appropriate credentials" that would ease their entry into German institutions and homes, as well as some kind of awareness program to inform the German population of the plan to relocate these children and the seriousness of not complying with the search efforts.[4] The lack of credentials, an oversight by the Third Army when initially granting UNRRA authority to locate and care for unaccompanied children, had not initially been a problem, but was increasingly proving to be such.[5]

As UNRRA intensified its efforts to screen German institutions, it found itself on a collision course with the newly resuscitated Landesjugendamt, which in turn was becoming increasingly vocal and organized in its protests against the removal of children it considered to be German. The Landesjugendamt did not object to the removal of children in principle; it was quite willing and eager for UNRRA to take responsibility for those children it considered to be of foreign nationality, if just to reduce its own financial burden. Indeed, if concrete evidence emerged that led to the conclusion that a child was not German, all the German agencies, including the private ones, were keen to have the child removed. This was made very evident in the case of one group of children in a Passau institution whose nuns had been stubbornly opposing their removal for twelve months. In an astonishing volte-face in early November 1946, the sister who ran the home requested that UNRRA take over responsibility for seven of the children as they had now heard from their parents in Poland.[6] It should be noted that the impulse was mutually shared, as UNRRA was just as keen for the Landesjugendamt to review those children who they had identified as unaccompanied, but whose nationality was uncertain, in order to identify those who might be German, for the same reasons. As early as June 1946, UNRRA was sharing information with the Landesjugendamt about children it had uncovered and who it suspected were German.[7]

Nevertheless, the German authorities and public were increasingly challenging UNRRA's right both to enter their institutions and homes and to remove children deemed non-German, and the Military Government was increasingly sensitive to the German complaints. The case of Sister Serafina and the Kallmünz nuns (discussed in an earlier chapter) was just the thin edge of the wedge. In that instance, when the twenty children had been removed from the Kallmünz home over the nuns' protests, the nuns had turned to the German authorities for help, arguing that the children were German and should be returned to them. By May 1946, their complaint had reached the Bavarian Red Cross, which then approached the UNRRA offices in Munich. The nuns, through the Catholic youth protection association with which they were affiliated, as well as a representative of the bishop of Regensburg, also protested to the Military Government in Regensburg. The Bavarian Red Cross explained that the nuns insisted that at least twelve of these children were certainly German based on what they knew of the children's history, although they admitted that the nationality of the other eight might be "questionable." In light of this, the Bavarian Red Cross demanded that the children be returned immediately to the home in Kallmünz, at which point "competent German official agencies" and UNRRA could determine the children's nationality through a "*mutual* clearing action [emphasis in original]." Only in this way, the Bavarian Red Cross argued, could "hardship ... be excluded and injustices against the parents and relatives of the children ... avoided."[8]

In another case, seventeen children had been evacuated from Yugoslavia to Germany, acknowledged as Yugoslavian by the Yugoslavian liaison officer, and plans were made for their repatriation. However, the German religious institution caring for them lodged a protest with the Military Government and the plans were put on hold, pending further investigation. In another instance, a child by the name of Koryman was recognized as a Pole by the Polish liaison officer, based primarily on verbal reports (the documentary evidence was admittedly thin). The child was removed from a German home, but when the foster family protested, the Military Government ordered the child's return, pending proof of nationality and a demonstration that UNRRA had the proper authorization for removal.[9]

At the heart of the matter was the question of Volksdeutsche or ethnic German children, yet another category of unaccompanied children for whom policy had not been formulated. The difficulty here lay in determining which children were actually Volksdeutsche and which were not. The children from Silesia posed a tricky problem, both because of their numbers – estimated to be several thousand in Germany – and the complicated nature of their story. As UNRRA understood it, and as the Polish authorities explained, Silesia had been German territory prior to the war, but had had a large Polish population living in it, people of Polish origin and nationality. During the Nazi regime, these people had been forced to take German citizenship in order to obtain food, housing, and employment. These people were those now referred to by the Poles as "Volksliste" (a modification of the term as it was used from the Nazi era; key was that the Polish version of the term applied to those *forced* to take German citizenship). Anyone in this category was welcome to reclaim Polish citizenship. There were, however, also the Volksdeutsche, people of ethnic German origin, who had declared themselves voluntarily to be citizens of the Third Reich. The Polish government had made it clear that these people would not be reinstated as Polish citizens. For those still in Poland, it was expected some would be interned; others probably would be expelled from the country. What this meant for those outside of Poland was unclear. Because of the paucity of documentation, it was unclear to the child welfare officers whether children from Silesia were Volksliste and therefore Polish or Volksdeutsche and therefore German – which had important ramifications in terms of the options available for their disposition.[10] The Landesjugendamt insisted that these children were German, based on the testimonies of the directors of the children's homes and the children's foster parents, who firmly maintained the children's German origins. The Landesjugendamt objected strongly to UNRRA's assertion otherwise and to the removal of the children to UNRRA facilities.[11]

Crucial to the argument was the reality that the methods used to determine the nationality of a child from this particular background were necessarily unreliable and subjective. As the children typically had no documentation, investigators had to rely on "less dependable factors" such as the children's statements about nationality, residence, place of birth, languages spoken, and the military service of family members. The spelling of names was taken as another indicator. Indeed, two of the key indicators (and often the only indicators) used by the Landesjugendamt were whether the child's name was German and whether it was born in a "German" area of Eastern Europe (such as Silesia or the Banat).[12] From UNRRA's perspective, this was extremely unreliable, as apparently many of the names of the children had been Germanized by the Nationalsozialistische Volkswohlfahrt (NSV, the Nazi People's Welfare Organization). Another measure used by the child search officers was the circumstances under which the children came to Germany: Were they forcibly removed from their homes? If so, they were likely to be non-German. Interviews with hundreds of children had identified certain key institutions in Upper Silesia that had served as collecting points for victims of the Germanization program (Lebensborn), such as Klosterbruck – yet another indicator, then, if a child had come through one of these children's homes. The children's body language and psychological reactions to questions about national-ity were also considered indicative. The German child, according to the child search officers, answered such questions freely and promptly. The non-German child often asserted its German nationality, but did so with embarrassment, hesitation, confusion, or a "frantic appeal to a member of the staff for help in making a reply." There was often considerable evidence of coaching on the part of the staff, from the officers' perspec-tive, and children suspected of being non-German often asserted that they were not Polish, but were German, before even being asked the question. In too many cases, children who insisted they were German, when removed from the home, were soon speaking fluent Polish and interacting freely with other Polish children.

In addition to this interrogative approach, UNRRA's Central Tracing Bureau was used in all cases as a way of locating parents and other family members. Often it was possible to reunite siblings, which also helped clarify a child's history and nationality, especially if the siblings were older. Once the information was compiled, UNRRA turned to the appropriate liaison officers for a final determination. Without firm policy from the occupation authorities or the Allied Control Authority, this was the practice that had evolved. It left UNRRA open, however, to challenges from the German authorities, who were just as inclined to read the scanty evidence available as demonstrating a child's German nationality as UNRRA was to read it as evidence of the opposite.[13]

The lack of definitive evidence was, in one sense, not as crucial an issue for UNRRA's staff as it was for the Landesjugendamt. UNRRA's staff argued that, for their purposes, if the information was enough to convince them that a child was not German, this was sufficient to warrant removal. Whiting, the UNRRA director for the US Zone, offered three cases that he believed vindicated UNRRA's perseverance:

> A girl, one of the group identified as Polish, wept upon removal from the German institution, insisted that she could not speak Polish. The moment she boarded the repatriation train, however, she began to speak Polish and identified herself completely with the Polish group. A three year old child taken from a German institution over protests of the German authorities was repatriated and immediately recognized in the Polish reception center as the child of a woman who had inquired just two days earlier when she might expect the baby back from Germany. In the case of two boys taken from a German institution with a group of 16, the pressure brought by the German authorities required two conferences with liaison officers. The night before the repatriation transport left German authorities called by telephone to reiterate the fact these boys were German and were not to accompany the transport. On arrival in Poland it was found that the father was living at the original home address in Poland and was daily expecting the return of the boys.[14]

UNRRA's policy was that its people did not make a definitive determination of nationality. From the beginning, that was the prerogative of SHAEF, and then the United States Forces European Theater (USFET), its successor. After the chaos of the summer of 1945, and when it became evident that there was going to be a sizeable residual population of displaced persons for the near future, USFET had become concerned about the serious drain on resources they posed at a time when those resources – housing, food, fuel – were scarce.[15] The question of who exactly qualified for aid became a very important one. Unfortunately, it was one that SHAEF had not anticipated, having failed to properly sort through the displaced persons admitted to the assembly centres over the summer months. By that autumn, there was serious concern that many who were receiving aid in the displaced persons camps did not qualify for it, including enemy nationals. Nor were the first efforts to sort the displaced persons successful, as it was very clear that neither the UNRRA nor military field personnel understood who qualified. By mid-November 1945, in an attempt to address this, USFET had issued a directive, "Determination and Reporting of Nationalities," laying out exactly who was eligible for assistance and who was not. The purpose of this directive was to clarify much of the confusion, although it was ultimately not completely successful.[16]

As explained in the directive's opening paragraphs, its purpose was to assist military personnel and UNRRA teams in determining the nationalities of displaced persons and to summarize standing policies and procedures for dealing with the various categories. This was because, based on the evidence provided by weekly reports from assembly centres, as well as other reports, "considerable confusion exists regarding the definition of nationalities and the assignment of individuals to their appropriate category. In many cases there has been a tendency to identify persons by reference to their religion, to geographical regions, to national sub-division, to ethnological groupings, and to other unrecognized categories, rather than by reference to the political state of which they are citizens or nationals."[17] The directive's purpose was to provide a comprehensive list of the acceptable categories of displaced persons. Note that it was USFET providing the list, one to be used by UNRRA, as well as by and military field personnel, in determining who among the displaced persons population was eligible for the aid UNRRA was providing, but USFET was funding. In the determination of that eligibility, nationality effectively was being assigned (by referencing the displaced persons "to the political state to which they [were] citizens or nationals"), as eligibility was restricted to displaced persons from a long list of acceptable nations (categorized as United Nations, neutral Nations, and "political entities," which included, for example, the Baltic states, Jews who do not wish to repatriate, persecutees, and the stateless) and distinguished from those deemed ineligible (categorized as members of ex-enemy nations).[18]

UNRRA was content to leave the determination of nationality to USFET. After all, it was not until October 1945 that it is possible to talk of UNRRA being operational in the field, precluding it from doing any screening of its own. Teams had been brought forward beginning in May, but they had been few on the ground, very inadequately equipped, and their role carefully circumscribed by SHAEF. For the summer of 1945 it was SHAEF that controlled the handling of displaced persons and was supposed to be making the determination of eligibility. In keeping with the policy that UNRRA did not determine nationality, those few UNRRA welfare workers who were in the field were instructed to take the displaced person's self-reported nationality at face value and to record that nationality on the DP2 (registration) card when admitting a displaced person to an assembly centre.

When UNRRA took over the displaced persons camps in the autumn of 1945, it expected that the camp populations would have already been purged of all those who were ineligible for assistance by USFET. According to the original agreement between UNRRA and SHAEF and the subsequent agreement with USFET, it was, after all, SHAEF's responsibility to evict ineligible displaced persons, not UNRRA's, and UNRRA had neither the resources nor the policing authority to manage any such evictions. UNRRA was especially keen to avoid being put in the position of having to determine who was a collaborator. This kind of determination would have required definitive proof of collaboration, from UNRRA's perspective, as denying aid based on only a suspicion of collaboration, it was felt, would "be contrary to UNRRA policy and could result in grave injustice."[19] From the beginning, UNRRA was keen to cede control over screening the displaced persons population to SHAEF. It was ultimately a vain hope, as SHAEF had done little sorting by the time UNRRA took over administration of the camps.[20]

Nor was this sorting going to be an easy task, as the USFET directive failed to recognize both the vagueness of certain of its categories of nationalities (thus leaving them open to interpretation and manipulation), and the basic difficulty of those in the field trying to determine the nationality of a displaced person who had no documentation. This meant that it was a certainty that there were many in the DP camps who should not be there, and as it became clear that the displaced persons were not going to go anywhere any time soon, it behooved USFET to screen the camp populations for any individuals who were ineligible for assistance.

During the last half of 1945 and most of 1946 there were repeated efforts by USFET at screening the camp populations – all ultimately unsuccessful. In each of two major screening exercises, UNRRA was largely sidelined. In the first attempt, it was to be a uniquely military effort, although the UNRRA camp directors were expected to assist as far as organizing the camps' inhabitants and providing rosters of names and facilities. Almost as soon as the operation got underway, certain quarters in UNRRA were questioning its efficacy.[21] The "untrained and unbriefed ... [and] disinterested" screening teams and boards were manifestly out of their depth, and the screening exercise soon collapsed.[22] The second screening attempt, in spite of coaching from UNRRA personnel (requested by USFET), was as disastrous, with the military personnel at sea in the face of the extremely complex problems of nationality determination confronting them.[23]

In frustration with the incompetence of the military screening teams, but recognizing the need to screen the camp population in order to reduce its size and to ensure that only those who deserved aid got it, UNRRA Germany twice tried to take control of the eligibility review process. First in European Regional Office Order No. 52 (issued on 24 June 1946) and then in European Regional Office Order No. 40A (a pared-down version of No. 52, issued on 9 July 1946), UNRRA asserted that it had "a very definite duty to assist military authorities in their task of determining eligibility for Displaced Persons care" and that there was no reason why UNRRA should continue to provide aid to those "obviously ineligible." Instead, it would provide its own list of those individuals it deemed eligible. USFET was willing to concede that, as a part of its function of administering the assembly centres, UNRRA had a duty to assist USFET in screening, but that was as much as it would allow.[24] By August 1946, USFET was even more blunt. As far as USFET was concerned, "directives and instructions of this [USFET] headquarters provide the basic policy and the eligibility conditions." If the General Council of UNRRA had passed a resolution that obliged it to offer care to those considered ineligible by USFET, "UNRRA must assume full responsibility for them including maintenance, care, housing and supply."[25] USFET would not fund the care or maintenance of anyone it did not consider within its definition of eligibility. Anyone else who UNRRA deemed eligible would have to be funded by UNRRA.

In the face of this financial threat, UNRRA quickly conceded defeat in the battle over determination of eligibility. The European Regional Office issued Administration Order No. 146, which stated explicitly that determination of eligibility would be carried out "in cooperation with U.S. Army screening procedures and not as a separate operation," that clear cases of ineligibility for UNRRA care would be referred to the Military Government for immediate removal, and "in case of conflict in policy between Military and UNRRA, military directives will control." Any conflict in interpretation would be referred to higher military-UNRRA echelons for resolution.[26] At the same time, the European Regional Office also issued Order No. 40G, politely but firmly urging the Military Government to expedite its screening, especially because the determination of a displaced person's collaboration with the enemy was a military responsibility, as was the removal of all ineligibles from the camps.[27] By late 1946, screening was clearly USFET's responsibility, not UNRRA's. This also held true for the determination of an unaccompanied child's nationality. UNRRA's role was simply to accumulate whatever evidence it could as to a child's nationality and, based upon this, draw a tentative conclusion as to possible nationality. The evidence was then to be turned over to USFET for a final determination of nationality. In practice, however, USFET had ceded the final determination to the national liaison officers accredited to it, as it was the liaison officers who determined whether the individual displaced person would be accepted as one of their nationals. For these reasons UNRRA argued that removal was not a definitive assertion of nationality, but only the first step in a process with several stages of review to it. The Landesjugendamt interpreted this differently, and the battles heated up over the course of mid- and late 1946.

One such battle erupted over a number of children at the Englisches Institut in Neuhaus. There were fourteen children, all from Silesia and all registered by UNRRA in April 1946. In the initial assessment, the children were recorded as being of German nationality, and on 7 May 1946, the Polish liaison officer had rejected them as Polish because of insufficient evidence. However, a month later, a second Polish liaison officer accepted them, at which point there was a meeting held on 21 June between the liaison officer, the UNRRA child welfare officers, and one of the sisters responsible for the home to determine the children's fate. The conclusion: the children were determined to be of Polish nationality. The decision was made to remove them from the institution and put them into an UNRRA children's centre, in anticipation of their repatriation.

When Anthony Kuharich of UNRRA Team 143 contacted Sister Reinelis, who was in charge of the institution, in order to arrange the children's removal, she now protested that the children were German and that she would not release them to him. She also complained bitterly about an earlier instance in which UNRRA had removed another sixteen children from the home after having determined that they were of Polish nationality, children Sister Reinelis also believed to be German. Indeed, she had argued that one boy's father had been about to be expelled from Poland as Volksdeutsch – proof, she argued, that he was German. Having been caught by surprise once, Sister Reinelis was ready this time, and she moved to mobilize her superiors at Caritas Landes Verband, who protested to the Office of the Military Government, Bavaria (OMG Bavaria) about both the earlier move and this one.

In response to these complaints, Kuharich interviewed the children himself. It is worth going into detail about his investigation, as it exemplifies the thin ground upon which many decisions about a child's future were being made. By the time of the interview, one child's future had already been determined – his mother had been located in

Mecklenburg, and he had already left to join her there (the files leave the question of his mother's [and therefore his] nationality unanswered). Of the remaining thirteen, Kuharich considered eleven to be German, having been born in territory that was part of Germany prior to 1939, but given to Poland at the end of the war. In addition, he stated that the children had insisted that they were German and that only German had been spoken in their homes. They all also insisted that they did not want to leave Neuhaus for a children's centre. Of the two remaining children, Kuharich initially speculated that one might possibly be Polish, based on his birthplace as reported on his DP2 card (the child was too young to remember either his date or place of birth). According to Sister Reinelis, however, the child's mother had put it in the Klosterbruck orphanage, and that was an orphanage reserved for German children. The second child, Kuharich felt, might possibly be Czech, since he was born in Ostrau, which was near the Polish and German borders. But this child insisted he was German and that only German had been spoken in his home. In the end, Kuharich concluded that all the children were German and recommended against their removal. Certainly he was swayed by Sister Reinelis's opinion and by her refusal to give up the children. Birthplace, testimony from the children as to the language used in their home, and the place where they grew up were all thin and contentious grounds for determining nationality. This also suggests an elision of two concepts, nationality and citizenship, with citizenship acting as a determinant of nationality – a flawed assumption to make in Central Europe especially, where ethnic minorities abounded (and still do). Birthplace, in such a situation, may serve as an indication of citizenship, but not nationality (read: ethnicity).

Eileen Davidson, an UNRRA child welfare specialist for the US Zone, who had ordered the children's removal, was taken aback by Kuharich's action. She doubted that Klosterbruck was strictly for German children, citing two other children, the Dlugolzinski brothers, who had been part of the May removal from Neuhaus and had also come through Klosterbruck. These boys had been returned to Poland in July, along with their sisters, where they were reunited with their father, who was certainly Polish. Impatient, Davidson made the point that there was an appeal procedure in place (established by USFET and OMGUS in light of the deteriorating relationship between UNRRA's Child Welfare Division and the Landesjugendamt). If the German institutions felt they had real evidence to the contrary, they were to submit it to the Kreisjugendamt (the county-level Youth Welfare Office) who would review it. If it deemed the complaint to have merit, that office would pass the complaint on to the Landesjugendamt for consideration by a committee of representatives of the OMG Bavaria, UNRRA, and liaison officers. So Davidson asked Kuharich to advise Sister Reinelis that she had one week in which to present her evidence to the local Kreisjugendamt, arguing that this was "ample time for Sister Reinelis. After all, these children were first registered by us [UNRRA] in October 1945. She must have her facts assembled by now."[28]

In September and again in late October 1946, Davidson requested permission from OMG Bavaria to remove the children. She pointed out that the German authorities had failed to submit any evidence as to the children's nationality, in spite of their names being reviewed by the Suchdienst (the German Search Service) – an added precaution requested by the Child Search Branch – which had reported that it had had no inquiries from these children's parents, suggesting strongly that they were, in fact, not German. Given that some of the children had siblings who had already repatriated to Poland, it seemed clear to Davidson that these children should be removed. Finally, in November, OMG Bavaria agreed – eight months after the children had been first registered.[29]

In another instance, Captain Sill of G-5 Intelligence, USFET, asked UNRRA to explain the removal of eleven children from St Joseph's Kinderheim in Kaufbeuren. This was a group that an UNRRA child search officer, Susan Pettiss, had discovered in October 1945 when first investigating German institutions in Bavaria. These children had also come from Upper Silesia. Subsequent investigation had determined that, of the fifty-three children in the institution, twenty-one were probably of Polish or Czech nationality. Of the remainder, the tentative conclusion was that they were either of doubtful or German nationality. Those considered Polish had been reported to the Polish liaison officer, Major Marian Langer, who had acknowledged them as Polish and asked for their removal. Sister Irmentraud had protested, arguing that none spoke or understood Polish and that they were German children who had been evacuated from German territory. When Langer heard of the complaints, he had requested that the children be returned to the Kinderheim. His logic was simple. Given that the children were all more than ten years old, and had been brought up as Germans, "we suppose it would be very difficult to change their minds. Our intention is to repatriate without any pressure." However, he never revoked his decision that they were of Polish nationality. As a consequence, before returning the children to the Kinderheim, a child welfare representative of the Polish Red Cross was asked to reinterview them. This representative confirmed the children's Polish nationality, and when Langer was informed of this, he retracted his decision. Sister Irmentraud appealed the decision to Director Max Schneller of the local branch of a Catholic youth welfare organization, the Katholisches Jugendfürsorge der Diözese Augsburg e.V., who then wrote to USFET to ask that the children be returned to the Kinderheim in Kaufbeuren, thus sparking Sill's October query.[30]

As late as December 1946, Dr Bamberger (of the Landesjugendamt) was still pursuing the case of the Kallmünz children, arguing that she had evidence that they were all of German nationality. Indeed, four of them had already been reunited with their German families. At the same time, she protested the earlier removal of an additional ten children from the same home (these ten children had been removed in May 1946, over the protests of the home's administration and of the Landesjugendamt).[31]

In October, the Landesjugendamt also submitted a particularly damning report to the OMG Bavaria of twelve other instances in which UNRRA had removed children from German institutions who the Landesjugendamt considered to be German or children they were actively tracing. In total, this involved a further sixty-eight children, sixty-two for whom the German authorities felt they had sufficient evidence to determine their German nationality, three of whom they considered definitely of a foreign nationality, and three of whom were still under investigation. To make matters worse, seventeen of the children had relatives reportedly asking for them; by mid-November, the Landesjugendamt had located another two mothers. In each case, Bamberger requested that the children be returned to their institutions.[32]

These battles between UNRRA and the Landesjugendamt were becoming very involved and time-consuming, fought out one child at a time. The process of determining the reality of a child's nationality had become increasingly complex and difficult, as the easy or obvious cases were, by now, resolved. The remaining ones were much more challenging, largely because of a lack of information. This made it easier for the Landesjugendamt to challenge UNRRA's determinations and harder for UNRRA to defend them. The Landesjugendamt was also becoming expert in using both the bureaucracy and a growing sympathy on the part of OMGUS to slow down, if not thwart the removal process completely, even if it was unable to definitively prove German nationality.

One result was that many children found themselves caught in limbo for protracted periods of time, as they awaited a truly final determination of their fate. Such was the case of a group of children in the Waldschule in Neustift.[33]

This particular case involved a total of nineteen children (all but two Polish, and many of them siblings). In August 1946, Eileen Davidson requested permission from OMG Bavaria to remove them from the Waldschule in anticipation of their repatriation, since the Polish and Yugoslavian liaison officers had accepted them as their nationals. By month's end, OMG Bavaria had granted permission for the removal of nine of them (the request had been submitted in two batches, the first containing these nine names). UNRRA's preference was to keep siblings together, if possible, so it chose to wait for the rest of the clearances. Meanwhile, the Landesjugendamt immediately informed OMG Bavaria that these children were being investigated as possible German children and that they should not be removed until that investigation was completed. In light of the protests, OMG Bavaria withdrew its permission and requested that Davidson submit all nineteen names to the Suchdienst, which she did. By mid-October, the Suchdienst reported that it only had information about one group of siblings in the batch, the five Steindor children. A Maria Steindor had inquired about the children, although the Suchdienst had no information about her relationship to them. Davidson again requested permission to remove all the children from Waldschule, with the exception of the Steindor children, suggesting that only they remain in the institution while Maria Steindor was tracked down and the nature of her relationship established.

The Landesjugendamt and the director of the school, Sister Perpetua, mounted a strong campaign to prevent this from happening. Even before the Suchdienst reported back, Sister Perpetua had written to the Landesjugendamt arguing that neither of the other two boys, Alois Przylutski or Heinrich Rollnik, should be removed. In each case, she argued, the boy was unable to reliably state his nationality, and there were no documents available to determine his nationality definitively. Both boys spoke only German; their parents had spoken German (in Przylutski's case, his parents also spoke Polish); neither boy had any known relatives in Germany. In both cases, Sister Perpetua maintained, "the boy wishes to stay in Germany and could be induced to return to Poland only by force."

Interestingly, this did not reflect the results of the initial interviews with the boys as recorded by UNRRA upon registration; Przylutski had been first interviewed on 28 May 1946, and Rollnick four days later. In that initial interview, Alois Przylutski had explained that, while he could speak a little German before being sent to a German children's home by the NSV in 1942, he and the other children in the home spoke Polish with one another "as often as possible" and were punished for it. Indeed, A. Rodesch, the UNRRA officer conducting the interview, had reported that Alois was very homesick, but was deeply afraid Poland would not allow him to return because he had forgotten the Polish language. He was, according to Rodesch and at least in May 1946, very keen to learn Polish again and to return to Poland.

The story of Heinrich Rollnik was more confused. Heinrich remembered his parents speaking only German in the home, but that his father spoke Polish very well. According to Heinrich, this was because his father was Polish and his mother was German. His older brother, Josef, who was living in another home in Oberlauringen, remembered both his parents speaking Polish and never German (the interviewer was inclined to give more weight to Josef's recollections, given that he was the older brother and "seems to remember everything better"). However, both brothers had agreed that their parents had Polish citizenship. As a result of Sister Perpetua's complaints, Bamberger formally protested to OMG Bavaria that Alois Pryzlutski and Heinrich Rollnik were German and should not be removed. (In this instance, ethnicity appeared to trump citizenship in the German calculations.) As a result of this impasse, in December 1946, the three boys' cases (Alois Przylutski together with Heinrich and Josef Rollnik) were referred to the Polish Plenipotentiary for the Vindication of Polish Children for confirmation of their Polish nationality, in spite of the Polish liaison officer having confirmed it already in the preceding summer.

What happened to the Rollnik brothers is not reported in the files, although we do know that they were still in a German institution as late as June 1947 and that the Landesjugendamt was still arguing that they should not be removed. Interestingly, by this time, the Landesjugendamt's argument had shifted. No longer claiming them to be German, Bamberger now argued that it would be inhumane to remove the children from the home and the close relationship they had with the staff there, or from each other. Alois Przylutski would not be reunited with his family until late summer 1948, after key identity documents arrived that July, including the following: Alois's birth certificate, a citizenship certificate testifying to his father's Polish citizenship, a certificate of loyalty to the Polish nation signed by his father, and a letter from the community office of Podlesic (his home town) testifying that his parents were considered Polish citizens. On 28 July, Alois was finally informed of his parents' whereabouts, a full two years after UNRRA first sought to remove him from Waldschule, And on 19 August, OMG Bavaria finally approved his removal.

The experience of the four Broll siblings (Antonia – the oldest, together with Nikolyj, Johann, and Karl) was similar. The three brothers had been identified in the August 1946 requests. Antonia had been discovered later, in a foster care arrangement with a farmer in Teufelsmühle, where she, Johann, and Karl were located. Although it was clear to UNRRA that the children were Polish, as their parents had been located in Poland, they apparently had been completely Germanized, and OMG Bavaria refused to permit their removal. Only in January 1947, after UNRRA received a letter from their parents in Poland, stating that they and their children were Polish citizens and that they wished their children to be repatriated, was UNRRA permitted to remove the children.

The five Steindor children found themselves in a similar state of limbo. In November 1946, Bamberger had written to the Public Welfare Branch of OMGUS to reassert that the Steindor children were German nationals, raised in formerly German Silesian territory according to both the director of the children's school in Neustift and their aunt, who had been recently discovered. Mrs Getrud Pawlitzek, the aunt, also insisted that the parents did not wish the children to return to Poland immediately, but to remain in the school until their father sent for them. In addition, an acquaintance of the children's father apparently had passed on a message to the children from their father that they should stay where they were, as he was currently a prisoner of war, having been in the Wehrmacht, and there was a distinct possibility that he might be expelled from Poland as a result. Meanwhile, the children insisted that their parents spoke German and that they did not want to return to Poland.

Nonetheless, UNRRA removed the children from Waldschule that winter, having been informed that their mother was in Germany. However, it proved impossible to track her down, which left the children caught. It was not until early 1947 that their father finally contacted UNRRA, requesting that they remain in Germany for the moment. He had finally been released from the prisoner-of-war camp but had found his home occupied by repatriates from the east with whom he was forced to live. With no clothing, no food, and no means to care for his children, and his wife (who was apparently in Poland, contrary to the rumours) desperately ill and in hospital, he could not provide for them. Meanwhile, their older sister, Hedwig, had been located. The decision was that she should be interviewed in order to get a definitive determination of nationality. Until that happened, the children were to remain where they were. Finally, in June 1947, the Steindor children, under the supervision of their eldest sister, Hedwig, were reunited with their father in Gross Strehlitz, Poland.

The Waldschule cases demonstrated several emerging trends that threatened to derail the child search process. First, the benefit of the doubt was increasingly tipping in favour of the German authorities. OMGUS was growing increasingly sympathetic to German complaints of rash and insufficiently substantiated decisions by UNRRA staff, and increasingly inclined to leave children where they were unless their parents had been located, whatever the nationality or citizenship. It was only when the parents of Alois Przylutski, the Broll children, and the Steindor children wrote to UNRRA – and in the case of Alois, submitted significant documentation – that OMGUS would entertain their removal from the German children's homes. The Rollnik brothers, with no parents claiming them, remained in the children's home until at least mid-1947. The standard of evidence required before OMGUS would be persuaded had risen sharply since child search began – only a direct request from a child's parents for the child's repatriation would do (and in the case of Alois, even that was not enough). The consequence of this for the children was that they found themselves trapped in a prolonged state of uncertainty about what their future might hold, from August 1946 when they were first identified as non-German by UNRRA to June 1947 and beyond – ten months or more; two years in the case of Alois. As the German institutions became more comfortable in their authority and better established, and with the Military Government's increasing impatience with UNRRA (which was evident to all) and increasing sympathy with the Germans, the process of extricating children from German institutions and homes had become interminable. A core dilemma was the difficulty in many cases of definitively determining a child's nationality.

The situation was untenable. On 6 November 1946, representatives from UNRRA, OMGUS, and the Landesjugendamt met to discuss how to better manage the situation regarding unaccompanied children of undetermined nationality. Part of the problem was that UNRRA and the Landesjugendamt were no longer willing to share information, even though each was uncovering children who would be of interest to the other. It was not just the Landesjugendamt that was refusing to cooperate with UNRRA, but also the other German institutions, such as Caritas. As Jean Troniak, now director of Search Team 1046, explained at the meeting, while Caritas had initially compiled a list of twenty-nine hundred names, 60 per cent of whom were reported to be from Upper Silesia, with the remainder from Poland, Czechoslovakia, Yugoslavia, and Bulgaria, it now refused to turn the list over. The issue was not that Caritas opposed the reunification of unaccompanied children in Germany with their parents, even if they were in another country. Rather, the Germans' fundamental concern, as it emerged, was straightforward – as the process of identification and nationality determination was often based on scanty evidence, mistakes were not uncommon. Caritas was reluctant to allow potentially German Silesian children to be repatriated to Poland unless Poland made clear that those children "would be returned to parents who were later discovered in Germany and found to be German nationals or refugees unacceptable to Poland." Thus, Caritas insisted that it should be involved in all decisions regarding the children's nationality, something UNRRA had been refusing to allow.

UNRRA had been just as uncooperative and obstructive, refusing to share key information about hundreds of unaccompanied children under investigation, especially their current location, in spite of repeated requests, seriously impeding the Landesjugendamt's tracing efforts as a result.[34] It was also inclined to refuse to return children already removed, even if new evidence suggested a mistake had, in fact, been made. This happened with four children in the children's centre at Prien. In November 1946, their father had been located in a Russian prisoner-of-war camp – on the face of it, prima facie evidence that he was German – and yet, as late as January 1947, Bamberger was politely, but pointedly, still requesting that they be moved from Prien to the Weihersmühle orphanage.[35] The Military Government was convinced that a clear decision on the Landesjugendamt's place in the decision-making process would do more than anything else to break down German opposition to the search for unaccompanied UN children.

The solution arrived at was straightforward, and a tacit recognition of UNRRA's straitened circumstances and looming deadline. Rather than UNRRA attempting to interview all children in German institutions, a task that would take far too long, Bamberger was to compile a list of all these children and their biographical information (such as was known): the child's name, birth date, birthplace, parents' names and last known address, and presumed nationality. These lists were to be sent to Cornelia Heise, Zone Child Search Officer, to be cleared through UNRRA's Central Tracing Bureau's files. The German authorities would also clear them through the Suchdienst and the Bavarian Refugee Commissioner. Once this was completed, there would be a conference chaired by the Public Welfare Branch of OMGUS "in order to determine future action relative to these children."[36]

Bamberger then issued a call to the various branches of the Caritas Verband to submit lists of all the children in their care. Apparently there was some concern on the part of the various levels of Caritas, because the call was followed by a letter from Mr Fritz, the Land director of Caritas, explaining the strategy to be adopted. Regarding contentious cases, he assured the complaining Caritas offices that he would pursue vigorously all appeals from the foster families and institutions, but he also urged them to pursue their appeals through the Landesjugendamt and the new review process and, most importantly, to not offer any form of practical resistance. Any instances of disputed identity should be reported to the Landesjugendamt immediately. In turn, the Landesjugendamt pledged to take seriously all justified complaints, and the agencies were urged to provide all evidence of a child's German nationality in its possession.[37] Begrudgingly and with much protest that the deadline was too short given their limited resources, the field offices complied, still convinced that the children who would end up on the list would turn out to be mostly German.[38] The German authorities had agreed to cooperate, but they did so reluctantly. They would continue to fight for the children they believed to be their own.

Misgivings

In this war of attrition between the Landesjugendamt and UNRRA over the matter of potentially Volksdeutsche children, it appeared that the Landesjugendamt was winning. Certainly, OMG Bavaria had strengthened its position when it essentially put the German youth welfare authorities on an equal footing with UNRRA, requiring the two to share information. The solution had also served to strengthen OMG Bavaria's control over the child search and identification process, by making its Public Welfare Branch the final arbiter regarding the children's ultimate disposition. UNRRA was finding its authority increasingly compromised, even while it continued to pursue its mission of identifying and settling as many unaccompanied displaced children as it could before its closure.

At the same time, while the upper ranks of the Administration insisted that all children presumed to be of United Nations nationality must be removed, a few UNRRA field workers were becoming less convinced. This was, in large part, due to the complexity of the situations they were now uncovering. In one instance, a baby was discovered in a German institution, the illegitimate child of a Norwegian woman, fathered by an SS officer. The mother had now returned to Norway and had made it clear that she did not want her child. The Norwegian liaison officer was sympathetic, believing that such a child would not be well received in Norway. However, he did not know what to do with the child who was technically a Norwegian citizen. Nor did UNRRA. In another situation, an illegimate child born of a Polish mother and French father was uncovered. The mother had left her child at a German farm and even had signed a release, turning her child over to the farmer. She had subsequently returned to Poland to join her husband and two legitimate children there. The German farmer wanted to adopt the child, but the Polish liaison officer was hesitant to contact the mother for her opinion (which was needed before an adoption could happen), because it was unclear whether her husband knew of the illegitimate child. In yet another case, a Ukrainian infant had been found in a German home. Its parents were unmarried and had repatriated to the Soviet Union, their address unknown. The German foster parents wanted to adopt the child. To make matters more confusing, it was unknown whether the child was a Soviet or Polish Ukrainian. Another Ukrainian girl, this one aged sixteen, was working on a German farm and wanted to stay in Germany, where she was happy and had a Ukrainian boyfriend, even though her mother had repatriated. By way of contrast, a fourteen-year-old Russian boy was found on a farm in Neu-Ulm. This particular boy, who had been an army mascot for the Soviet forces and originally from Leningrad, had ended up with a farmer who beat him regularly and who failed to provide him with adequate clothing. When Knut Okkenhaug, the child search officer, told the farmer that he needed to give the boy some warmer clothes, the farmer became abusive, complaining about how difficult it was now, and that he treated the boy better than his former master had. German police had removed another illegitimate Ukrainian infant from a German home because it was being ill treated and it was now in a German institution.[39] In cases of abuse, all agreed the children should be removed, but in cases where a child's parents had abandoned their child, even signed it over to the care of a German family (however irregular the process), was it right to remove that child and attempt to restore it to parents who had turned their backs on it? Opinions varied "on the importance to the child of the German family to which it has become attached in recent years, and which is often the only home the child has known," with no answer being reached.[40]

Making it more problematic for these workers was the growing disinterest of some national governments in getting their children back. Some, such as Poland and Czechoslovakia, remained adamant that they wanted all their lost children returned, but others had lost interest. One such was Belgium. In late 1946, Belgium informed UNRRA that it would no longer accept any Belgian children unless there was a relative or parent there who had actually made a written request for the child's return. The reason was that Belgium had no foster home program, and its orphanages were already overcrowded and substandard. As a result, the Belgian liaison officers had put the burden of proving the children's nationality on UNRRA, "rather than indicating any eagerness to claim Belgian children." This put UNRRA in a difficult position, and some child welfare workers were inclined to leave the children with their German families if Belgium did not want them back. However, it was unclear that this was appropriate. Moreover, there was the question of the Belgian children already living in UNRRA children's centres awaiting repatriation.[41] The effort to find these children seemed pointless to some. For the upper echelons of UNRRA, the possibility of not removing a child who was possibly a UN national was not acceptable, but cracks were beginning to develop in the facade.

OMGUS was becoming more firmly convinced that removal was bad policy. This emerging position was best articulated by Josephine Groves, an officer in OMG Bavaria's Public Welfare Branch. No child, she explained, should be disturbed until UNRRA had constructed complete after-care plans, including reunion with a relative – and the relative needed to have been located before the child could be removed. The psychic trauma of a sudden separation of the child from its German caregivers otherwise would be considerable and, to Groves, the child's interests were paramount. As well, if separation was inevitable, the German agencies needed time to prepare the German foster mother for it: "In this way O.M.G.B. [hoped] to demonstrate democratic procedure to the Germans generally and to show the contrast with the Nazi methods of seizure. In any case," she made clear, "O.M.G.B. was not a rubber stamp."[42] No child would be removed unless its future disposition had already been settled, that is, no sitting in UNRRA children's centres while possible solutions were explored – or not. Furthermore, the sensibilities of the German foster parents involved would be respected; to do otherwise would undermine the Americans' efforts to democratize the Germans. Just as the Germans were expected to respect due process and the law, so too were the occupying forces and their agents. The practical impact of this would be to leave Allied children with a German family or in a German institution for a considerable time, unless the registration teams were considerably augmented in order to handle the extra workload.

When Groves explained this position in a meeting with Eileen Davidson, now the UNRRA District 3 child search officer, and the Polish liaison officer, in which they were discussing some children they wished to remove from German care, the liaison officer exploded in rage, declaring he would not tolerate any delay and questioning OMG Bavaria's right and ability to challenge his decision regarding the children's nationality, a position with which Davidson had considerable sympathy. If they were not going to respect his decision, the liaison officer threatened to withdraw from the whole process – which would have brought the entire exercise in nationality determination, and thus settlement of the cases, to a grinding halt, as the liaison officer's approval was an integral step in the process. Groves made placating noises, but did not back down. Instead, she and the Polish liaison officer both promised to refer the deadlock to their respective superior officers.[43] Davidson was not the only one in the ranks of UNRRA who was concerned by Groves's position. Others in the field were just as concerned by what they considered to be the excessive attention paid to claims made by the Landesjugendamt regarding children already cleared by liaison officers.[44]

Certain Military Government offices were now insisting that only an officer from their Public Welfare Branch could authorize any child's removal, even a child whose United Nations nationality was not disputed. These officers, especially in OMG Greater Hesse, were adamant that the foster parent's or Landesjugendamt's consent was necessary before a child could be removed. Only in those instances when the child's parent(s) requested the child's removal and the parents accompanied the UNRRA child welfare officer to the home, and only if the persons caring for the child recognized the rights of the persons demanding the child's removal, was OMG approval not necessary. None of this was legal, in UNRRA's opinion, as the May 1946 USFET directive which governed its child search operations only required this consent at the point of repatriation or resettlement, not removal.[45]

The divisions were becoming overt, multiple, and complex in nature. They appear to be less a result of differing understandings of best practice in terms of child welfare, given that the majority of those working in the field in Germany were American-trained social workers well grounded in the casework approach, including both Davidson and Groves, but they were nonetheless diametrically opposed to one another's position on removal. What this diverse opinion demonstrates is the competing objectives of those who were involved in child search. Those in the field generally seemed particularly sensitive to the child's emotional state and needs, rendering them sympathetic to any child who fought its own removal from a foster family of whom it had grown fond, and to the often very real grief of the foster family, losing a child with whom they had established a close and loving bond. When the alternative for the child seemed less hospitable or less supportive than the existing foster arrangement, removal seemed cruel.

For Josephine Groves, it was not only inhumane to remove a child from a loving foster family, even if German, until a well-constructed alternative arrangement had been put in place (which did not include being moved to a children's centre), but it was also crucial from a larger, political perspective. OMGUS insisted that, if the German population was to learn to accept and respect democratic principles in its governance, then the occupying forces and UNRRA both must be seen to be abiding by them as well. Thus, the German foster families' concerns also had to be considered in the decisions made about their foster children. This latter concern was as important as the need for a concrete alternative plan for the child.

For Davidson and those others who argued that the children should be removed, the matter was straightforward. It was UNRRA's constitutional mandate to locate unaccompanied children and to restore them to their families, and if that was not possible, then to their homelands, if that could be determined. This was considered the optimal solution for each of these children, to be restored to their parents or immediate relatives, as only in that way could the children's emotional security be guaranteed. Second, but only still vaguely figuring in this particular position's argument, but one that would gain increasing weight, was a point that had been made presciently by Martha Branscombe during the planning discussions in 1944 – it was only in this way, by restoring a child to its family or to its country, that the child's legal identity would be secured. The debate, therefore, over what constituted the child's "best interests" was becoming increasingly complicated.

In the face of this growing debate, the upper levels of UNRRA remained firm in its resolve to remove those children deemed non-German. In early March 1947, Paul Edwards, the newest UNRRA director for the US Zone, wrote to the director of Civil Affairs at EUCOM, USFET's successor, requesting that it modify the directive for determining nationality so that "the removal from German private homes of children of undisputed UN nationality and their admission to UNRRA Children's Centres [be permitted] whether or not German authorities or the German foster parent consent to such removal."[46] He also objected to OMG Bavaria's interpretation of the caveat in the USFET directive of 11 May 1946 that a child must have "undisputed UN nationality" before the Military Government would authorize its removal. This had been interpreted to mean "the actual nationality of the child must be certain above any doubt." UNRRA, on the other hand, continued to maintain that "undisputed UN nationality" meant it was necessary only to demonstrate that the child was definitely not of enemy, ex-enemy, or neutral nationality, not that it was necessary to determine which of the United Nations nationalities the child held. The fact that the child was certainly of some United Nations nationality and not German should be enough to warrant removal. Once this was determined, argued Edwards, "there exists no sound reason to delay its separation from German surroundings, i.e. German institutions or private homes, and its admission into a children's center under the care of UNRRA for subsequent determination of positive nationality and repatriation to its home country ... [After all,] the longer a child remains in German surroundings, the more difficult would it become to establish its true nationality and to prepare the child psychologically for repatriation." Edwards asked EUCOM to inform OMG Bavaria to stop delaying removal of these children.[47] Edwards's request hit a stone wall, and OMG Bavaria continued its obstructionist tactics.

On 28 April, OMG Bavaria informed Cornelia Heise that OMGUS had requested its Public Welfare Branch to review all cases of unaccompanied United Nations children with an eye to drafting clear directives for the disposition of unaccompanied children. As a result, and because of "difficulties resulting from the current Military Government policy of approving removal from foster homes when nationality seemed clear," OMG Bavaria announced that, from that moment on, its Public Welfare Branch would withhold approval for the removal of any children from foster homes.[48] While UNRRA could continue to search for unaccompanied children, none could be removed. OMG Bavaria had effectively shut down child search operations.

In the face of these obstacles, the child search workers laboured to remove those children from German institutions and homes who had been previously cleared before OMG Bavaria had so arbitrarily suspended all removals, and to pursue lines of inquiry that were still open.[49] During the first half of 1947, in spite of the war between UNRRA and OMG Bavaria, some children were still approved for removal from German homes and institutions, at roughly the same rate as children's removal was denied (between February and the end of June, 146 cases of each). Even more children (211 cases) were referred to the German agencies by UNRRA after being identified as of German nationality.[50] In spite of these efforts, there was a sense of a job only half-finished, best illustrated in the statistics reported by the area teams in their summary activity reports for March 1946 to May 1947. In that time period, Area Team 1048 (Regensburg) alone had dealt with a total caseload of 1,714 cases in German institutions and homes (487 active as of 31 May, 468 dormant, 759 closed). The other area teams carried an additional caseload of 1,921 cases in the assembly centres (742 active, 1,179 closed), for a total of 3,635 cases. That meant that 468 cases remained dormant and 1,229 cases were still open as the teams shut down operations. Of the ninety-nine Landkreise, only eighty-seven had been investigated completely. An additional 3,837 unaccompanied children had been screened, but not necessarily registered, in the Landkreise that had been completely investigated. By June 1947, 103 requests for removal were on hold at the various Military Government offices in the US Zone.[51] Much remained unfinished.

Chapter Seven

Obstacle: The ACA Directive

The number of unaccompanied children remaining was small, only in the thousands, but they presented increasingly difficult challenges for the child search and welfare officers trying to reach a satisfactory resolution for each of them. Those challenges included the growing complexity of the children's cases and the inability of the United Nations Relief and Rehabilitation Administration (UNRRA) to definitively identify them or, in many cases, even to definitively determine their nationality. Complicating matters was the growing intransigence of the German authorities, who were firmly re-established by this time and functioning effectively, and who objected to the removal of children from German institutions and homes when their nationality was not certain. By early 1947, the battle over the children's removal had become a well-effected war, with the wholehearted support of the Office of Military Government, United States (OMGUS), and especially the Office of Military Government, Bavaria (OMG Bavaria), the state in which most displaced persons were located. OMGUS's determination to halt permanently the child search operations was made clear in the battle over what became known as "the ACA directive."

Underlying the growing tumult surrounding the disposition of these remaining unaccompanied children lay the fundamental issue of this inability to determine a child's identity. Failure to do so meant it was impossible to determine who was a child's putative guardian, as guardianship – in the case of a child without family to care for it – was determined by nationality. Without a guardian, there was no one to make a ruling on a child's ultimate disposition. Without a clear determination of nationality, the Landesjugendamt could challenge UNRRA's push to remove children it deemed to be non-German from its foster homes and institutions. Without a clear determination of nationality, a child's future was left uncertain.

There was one glimmer of hope in the midst of this growing storm, in the form of a sudden spark of interest at the level of the Allied Control Authority (ACA). The ACA's view of the problem was shaped by a bigger and ongoing debate about the determination of certain displaced persons groups' nationalities, and the question of what to do with those displaced persons whose nationality was uncertain. This issue of nationality determination applied more broadly than just to children, but it was the children who galvanized the conversation, led by the French member of the Allied Control Authority who first raised the question in early 1946. Without uniform legislation across the four zones on how to handle these children, the member argued, the only law that might pertain would be German law. His fear was that, if this was the default, the relevant German laws would clash with other countries' laws governing nationality, and the end result would be one or more members of the United Nations, as well as Germany, claiming that displaced person as their citizen. Not having policy in place to deal with this probable situation, the French member worried, could result in "serious controversy" if these children were unaccompanied and the country or countries claiming them as citizens desired to repatriate them.[1] With the end of UNRRA looming, the issue had become that much more urgent.

The French ACA member's concern struck a chord, and the Allied Control Authority instructed its Legal Directorate to draft quadripartite legislation addressing the problem. It also recommended that, until this legislation was implemented, "a provisional solution" should be put in place immediately.[2] A second effect was to galvanize the American Element at the Allied Control Authority. Lieutenant Colonel Abbott, the American member of the ACA's Legal Directorate, proposed a set of principles to be used in the determination of nationality for all displaced persons of doubtful nationality, including children (there seemed no reason, to Abbott's way of thinking, to restrict this to children only). These principles were straightforward and reflected an attitude that was becoming common to the American occupying authorities, namely, that this was an increasingly intractable problem in need of a quick and simple resolution. To that end, the set of principles was a rather blunt instrument. The principles were as follows:

1 A person born of legally married parents would be deemed to have the citizenship of the father or, if the father was not a citizen of any

state or not known to be a citizen of any state, including Germany, that person would be deemed a citizen of the country of his/her birth.

2   An illegitimate child would be deemed to have the citizenship of his/her mother, or if the mother was not a citizen of any state or not known to be a citizen of any state, including Germany, that child would be deemed a citizen of the country of his/her birth.

3   A person of unknown parentage who was born in a known country outside of Germany would be deemed to be a citizen of the country of his/her birth.

4   A person of unknown parentage born in Germany, or a person of unknown parentage whose country of birth is unknown, will be deemed a citizen of Germany.

One basic premise of Abbott's proposal was that no child (he set the age of majority at fourteen) should be removed from the care of a caregiver (defined as either a parent, natural or foster, or any "responsible person" who had been caring for the child), if such a separation "would be detrimental to the best interests of the child," whatever that meant (it was left unexplained).[3] If a child's current situation, even if in a German home or institution, was considered safe and secure, the child was to be left there. Second, and crucially, if a child's nationality was unknown, it would be presumed to be German. In fact, the proposal was going to grant these children German citizenship – a problematic proposition, as the Allied Control Authority had no such authority; only the German government, once resurrected, could grant German citizenship. The French member of the Legal Directorate objected strongly, as did the British and Soviet members, arguing that "Germany had committed a great number of crimes against humanity by the mass deportation of millions of people to Germany, and the children of such victims should not arbitrarily be given German nationality."[4] The American delegates resolutely refused to change their proposal, and the other powers on the Allied Control Authority refused to accept it, effectively shutting down any quadripartite discussion of the matter. This meant that each zone was going to have to determine policy at the zonal level. OMGUS's response was to move quickly to enshrine Abbott's proposal in an instruction to the US Zone.[5]

This new instruction would neatly resolve, so OMGUS believed, the increasingly contentious issue of the children of contested (read: undetermined) nationality, by deeming them German. It would also prevent the removal of such children from German homes or institutions unless the circumstances were considered to be physically harmful to the child. A shocking about-face, the new policy was a flagrant rejection of the claims of a number of national governments, notably primarily Communist bloc countries at this point, who argued that there were many thousands more of their children still to be uncovered and repatriated. It was also a draconian and marked reversal of the principles that had underpinned child search operations to date and to which the American military had subscribed until recently, that is, that every child was to be found and reunited with its family if possible, and returned to its homeland at a minimum. The new policy was also astonishingly blind to the implications of "deeming" nationality, an exercise with no legal justification or basis in law.

The reasons why OMGUS moved with such alacrity to enact the proposal at the zonal level were several. The first was financial. The displaced persons operations had become an enormous expense for the American occupying authorities, and there did not seem to be any obvious end in sight, as the remaining displaced persons population in Germany refused to repatriate and UNRRA's mandate restricted it to encouraging repatriation. This would change by late 1946, when the last extension of its mandate would allow UNRRA to consider resettlement options, but even then, they were few and far between and, by that time, too late. The American military's patience had worn very thin, and their conclusion was that the operations had become too costly and needed to be shut down.

Second was a growing frustration with the sheer volume of children still being uncovered who were not identifiable and likely never would be identifiable. It had been a year since the end of the war, and the Military Government was growing increasingly impatient, first, with UNRRA's inability to find a solution for all of the children uncovered and, second, with the growing "inventory" of children, as UNRRA continued to discover more and more children. If the displaced persons operations were truly to end, some kind of resolution had to be found for these children already located and whose nationality was not at all clear, and UNRRA had to cease finding and removing children to its care. The increasingly prevalent position among the American authorities was that, if a child was well taken care of, no matter what the circumstances, the child should remain where it was (i.e., in the German institution or home). This also had the advantage of avoiding the expense of having to maintain the child while trying to determine what to do with it. Increasingly, in the opinion of J.H. Whiting, UNRRA director for the US Zone, the Military Government seemed to look on the displaced persons, including the children, as a problem to be dealt with "from the rigid standpoint of military needs, and not as a matter involving human beings."[6] Military needs dictated that the displaced persons operations needed to be shut down.

This growing disinterest in the displaced persons question more generally, and the issue of unaccompanied children specifically, was due in part to the redeployment of experienced Military Government personnel who had dealt with the displaced persons since the summer of 1945 and had seen the horrific way in which the displaced persons had been treated by the Nazis. This personnel had been largely sympathetic. The new personnel replacing them did not understand the problem of and challenges facing the displaced persons. They had little sympathy for a group they dismissed as lazy, conniving, and often criminal, especially when held in contrast with an apparently energetic and hard-working German population. This dismissive attitude towards the displaced persons in general tainted the attitude towards the children.

In part explanation, too, the increasing pressure caused by the flood of German expellees coming into Germany meant that the Military Government was preoccupied elsewhere. The term "expellee" had been coined as a label for a very different group of refugees from the displaced persons. These refugees, more accurately described as forced migrants, were the subjects of a "whirlwind of revenge" (to use Pertti Ahonen's very powerful descriptor) in the immediate aftermath of the war. Across Eastern and Central Europe, spurred on by the mammoth border changes that had resulted from the postwar settlement, systematic policies of massive ethnic homogenization or cleansing were implemented. The purpose was to remove from within the boundaries of any particular country all persons who were not of the dominant ethnicity. Different nationalities were targeted: Poles, Ukrainians, Lithuanians, and Hungarians, as well as others; but most significantly, because it involved the largest numbers and because of recent history, Germans. These were both Germans who had migrated from Germany to various Eastern European countries as part of the grand Nazi colonization scheme for the east and ethnic Germans whose families had lived in these countries, in many instances, for generations. In total, between twelve and fifteen million Germans were expelled from various countries, most ending up in the four occupation zones of Germany. By 1950, there were some eight million German expellees in West Germany (17 per cent of the total population of the country); another four million in East Germany (24 per cent of the entire population). The German expellee experience was typically a nasty one – often they were rounded up summarily, shipped westward in cattle cars, and allowed to bring but one piece of luggage each. They were regarded as a potentially destabilizing element in their new homeland. The British, American, and Soviet occupation forces feared any hint of an insurrection. The Western powers also feared the expellees could be the core of a Communist revolution. Desperate to stabilize the internal situation in Germany, the occupation forces sought to ensure the successful and rapid integration of these millions into German society and the economy. The most immediate problem was to arrange feeding, housing, and medical care for the expellees, which was no easy task given the devastation of the German economy. The next task was their integration.[7] This problem distracted the American military from the numerically much smaller problem of the displaced persons and demanded resources that the displaced persons so far had been enjoying.

A third factor explaining the American impatience was the amount of physical space occupied by the displaced persons, both adults and children. Germany suffered from a serious housing shortage in the postwar period. Approximately 25 per cent of all housing stock had been destroyed or badly damaged during the war, with the damage much worse in the major cities, ranging from 50 to 90 per cent. Only 40 per cent of all German housing stock remained undamaged, and most of that was in rural areas.[8] The needs of the American military and civilian personnel had further aggravated what was already a dire shortage of space, as had the presence of the displaced persons population. With the arrival of the expellees, the shortage only became more acute. Housing repairs and new construction were unable to keep pace with the demand. In 1949, one estimate placed the housing shortfall at 6.5 million dwellings.[9]

At the same time as the expellee population grew, the American military presence was becoming increasingly permanent – something unanticipated at the war's end. Although most of the American troops had been demobilized, as the Cold War heated up, increasingly the United States viewed the three Western zones of Germany, united into one by 1949, as a potential bulwark against Soviet ambitions on the continent. This, it was determined, would necessitate a permanent American military presence in the new Federal Republic of Germany, as part of Western Europe's military defences, and the allocation of space and buildings for permanent military bases. The displaced persons, housed in large camps and often numbering in the thousands, occupied space considered ideal for conversion into military barracks. The need for space put the American military in direct conflict with the needs of the displaced persons.[10]

Further, to the immense frustration of the American Military Government, instead of declining as expected, the overall population in the displaced persons camps was actually growing, and not just the subset of unaccompanied children. As rapidly as people were repatriated from UNRRA centres, displaced persons from the community who had been denied admission for months due to lack of space, as well as newly arrived infiltrees, appeared at the gates, requesting admission.[11] This was driven in part by a decision made by the German authorities to reduce the size of and tighten up access to rations for "free-living" displaced persons (i.e., those living outside of the camps). Many displaced persons were suddenly being denied ration cards by the German food rationing authorities and so only now for the first time were appealing to UNRRA for care. As well, displaced persons living outside of the camps had always used a rough-and-ready identification card created by UNRRA as their form of identification. However, in May 1946, UNRRA had issued a new identification card to all inhabitants of the camps (and only inhabitants). The German authorities now insisted that only this new card was acceptable as proof of identification. Those living free were not issued these cards, and this meant that they now had no form of identification. To get the new card, they needed to be living in an UNRRA camp, forcing many of the free-living into the camps, many for the first time, and therefore onto the camp rolls.[12] By mid-June 1946, the population in UNRRA camps in the US Zone had actually grown by almost ten thousand to a total of 361,232 (50 per cent of the total number of displaced persons in the Western zones).[13]

Finally, the American Military Government was losing patience with UNRRA's apparent inefficiencies and ineffectiveness. It was a problem of which the upper levels of UNRRA's administration were well aware, although the solution, introducing a rigidly hierarchical, quasi-military structure, with all its rigours and supposed efficiencies, was not possible. First, UNRRA was a civilian organization, not military, in both its structure and its objectives, and its personnel could not be forced to adapt to a military-like administrative structure, in spite of their uniforms. UNRRA's operations were, by necessity, very loose and flexible, and very much about crisis management – addressing crises as they erupted. UNRRA was also a very lean organization, perpetually lacking the resources needed to pursue its mission effectively. The ever-present problems of inadequate transportation, a shortage of clerical support, and the lack of a reliable telephone network made it extraordinarily difficult for UNRRA generally, and child search especially, to do its job effectively. This all worked against the possible creation of any kind of tightly run, military-like chain of command.[14] Yet, the apparent lack of a clear chain of command and the independence exercised in the field and at the various lower levels made UNRRA's operations seem chaotic and inefficient to the Military Government. The considerable confusion in the field over who was responsible for what only reinforced the Military Government's conviction that UNRRA was inept.[15] Complicating the situation, the camps were constantly changing – relocating, consolidating, expanding, and contracting, ironically usually at the Military Government's behest – which made the appropriate allocation of personnel to teams difficult to predict.[16] UNRRA always seemed to be scrambling for staff, and staff was constantly shifting positions, locations, and responsibilities. The picture was of an organization that did not know what it was doing. In reality, it was an organization that found itself constantly trapped in a reactive posture – never able to take action, but restricted by circumstance, constraints, and practical limitations to reacting to crises as they erupted – a position that the Military Government either failed to recognize or for which it had little sympathy.

In early April 1946, the director of UNRRA District 2, R.C. Raymond, expressed concern about the changing attitude of the Military Government in a memo to Whiting. In it, he explained that, while on the whole, his relations with the Military Government in his district were good, he was increasingly concerned by the worsening attitude towards displaced persons: "It is apparent that the general intention is to try to be rid of the D.P. problem by Midsummer [sic] and to have the Displaced Persons either go home or live as German citizens ... In my opinion, the Army greatly magnifies the security problem presented by the D.P." and too easily blames the displaced person for any lawlessness in a community, "making him a sort of scapegoat." Displaced persons were too often and too easily reviled. According to Raymond, "the question of the status of the displaced persons and the program for their care has reached a critical stage."[17] Pressure from the Military Government to eliminate the DP "problem" only got stronger over the course of that spring, as it found itself increasingly hard-pressed to come up with enough space to accommodate all the displaced persons, infiltrees, and

German expellees. And the displaced person continued to be treated as "a second-class citizen and ... scapegoat."[18]

It was not just Raymond and District 2 who found the American Military Government's attitude alarming. The director of UNRRA District 5, S.B. Zisman, echoed Raymond's concerns. He found that, in his district, "there is a general approach on the part of M.G. that D.P.'s are not an M.G. responsibility in any way, that there is a general malpractice and inefficiency in UNRRA operations, and that the D.P. program has a low priority, if any, as against the needs of the Germans ... It is the observation of the District Director that M.G. officers are surrounded by German personnel and that the attitudes developed are, as a result, almost wholly one-sided – there is a failure to understand UNRRA's work and the position of the D.P.'s," especially on matters of law and order. Zisman found the Military Government officials to be "antagonistic and unco-operative," and in some instances, tension between the Military Government and UNRRA personnel was so thick that the situation was "potentially explosive."[19]

The increasingly hostile relationship threatened UNRRA's operations, both its general operations and child search specifically, dependent as it was upon the Military Government – for practical support in terms of supplies, transportation, policing, etc., and for policy decisions, as the practice was that the Military Government's policy prevailed in the US Zone and, if UNRRA's policies conflicted with the Military Government's, the Military Government policy was the default. If the Military Government was unsympathetic to UNRRA's mission, it could make it very difficult for UNRRA to operate. Meanwhile, UNRRA's child welfare and search workers were convinced that "there is now sufficient evidence both from ex-Nazi sources and from National Governments to establish the fact that organised raids were made on the countries adjacent to Germany for the purpose of removing large groups of children and bringing them to Germany where they were placed in German families and institutions." In the face of "National Governments [which] have been pressing for the return of their own children," UNRRA believed that action had to be taken to ensure the children's legal protection and the maintenance of the machinery necessary for their location, registration, and care.[20] Abbott's proposal patently did not do that.

UNRRA thus faced two serious challenges: OMGUS's determination to shut down its displaced persons operations quickly and OMGUS's determination to solve the problem of unaccompanied children of undeterminable nationality by deeming them German. UNRRA was just as determined to prevent either from happening, refusing to abandon those children who could not be identified because of the destruction of their records or whose history was so confused that it was impossible to establish their nationality, or to abandon those children with "physical and mental disabilities" – all children Abbott would have deemed German. Until their permanent disposition was sorted out, UNRRA staff in the field, at Central Head-quarters in Germany, and at the European Regional Office in London all believed that it was crucial that the children have the protection of a guardian and that the uncertainty of their nationality remain overt. It was also crucial that the type of service UNRRA had been provid-ing to date continue until plans for the children's ultimate disposition were formulated and enacted.[21]

The first impulse was to wrest control over policy from OMGUS by pushing the Allied Control Authority to issue policy directives on these questions, which OMGUS would then be obliged to enact. However, two attempts to galvanize the Allied Control Authority into action, first in March and then in May 1946, failed to achieve any results. UNRRA child welfare specialist, Eileen Blackey, sent by UNRRA Central Head-quarters in Germany to Berlin to make the case, was disheartened by the lack of consensus, as well as by the general incomprehension of the multitude of complex problems facing UNRRA in the field. Nonethe-less, she also astutely recognized that, while "there was no hope of securing quadripartite action on the major issues relating to unaccom-panied children," it was still important to stay abreast of the debate as it evolved at that level, for "while they may not end up as [ACA] directives, they may still greatly influence what may happen in a par-ticular zone."

Blackey's conversations with Lieutenant Colonel Abbott while she was in Berlin, however, were deeply disturbing. To her horror, Abbott was openly contemptuous of the plan for locating and identifying United Nations children now hidden in German families, arguing that "they should be left where they are unless they are being abused or poorly cared for," in spite of the demands from national governments that their children be found and repatriated. (How anyone would know if a United Nations child was being abused if it was never located was not clear.) Furthermore, Abbott refused to consider revising his pro-posal in any way, and he informed Blackey that, in fact, Colonel Mick-elsen, who was now the director of the Displaced Persons Division at the United States Forces, European Theater (USFET), had authorized his draft directive for use as a guide in the US Zone, even though it had not yet been officially released. (Blackey was also a bit frustrated with those same national governments because, while they were very vocal in their demands when communicating with UNRRA, they had not yet registered their demands with the Allied Control Commission, in spite of her repeated encouragement that they do so, thus weakening UNRRA's position.) [22]

Within two weeks, UNRRA Central Headquarters in Germany had crafted a lengthy letter to Mickelsen, arguing against Abbott's directive. It reiterated the chief concerns Blackey had already raised with Abbott, focusing on the two issues of deeming children of undetermined nationality to be German citizens and of the removal of children from German homes and institutions. The letter argued that the directive would effectively shut down the program to locate, identify, and repatriate these children and that this was plainly wrong. The letter did acknowledge

> The serious implications of removing children from the German families with whom they have been living for three, four or five years … [however,] it is recognized also that it is important to consider the lifetime destiny of these children. They are not Germans and should not be raised as such. Many of them have parents or relatives waiting for their return. Even those who have no close relatives still living have a right to their own identity and the protection of their own countries. It should be remembered [too] that the United Nations which have unaccompanied children in Germany have made firm demands that these children be located and repatriated.

Removal would "afford the children an opportunity to become reoriented in their own language [and culture] and to facilitate repatriation." While removal was something that had to be handled with the greatest skill and care, it was an option that had to be available.[23]

It was not just UNRRA's Central Headquarters in Germany that mobilized. The director of the Welfare and Repatriation Division of the European Regional Office, Selene Gifford, had the General Counsel's Office assist in drafting a second statement of the legal and social ramifications of the Military Government's directive for Central Headquarters, Germany's use in discussions with both the Zone Military Government and the Allied Control Authority. This statement called for a clarification and formal promulgation of policy by the Military Government and the authorization of UNRRA to act, where appropriate. Moreover, it declared that children in German homes and institutions who had been identified as United Nations children, "consistent with the desire of the United Nations for the recovery of their children," should be transferred into UNRRA custody, as should any neglected or deserted illegitimate children. A system of guardianship should be established, as well as procedures for determining nationality in doubtful or difficult cases; the European Regional Office recommended the creation of review boards for this purpose.[24] Central Headquarters Germany began to aggressively lobby the other zonal military authorities, with the aim of getting a uniform policy across the three Western zones.[25]

At the same time, OMGUS's Prisoners of War and Displaced Persons Division was becoming increasingly perturbed by the apparent discrepancies between USFET's policy regarding unaccompanied children and what UNRRA's child welfare workers were actually doing. The foundational document governing the handling of unaccompanied children remained the 11 May 1946 directive issued by USFET.[26] In spite of this directive's explicit instruction that a child was not to be separated from a parent, natural or foster, with whom it was residing or from any responsible person who was caring for it where such a separation would be detrimental to the best interests of the child, it was apparent to the Prisoners of War and Displaced Persons Division that UNRRA continued to remove children from German institutions and families, as well as from displaced persons foster families, in violation of this caveat. UNRRA was also failing to refer cases of removal and/or repatriation to the OMGUS for approval, as was required. Harry Messec, of the executive office of the Prisoners of War and Displaced Persons Division at OMGUS, directed USFET to "clarify" American policy and procedures to all concerned and for UNRRA Central Headquarters to be instructed to abide by them.[27]

At this point, a parallel low-grade turf war that had been brewing between OMGUS and USFET heated up, an inevitable collision given the way in which responsibility for the displaced persons had been allocated between them. USFET was responsible for the maintenance of the displaced persons population; OMGUS, for relations with the German population and government, and for maintaining law and order in the Zone. In late June, USFET, having previously wanted to shut down the displaced persons operations by 1 June, instead approached UNRRA to assist in writing a draft of a comprehensive policy directive or manual covering all the problems concerning the location and care of unaccompanied children. Ironically, as UNRRA's relations with OMGUS had deteriorated, they had improved with USFET, although it was being forced to assume more and more responsibility for tasks that were officially USFET's – such as finding housing for DPs displaced by the Military Government commandeering their camps, the management of repatriation, and drafting policy. In fact, one of USFET's objectives with this directive, contrary to the principles outlined by OMGUS but in keeping with an increasing delegation of responsibility for all things related to the displaced persons to UNRRA, was to expand the responsibilities of UNRRA's child search operations. USFET asked them to use the directive to delineate the responsibility of the Military Government and of UNRRA on the issues of "the determination of citizenship and a method of handling disputed claims, the program of location of children with attendant authorisation to search in German homes and institutions and to remove children from German care, and problems related to illegitimacy, abandonment, and adoption," all of which would require a solution to the vexing question of guardianship.[28] This was an opportunity, finally, to make a clear statement of the child search operations' mandate and procedures and to counter the extremely restrictive principles articulated by Lieutenant Colonel Abbott.

Before the draft directive could be completed, however, things came to a head in a meeting between representatives of OMGUS, USFET, and UNRRA that took place on 18 July 1946. The meeting had been precipitated by the growing number of complaints to the Military Government from Germans about the activities of UNRRA personnel in the field, especially concerning the search for unaccompanied children. UNRRA apparently had been engaging in what OMGUS called "unauthorized and legally questionable 'search and seizure' operations" of which the public welfare branches of the Land offices of Military Government were frequently unaware. Even worse, OMGUS accused UNRRA of removing children from German institutions and private homes without the Military Government's authorization. The UNRRA representatives bristled at these accusations. After all, they argued, UNRRA had continually pressed the Military Government to give them the necessary authorization, but to no avail. So, by default, UNRRA workers had been getting approval from local Military Government detachments for both entry into German institutions and any removal of children, and they always had either written or verbal authority from some agency of the Military Government or the tactical military authorities, as well as the approval of both UNRRA's US Zone director and Central Headquarters.

From the perspective of the UNRRA representatives at this meeting, the chief complaint of the Military Government was that

> after our interviewers have been in an institution, the staff is very much upset and the children are also disturbed. They feel that many children are interviewed who do not eventually turn out to be United Nations children and that this is a disrupting influence on the children. They were also inclined to feel that where children are living in individual German families and seem to be well taken care of and secure, these children should not be removed, unless, of course, they actually have parents back in their own countries.[29]

As the chief OMGUS representative there, Abbott explained in his minutes of the same meeting that he felt OMGUS had an obligation to also protect the legal rights of the Germans charged with the care and control of these children. This was a new twist to Abbott's arguments, namely, that the German caregivers had rights to be protected, rights that were at least as important as those of the children.

At the meeting, OMGUS announced that it wanted all search activities in the US Zone shut down until an adequate directive could be released clarifying all the points being discussed, including determination of nationality and authorization for both entering German homes and institutions and for removal of children. The UNRRA representatives reacted in fury at this proposition, as there was no way such a directive could be compiled quickly and to stop all child search activities for the interim would be "nothing short of disastrous." In the end, a compromise was struck. OMGUS would again seek a quadripartite decision on the principles of the determination of nationality, in order to get some direction on how to deal with children whose nationality was undeterminable. If nothing was forthcoming by 1 August, USFET would issue its own statement covering both the principles of determination of nationality and the issue of authorization for search and removal of children. While awaiting a directive, child search activities would continue, but there would be no visits to German institutions or homes without a written application for each visit being made to the Military Government's public welfare officer at the Land level. If, after a visit, it was determined that the child needed to be removed, a second application had to be made for authorization to remove the child. A child could only be removed if it was of undisputed United Nations nationality, or if the child was of doubtful or disputed nationality and not residing with either a natural or legal parent or close adult relative, or it was proven that neither natural parent was of enemy or ex-enemy nationality. Initially, the Military Government wanted to include all child tracing activities in this set of restrictions, but it was persuaded against this when it was pointed out forcefully that this would, essentially, stop all such work. At this point, Lieutenant Colonel Abbott proposed the directive he had drafted for consideration at the quadripartite level. Mr McCormack of USFET countered, stating that USFET was almost ready to propose its own directive – the one that UNRRA was in the midst of drafting.[30] The antipathy between OMGUS and USFET was now overt. This antipathy had always been brewing below the surface, but to have it aired so openly was a shock to all. It was also made clear that OMGUS wanted to shut down child search operations. Failing that, it intended to bury child search under an avalanche of paper and to obstruct its operations however possible.

OMGUS's position remained simple. Having been extended in March 1946 to just 31 December 1946, now a mere five months away, UNRRA's operations were due to end soon. Its strategy should have been one of trying to find a solution for those children already under its control, not trying to find still more children whose future was going to be very uncertain. OMGUS considered its own proposal – to leave the children where they were, if the care was adequate – an obvious and pragmatic one.

This also reflected a growing concern of OMGUS's, the protection of the rights of the Germans involved in these cases, especially the foster and adoptive parents. Indeed, immediately after the July meeting, OMG Bavaria informed its people that Germans were still allowed to appeal any case of removal "in which there is evidence that the child is not a member of the UN through the Kreis Jugendamt Office, which in turn [will refer] the matter to the Land Jugendamt Office for consideration and presentation to a committee comprised of representatives of UNRRA, the Land Youth Welfare Office and Public Welfare Branch, Military Government."[31] OMGUS feared that the interests of the German families and institutions were being lost in the drive to find and repatriate putative United Nations children. This was also, in part, a reflection of the Military Government's broader drive to democratize the German people. As the chief of the Youth Welfare Section of OMG

Bavaria's Public Welfare Branch, Josephine Groves, had explained earlier, if the German population and government were to be expected to embrace democracy and respect both due process and the rule of law, they had to see that they had recourse to both and that their interests were both protected and respected.

For UNRRA this solution was unacceptable and in violation of its mandate which required UNRRA, as it understood itself, to return all UN children to their families if possible, and their homelands if not – the children had a right to "their own identity." The unaccompanied children could not, in good conscience, be abandoned.[32] Second, OMGUS's solution was unacceptable because UNRRA was responsible not just to the American Military Government in the US Zone, but also to all the members of UNRRA's General Council, which included countries from the Communist bloc, many of which continued to demand that their children be located and repatriated. To stop child search operations would be to defy those to whom the Administration was accountable and, UNRRA feared, would resonate very badly on the world stage, earning howls of protest from those governments and widespread opprobrium. Finally, the OMGUS proposal would deny the children the legal protection that was their due. Deeming them of German nationality (a dubious assertion in the first instance, as the American Military Government had no right to arbitrarily assign nationality) would not make these children German citizens. The result would be a population of legal minors without any legal protection or rights – they would not be citizens of any country and so they would not be due any country's legal protection. This would place them in a perilous situation and needlessly so, felt UNRRA, when there was a possibility that their identity (and thus citizenship) might be discovered with adequate investigation. The child welfare and child search operations had to continue, so that every child had a chance of realizing its appropriate destiny and legal identity. OMGUS and UNRRA were set on a collision course.

USFET and OMGUS were also heading into a confrontation. USFET's response to OMGUS's intransigence was to quickly finalize its new directive on unaccompanied children. In this new directive, USFET claimed sole responsibility for the discovery, care, repatriation, and "otherwise dealing with" of unaccompanied children. It made clear that UNRRA would continue with its child search operations and pledged full military support for the effort. UNRRA's search personnel would have the authority to enter German institutions and homes to conduct their investigations and to make all necessary inquiries.

This latter point, in particular, was considered an affront to OMGUS's authority, as OMGUS, not USFET, was responsible for communications and relations with the German government and population. These UNRRA personnel would also have the authority to remove a child they considered to be an unaccompanied child, with the approval of the local Military Government detachment (USFET's local representation, not OMGUS's). The final determination of nationality would be made by the senior liaison officer, and any dispute over nationality would be referred to a review board to be established – consisting of one representative from the Displaced Persons Division, G-5, USFET; one from the Public Welfare Section of the Public Health and Welfare Branch of OMGUS; one from the UNRRA Child Welfare Branch in the US Zone; and one from the Judge Advocate General's office of USFET. The final arbiter on questions of adoption and repatriation would be USFET. This directive made clear that no child would be simply deemed German because of a lack of information. A child suspected of being a United Nations national would become the responsibility of USFET and UNRRA. This included any child (legitimate or illegitimate) born in or brought into Germany since 1 October 1938 and who had at least one parent known or suspected of being a United Nations national, as well as any child of unknown parentage and living with an adult relative (but not a parent), including any child of these categories who had been adopted or taken in by a German family or institution since 1 October 1938. An illegitimate child would be considered unaccompanied if abandoned or its custody relinquished by its mother. In this way, the directive curtailed OMGUS's role significantly, allowing OMGUS no involvement in child search other than on the review board to be established to deal with cases in which the child's nationality was in dispute.[33]

If this directive could be enacted, UNRRA's battle with OMGUS would be over and UNRRA could move quickly. For the interim, until the new directive was issued, and based on a recommendation made at the meeting, UNRRA Central Headquarters in Germany instructed UNRRA district child welfare officers in each district to compile a list of all the institutions and homes the welfare officers wished to enter in the next few weeks for submission to the public welfare officers for approval.[34] On 24 July, UNRRA's assistant chief of operations for relief services, C.H. Martini, forwarded the draft directive to UNRRA's headquarters in the US Zone for its approval and, hopefully, for speedy release by USFET.[35]

This was followed up, in August, with a cable from USFET clarifying the responsibilities of the various agencies operating in Germany regarding the care and control of displaced persons, with a special focus on OMGUS. The clarification infuriated OMGUS – not just Abbott, but also his superior, Sumner Sewall, director of the Internal Affairs and Communications Division – as the cable baldly stated that "written authority for the removal of children from German public or private care and control will be granted by Laender offices of Military Government upon request of UNRRA child welfare workers."[36] This implied, Abbott maintained, that the Military Government was obliged to deliver such written authority simply upon demand by UNRRA, with "no cognizance of any legal, moral, humanitarian considerations which Military Government is responsible for, especially in cases of nationality and/ or adoptions under German law still in effect." This gave UNRRA child welfare personnel "dictatorial powers" over Military Government personnel in the field, a patently unacceptable arrangement.[37] As Abbott pointedly insisted, UNRRA worked for OMGUS and operated under its sufferance, not the reverse – which was not technically true, as UNRRA was accountable to USFET, not OMGUS.

Sewall demanded USFET rescind the cable and replace it with one that more accurately reflected the results of the 18 July meeting as he understood it. The replacement should reiterate that blanket authorizations to enter German homes and institutions would not be issued, and that the procedure of investigation and removal would require two authorizations – one for entry and one for removal of the child. The requirement of two authorizations was important, in Sewall's mind, in order to allow "the German agencies … an opportunity to protest to Military Government if they feel that an injustice may be done. That such injustices are possible is recognized by all who are familiar with the program."[38] Implied was that the rights of the German people and their institutions also needed to be respected.

USFET buckled in the face of this pressure and rewrote the new directive, clarifying that no child was to be removed from any German home or institution by UNRRA without prior written approval of the Land office of Military Government concerned, because "certain legal questions frequently enter into the care and control of children with which tracing personnel are neither familiar nor empowered to adjudicate." The new directive also made clear that all cases involving the repatriation or resettlement of unaccompanied children from the US Zone had to have a complete registration at UNRRA Zone Headquarters before the Military Government would consider issuing an authorization for a child's release.[39] This was a significant concession, and one with serious repercussions for the child search operations.

Over the course of the fall of 1946, tensions continued unabated between UNRRA and OMGUS, as well as between OMGUS and USFET. OMGUS Headquarters was receiving numerous complaints from its Land public welfare branches that UNRRA continued to remove children from German institutions without their written authorization. UNRRA argued that it did have permission, but from USFET, not OMGUS. The logic was that UNRRA was administratively responsible to USFET, not OMGUS and, because the Military Government was not responsible for displaced persons, authorization for removal had to come from the tactical units, not the Land offices of Military Government – as per the 11 May 1946 USFET directive that had remained extant, by default, because nothing had replaced it.[40] It is evident that UNRRA was using this technicality to avoid dealing with the Land OMGs because, when permission was requested, the public welfare branches often denied it, either because of what the branches considered insufficient evidence of the children's nationality or, in the case of OMG Bavaria's Public Welfare Branch, which rejected fifteen of thirty-one requests in September, "because [it believed] the children are living with foster parents or close relatives who have been providing adequate housing."[41]

This was not a good long-term solution. Having OMGUS's cooperation would be preferable, as in the end OMGUS – and not USFET – managed relations and communications with both the German authorities, including the newly re-established Landesjugendamt, and the German population. Also OMGUS – and not USFET – provided the often-necessary support and assistance at the moment of removal, by both preparing the way with the German families and institutions in its role as interlocutor and facilitator and by providing security at the moment of removal, should the family or institution be reluctant to let the child go. UNRRA had no police force of its own that it could mobilize, should a removal be challenged physically. Having OMGUS liaising would also lend legitimacy to what was an increasingly contentious exercise. To that effect, the UNRRA's Headquarters in the US Zone pressed USFET to get a definitive decision from OMGUS on the issue of removal, and the Prisoners of War and Displaced Persons Division of OMGUS pressed USFET to declare itself. All the while, UNRRA continued to remove children.[42]

With his superior's approval, Abbott fought back. First, he requested that OMG Bavaria send him specific information regarding any instances of children whose removals were "legally questionable."[43] At the same time, he directed the OMG personnel in the field to force strict compliance with the 11 May USFET directive, specifically the requirement that UNRRA Zone Headquarters had to provide specific and detailed registration information on the children to be removed before authorization could be granted. If nothing else, the UNRRA workers would be buried with paperwork.[44] Abbott also resolutely refused to pass on lists of unaccompanied children that the German authorities had been compiling for his office since March 1946, although he was supposed to turn them over to either UNRRA's Tracing Bureau or Child Welfare Office in the US Zone. The lists were considered a key source of information and "the most authentic basis for determining the extent of the problem," yet Abbott would not forward them to UNRRA.[45]

In the face of the ongoing pressure from OMGUS, USFET rescinded its 11 May directive and issued yet another draft. In this latest iteration, USFET continued to assert that it had sole responsibility for the child search process and that it would make the final determination of a child's eligibility for assistance and whether or not a child would be removed. Removal would be effected if USFET determined the child was eligible and if it believed the child would be "specifically benefited with regard to health, environment and foreseeable future welfare." All tracing and compilation of information regarding known or possible United Nations children in German homes or institutions would be done by UNRRA's US Tracing Bureau, which it explicitly asserted was under USFET's jurisdiction. However, by way of a concession, USFET allowed that tracing would be coordinated between UNRRA and the Land offices of OMGUS; that the Land OMG public welfare offices would receive advance notice of entry into all individual German homes or institutions; and that the public welfare offices would be responsible for any child's actual removal. Thus, OMGUS's participation remained seriously restricted, namely, to the actual physical removal of a child from a German home or institution and to requesting a case be reviewed, while USFET insisted on maintaining ultimate authority and control regarding unaccompanied children.[46]

OMGUS's reaction was predictably dismissive. Messec, of the Executive Office of the Prisoners of War and Displaced Persons Division at OMGUS, complained that the new USFET directive still granted too much authority to tracing personnel by allowing them to enter German homes and institutions and to remove children from them without notifying the OMG offices prior to the action; that children could be removed "without due regard to the legality of such removals and/or the foreseeable welfare of the child concerned"; and that the directive failed to clarify what constituted eligibility for care in doubtful cases. OMGUS was insistent that tracing be taken out of the hands of UNRRA's child welfare personnel and be restricted to the US Zonal Tracing Bureau, which should be given the resources necessary for doing a more effective job of tracing (apparently not understanding that the Bureau was an UNRRA operation). Clearly, OMGUS did not think that USFET could or would do an effective job of supervising UNRRA's activities. With a spiteful flourish, OMGUS then forwarded to USFET a copy of a new draft of a quadripartite proposal that, it explained, had already been approved at the level of the Prisoners of War and Displaced Persons Directorate, and was under consideration at the Legal Directorate of the Allied Control Authority, in anticipation of being brought to the Coordinating Committee for consideration.[47]

This new draft of a quadripartite policy, quickly given the moniker of "the ACA directive," was a complete surprise to UNRRA – and presumably to USFET as well. UNRRA was shocked that the directive had already been approved at the level of the ACA's Prisoners of War and Displaced Persons Directorate without UNRRA being consulted. It was also shocked by its terms, because it was essentially the same as the proposal made in July and still contained the contentious clause that stipulated that "a child of unknown parents, born either in Germany or outside Germany in an undetermined country, will be assumed to possess German nationality." It also stipulated that the directive's principles would not be applied in such a way as to cause the child's separation from its mother with whom it is living; or from "a person caring for it, if such separation will be to its detriment, unless in either case, such separation is approved in advance by the Commander of the Zone in which the child is living." The two key provisions that had so incensed UNRRA earlier in the year had remained in the new draft.

Myer Cohen, UNRRA's acting chief of operations at Central Headquarters in Germany, immediately wrote to ACA's Prisoners of War and Displaced Persons Directorate and, once again, dispatched Eileen Blackey to Berlin. Both Blackey and Cohen made it clear to the members of the Prisoners of War and Displaced Persons Directorate that UNRRA had not been consulted on this draft directive, and given the impact that the directive would have on the work of UNRRA child welfare staff in the field and "upon the requests put to us by National Governments concerning their children," they argued it imperative that the Allied Control Authority consider UNRRA's opinion of the draft, given that certain major provisions were extremely problematic.

As this would be the first directive on the subject being issued by the Allied Control Authority, Cohen pushed for a preamble that provided for the location, removal, and repatriation of all children, including those whose nationality had been clearly established. To restrict its first, foundational statement on the issue to only children of undetermined nationality was counter-intuitive. Only once this basic principle was established would it then make sense to discuss the principles to be applied in special cases, such as when a child's nationality cannot be determined definitively, he argued. This would be a major coup for UNRRA if it happened, because it would establish the principle of location and repatriation for all children, including those of undeterminable nationality, and force their existence to be acknowledged (as one would not know if a child was of undeterminable nationality until after it was both located and tracing attempted and, once found, a child would be impossible to ignore or abandon).

Both Blackey and Cohen launched an attack on the provision that children of unknown parents born in Germany, or even outside of it, but resident in Germany, and of undetermined nationality, would be assumed to possess German nationality – most of these would be children of the Lebensborn program or of forced labourers, and now abandoned. Cohen argued that this would, in effect, penalize such children. He contended, instead, that it should be enough to establish that a child was simply *not* German. If this were the criterion for eligibility, then these children rightly would be entitled to United Nations care and protection even if it was not possible to establish with certainty their personal identity or specific country of origin at that moment. This also would give UNRRA time to determine their identity and nationality, necessary because many of the children being uncovered now were so completely Germanized that it was proving extremely difficult to determine their true nationality without thorough and lengthy investigation. If, however, a child was presumed German, this automatically rendered it ineligible for UNRRA services. This meant that UNRRA could no longer continue its investigation for further evidence, nor any tracing efforts, ending all possibility of reuniting the child with its family forever. For all practical purposes, these children would be treated as German nationals from thence forward. It would be impossible to preserve their theoretical claims to their true nationality and the privileges it might confer on them. Whether that was the actual intent of the proposed directive or not, its practical impact was potentially enormous for these children. This was not just an academic argument, but one with real implications.

Cohen's and Blackey's fears were justified. In a matter of just a few months, in early 1947, child welfare workers would come across three instances of groups of children whose nationality was uncertain, but believed to be Polish. UNRRA was not allowed to pursue its investigation, as it was claimed the children were German. Subsequently, all three groups were proven to be Polish, based on Nazi evidence discovered in Poland, concrete proof of the danger of the proposed policy[48] and justification for Cohen's suggestion that the directive be revised to allow any child to receive the benefit of UN care if the evidence suggested that it was of a non-enemy nationality, until definitively proven otherwise.

The second provision of concern in the new ACA directive was that dealing with removal. While Cohen had no objection to the provision that no child should be removed from its mother, he objected to the provision that no child should be removed from a non-parental caregiver. He wrote,

> It is our conviction that children who are determined to be of non-enemy origin, should be removed from German homes and institutions and placed under United Nations care. Under the existing plans for locating and identifying children, no child is removed from a German home or institution unless it was clearly established that he is of non-enemy origin. However, if children known to be non-enemy nationality are to remain in German institutions or homes, they will of necessity be lost in the German population. Too many United Nations children have been lost and too much evidence and information concerning them is still to be uncovered for us to feel that the decision contemplated in this directive is wise.[49]

Eileen Blackey also pointed out the incongruity of this section, as this was, after all, a directive designed to address the issue of children of undetermined nationality. If a child was living with its mother, then surely its nationality was known, so the child would not fall under the directive's purview? And if a child of undetermined nationality was to be assumed to be German, then there was no need for a statement talking about separating a child from the persons caring for it, because it would fall outside of UNRRA's mandate. Thus, this whole section seemed unnecessary, internally contradictory, confusing and, she feared, likely to result in the Military Government applying these restrictions to all children in the Zone, not just those of undetermined nationality.[50]

The British and French representatives on the ACA's Prisoners of War and Displaced Persons Directorate were sympathetic. Lieutenant Colonel Abbott, however, remained disinterested and uncooperative. He saw no reason why UNRRA should be consulted on the development of these policies and was not interested in any of the suggested revisions.

In late October 1946, UNRRA got another shock. Its Central Headquarters in Germany heard a rumour that the Allied Control Authority was considering releasing the ACA directive regarding unaccompanied children without revision, and that USFET was apparently unwilling to press the Displaced Persons Division of OMGUS to reconsider its position on the basis that the United States had already been committed to the existing draft by its representatives at the Allied Control Authority. USFET had found itself in an awkward position, as Colonel Mickelsen, chief of operations at USFET, was also chief of the Displaced Persons Division of OMGUS. As he had concurred in the ACA directive when it was brought up to ACA's Prisoners of War and Displaced Persons Directorate, he found it very difficult to now object to it. There was some solace in the fact that the British representative on the Directorate was not enthusiastic about the directive, but he had still signed off on it "in order to dispose of a problem which had been on the agenda for many, many months." There was the useful complication of a separate French paper on unaccompanied children which had passed the Coordination Committee, was still at the Legal Directorate, and which conflicted with the ACA directive. Neither could be released until they were harmonized. Nonetheless, the situation was critical.

UNRRA pressed USFET to communicate its objections. The hope was that this, combined with the objections channelled through the British representative, would result in enough pressure that the Allied Control Authority would feel compelled to reconsider. To that end, UNRRA's Central Headquarters in Germany also urgently requested that the European Regional Office make representations to the US State and War departments and to the British Home and War offices, opposing the directive in the strongest of terms: the directive was unrealistic given UNRRA's experience in the field; it would undermine the best interests of the children and infringe on the rights and interests of member governments of the United Nations; and it would expose the Administration to "opprobrium and censure of world opinion." Myer Cohen, who fortuitously was in Washington at the time, was instructed to contact Richard Winslow, the liaison officer for displaced persons in the State Department, and J.H. Whiting penned a detailed and scathing attack on the directive.[51]

Whiting was hard-hitting. He argued that the directive badly misrepresented the jurisdictional lines or boundaries, asserting as it did that OMGUS had authority on matters that were outside its jurisdiction. It was USFET that was responsible for the search for, identification of, and care of displaced persons, including unaccompanied children, not OMGUS. In fact, OMGUS had made it abundantly and repeatedly clear to UNRRA that its responsibility was for supervising the German government and German economy only. In matters not related to child search, such as supplies, OMGUS had insistently directed UNRRA representatives to USFET, with the explanation that it was with USFET that UNRRA had an agreement, not OMGUS. Any questions or concerns that needed to be addressed to OMGUS had to be channelled through USFET. UNRRA was accountable to USFET – and not OMGUS – and it was USFET's decision as to who should be authorized to conduct the child search. While it may have been within the purview of OMGUS to decide whether and when German homes could be entered due to its responsibility for supervising the German government and its economy, it was not up to OMGUS to determine whether the best interests of a United Nations child were served by removal, even if it had adequate personnel to do the job, which it did not.

OMGUS clearly did not understand the internal administrative structure of UNRRA, as was revealed in the proposed directive's declaration that the US Zonal Tracing Bureau worked for USFET, which it did not. The Tracing Bureau was an UNRRA unit staffed with UNRRA personnel and financed by UNRRA. OMGUS's concerns about the determination of eligibility and nationality were also inappropriate. UNRRA did not make a definitive determination of nationality, contrary to OMGUS's assertion. That was up to USFET and the appropriate liaison officers. UNRRA made a determination of nationality only for the purposes of care and custody: was the child German, United Nations, or possibly United Nations? Thus, why would it not be sufficient to make a determination of "not German"? And, just as UNRRA had always been making initial decisions for adults with no objections from OMGUS, why could it not be considered capable of doing the same for children?

Perhaps most significant from Whiting's perspective was that OMGUS appeared to have no comprehension of the challenges of working in the field. To require permission for both entry and removal on a case-by-case basis was unworkable. In order to successfully complete the search operations, practical experience in the field had shown the need for flexibility and freedom of movement, not only for the purpose of searching for children, but also for interviewing prospective informants regarding nationality and parentage. UNRRA was trying to abide by the terms of the July agreement, but had found "the mechanics provided in said agreement … cumbersome and difficult." While certain safeguards were necessary, "restricted by too many inconsequential measures the search is hampered and nullified."

Whiting also took great exception to OMGUS's insistence that a child should remain with any caregiver, even those without any legal claim on the child. In this matter, he stated bluntly, "we have a difference of policy." The concern was about the child's legal rights and protection. After due consultation, UNRRA had concluded that "a person who is merely caring for a child has no legal rights therein and should be given only a minimum of consideration, that a more important factor is the restoration of such child to its national care and that the only bar to such immediate removal would be the legal rights of a parent, natural or adopted, and the pseudo legal rights of a close relative plus the best interests of the child as determined by qualified professionals employed by UNRRA … that every effort should be bent to the discovery of that [the child's] government."

Whiting then concluded, "Is it or is it not the policy of the U.S. Government to restore to agreed nations the birthright that is rightfully theirs, the children lost by the nefarious practices of nazi agression [sic]? If it is, then with that premise of policy, a realistic approach should be adopted." Whiting declared that UNRRA was ready to cooperate fully with the US government, if it was so interested, but could only do so if it enjoyed the trust and confidence of that government and its representatives, and only if it could pursue its task using the policies it had developed based on the experience and information its staff had gained while working in the field. If this was not the case, if UNRRA did not enjoy the trust and confidence of the US government and its representatives, or its policies were not adopted (which seemed the case, given the onerous restrictions imposed on this operation), UNRRA would shut down its operations in the US Zone, including child search, and would do so in a very public manner.[52]

At the same time, Charles Alspach, UNRRA's deputy director of federal-state relations, recruited Ellen Woodward of the American delegation to the United Nations and the National Committee for Foreign Relief of the American Association of Social Workers to put pressure on the US State Department to press the Military Government, in turn, to support UNRRA.[53] Major General Lowell Rooks, incoming director general of UNRRA (he would replace Fiorello LaGuardia on 1 January 1947), telephoned and wrote to General Schulgen of the Civil Affairs Division of the US War Department, asking that the release of the ACA directive be delayed. Letters were also sent to the British, French, and Soviet embassies asking that the directive be delayed and the subject reconsidered at the next meeting of the UNRRA Central Committee, to be held on 4 December 1946 – which they agreed to do.[54]

UNRRA Central Headquarters in Germany also prepared a form letter for distribution to the repatriation missions of France, Belgium, Holland, Czechoslovakia, Yugoslavia, Poland, and the Soviet Union headquartered in Berlin, intended to mobilize them against the proposed ACA directive. In the letter, Central Headquarters listed the reasons why they should be concerned. It explained that among the reasons why the search for their children was taking so long was the intransigence and obstructionism of OMGUS which refused to turn over the lists of unaccompanied children identified by the German authorities, and which created serious obstacles to UNRRA's investigations and search by requiring separate permission for each time an UNRRA worker wished to enter an institution or home for the purposes of investigation and for each time an UNRRA worker wished to remove a child from a German home or institution, and who insisted that it must approve each removal separately.

While this should have been sufficient to concern them, Central Headquarters also warned that the Allied Control Authority was now on the verge of releasing a directive on the determination of nationality that, in UNRRA's opinion, would "have a detrimental effect on the identification and repatriation of unaccompanied United Nations children," especially the provision that deemed children of unknown nationality to be German, which would result in the loss of United Nations children to the Germans. If, suggested Central Headquarters, a mission was in disagreement with any portion of the proposed ACA directive, it should make its concerns known to the duty secretary of the Prisoners of War and Displaced Persons Directorate in Berlin. Central Headquarters then called on the repatriation missions to press their national governments to gather whatever information on its missing children it could as quickly as possible, so that the child search operations could be completed before UNRRA was replaced with a successor organization, and to press ACA's Prisoners of War and Displaced Persons Directorate to cooperate with UNRRA in its efforts to find their children.[55]

Finally, at the meeting of the UNRRA Central Committee in Washington on 4 December 1946, with the concurrence of the representatives of the occupying governments on the Committee, it was decided that it would insist that "a further consideration be given to UNRRA's view in ACA's consideration of proposed directive ... and before any directive ... is issued an opportunity be given to UNRRA Director-General and Central Committee to consider and comment upon its terms." Fiorello LaGuardia, director general (still), made it clear that he was strongly opposed to any foreclosure of "further examination and determination of true nationality of unaccompanied children presumed to be non-German and instead believed it imperative to enforce a policy for as long as possible that would facilitate the location and identification of unaccompanied children who may be nationals of one of the United Nations.[56] UNRRA was mobilizing all the forces at its disposal.

The aggressive campaign appears to have had an impact as, on 31 January 1947, the UNRRA director general's office was informed that both the US War and State departments had been in communication with United States European Command (EUCOM, the incoming successor to USFET) regarding policies affecting unaccompanied children. The State Department had even gone so far as to instruct EUCOM to "adhere to the recommendations made by UNRRA concerning provisions in the proposed directive of the Allied Control Authority."[57] Ever hopeful that finally a trans-zonal policy based on UNRRA's proposal might be in the offing, Cornelia Heise was instructed to keep in close touch with EUCOM for the near future, and Eileen Blackey met with Fritz Oppenheimer of the US State Department in Berlin. Sympathetic to UNRRA's argument, Oppenheimer took up the matter with both the Displaced Persons Division of OMGUS and the US Political Advisor's Office while there.[58] In light of this newfound sympathy, UNRRA began to press more vigorously for the issuance of a quadripartite directive. (It had begun to lose heart, fearing that any directive issued was probably going to be more detrimental than constructive.[59]) With this new support, the hope was that, if a directive could be put in place prior to UNRRA's termination, there was a good chance that it would shape policy regarding these children afterward. If not, the fear was that "the disposition of the problem may have some catastrophic results."[60] By mid-March 1947, the surge of hope had faded, as the proposed directive remained stalled at the Legal Directorate of the Allied Control Authority, blocked by the US Element (undoubtedly led by Lieutenant Colonel Abbott) and the need to reconcile it with the alternate directive proposed by the French Element several months previously.[61]

The fear remained that Abbott's directive would ultimately win out, if just because UNRRA was now mere months from closure. In a particularly nasty April meeting with Blackey, that this was Abbott's objective was made patently clear. In what was a rather heated confrontation, Abbott revealed his plan to finally bring child search under his control. He was going to have EUCOM request that OMGUS assume control of the US Zone Bureau of Documents and UNRRA's Tracing Bureau. This would bring the Tracing Bureau under the auspices of the ACA's Displaced Persons Division and Central Tracing Policy Board in Berlin – his office. Under a reorganization of child search and tracing at the zonal level, the newly combined Child Search and Tracing Section would become directly responsible to the Bureau of Documents and Tracing. This would have the effect of putting Cornelia Heise's child search operations under Abbott's control. And Abbott let it slip to Eileen Blackey that he expected that UNRRA would only staff the Tracing Bureau until 1 July, at which point it would probably be turned over to *German* authorities.[62]

In fact, OMG Bavaria had been planning for the German authorities to assume responsibility for the search and tracing of United Nations citizens since February 1947. Ironically, it was USFET that had started that conversation. While USFET had been responsible for the US Zonal Tracing Bureau, the Bureau had been funded and administered by UNRRA. With UNRRA's termination looming on the horizon, but no successor agency obvious, USFET was concerned that it would be left responsible for keeping the Bureau operating. In February, it had opened negotiations with OMGUS to assume responsibility for the Bureau, suggesting that, in this way, OMGUS could streamline the operation and turn over its daily operations to German personnel, while keeping it under American supervision, thus making it easier to more efficiently coordinate the efforts of the German and Bureau tracing efforts. (The Bavarian government had recently established a special division within the Ministry of the Interior and a central search service had been created, sponsored by the Bavarian Red Cross, the Innere Mission of the Evangelical Church, and the Caritas Verband.) OMGUS leapt at the opportunity.

The plan of the Internal Affairs Division at OMG Bavaria was to place responsibility for searching, tracing, and registering all German nationals, including expellees, and all United Nations nationals and ex-enemy displaced persons who remained in Germany, with the Länder governments, as it was expected that the problem of reuniting individuals and families would continue to be a major concern for at least another five years.[63] The effect would be to put all search and tracing responsibilities for all those displaced, German and non-German, in the hands of the Germans. Blackey was appalled.[64]

During the same meeting, Abbott angrily confronted Blackey over the long-awaited and long-stalled ACA directive. He was annoyed that UNRRA had blocked the directive and then mobilized the War and State departments, who had forced its return to him for revision. This would mean, he complained, an inordinate delay of months while it was revised and then resubmitted to ACA's Prisoners of War and Displaced Persons Directorate. By the time all that had happened and the directive was finally released, UNRRA would have long been out of existence, a ludicrous situation, he implied. So Abbott strongly suggested that UNRRA "refrain from doing anything to interfere with the development of a new paper," without actually explaining what the new revisions might look like. Blackey protested that UNRRA would be happy to support any directive that took into account the concerns it had raised regarding the earlier version, because it saw the value of some form of secure and uniform treatment of unaccompanied children across the zones. However, she explained, if the second attempt did not correct the problems of the first draft, "UNRRA will continue its efforts to prevent the release of such a directive." Blackey went on to argue that, if a EUCOM-level directive was not possible, then a zonal directive should be issued. Abbott argued disingenuously, and for the first time, that the US Zone could not release a directive on the determination of nationality "since this was a matter which can be settled only by quadripartite action." It was clear to Blackey that it would be "difficult to carry on an effective Child Search program in the U.S. Zone with the continued obstructions presented by Colonel Abbott."[65]

It was clear that this battle with Abbott was not going to be won, if just because he had the advantage of being able to outwait UNRRA's imminent closure, now definitively set for 30 June 1947. Blackey's mission, even while waging this fight, became to ensure that as many cases as possible got resolved and that child search not get shut down with UNRRA's closure. In late December 1946, personnel were assigned to the task of sorting out the files, which were in chaos, and expediting those cases that could be brought forward for either repatriation or resettlement, effectively trying to "clear UNRRA's desk" and prepare for the smooth movement of the files to the successor agency. Renee Thill was one such staff member, appointed child welfare consultant to the Child Welfare Department of UNRRA District 5 in December 1946. There, she found the paperwork in turmoil, with many files incomplete – a consequence of the shortage of personnel that had plagued UNRRA from the start, as well as the competing demands on that personnel's time and energies, with paperwork a low priority. Her mission was to bring order to the chaos, and to pursue aggressively all immigration possibilities for the children.

Working in UNRRA's favour were new opportunities for placing the children. Once the constitution of the International Refugee Organization (IRO) had been signed in December 1946, which allowed the nascent IRO to resettle displaced persons as well as repatriate them, UNRRA was given the option to consider resettlement possibilities for displaced persons. Although they were few, these new opportunities were pursued aggressively. By February, Thill had forwarded 218 cases to the US Committee for the Care of European Children (the only agency authorized to admit orphaned children to the United States) for consideration for resettlement in the United States (85 of which were rejected either because the child was over 18 years of age, the cutoff age, or because the child had relatives in Europe).[66] A further 26 cases were submitted to UNRRA's Eligibility and Emigration Office for consideration for other destinations, and 92 were submitted to the US consulate for consideration as they were outside of the mandate of the Committee for the Care of European Children.[67] Elsewhere, in UNRRA District 1, 186 children were registered as keen to emigrate to the United States, with 34 called into the American consulate for interviews in February alone and another 60 expected to be interviewed soon after.[68]

By late April, both the Committee for the Care of European Children and UNRRA's Child Search Branch were overwhelmed. The Committee's quotas were oversubscribed, with children whose applications were on file but not yet approved facing a wait of several months before they could be moved, and the future of its program uncertain because its mandate also was to end with UNRRA's, in June 1947.[69] Renee Thill remained busy – with 67 new cases in March and April 1947 and another 95 that April and May. In addition, she reported a "constant flow of children" at the office asking to register for emigration, under the mistaken belief that if they came to the office directly, their cases would be processed more quickly. Thus, while between December 1945 and May 1947, a total of 1,033 children were repatriated (734 of whom were Polish), and between October 1945 and May 1947, 1,146 emigrated (914 to the United States; 815 of whom were Jewish), many files remained open, at various stages of completion.[70]

Blackey's second task was to construct as comprehensive an overview of the state of child search operations as possible, in order to "point out the magnitude of the question in its true proportions, trusting that a successor agency would be in a position to carry out plans for the children once they were located," with special attention paid to those who might be a long-term responsibility and their needs.[71] With its termination only a few weeks away, UNRRA issued Field Order No. 19: UNRRA Policy Relating to the Registration, Care and Disposition of Unaccompanied Children, summarizing what it considered best practices as they had evolved in child search and tracing, as well as the state of policy at the moment of termination, as it understood it. Elsewhere, in summary and closure reports, the Child Search Branch argued forcefully that the operations needed to continue into the IRO period, but in order to be able to do that, the thorny issues of entry into and removal from German homes and institutions, protocols for dealing with contested cases of national identity, as well as the legal issues of adoption, guardianship, and illegitimacy needed to be addressed. In all instances, it was argued, action had to be taken to ensure these children's legal status and protection, which otherwise would be seriously compromised, especially in the cases of those children being left in German homes. At its core, the ultimate goal of Field Order No. 19 was to ensure the child's individual and national rights were protected.[72]

This marked a shift in UNRRA's position – from a goal of reuniting a child with its family, if possible, and at a minimum, of returning the child to its homeland, to ensuring its legal protection. It reflected both the reality that these remaining children were proving to be very difficult to trace (although reunifications were still happening) because of the lack of documentation and complexity of their cases, because of the Military Government's obstructionism, and because of the changing international climate. By 1947, then, UNRRA was starting to admit that some children might remain in Germany. This changed its focus of concern, shifting it to ensuring the child's legal protection. It was the logical extension of the argument UNRRA had made against the ACA directive proposed by Abbott – that it would leave these children vulnerable, as they would have no legal protection or identity.

The issue of legal protection was not yet a concern of OMGUS, as reflected in its own articulation of policy and best practice, compiled for the edification of its successor agency. The Military Government Regulation Title 20: Displaced Persons, Refugees, and Expellees, as this document was called, reaffirmed the tripartite division of responsibility for child search and welfare – with EUCOM responsible for all displaced persons operations, including child search and child welfare, and thus for any final decisions regarding the children's disposition; UNRRA's successor agency reporting to EUCOM and being responsible for locating unaccompanied children and investigating their identity on EUCOM's behalf; and the public welfare branches of OMGUS wielding close control over UNRRA's and its successor agency's ability to perform its tasks, whereby the agency's officers required Public Welfare's permission both to enter German institutions and homes in order to conduct their investigations (denial of which would completely stymy any investigation) and to remove children from those institutions and homes (denial of which would undermine the whole purpose of child search by making it impossible to either repatriate or resettle a child). Title 20 also reasserted that any child of undetermined nationality, unless "subjected to abuse or suffering because of inadequate care," would remain where it was until a decision was made with regard to its status by EUCOM and repatriation or resettlement had been authorized. No child could be repatriated or resettled without UNRRA or its successor demonstrating that the child was not residing with either a close relative or foster parent, or, if with such a relative or foster parent, that both the adult caregiver (whatever her or his legal relationship with the child) and the appropriate liaison officer approved of the child's repatriation or resettlement.[73] While there was no explicit mention of automatically deeming any unidentified child as German, there was also no mention of legal safeguards for the child.

The Central Tracing Policy Board of the Prisoners of War and Displaced Persons Directorate of the Allied Control Authority, in its own draft policy statement, "General Principles for Determining the Eligibility for Certain Measures of Protection, Care and Treatment of Children Brought into Germany or Born of Displaced Persons Within Germany," tackled this question directly. The Allied Control Authority declared that for those children of undetermined nationality and "when available evidence indicates that the child may later prove to be entitled to the protection of one of the United Nations," the child was to be treated as a United Nations displaced person until such time as a qualified judicial body or official agency ruled otherwise. There would be no deeming a child German if its nationality was undetermined; on this issue, the American Military Government had lost. However, at no time would the child be taken into protection if it meant separating the child from its mother, or from a United Nations national or person who was caring for the child if it was in the Zone Commander's opinion that the separation would hurt the child, or that the separation would violate the due process of law (reinforcing OMGUS's position on removal, by making it OMGUS's decision).[74] The policy battle lines were now well set, and this did not bode well for the nascent IRO.

Chapter Eight

Child Search under the IRO

One could be forgiven for thinking that, once the constitution of the International Refugee Organization (IRO) was passed by the General Assembly of the United Nations in December 1946, the transition from UNRRA to the IRO, in mid-1947, would be a straightforward exercise. Unfortunately, however, this was not the case. As late as April 1947, it was still not clear when the IRO would actually be functional, as this was conditional upon the accumulation of enough signatories to the constitution that the total financial contributions would equal at least 75 per cent of the overall budget. Thus, the constitution would only become effective in August 1948. Until that time, the Organization's responsibilities were carried out by the Preparatory Commission of the IRO; for simplicity's sake, in this work, we will refer to the successor agency as the IRO. The uncertainty about who would replace UNRRA and when continued well into 1947. This was only partially allayed in mid-April that year, when Arthur J. Altmeyer, executive secretary of the IRO, visited the US Zone of Occupation on a fact-finding mission. While in Germany, he made it clear that the IRO intended to pick up where UNRRA would leave off, on 30 June 1947, provided that the necessary funds were made available. However, at that point, Altmeyer and his immediate staff were the only employees, and they were operating on funds borrowed from the United Nations, with a few UNRRA personnel on loan to them. His expectation was that, while the IRO was not recruiting from UNRRA personnel at the moment, it would take over the personnel left in the field, in toto.[1] This was largely what actually happened, although at least within the child search operations, those who signed on with the IRO generally moved up at least one level in the administration. Nonetheless, that this would happen was not at all clear in early 1947, so Altmeyer's visit did little to defray the tensions or boost morale among UNRRA's field workers. It was all dishearteningly nebulous.

In addition, while the constitution had been struck in 1946, it was only in July 1947 that the IRO and the United States European Command (EUCOM) signed an agreement delineating the terms of IRO's work in the US Zone. The terms were very similar to those of the agreement between UNRRA and the United States Forces, European Theater (USFET) signed in February 1946. The overarching role of the new organization was to be a supportive one, as UNRRA's had been. The IRO remained responsible for the following: operating the assembly centres, including their control and administration; the coordination and supervision of the activities of all approved voluntary societies; the determination of which refugees were eligible for its assistance; the provision of medical care; the management and facilitation of both repatriation and resettlement operations; and the creation of an employment program for employable refugees (under the IRO constitution, refugees who had the opportunity to work but refused were to be denied assistance). The occupation authorities remained responsible for providing the following: accommodations, transportation, and basic supplies, including food, fuel, clothing, medical supplies for those in the IRO's care, furniture, bedding, and household equipment; security for the camps; adequate office space, warehouses, garages, and like facilities for the storage of IRO supplies and property; and suitable living accommodations for IRO staff, as well as communication facilities, postal services, and medical services for them. As for unaccompanied children, the IRO was to provide them with "all possible priority assistance, including normally assistance in repatriation in the case of those whose nationality could be determined."[2]

This division of responsibilities between the IRO and EUCOM largely echoed that between UNRRA and USFET (predecessor to EUCOM) but with certain key differences. The IRO was to give top priority to repatriation in the re-establishment (to use a term from the IRO's constitution) of displaced persons generally, but it was also allowed to explore resettlement opportunities for those who could not or would not be repatriated, including unaccompanied children. Second, it was clear from the tone of the IRO-EUCOM Agreement that the IRO was expected to resolve the displaced persons question expeditiously and to find a permanent resolution to the remaining displaced persons population, be it repatriation, resettlement, or integration into the German economy. It was now two years since the war had ended and time for these people to move on and build themselves a future. The displaced persons operations were to be shut down, and the mission of the IRO was to make that happen.

The impact on the child search personnel was devastating. It appeared that the Office of Military Government, United States (OMGUS) had inadvertently won the battle, because child search operations largely ground to a halt over the summer of 1947. Part of the explanation for the shutdown was that the Soviet Union had demanded the discontinuation of the Allied Control Authority's Central Tracing Bureau. It had been deemed advisable, therefore, "to declare [the] Allied Control Authority obligation" for tracing terminated and allow other "interested parties" to carry on the project at the zonal level.[3] The plan was to discontinue central tracing at the end of 1946 and to establish three zonal offices to tie up the loose ends. The result was that child search work in the British Zone ceased immediately (it had never been very extensive in the French Zone), and in the US Zone it was greatly reduced, although not completely halted.[4]

Child search operations that did continue in 1947 were desultory at best and increasingly plagued with problems. Complaints continued to come in from the field about the lack of direction from the Zone Headquarters, especially in the difficult problem of removal. IRO workers were being allowed into German institutions and homes for the purposes of search and tracing. Requests for permission to remove children from German institutions for repatriation, as well as finalized approvals and referrals to the German agencies of children found to be of probable German nationality continued to be submitted. German agencies continued to refer cases of children of apparently non-German nationality to the IRO.[5] The various Jugendamt offices continued to investigate children who UNRRA had identified as of doubtful nationality and, as long as it was operational, UNRRA continued to refer children deemed to be German to the Landesjugendamt.[6] However, the Public Welfare Branch of the Office of Military Government, Bavaria (OMG Bavaria) also continued in its policy of forbidding the removal of any children from a German foster home without the formal, written approval of the foster parents, resulting in few removals.[7]

Even when removals were approved, there were problems. Those removals were implemented typically by child care officers who had not been involved in the search and identification of the child being removed (that had been the responsibility of child search officers – a separation of responsibilities that had taken shape over the spring of 1947). These child care officers had little exposure to the child search process, its challenges or politics, and they generally walked into these situations blind, unprepared for the almost inevitable fear, anger, grief, and overt (sometimes violent) opposition to the child's removal. These officers tended to withdraw when confronted with the first hint of opposition. They were also inclined to identify with the foster family, sympathizing with the often very genuine grief and anger of foster parents faced with losing a child of whom they had grown very fond. These child care officers were patently unprepared for the task. The situation was unworkable and a source of growing frustration both in the field and at the zonal level.[8]

By September 1947, it was Deborah Pentz of the IRO Headquarters in Germany who finally raised the inevitable question of whether child search should be continued at all. As no government had been able to provide a reliable estimate of how many children had been removed for Germanization, and as all German institutions had now been visited and screened for unaccompanied displaced children, it was unlikely that many more would be uncovered, she argued. It made more sense to help those children already located to adjust to their current situation or to put the scarce resources into reuniting them with their parents or close relatives, as well as focus on assisting parents or relatives actively seeking a particular child or children. Her recommendation was to shut down the general search operations and scale them back to searching only for children who were specifically requested.[9] It was an argument with which many had sympathy. And so child search languished for much of 1947.

At the end of 1947, however, the IRO did a startling volte-face. The order was issued to resume tracing and general search, centralizing it in Arolsen in a new International Tracing Service. The zonal tracing offices would continue to operate, but the central organization would manage child search and tracing; maintain a master index of all children lost and found; centralize all tracing correspondence; establish a library of all documents pertaining to children; and assume responsibility for the centralized development and supervision of search and tracing plans and methods. Moreover, the IRO announced that it had decided to continue with the general child search operations, after all. Because the only extant child search operations (even if badly reduced in scope) were those in the US Zone, the IRO decided to organize the

Child Search Branch of the new International Tracing Service with the US Zone's child search and tracing section at its core.

The reasons for the change of heart are not clear, but the decision was made at the same time that the International War Crimes Tribunal in Nuremberg ruled on Case No. 8, commonly known as RuSHA (the Nazi regime's Race and Settlement Main Office), which had been responsible for the Lebensborn program. Much useful information had emerged during that trial, spurring a new interest in child search. As well, the IRO and the zonal authorities had remained under considerable pressure from various national governments, especially Eastern European ones, to continue the search, as well as from child search and care staff themselves, who believed there were still children undiscovered. While the new arrangements were ramped up, the field tracing staff continued their operations. These remained nominal for the interim, however, because of a serious shortage of staff (most having been dismissed or quit, because of the lengthy shutdown).[10]

Child Search Reprieved

The situation facing the resurrected child search operations was a serious one. Child search operations had been largely inactive for months, worsened by the serious shortage of staff. The IRO's Child Care Section now assumed control of thirteen children's centres with a total population of 1,792, but only three had IRO staff attached to them, and in each case, only one or two staff members. The new Child Search Section assumed responsibility for 2,840 unresolved files – including the children in children's centres, assembly centres, and free-living. Although there was a Zone child care officer, there were no longer any attached to any of the area teams. Child care was now assigned to the welfare officers instead, just one of their many tasks, despite the fact that there were over sixty thousand accompanied and unaccompanied children in their care. The IRO ordered the newly re-established Children's Emigration Section to review all resettlement applicants to ensure that they qualified – a backlog of 161 months of old cases left over from the UNRRA unit. Across the organization the staff shortage was felt sharply. The staff shortage also meant that child care operations had completely lost control over admission to the children's centres, and children were entering based on referrals from voluntary agencies, camp welfare officers, parents, relatives, and others. With no controls in place and little information on the children being recorded, this was causing havoc in the centres and enormous work for the child care workers who had to pick up the pieces afterward.[11] The temporary cessation of operations and the resultant loss of staff had thus critically undermined the child search operations. At the same time, the complaints about the length of time it was taking to clear cases were multiple and coming from every direction: OMG Bavaria, the US Committee for the Care of European Children, and the new resettlement missions.

As of October 1947, the staff shortage remained acute at every point. The Children's Emigration Section, consisting of just one staff person, was overwhelmed. The children's centres remained desperately short-staffed and unable to control the resident populations (with a resulting growth in delinquency among the youth in the centres).[12] The Zone's child care officer resigned in early November 1947 and was not replaced until January 1948. The delay in filling the positions was not because of a lack of interest (by June 1948, all but one of the positions was filled), but because it took time to recruit and because, significantly, the Military Government delayed issuing entry permits for months.

Child search operations were further hampered by a serious dearth of transport, which made it impossible to remove uncovered children or to carry out the investigations in the field that were core to their responsibilities. Broken-down cars had not been replaced, reducing one officer to hitch-hiking from his billet to the office, without any hope of visiting the field. In the Bremen area, it meant averaging three or four hours daily on the trams and trains in order to conduct the necessary site visits and investigations. Without transportation, "it is useless to apply for more personnel [as] their prospects of visiting, removing and investigating are ... grim."[13] The result was that child search operations remained largely at a standstill, and much of the territory still to be covered remained untouched.

Furthermore, child search operations also remained seriously compromised at a procedural level, as none of the fundamental policy and procedural issues of the UNRRA period had been addressed. Indeed, the gaps were largely entrenched in the agreement signed between the IRO and EUCOM. The IRO's child search operations had to conform to EUCOM policy, just as UNRRA's had had to conform to SHAEF, and then USFET policy. Because EUCOM had given little thought to child search, policy still necessarily defaulted to the 11 May 1946 USFET directive (the various replacement drafts had never got past OMGUS's objections, leaving this letter extant) – not a particularly satisfactory solution for any involved. While the IRO was, in the first place, responsible to EUCOM, OMGUS also continued to play a role in the child search operations and continued its obstructionist tactics. The low-grade war between them dragged on, along lines similar to those during the UNRRA years, but now between the IRO and OMGUS.

In an attempt to clarify both policy and procedure, the IRO issued Provisional Order No. 33 in November 1947, establishing what it considered to be its mandate regarding unaccompanied children. Provisional Order No. 33 stated clearly that the IRO's task was the identification, registration, classification, provision of care and assistance, legal and other protection, and the repatriation, resettlement, or re-establishment of children considered to be unaccompanied, that is, children 16 years of age or under; outside their country of origin or that of their parents; unaccompanied by a parent, legal guardian, or close relative; and presumed to belong to one of the categories of refugees or displaced persons that fell within the IRO's scope. Order No. 33 acknowledged that, while repatriation was "indicated as a normal solution" for an unaccompanied child, it was not always in the child's best interests, and therefore alternative solutions could be considered – a significant change that, it was hoped, would go some way to breaking the backlog of cases. Any resettlement schemes, however, had to be approved by IRO Headquarters in Geneva, with the exception of children being reunited with parents or close relatives in other countries.[14]

For the first year of the IRO's operation, Provisional Order No. 33 dictated the shape of child recovery in Germany. In July 1948, this was superceded by Provisional Order No. 75 (although it was not formally implemented until October 1948[15]), which reaffirmed the IRO's mandate to locate, register, and identify all unaccompanied children who fell within its mandate, and that its primary responsibility was to return these children to their countries of origin, although in each case, the child's best interests (left undefined) were to be taken into account.[16] With the Provisional Order No. 75, the International Tracing Service was made an independent operation and instructed to turn over responsibility for future planning for all the cases pending (approximately 1,000) to the IRO's Child Care Section. This would free up its people to focus on continued search, identification, and tracing. The Child Care Section was made responsible for confirming the children's nationality and status and planning for their future, be it repatriation, resettlement, or establishment in Germany, as well as enacting those plans.[17] However, the Child Care Section resolutely refused to accept these new responsibilities. Severely understaffed still, it had yet to establish effective control over the existing population in its centres. As a result, as late as June 1948, the cases had still not been transferred from the International Tracing Service.[18]

Provisional Order No. 75 rededicated the IRO to the task of locating and identifying all unaccompanied children in Germany who might fall under its mandate. Children whose nationality could be determined would be repatriated or resettled in accordance with the rights and wishes of their national government, with special consideration being given to children living with foster parents. No recommendation could be made that was contrary to a child's wishes (this was especially true for youths over 17 years old), or contrary to the wishes of the child's national government (enshrining the central role of the national liaison officer). If the child was not repatriated because of the child's objections, or if the national government refused the child, the IRO would then consider it for resettlement. The IRO reserved the right to consider individual offers of adoption from resettlement countries, as well as the option of allowing children of undetermined nationality to be considered for resettlement with their displaced persons foster family under the following conditions: if that family had been accepted for a specific resettlement scheme; if the family could prove that it would be able to provide for the child in the future; and if the family had applied for and met the requirements to legally adopt the child. Where a legal guardian or parent had been traced, decisions about the child's disposition would be made in accordance with the guardian or parent's wishes. No unaccompanied child could be placed in a foster home, either displaced person or German, for permanent care or with the prospect of permanent care, unless there was evidence of a blood relationship with the foster parents.

Unaccompanied children already in German foster homes could, in exceptional cases, be permanently established with those families, but only after careful investigation of their circumstances and provided that the following conditions held true: the child had not been forcibly removed from its original home; neither the child nor its parents had been persecuted by the Germans or its wartime allies during the war; and the child's initial placement with the German foster family had been done in good faith as a result of wilful neglect on the part of its biological parents, abandonment, or purposeful placement with that family by the parent(s) as confirmed with written documentation.

Children in German institutions were to be removed from those institutions immediately and placed in IRO children's centres. Where removal was not possible for health or other reasons, every effort would be made to formulate an alternate plan for care, with the caveat that the child not be placed by the German authorities in a German foster home. None of this was to be done without the proper approvals from the occupation authorities, but should the occupation authorities prevent the implementation of Order No. 75, the field was to alert the IRO Headquarters in Geneva immediately.[19]

These key provisions of the Provisional Order No. 75 make clear the principles upon which the IRO's child search operations would function and the increased latitude granted the International Refugee Organization. First, children would not be left in German institutions, although they could be left in German foster homes, depending on the circumstances. Second, the child's wishes would be respected – something generally practised by UNRRA, but never formally enshrined in policy. Third, the wishes of a child's national government (if nationality could be determined) would also be respected, as well as those of any legal guardians identified – a continuation of UNRRA policy, but one that would cause problems in the near future, especially if the wishes of any of the three parties clashed. Finally, a child's legal security was becoming increasing a paramount concern – whatever a child's final disposition, its legal identity and status had to be ensured. This was why the caveat that a foster family could only keep a child if they "met the requirements to legally adopt the child," and why, if legal guardians had been found, their wishes would rule. Order No. 75 also openly flouted OMGUS's wishes regarding the disposition of these children, which had not changed.

One consequence of the change in the distribution of responsibilities was that the International Tracing Service was soon swamped. Each month, 150,000 new cards were being added to the master index, and the working conditions deteriorated rapidly, with the predictable effect on output. The lack of office space was becoming quite serious by October 1948. The volume of material being processed by the Records Branch of the International Tracing Service, which was also suffering from a lack of space, was equally daunting – 719 lots of documents in October and November alone, including labour records; displaced persons records; prisoner of war records; birth, marriage, and death certificates; concentration camp records, and coming from a variety of sources – e.g., the two zonal divisions of the International Tracing Service; the IRO displaced persons operations in the US Zone; the IRO Interzonal Camp Grohn; the American Joint Distribution Committee's

offices in Paris, Berlin, and Kohne-Belsen; the Central Location Index in
New York; various national liaison offices; and various German offices
– all of which had to be indexed, cross-referenced, and filed. In those
two months, 212,331 displaced persons records were processed. Further
thousands of individual tracing requests were processed at the same
time, and over 329,000 location cards were created for the master index.
The Tracing Branch of the International Tracing Service, responsible for
tracing individual displaced persons, including children (which meant
the identification of the children, the establishment of their citizenship,
and locating their families) was just as swamped, processing over 11,000
cases in October and November.[20]

Marjorie Farley, newly appointed as child care field representative to
the International Tracing Service and responsible for the renewed child
search efforts in the new system, reported similar challenges. Much of
her and her child care officers' time was spent trying to straighten out
the records and determining the stage at which each investigation was,
as well as liaising with the OMG Bavaria and the various national consulates and voluntary agencies. Farley faced a number of minor frustrations, all of which were by now quite familiar complaints, but obstacles
nonetheless, including a shortage of office space, billets, transportation,
and telephones. Her primary objective, at that point, was to sort out
the cases and the records, rid the search program of as many clearly
ineligible cases as possible, and then focus her team's efforts on those
where there seemed a strong possibility of resolution, either because
they were close to being resolved or because the decisions seemed very
straightforward.[21]

Other challenges facing the child care officers remained. By the time
of a December 1948 child care workers' conference, these complaints
and concerns were well rehearsed. The Polish Red Cross had repatriated a child without consulting or notifying anyone, either military or
IRO. OMG Bavaria was continuing to be unhelpful in preparing the
Landesjugendamt and German foster families for the loss of a child
when removal was ordered, in spite of being mandated a thirty-day
period in which to prepare the family. The Landesjugendamt also continued to be obstructive, moving children from institutions to foster
homes without notifying the Child Care Section, and clearly uninter-
ested in identifying those possible unaccompanied children who were
living with either displaced persons or Germans.[22] Space remained an
issue, especially as the US Committee for the Care of European Children had requested that all children applying for its plan be processed

from children's centres. The Committee found that processing from the assembly centres was creating serious problems; for example, it was exceedingly difficult to determine a child's "true situation," and many of the applicants were found subsequently to have parents or to have lied about their ages. IRO's Child Care Section discovered that the Latvian Committee had been placing Latvian children from the British Zone with Latvian foster families in the US Zone without a proper investigation of the families, let alone the assistance or permission of either the IRO or EUCOM. The results were reportedly often tragic and, in at least one instance, had caused "irreparable damage" to the child.[23]

Adding to the difficulties was the complicated nature of the remaining cases. The number of children left in limbo by the lack of conclusive evidence as to their nationality or parentage was considerable, and the solution to their situations was not obvious, generating worries that these cases might never be resolved. For example, the Landesjugendamt had requested, yet again, the return of a group of children removed from the St Hedwig children's home in 1946 and still in an UNRRA, now IRO children's centre. These children had been on hold for two years, their repatriation delayed because of the lack of definitive evidence as to their nationality – there was not enough to convince the Military Government that they were Polish, but also not enough to determine that they were definitively German. The director of the Civil Affairs Division at OMG Bavaria, Albert Schweizer, pressed the Landesjugendamt to submit any additional evidence it had regarding the nationality of the children. Otherwise, the case, for which the IRO, Landesjugendamt, and OMG Bavaria were unable to reach a satisfactory conclusion, would have to wait for a decision from higher authorities – with the children left in uncertainty.[24]

Two children had been approved for removal to an IRO installation – Iwan Schykitka on 8 August 1947 and Anna Maria Jwaszkiwska in early 1947 (while UNRRA was still operating). In both cases, the removals had not yet taken place as OMG Bavaria did not believe their nationalities had been clearly determined, although the facts of each case suggested strongly that they were both Ukrainian.[25] In yet another instance, a child was uncovered in the care of Caritas Verband, about whom little was known – and that bit, contradictory. Maria Reckenai, born in 1943 (so 5 years old), was recorded as Polish, but her home address was in Hungary. The Hungarian Ministry of Social Welfare had rejected her repatriation, as no records for her parents could be found. It was unclear whether there were two children of the same name, but with different birth dates and birthplaces, or if it was the Hungarian authorities who were confused.[26] In October 1948, Martha Vondracek reported another thirty children who had been registered by the child search teams "in the very early days," but whose files were still incomplete, with no relatives yet identified. The Yugoslavian liaison officer had acknowledged them as Yugoslavian and certified them as able to return home, but it was still not clear whether they were truly Yugoslavian or Volksdeutsche. As such, the information was not sufficient to get permission from the OMG Bavaria to remove them without a written request for the child from a relative.[27] Some children were unable to repatriate because they were in quarantine, and some because their transportation was proving difficult to arrange. Still others refused to repatriate, such as one Italian youth who had repatriated to Italy in 1947, where he was reunited with an uncle, but only stayed a couple of days before running away and returning to the children's centre in Germany, refusing to repatriate again.

Finally, these children comprised a very fluid population that turned over regularly. The total number of outstanding cases was remaining roughly static, but the population's complexion was constantly changing, with children being steadily uncovered, even as others were re-established. And the expectation was that this would continue to be the case. Increasingly, many of these were children not normally eligible for IRO care, but ones that frequently came to the IRO's attention "in such a fashion as to make it difficult to refuse them. In most instances, the evidence of country of citizenship is so hazy that we feel justified in erring on the side of leniency."[28] This had the impact, however, of adding to the already alarming roster of unresolvable cases.

The lack of definitive answers meant that tensions had only worsened over the question of removal, with both the German authorities and the regional military governments. In April 1948, the Bavarian Ministry of the Interior was complaining to OMGUS that it was becoming increasingly difficult to work with the IRO, as some IRO officials were not observing the agreed-upon protocol. They were, instead, removing children from German foster homes and institutions without approval. This meant that OMG Bavaria was unable to give the Landesjugendamt the requisite thirty days' notice and the Landesjugendamt was unable to prepare the foster parents for the removal. Given that, in most cases, the child had been in the foster parents' care for a long time and the foster parents had become quite fond of the child, even to the point of adopting it in some instances, the lack of preparation meant serious upheaval and upset. The German authorities argued that it was "irresponsible to remove the child from orderly surroundings, the more so, as frequently the child cannot even be returned to his or her relations."[29]

The local military governments were losing patience with the IRO staff. In November, OMG Hesse decided that, while it had in the past trusted the IRO supervisory staff to ensure that the documentary evidence was sufficient to warrant granting IRO personnel approval to enter German homes and institutions to conduct investigations, given the liberties being taken by some IRO field personnel, it was going to have to assume responsibility for this function itself. OMG Hesse was particularly annoyed with Jean Troniak, who was now continuing his child search work under the auspices of the IRO, over his actions regarding the Gagatek children, and refused categorically to grant him future permission to enter German homes or institutions until he had been "properly briefed" by IRO Headquarters.[30]

The Gagatek incident was a particularly complicated one. There were three children, Anastasia (exact birth date unknown, although her mother and an illegitimate child were granted public welfare assistance in Poland on 19 August 1935; her father was purportedly Polish and had died during the war), Anton (born in Frankfurt on 18 May 1941; his father was also allegedly a Pole, but one who denied paternity), and Janina (born in Germany on 11 March 1945; her father was allegedly a French prisoner of war and remained unknown). The mother had been brought to Germany as a forced labourer in October 1939, bringing Anastasia with her. On 29 December 1947, the children were registered by the International Tracing Service and, on 19 January 1948, their Polish nationality confirmed by the Polish repatriation officer. The mother was reported to be illiterate, incompetent, and according to a psychiatrist, had "an incurable sickness of nerves, imbecility and post-encephalitis, and a right side hemiplegie [sic]." The mother was very fond of her children, it was reported, but incapable of caring for them. In 1946, she had been admitted to a "mental hospital" in Hesse, and then sent to an IRO psychiatric hospital, where she remained. Apparently by 1949, the mother was well enough to repatriate.

In fact, this case had been referred to the International Tracing Service by the Landesjugendamt in early 1947, because the Landesjugendamt was unhappy with the state of the foster home. During the war, the mother and children had been assigned to a German farmer in Oberursel by the name of Adrian Jamin, whose sister (who had trained as a nurse) had taken responsibility for the children's care when their mother was hospitalized, without compensation. This was a typical example of unaccompanied displaced children being placed informally with a German foster family. The children were in school, and after school, Anastasia looked after the children of a neighbouring family and Anton did light work on the farm of one of the farmer's relatives. Although the children were underweight and poorly clothed, they were in no worse shape than German children in that community, according to the welfare workers, and their condition was not considered the result of neglect. However and disturbingly, the farmer's sister had become passionately fond of the children, telling the youngest ones that they were her children by blood, and investing her emotional life in them. At the same time, she worked full-time and so was unable to supervise them adequately. Moreover, the investigation found that she was "a frustrated woman having caused trouble to many people," neurotic, and that she had treated the children's mother very badly.

The situation was not an ideal one, either in the opinion of the IRO worker doing the investigation (Jean Troniak) or the Landesjugendamt, and the decision was made that the children should repatriate to Poland with their mother. Nurse Jamin, as they referred to the sister, had objected strongly, launching into a long and tearful tirade. Complicating matters was a disagreement between the International Tracing Service and IRO's Child Care Section as to whether the children were accompanied or unaccompanied. ITS had requested permission from OMG Hesse to remove the children on the assumption that they were unaccompanied, but Troniak had assumed them to be accompanied and so removed them without getting clearance – over the sister's continued protest. They were put into the children's centre at Aglasterhausen. However, they were soon returned to the Jamin family at OMG Hesse's insistence, as "the children's removal [had] been done in contradiction with the Military Government regulations, as interpreted by OMGH." Although OMG Hesse recognized the children's nationality, it refused to approve their removal for repatriation "on the grounds that they found sister Jamin's house good enough for the children and do not want to remove them from a home where they think there is enough security to insecurity in Poland."[31]

This case illustrated a key clash in policy between the IRO and the Military Government. OMGUS refused to entertain removal of a child, even from a German foster family, if the foster parents objected. IRO policy, as set out in Provisional Order No. 75, would only allow unaccompanied children in German foster homes to remain there after careful investigation of the living conditions suggested that they were good (which they were not, by the Landesjugendamt's own admission) and only if the child had been placed with the foster family in good faith as a result of wilful neglect on the parents' part, abandonment, or voluntary placement by the parents, supported by documentary evidence – none of which applied in this case. The two positions were irreconcilable, although in the struggle to assert authority, OMG Hesse would win, as the IRO (like UNRRA before it) operated on the sufferance of OMGUS (who could shut down its operations by denying it access to the institutions and homes and by refusing to approve removals), even if it technically reported to EUCOM.

It did not help that the EUCOM was unclear about its general position regarding removal. EUCOM was uncertain as to how much weight should be given to a child's wishes in any decision made about its future, and it was uncomfortable with Provisional Order No. 75, at least regarding the criteria used to determine whether a child should be allowed to remain in a German foster home, as EUCOM policy expressly forbade leaving a child in foster care, even if placed there because of either neglect or abandonment. EUCOM's decision to defer to the US State Department for a policy statement meant the whole question would remain unsettled for the interim.[32]

Meanwhile, the German agencies' protests continued throughout 1947 and into 1948. By November 1948, Mr Ritter of the Bavarian Ministry of the Interior and a Dr Ladeson were both complaining that the number of children being repatriated by the IRO was climbing. Their concern was that some of these children had already been adopted and that "in mostly all cases, the foster parents object to repatriation." While they understood that the countries from which these children had been removed desired to have their children back, "such repatriations often are very detrimental to the children [they argued]. They mostly have become very attached to the foster parents and their repatriation is of great harshness to them." Especially in those instances where a child had no relatives in its country of origin or whose relatives did not care whether the child was returned, would it not be best for that child to leave it in Germany with the foster family?[33] This was a theme that would gain traction with time, namely, that it was cruel to separate a child from its foster family, even a German one, the only family the child had really known.

Various national welfare agencies were also still acting unilaterally, to everyone's frustration. In November 1948, IRO's US Zone child care officer, Eleanor Ellis, felt compelled to write to the IRO's Voluntary Societies Division to request that its chief remind the Polish Red Cross that it did not have the authority either to remove children from a home or institution, or to arrange a child's repatriation. Only the IRO had that authority and, while repatriation was always the first option considered, it was sometimes not the optimal solution for a child. Each case required careful and full investigation of all the circumstances, an investigation that had to be done by the IRO, and not the Polish Red Cross.[34]

OMG Bavaria, and especially its Youth Welfare Section, was feeling the sting of the criticism over the way in which removals were being handled. Having claimed responsibility for removals, it was now held responsible when they did not go well. Complaints were even being made to the Children's Bureau in the United States, which was tarnishing the personal and professional reputations of the personnel in the Youth Welfare Section. Doubly galling, OMG Bavaria also considered the process being practised as unprofessional, badly managed, and poor child welfare practice; its frustration was palpable, and shared by other regional military governments, such as Hesse.[35] The OMG Bavaria was also starting to lose patience with the Germans' growing lack of cooperation and intransigence, even if simultaneously it was growing frustrated with the IRO. It was particularly frustrating that, while increasingly objecting, loudly, to the removal of children they considered to be German, the German authorities were also increasingly reluctant to assume any responsibility for non-German nationals whose removal they had blocked, including children. German authorities had, in fact, inquired as to the possibility of getting financial assistance from the OMG Bavaria for those unaccompanied children who German foster parents wanted to keep (and so for whom the OMG Bavaria had withheld permission for removal), but who were in financial need – a request that got short shrift from Josephine Groves, of the Youth Welfare Section at OMG Bavaria.[36]

This was not the only instance in which Groves and the OMG Bavaria lost patience with what was becoming a very assertive Landesjugendamt. In response to a cluster of sixteen cases of removal and repatriation challenged by the Bavarian government – for having removed children from loving German foster families and repatriated them "again and again when parents do not want them" – Groves pointed out acerbicly that, in each case, protocol had been carefully observed and, in many cases, the natural parents had actually requested their child's return – which necessarily and quite properly trumped the foster parents' wishes.[37]

In yet another instance, in November 1948, when the Rektor for Caritas Verband, Franz Mueller, complained to the Military Government about IRO activities, the OMG Bavaria's frustration was as evident. Mueller complained that the IRO officials, who had been investigating the students at the Waldschule near Passau and even removing some children, did not have the proper authorizations from OMG Bavaria, nor was he happy with one IRO worker's reportedly very callous attitude towards a child with tuberculosis, and he could not believe that the Military Government would countenance the return of these children to the "Bolshevik East." (This was a second theme that would gain traction with time, namely, that it was better to leave a non-German child in a democratic Germany than to condemn it to a future in the Communist bloc.) Surely, he demanded, the Military Government could stop the disappearance of these children?[38] Albert Schweizer, the director of the OMG Bavaria's Civil Administration Division, was unimpressed that Rektor Mueller had stepped outside of "channels" to protest (all communication was supposed to be funnelled through the Landesjugendamt). And Schweizer proceeded to take apart the Rektor's complaint, case by case, clearly infuriated that the Germans were belabouring cases that had been settled, sometimes years earlier; others in which the Germans had no evidence to support their claim; and still others in which the children had already been reunited with their natural non-German parents. Schweizer pointedly reminded Mueller that, since July 1946, there had been an appeal process in place for German welfare agencies to challenge the IRO's (or UNRRA's) conclusions in individual cases and that it would be well worth the Rektor's time to acquaint himself with it.

Schweizer also made the point that fewer than seven hundred unaccompanied children had been repatriated from Bavaria to date, while another approximately three hundred had been identified as German by the IRO and turned over to the German agencies – so it was not that all children investigated were automatically removed and repatriated. Rather, the exercise was a careful vetting of the population, with due consideration being given to the possibility that a child might be German and, if so, turned over to the German authorities for care. Admittedly, given the length of time it took to investigate these cases and gather the documentation, there were some children who had been repatriated and were now being returned to Germany to reunite with parents who were discovered there; however, this number was quite small "in relation to the splendid work that is being done in reuniting children with their families or returning them to their homeland." The tone made clear that Schweizer did not appreciate Rektor Mueller's implied criticism of either the IRO's or OMG Bavaria's handling of child search operations.[39]

None of this is to imply that the Landesjugendamt and the IRO never cooperated. Indeed, there was considerable cooperation on one particular issue – ironically, it was also about children in German foster homes. By January 1948, both the IRO and the Landesjugendamt were becoming alarmed by the number of children discovered in inadequate, and sometimes actually dangerous foster care situations, as made clear in a comprehensive report compiled by Eileen Davidson, now deputy chief of the Child Search Section.[40] At its heart, the problem arose because the foster care arrangements in question were almost always the result of informal, ad hoc arrangements generally made during the war. These often were initiated by a child's mother who, as a forced labourer, had been unable to keep her newborn. Sometimes the consequences were tragic. Such was the case of Theresia Borek, born in 1942 in Germany to Polish forced labourers and then placed with a German woman by her parents, who had paid the woman to look after their daughter. When they were preparing to repatriate after the war, the parents went to collect the child, but as they reported to the IRO, the woman had disappeared with their daughter. The parents called eight times, but to no avail. Reports from the neighbours were alarming. Apparently the child spent "mostly all day with 4–8 dogs in a small room. This child is bitten often and sometimes cries over one hour. The house is dark, dirty and has bad odours ... When the German authorities called to remove the child, the woman escaped with her to the Russian Zone of Berlin, returning without her. When taken to court, it was felt that the woman was unstable, probably a psychopathetic [sic] personality. She was refused custody of the child. The child is still missing."

In many instances, like with Theresia, the conditions in which the children were living were quite poor and their health badly compromised as a result, sometimes so much so that it was German neighbours who called in the Landesjugendamt to do something about the situation. Jhore Andresen, for example, was a Norwegian boy born in 1942, living with a German foster family who apparently left him alone for the whole day with a big dog and their twelve-year-old daughter, who often teased and beat him. The situation was so bad that the neighbours all talked about the boy's living conditions and had eventually called in the Landesjugendamt, who removed the child and placed him with another foster mother "who took him out of pity." As another example, Anatoly Dzera, born in 1945 in Germany to a Polish Ukrainian forced labourer, had been placed with a German family within days of his birth "as her employer did not want to have the child around." A month later, the mother was killed in an air raid. The child was eventually referred to UNRRA in 1946, having been found in deplorable conditions, with untreated scabies and impetigo, the family being poor and "without hygiene."

Lebensborn children were still emerging as well, such as a Polish child, Lucie Deska, who was born in 1937. During the war, Lucie had been adopted by the Bauer family through the Lebensborn program. The German foster parents had divorced, and the foster father had remarried. The foster father's second wife had announced recently that she did not want to keep Lucie any more, as they now had three children of their own, and Lucie was proving "extremely difficult to manage" since she had been told the truth about her history. The foster father wanted the IRO to "relieve him of the child." Such was also the story of Herbert Norbeck, aged seventeen and from Norway, who had been placed in a foster home by Lebensborn. The foster parents were not certain they wanted to keep Herbert, as "he was disobedient and gave much trouble to [the foster mother's] father."

Whether Lebensborn or not, it was not uncommon for foster parents to call on the IRO to take over a foster child, generally because they could not or did not want to continue to care for it. Often this was because of the cost of the care, as the monthly allowance they were receiving from the Landesjugendamt was insufficient. This happened with Heini Bzdok, a Polish boy born in 1941 and separated from his mother in 1945 when the township was being evacuated; a family friend had picked him up and brought him to Germany. The foster parents had four children of their own, aged ten months to eleven years and, in 1948, were living in a refugee home on 80 Reichmarks a month – not enough to support the family and Heini; their wish was to return Heini to his parents. Klara Kraczkowska, now aged four and Polish Ukrainian, had been given to a German foster family because her mother had threatened to kill the baby. The foster mother was now approximately fifty years old, her husband worked in a factory, and they were living in poor conditions, receiving an allowance of only 25 RM monthly to care for Klara. It was the foster mother who requested that the IRO take over care for Klara, as "she will not be able to educate her later on."

Circumstances could make caring for a child too challenging. Renate Jendreszczyk, of undetermined nationality but from Silesia and born in 1944, had been brought to the Klein Kinderheim in Glogau, Silesia, in 1944. The child had been evacuated to Germany in 1945 with the entire home. Her current foster mother was given permission to take Renate when she was at the home collecting her own two children, who had been evacuated there. Renate was receiving good care, but the foster family, being Czechoslovakian expellees, were living in two small rooms. The foster mother was now pregnant and felt she could no longer keep Renate. In other instances, it was because the child proved unruly, like Hedwig Supalkowa, Czech and aged fourteen, who had been brought to Germany by German foster parents when they fled Czechoslovakia. She proved to be "very difficult to educate," and the foster parents were exasperated.

In a number of cases, it was actually the Landesjugendamt that initiated the request to the IRO. Michael Slaska, for example, was four years old and Polish, born in Germany, and placed with a German family by a German institution after his mother had abandoned him. The Landesjugendamt had referred the matter to the IRO, requesting that Michael either be admitted to a children's centre or that the Landesjugendamt be reimbursed for the child's living expenses, "since he is Polish." Bruno Lazirko, another Polish Ukrainian child, was born in 1944 and placed by his mother with a German family because she could not keep him on the farm where she worked. Again, it was the Landesjugendamt that referred the case to the IRO because it considered the foster family "unsatisfactory": the foster mother was a prostitute and receiving treatment "for a specific disease," while the foster father was in prison for theft. In fact, the Landesjugendamt had already removed Bruno and was prepared to prosecute the foster mother if she refused to give up care for him, but they wished the IRO to take on the child.[41]

By late 1947, then, the attitude of the Landesjugendamt had changed. The Landesjugendamt remained insistent that most of the children found in German institutions and homes were, in fact, German, and adamant that such children should remain in Germany. By 1947, however, it was willing to consider that there were many children, often Polish, who had been placed with German foster parents or in German homes and raised as German children, either as part of the Lebensborn program or as a result of ad hoc arrangements made by forced labourer mothers. Not only had the IRO provided documentary evidence to that effect, but the Landesjugendamt had also uncovered evidence of its own, as it pursued its own investigations of foster homes. In too many instances, German or not, the children were living in unacceptable circumstances, a result of having been placed without the proper home assessments. By September that year, the Landesjugendamt was preparing to launch a comprehensive review of all such ad hoc arrangements.[42] This would have the additional effect of winnowing out all non-German children who, now that the system of monthly fostering allowances had been reinstated, were a considerable expense. German children should remain under its care, the Landesjugendamt argued, including Volksdeutsche children, but non-German children would be turned over to the IRO.

Eileen Davidson's report had caught the attention of both the director of the IRO's International Tracing Service, Maurice Thudichum, and the chief of the Displaced Persons Branch of the Civil Affairs Division at EUCOM Headquarters. As a result of these discoveries, Thudichum informed EUCOM that his service was coordinating a detailed sample study by both German and IRO personnel of German foster homes in which it was reported that the children were receiving satisfactory care (it is not clear whether the Landesjugendamt's investigation was to be rolled into this one, or a separate investigation).[43] There was a growing recognition that, in the case of those children whose disposition was being held up because "it was contended that the German home offered the best solution for the child," it was important that the homes be investigated. By May 1948, even the Military Government had become sympathetic to this argument, given the overwhelming evidence that there were many children in inappropriate, unsatisfactory, even dangerous foster arrangements that had never been properly vetted.[44]

The appropriate solution, however, was still a matter of considerable argument. Again, the IRO's Child Care Section proposed what it considered would be the best practice for the "location, recovery, care, repatriation and resettlement of unaccompanied children." The Child Care Section insisted that its search officers be granted the authority to access German records and enter German institutions and homes for the purposes of investigation (a point of contention since 1946). Second, and still contentious, it continued to insist that it should be mandatory that any child considered to fall under the IRO's mandate be removed from a German home or institution in which it resided and that a child of unknown parentage born either in or outside of Germany, and for whom the evidence suggested that it may fall within the IRO's mandate, "shall be regarded as the concern" of the IRO (both also flashpoints in the past). The one exception would be a child placed in a German foster home or institution in accordance with a written statement from its parent or legal guardian, which was believed to have been given voluntarily; in this case, the parent's wishes would have precedence over those of the country of origin's representative. Finally, a special three-member review board should be created for dealing with disputed cases – so that these children were not left in limbo because of a lack of a route of appeal.[45]

OMGUS was predictably not impressed and fought a tough, rearguard action. It objected to the presumption that every child identified as "possibly within the IRO mandate" or as of "unknown parentage" be automatically removed from the German home or institution. If the home or institutional environment in which a child was located was found "detrimental" to the child's well-being, OMGUS had no objection to removal but suggested that it was nonetheless preferable to place the child in another home or institution in Germany, rather than in an IRO children's home or displaced persons centre.

OMGUS also objected to a new term introduced by the IRO – used whenever discussing the planning for a child's future – namely, "re-establishment." It was intended to reflect the expanded placement opportunities available to the IRO (repatriation, resettlement, and settling in Germany), but OMGUS declared the term vague, confusing, and threatening. The implication, according to OMGUS, seemed to be that, if the child could not be restored to its family or legal guardians, and if its nationality was undeterminable, the default solution was resettlement in any country willing to accept it. From the perspective of OMGUS's Legal Division, "such a practice [was] highly objectionable and closely analogous to the type of practices that the Nurnberg [sic] Tribunal held to be criminal ... Resettlement of adults who may desire to go to the United States, to Venezuela or to Patagonia, is one thing. Compulsory resettlement of children too young to know and express their own views on such resettlement is closely allied to what the Tribunal in the Rusha [sic] case described as 'kidnapping.'" Second, OMGUS continued to insist that all persons and their representatives interested in the removal of the child be given an opportunity to express their opinions, including those from the home or institution where the child had been living, that is the German foster family or the institution's administrators. Finally, it maintained that, before any removal, the environment of the home or institution had to be found to be detrimental to the child's interests (left undefined) by the (to be established) review board.[46] In spite of OMGUS's concern for children in insalubrious conditions, it was not ready to concede to the IRO's position.

It was in this latest battle of the ongoing war with OMGUS over child search operations that the principles underlying the IRO's commitment to them were most clearly articulated, as they had now taken shape. There had been a marked evolution in the IRO's understanding of the objectives of the child search operations since 1945. The IRO's first priority remained to reunite a child with its parents if possible, or with close relatives or a legal guardian – as had been the case since the search for unaccompanied children was first instituted. However, even this fundamental principle was now nuanced, and while reunion was still considered the ideal, it was now contingent on the legal rights of the child and relatives; on the willingness and ability of the family to care for the child; and finally, if the child was old enough, upon the child's own wishes. Reunion now was no longer considered, perforce, the optimal solution; it now depended upon these other factors. Where the child's parents or relatives could not be located, repatriation was generally still considered the first choice, as a child who returned to its own country "is thereby usually entitled to all rights a country affords its citizens, rights which are not guaranteed an individual when residing in a foreign country." Note here an important shift in the justification. No longer was it about preserving national identity, but about ensuring the child its rights as a citizen of its native country. For children who did not wish to repatriate or who were of undetermined nationality, resettlement was generally the option considered.

In all cases of resettlement, rather than sending the children indiscriminately to whatever country would take them (as OMGUS accused the IRO of doing), any country offering such a plan first had to convince the IRO that the child would receive adequate care and legal protection, have the opportunity to become a citizen, and have the opportunity to be adopted, rather than merely placed in a foster home – in this way, ensuring the child's full and legal integration into the host society – again, a caveat that had not been considered in 1945 or 1946. For this reason the IRO strongly objected to OMGUS's recommendation that a key prerequisite for removal was that the review board to be established "must" find the environment or institution in which the child was initially discovered to be "detrimental to the interests of the child."

To require this, argued Eleanor Ellis, US Zone child care officer, was "in our opinion tantamount to approving the kidnapping of children or their placement in German homes due to persecution of their families or relatives." Instead, she argued, it behooved the board to ensure that the current home was not detrimental to the best interests of the child and, key, that what was meant by "best interests" needed to be clarified:

> One cannot take into consideration only the child's immediate physical environment, i.e., the family relationships and adequacy of the home. Other questions must be answered. Can the family offer the child legal protection, so that his position as a member of the family is assured? What guarantee is there that the child in a foreign country will be given the opportunity to become a citizen? Will the child as a result of remaining in a foreign country lose its chance of becoming a citizen of any country, thereby becoming stateless? As a stateless person will he be entitled to a passport etc.? These questions, all related to the protective angle, are of paramount importance ... and must be considered.[47]

Resettlement, ironically, appeared a better means of providing this protection in many instances.

The argument made by Ellis, marked an important shift in logic – a key concern had become the legal security or protection of the child. Above all, whatever solution was pursued, the child's legal future had to be made secure. The notion of a child's best interests had moved beyond the initial practising definition of securing its physical and emotional health and security, which had been thought best restored and protected by returning a child to its family, to one that focused on the child's legal identity and future as well – looking towards the moment at which the child would become an adult and thus responsible for itself. The need to ensure, when that transition occurred, that the child was in as secure a legal position as possible, with the rights of a full citizen somewhere, was now recognized to be as important as its physical and emotional well-being.

EUCOM was becoming increasingly cognizant of the fact that a "foreign child is not assured the same legal protection as the German child," but it was not yet convinced of the logic of the IRO's argument, nor was it willing to embrace the consequences of accepting the IRO's proposed best practices.[48] The ultimate solution settled on was one that the IRO did not relish. In October 1948, the IRO's officers in the field reported the Military Government apparently had decided that the German

Youth Welfare Law was applicable to illegitimate unaccompanied United Nations nationality children, making the Landesjugendamt the guardian of illegitimate children – a violation of the IRO's mandate as it understood it.[49] In spite of the IRO's protests, by early 1949, without an alternative legal solution in sight, guardianship was conferred on the country of residence. Thus, in Germany, the Landesjugendamt became the default "collective guardian" for illegitimate children.[50] Alarmingly, there was considerable confusion even within the Jugendamt system, with some of the Jugendamt offices continuing to maintain that they did not have guardianship and others assuming they did. Thus, some children, including United Nations unaccompanied children, were, in all practical senses, without protection.[51] This decision simply stoked the IRO's desire to find, identify, and re-establish as many United Nations children as it could before its doors shut.

Limited Registration Plan

By early 1949, mild panic was beginning to set in. Not only had the child search operations not been wound up, but there seemed to be no sign that they might do so in the near future. Instead, children continued to be located, even as the IRO's officers were trying to clear old cases. Crucial policy issues remained unsolved, making it impossible to find a satisfactory resolution for many children. Too many cases remained open and the default resolution, to have them fall under Jugendamt protection, was not acceptable to the IRO. And there still existed a persistent belief that there remained many more children "out there" to be discovered – not just on the part of the Eastern European countries (who had always argued this), but increasingly on the part of the IRO, the Landesjugendamt, and EUCOM. All had come to realize that the haphazard approach to child search had left too much uncertain, and there was a growing, common suspicion that there existed an unidentified, "larger and more difficult case load, produced by the present very high birth rate, the lack of [a] sense of responsibility expressed by neglect and abandonment of children, and the lack of resettlement schemes providing for dependents."[52] Increasingly, a consensus was emerging that some kind of systematic review needed to be done in order to put this thorny question to bed.

A special test search project run in Land Niedersachsen of the British Zone with the cooperation of the German authorities, in which approximately forty-four presumably non-German children were registered, seemed to confirm these suspicions, as well as offer a model for a final review. The number of cases uncovered that required further investigation was quite large, and both new and useful documentary evidence had been uncovered in the process.[53] This was enough to convince the director of the International Tracing Service, the chief of the IRO's Child Search Section, and representatives from the American Military Government that the IRO should make a "concerted and intensified effort" to find and repatriate all non-German children, but with one caveat: it had to be done within a limited period of time (the time frame proposed was 12 to 18 months). This would be the definitive and final search. In answer to the prickly question of who would determine the child's future, it was decided that, in the absence of a parent, the government of the nation of which the child was a citizen would be deemed "competent to make decisions for the child." The occupation authorities would act on behalf of those children without a recognized governmental representative in Germany (i.e., the Baltic and Ukrainian children, as well as those of undetermined nationality and the few remaining Jewish children). The Child Search Section was given the responsibility of not only locating these children, but also of continuing their investigation through registration and documentation, and it was instructed to remove uncovered children from German care, if appropriate. EUCOM also agreed to issue a directive stating its policy regarding child search, in order to bring military and IRO policy into line.

The result was the Limited Registration Plan (also soon known as the Recovery Program), which mandated the registration of *all* children in German institutions and foster homes, as well as those who had been adopted since the beginning of the war. It would include all children who had been in foster care up to two years before the registration, but released from foster care because they had reached the age of majority.[54] This would be done, in the first instance, by the Jugendamt offices using special forms created expressly for this operation. This flew in the face of observations made during the trial run in Niedersachsen that relying on the German authorities' reporting, no matter how carefully managed and planned, was an error. Whether by accident or design (and it was probably a bit of both), the German authorities and their information had proven as unreliable as it had in 1945 and 1946. The answer, based on the experience in Niedersachsen, instead lay in "a method which would provide automatically for a check on *every* [emphasis added] child's case, German or Allied." The concession was, in all likelihood, recognition of the reality of the situation – the IRO just did not have the manpower to do this itself. In order to mitigate this, once the institutions had completed the forms, they would be turned over to child search officers who then would canvass each institution and determine whether the child fell under the IRO's mandate. If so, the officer would then register the child. The forms for both adopted and foster children were to be directed to the International Tracing Service where the information would be checked against its records. Any questionable forms would be returned to the relevant Jugendamt offices for "completion." Once the data were considered accurate, the files would be divided into two groups: those of children whose parents were undoubtedly of German nationality or who appeared to be accompanied by their natural parents and those of children whose circumstances were "doubtful." This latter group would then be assigned to the child search officers for further investigation.

It was estimated that this would involve registering between three hundred thousand and four hundred thousand children in the Western zones, four thousand to eight thousand of whom the IRO expected would fall within its mandate. This was an enormously ambitious project, the success of which would hinge on the cooperation and effectiveness of the Jugendamt offices in the first instance, and the efficiency of IRO's child search staff at clearing the cases, in the second. It also presumed that there would be no objections to screening by IRO staff both of children who were clearly German and children whose nationality was being debated – not something that could be guaranteed. To make the project more challenging, the timelines were quite tight. Registration was to be completed by September 1949. The child search program was to terminate in October 1949. With the IRO scheduled to close operations in June 1950 and the International Tracing Service tentatively being shifted to the United Nations, all residual work had to be completed by then. From the very start of this newest program, it was considered inevitable that there would be a residual group of children for whom plans could not be completed by the IRO, and all acknowledged that plans would have to be made for this remnant. The Recovery Program was a prospect that filled some in the field with dread in the certainty that it would overwhelm their resources.[55]

On 16 February 1949, OMGUS finally approved the Limited Registration Plan in principle and instructed the Landesjugendamt offices, the Kreisjugendamt offices, and all German child-caring agencies and institutions, as well as the various branches of the German Guardianship

Court to provide the IRO with the required information; as one of OMGUS's functions, it was to act as conduit for communication with the German authorities. The Land OMGs were directed to submit reports of all children among the German population under seventeen years of age and living in foster homes or institutions (both public and private), and who had been adopted after 1 September 1939, although this was not quite as comprehensive a sweep as originally anticipated. Importantly, however, OMGUS did not stipulate any details of the procedure, something that was instead to be thrashed out in a conference between the Land Military Government public welfare adviser and representatives from the Child Search Section in the US Zone, the International Tracing Service, and the various German authorities (the ministries of the Interior, Culture, and Justice) involved.[56] The initial agreement reached was that the International Tracing Service and the child search representatives would work with the German authorities to devise a mutually satisfactory plan with the proviso that, if any participant felt the agreement was not being followed, they would contact the Public Welfare Branch of OMG Bavaria "for further planning and solution."[57] OMG Bavaria, thus, would be the referee.

When the announcement was made, the reaction from Eastern Europe was predictably unenthusiastic. When the Polish Red Cross was informed of the plan, it was unimpressed, stating that both the Polish Red Cross and the Polish government had expected to be consulted in the conception of the Plan, not presented with a fait accompli.[58] For its part, the Yugoslavian Mission also protested that it could not believe the International Tracing Service could do an effective job of reviewing the submissions from the German functionaries without the aid of a Yugoslavian representative.[59] From the outset, then, the Limited Registration Plan was the object of criticism.

To facilitate the Recovery Program and address the space issues still plaguing the Child Care Section, the IRO established a Children's Village in Bad Aibling in January 1949. The initial purposes of the Children's Village were to provide temporary care for children who needed it due to a family emergency, such as a parent falling ill and being unable to care for his or her children (up until now, these children were either being cared for in a hospital or in area nurseries, neither of which was considered an optimal solution to the situation[60]) and to provide care for children and selected youth who had been approved for re-establishment. The Village also would offer casework, as well as legal and welfare services as appropriate.[61]

Within months of launching the project, it was clear that the process flow was not as efficient as first hoped and that the Child Search Section was again inundated. The first obvious glitch was that child search officers were conducting home investigations (intended to determine if the child's living conditions were adequate) before it was known whether the child being investigated was eligible for IRO care, because this particular question was handled by the Control Centre at the International Tracing Service, whose review followed the home site visit. If the child subsequently proved ineligible, the time and effort put into the home investigation was wasted. The order of the steps was reversed, but not before several months had been lost.[62] To further improve efficiency, certain categories of children were identified as not requiring registration, as long as their legal status was clear and the documentary evidence complete (in anticipation of possible appeals). This included children who were over fourteen and for whom all the evidence suggested they were German; children legally adopted before the war and still with their adoptive parents; children born in Germany before the war who were, as of 31 December 1947, full orphans with the foster parents with whom they had been placed prior to the war or foundling children (to use their term) for whom the *pre-war* authorities could not locate any relatives; children adopted after the war with the consent of both parents, if the child was legitimate, or the mother, if the child was illegitimate; any foundling children located after 1 January 1946 unless the evidence suggested they might not be German; and children who were expelled from their countries of origin to Germany after the war, together with their parents, but then became separated from them.[63] The requirement that the documentary evidence be convincing, however, was a difficult standard to meet.

Adding to the inefficiency was the half-hearted cooperation of the German youth welfare authorities. Although the Landesjugendamt worked hard to help with the survey (it saw value in getting the matter settled definitively), the lower Kreis and city Jugendamt offices, as well as many of the children's homes, were less committed to the project. In spite of careful instructions being issued in early April 1949 with a deadline for the information to be submitted to the Landesjugendamt by 15 May, as late as mid-June, many were pleading for extra time to compile the information. The institutions and various Jugendamt offices had been instructed to report all children for whom they were providing care as of that date, as well as all children who had left the institution since 1 June 1945, whether because of having reached the age of fourteen (the age at which they no longer qualified for youth welfare support) or other reasons, whatever the child's presumed nationality or whether the child had parents or not.[64] Many children's homes did not see the point, as they did not deal with those who might be United Nations children – such as the Kindererholungsheim Scholss Seeburg which provided only temporary care for German children from Munich brought to the home by their parents, or unmarried mothers. Others did not even deal with children, but with youths over the age of fourteen – and so did not think they needed to complete the forms.[65]

The task was an overwhelming one even for those who did handle the right age group and potential population, faced as they were with the compilation of information for sometimes thousands of children who had passed through their doors. Many Jugendamt offices and institutions ran out of forms, delaying reporting. Sometimes, the information supplied was too vague to be of use – for example, reporting a child's address as the Kreis and Land, but no actual street address.[66] Some offices, such as the Munich Jugendamt, complained that it was impossible to provide accurate numbers because almost all the records of children under its care in 1945 had been lost in the fires caused by the air raids of 1944 and 1945. While the office had tried, over the preceding year, to reconstruct its index of all "welfare children" in the city by appealing to all the family welfare workers, the schools, and the police to inform them of any children they knew about, it became clear that there were many foundlings in Munich living (or having lived) with foreign families but never registered with the Jugendamt. Thus, while the Jugendamt could provide a reasonable estimate of numbers in its care for the statistical report, it was going to be difficult to report accurately or fully the biographical data of those currently receiving welfare, as requested, and impossible to provide information about those discharged or who had left Jugendamt care since 1945 (a claim echoed by the Kreisjugendamt in Starnberg, for one). The whole exercise was a costly one, in terms of personnel needed to compile the information, such as it was. Who, asked the Munich Jugendamt, was going to pay for these extra costs?[67] As late as October 1949, the Landesjugendamt was still pursuing regional offices for their reports, and the International Tracing Service was returning incomplete forms for completion.[68] The reservations expressed by the Child Search Section about relying on the Jugendamt offices to conduct the initial registration and data compilation had proven prescient.

The review was running into another challenge as well: a lack of cooperation on the part of the children, especially the youth. The continued shortage of staff in the camps had translated into very little control over the children and youths. Youths, especially, were inclined to leave the camps for extended periods of time, without letting anyone know, and to ignore calls to register or attend counselling interviews.[69] This made it difficult to review a camp's population quickly or efficiently, or with a sense that, indeed, every child had been identified and registered.

Another factor slowing down the operation was a growing need for counselling, a result of the nature of many of the new cases being registered. Registration was uncovering a number of situations in which a child's family circumstances and environment were very complicated, as well as "potential hard core cases of children who are neglected because of illness, moral laxity, or general inadequacy of parents," requiring careful and extensive investigation and counselling. Adoptions and guardianship arrangements were being uncovered that had been arranged over the preceding three years without either the IRO's or UNRRA's knowledge, largely (it was argued by Eleanor Ellis) because of the complicated and contradictory laws surrounding the matters – both Military Government and German. This meant that increasing numbers of child care officers, who were supposed to be carrying out the Recovery Program, were being diverted into counselling.[70] In fact, in Area 7, which theoretically had eleven child care officers engaged in the registration exercise, only one remained working on the Recovery Program by September 1949. The other ten were now devoted to counseling full-time. This had effectively shut down the Recovery Program in the area, and by all reports, the situation was as desperate in other parts of the US Zone. The overworked child care officers were swamped dealing with urgent crises that erupted daily and distracted them.[71] This was further complicated by a sudden and unexpected influx of refugees from Czechoslovakia (a consequence of the Communist coup in that country in early 1948), including a number of youths, and many in the field resented having to now deal with these new refugees.[72]

In spite of the promise of relief, the child care officers continued to do counselling work into November 1949. In Area 3 this meant that there were only two workers available to work on recovery cases, with 197 International Tracing Service cases outstanding, as well as ten new cases monthly (on average) and a further 145 foster homes still to investigate.[73] In January 1950, E. Starner, the Child Care officer for Area 5, was reporting a similar state in her district: the counselling caseload was actually increasing as more and more difficult cases were emerging, such as children who could not emigrate because of physical and/or mental disabilities and adopted children who did not meet the requirements for emigration to the United States.[74]

The growing backlog was leaving a distressing number of children in a difficult and anxious situation, with their futures unknown.[75] This ate at the child care workers, as well as at the children, as Yvonne de Jong, a child welfare consultant at the IRO Headquarters in Geneva, astutely observed in an October visit to Bad Aibling Children's Village. Rumours were feeding off one another, permeating and infecting both staff and children. The displaced persons staff were experiencing their own difficulties in trying to emigrate; even for the most likely candidate, child or adult, resettlement was a long, drawn-out, uncertain affair. Their fears, frustrations, and rumours affected the children badly, influencing their dreams, attitudes, behaviour, and conversations. They were all, in spite of a misleading appearance of maturity, understandably "terribly insecure."[76]

Increasingly, it was becoming clear that initial fears were going to prove true – that, indeed, there was no way in which the Limited Registration Plan could be completed and all files closed by the time it was supposed to be finished or even before the IRO was to close down its operations. As also had been feared, a large number of children were being discovered who had never been identified previously, but who clearly fell within the IRO's mandate. In the end, under the Limited Registration Plan, the IRO reviewed 340,000 cases, of which 205,000 had required field investigation (180,000 of them in institutions and 25,000 in foster homes or adopted). As of June 1950, 1,500 had been registered as potentially within the IRO mandate. An additional 800 new cases had been registered in 1949 alone, these uncovered through individual tracing efforts (not the Limited Registration Plan). During 1949, a total of 1,624 inquiries for unaccompanied children had been resolved (as many as had been resolved in the preceding three years), but other inquiries had continued to come in, leaving a balance of 18,945 files outstanding, involving thirty nationalities, at the end of 1949 (new registrations, plus outstanding files). About two-thirds of the unaccompanied children had been found in foster families. As of 31 May 1950, 2,313 unaccompanied children had been registered as within the IRO's mandate; since 1 July 1947, 1,749 children had been repatriated and 3,088 resettled. At the same time, new cases continued to be uncovered, although there was a constant and large turnover in the caseload, with most cases being cleared within four to six months. The result was that the total number of unaccompanied children under care at any moment remained remarkably consistent. The expectation was that, in the end, there would be 12,500 cases uncovered by the Limited Registration Plan but whose files either would not be completed or for whom plans would not be finalized before the IRO's termination.[77] It appeared that people's suspicions were correct. There had been many more children to be found, and there would not be enough time to complete the exercise given the resources available. In February 1949, the IRO's General Council had decided not to allocate additional funds to child search operations for the organization's third financial year. The logic was that there were enough funds to see the program through to 30 June 1950, at which point all care was to cease except for those refugees already in the pipeline for either resettlement or repatriation and those still requiring finalization of plans to transfer them to institutional care in Germany.

The situation required a careful reallocation of resources for child search operations, in order to give them enough time to register all the children presumed to be non-German and to allow a few more children, whose nationality, identity, and eligibility under the IRO could be definitively established, to be transferred to the Child Care Section and into the pipeline. The plan was that everything would be completed by 31 July 1950: all children presumed to be non-German registered; the archives and master index of all documentary evidence completed; the establishment of the identity and nationality of children, and the tracing of their relatives, as much as possible done; and all individual queries about children received by 31 July 1950 checked against the Master Index. The Child Search Section would be liquidated by the end of August 1950. While this meant that not all children's cases would be resolved (the residual load would be dismayingly large), it was going to have to suffice.[78]

The Evolving Debate: Legal Security

All of these plans, of course, were contingent upon being able to move the children into the pipeline. It was pointless to register children and devote the resources to determining whether or not they were within the IRO's mandate if they could not then be removed from the German homes and institutions. Yet, this is the exact position in which the IRO found itself by early 1950. The low-grade war between OMGUS and the

IRO had continued all the while, and OMGUS had continued to block many applications to remove children from German foster families and institutions. The IRO remained hamstrung. The Länder OMGs used the excuse that a promised directive from EUCOM that was supposed to clarify the principles that would shape removal policy had not yet been released to justify both withholding a decision on all requests, and to suspend all removals already approved, but not yet enacted.[79]

The position of OMGUS remained largely the same: extremely reluctant to remove a child from a foster home if the foster parents objected, even in instances when the child's nationality had been definitively established, with the possible exception of the IRO having located the child's natural parents. To do otherwise, OMGUS continued to argue, would have a detrimental effect on the process of democratization in Germany. The removals had to be seen as based on the democratic principles of the due process of law, regardless of the legality or illegality of the process that put a child in that home or institution in the first place. To do otherwise would make a mockery of the democratic values that the Military Government was trying to instil in German society. Thus, every German family and institution was due a fair and impartial hearing. This had the effect of adding yet another layer of complexity to the resolution process and threatened to bog it down, as all the child care officers in the field realized, because the foster parents, as a rule, had "a definite stake in the retention of allied children."[80]

Ominously, however, the public welfare branches of Military Government had also begun to extend their review of applications for removal to include an evaluation of whether they considered it in the child's best interests, although they seldom explained exactly what they meant by the term "child's best interests." They had always framed their position in those terms, but now the Public Welfare Branch was taking a more active role in the determination. It was now deciding on whether a child should be removed or not, not just on the strength of the IRO's research, but increasingly on the strength of independent German sources of information (considered dubious at best by the IRO) and an evaluation of the future plan devised by the IRO for the child. If the public welfare personnel did not deem the future plan appropriate, they denied removal.

The IRO protested that the Länder OMGs were overstepping their mandate – which was to ensure that children were not removed from homes through error. Indeed, insisted the child care representative, the Military Government "must accede to an IRO request for removal of a child who has been established by IRO to be a United Nations orphaned, abandoned or unaccompanied child," as the IRO was the judge of whether a child fit its mandate, not the OMGs. This, of course, went to the heart of the battle between the IRO and the OMGs and was not something the public welfare branches were willing to concede easily.

OMGUS argued that it was not a "rubber stamp," but that it had both the right and the responsibility to investigate the legal validity of any IRO claims. The IRO was deemed responsible for this class of children, but military regulations did not mean that all such children "may be summarily repatriated or resettled by IRO authorities." The IRO did not have the authority to "disturb settled legal relationships between children and their natural or adoptive parents or other legal guardians." Ultimate responsibility for the final resolution of a child's case lay with the OMGs.[81] And so the turf war continued as each side became more entrenched.

Some removals did happen over 1949, although they were few in number. When they did happen, the German popular reaction was increasingly and belligerently angry. The social affairs adviser for the director of the Public Welfare Branch at OMG Bavaria, James Campbell, brought two cases in particular to the attention of the Public Welfare Branch to demonstrate the point: Marian Gajewy and Zofia Schink. Marian Gajewy was a Polish child who was born in September 1935, but placed with the Dengler family in Esslingen by Lebensborn in November 1944. Dengler had been a member of the Nazi Party and other party and SS organizations. Marian's aunt had now requested the boy's repatriation, and OMGUS had approved his transfer to Bad Aibling in July 1949. However, news of his removal soon spread in Esslingen, where he had been attending high school, "and [it] was resented by the population which did not understand that the child should be transferred after having been with his foster-family for almost 5 years out of which 4 years were of occupation. The Landrat protested ... and ... presented credible information to the fact that the child is Volksdeutsch and that his aunt in Poland agrees to the child's stay with the Dengler family."[82]

Zofia Schink was born in April 1935 and confirmed as Polish by the Polish liaison officer. She was unaccompanied in Germany and had only been placed with her current foster family by the local Jugendamt on 11 June 1946. Based on letters from her mother requesting the child's return, the IRO got permission to remove her on 15 June 1949. At this point, her foster father complained that the child could not remember her mother, who was, in reality, her stepmother. Her father, he claimed, had served in the German Army and was now in England. In this case, the Bavarian Ministry of the Interior had become involved, asking OMG Bavaria to reconsider the case "since the child is well taken care of by her foster-parents, the Ebner family in Ludwigsburg, who have no Nazi background ... [arguing] that the transfer of the child to Poland would be tragical [sic] for the child as well as her foster-parents." Given the level of German government now getting involved, Campbell argued, an appeal board was needed immediately, and it should include a representative of the Public Welfare Branch, as well as provide an opportunity for the German authorities involved in the case to address it.[83]

There was also growing sympathy for the Germans' position in some parts of the IRO, to the dismay of those further up the administrative ladder – in part because removals were often very upsetting for all involved, including the child care worker. Mrs Laursen, a sub-area child care officer based in Rosenheim, had one particularly difficult removal which shook her resolve. She was instructed to move Anna Jurek, aged six, from her foster home to Bad Aibling. Although she gave both the Jugendamt and the foster parents a week's notice, when she arrived at the home, the foster father resolutely refused to allow her to take the child. After an hour's conversation, she gave up and approached the local military police. They gave her one officer to accompany her and instructed her to bring along a German police officer as well. Laursen wrote to her supervisor:

> I hope you understand the whole situation. – it was a little village, and the whole population was looking on and the foster-father was saying that we are using the same terror means as the Kommunist [sic] in East-Europe, to what I in one way agree. Our work in IRO is a humane one, or should be, but I feel in many of our ITS cases, it is not considered to be such a one. The child was 6 years old, and she is so big now, that she will never forget that she once in her life was taken by a policeman from these people she called father and mother, because she has been living with them since she was 8 days old ... I don't 'love' the Germans, because of what they have done to my country, but now there is peace, and our social work should consist in showing the world that we are trying to do it better.[84]

In her response to this groundswell of opposition to removal from within her own ranks, Eleanor Ellis, the US Zone child care officer, offered the clearest articulation yet of the evolution in the IRO's logic for continuing to push for removal. Although she recognized that the removal of a child from German care was always a difficult psychological experience for a child, Ellis argued that it must be realized that this policy decision was not the IRO's but that of its member governments. More importantly, it had to be realized that, in most cases, leaving a child in foster care was particularly hazardous for the child. This was not necessarily because the family was not a loving one, but because it was almost impossible for the child to achieve "full establishment into German citizenship." A child might have identification papers, but this was not the same as having the full protection of the German government. There was also the concern that any child left in the German community was a potential public charge, dependent on limited German welfare resources that were, in the first instance, directed to Germans. Given that few children would ever gain German citizenship, after careful consideration by the United Nations and their governments, the consensus was that it made more sense to either repatriate these children or re-establish them outside of Germany, where their legal rights could be established definitively.[85] As Ellis had argued elsewhere, besides the "basic human right [of every child to have] full knowledge of his background and origin," all support and access to benefits was contingent upon one's citizenship or nationality, or even religious faith. It was, Ellis maintained, "not only important to the child to know who he is, it is to the *State* [emphasis in original]." It was crucial that a child's legal status be determined definitively because otherwise that child's access to the rights and benefits of a citizen of any country was in doubt.[86] Increasingly, the central argument had become the legal security of the child.

By 1949, there were now three components to the definition of a child's best interests – physical, emotional, and legal security – the latter two of which were proving increasingly contentious. While it was easy to decide whether a child was in good health and was being provided with adequate sustenance and hygiene, the question of how best to ensure the child's emotional security was less clear-cut. Whether it was better to leave a child in the family or institutional situation in which it had been living, sometimes for years at this point, and in which the child seemed to be content, or to remove the child to return to the often-shattered family from which it had been torn so many years earlier, or to an institution in the homeland in order to help the child develop or re-establish a sense of its national identity, was a subject of considerable and heated debate. The third component, a child's legal identity and security, while relatively new to the discussion, was subject to as heated a debate – largely around the question of how crucial it was to ensure a child would enjoy full citizenship rights wherever it ended up. Both of these debates crystallized around the argument as to when or if a child should be removed from a German foster family or institution, and the IRO and OMGUS remained at odds over them. Just as the IRO continued to be determined to get unaccompanied displaced children out of German homes and institutions, OMGUS continued to be as determined that they remain there, if it was a healthy and reasonably secure environment.

This expansion in the IRO's notion of what was in a child's best interests was also fed by a growing concern about the implications of the occupying authorities' plan to grant increasing legislative and judicial powers to the nascent West German federal government and Länder. This plan was crystallized in the Occupation Statute of 12 May 1949, the first step in the transfer of power to what would ultimately be a full-fledged and independent German administration and enacted in September 1949. The Statute's purpose was to grant the German federal state and its Länder full legislative executive and judicial powers in accordance with the Basic Law for the Federal Republic of Germany (which came into effect on 23 May 1949) and the Länder constitutions, with certain caveats, including an option for the occupation authorities to intervene if they did not approve of the application of those powers. The Occupation Statute was meant to be a trial for a period of year, at the end of which its provisions would be reviewed in light of the year's experience and with an eye to possibly expanding the German authorities' jurisdiction.[87]

How this transfer of powers would affect the right of the IRO to operate in West Germany, or the status of the displaced persons, which had always been derived from American authority in its Zone, was uncertain. It was not clear that the rights, privileges, and immunities that either the IRO or the displaced persons had enjoyed under the occupying forces' jurisdiction would continue under the auspices of the emerging German administration. The IRO, therefore, aggressively lobbied the Military Government to ensure that it would be able to continue all its operations as before; that the displaced persons be protected from discrimination, their special status preserved for at least an intermediate period; and that the IRO be involved in all negotiations dealing with the proposed Occupation Statute that might have an impact on it or on displaced persons.[88]

Of special concern were elements in the West German Civil Code that, if applied to the displaced persons, would put them in a difficult position, especially the children. Because there was no reciprocity between Germany and most displaced persons' home countries, the German Civil Code made clear that displaced persons were subject to the laws of their home country. This meant, when they needed any kind of a legal ruling, they would have to obtain it from their national consuls – a patently difficult situation for the displaced persons remaining in Germany by this time, most of whom were very leery of approaching their consuls or who had been denied their country's protection. (One such example would be of a Yugoslavian, recognized to be of that nationality, but who had refused to return to Yugoslavia and thus had lost that government's protection.) For unaccompanied children, it meant that, for someone to acquire guardianship of the child, that person had to do so with the approval of the child's native government – complicated in the best of circumstances, problematic if there was no recognized liaison officer. For unaccompanied children of undetermined nationality, the situation was even murkier. The complexities of national adoption laws, such as in Germany and Poland, for example, meant that it was virtually impossible to reconcile them, and thus impossible for a non-German child to be adopted by anyone. Some countries, including Poland, refused to recognize marriages between displaced persons contracted in Germany, with the corollary impact of rendering illegitimate any children of such a marriage – which made resettlement impossible for the family unit. And the question of whether the Landesjugendamt could be appointed guardian of an illegitimate displaced child was still apparently unsettled, in spite of OMGUS's pronouncement, as some among the legal counsel contended that the German Civil Code only permitted this for illegitimate German children.[89] This situation threatened to make resettlement of many unaccompanied children next to impossible and to undermine efforts to encourage resettlement of displaced persons family units by making it impossible to put their family's status on the firm legal footing required before emigrating.

With the transfer of power, the role of the American Military Government also changed fundamentally, from de facto government of the region to adviser to the new West German government, encapsulated in the winding up of OMGUS and its replacement with the High Commission for Occupied Germany. While it retained many of the functions and activities of both the US Group on the Allied Control Council and OMGUS, the relationship of the High Commission for Occupied

Germany with the newly establishing German state was a very different
one. This meant that the Military Government could no longer require
action on the part of the German authorities – it could only suggest it.
This might have had its advantages in that the IRO and OMGUS had
been at war over child search for years now, but it did mean that the IRO
was left having to negotiate with the German government on behalf of
its charges. At least with OMGUS, the IRO had had a formal arrangement and a contract that obliged OMGUS, however begrudgingly, to
support the displaced persons and the IRO's operations. The IRO had
no such agreement with the German government, which left its position, and the position of its charges, disturbingly nebulous.

From the occupation authorities' perspective, this was a temporary
glitch. They continued mistakenly, perhaps naively, to believe that the
concept of displaced person as a category would simply disappear with
the closure of the IRO, and displaced persons would then simply "be
regarded as Germans" (it would have resolved all the problems neatly,
had that been the case). This was patently not true, at least in terms
of legal status, but this point apparently had evaded the occupying
authorities. Nor did it recognize that many of the displaced persons
would resolutely resist assuming German nationality, even if given the
option. Finally, there was great reluctance on the part of the German
authorities to the notion of granting the displaced persons any kind of
lasting special status.[90]

The IRO's legal counsel explored various solutions to the problem of
the displaced persons' legal status: declaring them stateless, exempting
them from specific pieces of German legislation, or unilateral naturalization by the occupation authorities. None of these were considered
viable. Declaring them stateless would be a dangerous precedent, as
they were not technically stateless, and it would have the unwelcome
result of increasing the size of a population who posed enormous legal
and diplomatic, as well as social and economic challenges. Exempting
them from a list of pieces of legislation that compromised their status
was dismissed as cumbersome, as no list would be exhaustive and also
would require constant monitoring and updating. Unilateral naturalization as Germans by the occupying authorities would fly in the face
of efforts to re-establish a sovereign German state that should then have
control over who is admitted to its citizenry. It was anticipated that this
would also elicit a violent public reaction in Germany, which would
undermine any possible long-term solution and make any ultimate
integration of displaced persons into German society and economy

extremely difficult. The best alternative in the minds of IRO's legal counsel was to have German law regarded as the domestic law for both displaced persons and refugees – that the laws of the country of current residence would apply to the displaced person, at least regarding their personal status – with protection for certain of the displaced persons' special privileges, including that the IRO or its successor have the right to protect the displaced persons' legitimate interests, especially to provide legal and political protection. For unaccompanied children, this would make them the responsibility of the Landesjugendamt.[91]

The interim solution reached was a non-solution. The Occupation Statute treated the refugee and displaced persons question as a "reserved subject" (one of nine areas of responsibility or "subjects" retained by the occupation authorities) to be reviewed again in twelve months after its passage. Those displaced persons who were de jure stateless (i.e., legally so) were to be governed by the laws of Germany; those who were only de facto stateless (i.e., had a nationality but were "unable or unwilling to avail themselves of the protection of [their] government") were to be governed by the laws of their country of origin. This left the latter unable to sort out their family affairs, as the German courts had no authority to deal with their problems regarding marriage, divorce, legal capacity, guardianship, adoption, etc. Not only did this leave the displaced persons in limbo, it deeply compromised their ability to participate in any resettlement schemes, as those required that these questions be addressed before they would entertain a candidate. For the children, it threw them back on their national governments' representatives, if they had a national government. The result was that it threatened to swell the ranks of those who would have to remain in Germany. It also meant that the particular challenges of the unaccompanied children were not addressed.

The occupation authorities were reluctant to consider the possibility of granting the displaced persons any special status; however, they also realized that there were going to be displaced persons who could not be resettled and so would have to be absorbed into the German economy and society. This transition would need to be managed carefully as there was considerable concern about how receptive the German state and the German population would be to the idea.[92] For this reason, the Military Government reluctantly agreed that measures had to be taken to guarantee the legal position of any displaced persons who were going to remain in Germany. The challenges to doing so were several. First, only a very small percentage of the remaining displaced persons, it was estimated, would be interested in acquiring German citizenship. Second, it was not clear that those who were willing to do so would be welcome. (When asked what he thought would be the displaced persons' status after the termination of the IRO, one legal adviser replied, "Verfluchte ausländer" or "damned foreigner.") Finally, no solution would be durable that was not agreed to by the new German government. Therefore, it was urgent to get some kind of guarantee from the nascent German government that it would not use its new powers to deprive displaced persons of the rights they currently enjoyed. This, it was argued, was not intended to establish a privileged status for the displaced persons, but to ensure that they were treated as equals to German citizens. The proposal was to try to persuade the German authorities to regularize the displaced persons as part of "the family of nations ... dealing with a problem which was common to other western European countries" and to point to various international conventions on the matter as guidelines. Meanwhile, an interim solution was needed to regularize the displaced persons' personal status and family affairs.[93]

The question was no less urgent for unaccompanied children. In some ways, it was more so as these were, it will be remembered, minors legally incapable of making decisions for themselves, and therefore theirs was a particularly precarious situation. This was the context that explains the increased concern about the legal security of children: the looming closure of the IRO and the emerging West German government, together with the gradual relinquishing of responsibility for the displaced persons by the occupying authorities. If the West German government could not be trusted to protect the children, the legal rights of any children who had to remain in Germany had to be set in stone; they needed to be identified and their situations made stable. If the Jugendamt was to assume legal responsibility for all remaining unaccompanied children, then the number of such children needed to be reduced as much as possible.

Chapter Nine

The Residual

The challenges facing the people in the Child Care Section of the International Refugee Organization (IRO) as they confronted the reality of the anticipated residual load of unaccompanied United Nations children, as well as the impending closure of the IRO itself, were several. Child care staff needed to aggressively pursue all resettlement options, which meant completing as many of the open files as possible and finding viable opportunities for the children. It also meant that a solution was needed to the deadlock over removals, for there were many children for whom resettlement or even repatriation was a viable alternative, if only the Office of Military Government, United States (OMGUS) would approve their removal from German foster homes and institutions. Finally, child care staff needed to find solutions for the children whose files would remain open when the IRO closed its doors. These included children who simply did not qualify for a resettlement program because they were of the wrong age (perhaps too old, as many programs had a cut-off age of the early teens, leaving behind those in their late teen years but under the age of 17); because, while they were technically in only temporary care at IRO installations such as Bad Aibling, their parents were never going to be able to resume responsibility for them (often due to mental or physical health issues); or because they were not attractive to either resettlement missions or their own national governments because of physical and mental disabilities. This meant the Child Care Section was going to have to work with the Landesjugendamt and the new West German government to arrange for the inevitable absorption of the children for whom alternatives could not be found, including those in temporary care and the physically and mentally challenged.

To help make all this happen, an extension in the life of the IRO would be enormously useful. With a date of 30 June 1950 for the end of the IRO's operations, and the August 1950 liquidation date for the Child Search Section on the near horizon, trying to find reasonable and secure solutions to the remnant cases was going to be almost impossible otherwise. The IRO had indeed been pressing for an extension for the child search operations, and fortuitously several factors came together to make this an attractive idea to others as well. If children were going to be turned over to the German authorities for permanent care, the US High Commission for Occupied Germany (HICOG) feared that the Germans would rightly balk if the number to be transferred were too large. If the IRO's operations were extended to 31 March 1951, however, there was a very real possibility that many of the displaced persons remaining in the IRO camps, both adults and children, could be expected to "find an immigration outlet." This meant that HICOG could argue to the Germans that they would face "a relatively small 'hard-core'... [when] the IRO is scheduled to disappear from the scene," a much more palatable prospect.[1] This compromise, it was hoped, would allay German fears and go some distance towards preventing a German refusal. It would also spare the German government assuming responsibility for the IRO resettlement program which it would inevitably have to take on if the IRO terminated operations before all displaced persons in the resettlement pipeline had been processed – a task for which the Germans were not prepared and in which they had no expertise or experience. It would also, as pointed out in a confidential memo to the US Department of Political Affairs in Geneva, deny the Soviet Union the opportunity to yet again criticize the IRO (and by implication, the United States), as had happened in Austria, for having "thrown upon ... taxpayers [an] unwarranted burden for support [of] persons whose voluntary repatriation [was] obstructed by such authorities." This had created "serious internal economic and political problems in Austria," which would be good to avoid in Germany. Therefore, the American government was willing to assist the IRO in finding additional funds sufficient to continue its displaced persons operations until 31 March 1951, if just to avoid this happening.[2]

A second reason for extending the IRO's mandate was a last-minute reprieve that seemed to be taking shape in the United States. There, legislation was pending that would permit the admission of possibly forty thousand more displaced persons at this late point, and establish a new special visa quota for five thousand children adopted by American employees in Germany. An extension would make it possible to take advantage of this last-minute opportunity. If the IRO were shut down on 30 June, the displaced persons would almost instantly be evicted from the camps, with serious consequences. Without the IRO's bureaucracy in place and with the displaced persons scattered across the US Zone (the inevitable result of closing the camps), trying to allocate these new visas would be much more complicated. Better to keep the displaced persons in the camps and take advantage of the IRO's expertise, knowledge, and records until this was done. If this meant extending the IRO's funding, it was worth it.[3] In June 1950, HICOG formally confirmed that it would continue providing logistical support to the IRO and the voluntary agencies without change until 1 April 1951.[4] (Like UNRRA, the IRO would be granted several more reprieves, always at the last moment, its period of operation being extended twice more: to 30 September 1951, and then 1 January 1952 – all for the same reason, to give the IRO more time to re-establish the remaining DP population, adult and child, and eliminate the residual load.) By October 1950, the HICOG was ready to revise the Occupation Statute and remove "displaced persons" from the list of reserved subjects, contingent upon a successful resolution to the question of the displaced persons' legal status in Germany, among other things.[5] In March 1951, HICOG submitted a formal request that the Federal Republic of Germany assume responsibility for displaced persons remaining within its territory at the end of the IRO's operations.[6]

The self-defined mission of the IRO became, at this point, to "establish," to use its words, as many children (as well as displaced persons more generally) as possible. The reprieve also would give it time to reach agreements with the West German authorities about the care, the legal status, and the legal rights of the displaced persons once they became a German responsibility – a complicated and drawn-out set of negotiations.[7]

Resettlement

One of the options for the resolution of the remnant children's cases, considered the most preferable by IRO's Child Welfare Section, was resettlement. It had become an option in the last year of UNRRA's operations (since mid-1946), but for children resettlement had been limited primarily to the United States and only under the auspices of the US Committee for the Care of European Children. The Committee had been approved by the American government as the sole agency authorized to admit orphaned children to the United States. However, eligible candidates were further restricted to those whose sole surviving relatives were in the United States; those who had been "disclaimed" (or rejected) by the national liaison officer of the only country in which they could claim nationality; those of unknown nationality or of a nation without a liaison officer in Germany (such as the Baltic countries); and Jewish children who had expressed a "decided preference" for going to the United States. It was emphasized in the administrative order authorizing the operation of the Committee in Germany that any child referred to the Committee had to be clearly a candidate for one of these categories, with no ambiguities.[8]

In spite of the Committee's authorization, UNRRA had never managed to truly reconcile itself to resettlement. While it worked quite willingly with the Committee to identify and process children who fell within the Committee's mandate, UNRRA's priority had remained (in fact was required by its constitution to remain) repatriation – even as all involved came to acknowledge that repatriation was an increasingly unattractive option among the displaced persons, including the children. Indeed, with the introduction of resettlement as a viable and legitimate option, all also understood that this would further undermine any repatriation efforts among the remaining displaced persons population, who were quite hostile to the notion. UNRRA had had to tread a careful line between cooperating actively in the pursuit of resettlement options and trying to "soften [resettlement's] deterrent effect on [the Administration's] continuing and priority function of repatriation."[9] The Committee had also not moved a significant number of children by the time that UNRRA ceased operations. In March 1947, Cornelia Heise reported that a total of 842 children had taken advantage of the program, most of them Jewish.[10] The only other movement of significance was that of Jewish infiltree children, although without much assistance from UNRRA, as part of the ongoing and illegal exodus to Palestine.

There were options other than the United States for resettlement, but usually these were not available to children. Numerous national governments, especially the United States, Canada, Australia, and New Zealand, but others as well, were interested in the displaced persons, but they looked upon them as a potential source of labour for their recovering economies. Thus, the focus of the various national resettlement missions sent into the displaced persons camps by the various governments was primarily on the adult population who would be employable upon arrival, could make a contribution to the national economies, and who would thus not prove a financial burden to the state. None were keen to take on displaced persons who could not support themselves. As a result, priority was always given to adult displaced persons who were single (and thus had no dependents) and immediately employable, typically in occupations specified by the governments.

However, due to the publicity and public concern surrounding the plight of unaccompanied children, many national governments also made a nominal exception for this particular group of displaced persons as a humanitarian gesture – nominal in that, while a number of governments agreed to allocate a certain number of visas to unaccompanied children, the visas were in the dozens or hundreds at most, and the programs were very carefully constructed to ensure that the children posed as minimal a burden on the state (who would be directly or indirectly assuming responsibility for them) as possible. After all, these children would be dependent, fully or partially, upon the state for support until adulthood – either because they were in school full-time or in training, for example, as an apprentice in a trade. Furthermore, as legal minors, it would be the state, or some representative of it, that would be legally responsible for them. These particular schemes were always small in scale and selective in their target candidates.

The IRO was much more keen on resettlement as an option, given the hostility of the remnant displaced persons population, adult and child, to repatriation. While its official mandate was to pursue repatriation first, it was given the freedom to pursue resettlement options equally (unlike UNRRA). In practice, although repatriation was always available and continued to happen at a desultory pace, resettlement was the option of choice. The United States was, by far, the preferred destination of the vast majority of displaced persons. When, on 19 June 1948, to the IRO's great relief, the US Displaced Persons Act of 1948 was passed, a solution seemed to suddenly open up. The Act allowed two hundred thousand displaced persons and refugees to apply to emigrate to the United States, with three thousand visas being set aside specifically for displaced orphan children under the age of sixteen and assigned to the US Committee for the Care of European Children. To qualify, the children had to have been orphaned due to the death or disappearance of both parents and must have been in Germany before the effective date of the Act. The window was small, with the visas set to expire in two years, but the American authorities were very keen on the Act, in spite of its restrictions, if only because it offered a means for reducing the size of the remnant displaced persons population, thus reducing the cost of that population's maintenance to both American and German taxpayers.[11] The IRO was also pleased, although the child care workers did fret that, like so many other programs, it excluded youths aged sixteen and seventeen.[12]

Responsibility for implementing the new law's provisions was assigned to a new Displaced Persons Commission, a three-member body chosen by the President of the United States.[13] The Commission swung into action quickly and, just as quickly, it and the IRO began to bicker, with the Displaced Persons Commission accusing the IRO of being slow, cumbersome, inefficient, and understaffed, and the IRO accusing the Displaced Persons Commission of having unrealistic expectations and no understanding of the nature of fieldwork, where it was difficult to complete cases in a timely fashion because of the realities of the displaced persons' lives.[14]

By June 1950, all were becoming rather exasperated. The window for this tremendously important source of resettlement opportunities for the children was set to expire that month. The mounting frustration was due to the tedious pace at which children were being processed for admission to the United States, which meant that many of those visas were in danger of being lost. At the last minute and in the midst of a flurry of lobbying, on 16 June 1950, the Displaced Persons Act was extended to 1 July 1952. The extension created a new special non-quota immigration visa (i.e., it fell outside the standard national quotas imposed on the numbers of immigrants from any particular country allowed into the US in any one year), available to both adults and children, and it established a special sub-class of five thousand visas, created specifically for orphans or unaccompanied children under the age of ten at the time the visa was issued who, by 30 June 1951, had in hand assurances from the child's guardian or sponsoring agency that adoption or guardianship proceedings would be initiated in the United States and that the child would be cared for properly.[15]

This last caveat threatened to create even further complications. By this point, 1950, having the German courts rule on adoption cases had become accepted practice. In December 1947, OMGUS had issued Military Government Law No. 10, allowing German courts to rule on adoptions of both German and United Nations children, if so authorized by the Land Office of Military Government (OMG). It also simultaneously instructed the directors of each Land OMG to grant German notaries a general authorization to "attest, authenticate or witness adoption contracts." (In the case of United Nations national children being adopted, the courts were instructed that they had to receive the consent of European Command (EUCOM) to the adoption as well.) It was done begrudgingly, as the challenges facing American personnel determined to adopt a child in Germany were daunting, but OMGUS felt compelled. In mid-January 1948, the process was modified in order to address a glitch that had quickly emerged.

Crucially, one of the German courts' tasks was to ensure that the adoption met the legal adoption requirements of both Germany and the country of the adopting parents.[16] For their part, in the case of adoptions by German nationals, German courts focused solely on the contractual aspects of a case and so would accept any adoption that met the formal requirements of the law and was approved by their Guardianship Court. In the case of a prospective adoptive parent who was not a German national, however, the law required that the adoption satisfy all the requirements of the adoption laws of the adopter's permanent residence. In the United States, comprehensive social investigations of the prospective adoptive parents and their home were also required. In this case, because they were unable to ensure a proper investigation was done, the German courts' practice was to refuse to consider the case, arguing "they would not do more for a foreign national than for a German national."

The solution arrived at had been to use an Adoption Review Board, to be established by HICOG, as a substitute for the social or home investigation.[17] The process that had evolved was as follows. If an American wished to adopt a child of a United Nations nationality in Germany, they applied to the appropriate German court. That court referred the case to the Military Government for approval before ruling on it. If the Adoption Review Board approved an adoption, this was deemed to be "sufficient proof that state laws have been complied with." The various American state governments had already accepted this practice, as they were not in a position to investigate residents living in Europe. While this was not considered ideal, the investigations carried out in the name of the Adoption Review Board were considered to meet the minimum requirements.

The problem created by the amendment to the Displaced Persons Act was that it required the Displaced Persons Commission to demonstrate that the child would be adopted and cared for properly. The fear was that the German courts would interpret this to mean that they could not release children without a "properly approved adoption contract." If this amendment were implemented, HICOG now would be obliged to conduct social investigations, for which it had neither the resources nor the budget. Each investigation, it was estimated, would require two man-days, on average, and the expectation was that there would be approximately five hundred cases coming forward in the coming year. This would amount to the need for an additional four professionals – a cost that HICOG was unwilling to bear.[18] If the German courts decided to cleave closely to the wording of the Displaced Persons Act, as some did, it could derail the scheme.

Another glitch was that the sub-class of visas was not limited to orphans from Germany, but was open to displaced orphans from a number of countries, comprising a lengthy list that had recently been expanded to include children from Greece (a response to the civil war raging in that country by this time, which had resulted in extensive displacement). Thus, unaccompanied children in Germany were competing for a limited number of spots with children from various other countries.

A third and growing concern in the United States was how well the children were integrating into American society. The lack of support available in the United States for those who adopted these children, and the individual states' exclusion from the selection and placement process was proving a problem. These children arrived necessarily without the same level of rigorous investigation that a child adopted from within the United States underwent, so the child's suitability was uncertain. The risk in adopting a child from a different culture and language was a particular worry for many social workers in the United States. The basic dilemma was that, if a placement did not work well, there were few options for either the child or the adoptive parents. Although the Displaced Persons Commission was responsible for the initial placement, it was the responsibility of local American agencies to make any new plans, both because the Displaced Persons Commission was a temporary agency scheduled to cease operations on 31 August 1952 and because it had never been authorized to provide support beyond the initial placement. Suggestions that the American agencies should be more involved in the selection of placements from the beginning, however, received short shrift.[19]

The key underlying reason for the panic about the expiring visas, however, was that the processing of files was taking exceedingly long. From the beginning, the Displaced Persons Commission blamed the IRO for the slow pace. In July 1950, in a fit of either pique or frustration, the coordinator for the Displaced Persons Commission's operations in Europe, Alex Squadrilli,[20] resigned in protest, convinced that, after having won an extension of the Displaced Persons Act, it would be wasted due to "administrative controversy and ineptitude," costing some thirty thousand displaced persons the opportunity to resettle in the United States.[21] This was a concern echoed strongly by his successor, Harry Rosenfield, who complained in November 1950 to J.D. Kingsley, the director general of IRO Geneva, about the growing backlog in cases with the IRO. By his count, on 1 November there were 8,213 cases (involving approximately 16,000 people) at the IRO for documentation, a backlog that had been growing steadily since August. In fact, he pointed out, 54 per cent of that backlog had been with the IRO for over two months, and 1,499 cases, for over six months. The situation was appalling, he complained, and something had to be done if the Displaced Persons Commission and the IRO were to complete their tasks.[22]

Contrary to the accusations, however, it soon became clear that the backlog was not the fault of the IRO. The Office of the Land Commissioner Bremen (OLC Bremen, formerly OMG Bremen), concerned about the growing overcrowding in the embarkation camps, Grohn and Tirpitz, in Land Bremen, had launched its own investigation of the situation, as the growing population in these camps was becoming increasingly restive, waiting for transportation to the United States. OLC Bremen identified several reasons for the decline in numbers moving out. Chief was the American government's much more stringent security review required of a displaced person before being cleared for transport. What once took under a month now took two or three months. In addition, the IRO had lost access to four US Navy ships, as they had been reassigned because of the North Korean invasion of South Korea on 25 June 1950, the first major armed conflict of the Cold War and a source of deep international tension. The United States had become involved on the side of South Korea immediately, and the reallocation of military resources from Europe to the Pacific theatre was one result. Finally, the Displaced Persons Commission had suffered an extraordinary turnover in staff (almost 50 per cent had resigned after Squadrilli left), and the new recruits were both untrained and inefficient, creating tension and dissatisfaction in the organization and resulting in a very ineffective operation. Thus, the slowdown in displaced persons immigration to the United States, in the opinion of OLC Bremen, was the result of administrative failure, rather than something more "substantive," with the result that "the IRO will find itself sorely taxed to liquidate its program by March 31, 1951."[23]

This sentiment was echoed strongly by others, including a special eleven-member advisory committee representing both American voluntary agencies and various representatives from state-level branches of the Displaced Persons Commission sent in July to investigate the slowdown. It was pointed out that the breakdown in the operations of the Displaced Persons Commission threatened not just to stall the resolution of the displaced persons problem in Germany and thus delay the termination of the IRO (Kingsley was already requesting another extension), but also to compromise the operations of HICOG more generally, through the creation of a bottleneck in the flow of the displaced persons out of Germany. Internal dissension and a dysfunctional organizational structure, as well as serious administrative constraints imposed on the European coordinator by the Displaced Persons Commission, had brought the Displaced Persons Commission's operations almost to a standstill. According to Kingsley, while the IRO resettlement centres had handled up to eighteen thousand visaed persons monthly in the past, the problems in the Displaced Persons Commission had reduced that flow to seventy-four hundred in July and even fewer in August 1950. He warned that, if this continued, the Displaced Persons Commission would fall well short of its goal by approximately forty thousand immigrants. It also meant that barrack space desperately needed by EUCOM for an incoming forty thousand new troops was not available – as it was currently occupied by the backlog of displaced persons. The Displaced Persons Commission had lost the confidence of HICOG, the IRO, and the voluntary agencies in Germany, as well as the displaced persons themselves. It was clear that this situation required immediate intervention from the highest office, namely, that of the President of the United States, to ensure that the Displaced Persons Act was successfully implemented.[24]

By March 1951, Rosenfield had been replaced, and Robert Corkery[25] had become European coordinator for the Displaced Persons Commission. Corkery put the situation back on track. In his "pipeline report" of 1 March 1951, Corkery reported that, of the total caseload, 25 per cent had been determined to be dead files or rejections for various reasons, and so had been eliminated from the pipeline. Regarding the remaining 75 per cent (34,842 cases), 20 per cent were inactive due to medical reasons, security clearance issues, outstanding interviews, or missing documentation. The remaining 54 per cent were moving through the system in a timely manner, with only 700 of them being in the system for more than three months. Of those deemed inactive, there were cases that were continuously moving into the active category as circumstances changed and information became available. In conclusion, Corkery reported, he expected that there would be a need for approximately 61,700 visas, of which he expected to issue approximately 27,678 by 30 June 1951, leaving 34,022 outstanding – an improvement, perhaps, but not a promising prospect. For the children, the consequences were dire. As of March 1951, only 147 children had been issued visas under the Displaced Persons Act.[26] It appeared that the IRO as a whole, in spite of best efforts by the Child Care Section, was more interested in moving out adult displaced persons than children. Certainly this is how it appeared to George Warren, adviser on refugees and displaced persons for the US State Department.[27]

Other officially sanctioned resettlement options for unaccompanied children also began to open up by mid-1948. By that point, the Canadian Jewish Congress had offered to sponsor a thousand Jewish orphans up to eighteen years of age. A second Canadian scheme proposed to resettle a thousand Roman Catholic children aged five to twelve. There was also a Swedish resettlement scheme offering space for 150 Protestant children up to ten years of age, under the auspices of the Swedish Save the Children Fund. The New Zealand government offered to take in a hundred children aged five to twelve, preferably Baltic in nationality. In addition to a plan created by the Australian branch of the American Joint Distribution Committee to bring four hundred Jewish orphans aged between six and seventeen to Australia, the Australian government proposed a second scheme for youths aged sixteen to eighteen, with an initial quota of 150, but soon raised to five hundred. This last plan generated considerable excitement, both because of what it offered (foster home placement, legal protection through the appointment of a guardian upon arrival, access to either higher education or vocational training, assistance in finding suitable employment, and full care where necessary until age 21[28]), and because it addressed an otherwise very difficult group to place – older youth. When news reached the Children's Village and displaced persons community, approximately 140 boys and a few girls promptly expressed an interest in applying, and Eleanor Ellis, US Zone child care officer, estimated they would get at least seventy-five to one hundred more applicants over the ensuing six months. At this point, if the child was eligible and of "an age to express a wish," the child was free to choose between schemes.[29]

Although eligibility was sometimes a challenge (resettlement missions often imposed age, gender, nationality, and religious requirements on the pool of candidates they would consider), with these schemes, children were moving out steadily, if still not in great numbers. In September and October 1948, the first large group of children had left for the United States.[30] In March 1949, twenty-four children were presented to the US Committee for the Care of European Children, four were presented to the New Zealand Commission, several repatriated to France, another group was processed for repatriation to Poland, and several more applications for Canada were finalized.[31] By August 1949, the Committee had obtained clearances for 111 children from EUCOM (although only 34 of them had been called forward for visa approval). Forty-eight more had already left for Australia, with another sixteen applications in process and another sixteen admitted to the Children's Village in anticipation of filing applications for Australia.[32] The last group of Jewish unaccompanied children left for Israel in December 1949, and Dorfen, the last centre for such children, was closed.[33] In March 1950, there was a marked spurt in resettlement. Several large groups were called forward for processing for Australia, and all the pending cases for the United States had been called to the Resettlement Centre for examination.[34] As well, by late 1949, three new resettlement plans had been approved and one expanded: the Canadian Plan for Jewish Orphans was granted additional visas, a new plan was introduced to bring Catholic children aged five to fifteen to Canada, and another to bring any unaccompanied child between the ages of five and twelve to New Zealand.[35]

It was a steady pace, but not the flood that child care workers had hoped for, and some schemes came to naught. Only three children were referred (all were accepted) to the New Zealand mission in the end, and New Zealand soon appeared to lose interest. The Canadian scheme, while generating more interest, still imposed serious restrictions on eligibility, largely in terms of age, curtailing the numbers eligible. By August 1949, only five had been moved to Canada, and the expectation was that they might average between five and ten referrals monthly. The two schemes that focused on Jewish children, those sponsored by the Canadian Jewish Congress and the Australian branch of the American Joint Distribution Committee, had little prospect of relieving much of the pressure, as there were few Jewish unaccompanied children remaining in the US Zone by this time. The Swedish scheme, for its part, never became operational in the US Zone.[36] Some countries, as well, were losing interest in the repatriation of even their own children – France, for example. In that case, the French Red Cross (the agency designated to sponsor French children for repatriation) announced that it no longer wished to carry this responsibility. It was only after a lengthy and fruit-less discussion with the French government that the IRO finally per-suaded the Social Service Aide d'Emigrants to act as sponsor.[37] In other cases, resettlement schemes were closing. In July 1950, for example, the Australian scheme for unaccompanied youth was cancelled, although individual applications continued to be considered.[38] It was an uphill climb.

Contributing to the slow pace were some very practical problems – a shortage of personnel, accurate information, and transportation (by now, a too-familiar refrain). It remained very difficult to get accurate statistics from the field. This was an ongoing problem for IRO Geneva, which was responsible for managing the resettlement plans, as it could not respond easily to queries from immigration officers from various countries without reliable numbers. Resettlement missions wanted accurate information regarding different age groups and sexes imme-diately, as they often had a limited window of opportunity and strict quota limits. Over- and under-estimations of numbers in the different categories of children and youths available had a deleterious impact, affecting "not only the success of a scheme but also [creating] a most confusing situation with regard to resettlement opportunities of other special groups who could otherwise benefit by uselessly reserved visas."[39] The additional fear was that a long-unfilled quota would erro-neously suggest disinterest in a scheme, when the true challenge was that the conditions imposed, such as age restrictions or religion, made it difficult to find candidates. The concern was that unfilled quotas could be withdrawn easily, and representatives of the schemes would lose heart when the IRO was unable to give them a sense of how many chil-dren might qualify for their particular offer.[40] The actual repatriation process was often excruciatingly slow, taking months for the paper-work and the entry permits to be processed – in part due to a shortage of qualified staff, but also because of the complicated nature of negotiating with all the various entities involved in every case, including the child's national government, the IRO child welfare worker, HICOG, the spon-soring agency, and the recipient government. Lining up all the approv-als was a tedious, painstaking task.[41] The general shortage of shipping meant that there was a considerable backlog in visaed displaced per-sons, adults and children, at the embarkation centres, a key bottleneck in early 1949 especially. Complicating this was the disorganization in the management of the shipping, often resulting in too short notice, which gave the field offices too little time to coordinate the potential emigrants. Making things worse was a shortage of qualified personnel capable of dealing with the complications of international resettlement and of escorting the children overseas.[42] The combined impact was to put a brake on what little momentum there was.

There were occasional moments of hope, as in January 1951, when Eleanor Ellis received notice that New Zealand was going to sponsor a new scheme for unaccompanied youth, aged fifteen to seventeen, and would be sending a team in April 1951. They were looking for youth who were physically fit, free of infectious diseases, and suitable for placement as trainees in various trades, principally as apprentices for railway repair work near Wellington. Unofficially, the rumour was that they were only interested in cases unsuitable for other mass schemes. Best estimates were that there were forty-two youths who might qualify.[43] In December 1950, the IRO signed an agreement with the National Catholic Welfare Conference, effective April 1951, to allow it to sponsor the emigration of unaccompanied children of the Catholic faith to the United States under the auspices of the Displaced Persons Act (thus taking advantage of outstanding visas and taking some pressure off the Committee).[44] This was especially promising because it would permit the Committee for the Care of European Children (which was swamped) to focus on non-Catholic children.[45] Like earlier schemes, however, the numbers of children involved in these were in the dozens, not hundreds. There was a steady trickle out of Germany, but only a trickle.

The Children's Court

At the same time, by October 1950, a solution of sorts was found for the vexatious issue of removal, and this was the HICOG Law No. 11: Repatriation and Resettlement of Unaccompanied Displaced Children. The objective was to get a clear ruling on a child's status and nationality, and in so doing, allow the child's removal and resettlement or repatriation. The purpose of the law was to provide a final, definitive judgment on all contentious cases in which the evidence of a child's nationality and the re-establishment plans constructed for a child by the IRO were contested by others, primarily German foster parents and institutions (including the Landesjugendamt) and HICOG Law No. 11 provided for the creation of a special Children's Court within the American court system that was still operating in Germany (having been established by SHAEF upon occupation of Germany). The purpose of the Children's

Court was to deal with contested cases of resettlement or repatriation of unaccompanied children under the age of seventeen. An individual or agency considering itself to have an interest in a particular child's welfare merely had to file a petition to the court to institute a hearing. The court would then summon to a hearing all parties of interest which could include the IRO; the child's nearest adult blood relation; any blood relation of the child who had expressed a desire to have custody of the child at any point in time; any foster parent, any person, agency or organization who had had custody of or responsibility for the child at any point; and the Landesjugendamt. Once the invitations were issued, the parties of interest were given the opportunity to present their positions to the court in writing. The court would then appoint a guardian ad litem to represent the child – a guardian appointed solely for the purposes of the court hearing. The court's task was to determine whether the child was in fact an unaccompanied displaced child and whether it was in the child's best interests to be established in Germany, or to arrange repatriation or resettlement.[46]

This was a solution that the IRO was very keen to see implemented, and for which it had been pressing since 1949,[47] for several reasons. The Children's Court would be a means of resolving the outstanding cases that had been left in limbo for so long, to the consternation and concern of all, and to the great distress of the children and their caregivers. The court had the added advantage of its legal status – in this way, its decisions would be definitive, with the force of law behind them. Resorting to the Children's Court would also address that concern repeatedly trumpeted by OMGUS, namely, that the Germans must see the "tools of democracy" being applied in the resolution of conflict.[48] Another advantage to implementing HICOG Law No. 11 would be that it would rule whether the German courts and agencies had jurisdiction over a particular child. By implication, then, they did not have such jurisdiction until the Children's Court had decided so – thus resolving the thorny question of the Germans' authority over unaccompanied children.[49] HICOG, for its part, was pleased that both foster parents and the Landesjugendamt were on the list of participants. The German families' and authorities' right to a voice in the decisions made regarding the children finally had been formally recognized. Finally, both EUCOM and the US State Department liked the fact that the Children's Court would have the weight of law behind it and its decisions (unlike a review board).[50]

Thus, the delay in passing HICOG Law No. 11 to establish the Children's Court, and then in getting it operating, caused the IRO considerable angst. The backlog in unresolved cases threatened to explode.[51] With the announcement of the pending establishment of the court, HICOG began withholding decisions on an increasing number of cases deemed too complicated, preferring to wait until the court could rule on them, thus adding to the backlog.[52] The American authorities also decided that, in the interim, no child could leave the zone using clearances that had been granted prior to the court's establishment, so even cases that presumably had been closed were now in question.[53] The IRO estimated that, by December 1950, there could be at least two hundred petitions filed with the new court, in addition to many cases that had been closed previously but that likely would be appealed.[54]

The Children's Court was only finally established due to the efforts of the chief justice of the US District Court in Bavaria who took it upon himself to develop the procedures for petitioning.[55] Even with this, the court was quite slow in becoming operational. As of early March 1951, no cases had yet been processed by the Children's Court.[56] Not only the IRO field staff were frustrated. The US Committee for the Care of European Children, as well as various sectarian agencies, including the National Council of the Churches of Christ, Church World Service, and the Centre Quaker International de Genève, were deeply concerned by the delays. For the Committee especially, the threat loomed that the US Displaced Persons Act, upon which it depended for visas for the children it brought to the United States, would expire before the children whose files it had already processed would be granted visas (the Act was due to expire on 30 June 1951). Given this, the Committee was now reluctant to process any more candidates for emigration to the United States without having a release from the Children's Court in hand.[57] By March 1951, Theodora Allen of the Committee had become quite vocal, contacting Guy Swope, chief of the Displaced Persons Division of HICOG, as well as others in both HICOG and the IRO, to express her "grave concern about not being able to move the unaccompanied children who were visaed and whom [the Committee] had nominated for US Committee assurances," making clear that she spoke, not just for her organization, but for the Council of Voluntary Agencies in the US Zone as a whole.[58]

The reasons for the excruciatingly slow pace of the work were several. There were serious logistical challenges created by the way in which the law and the process of review required had been constructed. These slowed down the processing of the files significantly. For one thing, there were ambiguities in HICOG Law No. 11. It was unclear which children were considered to fall within the purview of the Children's Court. Children were being caught in its mesh to whom the IRO did not think the HICOG law applied – such as a number of children who were currently living with their grandparents, but because of the grandparents' circumstances (either ill health or financial straits) they were to be reunited with their parents overseas, with the grandparents' approval. In each such case, the parents had resettled earlier, at a time when it had not been possible to take their children with them. These children, then, were not truly unaccompanied and their documentation was in order. Nonetheless, the HICOG refused to allow even these children to be moved before their cases were heard before the Children's Court.[59] The catch was that, to be processed by the Committee, these children had to be moved into Bad Aibling Children's Village, which, according to the Land commissioners, technically rendered them temporarily unaccompanied.[60] This had the impact of adding a number of new cases to the caseload (needlessly so from the IRO's perspective).

The response of the IRO to the ambiguities was to read HICOG Law No. 11 quite literally, resulting in the IRO submitting petitions for every open case on its desk, identifying as necessary parties in interest every person who had had any responsibility for a child at any point, requiring the court to then issue a summons to each and every one of them. The reaction was both a reflection of the IRO's general distrust of HICOG and two specific concerns: that a case would be thrown out for failure to meet the letter of the law and that if any cases were settled outside the Children's Court, the court would lose its authority and the IRO would lose its last venue for finding closure for cases that had been held in stasis for so long. This had the impact of adding to the delay by increasing the volume.[61]

There was also the challenge of bringing together all the parties of interest involved in the case: the IRO; the child's nearest adult blood relation; any blood relation of the child who had expressed a desire to have custody of the child, either currently or in the past; any foster parent; any person, agency, or organization that had had custody of or responsibility for the child at any point; and the Landesjugendamt. The spirit of the law was to ensure that everyone concerned with the case would have input, with the aim being to prevent later complaints and appeals, but logistically it was enormously difficult to implement. The law required that the summonses to appear be delivered in person, without exception. In postwar Germany, even if it was now 1951, this was tremendously difficult. Those delivering the summonses first had to locate the parties of interest and then hand-deliver the summonses to them, sometimes necessitating considerable travel. And what was to be done if a party's address was unknown? Or what if the individual was now located outside of Germany? It also required compiling a list of all persons and agencies who had had either "actual or constructive custody" of the child in question at any point, a difficult task given how children often moved around, thus creating additional delays. The Children's Court required the specific IRO officer(s) responsible for compiling the case materials to attend, which was also difficult given the constant turnover and reduction in the IRO staff; many had left both Germany and the IRO. The summons had the potential to create enormous difficulties for some of those summoned, for example, an illegitimate child's biological mother who did not want her present family to know about the child's existence; such a summons could have a devastating impact on her life without necessarily helping the child's case.[62] In addition, there was the challenge of getting the parties of interest to the court to attend the hearing. Five of the first twenty cases heard were held back pending requests that a parent appear before the court.[63]

Nor did the court accept a practice that had become common for those parents who had chosen to turn responsibility for their children over to the IRO. The IRO had arranged, in many cases, to get notarized statements from the blood relatives attesting to that effect, and had based the children's treatment as unaccompanied on that statement. Yet, the Children's Court required that this exercise be repeated in order to send out summonses. Frequently, the parents or relatives, when contacted, were only confused by the summons, especially those who believed they had done all that was necessary officially to settle their children's future plans. They could not understand why the question was being opened up once again. While it was possible to get the parents to sign an Appearance of Party form, waiving their right to appear and confirming their position on the child's future, this required time and resources – all of which meant further delays. Moreover, it was unclear what the court would do if one of those parties returned and contradicted the instructions they had earlier given. The IRO argued that it would be more efficient and more certain to rely on the records that existed, rather than formal summonses, to determine the parents' intentions.[64]

Third, the list of parties of interest quickly expanded. By January 1951, the Polish Red Cross demanded that it be allowed to participate in the hearings. In fact, the US State Department had anticipated this and initially had recommended that a child's national liaison officer should be included (with the exception of Baltic and Polish Ukrainian children), in the interest of heading off the inevitable protests that would otherwise erupt. The IRO had objected, worried at the delays this could introduce to an already lengthy process. As a compromise, the State Department allowed it to be left to the court's discretion whether to call a national representative in any particular case.[65] This added another level of complexity to the court proceedings, however, as well as another potential source of delay, as the liaison officers were to be granted thirty days to review a file after being summoned.

Nor was it clear to the IRO why the Landesjugendamt needed to be present at hearings for children who had never fallen under Landesjugendamt care, nor were staying in Germany. The IRO argued that it only made sense if the child was to be established in Germany and would become the Landesjugendamt's responsibility. Otherwise, this merely added needless complication. It was also galling to have the Landesjugendamt checking the IRO's investigations and conclusions, thus implicitly raising questions about the IRO's judgment.[66] And the IRO personnel bristled at the considerable weight given by the court to the opinions of the Landesjugendamt. [67]

Fourth, the guardians ad litem, who were typically German lawyers, only confused matters further, according to Allen, of the US Committee for the Care of European Children, as they were neither professionally trained in the social and psychological aspects of children's cases, nor did they "always appreciate or understand the problems of displaced persons living in Germany and the IRO resettlement programs for children in other countries."[68] Whether qualified or not, the guardians ad litem added yet another layer of complexity to the process. By way of example of the manner in which they could derail the proceedings, one might consider two cases managed by a Dr Franz Gonnsler, one of two guardians ad litem appointed by the Munich Children's Court. In each instance, Gonnsler challenged the IRO's recommendations. The IRO had recommended that these children be repatriated to Poland. In the first case, while he did not question the nationality of the child, Janina-Marie Bereznicka (born 8 August 1945 and living in a German children's home in Augsburg), he objected to the plan because there were no close relatives in Poland requesting her return, she only spoke German, and

> most important of all, [because] he is acting for the welfare of the children
> [he] has been appointed to represent and consequently he cannot con-

cur in a recommendation for repatriation to an "eastern country." In his opinion, it is for a child's best interest to be reared in a "western country" where education is along the lines of political freedom. When asked, "Will you, then, oppose every case in which a recommendation has been made for repatriation to any Eastern country?", he first replied, "Yes" and then modified his statement by saying that there could be possible exceptions in cases in which it can be definitely proved that parents have made recent requests for the child's return.

Gonnsler did not question the child's nationality, but argued that "even Polish children should not be subjected to the political influence and type of education that now prevails in Poland."[69]

In a second case involving a Polish child who the IRO had also planned to repatriate, Gonnsler was as adamantly opposed. The IRO had been trying to remove this child from what was considered an unsuitable foster home for over a year, after gaining permission to do so from the OLC Bavaria. However, each time OLC Bavaria officers visited the home, the foster mother hid the child. Again, Gonnsler "expressed in considerable detail his objection to sending a child into an 'eastern' country," challenged the notion that the foster home was inappropriate, and objected to removing a child from "an environment to which they are accustomed." Thus, Gonnsler announced, he intended to delay the hearings while he conducted his own investigations – dismissing the months and years of investigation done by the IRO, to the fury of Starner, the child care officer responsible for these cases.[70] Thus, the guardians ad litem had the potential to cause, and were often a source of, additional delay as the case files were dissected and reinvestigated.

Fifth, part of the problem lay with the case files themselves. From the beginning, the Legal Division of the IRO was frustrated by the child care staff and the state of the files submitted. These were often inadequate and incomplete, rife with inconsistencies. Lacking the resources to double-check the materials, Legal insisted that the child care staff ensure that the files forwarded were accurate and complete – or risk embarrassing in court both the Legal Division and the IRO more generally.[71] The difficulty lay in the fact that the Children's Court required information that had not been needed before, because of the "rigidity of the law." These files had been prepared by social workers and for very different purposes, so even if they had been complete and well organized, they would have remained inadequate for the court's purposes. This meant considerably more work in preparing the files for the court hearing. The IRO child care staff were as frustrated with the Legal Division's counsel who, they felt, failed to recognize the value of the work they had done on the files or for the children, or the social and psychological needs of the children.[72]

Sixth, other delays were built into the process. A twenty-day delay was mandated between the filing date and the hearing date, to allow the various parties of interest time to respond. In addition, should any parties of interest wish to appeal a decision, they had twenty days from the date of the decision to do so, which would mean an additional twenty days before a second hearing or the case finally closing. If, therefore, any case was challenged, it could mean enormous logistical complications.[73]

Seventh, the courts themselves were slow to get operational. By September 1951, there were eleven area children's courts in operation – Bremen, Berlin, Marburg, Frankfurt, Mannheim, Stuttgart, Augsburg, Munich, Regensburg, Ansbach, and Würzburg – and they had all agreed to sit weekly in order to deal with the backlog of cases. However, in practice, only the Munich court was hearing cases regularly, and several of the others had no cases before them at all.[74]

Eighth, the shortage and calibre of the IRO's legal staff assigned to the cases did not help matters. Initially, the IRO put only one lawyer on this task, Mr Toliszus, with one secretary to assist him. They were soon, predictably, overwhelmed. While the Child Care Section and the Legal Division soon realized this error and pledged more assistance for Toliszus, they had difficulty finding additional staff to assign at a time when the IRO was gradually reducing its staff.[75] The one person added to his staff from Child Care to help draft petitions, Marjorie Farley, proved not to be a great improvement as she and Toliszus often disagreed heatedly on how best to present a case, creating further delays while they wrangled over the wording of the summaries and petitions.[76]

At the heart of the problem was the incompetence of Toliszus (the peril of having only one person managing the IRO's part of the process). Although he was trained in law in the United States, he was clearly out of his depth as the IRO's legal representative, proving very ineffective, disorganized, and poorly prepared in the courtroom, to the judge's immense frustration. Too often, based on the comments of an IRO staff member (by the name of Bergman) sent to observe him in action, Toliszus did not have a good grasp of the files in front him, was lacking the necessary documentary evidence, or could not locate it in the files. The judge presiding over this particular hearing was clearly sympathetic to the cases at hand and with the mission of the court, but he eventually lost his temper with Toliszus's lack of preparedness, which was wasting precious time.[77]

Finally, both the IRO and Theodora Allen of the US Committee for the Care of European Children were increasingly concerned about the way in which the process required the close interrogation of the children themselves, often with devastating impact. The guardians ad litem, not trained to work with children nor terribly sympathetic to the children's experiences, easily upset the children when interviewing them. The experience in the first hearings of the Children's Court was even worse as the children, parents, and witnesses all testified in each other's presence, and in the presence of newspaper reporters and photographers in an open courtroom. Everyone involved was quite upset about having the children in the courtroom while the witnesses gave their testimonies (frequently devastating for the children, as they listened to both their pasts and their futures being dissected), and that the children were forced to answer the judge's questions – often painful ones – in front of the crowd. Inevitably, details of the children's histories were reported in the press, adding to the children's distress. The whole experience left them extremely distraught. In one case, reported the staff at Bad Aibling Children's Village, after his hearing, a five-year-old boy suffered such serious nightmares and hysteria that he had to be removed from the Village and presumably hospitalized. In another, a fourteen-year-old girl, "having been branded in the court as an illegitimate child, had crying fits on her return to the Village." As Allen protested, "You only have to review one of the children's records to realize the many painful tragedies they have had in their short lives and the painful experiences they have had in separating from the various members of their families. It would seem to us that these children should be spared all such direct questioning, especially when they have such close relationships with their caseworkers who are well able to represent them in any situation."[78] For those children waiting for their hearing, the delays were interminable.[79] Furthermore, the delays, uncertainty, and horror of the courtroom had all combined to undermine any sense of security or hope for the future among the children and their parents and relatives, or so reported Theodora Allen.[80] The child's interests seemed lost, according to one observer, while the social workers, lawyers, guardians ad litem, and judge squabbled with one another.[81]

It was a cumbersome system, indeed. By April 1951, there was finally a steady flow of cases moving forward,[82] but there were still 476 unaccompanied children to be re-established, with twenty-six weeks remaining to the final, definitive deadline. To hear all of these cases, 18 would have to be cleared weekly – a seemingly impossible target given the existing system.[83]

All of this confusion had inevitably made it into both the German and international press, badly tarnishing the reputation of the IRO, as it was being blamed for the fiasco. The negative impact on the staff's morale was significant.[84] HICOG was much more complacent about the pace and the reaction in the popular press, explaining to the State Department when queried in April that there were over a hundred cases already filed with the various area courts and in the midst of processing, with priority being given to those children with visas to the United States. Although it had sympathy for the "desire for haste on [the] part of IRO and US Committee," HICOG felt that implementing the court procedure had, "while slow, effectively stopped bad publicity [in the] German press [about] alleged injustices [to] German and other foster parents" – the priority of HICOG remaining the German perception of the whole process.[85]

Meanwhile, Theodora Allen continued to protest loudly to every level of every agency possible, pushing everyone to do something about the situation, and stirring up a "political rumpus" in the process. Other voluntary agencies, as well as branches of the US government, were becoming equally concerned and equally vocal.[86] As of 25 April 1951, with only seventy-six days until termination, the situation was becoming serious. Of the 217 cases prepared by IRO's Child Welfare Section, 188 had been referred to IRO's Legal Division, of which only 116 had been completed. Of those, a mere 104 had been submitted to the Children's Court, less than half the total number of cases prepared, and less than 25 per cent of all unaccompanied children in the US Zone. While the dates had been set for thirty more case hearings (thirty having been held to date), the promised weekly sittings were not happening, with sometimes several weeks passing between them. In addition, the question was still open as to whether to consider as unaccompanied a child living with grandparents or close relatives and who was to be resettled overseas with its parents, as was the question of a child living with its parents who had released the child for resettlement, with the Offices of the Land Commissions insisting that there had to be court releases before any such child could leave the US Zone.[87] To Allen's fury, both Swope, who was chief of the Displaced Persons Division of HICOG, and IRO Geneva dismissed Allen's fears, arguing that they were certain the courts would be able to handle the cases in time.[88]

One immediate consequence was that IRO's Child Welfare Section reorganized its approach to the files, as well as prioritized the cases. Eleanor Ellis coached the child care workers to ensure the files were as complete as possible, that the recommendations were simple and restricted to one of three alternatives (so as not to confuse the matter): establishment in Germany, resettlement, or repatriation. She pushed for more careful tracking of the files' progress through the area children's courts, so that everyone knew exactly what was happening with each child and where each file was in the system (information that had not been tracked previously). She was still hopeful that the IRO would be successful in most of its cases as, out of fifty-six now heard, only two had been denied and many held up only for the lack of one witness. If the cases were prepared more carefully and their flow through the children's courts managed more effectively, she hoped this would speed things up. The staffing shortage in the Legal Division's office was also addressed with the secondment of a class I legal officer to the US Zone from Austria and the postponement of the loss of one child care worker at Bad Aibling until at least the end of July, so that this worker could be assigned to the time-consuming preparation and presentation of case files.

Ellis instructed her staff to give top priority to cases that could be cleared easily, with priority to those with visa expiry dates looming, and for those intended for resettlement in the United States, followed by those meant for Australia (another program that was soon to expire), and only then other countries. The next priority would be cases for repatriation, and then only finally should they work on cases for settlement in Germany. The logic was straightforward – if a child was to remain in Germany, it was less critical that its case be closed before the IRO's termination, as the result generally would be the status quo either way. And the IRO set a cut-off date of 30 June for the acceptance of new cases (defined as cases in which neither the child nor the parents had been previously declared as within the mandate – a waffling definition that left the way open for new cases to be accepted if they had been handled by the IRO at any point earlier).[89]

A second immediate consequence of Allen's persistence was that HICOG finally decreed that decisions by the Children's Court were unnecessary for cases where parents or close blood relatives resided in the US Zone – eliminating the need for court releases before issuing exit permits for the technically temporarily unaccompanied children. This had the immediate impact of removing an estimated thirty to forty cases from the courts' dockets (although the news was slow in getting to the field, to the frustration of the agencies trying to get "their" children released for resettlement).[90]

Third, HICOG amended the law governing the children's courts slightly, allowing the hearings to be held informally, in order to reduce the stress on the children involved (with the children kept out of the courtroom and instead interviewed separately by the judge in chambers) and to accept the IRO's records and written materials as evidence.[91]

Meanwhile, the 30 June deadline came and went, and the courts continued to sit – some more effectively and more often than others.[92] The best estimate was that the majority of the current caseload would only be resolved by 30 October 1951 with the hope that all cases going to a hearing would at least have had their first airing in Children's Court by the end of July.[93] The expectation was that 135 resettlement cases and 54 repatriation cases would be left outstanding, based on the numbers as they stood on 30 July. Meanwhile, cases of children being established in Germany were being finalized and transferred to the Landesjugendamt as quickly as possible.[94]

Contributing to the ongoing delay was a belated interest on the part of Eastern European countries in the procedure. In late June 1951, the Polish government finally registered a formal diplomatic complaint about HICOG Law No. 11, stating that this law violated "the rights of the Polish State to take care of displaced Polish children" – instead, it charged, the fate of these children was being decided exclusively by American courts, with mandatory German participation (by the Landesjugendamt). Clearly, this was a shameful attempt "to create a semblance of legality for sending Polish children to the United States, which has been practiced for a long time" – "a kidnapping system with a legal facade," as paraphrased by Louis Stephens, general counsel for the IRO. As such, the Polish government stated that it would not recognize the validity of the children's courts or their decisions.[95] At the same time, these governments, Polish and others, insisted on participating in the hearings as necessary parties of interest, which meant that these cases (which comprised a majority of those outstanding) had to be adjourned for thirty days while the petitions were submitted to them for review. It was unclear whether any representative would actually show up in court at the time of the hearing, or what kind of arguments they might make, but it did have the effect of acting as a further drag on the proceedings.[96]

Also contributing to the delay was an extension to the Displaced Persons Act that was passed by the US Congress, moving the deadline for visas for unaccompanied children to 30 June 1952, as well as granting yet another extension to the life of the IRO, tentatively to 1 January 1952, when its funding was expected to run out. Both of these extensions had the problematic impact of reducing the pressure to clear the cases quickly, although by this time the blame for the slow pace was being largely laid at the feet of the children's courts, which were moving at a glacial pace, rather than the IRO.[97]

By early November 1951, 279 cases had been submitted, approximately the total number of cases originally anticipated when the Children's Court system was first established. Of those, 42 had been deemed outside the court's jurisdiction, for a variety of reasons (e.g., the child reaching the age of majority or reuniting with its parents or relatives). That left 237, all of which had been filed with the courts by this point. Of those, 178 had been finalized, leaving 59 cases pending with just under two months to go – and the bulk of these involved children from Czechoslovakia, the Soviet Union, and Poland. How these were handled would determine whether the final caseload could be cleared quickly.[98]

By the end of January 1952, one month later than the supposedly final deadline, the whole process had finally finished, if rather anticlimactically. At that point, Ellis was reporting that all cases of unaccompanied children had been "disposed of." A number had been resettled or repatriated; others were established in Germany. Plans for a total of fifty-six children had not managed to get finalized before the process ground to a halt, either because the Child Care Section was unable to complete its investigations, because they had been cleared for departure but had not been able to leave before the IRO shut down operations, or because their cases were still pending in the courts. These fifty-six children were transferred to voluntary agencies that agreed to assume responsibility for their ultimate disposition. It was in this way that the remnant had been disposed of. It was a messy and inconclusive end for these few remaining cases that dragged on for months. In March 1952, Hugh Hinchcliffe, formerly the chief legal adviser for the IRO in the US Zone, was still shepherding the cases of thirty-four children, now on a strictly voluntary basis.[99]

This had been a clumsy, agonizing and drawn-out affair that left a sour taste in everyone's mouths. Nor did the Children's Court settle all the outstanding cases. There were still a number of children who lay outside its jurisdiction and yet needed re-establishment, those for whom neither repatriation nor resettlement was an option. The military's disinterest and the IRO's lack of resources would shape the resolution of their fate as well, in the same agonizingly slow and haphazard manner.

Transfer into the German Economy

There remained yet another category of unaccompanied children for whom the IRO desperately wanted to make arrangements prior to its closure. In September 1950, the field was instructed to begin the process of transferring into German care those children whose prospects for either repatriation or resettlement were "limited."[100] These were all children whose circumstances – either legal or physical – made it impossible for them to either repatriate or resettle outside of Germany, chief among them figured children with physical and mental disabilities. By late 1950, the imperative to find a permanent solution for these children that would safeguard their rights overrode the desire to complete their files and thus definitively identify the children and their nationalities. For these children, that solution would have to be establishment in Germany.

From the IRO's perspective, it was imperative that negotiations with the German authorities begin quickly and especially that both the children's legal status be sorted out and the Landesjugendamt's legal authority to care for these children be clarified and enshrined in law – neither of which was clear at this point. It was also imperative that the negotiations begin soon because the Landesjugendamt was both understaffed and, in the opinion of the IRO, lacking in what it considered properly trained child welfare workers. The Child Care Section wanted to ensure that it participated in the development of the German plans for the children's future, which meant the plans needed to be drafted before the IRO closed down its operations.[101]

Thus, while pursuing resettlement opportunities for children who qualified, as well as pushing cases through the Children's Court (and, in that way, freeing up as many children for resettlement as possible), the IRO was simultaneously constructing plans for those children who could not be resettled within its lifetime. These included several special groups of unaccompanied children: children with physical and mental disabilities; the illegitimate children of black American fathers, known as Mischlinge; those in so-called temporary care, but who were almost certain to be there when the IRO ceased operations; and a handful of youth, either too old or too young to qualify for resettlement. These were the most vulnerable, children who were attractive to neither resettlement missions nor their national governments (if known), and whose legal guardians had abandoned them.

Few countries were willing to consider physically and mentally disabled children for resettlement, as they would be a long-term, if not permanent drain on national coffers. (This held true for disabled adult displaced persons as well, of whom there were an estimated 20,000.[102]) Alternate provisions had to be made. It was a group that had been largely ignored to date, only drawing the attention of the IRO and the Military Government in any real sense in 1949. What forced the question initially were the increasing number of instances coming to light of families who had been prevented from resettling because of mentally or physically challenged children. In each case, although often with much anguish, the family had agreed to place the child in an institution (thus freeing the rest of the family to resettle), but the IRO had been unable to find an institution willing to accept them. Until a plan could be made for these children, the families were unable to leave. Making it even more difficult, this was often not realized until just days before departure, creating chaos, panic, and despair. Neither solution – that the family not emigrate or that the child be left behind – was attractive, and the lack of warning added to the chaos and complications. Although the IRO considered the possibility of sending these children to the United States under separate assurances, sponsored by the US Committee for the Care of European Children perhaps (and, in fact, some sponsoring agencies had been surreptitiously doing just this, in a few instances), this was not ideal, as there was no guarantee that the child, once moved to the United States, would be able to reunite with its family there.[103]

The nature of the resettlement opportunities for adults that were opening up by late 1947 and early 1948 created yet another abuse of temporary care. As explained earlier, few resettlement missions were willing to take families, especially with young, unemployable children, able-bodied or not. These missions were primarily interested in finding workers for their national labour markets and generally gave preference to single men and women. Thus, some parents wanted the IRO to care for their children while they resettled, with the intention of sending for their children once they were established in the new country. The IRO was leery of this abuse of the temporary care option because of the problems of trying to reunite the children with their parents after they had left Germany and the danger that the children might never be sent for, rendering them effectively abandoned. While there was sympathy for the families' plight, the IRO was reluctant to do this for more than a few, select cases. Past experience had taught its welfare workers to be cautious. Nevertheless, as resettlement opportunities had improved, child care workers also had found that their temporary care facilities were being increasingly abused by parents, especially unmarried mothers, who used this as a vehicle to abandon their children. Little or no planning could be done for a child summarily abandoned on the IRO's doorstep. The growing fear was that the IRO was going to become a dumping ground for "forgotten" children. By 1949, the Child Care Section was of the opinion that it was better to address the problem proactively and find a solution that allowed the IRO to control events.

One such case will serve as an example. In late 1948, the attention of the Child Care Section was drawn to the case of a child, legitimate, born of an Irish mother and German father. Although married at the time the child was born, the parents later divorced, at which point the mother regained her Irish citizenship (which meant that she and her children now qualified for IRO assistance). She and two of her children had returned to Ireland, but she had left behind a third child due to his health – he was unable to walk and was left in a German orthopedic hospital, where he stayed for almost a year. He was then admitted to an IRO children's centre, awaiting the orthopedic devices he needed. Meanwhile, the child care worker in charge of his case had written his mother repeatedly to inquire as to what plans she might have for her child, with no response. It was not an uncommon situation, and echoed a similar problem that had emerged years earlier – of parents who abandoned their foster or adopted children in IRO installations because they could not resettle as a family unit.[104]

What truly focused Child Care's attention on these particular children, however, was an early 1949 request from the Belgian charitable organization, Secours-International (a part of Caritas), for information on them, including how many there were and what their specific issues were. Secours-International was considering making "a firm offer for a certain selection of children who could be permanently resettled in Belgium in specialised institutions where adequate treatment and training could be given."[105] It was a prospect that greatly interested Eleanor Ellis, and she immediately ordered a survey of the areas, as they had as yet no idea of the scale of the problem.[106] While she awaited the results of the survey (which were due by the end of April), she sent IRO Geneva a sample list of cases to pass on to the Belgian organization, explaining that she knew of at least twenty-five children in this situation, including one unaccompanied Latvian child, aged nine, for whom an immediate plan was needed. This girl was in a German hospital, but had to be moved, as the IRO could not afford her care there. The exact nature of her problem was unknown, as the diagnosis was in German and needed to be translated, but Ellis did know that the girl could talk and take care of herself with assistance. The other sample cases were of children much less able, generally with diagnoses of "idiocy" (the term used at the time) and considered unable to care for themselves at all. These children ranged in age from six to sixteen, and in every case, were preventing the rest of the family from resettling.[107]

By late May 1949, still not having received the survey results and clearly worried that the opportunity in Belgium might evaporate, Ellis sent IRO Geneva an advance report of the cases that she knew about, plus a sense of the numbers that might be involved. She explained that currently she knew of forty children, twenty-six of whose families, she felt, would consider the Belgian scheme and whose names could be referred to Belgian Caritas immediately.[108] By August 1949, the areas had finally reported, identifying a total of fifty-three such children.[109] At this point, the IRO's Medical Department was also drawn into the conversation, as it was decided that it should be involved in determining the best permanent solution for each child. Pressure was mounting for a solution, now that people's attention had been turned to these children, and it was finally realized that neither resettlement centres (where the children were often abandoned) nor the children's centres were equipped to deal with the special needs of these children, nor did they want to lose the Belgian opportunity.[110] Ultimately, the Belgian scheme proved less successful. It took until April 1950 for Secours-International to offer to take in just twenty-four mentally challenged children, accompanied or not, who had to be under fourteen years of age, if male, and under eighteen, if female.[111] Only nineteen ended up applying for the program, although the IRO informed as many families as possible of the opportunity.[112] Even then, the process dragged on. As late as October 1950, while the documentation and exit permits were all in order, few Belgian visas had been issued, nor was it clear when they would be available.[113]

By late 1949, the challenge posed by these particular children was definitely a focus of attention. Although the number was not large, more and more were being uncovered daily as the registration exercise continued and, from the perspective of the IRO workers, in all good conscience, they could not be abandoned. With no other opportunities arising besides the Belgian offer, and with it stalling, the German alternative seemed a much more viable option, indeed, the only real option.

The two chief issues that shaped the conversation with the Germans were straightforward, if not easily resolved: the question of what facilities were available and whether they met acceptable standards, and who would pay for the children's care once the IRO had ceased operations. (The IRO had pledged to pay for the children's care as long as it existed.) Initially, the IRO's Medical Department was only able to locate a few individual spots in various German institutions, such as the Heil- und Erziehungsanstalt in Idenstein, which was, however, considered to be an unsatisfactory situation. Then, in December 1949, the Medical Department discovered the Landes Heil und Pflege Anstalt Phillips hospital in Goddelau, which was ready to accept children immediately and could take a large number. Goddelau was an institution that specialized in children with mental disabilities and, with a capacity of twelve hundred beds, it was willing to take on all seventy cases of children that the Child Care Section had on its files. Upon inspection, it made an excellent impression. Dr Belinfante, chief of the Health Department, was ecstatic and requested that the funds be made available immediately for the children's maintenance in the hospital (the IRO would cover the costs until 30 June 1950), as "this is by far the best offer we have had so far from any German Mental Hospital."[114]

Further inspections and reports from parents, in fact, led to mixed impressions of that institution – some reporting that the facilities and care were fine; other parents condemning Goddelau as horrible and removing their children, claiming they came out of the hospital thin, underfed, and ill. In the end, rather than abandon Goddelau, the IRO decided to invest considerable sums into renovating a wing of the hospital for the IRO's use, bringing the accommodations up to standard, because Goddelau was both large enough and still better than any other institution that the IRO had seen. This would also allow the IRO's children to be kept together, which was important to the child care staff. As well, the doctor in charge of the hospital seemed very anxious to help in the effort – something not to be taken lightly. By late January 1950, the hospital had taken in nineteen children from the US Zone, and referrals continued to be processed. By all accounts, and in spite of the earlier concerns, care at the hospital was excellent.[115] This was an auspicious beginning.

By May 1950, negotiations between the IRO, HICOG, and the Bavarian government over the Bavarians' assumption of control of other chronic care institutions were ongoing, with three hospitals (Amberg, capacity 525 of the chronically ill; Regensburg, capacity 300 of the chronically ill; Dorfen, capacity 40 of physically challenged children) to be turned over to the Germans before 1 July 1950.[116] It was slow going, as the German authorities and agencies insisted on doing their own assessments of the IRO institutions they were being invited to assume.[117] In a number of instances, the IRO facilities were considered inadequate or only just, and there was considerable discussion about whether it made more sense to renovate the existing facilities, find a better installation, or distribute the hospitals' inmates among existing German institutions.[118] Although the IRO had pledged funds to renovate the facilities, this did little to allay the Germans' concerns, and the negotiations were lengthy.[119]

The second concern was another contributing factor to the lengthy negotiations: the question of financing these children after the IRO ceased operations. These children were going to need very expensive long-term care, possibly lifetime care. Although the numbers were small, the costs would be prohibitive. While the Germans recognized that they were going to have to assume responsibility for them (which the Landesjugendamt estimated would be for approximately 80 children, either "feeble-minded" – to use another term of the time – or with tuberculosis), they were determined to ensure that the costs were well managed. This would require the children to be spread out among a number of German institutions. This was because the German institutions were funded at the district, or Kreis level. Having all the children in one installation would place an enormous and unacceptable financial burden on the local district in which it was located. In addition, spreading the children out would facilitate their integration into German society, their new home, as well as into the youth welfare system of the country – something that would not happen if they remained as a group in one institution. Placing children with German children dealing with the same issues, physical and mental, would be more efficient in terms of the provision of care, which would also help defray the costs. The one concession the Landesjugendamt offered was a pledge to establish an agency to monitor the children's care and education and to ensure continued contact between the child and its family.[120]

This solution did not sit well with many of the IRO's child care staff, who were concerned about the children being lost in the system and thus losing any chance of future resettlement or repatriation. They pleaded that opportunities to resettle these children outside of Germany be pursued at all cost – but to little avail.[121] The reality of the IRO's looming deadline meant that this was now impossible, and the German option was the only one. Better to ensure that the German arrangements were as good as could be than to wait in hope of a better opportunity appearing.

Another group that was a growing concern, in this case especially from the perspective of the Landesjugendamt, were the illegitimate children of black American soldiers who had been abandoned in Germany by their mothers, both German and displaced persons. These children had not been acknowledged by their fathers, and the US military still resolutely refused to pursue the fathers on the German youth welfare authorities' behalf. The Landesjugendamt and the IRO child welfare staff were both convinced that these children faced a difficult future if they remained in Germany, because of their skin colour. It would be preferable, the Child Care Section argued, if they could be found adoptive homes in the United States, under the auspices of the Displaced Persons Commission perhaps. The numbers, while not known, were thought to be relatively small – approximate thirteen hundred in Bavaria, where they believed the largest number to be located. Whatever the number, it was thought that a special effort to find homes for them in the United States was warranted as "Child Welfare Officers in Europe [believed] that Negro-families desiring to adopt in the states often prefer light children and these children would qualify inasmuch as they are mulattoes."[122] After consultation with the US National Association for the Advancement of Colored People (the NAACP), however, it was decided that a separate program for illegitimate black children would be inadvisable, especially one that emphasized the illegitimacy of the children, as this would make them much less attractive. Instead, the suggestion was that the children should be handled through the larger resettlement program, but that the Displaced Persons Commission should send its press releases to the major black newspapers in the United States.[123] This was done, and the black press gave considerable and sustained attention to the matter. Many black families were interested in adopting these children, although few could afford the children's transportation costs. Nonetheless, significant obstacles still existed. Many mothers refused to release their children for adoption;

the Displaced Persons Commission was not interested in pursuing these options, preferring to focus on white children; some American voluntary agencies raised concerns about the difficulties these children would have in adjusting to life in a black community in the racially discriminatory United States. In the end, by 1968, some seven thousand black unaccompanied children had been adopted by American parents.[124]

Another group for whom special arrangements needed to be made were children in long-term temporary care. These were the children in the IRO's children's homes, increasingly Bad Aibling (as the homes had been consolidated), who were technically accompanied, in that their parents were alive and in contact with them (albeit often tenuously) but unable to take responsibility for them. In some instances, it was because the parent was in prison, but in most cases, it was because the parent was in an institution himself or herself, because either physically or mentally ill. The IRO had been working with various voluntary agencies, vainly petitioning them to take on responsibility for these children. There was also another category of temporary care: children who were in IRO hospitals, usually because they had tuberculosis. In both cases, the hope was that these children would be only a short-term responsibility for the German authorities, although the children with tuberculosis were more certain of eventually being released from nominally temporary care than were the children whose parents were institutionalized.

In January 1951, discussions were held between the IRO, OLC Bavaria, and the Public Health Department of the Bavarian Ministry of the Interior about the possibility of turning over three IRO tuberculosis hospitals (Gauting, Amberg and Kempten – Kempten being the children's hospital) to the Germans, with approximately twelve hundred adult cases of tuberculosis and two hundred to three hundred children. There was some urgency to the question, as the IRO was trying to draw down its staffing commitments at the hospitals. As was the case in the discussions about the physically and mentally challenged children, the negotiations were slow – in part, as with the disabled children, because of the state of the IRO facilities; in part because of the need, first, to find a German agency to take on this responsibility, which entailed less of a commitment than the disabled, but a commitment nonetheless.[125]

Complicating the matter was a disagreement in principle between the German youth welfare agencies and the IRO. The German authorities saw an advantage to distributing the children across a number of institutions, or even across Länder and, by so doing, defraying the cost across a number of budgets, but in this case, the IRO strongly preferred to keep these particular children together in one place. There were several reasons. The children with tuberculosis, unlike adults with tuberculosis, were likely to recover within a few months, at which point, they would be eligible to resettle, an option the IRO wished to keep open for them; keeping the children together in one place, be it Kempten or another institution, would make it much easier for this to happen. Second, the investigations of many of the children in temporary care were not yet complete, and keeping them together would facilitate this as well; it would also make it much simpler to maintain contact between parents and children. The IRO hoped that the Germans could be persuaded to take over Kempten as it existed, suggesting that it could be to their advantage – Kempten only had 148 children in it as of 1 January 1951, but a capacity of 310, meaning that there would be approximately 160 beds available for German children with tuberculosis.[126] This hope was complicated, however, by the news that the Military Government wanted Kempten for its troops (space appropriate for the housing of troops being quite scarce).

The story of the transfer of the children at the Kempten Tuberculosis hospital followed a familiar, if rocky path, and the hope of keeping the children together proved a vain one. In this case, the National Catholic Welfare Conference agreed to assume responsibility for the children, in conjunction with its German counterpart, the Katholische Jugendfürsorge-Verein. As early as April 1951, the Conference expressed a readiness to start the process of transferring children from Kempten to German long-term care institutions. At that point, it anticipated that, of the 110 cases in Kempten, some 63 would have been discharged by the time the hospital closed in October 1951. However, to the Conference's frustration, as of November 1951, only 22 children had been referred to the organization. With only weeks to go before the hospital was finally to close, little had been done to find places for the majority of the children still in the hospital. In addition, and as frustrating, the institutions caring for those children the Conference had already placed were still, months after admission, waiting for payment for their care. The Conference was blunt when it warned the IRO that it could assume no financial responsibility for the children's care. (In fact, by this time, the financial obligations for the children had been assumed by the German state, which was apparently having difficulty meeting those obligations.)[127]

As well as assuming responsibility for the various institutions caring for children with mental and physical challenges and for such
children still residing with their families (estimated to number 155 in
mid-1950), and for children hospitalized with tuberculosis, the Germans were faced with assuming responsibility for children in long-
term temporary care (an oxymoron if ever there was one), healthy
accompanied children but whose parents were unable to care for
them. By mid-1951, most of these latter children had been gathered in
the Children's Village in Bad Aibling. The German plan was to place
all these children either in a German institution or with foster parents,
until such time as their parents could once again provide care, if that
became possible.[128]

The future of Bad Aibling Children's Village had been in doubt for
some time. The original decision had been that the Village, now the
main children's home still operating, would continue to operate after 30
June 1950 as a centre for temporary care, with the remaining children's
centres being consolidated into it. Investigations and planning would
continue for these children, as would individual casework, for as long
as possible. The IRO would continue to run the Village until they literally ran out of funds, at which point it would be turned over to the
Landesjugendamt.[129] By September 1950, the sense of urgency was palpable, especially as the numbers in the Village had remained static, with
354 children in residence, although 100 children were now documented
for the United States and likely to actually get moved. Another 100 were
there for temporary care, of whom it was estimated that approximately
80 would actually return to their families. This left 154 children in the
Village for whom a solution had to be found. For many, if not most, it
appeared that re-establishment outside of Germany would be a "practical impossibility," as there had been considerable effort made to resettle
these children with no success. The welfare staff at Bad Aibling now
favoured arranging for the children's establishment in Germany as
quickly as possible, so that they could ensure the arrangements were
suitable. Otherwise, it could mean "the abandonment of an indeter-
minate number of children at the time of closure of this Program."[130]
The Child Care Section was directed to begin transferring the cases to
the German youth welfare services, and Bad Aibling was scheduled
to make its final admission at the end of 1950. At the same time, all
child welfare and child care staff were to be merged into one unit, now
focused on the Recovery Program (see previous chapter), with an eye
to the program's gradual liquidation.[131]

Other, small groups posed similar challenges. There were children who had been discovered through the Limited Registration Plan, identified as within the IRO's mandate and registered as such (expected to number 200 in the end), but who had proven impossible to establish because crucial information was lacking – such as their nationality, identity, citizenship, or the location of relatives. As a result, no conclusive decision could be made as to their future. These cases were also to be transferred to the Landesjugendamt, although what would happen to them was unclear. Another group, who had also ended up in temporary care, were the illegitimate children of women who had had extramarital affairs after their husbands had gone overseas. As the IRO was winding up, these women were now preparing to join their husbands, who usually were not aware of the child's existence. In most instances, the women did not want to take the child with them.[132] Yet a third group, by this time numbering some 50 in the US Zone, were unaccompanied youths aged fourteen and fifteen, for whom there were no resettlement opportunities. This was a particularly difficult group to place because of their age.[133] These youths ended up being transferred to the German system as well.[134] Meanwhile, children continued to drift into the Village, in spite of best efforts to close its doors to new cases. This all meant that, as of the end of July 1951, there were still 235 children in residence. Of these, 98 were in "the pipeline," approved for resettlement but not yet moved out – most going to the United States. Thirteen were waiting to repatriate (4 to the USSR, 4 to Poland, 3 to Czechoslovakia, one to Italy, and one to France). A further 5 were to be resettled in Germany; 106 were there in temporary care; 3 were without any plans; another 3 (presumably Children's Court cases) were considered pending; and then there were 7 described as "stray cases" – possible resettlement cases.[135]

In the end, Bad Aibling's operation was extended yet again, to a new closure date of 30 September 1951. Any children remaining at that point were to be moved to Feldafing temporarily, and into German institutions or resettled overseas by 31 December (estimated to involve between 80 and 140 children).[136] There were several reasons for the transfer to Feldafing, a village near Munich. Bad Aibling had been identified as a military requirement over a year earlier, and a military unit was on stand-by, waiting to occupy it as soon as the children moved out. More importantly, moving the children to Feldafing would move them to a facility that was more appropriate for their decreased numbers, less expensive to run, and would place the children closer to a number of processing centres, as well as consulates and other key functions. The American Friends Service Committee was agreeable to moving with the children and continuing its work with them, in conjunction with the Paritätsicher Wohlfahrtsverband, a well-established German interdenominational voluntary agency which had agreed to take over responsibility for the children as long as necessary. The actual transfer happened over the month of October, and the German agency finally took over the institution as of 1 November 1951.[137]

Closure of the IRO

The lifespan of the IRO was extended one more time, to the end of 1951. This was the final extension, and the IRO's funding was fast running out. The remaining objective of the child care staff became to clear as many cases, especially those backlogged, so that there would be no children "whatsoever" dependent on just the IRO for care after 31 December 1951.[138] It was a naive goal, recognized as unattainable well before that date. Aside from the cases that were late in being processed through the Children's Court and which Hinchcliffe had volunteered to shepherd through to conclusion, the estimates as early as October were that there would be 141 children scheduled for repatriation or resettlement but who would not be transported before the end of the year, 75 of them destined for the United States. The IRO would be able to guarantee transportation until 31 December, but after that, it would depend on the state of its funds.[139] There was inevitably going to be some cleaning up afterwards, and it would have to be done with a skeleton staff and minimal financial resources.

Even this was threatened when the Displaced Persons Commission was informed in October 1951 that HICOG was planning to withdraw most of the logistical support it had been providing to both the Commission and the numerous voluntary agencies upon which it vitally depended. The funds of the Displaced Persons Commission were completely inadequate to cover these expenses which meant that, as soon as support was cut off, the Commission would have to cease operations – with some sixty thousand visas still available and unassigned, and visaed children left stranded in Germany. The prospect threw the Displaced Persons Commission into panic.[140] In response to urgent queries, the US State Department stepped into the breach and reassured the Commission that its funding would not be summarily cut. If necessary, the State Department promised to replace those funds, although it could not help the associated agencies.[141]

In fact, as of 11 December 1951, it appeared that even this would not be enough, as the IRO lacked the funds to transport even the visaed displaced persons, adults and children. The estimate was that a total of eighteen thousand adults and children would be trapped in Germany as a result, even with the Displaced Persons Commission still functioning.[142] There was a mad scramble once again, and in a last-minute reprieve, the State Department gave the IRO enough money to cover the cost of two transport ships for the month of January 1952, with the possibility of access to another three ships.[143] Its objective in doing so was clear – the goal was to reduce by as much as possible the number of displaced persons to be turned over to the German government, thus making the German assumption of responsibility as palatable as possible.

The Landesjugendamt expected to be given responsibility for a total of 780 children, when all was settled.[144] By mid-1952, the West German authorities had finally figured out how they were going to manage this new responsibility. The federal minister of the interior created a Special Committee for Unaccompanied Children, operational as of 2 July 1952 and charged with maintaining the records of the children, as well as working with the International Social Services to advise and assist the various agencies with legal responsibility for the children in providing the necessary services.[145] The primary purpose was to ensure that the tracing of relatives, especially abroad, would continue efficiently and effectively, and to ensure that the children were treated fairly under German law and in German courts. At the same time, the records of the International Tracing Service were moved to a new headquarters in Arolsen, Germany.[146] As late as May 1952, child welfare officers were still working with the Displaced Persons Commission, German agencies, and German government in processing children who had been sponsored for resettlement. This was a tremendously time-consuming and complicated effort for the remaining hundred-odd children, involving child search officers, German voluntary agencies, the German courts, individual German guardians, and American consulates in coordinating the children's processing and actual transportation by air.[147]

It was a story that ended, to borrow T.S. Eliot's words, "not with a bang but a whimper." It was a long, agonizingly drawn-out exercise of sorting out the children's futures one child at a time, consuming enormous amounts of time, energy, and resources in the process – much as

Olive Biggar had fatefully predicted in late 1945, when the child welfare staff first contemplated launching a child search operation. With the repeated extensions of both the United Nations Relief and Rehabilitation Administration and the IRO, and the slow resolution of cases, sometimes one at a time, when the operation finally ended in 1952, it had a rather anticlimactic feel to it.

That said, one could also look on the saga in a rather different light. In spite of the concerted and sustained efforts of key elements in the American Military Government, and especially those of Lieutenant Colonel Abbott and the OMG's Public Welfare Branch, to restrict the child search operations, and even to shut them down completely, the operations had continued. Children continued to be uncovered, identified (or not), re-established, even reunited with family members, right up to 1952, a full seven years after the Second World War had ended, testament to the complexity of the exercise, and the politics surrounding it. While the numbers of those involved are lamentably unreliable, an estimated forty thousand unaccompanied children passed through UNRRA and IRO care, almost all of whom were successfully re-established – either through repatriation, resettlement, or absorption into the German economy and society. This was, in itself, testament to the dogged determination of the child search and child care staff whose goal was to not leave a single child behind. In light of the formidable challenges faced by these child search and welfare workers from the beginning, it is truly remarkable that they achieved all that they did.

Chapter Ten

Nationality

Underlying much of the increasingly acrimonious debate over the fate of the unaccompanied children was the challenge of determining a child's nationality. Running like a thread through all the arguments over the children's future was the issue of what to do with a child whose nationality could not be definitively determined: who would speak for the child, who would determine its ultimate fate, and to whom did the child "belong"? Nationality had proven to be a contentious and ill-defined concept. Too often, nationality (read: ethnicity) and citizenship were conflated by the people doing the determining, while the people whose nationality was being determined often insisted that the two concepts were quite different. Politics complicated and even distorted the distinction, or conversely, resulted in an obstinate refusal to acknowledge that there was a distinction. The privileging of one over the other had important consequences for every displaced person, but especially for displaced unaccompanied children whose fate was determined in a very real and inescapable way by the nationality ascribed to them.

The presumption on the part of the Allied forces and the United Nations Relief and Rehabilitation Administration (UNRRA) was that states and nations, by the mid-twentieth century, were now aligned – that political borders matched ethnic boundaries. The theoretical norm may have been that European states were ethnically homogeneous; in practice, however, that was patently not the case, not in Western Europe (as examples, think of the Catalans in Spain, the Flemish in Belgium, the Sami in Scandinavia) and certainly not in Eastern Europe. Indeed, the disintegration of the European empires (German, Russian, and Austro-Hungarian) by the end of the First World War had created a number of new Central European states, each of which had a very mixed population ethnically, with their various elements cohabiting uneasily at the best of times. With the strain of the interwar years and then the Nazi occupation, which privileged certain ethnic groups (especially the Volksdeutsche) and had devastating consequences for others (especially Jews), those pre-war and wartime ethnic tensions roiled across the postwar landscape and played out in the form of an orgy of ethnic cleansing in the summer of 1945 and into 1946. Many Eastern European countries seized the opportunity to purge themselves of those deemed ethnically, as well as politically unsuitable, especially, but not only the Volksdeutsche. The governments of countries whose borders had shifted were as keen to ensure that their new territories were appropriately populated with the "right" ethnicity in order to establish and entrench their control. Millions of people found themselves without a home or citizenship. Further hundreds of thousands found themselves citizens in new countries – without ever having left their homes.

Initially, the implications of these shifts were missed by both the Allied authorities and UNRRA. Neither had seemed aware of the deep ethnic tensions that permeated Central Europe. In hindsight, the early planning was remarkably naive on this front. In the first plans, drafted in 1944 but brought to the field in 1945, the objective was simply to separate enemy from "non-enemy refugees," to use the terminology of the Supreme Headquarters, Allied Expeditionary Force (SHAEF). For UNRRA's purposes, aid was to be extended to refugees of United Nations nationalities, that is, citizens of United Nations countries, which roughly correlated with SHAEF's non-enemy refugees. The purpose was to ensure that no international humanitarian relief went to the enemy population; their care was to be the responsibility of their own governments, however inadequate their resources might be. A second assumption was that all the people who had been displaced by the war would be keen to return home as quickly as possible, and the challenge, therefore, would be one of controlling their exodus, not of having to persuade them to go. Thus, as SHAEF's forces moved across Western Europe and into Germany, the refugees were simply sorted into Western Europeans and Eastern Europeans and marshalled westwards and eastwards as appropriate, to put them closer to home in anticipation of their repatriation.[1]

The only other group singled out at this point was Soviet citizens. A corollary document to the Yalta Agreement, known as the Halle Agreement, required that all Soviet prisoners of war and civilians be repatriated to the Soviet Union, whether they wished to return or not. This repatriation movement, involving some 2.5 million people, dominated the spring and summer months of 1945. Although most returned willingly, a significant minority refused, many of them protesting their forced repatriation volubly and sometimes violently, to the shock of the American troops forcing them onto trucks and trains. A significant number of those protesting argued that they were, in fact, not Soviet citizens. A question, and harbinger of coming confusion, quickly emerged from the field that would have long-term implications, namely, who exactly was a Soviet citizen? There had been considerable territorial shifts in Eastern Europe, with great swathes of it absorbed into the Soviet Union, including Poland, the Ukraine, and the Baltic republics, and great stretches of Germany absorbed into Poland. These territorial changes raised questions about the citizenship or nationality of displaced persons from these transferred territories: was a person from a former Baltic republic a Soviet citizen? Was a Pole from east of the Curzon Line (the new Polish-Soviet border) a Soviet citizen? Was there such a nationality category as Ukrainian? This was the first inkling for SHAEF and UNRRA that determination of nationality was going to be a more complicated matter than anticipated.

This became a critical question as a result of another key decision made late in the summer of 1945: to not repatriate anyone against their will, with the exception of Soviet citizens proven to be so. Early that April, the American government had made it clear to the US War Department and to SHAEF that it understood the Halle Agreement to oblige them to return to the USSR all Soviet military personnel held as prisoners of war by the Germans and liberated from German prisoner of war camps, all liberated civilians who were Soviet citizens, and all Soviet citizens captured in German uniforms other than those who demanded to be treated as German prisoners of war. However, as the American Government had not recognized the absorption of the Baltic states or eastern Poland into the Soviet Union, people from these territories would not be forcibly repatriated to the USSR "unless they affirmatively claim Soviet citizenship."[2] Military commanders were instructed to ensure that individuals were Soviet citizens before turning them over to Soviet representatives.[3] Unless a Latvian, Lithuanian, or Estonian affirmatively claimed Soviet citizenship, he or she was not to be repatriated to the USSR, the Soviet Zone of Occupation, or their district of former residence.[4] This question of whether a displaced person was a Soviet citizen or not became all-important when many individuals denied their putative citizenship and protested their forced repatriation.

The instruction was not well understood in the field, creating much confusion. The Latvian minister of France and also a councillor of the Lithuanian delegation in Paris, for example, reported several instances of violation of the decision. In one case, a Soviet repatriation commission had visited displaced persons camps near Vorarlberg in Austria and informed the Baltic displaced persons there to pack in preparation for repatriation. When they refused to do so, the Soviet representatives informed them "they had no right to express their will." The result was very real panic among the Baltic displaced persons, who felt threatened with repatriation at any moment. In another incident, on 14 May 1945, Mr and Mrs Ernescks, Estonian citizens, were turned back when trying to cross the Elbe River to the western side by a Captain Jacobs, who was in command of the American forces at Bertingen and who argued that they were Soviet citizens. It was only thanks to a commander of a group of French repatriates that they got to France. Ironically, once there, they were promptly turned over to the Soviet consulate in Maubeuge. The Latvian minister and the Lithuanian councillor called on the Allies to give all possible assistance and protection to the Balts, including allowing them, if they wished, to emigrate freely and to keep them out of Soviet hands.[5]

The list of categories being used by the central authorities – which consisted of three at this point: non-enemy or United Nations displaced persons, Soviet citizens, and those not affirmatively claiming Soviet citizenship – was clearly of little help to those in the field actually trying to sort the displaced persons. There the situation was much more complicated, as reflected in repeated memos asking for direction on how to deal with a more diverse list of nationalities confronting them, including Soviet, Estonian, Latvian, Lithuanian (these latter three often being lumped together as "Balts"), Polish, Ukrainian, the stateless (an odd one to see in a list of nationalities, admittedly), and Jewish. What was to be done with a Soviet or Polish Jew? More confusingly, what of German Jews? Were they Jewish or German? Did they qualify for assistance? And what about the stateless? Or what about the Volksdeutsche – those of ethnic German origin from outside of Germany, many of whom had acquired (voluntarily or not) German citizenship during the Nazi regime? Finally, given the decision that no displaced persons would be repatriated against their will, what was to be done with those displaced persons who refused to repatriate because of political reasons, such as

Poles, Ukrainians, Balts, or Yugoslavians? Even more alarmingly, what of the displaced persons whose governments were refusing to allow them to return (and there were many individuals emerging who were caught in this particular situation)?

By mid-November 1945, in an attempt to address the confusion, the United States Forces, European Theater (USFET) issued a directive entitled, "Determination and Reporting of Nationalities," intended to lay out exactly who was eligible for assistance and who was not, and end the "considerable confusion [that] exists regarding the definition of nationalities and the assignment of individuals to their appropriate category." As the drafters pointed out, "There has been a tendency to identify persons by reference to their religion, to geographical regions, to national sub-division, to ethnological groupings, and to other unrecognized categories, rather than by reference to the political state of which they are citizens or nationals." The purpose of the directive was to provide a comprehensive list of the acceptable categories of displaced persons. Importantly, it also had the effect of conflating nationality and citizenship, although political expediency shaped certain categories as well.

First, the directive provided a list of which nations were considered United Nations, neutral nations, and ex-enemy nations. There were also two, more ambiguous categories: "Political Entities" and "Special Categories." Thus, it began with the "United Nations," whose nationals were eligible for assistance – fifty-one in all.[6] The neutral nations were Afghanistan, Eire, Finland, Portugal, Spain, Sweden, and Switzerland. There was a separate category for the Baltic republics (Estonia, Latvia, and Lithuania) called "Political Entities." Next came the "Ex-Enemy Nations": Austria, Bulgaria, Germany, Hungary, Italy, Japan, Romania, and Siam. Finally, "Special Categories" consisted of "persecutees" (defined as those who had been discriminated against based on race, religion, or activities in favour of the United Nations and made up of two subcategories: Jews and other persecuted persons of ex-enemy nationality), and the stateless.[7]

This directive acknowledged the complexity of the situation, but it was flawed in several ways. For one, it equated nationality and citizenship, failing to recognize the reality of Eastern Europe, where the two were sharply distinct. As an UNRRA reports officer succinctly put it, "It is my experience that Eastern Europeans customarily distinguish between nationality (in their eyes an ethnic concept, based on cultural factors) and citizenship (corresponding to the concept of nationality,

[but] based on legal status following political boundaries)."[8] Nationality and citizenship were not necessarily the same. This flaw was of consequence, as it offered no solution for any displaced persons who repudiated their ascribed citizenship and insisted on being registered according to their nationality (read: ethnicity). Nor did it address the question of what to do with people who were rejected by their country's government, even though they were citizens of that country. Policy decisions continued to be made on the fly that had serious ramifications for the handling of the displaced person population in general, and unaccompanied children especially. The failure of the November 1945 directive to distinguish between nationality and citizenship, the impact of the emerging Cold War, and the refusal to effect clear policy for dealing with these special cases created confusion and conflict that left many of the remaining displaced persons, and above all, many unaccompanied children, trapped with no clear way out of their dilemma created by the ambiguities surrounding their national identity.

Jewish Displaced Persons

Initially, Jews had not been identified as a specific group of displaced persons qualifying for United Nations displaced persons care. Instead, Jews had fallen within the broader category of "the persecuted," which included concentration camp survivors, but encompassed all those who had been persecuted by the Nazi regime or its allies for reasons of race, religion, or political activities in favour of the United Nations. As the definition makes clear, this category was to apply to all survivors of Nazi persecution. The effect was to lump Jewish concentration camp survivors in with resistance fighters, Jehovah's Witnesses, Communists, Socialists, and others. Even SHAEF's Administrative Memorandum No. 39, issued in November 1944 and revised in April 1945, and which formed the foundation for the determination of care for displaced persons, made no mention of Jews as a category of displaced persons, enshrining the policy of considering them simply among the persecuted. As explained in SHAEF's *Handbook for Germany*, "as a general rule, military Government should avoid creating the impression that the Jews are to be singled out for special treatment, as such action will tend to perpetuate the distinctions of Nazi racial theory."[9] Instead, inclusion in this category was determined by one's treatment at the hands of the Germans, making it an unusual and very different kind of category and, in some ways, a catch-all category.

This had several important implications for the Jewish survivors. First, this categorization meant that Jewish displaced persons received no extra or special care, in spite of their particularly dire condition, having been the special target of the Nazi regime and subjected to particularly brutal conditions in the concentration camps. Second, as they were not considered a distinct category, Jews were initially placed in assembly centres and displaced persons camps with other displaced persons of their nationality or citizenship, for example, Soviet Jews with Soviet displaced persons, Polish Jews with Polish displaced persons. This often had the effect of putting Jews in the same camps as their earlier guards and tormentors, to the great and understandable distress of the Jewish displaced persons. Third, it meant that, as "Jewish" was not considered a separate category or group, these displaced persons did not have their own liaison officers to protect their own particular interests and advocate on their behalf.[10] Fourth, it meant that the status of German and Austrian Jews was unclear. German Jews, once released from the concentration camps, often found themselves left to their own devices, forced to appeal to German authorities for assistance, a particularly upsetting and infuriating situation.[11] The result of this decision was to grant Jewish displaced persons the same level of care as for the other displaced persons, but no more. Jewish relief organizations were not allowed to provide any assistance for Jewish displaced persons until mid-summer 1945, as they were not recognized as representatives of any national government and so could not be accredited.[12]

This situation was corrected only after pressure was brought to bear on the American government by US Army rabbis, American soldiers, and a number of powerful American Jewish organizations that mobilized and galvanized American public opinion by sending home news of the horrific conditions.[13] In the wake of a particularly damning report by Earl Harrison, who inspected the displaced person camps in Germany in July 1945 at Washington's behest, SHAEF made two changes. First, they immediately improved the living conditions and standard of care for the Jewish population. Second, they recognized Jews as a special group. As Harrison argued, because they had been more severely victimized than the non-Jewish displaced persons, Jews had to be recognized as a separate group with greater needs: "The first and plainest need of these people is a recognition of their actual status and by this I mean their status as Jews."[14] By dint of their treatment at the hands of the Nazis, the Jews had been forged into a new, separate identity, that of "Jew." In effect, "Jewish" had become a nationality and had to be recognized as such.

The response to the investigation had been swift. In a meeting on 25 July 1945, even before Harrison had officially submitted his report to the President of the United States, deputy military governor of Germany, General Lucius Clay, informed the Army commanders that "Jewish displaced persons would be provided for on the basis of nationality and not on the basis of religion."[15] If those of the Jewish faith desired to be repatriated to the country "of which they are nationals," they would be treated as citizens of that nationality and placed in the same assembly centres as other displaced persons of that nationality. If they were without a nationality or chose not to repatriate to their country of origin (with the exception of Soviet Jews), Jews would be treated as stateless and non-repatriable. Importantly, Jews would be put into separate Jewish assembly centres.[16]

Therefore, as of the November 1945 directive of determining nationality, there were two further significant changes in the handling of Jewish displaced persons. Jews were now a category separate from the other persecutees, e.g., resistance fighters or Jehovah's Witnesses. Second, Jews were the one category of displaced person essentially allowed to choose whether or not to reassume their pre-war citizenship: Jews could either opt to be repatriated to the country "of which they are nationals," which meant that they would be treated as citizens of that country and placed in the same assembly centres as other displaced persons of that country, or, if they were without citizenship or chose not to repatriate to their country of origin (with the exception of Soviet Jews), choose to be treated as stateless and non-repatriable.[17] As the directive explained, "Persons of Jewish faith who desire to be repatriated to the country of which they are nationals will be classified as citizens of that country. Those Jews who are without nationality, or those Jews (not Soviet citizens) who do not desire to return to their country of origin, will be reported as 'Jews'" – not stateless, but "Jews." This special categorization marked the formal encoding of a unique status and treatment granted to Jewish displaced persons.

What this allowed, besides the establishment of Jewish assembly centres and camps, was the appointment of Jewish liaison officers (initially in the form of the Office of Special Advisor on Jewish Affairs to the Military Governor of Germany, soon replaced by the Jewish Agency for Palestine). It also meant that, as the infiltree population of Jews moved into Germany, they could remain together and move through the Jewish camps in Germany with little difficulty, including the kibbutzim of unaccompanied children. Finally, it also meant that Jewish unaccompanied children would be under the protection of Jewish liaison officers and agencies.

The special treatment was echoed in the policies of various Eastern European governments regarding "their" Jewish children. While Poland, Yugoslavia, Czechoslovakia, and Hungary generally insisted upon the return of all "their" children, from the beginning they were willing to allow both the adoption of Jewish children of their nationality/citizenship located in Germany by people of other nationalities/citizenships and the resettlement of these same children, rather than requiring their repatriation, if that was what they preferred.[18] Their reasoning was not made clear. Their lack of interest, however, in getting back Jewish children could be explained as a reflection of the broader anti-Semitism that swept Eastern Europe in the immediate postwar period. It also explains why these governments failed to protest the movement out of their territories and into Germany of Jewish children as part of the infiltree movement, the only loss of "their" children that was not vehemently protested. This did, however, have the effect of confirming the new nationality that had been embraced by the occupation authorities – that of Jewish. A new ethnicity had trumped citizenship.

Baltic Displaced Persons

The crux of the problem for the Estonian, Latvian, and Lithuanian displaced persons lay in the invasion and occupation of these states by the USSR and their subsequent absorption into that country in 1940. In September 1940, a decree was passed by the Presidium of the Supreme Soviet granting Soviet citizenship to the people of the new Latvian, Lithuanian, and Estonian Soviet Socialist Republics.[19] From the perspective of the Soviet Union, this made all Baltic displaced persons Soviet citizens and so, according to the terms of the Yalta Agreement, to be repatriated to the USSR whatever their personal wishes. However, neither the United Nations nor the US government had ever recognized that absorption and so, as early as April 1945, the United States refused to repatriate any displaced persons from those three former republics "unless they affirmatively claim[ed] Soviet citizenship" or to turn them over to Soviet control.[20] These instructions were not always well understood in the field, with many Baltic displaced persons continuing to be treated as Soviet citizens, to the consternation and dismay of the displaced persons and their representatives, both governmental, in the form of representatives of their national governments based in London, and the emerging displaced persons organizations. The USSR, for its part, continued to insist that all Baltic displaced persons were Soviet citizens. With 82,555 Baltic displaced persons in assembly centres in the US Zone as of November 1945, this was not a question that could be ignored.[21]

Ultimately, the US State Department prevaricated. The United States continued to refuse to recognize the absorption of the Baltic republics into the USSR, and so would not acknowledge these displaced persons' purported Soviet citizenship. The United States was not, however, prepared to take action to liberate the Baltic republics either.[22] The language in USFET's nationality directive reflected this impasse, stating "the category 'USSR,' includes all Soviet Republics." However, it also baldly observed in the next sentence, without amplification, "The incorporation of Estonia, Latvia and Lithuania into the Soviet Union as republics has not been recognized by the United States Government." And there it stood.[23] This did little to resolve the issue of the Baltic displaced persons. They were left in limbo – not Soviet citizens, but also not citizens of any other nation. This was the implication of the three republics' categorization as "Political Entities" in the directive. They were not United Nations, and they were not neutral nations. They were, in fact, not recognized as nations at all, but as some other, ambiguous, ill-defined "political entity," about which no decisions were going to be made any time soon. Meanwhile, for the Balts in the displaced persons assembly centres, this meant not only that they would not be forcibly repatriated to the Soviet Union, but also that their future was quite undecided, as it begged the question of their status. If they were not Soviet nationals, how should they be treated: as nationals of Latvia, Estonia, and Lithuania (which was a diplomatically problematic option) or as stateless?[24] Would recognizing their nationality (Estonian, Latvian, Lithuanian) be tantamount to legitimizing their claim to Estonian, Latvian, and Lithuanian citizenship, rather than Soviet citizenship? As well, one practical consequence was that the Baltic displaced persons did not have representatives or liaison officers, as the only government that could provide such was that of the Soviet Union.[25] This had important ramifications, especially for unaccompanied Baltic children.

Given the lack of direction from SHAEF, a de facto practice cum policy evolved in the field: to treat clearly non-Volksdeutsche Estonians, Latvians, and Lithuanians as eligible for UNRRA care "on the ground that they are to be regarded either as Soviet subjects (thus United Nations nationals) or as de facto stateless." The Baltic Volksdeutsche would be treated as Germans and refused care. Differentiation between the two was the responsibility of the Military Government (UNRRA steadfastly refusing to accept responsibility for the determination of any displaced person's nationality). In no case was the Soviet liaison officer to be consulted, either formally or informally, until Washington's views on the Baltic republics were made clear.[26]

Unaccompanied Baltic children faced the same challenge as the adult Baltic displaced persons, but with more serious consequences. Those not deemed to be German were trapped. As the absorption of their countries of origin into the Soviet Union had not been recognized by the American government, SHAEF did not consider them the responsibility of the Soviet repatriation officers and, indeed, denied these officers access to the children. However, because the American government had also refused to recognize the Baltic republics as still independent states, it refused to authorize any Latvian, Lithuanian, or Estonian liaison officers. It meant that Baltic unaccompanied children had no one protecting or advancing their interests in Germany. This was a problematic situation, as a liaison officer's approval was needed for any decision regarding the children's fate. Without a liaison officer, literally nothing could be done for or with these children. Without a liaison officer, there was no one to advocate on their behalf, as they, being minors, were denied any voice in their own affairs. The Latvians in the Esslingen camp proposed the creation of a committee to advise UNRRA in making decisions about Latvian children, especially in light of emerging resettlement possibilities, but the idea did not gain much traction.[27] As a result, these children remained in the children's centres – not stateless, but without a liaison officer to speak for them, and so unable to move forward.

The situation proved increasingly untenable. In October 1946, to break the impasse, UNRRA's European Regional Office instructed the field to abide by UNRRA's Resolution 92 (issued in March 1946) which required UNRRA to consult with the accredited representative of the Soviet Union in cases involving displaced persons of Latvian, Lithuanian, and Estonian origins. This was a controversial move, for it contravened the policy of both the American and British occupying authorities, who only recognized the Soviet liaison officers' authority over those Baltic displaced persons who wished to repatriate and forbade consultation with those liaison officers on general questions concerning Baltic displaced persons. As for unaccompanied Baltic children, the Military Government considered them to be its responsibility and refused to allow Soviet liaison officers to even comment on decisions made about these children. The instruction put the field personnel in an impossible situation. If consulted, it was clear that the Soviet liaison officers would not approve anything other than repatriation for the children, arguing that the children were too young to have a voice in the decision, but UNRRA would not repatriate the children against their will. The stalemate was an especially frustrating one as opportunities were finally starting to open up for emigration to the United States under the aegis of the US Committee for the Care of European Children, which had stepped up its operations in Germany that autumn. In an act of quiet rebellion, the field personnel's solution was to not refer any cases to the Soviet liaison officers, unless the child or its parents, who had been located in the homeland, specifically requested repatriation, in spite of their instructions. However, this still left unresolved the question of who could clear the children for emigration, leaving the possibility of resettlement remote.[28]

As late as May 1947, the impasse continued. Although their number was small – approximately ninety – the children who remained were older, adamantly anti-Communist, and resolutely determined not to repatriate.[29] The United States continued to refuse to recognize the Baltic displaced persons as Soviet citizens. UNRRA's field workers refused to refer cases to the Soviet liaison officers.[30] At this point, the upper echelons of UNRRA finally realized that their instructions to refer the children to the Soviet repatriation officers had been ignored. Furious, the director for the US Zone, Paul Edwards, was pointedly told to instruct the field staff to refer the files of Baltic children to the Soviet liaison officers.[31] Edwards, equally furious, but with Zone Headquarters, immediately wrote to G-5 Section of the European Command (EUCOM) asking if, in light of the fact that his people needed EUCOM's approval for all children leaving the US Zone, EUCOM could clarify what its policy would be on releasing these children for repatriation to the Soviet Union. After all, there was not much point in turning the files over to the Soviet repatriation officers who would insist that the only possible resolution was repatriation if EUCOM would then refuse to allow it. The answer was blunt: the children would not be released.[32]

As a solution, any final decision on the fate of these particular children, be it repatriation, resettlement, or establishment in Germany, was made the responsibility of EUCOM alone. By October 1947, however, EUCOM was becoming quite worried as very few Baltic or

Ukrainian children were being referred to it for clearance, especially as it was receiving reports that Soviet liaison officers were still being consulted by IRO field workers.[33] Furthermore, complaints were coming in from various voluntary agencies pushing various resettlement opportunities for Baltic children and becoming frustrated with what they considered the apparent determination of the International Refugee Organization (IRO) to repatriate Baltic children to the Soviet Union rather than allowing them to resettle.[34] These were youths aged twelve to seventeen, the agencies argued, who were "mature beyond their years, because of the hardships they have undergone, political as well as otherwise" who had a "terror of being returned to their countries of origin." The agencies demanded that EUCOM issue a directive clarifying its policy regarding this group of children, namely, that like with Jewish children, only releases from EUCOM were acceptable, not ones issued by Soviet liaison officers.[35] EUCOM reissued blunt instructions to the IRO that all Baltic unaccompanied children required EUCOM clearance, and only EUCOM's. If the IRO was consulting the Soviet liaison officers, this needed to stop.[36] IRO Geneva promptly denied that anyone had sought clearance from the Soviets in the past year. The lack of applications, it explained, was instead a result of the fact that there were simply very few such children remaining in the camps – in October 1947, there remained only thirty awaiting visas from the American consuls.[37]

Nonetheless, the remaining thirty were proving to be a stubborn problem. Finally, in May 1948, a decision of sorts was reached. In an informal meeting of representatives from the American, British, and French governments, it was determined that the IRO would only repatriate those children of these nationalities when there was satisfactory documentary evidence that the parents were alive and still resident in the Baltic countries. The Soviet repatriation officers would not be recognized as the children's national representatives, nor would they be allowed to claim the children as Soviet nationals. It was an odd resolution, because repatriation of these children would turn them over to Soviet control, even if the liaison officers had no say in their repatriation. It would also have the effect of declaring them Soviet citizens, without formally acknowledging it. In reality, however, this did not change much, as there was very rarely any evidence of the existence of parents in Baltic or Ukrainian territory, so the issue was moot.[38] What it did do, or at least attempt to do, was mollify the Soviets and Eastern Europeans without truly risking much. Interestingly, this compromise effectively gave primacy to the principle of reuniting families, while evading the tricky issue of citizenship. Ethnicity had, in this instance, trumped citizenship.

Yugoslavian Displaced Persons

The estimated seventy-eight thousand Yugoslavian displaced persons (as of June 1945[39]) posed a slightly different kind of problem for those responsible for their care. There were two complicating factors affecting the disposition and the identity of Yugoslavian displaced persons: politics and ethnicity. The political factor was a result of the civil war between the Royalist Chetniks and the Communist Partisans that had raged in Yugoslavia at the same time as the war with Germany and after, which ended with the Communists seizing power and establishing the Socialist Federal Republic of Yugoslavia, as well as the very brutal Nazi occupation of the country, in which a number of Yugoslavians had collaborated. The ethnic factor was the presence of a now unwelcome ethnic minority both in Yugoslavia and among the Yugoslavian displaced persons – the Volksdeutsche. Largely ethnic Germans whose families had lived in Yugoslavia for generations, these people had been singled out for favourable treatment by the Nazi occupiers, and many of them (although not all) had actively collaborated and benefited from their country's occupation. Now, they faced a hostile regime.

The newly formed Yugoslavian government under General Tito declared itself keen to repatriate all of its displaced persons as quickly as possible, and in fact it was the first nation from outside of SHAEF's operational area to petition to send a mission into Germany to deal with its people. Initially, it should be noted, the new Communist government made no distinction between Volksdeutsche and non-Volksdeutsche Yugoslavians (SHAEF, however, first wanted to screen the population for collaborators).[40] By the end of June 1945, Yugoslavian liaison officers were in place and ready to assist their nationals in repatriation.[41]

It seemed, at first, that this would be a straightforward exercise, in the same way that repatriation of the Soviets had initially seemed straightforward. But matters soon became complicated. It emerged that among the Yugoslavian displaced persons was a significant contingent of men who had served in the former Royalist Yugoslavian Army, loyal to the now-dethroned King Peter, or who had fought against Tito's forces, as well as against the Nazis. Thus, they were not technically collaborators, but their status in the new Communist Yugoslavia was uncertain, their welcome even more so. They themselves were reluctant to return, justifiably fearing persecution at the hands of the new regime if they did.

On 25 August 1945, the Yugoslavian government threw down the gauntlet and passed a law decreeing that certain categories of persons, having failed to participate in the mass repatriation program, would forfeit their Yugoslavian nationality if they failed by a certain date "to declare their readiness to be repatriated." Those categories were the following: officers and non-commissioned officers of the former Yugoslavian Army; prisoners of war and internees; and members of the military formations who had fought against the Yugoslavian Liberation Army and left Yugoslavia either with the withdrawing enemy or before that time. The Yugoslavian government stated that it would consider the mass repatriation to be completed by 15 October, setting a deadline of 15 December 1945 for these people to declare their intentions or lose their nationality (in reality, their citizenship).[42] As it was now policy not to forcibly repatriate displaced persons, and Yugoslavian displaced persons were considered to be UN displaced persons anyway according to USFET's directive on determining nationalities, suddenly tens of thousands of Yugoslavians were going to be rendered stateless, making them twice dependent on UNRRA and OMGUS aid for the foreseeable future – as Yugoslavian United Nations displaced persons in the first instance and as stateless in the second.

Yugoslavia had also, by this point, taken an increasingly hard stance against its ethnic German population, which numbered approximately two hundred thousand at the war's end. As early as November 1944, all German-speaking people in the cities had been expelled to rural towns, and all who had been involved with the wartime German administration or army had been interned in provisional concentration camps, under horrific conditions. At approximately the same time, the government declared that it was expropriating the property of the German-speaking population. By March 1945, this population had been ghettoized in what were euphemistically called "village camps." The goal was to ethnically cleanse all Yugoslavian territory of ethnic Germans, ideally by expelling them to Germany. The Potsdam Conference had given approval to the wholesale expulsion of ethnic Germans from Poland, Czechoslovakia, and Hungary, and while Yugoslavia had not been explicitly mentioned, its government had concluded that Potsdam gave it grounds to do the same.

In January 1946, the Yugoslavian government began pressing the Allied Control Commission to allow it to resettle its Germans in

Germany. On 8 February, it closed its borders to repatriates, forbidding any more Yugoslavians to return home from Germany. The logic was that those who had been willing to return had done so already. Those who remained in Germany were, it was assumed, hostile to the new regime and so not welcome. The only exception made was for those officers and non-commissioned officers who had served in the former Yugoslavian Army and who agreed to declare their willingness to return to Yugoslavia and to place themselves at the disposal of those authorities dealing with repatriation efforts by 16 April 1946, otherwise they, too, would lose their Yugoslavian citizenship.

Neither the United States nor Great Britain was interested in absorbing an additional two hundred thousand expellees, whether Yugoslavian or German, as they were overwhelmed by the expellees and displaced persons already in Germany, as well as by the flood of infiltrees streaming in. Both refused the Yugoslavian government permission to expel its ethnic Germans (although it appears that there may have been some accommodation reached about expulsions to Austria). Aside from twenty thousand to thirty thousand who were turned over to the Soviets as forced labourers, few escaped Yugoslavia. By 1947, the Yugoslavians would lose patience with the Americans and British and begin to "facilitate" the ethnic Germans' "escape" to Germany. However, in the summer and fall of 1946, Yugoslavia was still expecting to receive permission to openly expel its ethnic Germans.[43] The Yugoslavian unaccompanied children found themselves caught between these two competing drives – the first, to return all loyal Yugoslavians to Yugoslavia and quickly, and the second, to expel all Volksdeutsche just as quickly. It was no longer about repatriating all Yugoslavians. It was now about a selective repatriation of those deemed politically, as well as ethnically acceptable.

The implications of this for the children were twofold. First, some means of determining which children were to be considered Yugoslavian, as opposed to Volksdeutsche, had to be established and second, for those children whose parents were considered Volksdeutsche and facing apparently imminent expulsion, a decision had to be made as to whether it was better to keep the children in Germany and reunite them with their parents after expulsion, or return them to Yugoslavia only to have them returned to Germany, with their parents, almost immediately. If the former was the option chosen, it begged the question as to whether UNRRA would be allowed to continue to care for them pending reunion with their families, even after they were determined to be

Volksdeutsche and therefore technically outside of UNRRA's mandate. Or should these children be turned over to the German authorities?[44] The answer was not obvious. Technically, they should have been turned over to the Landesjugendamt as soon as their Volksdeutsch status was determined. From a humanitarian perspective, the answer was less clear-cut. To tear them from their current situation, be it foster home or children's home, and put them in a strange, temporary placement for what promised to be a matter of just a few months, seemed to many to be harsh, disruptive, and counterproductive.

Even more vexing were those Yugoslavian unaccompanied children whose ethnicity could not be definitively determined – the evidence being too scant to determine if they were Volksdeutsche or not. These children got caught in the wrangling between the Landesjugendamt, the American Military Government, UNRRA, and then the IRO. These were among the children who remained trapped in the children's centres for years, awaiting a decision on their purported nationality and therefore, their ultimate fate.

One group of seventeen Yugoslavian children in particular encapsulated much of the complexity of these cases. Identified as Yugoslavian by the Yugoslavian liaison officer, the seventeen were removed from a German orphanage in Weihersmühle to the UNRRA children's centre in Kloster Indersdorf in March 1946. In a salvo of the battle over removals, the German authorities mobilized. The director of the orphanage objected strongly to the Landesjugendamt, who protested the removal to the offices of the Public Welfare Branch of the Office of the Military Government, Bavaria (OMG Bavaria). The Evangelical Council of Bishops also complained, arguing that these children had come from a Yugoslavian orphanage that was expressly established to care for German nationals and that they were therefore Auslanddeutsche (foreign Germans, literally) or Volksdeutsche. The Bishops' Council also claimed that the children's parents were actually in Austria, having been expelled from Yugoslavia as Volksdeutsche. Sympathetic to the complaints, OMG Bavaria cancelled the children's repatriation and instructed UNRRA to reopen the files, arguing that the evidence supporting the asserted nationality was insufficient.

The liaison officer was himself hesitant to force the repatriation of the children, as they were openly reluctant to return to Yugoslavia. While he was willing to make his pitch for repatriation, he made it clear that he would not require them to repatriate against their wishes, in spite of them being minors. In the subsequent investigations, UNRRA and the Council of Bishops were able to locate relatives of thirteen of these children in Austria, and the conclusion was that, indeed, these thirteen were Volksdeutsche. However, none of the relatives were in a position to care for the children and were, in fact, expecting to move to Germany soon themselves. So, in spite of determining them to be Volksdeutsche and therefore outside of UNRRA's mandate, the children remained where they were, now UNRRA's Prien children's centre, pending a final decision, "particularly as this will be in many respects a test case and the children should not be subjected to another move." At this point, however, the Yugoslavian liaison officer (who had changed by this time) decided he wanted to revisit the cases one more time before making a final decision. Lieutenant Colonel Robert Reese of the Public Welfare Branch, frustrated with the inordinate delays (the children had now been in an UNRRA centre for eight months and were not coping well with the uncertainties), could not understand why the Yugoslavian liaison officer still had any say in the matter if the children were Volksdeutsche and therefore not Yugoslavian. His supervisor, Mr Miniclier, the senior public welfare officer at OMG Bavaria, was as flummoxed by the situation and decided to take the question up the chain of command for clarification. UNRRA, meanwhile, was working hard to complete the investigation and get a ruling from the liaison officer. As late as February 1947, a full eleven months later, the children were evidently still in Prien, as Dr Bamberger of the Landesjugendamt was, at that point, requesting that four of the children be returned to the Weihersmühle orphanage because their father had been located in a Russian prisoner of war camp.[45]

Several lessons are to be drawn from this sad affair, which was all too common a situation. The lack of evidence as to the children's ethnicity cum nationality meant, given the climate in which the cases were being discussed (it was late 1946 and early 1947, when the war over removals between the Office of Military Government, United States (OMGUS), UNRRA, and the Jugendamt was full-blown), some were stalled until family members could be located, the only evidence of nationality acceptable at that moment. It meant, for example, that the children who had been admitted to Kloster Indersdorf in March 1946 remained in UNRRA's children centres until at least the spring of 1947, that is, at least another year. Even after family members were located, the children could not be reunited with them, as the adults were in no position to support the children or were due to be moved to Germany. It made no sense to send the children elsewhere only to have them return to Germany almost immediately. Those children who were found to be Volksdeutsche remained in the UNRRA children's centres, this being considered more humanitarian than the upheaval that would come with moving them temporarily into Jugendamt facilities while awaiting their families' arrivals. Finally, the liaison officer's position on these cases was revealing, as was that of Reese. Although the first liaison officer accepted these children as Yugoslavian, he was unwilling to repatriate them against their will – contrary to the ardent demands of his national government, which still insisted, at least on the world stage if not in practice, that it wanted all of its children back. Here, political orientation trumped nationality and citizenship. OMG Bavaria's confusion was also revealing: with Reese, on the one hand, arguing that, if the children are Volksdeutsche, the Yugoslavian liaison officer had no right to rule on the children's disposition, and Miniclier, on the other, uncertain as to what their Volksdeutsche status did to their citizenship. Clearly, at least in late 1946, even OMGUS did not have a good sense of how to handle the Volksdeutsche issue: how should a child be identified, by its ethnicity or by its citizenship? The answer had important implications for the child, determining which liaison officer would make the decision, to which country the child might be repatriated, and who might be able to adopt it.

The shift from the UNRRA to the IRO did nothing to resolve the situation. Technically, such children did not fit into the IRO's mandate either, as its constitution specifically stated that persons of German ethnic origin, having fled to Germany or having been moved to Germany, were not a concern of the IRO. However, when a child's nationality was not clear because the information was inconclusive, the file remained with the IRO. The result was that the IRO ended up with a number of files it could not close. In July 1948, Charlotte Babinski, an IRO child care officer, reported that she still had an estimated sixty to eighty cases pending that were Yugoslavian Volksdeutsche children. In some (not necessarily Babinski's files in particular), these children had been registered months, if not years previously, but with still no decision as to their nationality: Yugoslavian or German. Politics, confusion around the concept of nationality, and a lack of convincing documentation meant that a number of children remained caught in the camp system for years.

By this point, the IRO Headquarters in the US Zone was inclined to dismiss these children as outside of its mandate and therefore not the IRO's responsibility, as was EUCOM.[46] The director of the International Tracing Service, Maurice Thudichum, begged to differ. While the IRO's constitution may have stated that, generally, persons of German ethnic origin were not its responsibility, within the constitution's definition of refugees and displaced persons who were eligible there was a particular clause that made these children an exception: "the term 'refugee' also applies to unaccompanied children who are war orphans or whose parents have disappeared and who are outside their countries of origin. Such children, sixteen years or under, shall be given all possible priority assistance including, normally, assistance in repatriation in the case of those whose nationality can be determined." Thus, unaccompanied *children* of ethnic German origin *did* fit within the IRO's mandate. As was brought out in the War Crimes Trial No. 8 (Race and Resettlement Case, or RuSHA case), Thudichum argued, the Nazi regime had

> indiscriminately labelled all children who pass the physical exam of the Race and Resettlement Office ethnic German children and removed them forcibly to Germany. The examination ... did not deal with the origin of the child but was merely concerned with physical characteristics ... The defendants in question used the term "ethnic German" in connection with those children ... The Tribunal, however, classified those children, from the evidence before them, as Poles, Yugoslavs etc. and ruled that they were nationals of countries other than Germany.

In light of this, the director of the International Tracing Service concluded, "We do not see how the IRO could possibly exclude those children from the services of the Child Search Branch." Every unaccompanied child whose origin is presumed to be non-German was eligible for the services of the International Tracing Service.[47] Thudichum's argument apparently was persuasive, as the files remained open, if not active. Although attitudes towards the Volksdeutsche had hardened, the door was still left open for Volksdeutsche children who were considered by at least some to be a special case. Once again, their lack of agency – having been removed forcibly to Germany, rather than moving of their own volition – meant that they required special consideration as victims of Nazi oppression. As such, even if they technically fell outside of the IRO's mandate based upon their ethnicity, as children, they were to be considered nationals of their countries. In this case, citizenship trumped ethnicity.

Polish Displaced Persons

The Polish displaced persons' situation echoed the Yugoslavian, with two additional twists. According to USFET's November 1945 directive on determining nationality, similar to all displaced persons, Poles were to have their claims of citizenship screened by a Polish liaison officer. If deemed Polish, the assumption was that they would return to Poland. Those who were denied permission to return to Poland because they were of ethnic German origin would also be denied classification as United Nations displaced persons and turned over to the German authorities for care. Those who were eligible for repatriation, but refused, would be granted United Nations displaced persons status and receive the appropriate care. What muddied the waters in the first instance (the first twist) when dealing with this particular group of displaced persons, and especially with Polish unaccompanied children, was the existence of two competing governments, each claiming to represent the Polish displaced persons – the Polish government in exile based in London and the Polish Provisional Government of National Unity (the Lublin government) in Warsaw. At the war's end, it was the Polish government in exile that was internationally recognized as the legitimate government of Poland. This Polish government had fled Poland when it was invaded by and divided between Germany and the Soviet Union in September 1939, finally settling, like so many other exiled governments, in London in 1940. There it had operated as the official government of Poland for the duration of the Second World War and had been recognized as such diplomatically. Furthermore, the Polish armed forces had been reconstructed under British military command and fought beside British troops throughout the war. As a result, the British government felt a particular debt of gratitude to the Polish forces, as well as a special responsibility for Polish displaced persons and to the Polish government in exile, which shaped the British position regarding the Polish displaced persons in the immediate postwar period.

Meanwhile, in the last year of the war, a Soviet-sponsored Communist government had been established in Poland after the Red Army liberated the country from German occupation; this was the Polish Provisional Government of National Unity. It was made up of Polish Communists who had fled to Moscow, rather than westward, and who were loyal to the USSR. This new government had the sanction of Moscow and claimed to be the legitimate representative of the new, resurrected

Poland. Thus, at the war's end, there were two possible governments of Poland – one based in London, which loathed the Soviet Union as much as Nazi Germany for having dismembered and occupied the country in 1939, and a pro-Soviet Communist government based in Warsaw. When liaison officers were first appointed in the Western-occupied zones of Germany, they were drawn from the staff of and appointed by the London-based government. These liaison officers generally were hostile to the Warsaw government and actively opposed to the Polish displaced persons' repatriation to a Communist Poland. In the first months, a large number of Poles repatriated voluntarily, but when the dust settled, Poles still made up the largest number of displaced persons refusing to return home. In a G-5 survey, it was estimated that there were over half a million Poles in the SHAEF Zone, while, in a report to the US Secretary of State sent in mid-July 1945, the number given was 648,000.[48] However many there were, these Poles were vehemently hostile to the Soviet Union and the new Communist regime in Poland. They were not averse to returning to Poland, but would only do so when the Communist regime had been ousted and Soviet control of Poland ended. Many of the London-appointed liaison officers actively encouraged this hostility.

The situation became more complicated on 5 July 1945 when, bowing to the inevitable, both the United States and Great Britain officially terminated their diplomatic recognition of the Polish government in exile and recognized the Polish Provisional Government of National Unity in Warsaw as the legitimate government of Poland.[49] This complicated the matter of repatriation considerably on a number of fronts, but two immediate issues that arose were those of the disposition of the remaining anti-Communist Poles in Germany and the London-appointed liaison officers. Rather naively, the Americans still hoped that the displaced persons would all go home, which would have solved the problem. Over the course of the remaining summer months and into the autumn of 1945, the American Military Government worked to encourage the Polish displaced persons to return to Poland voluntarily, arguing that they could do more to shape their country's future if they returned to their homeland than they could by staying in Germany.[50] This effort was hampered, however, by the ongoing rivalry between the London Poles, as they were known, and Warsaw's representatives, by Warsaw's failure to bring forward its own liaison officers, and by the mounting anti-repatriation activities among displaced persons.

Through that July and August, tensions within the Polish displaced person population rose as an anti-repatriation campaign among the displaced persons took shape, in the form of newspapers, pamphlets, posters, and rumours urging Poles not to repatriate to a Communist Poland, aided and abetted by the London Polish liaison officers. In spite of this, the American Military Government decided to retain the original liaison officers until such time as Warsaw chose to replace them, as much out of expedience as anything. USFET was not opposed to their replacement with Warsaw appointees, but until Warsaw saw fit to bring forward replacements, someone had to be responsible for the Polish displaced persons. To dismiss them before replacements were in the field would, USFET explained, "inconvenience military authorities and result in unnecessary distress for Polish nationals."[51]

It took until late September 1945 for Warsaw to act. The liaison officers in the field were instructed that they would now have to declare their allegiance to the Polish government in Warsaw or face the possibility of dismissal.[52] It was not, however, clear that Warsaw had sufficient personnel to replace all the London Poles, or was willing to spare them. In the end, a compromise was struck, officially in order to not upset the "very satisfactory liaison machinery" that was already in place. More importantly, the fear was that abruptly removing the London-appointed liaison officers would have ignited the smouldering resentments in the camps and destroyed any chance of persuading the Poles to repatriate. Yet the London appointees could not be allowed to operate unsupervised, as they, too, undermined the repatriation effort. Thus, responsibilities were divided between the Warsaw and London Polish liaison officers. The Warsaw appointees were given responsibility for verification of nationality and for repatriation; the London appointees were assigned responsibility for the administration, control, welfare, and discipline of Poles in the displaced persons assembly centres.[53] Inevitably, the two sets of liaison officers worked at cross-purposes. For the unaccompanied children, this was a critical point: it was now the Warsaw liaison officer who determined if they were Polish or not, and therefore if they would be repatriated or not. But it was the London Poles who cared for them on a daily basis, giving them considerable influence over the children, at a moment when UNRRA would not consider repatriating a child who was opposed to being repatriated; these liaison officers used their access to encourage the children's anti-Communist sentiments and their reluctance to repatriate. The children, then, became fodder in the battle between the London and Warsaw Polish liaison officers for the hearts and minds of the Polish displaced persons, as well as fuel for a growing propaganda war between East and West.

To make matters more complicated, the second twist was the question of who exactly was a Pole – a question crucial to the fate of unaccompanied children. This second dilemma was a result of the border changes between the USSR and Poland, by which the USSR had formally annexed the huge swathe of eastern Polish territory it had occupied in 1939 and which had been internationally recognized as Soviet territory (unlike the annexation of the Baltic republics) under the terms of the Yalta Agreement of February 1945 (and confirmed as the Soviet-Polish border in a treaty signed between the USSR and Poland on 16 August 1945). This territory lay east of the Curzon Line, which stretches south from Grodno, through Brest-Litovsk, and follows the Bug River to the Carpathian Mountains. This shift in territory meant that all those resident in the formerly eastern Polish territory were now Soviet citizens. The question was whether that rendered all Polish displaced persons from east of the Curzon Line, but currently in displaced person camps in Germany, Soviet citizens or whether they remained Polish citizens.[54] If deemed Soviet, according to the terms of the Yalta Agreement, these displaced persons faced forcible repatriation in the first months after the war's end. While that threat had disappeared by early 1946, the fear remained palpable, and for the younger unaccompanied children who were subject to the decisions of the liaison officer responsible for them and who were denied a voice in the decisions made about their future, still a potential reality. For this reason, the Poles in the displaced persons camps who came from formerly eastern Poland continued to insist that they were Polish whenever asked for their nationality. However, while SHAEF refused to forcibly repatriate anyone, this did not mean that the United States accepted their professed identities.[55]

For the children, the question was particularly fraught. The children from Silesia posed an especially tricky problem, both because of their numbers – estimates were there were several thousand in Germany – and the complicated nature of their story. As UNRRA understood it, and as the Polish authorities had explained, Silesia had been German territory prior to the war, but had had a large Polish population living in it, people of Polish origin and nationality. During the Nazi regime, these people had been forced to take German citizenship in order to obtain food, housing, and employment. Now the Poles referred to these people as "Volksliste" (a modification of the term as it was used by the Nazis). Key to the Polish use of the term was that it referred to those who had been *forced* to take German citizenship. Anyone in this category was welcome to reclaim Polish citizenship. There were the Volksdeutsche, however, who were former Polish citizens of ethnic German origin who had voluntarily declared themselves to be citizens of the Third Reich. These people were not permitted to reclaim their Polish citizenship although their ultimate fate was not yet determined. Some of them, it was expected, would be interned; some would probably be expelled from Poland. Thus, it was not clear whether children from Silesia were Volksliste and therefore Polish, or Volksdeutsche and therefore German.[56] (It was a similar situation with Yugoslavian, Czechoslovakian, and Hungarian children of the same ethnic background.) The Landesjugendamt insisted that these children were German, based on the testimonies of the directors of the children's homes and the children's foster parents, who firmly maintained the children's German origins, and objected strongly both to UNRRA's assertion otherwise and to the children's removal to UNRRA facilities.[57] These were the children over whom the Landesjugendamt, UNRRA, the IRO, and the American Military Government, as well as the Eastern European governments (especially the governments of Poland, Czechoslovakia, Yugoslavia, and Hungary) were arguing, and the dispute continued because of the lack of convincing evidence, the failure to address the distinction between ethnicity and citizenship, and the impact of international politics. This may not have been a numerous population, but it proved stubbornly resistant to resolution, and one that threatened to make the objective of permanently "establishing" every displaced person, adult and child, elusive.

The matter was further muddied by the Polish government's continuing indecision. It took until November 1946 for the Polish government to provide any formal statement of how to deal with this population. While it refused to provide either UNRRA or the American Military Government with a copy of the Polish-Soviet treaty governing the new citizenship rules, it did, finally, provide a formal letter of explanation. In it, the Polish government explained that persons of Polish nationality formerly domiciled in territories east of the Curzon Line ceded to the Soviet Union would retain their Polish citizenship and were "welcome back and where necessary provided housing, farmland, etc."[58]

Finally, in late May 1947, Poland issued a set of instructions specifically for the determination of the nationality of unaccompanied Polish children. The basic premise was that all doubtful cases were to be presumed non-German, and any such case that was in dispute should be settled by "an arbitrage of Liaison Officer or Consular Officials of the concerned nations." In principle, no non-German child was to be left in the hands of a "German tutor," and all effort was to be focused on determining the quickest way of removing Polish children from German institutions. Minors either born or found in the Polish republic were considered to be Polish citizens, as were children whose parents were Polish (legitimate children took the nationality of their father; illegitimate children, that of their mother, unless acknowledged by their Polish father). Children of mixed marriages that had ended in divorce during the war were also considered Polish citizens (as the Polish government refused to recognize the legality of German courts' decisions), if the mother was Polish, willing to reassume her Polish nationality, and if she had not "committed any disgraceful deed with regard to the Polish Nation." If the mother was unable to return, a child under the age of sixteen could still repatriate "to become [a] Polish Citizen and to manifest their Polish Nationality by their behaviour." Still other categories of children were given the opportunity to claim Polish citizenship. Children of Russian, Ukrainian, White Russian, Ruthenian, and Lithuanian nationalities aged sixteen or older who stated that they were willing to be Polish citizens and "prove by their behaviour that they belong to the Polish Community" could be considered. Note the shift in Polish thinking. The Polish government was no longer concerned with simply getting all Polish children back; it had become more selective. Now it only wanted back those children who were either young enough to adapt to the new society or who were sympathetic to the new regime. The rebellious were not welcome.[59] As in the Yugoslavian case, political reliability trumped both nationality and citizenship.

Ukrainian Displaced Persons

The Ukrainian displaced persons found themselves in a particularly vulnerable position, different from that of the other categories discussed so far. Unlike the others, "Ukrainian" was not recognized as a nationality, in spite of Ukrainian displaced persons' determination to claim it as such. Rather, Ukrainians were considered citizens and therefore nationals of various countries: typically Polish or Soviet, although also Czechoslovakian, Romanian, Yugoslavian, as well as American and even Iranian.[60] In the Ukrainian case, citizenship trumped nationality, as both SHAEF and UNRRA steadfastly refused to recognize Ukrainian as a legitimate nationality category. When the Ukrainian displaced persons pressed their claim, the occupation authorities' attitude hardened quickly and in an unfavourable direction. Although as late as June 1945, SHAEF was informing those in the field that individuals claiming Ukrainian nationality and denying Soviet or Polish citizenship were not to be repatriated forcibly, by mid-July, its position had changed markedly. SHAEF now declared that "Ukrainians are not recognized as a nationality" and so would be handled according to their citizenship, be it Soviet, Polish, or Czechoslovakian, or of some other country, or as stateless persons (if they were such). Those "styling themselves as Ukrainians who are Soviet citizens displaced by reasons of war," identified as such by the military commanders and Soviet repatriation representatives, were to be repatriated to the Soviet Union "without regard to their personal wishes," including unaccompanied children.[61] This was forcefully reiterated in a cable sent to the field in August.[62]

As a result, in the summer of 1945, Ukrainians from east of the Curzon Line were being rounded up for forcible deportation (unlike the Poles), deemed Soviet citizens. The Ukrainians' response was as strong as it was predictable. They protested vehemently against their forced repatriation, to either Poland or the Soviet Union. Rumours were flying about the treatment of those who had returned, and they were not pleasant: Polish Ukrainians in Poland were being expelled to the Soviet Union, so it was said, causing a "resurgence of the traditional antagonism" between the Ukrainians and the Poles, which the Polish and Soviet authorities were allowing to escalate. Violence was not uncommon.[63] The rumours only served to further reinforce these displaced persons' determination not to repatriate.

Although USFET's November directive on determining nationality eliminated the threat of forcible repatriation, it reasserted that individuals should be dealt with according to their "nationality status" (read: citizenship) or as stateless persons.[64] As Sir Frederick Morgan, chief of UNRRA's operations in Germany, explained to the director of the US Zone at this time, Jack Whiting, Ukrainians born west of the Curzon Line were to be counted as Poles and those born east of the Curzon Line as Soviet citizens.[65] This did not stop those counting heads in the assembly centres from adulterating the census forms received from UNRRA's Statistics Branch, adding in new categories, including Ukrainian. They had little choice, in fact, as they were required to record whatever nationality the displaced person claimed, not what nationality they, the registrar, wished to ascribe to the displaced person. If any displaced persons refused to reveal their citizenship and the registrar was suspicious of their claimed nationality, the best the registrar could do was put such persons in the "undetermined" or "doubtful" column on the form (the two words were used interchangeably) – a problematic solution, as the numbers in that column ballooned and became a misleading measure of the truly undetermined or doubtful. Nor did USFET's pledge to end forcible repatriation do much to allay the Ukrainian displaced persons' suspicions and fears, especially since they were still to be recorded according to their citizenship, rather than nationality. They might not be forcibly repatriated, but Ukrainians were still considered Soviet or Polish citizens, meaning their liaison officer was the Soviet or Polish one.

Matters were further complicated by the population exchanges happening between Poland and the Soviet Union at the same time. The two countries had signed a treaty allowing both ethnic Poles and Jews who were Polish citizens before 17 September 1939 but were at present residing in what had become Soviet territory (the former Polish territory east of the Curzon Line) to return to Poland if they wished to do so. As well, any Soviet citizens residing in Polish territory who wished to return to the Soviet Union were permitted to do so. This was deemed also to apply to displaced persons currently in Germany but of Polish or Soviet nationality who had resided in those territories prior to the territorial exchange. There was also a provision permitting Russian, Byelo-Russian, Ruthenian, Ukrainian, and Lithuanian nationals to change their citizenship to Soviet from Polish should they wish to do so; however, the Soviet Union allowed only Soviet citizens of Polish and Jewish nationality to change their citizenship to Polish.

This meant that those of Ukrainian nationality who had had Polish citizenship in 1939 had now lost it, and had simultaneously acquired citizenship in the Ukrainian SSR (part of the Soviet Union). In fact, those people of Ukrainian nationality *currently* residing within the current borders of Poland were being transferred "without compulsion" to the Ukrainian SSR (they ostensibly had the right to opt out of the transfer, but few did, or so the Poles reported). Ukrainians who were currently living outside the new borders did not have the option to retain their Polish citizenship. Exceptions were technically possible "when the whole family has been brought up in a thoroughly Polish 'frame of mind,' i.e., (apparently) feeling genuine allegiance to Poland," but how an UNRRA worker was to determine whether or not a family was of a thoroughly Polish frame of mind was unclear, as was how one might articulate its measurement in a directive for the field.[66] Polish

Ukrainians living in the displaced persons camps, whether from east or west of the Curzon Line, had lost their Polish citizenship and would be sent to the Ukrainian SSR, even if they were first repatriated to Poland. In fact, by early 1947, the Polish government was refusing to accept any Polish Ukrainian displaced persons, either adults or children, for repatriation to Poland. The population transfers to the Soviet Union had not gone smoothly, no matter the government rhetoric, and had led to riots and other disturbances and forms of resistance. There was no desire to add more reluctant transferees to the population. The Polish government argued that, as Soviet nationals, the Polish Ukrainian displaced persons should instead be dealt with directly by the Soviet Union.[67] This instantly rendered a sizeable number of displaced persons unrepatriable, as it was recognized that they would never agree to go to the Soviet Union. It did not, however, determine whether they were eligible for assistance.

In the process, the Polish government had made a clear distinction between its citizens based on ethnic lines. This rendered things much more difficult for UNRRA and the Military Government, as they now had a definitely unrepatriable population identified by its ethnicity, an ethnic identity whose legitimacy UNRRA and the Military Government had been steadfastly denying, but which now had the formal sanction of its one-time national government. To identify the Polish Ukrainians among the displaced persons now became an urgent matter, in order to know how many could no longer be considered repatriable. The problem, of course, was that UNRRA had no idea how many Polish Ukrainians it had in its camps, as it had been telling its people repeatedly not to count them. As a result, the reporting was completely unreliable. This was especially embarrassing because various Ukrainian organizations had been pressing UNRRA for some time to recognize the size of the Ukrainian problem, quoting a figure of three hundred thousand Ukrainians in Europe but outside the Soviet Union who needed assistance, a number UNRRA was unable either to confirm or refute.[68]

A close look at the "Summary of D.P. Population, District No. 5, as of 28 December 1946" compiled by the Statistics and Reports Branch at District 5 UNRRA Headquarters in Munich, is a revealing glimpse of the resulting confusion. The summary, put together by a mid-level office, reflected which nationalities were now deemed acceptable to report (the total number of displaced persons reported was 123,552). The list was extensive, with eighty-eight categories in all, eleven of which were some variant of Ukrainian. "Jews" were one category and the first on the list, but were broken down by nationality (read: citizenship) into four sub-categories (Polish, Hungarian, German, Other). Unlike the category of "Jewish," however, "Ukrainian" was scattered throughout the report, seemingly randomly: Polish Ukrainian, Ukrainian Undetermined, Ukrainian, Russian Ukrainian, Ukrainian Stateless, Ukrainian Czech, Ukrainian Romanian, Ukrainian French, Ukrainian Yugoslavian, Ukrainian American, and Ukrainian Iranian.[69] The plethora of categories and the randomness of their appearance throughout the report testifies to the confusion that reigned. As well, the repeated inversion of citizenship and nationality in the column headings (Polish Ukrainian versus Ukrainian Czech – in some cases, then, the noun being Ukrainian, with citizenship as an adjective; in others, the citizenship functioning as the noun and primary identifier) suggests that the conflation of citizenship and ethnicity was still common. Unlike Jewish and the other generally accepted nationality categories, this one was still in the making. The confusion was a reflection of the failure to answer a fundamental question that plagued the entire exercise: how was one to deal with an ethnicity that had no tangible geopolitical manifestation? For its part, the US Department of State, even as late as March 1947, remained uncertain about how to treat these displaced persons and instructed the Office of Military Government, United States (OMGUS) to consider them Polish nationals, not Soviets, but to grant both Polish and Soviet liaison officers access to them for purposes of voluntary repatriation, at its discretion.[70]

Technically, then, unaccompanied Ukrainian children should have been referred to the Soviet and Polish liaison officers for clearance and repatriation, but UNRRA chose not to deal with the Soviet liaison officers for two reasons. First, most of these children were, in fact, youths and they flatly refused to be repatriated as Soviet citizens – they considered themselves Poles. Second, EUCOM unofficially, but very strongly discouraged the referral of these cases to Soviet liaison officers (not going as far as it had with Baltic children, but having a similar effect). In instances when the children were eligible for emigration to the United States, now finally an option, UNRRA divided the group into two. For those children who might be considered acceptable as Polish citizens, their cases were referred to the Polish liaison officers. For those who might be Soviet citizens, rather than refer them to the Soviet liaison officers, EUCOM assumed for itself responsibility for releasing these children for emigration, as it had for Baltic children.

At last, in May 1948, at the same informal trilateral meeting of representatives of the American, British, and French governments where the plight of Polish unaccompanied children was discussed, it was decided that the IRO would only repatriate those Ukrainian children for whom there was sufficient documentary evidence that their parents were alive and resident in Polish Ukraine. Like the Polish children, the Soviet repatriation officers were not to be recognized as the children's national representatives, nor would they be allowed to claim the children as Soviet nationals. And the expectation was the same as that for such Polish children – that few would actually have parents in Ukraine, so few would face the possibility of repatriation.[71] In this way, ethnicity ultimately trumped citizenship, although in this instance, it was a near thing.

Stateless and the Doubtful or Undetermined

There remained one more special category articulated in USFET's November 1945 directive on determining nationality, namely, that of "stateless." Stateless included all those, except Jews and persecutees, who were "de jure or de facto ... deprived of the protection of a government." The difficulty, as was becoming the norm for questions concerning eligibility, was defining who could be considered stateless. Many displaced persons self-identified as such, especially Eastern Europeans (e.g., Ukrainians and Balts) – an easy way, it seemed to them, to avoid being identified as a citizen of a former homeland to which one did not want to return in the present circumstances. One particularly intriguing instance was a group of four hundred Kalmycks in a displaced persons camp who had been scattered across Europe before the war and forcibly moved to Germany by the Nazis; none of them wanted to return to their various countries of birth and citizenship, but instead, they wanted to emigrate en masse to their ancestral home, Mongolia, and they "therefore declare[d] themselves to be 'stateless.'"[72] In the first months in the field, as UNRRA workers were frantically registering thousands upon thousands of displaced persons who had no identification papers or documentation of any kind, and so had to accept their self-identification at face value, it was easier to accept their claim to stateless status than to ferret out the claimants' true nationality.

The most clear-cut example of the stateless was those people who had been deemed such during the interwar years. This included both White Russians (Russians who had fled Russia at the time of the Russian Revolution and so did not enjoy the protection of the Soviet Union before the outbreak of the Second World War, but also had not acquired another nationality) and other individuals holding Nansen passports. These identity documents had been issued by the League of Nations as a result of territorial changes after the First World War, combined with the impact of a series of citizenship laws passed in Europe after the war. These were for individuals who had suddenly found themselves without citizenship, and thus without the protection of any state. Their lack of any documentation had made it impossible for them to establish any kind of normalized, legal relationship with their host countries, or even to leave those countries if they wished. The Nansen passport had been created in order to give them some semblance of a legal identity. These people, then, were considered stateless. This had effectively given these refugees some degree of the kind of legal protection that comes with citizenship. However, the practice that began to emerge in the field after the Second World War was to consider all those who were non-repatriable as stateless, although the term was used inconsistently. The concept of statelessness clearly had created considerable confusion both in the field and at the various headquarters, and it especially complicated the collection of statistics.[73] This confusion led to a request to UNRRA's Legal Division for clarification and direction.

Although it was quickly apparent to the Legal Division that the concept of statelessness was poorly defined in international law, it was also clear that only an act of government could result in statelessness. Individuals could not unilaterally shed their nationality, although individuals could render themselves stateless by failing to comply with some national law or treaty provision (e.g., being required to register by a certain date and failing to do so), or because of gaps in international agreements, the implications of divergent nationality laws, or acts of government. However, the mere absorption of one state by another, as in the instance of the Baltic republics, did not result in statelessness (as some Baltic displaced persons were wont to claim). Instead, citizens of the first state (e.g., Estonia) lost that nationality (read: citizenship) and acquired the nationality (read: citizenship) of the absorbing state (i.e., they became Soviet citizens in this case). The definition of stateless was to apply to those who "in law or in fact, lack the protection of a government." Note that the stateless may have lost the protection of their government (read: citizenship), but they could not be said to have lost their nationality (read: ethnicity). Voluntary "expatriation" was not in itself sufficient to create statelessness.[74]

The difficulty that had arisen nonetheless was, in part, because there were effectively two kinds of stateless displaced persons. As P.N. Carter, legal adviser for UNRRA Germany explained, there was de jure state-lessness, which was a condition resulting only from

> Sovereign Acts, either law or treaty. Personal renunciation of nationality, whether by word or deed, unless given such effect by law, is irrelevant ... De jure statelessness is a status imposed by law and exists irrespective of the existence of evidence in the possession of the person claiming such status or even his knowledge ... De facto statelessness [as used by the Military Government] contemplates a person who, although he has not by law or treaty, been deprived of his citizenship, lacks in fact, for political or other reason, the protection of a Government.

De jure statelessness was most commonly proven by the possession of a Nansen passport or other League of Nations documentation; de facto statelessness would not have any documentation.[75]

Lack of documentation was a part of the challenge. The bigger challenge, however, was determining at what point an individual had been deprived of his or her citizenship. This was not as easily done as might at first be expected, for often the loss of citizenship was determined by one's place of residence as of a certain date. J.B. Krane, chief of the Reports and Analysis Branch of UNRRA, raised this particular quandry in the context of the Ukrainian question: Was a Ukrainian determined to be Polish (or not) based on the national status of the area in which the Ukrainian lived as of the time of his or her birth, as of 1 September 1939, or some other date, such as his or her place of residence on 1 September 1939?[76]

It was not clear what reasons were sufficient to achieve this condition of statelessness or who could make the declaration. Unlike in the interwar years, there was no intergovernmental machinery that had the authority to declare an individual stateless.[77] In addition, it was unclear whether rejection by a liaison officer was tantamount to a rejection by a state of an individual's claim for nationality.[78] Determining whether any displaced persons who did not have stateless status prior to the Second World War had been rendered stateless by the consequences of the war and its territorial settlements was not obvious. For unaccompanied children, lacking documentation and unable to provide much information about their families, the determination was even more difficult. Part of the problem, too, was that a considerable portion of the remaining displaced persons population did not themselves know for certain what their citizenship was any longer, due to the border changes. At least the

Baltic republics had remained intact as geopolitical entities within the Soviet Union, so there was little confusion about whether someone was from those regions or not. But it initially was unclear, as already seen, how to classify a displaced person of Ukrainian ethnicity who was from near the Curzon Line.

By 1946, the definition of statelessness had been both clarified and delimited, restricted to those who had lost their nationality as a result of the peace treaties following the First World War and the border shifts that resulted from them; those whose governments had passed laws which denationalized them, usually as a consequence of what their governments deemed "bad conduct"; and those whose naturalization was cancelled due to changes in nationality laws. Deemed stateless, then, were those individuals who did not enjoy the diplomatic protection of any state, who had lost their citizenship. Statelessness arose, when the "state removed itself from the individual."[79] The list of who qualified as stateless was now carefully restricted.

It left many unaccounted for, however. Were Polish Ukrainians who were denied their Polish citizenship as well as the right to return to Poland (whether they wanted to go or not) by the Polish government now rendered stateless, given that they had been granted Soviet citizenship in the process? What about those Poles who did not wish to return to Poland? Crucially, what about those displaced persons, like the Yugoslavians and Polish Ukrainians, who were denied permission to repatriate by their national governments? What about the Ukrainians from lands ceded to the Soviet Union but who were only considered Soviet citizens if they affirmatively claimed it, and of undetermined nationality if they refused? Some of the latter had received documents from a US Army Officers Board in September 1945 that read, "After examination ... as to the applicability of the Yalta Agreement this individual has been found not repatriable under its provision and is therefore considered stateless."[80] At the heart of the matter was a key question: at what point did someone who was non-repatriable become stateless, as becoming non-repatriable could be either voluntary or involuntary?

This had important ramifications not just for counting heads, but ultimately for determining what to do with these people. It did not help that this category had become a catch-all containing, as the chief of the Reports and Statistics Branch, J.B. Krane, complained, "persons with recognized legal 'Statelessness,' persons with good claims to legal 'statelessness,' and persons in merely self-declared 'stateless' category." The problem, according to Krane, was that at this time almost any displaced person in Germany had as much right to claim de facto statelessness as those non-Nansen displaced persons currently counted as stateless. Failing to distinguish between them would only make their final disposition that much more difficult to determine.[81] "Undetermined" or "doubtful" was as unsatisfactory an alternative. By late 1946, the upper ranks of UNRRA, reaching as high as the Central Committee of the General Council, had lost patience. This long after the war was over, they felt, there was no reason for having an "undetermined nationality."[82]

Although it had soon become clearly unwise to allow displaced persons to so self-identify, at the same time it remained unclear exactly who was to be considered stateless, at what point someone who was non-repatriable should be considered stateless, or even who had the authority to declare an individual stateless, and based on what evidence.[83] The simple answer was that displaced persons only became stateless when their government had formally rejected them as citizens. Displaced persons who refused to repatriate did not become stateless because of that choice, as they had not been rejected by their national government; they therefore retained their original nationality (read: citizenship).[84] This did not resolve the problem, however, of what to do with those individuals who had been refused permission to repatriate, those who chose not to provide an identity, or, in the case of the unaccompanied children, those who were unable to do so.

The drive became, at least for UNRRA, to be far more cautious in allocating the classification of stateless to a displaced person. This caution took two forms. The first was to narrow the definition of stateless to those displaced persons whose national governments had denied them the protections of citizenship in their states and to attempt to differentiate between the de jure stateless (e.g., holders of Nansen passports) and the rest. Increasingly, the preference became to classify the remainder according to their citizenship or, if that was unclear or unknown, their place of residence as of a certain date, as a substitute. Both, of course, remained problematic for a small, but not to be ignored population. The use of the last place of residence could be especially misleading, argued Rhea Radin, chief of the Welfare and Repatriation Division at UNRRA in Washington. As she pointed out, the Nazis brought to Germany and Austria from the occupied territories almost all the foreigners in those countries. Many were exiles from their original countries and unable to claim permanent residence in any country. Showing the last country of residence for this particular group might lead to considerable confusion. A similar dilemma arose when dealing with Jews who were listed as undetermined, because it was equally difficult to establish what was their permanent residence. Many had moved through several countries over the course of the Nazi regime, and so using their last place of residence as a substitute for citizenship obscured the reality of the forced nature of their displacement.[85] Nor did it take into consideration those born in Germany to foreign parents.

Second was the growing preference to use citizenship as the definition of nationality, rather than using ethnicity. By late 1948, the IRO was instructing the field to break down the number of displaced persons in the centres by nationality. However, these instructions explicitly equated nationality with citizenship: "The use of the term 'national' in UNRRA resolutions is equivalent to the term 'citizen' in American practice, i.e., country of citizenship and nationality are synonymous, both refer to a legal claim upon a country. Under 'nationality' racial or religious groups should not be reported; Jews should be reported under the country of which they claim citizenship." "Former" nationals of Estonia, Latvia, and Lithuania were to be reported separately "until further notice." The field workers were also instructed to report separately "other persons who have been obliged to leave their country or place of origin or former residence, or who have been deported therefrom, by action of the enemy, because of race, religion or activities in favor of the United Nations." As well, the stateless were to be reported separately, but limited to those with Nansen passports or for whom it has proven "beyond all possible doubt" that the individual cannot establish a claim to citizenship in any country. By 1948, citizenship had largely trumped ethnicity, at least for the purposes of counting heads.

Citizenship had the benefit of being somewhat easier to determine than ethnicity, theoretically at any rate, and would result in every displaced person having a clear relationship with a state, or at least citizenship would serve to reduce the numbers of displaced persons without such a link. Citizenship did not, however, resolve the tensions that arose when nationalities (read: ethnicities) were denied recognition and, thus, legitimacy.

The final category in USFET's November 1945 directive on determining nationality pertained to those who remained impossible to classify or who fell outside of any of the categories prescribed. These were the doubtful or undetermined (the two terms were used interchangeably) – either the unidentifiable (not an unusual condition among unaccompanied children) or the displaced persons who refused to admit to a nationality that was recognized by UNRRA and the American Military

Government (Ukrainian being a common example). This was the category to which all the questionable cases were assigned, and it quickly became an impossible hodge-podge and a particularly problematic category for the authorities, as the options for this particular subgroup's disposition were not obvious. Its existence effectively represented the inconsistencies and flaws in the understanding of nationality and citizenship – and the distinction between the two, no matter how much the authorities wanted to ignore such a distinction.

Observations

The conflation of ethnicity and citizenship in the term "nationality" as it was then used (or abused) resulted in, at first glance, a confusing and inconsistent categorization of the displaced persons, with important consequences for unaccompanied children. Nationality was used to denote everything from ethnicity to citizenship, making the term useless for those attempting to classify individuals in any consistent or rigorous way, but tremendously useful for those (e.g., governments) wishing to classify individuals in a manner that suited their own purposes (e.g., to exclude or include specific individuals or groups). A closer look, however, reveals something of a pattern in the prioritization of determinants that is revealing. The net effect was to allow governments to sort the displaced persons according to domestic priorities, selecting those they preferred to have return to their homelands, and creating an opportunity to reject those deemed unsuitable for either ethnic or political reasons. It facilitated an impressive project of recategorizing a subset of national populations within the displaced persons population as a whole, a part of the bigger project of purging happening among a number of Eastern European populations who had not been displaced, resulting in the reconfiguration of national populations along both ethnic and political lines.

The first filter appears to have been whether a national government recognized a displaced person as its citizen. This should have been a straightforward exercise but, as we have seen, it was anything but that. Aside from the pervasive problem of individuals lacking sufficient documentary evidence to demonstrate their citizenship status, the fluid situation of the immediate postwar years, especially the shifting borders, and the lack of clarity surrounding the term "nationality" permitted certain governments to redefine or recalibrate the criteria for inclusion in their national communities and, in so doing, purge their citizenry of those no longer considered acceptable. The drive to reclaim citizens from within the displaced persons population generally, and from among the unaccompanied children specifically, competed with a simultaneous desire to ethnically cleanse those same citizenries. Yugoslavians were Yugoslavian citizens, unless they were Volksdeutsche, which meant the Yugoslavian government now deemed them to be German citizens. Poles were considered Polish citizens, unless they were Ukrainian, in which case the Polish government deemed them Soviet citizens or, if found to be Volksdeutsche, then German citizens. Displaced persons from the Baltic republics were now technically Soviet citizens and, if they voluntarily opted to adopt that citizenship, were allowed to do so; however, if they objected to such a reclassification, they were not considered Soviet, but instead were categorized as Latvian, Lithuanian, and Estonian (by the Military Government, UNRRA, and the IRO, in this instance) – categories now considered nationalities (read: ethnicities), but not citizenships. Their actual citizenship, it should be noted, remained unclear. Ukrainians were not allowed the Baltic displaced persons' luxury of choice until a late reprieve, but for much of the period in question, were considered to be Soviet citizens, although not forced to repatriate. In the end, because they would not be forced to repatriate, Ukrainian became a category of classification and a recognized nationality, but importantly not a category of citizenship. For the stateless, the pressure was strong to determine an individual's citizenship, in an effort to winnow the ranks of what promised to be a category of displaced persons whose legal status would continue to be ambiguous and precarious.

In the process used to sort the displaced persons that emerged over time, priority went to the state. The individual state made the first determination through its agents, the national liaison officers, and it was a determination of citizenship, although termed nationality. In the process of confirming (or denying) citizenship in the first instance, ethnicity could then come into play, a reflection of a widespread desire to more narrowly restrict citizenship to an ethnically homogeneous population. A displaced person might be considered Yugoslavian at first glance, for example, and that individual may have enjoyed Yugoslavian citizenship prior to the war, but then may well lose it if deemed subsequently to be Volksdeutsche. Instead, that displaced person might gain German citizenship. In the case of Polish Ukrainian displaced persons, they lost their Polish citizenship and gained Soviet citizenship, with Ukrainian ultimately being recognized as a nationality category.

This was small consolation for the Ukrainian displaced persons, who struggled to assert their ethnic identity in a world determined to ascribe to them an internationally recognized non-Ukrainian citizenship. For Polish displaced persons, they were deemed Polish citizens in the first instance (whether from west or east of the Curzon Line), unless they were of Ukrainian or German ethnicity, in which case they gained either Soviet or German citizenship.

In every instance, the drive on the part of UNRRA and the IRO was to ensure that each displaced person had citizenship in some country, and so ensuring each had a state responsible for him or her. Pressure was applied to determine citizenship, if not ethnicity, for even those displaced persons who fell into the category of stateless. The impetus to provide what could be construed legal security, a legal identity, had become paramount and trumped ethnicity in most instances. Even where some individuals' ethnicity cost them their pre-war citizenship, concerted efforts (and often contortions) were made to arrange an alternate citizenship for them. "Stateless" was considered to be a very undesirable condition in a world that increasingly required every person to have a clear, unambiguous legal identity that, for example, could be embodied in a passport. All individuals had to have a state responsible for them, their care, and their actions.

The one exception to this rule was Jewish displaced persons. This particular group of displaced persons were allowed to choose for themselves between their pre-war citizenship and their new ethnicity, a recognition of the horrific treatment they had endured at the hands of the Nazis, of the way in which their new identity as Jews, separate from any citizenship, had become effectively a new ethnicity, and a reflection of the continuing, latent anti-Semitism in Europe. For those national governments whose Jewish population rejected their pre-war citizenship, this appeared to solve the problem of reintegrating the Jewish displaced persons. Instead, it was an easy "out" – if a Jewish displaced person refused to resume his or her pre-war citizenship, then that state was no longer responsible for that displaced person, nor would the displaced person return to his or her prewar homeland. Note that the assumption made by all, both Jewish and non-Jewish, was that the Jewish displaced persons who denied their pre-war citizenship would resettle elsewhere, very likely outside of Europe, and quite probably in Palestine – whatever the British felt about it. Indeed, the movement of Jews, whether displaced persons or infiltrees, through the US Zone and on to Palestine was facilitated by everyone involved with the displaced persons. This was one group whose resettlement off the European continent was not contested by anyone, save the British government – who did not want their Mandate in the Middle East to be destabilized by a flood of illegal Jewish immigrants.

The second filter was what one might term "political reliability." For the newly established Communist regimes, it was important that the returning displaced persons be of the "right" political frame of mind, that is, sympathetic to the new regimes. Those displaced persons who demonstrated hostility towards the new regimes in the Eastern bloc were not welcome to return (with the initial exception of Soviet displaced persons, who were forced to repatriate in the first months after the war's end, but whose forced repatriation soon ended). Even children, who were generally considered malleable and therefore presumably ideal candidates for repatriation, as they could be re-educated into becoming good and loyal citizens, were not welcome if they were old enough to have formed opinions hostile to their putative national governments. If a child was anti-Communist, the liaison officer's inclination was to not require its repatriation. Note here that being politically unreliable did not lose displaced persons their citizenship nor did it cost them their ethnicity, it just lost them the opportunity to repatriate. Non-German Yugoslavians did not lose their Yugoslavian ethnicity, but they did lose their citizenship if they refused to repatriate. This was confusing enough in a world that required every individual to have a legal identity linked to a national state, but unaccompanied children found themselves in an even worse position if they were determined to be politically unreliable. Polish children remained Polish citizens, but persona non grata – so not encouraged to repatriate – but still able to be held hostage by their liaison officers. The debate over nationality determination was further complicated by this extra layer of concern, namely, that of an individual's (including a child's) political reliability. The combination of these different factors meant that liaison officers held inordinate power over the fate of a displaced person, and especially that of an unaccompanied child, a fate that was never a certainty. Again, priority went to the state.

These national governments also could, and did, use these children (whether they actually wanted them returned or not) as fodder in the escalating propaganda war between East and West. There was clearly much political capital to be made by the various Eastern bloc countries out of the West's apparent failure to locate and repatriate "their" children, both internationally and domestically. As relations between East and West deteriorated through 1945 and 1946, Eastern European criticism of the Western Allies' and UNRRA's failure to restore the Eastern European children to their families and homelands was a common theme in a battle waged both in the international press, and as importantly, in the various countries' domestic press. It was an issue that apparently played particularly well for domestic consumption, as the Cold War escalated. Major General Prawin, minister plenipotentiary and chief of the Polish Military Mission, stated bluntly in one of his many letters of complaint (as did similarly placed representatives from the other Eastern European governments), that what had been three years' of tracing at the moment of this particular missive had yielded "strikingly poor" results, with only a few score Polish children being repatriated, of the tens of thousands of Poles estimated to be remaining in the US Zone alone. Prawin condemned the inefficiency of the tracing methods, the obstructiveness of the German institutions and individuals, and he warned of the "voices of thousands of mothers expecting ... something essential be done to ... give them back their babies."[86] This became the dominant narrative in the Eastern European press and in Eastern European condemnation of UNRRA and IRO operations through diplomatic channels. As a weapon of the Cold War, the perceived failure of the child search operations was too powerful to not mobilize, made possible by the privileging of the various state governments in the decision-making process surrounding the disposition of unaccompanied children and by the lack of clarity surrounding the idea of nationality.

It would be a mistake, however, to say that citizenship trumped nationality (read: ethnicity) in the debate over identity, which at first glance, might be the inclination. To say this would be to ignore the extraordinary treatment of Jewish displaced persons, who were given the choice to reject their citizenship as an identity and instead to opt for a newly created one, an ersatz nationality, that of "Jewish" – a category that came without citizenship and did not really reflect a true ethnic identity in the then-accepted sense. It would belie the decision to deny the pre-war citizenship of the Volksdeutsche and instead to impose a German identity, and presumably citizenship, on these children. It would fail to recognize that political reliability could trump both citizenship and ethnicity. Instead, what we have seen is that the confusion over these two concepts – ethnicity and citizenship – created an opportunity for various states to use them interchangeably and to the advantage of their own domestic agendas. The pliability of the term "nationality" simply facilitated this.

The way in which nationality was used flies in the face of a considerable body of literature that has developed over the past decades around the concepts of "nationalism" and "national identity" – what the terms mean, how they take shape, what are their origins, how are they defined. Ironically, none of this theory is of much use in trying to understand how the term "nationality" was used by the various agencies ostensibly trying to determine the unaccompanied displaced persons children's nationalities so that they could be returned "home." Instead, "nationality" was a political tool, a rhetorical device, used by the various agencies involved to achieve their various goals. Ultimately, "nationality" was abandoned in favour of "citizenship" – a legal identity, separate from any "ethnic" identity – although the abandonment was never acknowledged. Occasionally, the two terms were conflated, but only by accident, not design. Instead, while the agencies ultimately settled on a guarantee of citizenship as the criterion for the "establishment" of a child, they continued to assert that they were respecting the national identity of the child. Nationality was a tool, rather than a principle. Nationality also had the effect of codifying national (read: ethnic) identities – rendering some legitimate and others illegitimate (e.g., Polish versus Ukrainian). These decisions would reverberate through the Cold War years and beyond.

The consequences for unaccompanied children were life changing. Although "nationality" may have been very poorly understood at the time, and so could be used to mean a variety of things, "citizenship" meant something very definite. "Citizenship" was well understood, clearly defined in law, and had significant legal implications. The shift to citizenship was crucial for the unaccompanied children, because it determined whether a child would be repatriated to its homeland (whether born there or not), resettled elsewhere (as an immigrant to a country such as Canada, the United States, or Australia), or "established" in West Germany.

Conclusion

When, in early 1946, the decision was made to launch an organized and comprehensive search for unaccompanied children, the expectation was that this would be a straightforward exercise – labour intensive, but straightforward. It was gradually realized, however, that there were possibly thousands of children scattered throughout the German countryside, in German foster homes and institutions, who were potentially United Nations unaccompanied children. Although the prospect became more daunting, the belief was that this would just require the search teams to be more efficient and thorough – that it might take some time, but the actual locating of children would not be difficult. At first, there was tremendous goodwill on the part of the Office of Military Government, United States (OMGUS) and of the United Nations Relief and Rehabilitation Administration (UNRRA), with all agreed that children separated from their families should be reunited with them, if at all possible. With their physical security (food, shelter, and medical care) addressed within the first months of occupation, the focus shifted to the children's emotional security and the need to secure their emotional well-being, which was thought best restored through reuniting children with their families. There was also tremendous sympathy with the demands made by various national governments for the return of "their" children. This fit with the expectations of the Allies that all displaced persons would be repatriated, and it resonated with the child welfare workers' belief that the best possible solution for any unaccompanied children was to restore them to their families, and where that could not be done, to their homeland and culture: The principle shaping child search initially was "reunion if possible, repatriation certainly."

Not many people had a sense of the potential scale of the undertaking or of the complexities that would arise. As it turned out, the pressures shaping and hindering the resolution of the question of unaccompanied children were multiple and complicated due to a plethora of obstacles. The lack of resources nearly stopped the child search and tracing operations before they even began, and a lack of resources continued to plague the operations until their conclusion in 1952. A persistent shortage of basic supplies like paper, pens, typewriters, billets, office space, and access to telephones, as well as chronic understaffing and a lack of reliable transportation made it exceedingly difficult for child welfare and search officers to do their job effectively and efficiently, especially when the search moved out from the assembly centres and into German institutions and homes. Without paper or a pen or a typewriter, it was not possible to compile a child's file, let alone begin tracing the child's history or family. Without reliable transportation, it was impossible to visit the numerous German institutions and homes in the US Zone of Occupation in order to search for children or to transport them, once they were located. Without adequate contingents of personnel, information uncovered could not be processed or followed up, and uncovered children remained untraced, families not located, files in shambles, and children in limbo.

Once a child was found, trying to determine its identity was onerous. Especially in the case of the youngest, the children themselves often were unable to provide any information about their families or their identity. Few had much in the way of reliable memories and even fewer had documentation, making the compilation of convincing evidence of a child's origins complicated, and often impossible. That many of these children were born and/or raised in Germany, and so spoke only German, made matters even more difficult. Getting beyond the presumption that a particular child was not German and to a definitive identity based on convincing evidence was a tricky, imprecise, and time-consuming exercise.

The international agencies' independence of action doing this work – no matter what their constitutions may have declared – was seriously restricted in two ways. First, both UNRRA and the International Refugee Organization (IRO) were accountable to their General Council. For UNRRA, this comprised a total of forty-four different member countries, spanning the globe; for the IRO, it was a slightly smaller roster as its membership did not include the Communist bloc countries, although the IRO, like UNRRA, was also ultimately responsible to the

United Nations and its councils. This affected the agencies' understanding of their mandates, making them aware of a need to balance the competing, often conflicting demands of their various "bosses." As the Cold
War hardened, this became increasingly difficult. For the IRO, there was
some reprieve from the impact of the Cold War when the Soviet Union
and its satellite states decided not to join it, but those countries nevertheless remained very vocal members of the United Nations General
Assembly and used that as a platform to vilify the IRO and the governments who did participate in that organization.

Second, and of greater significance perhaps, both organizations
were dependent upon and beholden to the occupying authorities in
the Zone of operation. UNRRA's very entry into the field had been
delayed because of the reluctance of the Supreme Headquarters,
Allied Expeditionary Force (SHAEF) to countenance a large, independent, civilian-run international organization operating in its zones, in
all likelihood getting underfoot and creating needless complications.
Even when SHAEF finally invited UNRRA into Germany, if only out
of sheer desperation, its deep distrust of all things civilian meant it
had little sympathy or respect for the nature of UNRRA or its mandate, especially after the first months. SHAEF made it very clear from
the beginning that UNRRA, and later the IRO – under SHAEF's successor, the United States Forces, European Theater (USFET), and then
European Command (EUCOM) – operated in the field on its and the
Military Government's sufferance. UNRRA and the IRO functioned
with their permission, and they were accountable to SHAEF (and its
successors), and then the Military Government in each Zone. They
required formal permission from the military authorities to operate
in the Zone, and were dependent upon the Military Government for
everything from uniforms and billets to messing facilities and transportation. The Military Government provided the camp facilities and
supplied provisions for the displaced persons. The American Military
Government's priority was seldom the displaced persons, certainly
not after early 1946, and it had little appreciation of the challenges
and needs of this diverse population. The result was that UNRRA
and then the IRO continuously functioned with inadequate resources
or support. From the beginning, this was a prickly, often dysfunctional relationship that took the form of a turf war between OMGUS
and UNRRA, then the IRO, with OMGUS deliberately working to
undermine the child search operations specifically. At the same time,
the shared governance structure in the Zone's military occupation

government, with responsibilities split between USFET (then EUCOM) and OMGUS, meant a turf war was almost inevitable, further complicating and undermining child search.

The nature of this relationship with the military authorities not only made challenging the practical implementation of the agencies' mandates, but also compromised the agencies' independence of operation, as it meant that the occupation authorities determined the agencies' policy in the Zone and determined the parameters of their work. Because the Allied Control Authority – the quadripartite council created to coordinate policy across the four occupation zones of Germany – was hamstrung by its structure and by the hostility that existed between its members, policy determination defaulted to the various zonal occupation authorities. This meant that the American Military Government determined the policy governing the agencies' operations for the US Zone (or chose to leave it undetermined). Both UNRRA and the IRO were, in practice, very much working for and beholden to the Americans, despite their constitutional structure. Without American cooperation and support, neither could function. As was seen in the dispute over removing children from German homes and institutions, when the American Military Government chose not to support UNRRA, its operations could grind to a standstill. This dependency governed UNRRA's and the IRO's efforts and decision-making at every level and inevitably shaped both, whether it aligned with the broader mandate set by the agency or not.

Second, there were a number of policy issues that threatened to derail the child search operations. Because the occupation authorities refused to rule on key issues, the re-establishment of unaccompanied children was further complicated. It was unclear how to deal with illegitimate children, as well as those who had been or promised to be abandoned by their parents. It was unclear if a child could be adopted and, if it could, by whom. The question of the age of majority was never resolved formally: at what age could a child participate in the decisions made about its future or veto a decision made on its behalf? Crucially, the Military Government refused to address the matter of guardianship. Without a legal guardian, these children had no one to speak for them or to make decisions on their behalf. It was a policy question that UNRRA had pressed continually, to no avail. The Military Government's refusal to make a determination and UNRRA's (and then the IRO's) reluctance to assume that responsibility because of the temporary nature of these organizations, meant that the default became the national liaison officers – and this was not a foolproof solution, as has been seen. This meant that not all children had a guardian, and that many had a guardian whom they did not want. Underlying these policy conundrums was the issue of nationality, whatever that term meant to its user: if a child's nationality could not be determined, or if the child was of a nationality that had no liaison officer representing it, the child fell through the cracks, trapped in the system, sometimes for years.

With time, the list of different parties interested in the children grew, just as the agendas of these various parties diverged, creating additional complications. The increasing reluctance on the part of the American Military Government to permit the removal of any child whose nationality was not definitive was fed by a mounting and effective campaign against removal waged both by the German authorities and the German population generally. The impact was to effectively shut down the child search and tracing operations at a critical juncture by denying the child welfare and search officers access to the children and to their records, such as they were. It was an ongoing battle between UNRRA, on the one hand, and the American and German authorities, on the other, culminating in the lengthy battle over a proposed ACA directive, which would have resolved the problem of the remaining unaccompanied children by deeming German all those children whose nationality was not clear. Lobbying by the IRO, international pressure, especially from the Eastern European countries, a belated trial in the war crimes trials, and a change of heart on the part of the Landesjugendamt, which was concerned about the questionable informal fostering arrangements struck during the war, finally brought about the Limited Registration Plan (Recovery Program) – one last effort to locate and identify all remaining unaccompanied United Nations children before the IRO closed its doors forever. Even with that effort, several hundred children remained whose ultimate fate was unclear, as resettlement options evaporated and their identities remained uncertain. The Children's Court, set up by this plan, went some way to settling the disputes between the IRO, the German families and Landesjugendamt, and the Military Government over what was the appropriate resolution for these children, but even with the court's establishment, the process remained cumbersome, acrimonious, and slow. Nor did all of the remaining children's cases go through the court. There remained some children, primarily the physically and mentally challenged, whose cases were resolved outside the court system. These were children who were never going to leave Germany. Instead, the solution ultimately settled upon was to move them into German institutional care.

Over the course of the seven years, 1945 to 1952, when the last of the unaccompanied children were "established," each of the interested parties' understanding of what they believed was in the children's best interests evolved. UNRRA's initial mandate vis-à-vis all unaccompanied children was to locate and identify them, reunite them with their families if possible, and if not, repatriate them to their homelands. This was in keeping with the social welfare principles that dominated the profession of social work in the United States at the time, and so was considered best practice. It was believed that this was the best way to ensure a child's physical security (its physical health and well-being) and its emotional security (its psychological and emotional well-being). A child was best raised in the bosom of a loving family, ideally by its mother, rather than in an institution, no matter how good the child's current home.

This belief dovetailed neatly with the demands of the governments of Eastern Europe, which maintained that thousands of their children had been kidnapped by the Nazis as part of the Lebensborn program, taken as forced labourers, or been born to forced labourers. They insisted that UNRRA must locate "their" children as quickly as possible and return them home. To do otherwise was unacceptable, as it would mean that Germany had really won the war. By keeping the children, it would be Germany who would benefit from this future labour force.

OMGUS was initially sympathetic to the desire to reunite the children with their families or their homeland, but its enthusiasm for the search for unaccompanied children quickly waned. The primary objective of OMGUS became to resolve the broader displaced persons question as quickly as possible, which entailed re-establishing them permanently, including the children, so that the displaced persons camps could be closed. Having assumed initially that all displaced persons would return home within a matter of months after the Second World War in Europe came to an end, OMGUS was flummoxed, then increasingly frustrated, by the continued presence of a remnant of hard-core displaced persons who either would not or could not go home. Displaced persons camps were costly affairs, paid for by the Military Government. OMGUS was concerned that the remaining displaced persons seemed to have settled into the displaced persons camps permanently with little inclination to move on any time soon. The Military Government was also increasingly frustrated with the displaced persons' refusal to integrate into German society and, from its perspective, assume responsibility for themselves and their future, preferring to live at the American government's expense. This concern over the rising and ongoing cost of maintaining the remnant displaced persons population shaped OMGUS's reaction to the child search operations. The American Military Government became concerned as the number of children whose nationality could not be definitively determined grew. As it was unclear what exactly was to be done with them, OMGUS feared these children would turn into a long-term liability. Instead, it proposed that as long as a child was healthy, happy, and well-cared-for, it should be left where it was, even if that was a German institution or home. And it proposed that these children be "presumed to be German," which would have solved its problem – but which horrified UNRRA.

The Military Government was also preoccupied with the vastly larger number of German expellees flooding into Germany, the result of the wave of ethnic cleansing that swept the Eastern bloc countries in the immediate postwar period. These refugees threatened to destabilize an already shaky economy and society and were a greater concern for the occupiers. This became a far more pressing issue for the occupation authorities, and the displaced persons question – including child search – slipped down the list of priorities.

Third, the occupiers were more concerned with fostering a new and democratic German state than with the pursuit of social justice for unaccompanied children, and they saw an opportunity to provide an object lesson in the rule of democracy and of law in the confrontations over the removal of children from German foster homes and institutions. In the battle between the Landesjugendamt and UNRRA (then the IRO) over the removal of children from German foster homes and institutions, and in the groundswell of opposition on the part of the German population, OMGUS saw an opportunity to provide a lesson in democracy for the German population and government.

Finally, there was the vexing issue of space. The displaced persons, both adult and child, were in accommodations that the American military forces wished for themselves. At the same time that the displaced persons question was plaguing the Military Government, West Germany was emerging as a key bulwark in the emerging Cold War. Under the auspices of the new North Atlantic Treaty Organization, the American government had pledged to maintain a military presence on the European continent, including in West Germany. This would necessitate the allocation of space and buildings for permanent military bases. The displaced persons, housed in large camps often numbering in the thousands, were taking up space considered ideal for conversion into military barracks. This need for space put the American military in direct conflict with the needs of the displaced persons.

For its part, while the Landesjugendamt had no objection to UNRRA or the IRO assuming responsibility for all United Nations children in German care, if just as a way of alleviating its financial obligations, it was also determined that neither UNRRA nor the IRO take any children it thought were German. Moreover, the Landesjugendamt was not convinced that UNRRA was doing an adequate job of determining the children's nationality before removing them. The Landesjugendamt, and the German press and population at large, became increasingly vocal in their objections to removals they considered suspect. Rather than allow UNRRA to act unilaterally, OMGUS chose to give the German families, institutions, and Landesjugendamt a voice in the decision-making process – as an object lesson in democracy and the rule of law. If this meant leaving children whose nationality was not certain in German foster homes and institutions, and if this meant further complicating (and thus dragging out) the decision-making process by involving even more interested parties in it, so be it. OMGUS considered this an acceptable cost.

By 1947, for their part, UNRRA's and then the IRO's understanding of their priorities had shifted significantly, in part because of the threat made by OMGUS both to shut down the child search operations and to leave many of the children in Germany. Increasingly, their chief concern became the legal status of such children. If United Nations children were simply left with their German foster families or in German institutions, and no arrangements were made to establish a legal identity for them, such as through adoption, then these children would face serious legal discrimination when they reached adulthood. If not granted citizenship of some country, they had no legal identity – they were legal non-persons. Presuming them to be German, as OMGUS was blithely willing to do, carried no legal weight. Nor could OMGUS direct the German state to assume responsibility for these children. As an independent sovereign state, Germany could only be asked to do so, and it could refuse. By this time, the IRO, like UNRRA before it, had become as concerned about the children's legal security as it was about their physical and emotional security. This explains the IRO's push to resettle as many of the children as possible, as the German government was reluctant to commit to granting any of them citizenship.

At the heart of much of this exceedingly acrimonious and multifaceted debate over the disposition of the unaccompanied children was the issue of determining nationality. Even with documentation, a child's nationality was not always obvious given the shifts in borders and thus citizenship in Central Europe and the privileging of certain ethnicities over others, certain ethnicities over citizenship, certain citizenships over ethnicity, and not uncommonly, political reliability over both ethnicity and citizenship. Nor was the concept of nationality well understood. "Nationality" was a very pliable term at the time, being mobilized for a variety of purposes, few of which had little to do with ethnicity, the closest approximation of the term's use in the theory. Just as it was sometimes unclear what the right classification should be for adult displaced persons, so it was for the unaccompanied children. However, matters were made that much more complicated for unaccompanied children, as they needed the approval of a national liaison officer before they could be determined to be of a particular nationality. That final determination of nationality (read: citizenship, as no ethnicity that did not equate to some recognized citizenship status was granted a liaison officer to represent it, with the exception of "Jewish") was ultimately, then, the decision of the liaison officer who often based his decision as much on political imperatives as on the evidence in a child's file. If a child was reluctant to return, and especially if the child was obviously anti-Communist (as most came from Eastern Europe), its putative nationality could be and most commonly was denied, leaving the various international agencies in a bind. If the child was not that nationality for political reasons, what then was its nationality (read: citizenship)? International law made no accommodation for this situation, now that Nansen passports were out of use. And for those unaccompanied children for whom there was no liaison officer, because their nationality (read: citizenship) had not been recognized internationally – like the Ukrainians and the Balts – it meant little could be done to resolve their disposition.

The unaccompanied Volksdeutsche children were a special example of this dilemma. Born citizens of a country other than Germany, but of German ethnicity, it was initially unclear whether these children were the responsibility of UNRRA (or the IRO), or what their disposition should be – which took priority: citizenship or ethnicity? The question was never adequately resolved, and these children proved the most difficult cases to settle. It was largely Volksdeutsche children whose case files remained open into the late 1940s and even early 1950s, as the various agencies involved quarrelled over their nationality and the appropriate resolution for their situations.

The long and acrimonious debate over how to handle the remnant population was fodder for the Eastern European propaganda machine. As has been made clear, although the Eastern European governments did not want all their children back, they did make much of UNRRA's (and the IRO's) failure to find and return their children, and used that apparent failure to embarrass the Western occupying powers to great effect.

But there was more feeding this public anger over the failure to have the children returned than the delight of having discovered a way to truly embarrass the new enemy. There was also a very real desire to get "their" children (the non-German children) back. This had been evident as early as the first months after the war ended, when the Polish Red Cross sent representatives into Germany to locate Polish children who had been kidnapped by the Lebensborn program, independent of both UNRRA and SHAEF. The Polish Red Cross considered it a travesty that Polish children might remain in German families or institutions any longer than absolutely necessary – every day left there eroding their links to their homeland: their language, religion, and national identity – and becoming more and more German. This was, they argued, a humanitarian disaster. It was also a very real national disaster, as the children represented their country's future, both its future labour force and its future citizenry and key to the nation's future prosperity. This sentiment was shared by others, notably, Yugoslavia, Czechoslvakia, and the Soviet Union. For countries that had been physically devastated by the Nazi occupation, it was thought crucial to get back every individual person who might be able to contribute to rebuilding their country, either immediately or in the future. For a country that had seen its population decimated by the war and occupation, every citizen it could regain was crucial to the country's future strength and well-being. Thus, there was the drive to regain the children. From the very beginning, and well before one can speak of a cold war, the various Eastern European governments – Polish, Soviet, Yugoslavian, Czechoslovakian – were pressing both UNRRA, and later the IRO, to locate "their" children and return them to their families and homelands as soon as possible.

The desire to get "their" children back was also a reflection of a longstanding belief that children were the "collective property" of the state, to borrow Tara Zahra's evocative turn of phrase.[1] This notion both that a nation's children were of value to the state and that children were in some way the property of the state was one that had been taking shape since the mid-nineteenth century. Perhaps the first manifestation of the state's recognition of children and youth as requiring its special attention and protection came in the mid-nineteenth century with a drive led by middle-class reformers to protect children employed in mills and factories – the child welfare movement, which resulted in the first labour laws in Europe. These laws, a result of middle-class outrage at the horrific conditions in which working-class children were forced to labour, were passed to prevent the gross exploitation of those children.

By the late nineteenth century, most European states had also realized the necessity of creating a state-run secular education system in order to educate their nations' children both as future workers (who needed at least the rudiments of reading, writing, and arithmetic in order to function as fully contributing workers in what were rapidly industrializing economies) and as future voters. Now that the franchise had expanded greatly in many parts of the European continent, and much larger swathes of at least the adult male population had the vote, children and their education became very important – to make them effective workers, but also to teach them how to exercise their newfound electoral responsibilities appropriately. This could not be left to happenstance. Instead, this future electorate needed to be properly moulded – taught duty, punctuality, discipline, respect for authority, and patriotism. As well as literacy and numeracy, these future voters needed to be taught to be good and loyal citizens. By the last decade of the nineteenth century, most European states had compulsory state-run primary education.

Finally, in the nationally "ambiguous" Central European territories, where nationalities commingled and intermarried, and where national boundaries and ethnic divisions did not align, and where, as so ably demonstrated by Tara Zahra, national identities were worn lightly, if at all, children became important weapons in the battle to establish the legitimacy of national identities – manifested first and foremost through a battle fought through the state-sponsored and -administered education system. By the turn of the twentieth century, most states of Europe had recognized children as an important form of economic and political capital and had asserted considerable state control over key aspects of their lives, ostensibly for the protection of the children, but as much for the advantage of the state.

Throughout the first half of the twentieth century, the importance of children to the European states continued to grow. Almost uniformly, concerns mounted over a marked and almost universal decline in birth rates. Not only did this threaten the national economies, it threatened the nations' military strength. The result was a raft of social welfare programs, centring on systems of family allowances intended to encourage families to have more children by offering financial incentives. At the same time, there was a growing concern about the underemployment of male youth and a perceived rise in juvenile delinquency, and the threat this posed to social stability and the moral order. This was linked closely by contemporaries to a perceived breakdown in the family, which nonetheless continued to be understood to be the cornerstone of social stability. In most parts of Europe, the philanthropic and religious resources that had previously attempted to address this moral threat were no longer considered adequate. As a result, a welter of state-sponsored institutional responses was constructed in order to re-educate and thus salvage these wayward youth (at a time when every child was needed) in order to preserve the nation's moral health, as well as to rescue the family.

By the end of the First World War, the loss of human capital – in terms of both the mind-numbing death tolls and the lives maimed both physically and psychologically – meant that the European states' concern about both the quantity and quality of their children was exacerbated. The massive recruiting of the war years had made clear to all, as well, the poor physical condition of the working-class populations of Europe. In the interwar years, the states' drive to protect, nurture, and promote the birth of Europe's children continued even more strongly. With the rising threat of another war, children became increasingly important as a matter of state security.

The rise of fascist and quasi-fascist regimes across Europe resulted in even more state resources being focused on this segment of the population. Children and youth were not only the future of the national economy. For the new regimes whose ultimate goal was to construct a new fascist society, children and youth were key recruits to their cause – they would be the future of the new fascist states. These states used monolithic youth organizations to usurp parental control over their children, appropriating it for themselves. By the end of the Second World War, it was a commonplace that the state had a strong claim to "its" children and a vested interest in their upbringing and future, equal to and sometimes surpassing that of the children's parents. It was also a commonplace that the parents' rights over their children could and would be superceded by those of the state, if deemed necessary as a matter of the state's security.[2] Thus, by 1945, the state's collective right to its children, indeed as Zahra argues, the idea that children were a form of "national property," was well entrenched, even normative. This gave legitimacy to the Eastern European states' claims to "their" children in the postwar period.

Denying a child to a state would be difficult to justify. The American Military Government and at least one of the guardians ad litem of the Children's Court made the argument that it was better to leave the children in Germany, even if they were not German, than to return them to a Communist-controlled state. But this was an argument that was made only informally, never in a court or public forum. Instead, the children's anti-Communist sentiments were used as justification for a decision not to repatriate them. Making it the children's choice whether to repatriate or not appeared to take the matter out of the hands of the occupying powers, when the outcome was patently clear to all – the children seldom hid their hatred of all things Communist. Making it the children's decision was very different from one state denying another its children. In other instances, the Western powers paid lip service to the principle of a state's right to its children, but then quietly worked around it to resettle the children, rather than repatriate them.[3]

Note that this did not mean a state could not reject a child identified as one of its own. In spite of the apparently desperate determination to get back "their" children, there were some children some states were willing to leave in Germany, namely, the politically unreliable and the Volksdeutsche. While the Eastern European countries ostensibly wanted all their children back, in reality they did not want political rebels and they did not want the ethnically incompatible. In both instances, time and again, when a liaison officer was confronted with such a child, he prevaricated, flatly denied the child, or worse still, refused to make a decision as to a child's nationality or disposition. This did not prevent those governments from using the children's failure to repatriate as a rhetorical cudgel with which to batter the Western powers, nor did it mean that they cooperated in the pursuit of an alternative solution to the children's plight. Rather, the Eastern European states also often proved quite obstructionist, refusing to repatriate children, but also refusing to sign off on an alternative solution, leaving the children mired in the displaced persons centres in Germany.

The system for determining the fate of the children that had emerged by default, for lack of more proactive policymaking on the part of the occupation authorities, had resulted in this impasse. Allowing the

liaison officers to become the children's guardians and thus responsible for both the final determination of their nationality, as well as
their disposition, gave the Eastern European liaison officers and their
governments tremendous power to obstruct the successful resolution
of the children's cases. By so doing, they were able to create considerable difficulty and some embarrassment for the occupiers, as well as
for the international agencies dealing with the children. It meant that
these children were forced to remain in the children's centres until they
reached an age at which they entered adulthood or until the Military
Government decided to ignore or circumvent the liaison officers. The
thwarted ACA directive – the objective of which would have been to
simply leave children in German institutions and foster homes and
deem them to be German – was one such attempt to break free of this
Gordian knot. The Children's Court was another vehicle for doing so,
as was settling the last remaining children in Germany permanently.
The effective, if belated assumption of the role of guardian for Baltic
and Ukrainian children by EUCOM was yet another "work-around."
All of these tactics were responses to the worsening relations between
East and West, with the unaccompanied children caught in the middle
of the fight. Each side argued that its solution – repatriation, from the
perspective of the Eastern bloc countries; resettlement or establishment
in Germany, from the perspective of the Americans – was supposedly
in the children's best interests. In reality, each camp's solution was in its
own best interests, and not clearly in the children's, and it left the children vulnerable to the vagaries of both the liaison officers and the Cold
War. In this situation, the international agencies' objective and sense of
what was in the children's interests changed over time from ensuring
the children's physical security (their physical health and well-being)
and their emotional security (best achieved through family reunion) to
establishing the children's national identity, and thereby ensuring their
legal security.

This goal was made more difficult by the numerous older children
who refused to repatriate and whom the agencies and the Military Government would not force to repatriate. It was further undermined by
the case of the unaccompanied children whose nationality could not
be determined. To repeat a point, the Military Government, fearful that
it would prove impossible to find a solution for this group (although
small in number, threatening to grow in size), pushed to leave them in
place in Germany, wanting to deem them to be German – a solution
with no legal validity. The authorities also fought hard to shut down

the child search operations, if just to prevent the uncovering of more children of undeterminable nationality. Crucially, this was the battle that convinced UNRRA that the children's legal security needed to be a primary consideration when deciding on the disposition of the children. This shift in thinking had been taking shape over time, but the battle over the doomed ACA directive crystallized it. The fear was that if the children were simply left where they were in Germany without being given a legal identity in the form of citizenship, or some other legal resident status, their future would be seriously compromised, especially upon reaching adulthood. Without being granted citizenship somewhere, these children would be legal non-persons, with no state assuming responsibility for them and no state to act on their behalf. They would be subject to the whims of the humanitarian instincts of whichever state in which they resided, with no protections. This was an unacceptable solution, and resulted in both UNRRA and the IRO concluding that the children's legal security must be the key priority. Thus came their drive to resettle as many of the children as possible, as there was no assurance that any remaining in Germany would be granted any form of legal status in that country. The goal was to gain citizenship or some form of legal status in some country for each of the remaining children and, in so doing, secure their future.

In a world in which, since the French Revolution, the state had become increasingly institutionalized, to paraphrase John Torpey, it was essential that the unaccompanied United Nations unaccompanied children be given an identity recognized by governments.[4] Since the French Revolution, as Torpey and others have argued, the state in Europe has grown larger and more "administratively adept," its bureaucratic infrastructure expanding with the growth of a network of institutions which is its physical, tangible manifestation. At the same time, and feeding this intensification of administrative infrastructure, was a desire on the part of the state to assert ever greater control over its population, in order to better extract resources from it, be it in the form of military service, taxes, or labour; to facilitate law enforcement; to exclude, surveil, and contain undesirables; or to supervise the growth, distribution, and composition of populations within its borders.[5] To do this, a state needed to be able to effectively distinguish between its citizens (from whom it could legitimately claim resources) and non-citizens (whom it may well wish to exclude from its territory, or whose freedom while in its territory it may well wish to restrict). This required registration – as one otherwise could not discern a person's nationality – epitomized by the passport. In the late nineteenth century, this interest on the part of European states in registering their population was further driven by economic crises, which demanded control over the flow of labour, by a perceived need to identify who among a state's residents was eligible for military service as the threat of war grew, and by questions of who qualified for access to the new state-funded social welfare programs that were being established. This trend continued over the course of the first half of the twentieth century, under the pressure of the two world wars, which bred a growing fear of espionage and of possible fifth columns. The desire to control individual entry into a state's territory mounted, and states became increasingly determined to establish a "monopoly over the legitimate means of movement,"[6] that is, to claim for the states exclusive control over which types of persons would be permitted to move within or across their borders, and how, when, and where they would be permitted to do so. Passports and other forms of government-sanctioned identity documents were central to this effort. By the mid-twentieth century, the European states (and most Western states) had constructed effective and pervasive bureaucracies to do just that – to manage a regime of identification, both its production and its scrutiny.[7] As Torpey aptly put it, "Once it is possible for everyone to have a document, then it can become a requirement."[8]

With that documentation, individuals were given an "identity," one recognized by the state. That identification with a particular state did several things. It gave the state the right to extract resources from the individual. It guaranteed the individual certain rights, privileges, protections, and supports from that state, both within and outside of the state's physical borders, that were not available to non-citizens. It also, and the passport was central to this, gave the state a monopoly over the legitimate means of movement (which is why, today, we can have illegal migration, a concept that would have made no sense in the nineteenth century[9]). In this process, too, Benedict Anderson's "imagined communities" were codified and institutionalized, anchored in law and in policy.[10] At the same time that the state was defining its membership (and simultaneously determining who would not be a member), it was also constructing a national identity.[11] By denying membership to some and extending it to others, the state articulated the parameters of its "imagined community," made it concrete, and took an important step towards articulating its particular national identity. At this point, it was now possible to restrict access to state resources (e.g., social welfare, education, and health care) to the state's members only. It thus invited, even required, categorization of and differentiation of treatment between various residents in the state's territory.

The aftermath of the First World War highlighted the flaws inherent in this system of universal registration and mutually exclusive citizenries. There were many individuals, beginning with the Russian refugees fleeing the Russian civil war (known as "White Russians"), but quickly followed by others, who had no state, or more accurately, who had had their citizenship revoked by their putative government, rendering them literally "stateless" (another term that would have made no sense in the early nineteenth century). These were people whose plight was, in the words of Hannah Arendt, "not that they [were] not equal before the law, but that no law exist[ed] for them; not that they [were] oppressed but that nobody want[ed] even to oppress them."[12] Denied membership by their pre-war home government, these people fell into an administrative and diplomatic no-man's-land. The new identification regime that had emerged and which required every person to have formal identity documentation made no accommodation for those without identification or whose identification had been revoked by their government. The solution in the interwar period was the Nansen passport. Its original purpose was to provide a travel document to White Russians who had had their citizenship revoked by the new Communist regime. In the end, fifty-two countries recognized the document as a legitimate piece of identity. The Nansen passport gave its bearer a form of identification, but crucially, it failed to grant its bearer citizenship in any country, nor did it guarantee either re-entry into the bearer's initial host country or entry into another country. The Nansen passport was a band-aid solution for an intractable problem, created by a world in which every person was expected to be a member of some specific state, and only went some way to solving the very real problem facing these refugees – the lack of a legal identity. The basic premise remained: every individual needed to be a citizen of some country and was expected to have documentation to verify that citizenship. Indeed, the Nansen passport confirmed the premise. The fact that the League of Nations' solution to the dilemma of the Russian refugees was to create a form of travel and identity document and to cajole a total of fifty-two countries into recognizing it as an alternative to a normal passport is testimony to the new norm – that everyone needed some such form of identification.

It was in this context, a world in which every individual was expected to have a state that claimed him or her as theirs and in which every individual was expected to have a formal, legal national identity granted by some state, the unaccompanied children – and especially those of undetermined and undeterminable nationality – posed a serious conundrum. This is why UNRRA, and even more so the IRO, were so determined to ensure that the children had legal standing somewhere. It was a position with which the American Military Government had little sympathy, disinterested in the children's plight as increasingly it had become and inclined as it was to trust the German government's humanitarian instincts. In the grand scheme of things, one might suppose it was thinking that these were only a few hundred children. Amid the sea of refugees, they were not even the proverbial "drop in a bucket." Add to that the fact that the displaced persons question had, by 1949, become a non-issue for the Americans, focused as they were on buttressing Western Europe and especially Germany as a bulwark against the Communist threat on the other side of the Iron Curtain that now sliced through Germany, and one might understand, if not excuse, their wish to be done with the displaced persons and especially the knotty problem of unaccompanied children. The impact of this choice, ultimately, was to give primacy to citizenship over ethnicity, without resolving the question of what to do when citizenship could not be determined or was denied.

What else becomes evident is the vulnerability of the unaccompanied children and their role as pawns in a greater game. While all involved in their care at least paid lip service to the children's personal needs, and especially to their emotional and psychological needs, in the end, politics often seemed to trump the personal, state interests taking primacy over the children's interests. This is made most clear in the cases of those unaccompanied children who remained in the displaced persons centres or children's centres for years, as the various authorities argued over their nationality and disposition – a situation that no one could claim was in the children's best interests, but instead suited the various national governments', as well as the Military Government's particular interests at the time. Because it was unclear exactly what was in the children's "best interests," because this term is a deeply subjective one and culturally constructed, and so decidedly open to debate, everyone involved in the discussion around unaccompanied children – UNRRA, the IRO, OMGUS, the Landesjugendamt, the German people, and the displaced persons themselves – could claim to be acting in the children's "best interests."

The study of unaccompanied children in the US Zone of Occupation in Germany makes clear the complexity of the issue of nationality, both because of the multinational nature of this subset of the displaced persons population and because no decision could be made about a child's fate without first determining the child's nationality. Their very existence forced the issue. The modern concept of nationality was a relatively new one at this point, born in the nineteenth century and given tremendous political force with the settlement of the First World War, through President Woodrow Wilson's famous Fourteen Points and the concept of national self-determination articulated therein. Nationalism and national identity became legitimized as political goals and claims. What actually was meant by the term "national identity" was unclear, however. Indeed, the incredibly rich and ongoing debate among academics over the roots, causes, manifestations, and definition of nationality that has evolved over the decades since is an effective demonstration of the complexity of the concept. Small wonder that no one was especially clear in the 1940s as to what constituted a nationality, and which "nationalities" were truly such.

The complexity was not initially recognized, it should be noted. Instead, it was thought a straightforward way of sorting the displaced persons and especially of determining the disposition of unaccompanied children. The use of liaison officers as de facto guardians seemed an easy solution and indeed it worked for many of the children. Citizenship became the default solution in many instances, based on the assumption that nationality and citizenship obviously aligned. However, for those children whose nationality was not obvious, for those without a liaison officer because their nationality was not recognized as legitimate, for those who denied their putative liaison officer, and for those who were denied by their putative liaison officer the issue became a quagmire. If citizenship was the default, then any individuals whose citizenship was unknown, not recognized, or denied, found themselves adrift, and the authorities found themselves at a loss, or at least UNRRA and the IRO did. What was to be done with a displaced person who was clearly of a particular citizenship (e.g., Polish), but who was denied by the Polish liaison officer? It was not as if that displaced person's file could be taken to another national liaison officer for consideration as a national of that country (e.g., France). It was a bizarre quandary.

Technically, displaced persons were not allowed to self-select their citizenship; only a government could grant or deprive an individual of citizenship. In practice, this was breached regularly, by other governments and even by the displaced persons themselves. The litmus test was the treatment of the unaccompanied children of these various nationalities, as they were legally minors and therefore could not choose for themselves how they wished to be regarded. For example, while adult Baltic displaced persons could choose to be considered Soviet citizens, they also could choose not to be so considered, at which point the American occupation authorities denied the Soviet liaison officers access to them. As a matter of course, Soviet liaison officers were denied access to unaccompanied Baltic children, even though this left these children in administrative limbo. Ultimately, by 1950, five years after the Second World War had ended, the solution was to put these children under EUCOM's authority (with the pro forma action of consulting the Soviet liaison officers on the children's disposition, knowing full well that the Soviets would not be interested in this, by now hostile remnant). Although the occupation authorities never formally or officially articulated these policies, these were the practices put in place.

The challenge came when citizenship and nationality did not align. This was much more common than was anticipated in 1945, in part because of the multi-ethnic nature of Central Europe and in part because of the shifting borders. It had become a much more salient issue by this time, as nationalism had become a potent political force in the twentieth century. Indeed, the very fluidity of the borders at the time encouraged nascent nationalist movements to assert their claims to territory. The widespread ethnic cleansing of the immediate postwar months, as various national governments rounded up and shipped out their ethnic minorities, especially the Volksdeutsche, kept the issue of national identity and its lack of congruency with citizenship at the forefront. Indeed, it highlighted the incongruency, as well as kept alive the issue of nationality and especially that of the privileging of some nationalities over others. The Cold War only served to stoke the flames, as governments, and the occupation authorities used nationality and its denial or enforcement as a weapon in the escalating conflict. Nationality became a weapon in the war between East and West, to be recognized or not as suited the needs of the government doing the recognizing. Throughout this period, nationality and citizenship were confused, sometimes inadvertently, sometimes purposefully, by both the authorities and by the displaced persons themselves. A slippery term, "nationality" was easily manipulated for political purposes, with some claimed nationalities being denied and others acknowledged (even created, as one might plausibly argue in the case of the newly recognized "Jewish" nationality category), as it suited a particular power's political interests. Small wonder that beleaguered field workers and administrators often defaulted to citizenship as a shorthand for nationality, no matter how imperfect a fit it was. Small wonder, too, that various national governments were able to use nationality as a political tool to purge their populations of the racially and politically unacceptable, because the term was so amorphous.

In dealing with unaccompanied children, the two conundrums of certain nationalities not being recognized as legitimate, but for whom the alternatives were politically unpalatable (either for the displaced person or for the national government involved), and of children for whom a nationality simply could not be definitively determined meant that "nationality" became a problem, rather than a solution, for those trying to re-establish the unaccompanied children permanently. Because they were legally minors, the issue of guardianship was a crucial one – who was legally able to speak for them and to make decisions regarding their disposition? If a government would not recognize a child as its national, thus denying that child citizenship; if the occupying authorities did not recognize or denied a government's claim on a child; if a child was hostile to the notion of repatriating to its putative homeland, and therefore would not be repatriated, what was its legal status? If a child's national identity, either ethnic or citizenship, was not determinable, what was its legal status? And in each case, who then spoke for the child, as the child was not legally able to speak for itself? The answer to these questions and to the issue of guardianship, given the reliance on liaison officers and citizenship, was closely, intimately tied to that of nationality determination. These very thorny problems, and the failure to resolve the issue of what constituted "nationality" plagued the efforts to re-establish these unaccompanied children from the beginning of UNRRA's operations in Germany until the end of the IRO's tenure. Increasingly, citizenship became the default measure of a child's nationality, although there remained numerous instances where citizenship was not, could not, be the solution. Yet, at a time when an individual's legal identity was essential for effective functioning in the modern world, the children's legal security – ensured by the establishment and recognition of their citizenship in some country – was seen as crucial, at least by UNRRA and the IRO. Even the occupation authorities, in the battle over the ACA directive, acknowledged this when they decided that children of undetermined nationality would be deemed German, although they failed to consider the ramifications of this particular, awkward, and unworkable solution.

This fundamental dilemma, the inability to conclusively determine the nationality of a certain number of unaccompanied children, resulted in a long, acrimonious, and confused debate over what constituted nationality and how it might be determined. It shone a light on the importance of a legal identity in the twentieth century, and crystallized the competing agendas of the various bodies involved in caring for and determining the disposition of unaccompanied children in postwar West Germany. In that debate, it became apparent both that the notion of nationality was poorly understood and that any abstract principles that might have governed nationality determination were secondary to the political concerns and objectives of those involved in the determination. Instead, primacy was given to the politics of the moment, at the expense of consistency and of principle. In that fractious debate, the children's best interests were regularly invoked, but just exactly what were the best interests of the children was never certain. It was, like most things, a construct, rather than an absolute. The "best interests" of the children were determined by the values, needs, and expectations of the person or entity doing the determining, and these shaped that particular definition of what was considered the appropriate solution for a child bereft of a legal guardian. National interests made children into both the spoils of hot war and the pawns of cold war.

Abbreviations

ACA	Allied Control Authority (also known as Allied Control Council or ACC)
ACC	Allied Control Council (also known as Allied Control Authority); Allied Control Commission
AJDC	American Joint Distribution Committee
BAOR	British Army of the Rhine
BKC	Bavaria Land Commissioner
CAD	Civil Affairs Division or Department
CC	Control Council
CCOS	Combined Chiefs of Staff
CDPX	Combined Displaced Persons Executive
CG	Commanding General(s)
CHQ	Central Headquarters
CO	Commanding Officer
COS	Chief of Staff
CRX	Combined Repatriation Executive
CTB	Central Tracing Bureau
DLEG	Legal Directorate
DPBr	Displaced Persons Branch or Displaced Populations Branch
DPC	Displaced Persons Commission
DPOW	Directorate of Prisoners of War and Displaced Persons
DPs (UNDPs)	Displaced Persons (United Nations Displaced Persons)
DPX	Displaced Persons Executive
EMD	Eastern Military District

ERO	European Regional Office
ETOUSA	European Theater of Operations, United States Army
EUCOM	United States European Command
HIAS	Hebrew Immigrant Aid Society
HICOG	Allied High Commission for Occupied Germany; US High Commissioner for Germany
HQ	Headquarters
IA&CD	Internal Affairs and Communications Division (OMG)
IGCR	Intergovernmental Committee on Refugees, also ICR
IRC	International Red Cross
IRO	International Refugee Organization
ITS	International Tracing Service
JAFP	Jewish Agency for Palestine
JAG	Judge Advocate General
JCS	Joint Chiefs of Staff
JDC	Joint Distribution Committee, i.e., American Joint Distribution Committee
LO	Liaison Officer
MG	Military Government, Military Governor
MGR	Military Government Regulation
NAACP	National Association for the Advancement of Colored People
NCWC	National Catholic Welfare Commission or Conference
NSV	Nationalsozialistische Volkswohlfahrt (the Nazi People's Welfare Organization)
OAG	Office of the Adjutant General
OCS	Office of the Chief of Staff
OGS	Office of General Staff
OLC	Office of the Land Commissioner
OMGB	Office of Military Government, Bavaria (regional level of OMGUS)
OMGUS	Office of Military Government, United States
Ops.	Operations
OSE	Oeuvre de Secours d'Enfants
OWI	Office of War Information
PAD	Political Affairs Division

PCIRO	Preparatory Commission for the International Refugee Organization
POW&DPBr	Prisoners of War and Displaced Persons Branch
RuSHA	Rasse- und Siedlungshauptamt (SS Race and Resettlement Office)
SCAEF	Supreme Commander, Allied Expeditionary Force
SHAEF	Supreme Headquarters, Allied Expeditionary Force
SOS	Secretary of State
UNRRA	United Nations Relief and Rehabilitation Administration
USFET	United States Forces, European Theater
USGCC	US Group Control Council
WMD	Western Military District

Notes

Introduction

1 Liah Greenfeld, *Nationalism: Five Roads to Modernity* (Cambridge MA: Harvard University Press, 1992), 11–13.

2 A variant of this thesis was previously proposed in Lynne Taylor, "'Please Report only *True* Nationalities': The Classification of Displaced Persons in Post–Second World War Germany and Its Implications," in David Cesarani, Suzanne Bardgett, Jessica Reinisch, and Johannes-Dieter Steinert, eds., *Landscapes after Battle*, vol. 1, *Survivors of Nazi Persecution in Europe after the Second World War*, 49–50. (London: Vallentine Mitchell, 2010).

3 E.M. Kulischer, *Europe on the Move: War and Population Changes 1914–47* (New York: Columbia University Press, 1948); J.B. Schechtman, *European Population Transfers, 1939–1945* (New York: Oxford University Press, 1946); Malcolm Proudfoot, *European Refugees, 1939–1952: A Study in Forced Population Movement* (London: Faber and Faber, 1957).

4 Michael R. Marrus, *The Unwanted: European Refugees in the Twentieth Century* (New York: Oxford University Press, 1985).

5 Jessica Reinisch and Elizabeth White, eds., *The Disentanglement of Populations: Migration, Expulsion and Displacement in Post-war Europe, 1944–49* (Basingstoke: Palgrave Macmillan, 2011), xv.

6 See, e.g.: Georges Coudry, "La rapatriement des ressortissants soviétiques de 1945 à 1947: Avatars de la reciprocité," *Guerres mondiales et conflits contemporains* 45/178 (1995): 119–40; W.W. Isajiw, Y. Boshyk, and R. Senkus, eds., *The Refugee Experience: Ukrainian Displaced Persons after World War II* (Edmonton: Canadian Institute of Ukrainian Studies, 1992); Johannes-Dieter Steinert, *Deportation und Zwangsarbeit: Polnische und sowjetische Kinder im nationalsozialistischen Deutschland und im besetzten Osteuropa*

1939–1945 (Essen: Klartext Verlag, 2013); Milda Danys, *DP: Lithuanian Immigration to Canada after the Second World War* (Toronto: Multicultural History Society of Ontario, 1986); Pranas Gaida et al., *Lithuanians in Canada* (Toronto: Lights Printing and Publishing, 1967); Bronis Kaslas, *La Lituanie et la Seconde Guerre mondiale* (Paris: Maisonneuve and Larose, 1981); Antanas Kucas, *Lithuanians in America* (Boston: Encyclopedia Lithuanica Press, 1975); Pamela Ballinger, *History in Exile: Memory and Identity at the Borders of the Balkans* (Princeton, NJ: Princeton University Press, 2003); Yury Boshyk, ed., *Ukraine during World War II: History and Its Aftermath* (Edmonton: Canadian Institute of Ukrainian Studies, 1986); Mark R. Elliott, *Pawns of Yalta: Soviet Refugees and America's Role in Their Repatriation* (Urbana, IL: University of Illinois Press, 1982); Anna D. Jaroszynska-Kirchmann, *The Exile Mission: The Polish Political Diaspora and Polish Americans, 1939–1956* (Athens, OH: Ohio University Press, 2004); Lubomyr Y. Luciuk, *Searching for Place: Ukrainian Displaced Persons, Canada, and the Migration of Memory* (Toronto: University of Toronto Press, 2000); Philippe Ther and Ana Siljak, eds., *Redrawing Nations: Ethnic Cleansing in East-Central Europe, 1944–1948* (Lanham, MD: Rowman and Littlefield, 2001); Ekkehard Völkl, "Ukrainische Emigration in Bayern 1945–1949," in Hermann Beyer-Thoma, ed., *Bayern und Osteuropa: Aus der Geschichte der Beziehungen Bayerns, Frankens und Schwabens mit Russland, der Ukraine und Weissrussland* (Wiesbaden: Harassowitz, 2000).

7 See, e.g.: Angelika Königseder and Juliane Wetzel, translated by John Broadwin, *Waiting for Hope: Jewish Displaced Persons in World War II Germany* (Evanston, IL: Northwestern University Press, 2001); Michael Brenner, *After the Holocaust: Rebuilding Jewish Lives in Postwar Germany* (Princeton NJ: Princeton University Press, 1997); Y. Michal Bodemann, ed., *Jews, Germans, Memory: Reconstructions of Jewish Life in Germany* (Ann Arbor, MI: University of Michigan Press, 1996); Gerard Daniel Cohen, "The Politics of Recognition: Jewish Refugees in Relief Policies and Human Rights Debates, 1945–1950," *Immigrants and Minorities* 24/2 (2006): 125–43; Dan Diner, "Jewish DPs in Historical Context," *Birth of a Refugee Nation: Displaced Persons in Postwar Europe, 1945–1951 – Workshop Draft Papers*, 20–1 Apr. 2001; Leonard Dinnerstein, *America and the Survivors of the Holocaust* (New York: Columbia University Press, 1982); Jay Howard Geller, *Jews in Post-Holocaust Germany, 1945–1953* (Cambridge: Cambridge University Press, 2005); Yosef Grodzinsky, *In the Shadow of the Holocaust: The Struggle between Jews and Zionists in the Aftermath of World War II* (Monroe, ME: Common Courage Press, 2004); Atina Grossmann, *Jews, Germans, and Allies: Close Encounters in Occupied Germany* (Princeton NJ: Princeton

University Press, 2007); Anna Holian, "The Ambivalent Exception: American Occupation Policy in Postwar Germany and the Formation of Jewish Refugee Spaces," *Journal of Refugee Studies* 25/3 (2012): 452–73; Arieh J. Kochavi, *Post-Holocaust Politics: Britain, the United States, and Jewish Refugees, 1945–1948* (Chapel Hill, NC: University of North Carolina Press, 2001); Hagit Lavsky, *New Beginnings: Holocaust Survivors in Bergen-Belsen and the British Zone in Germany, 1945–1950* (Detroit, MI: Wayne State University Press, 2002); Zeev W. Mankowitz, *Life between Memory and Hope: The Survivors of the Holocaust in Occupied Germany* (Cambridge: Cambridge University Press, 2002); Zorach Warhaftig, *Uprooted: Jewish Refugees and Displaced Persons after Liberation* (New York: Institute of Jewish Affairs of the American Jewish Congress and World Jewish Congress, Nov. 1946); Idith Zertal, *From Catastrophe to Power: Holocaust Survivors and the Emergence of Israel* (Berkeley, CA: University of California Press, 1998); David Bankier, ed., *The Jews Are Coming Back: The Return of the Jews to Their Countries of Origin after WWII* (New York: Berghahn, 2005); Margarete Myers Feinstein, *Holocaust Survivors in Postwar Germany, 1945–1957* (Cambridge: Cambridge University Press, 2010).

8 Atina Grossman, *Jews, Germans, and Allies: Close Encounters in Occupied Germany* (Princeton, NJ: Princeton University Press, 2007).

9 Mark Wyman, *DP: Europe's Displaced Persons, 1945–1951* (Philadelphia: Balch Institute Press, 1989); Wolfgang Jacobmeyer, *Heimatlosen Ausländer: Die Displaced Persons in Westdeutschland, 1945–1951* (Göttingen: Vandenhoeck & Ruprecht, 1985).

10 Gerald Daniel Cohen, *In War's Wake: Europe's Displaced Persons in the Postwar Order* (New York: Oxford University Press, 2012).

11 Anna Holian, *Between National Socialism and Soviet Communism: Displaced Persons in Postwar Germany* (Ann Arbor, MI: University of Michigan Press, 2011).

12 Adam R. Seipp, *Strangers in the Wild Place: Refugees, Americans, and a German Town, 1945–1952* (Bloomington: Indiana University Press, 2013).

13 See, e.g.: John Willoughby, *Remaking the Conquering Heroes: The Social and Geopolitical Impact of the Post-War American Occupation of Germany* (London: Palgrave, 2001); Julian Bach, *America's Germany: An Account of the Occupation* (New York: Random House, 1946); Judah Nadich, *Eisenhower and the Jews* (New York: Twayne, 1953); Earl F. Ziemke, *The U.S. Army in the Occupation in Germany, 1944–1946* (Washington, DC: Center of Military History, United States Army, 1975); O.J. Frederiksen, *The American Occupation of Germany, 1945–1953* (Historical Division, Headquarters, United States Army, Europe, 1953); Harold Zink, *The United*

States in Germany, 1944–1955 (Westport, CN: Greenwood Press, 1957); Michael Balfour, *Four-Power Control in Germany and Austria, 1945–1946* (London: Oxford University Press, 1956); W. Friedmann, *The Allied Military Government of Germany* (London: Stevens & Sons, 1947); Robert Wolfe, ed., *Americans as Proconsuls: United States Military Government in Germany and Japan, 1944–1952* (Carbondale, IL: Southern Illinois University Press, 1984); Detlef Junker, ed., *The United States and Germany in the Era of the Cold War, 1945–1990*, vol. 1, *1945–1968* (Cambridge: Cambridge University Press, 2004); Edward N. Peterson, *The American Occupation of Germany: Retreat to Victory* (Detroit, MI: Wayne State University Press, 1977); Roger Morgan, *The United States and West Germany, 1945–1973: A Study in Alliance Politics* (London: Oxford University Press, 1974); Paul W. Gulgowski, *The American Military Government of United States Occupied Zones of Post World War II Germany in Relation to Policies Expressed by Its Civilian Governmental Authorities at Home, during the Course of 1944/45 through 1949* (Frankfurt am Main: HAAG + HERCHEN Verlag, 1983); Forrest C. Pogue, *United States Army in World War II: The European Theater of Operations – The Supreme Command* (Washington, DC: Office of the Chief of Military History, Department of the Army, 1954); Jeffry M. Diefendorf, Axel Frohn, and Hermann-Josef Rupieper, eds., *American Policy and the Reconstruction of West Germany, 1945–1955* (Washington, DC: German Historical Institute, 1993); Richard L. Merritt, *Democracy Imposed: U.S. Occupation Policy and the German Public, 1945–1949* (New Haven, CT: Yale University Press, 1995); John Gimbel, *The American Occupation of Germany: Politics and the Military, 1945–1949* (Stanford, CA: Stanford University Press, 1968); Thomas Alan Schwartz, *America's Germany: John J. McCloy and the Federal Republic of Germany* (Cambridge, MA: Harvard University Press, 1991).

14 Sharif Gemie, Fiona Reid, and Laure Humbert, with Louise Ingram, *Outcast Europe: Refugees and Relief Workers in an Era of Total War, 1936–48* (London: Continuum International Publishing Group, 2012); Susan Armstrong-Reid and David Murray, *Armies of Peace: Canada and the UNRRA Years* (Toronto: University of Toronto Press, 2008).

15 George Woodbridge, ed., *UNRRA: The History of the United Nations Relief and Rehabilitation Administration* 3 vols. (New York: Columbia University Press, 1950); Louise Holborn, *The International Refugee Organization: A Specialized Agency of the United Nations – Its History and Work, 1946–1952* (London: Oxford University Press, 1956).

16 By way of a sampling, see the following: Janet Pack and Margaret Weis, *Lost Childhood: Children of World War II* (New York: J. Messner, 1986); Lynn H. Nicholas, *Cruel World: The Children of Europe in the Nazi Web*

(New York: Knopf, 2005); Howard Greenfield, *The Hidden Children* (New York: Ticknor and Fields, 1993); Simone Gigliotti, *The Young Victims of the Nazi Regime: Migration, the Holocaust, and Postwar Displacement* (London: Bloomsbury Academic, 2016); Sue Saffle, *To the Bomb and Back: Finnish World War II Children Tell Their Stories* (New York: Berghahn, 2015); Julie K. deGraffenreid, *Sacrificing Childhood: Children and the Soviet State in the Great Patriotic War* (Lawrence, KS: University Press of Kansas, 2014); Sarah Lew Miller and Joyce Block Lazarus, *Hiding in Plain Sight: Eluding the Nazis in Occupied France* (Chicago, IL: Academy Chicago, 2012); Steinert, *Deportation und Zwangsarbeit*; Dan Bar-On, *Legacy of Silence: Encounters with Children of the Third Reich* (Cambridge, MA: Harvard University Press, 1991); Martin Gilbert, *The Boys: The Story of 732 Young Concentration Camp Survivors* (New York: Henry Holt, 1998); Patricia Heberer, *Children during the Holocaust* (Lanham, MA: AltaMira Press, 2011); Vera K. Fast, *Children's Exodus: A History of the Kindertransport* (London: I.B. Tauris, 2011); Nicholas Stargardt, *Witnesses of War: Children's Lives under the Nazis* (London: Pimlico, 2006).

17 Tara Zahra, *The Lost Children: Reconstructing Europe's Families after World War II* (Harvard, MA: Harvard University Press, 2011).

18 Ibid., 88.

19 Ibid., 119.

20 Ibid., 147.

1 UNRRA Gets Started

1 Cited in "Long Range Plan for Refugee Care," *New York Times*, 18 Oct. 1939.

2 Gerard Daniel Cohen, *In War's Wake: Europe's DPs in the Postwar Order* (Oxford: Oxford University Press, 2012), 3–4.

3 Article 10, Covenant, League of Nations.

4 David MacKenzie, *A World Beyond Borders: An Introduction to the History of International Organizations* (Toronto: University of Toronto Press, 2010), 37.

5 "The Nobel Peace Prize 1938." *Nobelprize.org*. Nobel Media AB 2013. http://www.nobelprize.org/nobel_prizes/peace/laureates/1938/ (consulted 21 May 2014).

6 Michael R. Marrus, *The Unwanted: European Refugees in the Twentieth Century* (New York: Oxford University Press, 1985), part II, ad passim.

7 Susan Armstrong-Reid and David Murray, *Armies of Peace: Canada and the UNRRA Years* (Toronto: University of Toronto Press), 2008, 19–20; George Woodbridge, ed., *UNRRA: The History of the United Nations Relief*

and Rehabilitation Administration (New York: Columbia University Press, 1950), I: 13.

8 Tommie Sjöberg, *The Powers and the Persecuted: The Refugee Problem and the Intergovernmental Committee on Refugees (IGCR), 1938–1947* (Lund: Lund University Press, 1991), 14.

9 Ibid., 146.

10 Ibid., 126–41,153–65.

11 Forrest C. Pogue, *United States Army in World War II: The European Theater of Operations – The Supreme Command* (Washington, DC: Office of the Chief of Military History, Department of History, 1954), 84.

12 Malcolm Proudfoot, *European Refugees, 1939–1952: A Study in Forced Population Movement* (London: Faber and Faber, 1957), 114–15.

13 RG 331, Supreme Headquarters, Allied Expeditionary Force (SHAEF), Office of the Chief of Staff (OCS), Secretary, General Staff, Decimal File May 1943–Aug. 1945, Entry 1, Box 88, 383.7 vol. 1 (Refugees and Displaced Persons of European nationality): cable WX-56221, AGWAR/Combined Chiefs of Staff, to AFHQ for Wilson, 26 June 1944. Here and throughout these notes all archival documents beginning with RG (Record Group) are from the US National Archives and Records Administration (NARA), College Park, MD.

14 Resolution 57, "A Proposal Transmitted by the Committee of the Council for Europe in the Minutes of Its Sixth and Seventh Meetings," in Woodbridge, *UNRRA*, III: 136–5.

15 RG 331, OCS, Secretary, General Staff, Decimal File May 1943–Aug. 1945, Entry 1, Box 88, 383.7 vol. 1 (Refugees and Displaced Persons of European nationality): cable, S-63942, SHAEF Main, to HQ Central Group of Armies Rear for Bradley, 25 Oct. 1944.

16 RG 260, Records of the Occupation Headquarters WWII (OMGUS), Civil Administration Division (CAD), PW&DP Branch, Records Relating to DPs in Germany and Other Countries, 1945–49, Box 148, 080 UNRRA: B.L. Milburn, Brigadier General, USA, Acting Director, US Group C.C., Division 'B', to General C.W. Wickersham, 16 Sept. 1944; "Draft Agreement to Regularize the Relations between UNRRA and SCAEF during the Military Period," 19 Sept. 1944; L.W. Charley, Lt. Col., Director DP Branch, to Chief Staff Officer, 19 Sept. 1944; "Participation of UNRRA in the Displaced Persons problem in occupied Germany"; F.D. Stephens, Lt. Colonel, GSC, US Group C.C., Division 'B', Displaced Persons (DP) Section, to General Milburn, 19 Sept. 1944; B.L. Milburn, Brig. General, USA, Acting Director, Division 'B', US Group C.C., to Acting Deputy, US Group C.C., 21 Sept. 1944.

17 RG 260, Office of the Adjutant General (OAG), Gen. Correspondence and Other Recs., 1945–49, 390/40/21/2: Box 92, AG 383.7 DPs, vol. 1, Office of Military Government (OMG), 1945–46: "Outline Plan for Refugees and DPs (All Operations)," 3 June 1944.

18 RG 260, OAG, General Correspondence & other records, 1945–49, 390/40/21/2, Box 92, AG 383.7 Displaced Persons, vol. 1, OMG 1945–46: "Outline Plan for Refugees and Displaced Persons (All Operations)," 3 June 1944.

19 RG 331, Office of the General Staff (OGS), G-5 Division, Secretariat, Numeric File Aug. 1943–July 1945, Entry 47, Box 12, Internal Affairs Branch SHAEF G-5/651/1 Liaison Officers - General: AH Moffitt Jr., Lt Col, GSC, Acting Chief, Displaced Persons Branch (DPBr), G-5 SHAEF to ACOS, G-5, 6 May 1944.

20 RG 260, CAD, PW&DP Branch, Records Relating to DPs in Germany and Other Countries, 1945–49, Box 151, 092 Polish Military Mission: Chief, Polish Military Mission to Major-General A.W. Gullion, Chief of DP Branch, G-5 SHAEF, 12 Sept. 1944.

21 RG 331, OCS, Secretary, General Staff, Decimal File May 1943–Aug. 1945, Entry 1, Box 88, 383.7 vol. 1 (Refugees and Displaced Persons of European nationality): cable Q-10794, HQ 12 Army Group Rear to SHAEF FWD, att G-5, 13 Sept. 1944; cable S-60046, SHAEF Main to 12 Army Group Rear, 18 Sept. 1944.

22 RG 331, HQ 6th Army Group, Special Staff, Adj Gen Section, Decimal File 1944, Entry 242, Box 97, 383.7-1: cable S-63003, Eisenhower to Commanders of all Army Groups, SHAEF Mission to France, Belgium, Netherlands, Luxembourg, 19 Oct. 1944.

23 RG 260, OAG, General correspondence & other records, 1945–49, 390/40/21/2 Box 92, file AG 383.7 Displaced Persons, vol. 1, OMG 1945–46: SHAEF to HQ, 21 Army Group and Commanding Generals of 12th, 6th Army Groups & Communications Zone, 4 Nov. 1944.

24 RG 331, OCS, Secretary, General Staff, Decimal File May 1943–Aug. 1945, Entry 1, Box 88, 383.7 vol. 1 (Refugees and Displaced Persons of European nationality): cable S-67825, SCAEF to 6th Army Group for G-5 for Parkman; SHAEF Mission to France for G-5; SHAEF Rear for G-5 for Frost, 22 Nov. 1944.

25 PAG 4/1.0.1.0.0:31, Displaced Persons general file no. 1 Nov. 1943–Jan. 1945: Herbert H. Lehman, Director General, UNRRA to Fred K. Hoehler, UNRRA, London, 8 Sept. 1944. Here and throughout these notes all archival documents beginning with PAG are from the UN Archives, UNRRA Archives, New York City.

26 Ibid., Hoehler to Lehman, 26 Sept. 1944.

27 Ibid., Hoehler to Director General, UNRRA (Lehman), 1 June 1944.

28 Ibid., Hoehler to Tom Cooley II, 12 Oct. 1944.

29 RG 331, OCS, Secretary, General Staff, Decimal File May 1943–Aug. 1945, Entry 1, Box 88, 383.7 vol. 2 (Refugees and Displaced Persons of European nationality): cable S-85009, SCAEF to CG 12 Army Group Rear for G-5, 14 April 1945; cable Q-13972, Bradley, 12th Army Group Rear to SHAEF Main, 12 April 1945.

30 Ibid., R.W. Barker, Major General, GSC, AC of S, G-1 SHAEF to Chief of Staff, 6 Nov. 1944.

31 RG 331, OGS, G-5 Division, Secretariat, Numeric File Aug. 1943–July 1945, Entry 47, Box 50, Displaced Persons Branch. SHAEF/G-5/2708/1. Countries - Czechoslovakia - DPs: R.H.S. Venables, Brigadier, DPWX, G-1 FWD to EACS Main, 13 April 1945; G.E. Tritton, Major for Lt-General, EACS Main to PWX Branch, G-1 FWD, 16 April 1945; R. Harden, Lt. Col. for Major General i/c Administration 21 Army Group to SHAEF FWD G-1 Division PWX, 10 April 1945.

32 Ibid., Box 49, Displaced Persons Branch, SHAEF/G-5/2706/1, Countries - Poland - DPs: V.R. Paravicini, Lt. Col., Chief Allied Liaison Officer, G-5, DP Branch, SHAEF to Executive, Captain Neiman, 1 May 1945.

33 RG 331, OCS, Secretary, General Staff, Decimal File May 1943–Aug. 1945, Entry 1, Box 89, 383.7 vol. 3 (Refugees and Displaced Persons of European nationality): cable W-76505, Joint Chiefs of Staff to Eisenhower, 3 May 1945.

34 RG 331, OGS, G-5 Division, Secretariat, Numeric File Aug. 1943–July 1945, Entry 47, Box 49, Displaced Persons Branch. SHAEF/G-5/2706/1. Countries - Poland - DPs: Alec Randall, Foreign Office, London to C.E. Steel, SHAEF FWD, 15 May 1945.

35 RG 260, CAD, PW&DP Branch, Records Relating to DPs in Germany and Other Countries, 1945–49, Box 177, 319.1 Reports-DP: H.L. Fuller, Lt. Col., A/Chief, DP Branch, PW&DP Division to Acting Director and Deputy, PW&DP Division, 24 April 1945.

36 Ibid., Box 148, 080 UNRRA: L.W. Charley, Lt. Col., Director DP Branch, to Chief Staff Officer, 19 Sept. 1944; "Participation of UNRRA in the Displaced Persons problem in occupied Germany."

37 RG 331, OCS, Secretary, General Staff, Decimal File, May 1943–Aug. 1945, Entry 1, Box 88, 383.7 vol. 1 (Refugees and Displaced Persons of European nationality): cable WX-39006, Combined Chiefs of Staff, to Eisenhower, 30 Sept. 1944.

38 PAG 4/1.0.1.0.0:31, Displaced Persons general file no. 1, Nov. 1943–Jan. 1945: Hoehler, Director, DPBr, UNRRA to General Grasett, 21 Sept. 1944; Hoehler to Sir Frederick Leith Ross, 9 Oct. 1944.

39 "Agreement to Regularize the Relations between the SCAEF and UNRRA during the Military Period," signed by General Dwight D. Eisenhower and Herbert H. Lehman, 25 Nov. 1944, in Woodbridge, *UNRRA*, III:180–1.

40 PAG 4/1.0.1.0.0:32, DP File no. 2: SHAEF Administrative Memorandum No. 39: DPs and Refugees in Germany, General Eisenhower, SCAEF, 18 Nov. 1944.

41 "Agreement to Regularize the Relations between the Supreme Commander, Allied Expeditionary Force, and UNRRA during the Military Period," in Woodbridge, *UNRRA*, III:180–1.

42 RG 331, OCS, Secretary, General Staff, Decimal File May 1943–Aug. 1945, Entry 1, Box 88, 383.7 vol. 1 (Refugees and Displaced Persons of European nationality): T.J. Davis, Brigadier General, USA, Adjutant General, SHAEF to "All concerned," 18 Dec. 1944.

43 RG 331, OCS, G-3 Division, General Records, Subject File 1942–45. Entry 23, Box 18, Displaced Persons on the Continent: cable S-79118, SCAEF to CG 6th Army Group for G-5, 14 Feb. 1945; cable S-79117, SCAEF to 21 Army Group Rear, 14 Feb. 1945.

44 PAG 4/1.0.1.0.0:32, DP file no. 2 Displaced Persons Nov. 1944–Jan. 1945: S.R. Mickelson, Brigadier General, Chief, Displaced Persons, Refugee and Welfare Branch, G-5 SHAEF to Hoehler, Director, DP Branch, ERO, 2 Dec. 1944.

45 RG 331, OCS, G-3 Division, General Records, Subject File 1942–45, Entry 23, Box 18, Displaced Persons on the Continent: cable S-80241, Eisenhower to Civil Affairs Division, 25 Feb. 1945.

46 PAG 4/1.0.1.0.0:32, DP file no. 2 Displaced Persons Nov. 1944–Jan. 1945: Hoehler, ERO to Tom (Cooley), 19 Dec. 1944.

47 RG 331, OGS, G-5 Division, Secretariat, Numeric File Aug. 1943–July 1945, Entry 47, Box 51, Displaced Persons Branch. SHAEF/G-5/2723. UNRRA - Agreements & Relationship Between SCAEF and UNRRA: Fletcher C. Kettle, UNRRA Liaison Officer, SHAEF to T.T. Scott, Director, DP Division, ERO, 25 Feb. 1945.

48 RG 331, OCS, G-3 Division, General Records, Subject File 1942–45, Entry 23, Box 18, Displaced Persons on the Continent: cable S-80241, Eisenhower to Civil Affairs Division, 25 Feb. 1945.

49 RG 260, CAD, DP&PW Branch, Box 138, 001.0 Meetings: minutes, 18th meeting of Standing Technical Sub-Committee of Displaced Persons for Europe, UNRRA, 8 May 1945; PAG 4/1.3.1.1.2.1:1, Guide - Welfare: *Welfare Guide: Services to United Nations Nationals Displaced in Germany*, UNRRA - Welfare Division (Paris-London-Washington), 15 March 1945.

50 RG 260, CAD, PW&DP Branch, Records Relating to DPs in Germany and Other Countries, 1945–49, Box 148, 080 UNRRA: PE Barringer, Major

FA Liaison Officer PWDP (Rear) to DP Br., PWDP Div US Group CC, 27 March 1945.

51 RG 331, OCS, G-3 Division, General Records, Subject File 1942–45, Entry 23, Box 18, Displaced Persons on the Continent: cable S-83279, Eisenhower to G-5 DP Branch and UNRRA, 27 March 1945.

52 Ibid., cable S-83356 Eisenhower to Combined Chiefs of Staff, for Combined Civil Affairs Committee, 28 March 1945.

53 Ibid., cable W-42470 Hilldring to Eisenhower for SHGE, 24 Feb. 1945.

54 Ibid., cable S-80241 Eisenhower to Civil Affairs Division, 25 Feb. 1945.

55 Ibid., cable FWD-17969 Eisenhower to WEPVEE 5, EXFOR Main G(SD), 18 March 1945.

56 RG 331, OGS, General Staff, G-5 Division, Secretariat, Numeric File, Aug. 1943–July 1945, Entry 47, Box 51, Displaced Persons Branch. SHAEF/G-5/2723. UNRRA - Agreements & Relationship Between SCAEF and UNRRA: Hugh Jackson, Deputy Director General for Regional Liaison, UNRRA HQ (Paris) to Lt General W.B. Smith, Chief of Staff, SHAEF, 31 March 1945.

57 RG 331, OGS, G-5 Division, Secretariat, Numeric File Aug. 1943–July 1945, Entry 47, Box 51, Displaced Persons Branch. SHAEF/G-5/2723. UNRRA - Agreements & Relationship Between SCAEF and UNRRA: W.B. Smith, Lt. General, US, Chief of Staff to Hugh R. Jackson, Deputy Director General for Regional Liaison, UNRRA, Paris, 17 April 1945.

58 RG 331, OCS, G-3 Division, General Records, Subject File 1942–45. Entry 23, Box 18, Displaced Persons on the Continent: cable FWD-18169, SCAEF to GENORD PARL 2, 25 March 1945.

59 Ibid., cable S-83356, Eisenhower to Combined Chiefs of Staff, for Combined Civil Affairs Committee, 28 March 1945.

60 RG 331, OGS, G-5 Division, Secretariat, Numeric File Aug. 1943–July 1945, Entry 47, Box 51, Displaced Persons Branch. SHAEF/G-5/2723. UNRRA - Agreements & Relationship Between SCAEF and UNRRA: W.B. Smith, Lt. General, US, Chief of Staff to Hugh R. Jackson, Deputy Director General for Regional Liaison, UNRRA, Paris, 17 April 1945.

61 RG 260, CAD DP&PW Branch, Box 138 001.0 Meetings: minutes, 18th meeting of Standing Technical Sub-Committee of Displaced Persons for Europe, UNRRA, 8 May 1945.

62 RG 331, OGS, G-5 Division, Secretariat, Numeric File Aug. 1943–July 1945, Entry 47, Box 50, Displaced Persons Branch. SHAEF/G-5/2708/1. Countries - Czechoslovakia - DPs: A.H. Moffitt, Jr., Col GSC, Executive Officer, G-5 DPBr, SHAEF to Political Advisor (British), SHAEF FWD, 8 June 1945.

63 Ibid., Box 47, Displaced Persons Branch. SHAEF/G-5/2701/1 Countries - France - French DPs: F.W. Jones Jr, Major, AGD, Adjutant General, SHAEF Mission (France) to Supreme Commander, AEF (Main), att: G-5, DP Branch, 26 June 1945; OCS, Secretary, General Staff, Decimal File May 1943–Aug. 1945, Entry 1, Box 89, 383.7 vol. 3 (Refugees and Displaced Persons of European nationality), cable MF-14700, SHAEF Mission France, Lewis to SHAEF Main, 19 June 1945.

64 RG 260, CAD, PW&DP Branch, Records Relating to DPs in Germany and Other Countries, 1945–49, Box 176, 319/1 Reports Congressional Committee: Bi-monthly progress Report No. 1, 8 June 1945–30 June 1945, DPBr, PW&DP Division, Headquarters US Group CC, US Army.

65 Ibid., Box 139, 001 Staff Meetings USGCC: minutes, staff meeting, US Group CC, 15 July 1945.

66 RG 260, OAG, General correspondence & other records, 1945–49, 390/40/21/2, Box 92, AG 383.7 Displaced Persons Reports, OMGUS 1945–46: Eric Fisher Wood, Brigadier General, GSC, Office of Deputy Director to Commanding General, US Group CC, 23 July 1945 (includes annexes).

67 PAG 4/3.0.11.3.1:2, Reports, Miscellaneous, Surveys, Inspections July 45–Dec. 45: "Observations of Fifteen Displaced Persons Camps in US Zone," by Joseph P. Harris, 20–26 July 1945; Susan Pettiss, *After the Shooting Stopped* (Victoria B.C: Trafford Publishing, 2004), ad passim; PAG 4/1.3.1.1.1:24, F400.3 Germany Summaries & Notes on DP Operations: "Item 4. On the Agenda: Brief interim report on UNRRA's participation in Displaced Persons operations in Germany (SHAEF Area.)," Twenty-third meeting, Standing Technical Sub-Committee on Displaced Persons for Europe, 5 July 1945.

68 *The US Army in the Occupation of Germany, 1944–1946* (Washington, DC: Government Printing Office, 1975), 425–33; Oliver J. Frederiksen, *The American Military Occupation of Germany, 1945–1953* (Historical Div., HQ, US, Europe, 1953), 29–32; Earl F. Ziemke, "Improvising Stability and Change in Postwar Germany," in Robert Wolfe, ed., *Americans as Proconsuls: United States Military Government in Germany and Japan, 1944–1952* (Carbondale, IL: Southern Illinois University Press, 1984), 59–64.

69 RG 260, CAD, DP&PW Branch, Box 138, 001.0 Meetings: minutes, 15th Weekly Meeting between Control Commission for Germany (British Element) and US Group Control Council, 27 April 1945.

70 RG 331, OGS, G-5 Division, Secretariat, Numeric File Aug. 1943–July 1945, Entry 47, Box 51, Displaced Persons Branch. SHAEF/G-5/2723. UNRRA - Agreements & Relationship Between SCAEF and UNRRA: H.H. Newman,

Col. AGD, Acting Adjutant General, G-5 SHAEF to Commanding General, 12th Army Group, 16 June 1945.

71 Ibid., "UNRRA-Military Program for the Control and Movement of Displaced Persons after the termination of Combined Command," 22 June 1945, no author; RG 260, CAD, PW&DP Branch, Records Relating to DPs in Germany and Other Countries, 1945–49, Box 140, Headquarters US Group CC - Policy Book - PoW&DP Division: memo to Commanding Generals, Eastern Military District (EMD), Western Military District (WMD), Bremen Enclave, US Sector Berlin, Communications Zone, USFET, 23 June 1945 (revised).

72 RG 260, CAD, PW&DP Branch, Records Relating to DPs in Germany and Other Countries, 1945–49, Box 148, 080 UNRRA: cable S-13155, Eisenhower to AGWAR, 21 July 1945.

73 Ibid., Box 139, 001 Staff Meetings USGCC: minutes, held on 28 July 45, Hochst, Germany.

74 S-0425–0041, Reports Branch file 6, R.B. Lovett, Brigadier General, USFET HQ to Commanding Generals: EMD, WMD, the Berlin District and the Theater Service Force, European Theater, 5 Sept. 1945. Here and throughout these notes all archival records beginning with S-XXXX–XXXX are from the UN Archives, UNRRA Archives, New York City.

75 RG 260, CAD, PW&DP Branch, Records Relating to DPs in Germany and Other Countries, 1945–49, Box 148, 080 UNRRA: cable S-13155, Eisenhower to AGWAR, 21 July 1945.

76 PAG 4/3.0.11.3.1:13, Aug.–Dec. 1945: Alex E. Squadrilli, Deputy District Director, WMD UNRRA to Alvin Guyler, Zone Director, US Zone UNRRA, 29 Sept. 1945.

77 PAG 4/3.0.11.3.1:3, Directives UNRRA: HQ WMD and 7th Army Area Heidelberg, Squadrilli, Deputy District Director, UNRRA WMD to all Team Directors and Field Supervisors, 17 Oct. 1945.

78 Ibid., Western Military District, June 1945–Dec. 1945: Charles McDonald, District Director, UNRRA HQ, WMD to Guyler, Zone Director, UNRRA HQ, US Zone, 29 Nov. 1945.

2 Unaccompanied Children

1 RG 260, PW&DP Branch, Recs Relating to Displaced Persons and Their Movements, 1945–49: Correspondence July 1949 Thru Correspondence Misc, Box 121, Correspondence - Misc: directive, "Care and Protection of Displaced Children Uncovered in Germany", H.H. Newman, Col., AGD, Assistant Adjutant General, for Supreme Commander, SHAEF, 6 March

1945; RG 331, OCS, Secretary, General Staff, Decimal File May 1943–Aug. 1945, Entry 1, Box 88, 383.7 vol. 2 (Refugees and Displaced Persons of European nationality): A.E. Grasett, Lt. General, Assistant Chief of Staff, G-5 SHAEF to Chief of Staff, 28 Feb. 1945; T.J. Davis, Brigadier General, USA, Adjutant General, SHAEF to HQ 21st Army Group; Commanding General of 12 Army Group, 6 Army Group and Communications Zone, 22 Feb. 1945.

2 The Child Welfare Division was a separate division from the Welfare Division, as well as from the Displaced Persons Division. In addition, there was a Child Welfare Section of UNRRA's Central Headquarters. UNRRA's organizational structure was a fluid one, in part a result of the speed at which it expanded, resulting in overlapping responsibilities.

3 PAG 4/1.3.1.1.0:11, P.300.4B Unaccompanied and/or Stateless Children: Martha Branscombe to Sir George Reid, 6 Dec. 1944; P.300.4 Categories – Children: "Report on Unaccompanied Children," by Expert Commission on Services, Standing Technical Subcommittee on Displaced Persons for Europe, UNRRA, 20 July 1944 (revised 22 July 1944).

4 PAG 4/1.3.1.1.0:11, P.300.4 Categories – Children: Hoehler to Oscar Schachter, 16 May 1944; Oscar Schachter to E. Longley, 20 May 1944; Elizabeth Longley to Oscar Schachter, 22 May 1944.

5 Ibid., "Report on Unaccompanied Children," by Expert Commission on Services, Standing Technical Subcommittee on Displaced Persons for Europe, UNRRA, 20 July 1944 (revised 22 July 1944).

6 PAG 4/1.3.1.1.0:11, P.300.4 Categories – Children: "Social Welfare Services for Children and Mothers in Assembly Centers," lecture material, ERO Training Center, 28 Oct. 1944.

7 PAG 4/1.3.1.1.0:15, P410.12 21 Information, Advice, Counselling Casework: "The Treatment of Individual Social Difficulties in Assembly Centres," revised draft, Welfare Division ERO, 12 Dec. 1944, probable author, Marjorie Bradford; comments on memorandum by Bradford, 30 Oct. 1944, and by A.T. Macbeth Wilson, Lt-Col, 1 Nov. 1944.

8 PAG 4/1.3.1.1.0:11, P.300.4 Categories – Children: "Social Welfare Services for Children and Mothers in Assembly Centers," lecture material, used at the ERO Training Center, 28 Oct. 1944; "Social Welfare Services for Mothers, Children and Young Persons up to 18 Years of Age," by Subcommittee on Welfare for Europe, UNRRA, 19 Dec. 1944.

9 PAG 4/1.3.1.1.2.0:3, Complete Set of Papers on Welfare Services Prepared in ERO.

10 PAG 4/1.3.1.1.0:11, P.300.4B Unaccompanied and/or Stateless Children: Branscombe to Sir George Reid, 6 Dec. 1944.

11 PAG 4/1.3.1.1.2.1:1, Guide, Welfare: *Welfare Guide: Services to UN Nationals Displaced in Germany*, UNRRA Welfare Division (Paris-London-Washington), 15 March 1945.

12 Aleta Brownlee had already served with UNRRA as a welfare specialist on the Yugslavian Mission in 1945 and in Vienna as director of child welfare in Austria. See www.oac.cdlib.org/findaid/ark:/130303/tf4t1nb0jj (consulted 5 July 2010).

13 PAG 4/1.3.1.1.0:11, P.300.4a Categories – Unaccompanied Children: Branscombe and Anne Wood to Sir George Reid, 14 April 1945.

14 PAG 4/3.0.11.0.1:3, 2 Child Welfare: cable S-12437 USFET Main to AFHQ for Alexander, 14 July 1945; cable 2085, ALCOM to USFET Main, 19 July 1945.

15 Ibid., unnumbered cable, CG USFET Rear, 20 July 1945.

16 Ibid., cable N2524 SHAEF Mission Netherlands to USFET G-5, 13 July 1945.

17 Ibid., cable S-14593 USFET Main, CDPX, to 3rd Army and 7th Army, 30 July 1945.

18 PAG 4/1.3.1.1.0:11, P.300.4B Unaccompanied Children and/or Stateless Children: Barrett to Shepperson, 6 May 1945; RG 331, HQ 6th Army Group, Special Staff, Adj. Gen Section, Decimal File 1944, Entry 242A, Box 188, 383.7-II: cable EX-16196, 6th Army Group, Devers to 1st French Army, Cinquième Bureau, 9 June 1945.

19 PAG 4/1.3.1.1.0:11, P.300.4a Categories – Unaccompanied Children: untitled report by Langrod, Repatriation Section, Displaced Persons Division (DP Division), UNRRA ERO, 7 Feb. 1945.

20 Ibid., Branscombe and Anne Wood to Sir George Reid, 14 April 1945.

21 PAG 4/1.0.1.0.0:5, Children Unaccompanied and Displaced, 1947: Benjamin E. Youngdahl, Processing Center Section, SHAEF DP Branch to Sir George Reid, Tom Scott, and Fletcher Kettle, 7 May 1945.

22 Ibid., cable 1470 from Lehman, 23 May 1945.

23 Ibid., cable 1563 from London, 15 June 1945.

24 PAG 4/1.3.1.2.0.0:2, DPs (Children): M. Craig McGeachy to Roy Hendrickson, 21 May 1945.

25 PAG 4/1.0.1.0.0:5, Children Unaccompanied and Displaced, 1947: M. Craig McGeachy to the Director General, 4 June 1945.

26 PAG 4/1.3.1.1.0:11, P.300.4B Unaccompanied Children and/or Stateless Children: Branscombe to M. Craig McGeachy and Gay B. Shepperson, 21 May 1945.

27 PAG 4/1.0.1.0.0:5, Children Unaccompanied and Displaced, 1947: Hoehler, UNRRA, Washington, to Governor Lehman, 7 June 1945.

28 PAG 4/1.3.1.1.0:11, P.300.4B Unaccompanied and/or Stateless Children: "Europe Vies for Orphaned Jews: Seeks Them to Build Population,"

by Carl Levin, *New York Herald Tribune*, 9 June 1945; PAG 4/1.0.1.0.0:5, Children Unaccompanied and Displaced, 1947: Hoehler, UNRRA, DP Division, Washington, to Governor Lehman, 7 June 1945; cable 1563, from London, 15 June 1945; PAG 4/3.0.11.0.1:3, 2 Child Welfare: cable S-13578, CDPX, USFET Main to Commander in Chief, 21 Army Group, Commanding General Third US Army, Commanding General 7th US Army, Headquarters 1st French Army, undated.

29 PAG 4/1.3.1.1.0:21, R+W Div., Child Welfare 620.1: Hoehler, Dir. DP Div., to Tom Scott, ERO UNRRA London, 15 June 1945.

30 Ibid., Hoehler, Dir. DP Div., to Tom Scott, ERO UNRRA London, 15 June 45.

31 PAG 4/1.0.1.0.0:5, file 2 Children – Unaccompanied and Displaced, 1947: Martha M. Biehle, American Resident Representative, IGCR, to Hoehler, Director, DP Division, UNRRA, 16 June 1945.

32 PAG 4/1.3.1.1.0:11, P.300.4a Categories – Unaccompanied Children: C. [Conrad] van Hyning to M.A. Menshikov, 18 June 1945.

33 The Commission had been created by the American government in 1942 "to review all aspects of the needs of children in wartime." Its primary focus was on dealing with issues revolving around children within the United States, but in this instance, it was asked to review UNRRA's operations insofar as they dealt with children. *United States Government Manual 1945* (1st ed.), Division of Public Inquiries, Office of War Information, Department of Labor, 418.

34 PAG 4/3.0.11.0.1:3, Child Welfare: A Committee of the National Commission on Children in Wartime, appointed to consider problems of children in liberated countries, to Herbert H. Lehman, Director General, UNRRA, 12 June 1945.

35 Ibid., Welfare Division, Headquarters, to Chief Welfare Officers, Regional, Area, and Field Offices, 19 July 1945.

36 PAG 4/1.3.1.1.0:12, P.300.12 Stateless: Hoehler, Director, DP Division, to Merrill Rogers, Chief, Writers Section, 6 July 1945.

37 PAG 4/1.0.1.0.0:5, Children – Unaccompanied and Displaced, 1947: "General Policies of UNRRA and Current Operations Relating to the Welfare of Children," Working Committee on Children, 19 June 1945; PAG 4/1.3.1.1.0:27, Working Committee on Children of Standing Tech. Sub Comm: resolution, TWE(45)41, United Nations Relief and Rehabilitation Administration - Working Committee on Children - Standing Technical Committee on Welfare, 20 June 1945.

38 PAG 4/1.3.1.1.0:27, Working Committee on Children of Standing Tech. Sub Comm: Hoehler to Commander Jackson, 26 June 1945.

39 PAG 4/3.0.11.0.1.3:8, Switzerland: Don Suisse pour les Victimes de la Guerre to J.A. Edmison, Chief UNRRA Liaison Officer, G-5 SHAEF, 4 June 1945.

40 Ibid., "Report Concerning the Buchenwald Children Now at Bad-Gurnigel," by A. Bohny, Swiss Red Cross, 5 July 1945.

41 Ibid., "Memorandum on the First Children Transport from Buchenwald," Don Suisse, 6 July 1945.

42 Ibid., C.H. [Charles] Alspach, DP Representative, UNRRA Geneva, to J.A. Edmison, Chief UNRRA Liaison Officer, SHAEF Frankfurt, 20 July 1945; Marianne Flügge-Oeri, Don Suisse, Berne, to Alspach, UNRRA Delegate, Geneva, 25 July 1945.

43 Ibid., Alspach to R. Olgiati, Don Suisse, 27 July 1945.

44 Ibid.

45 Ibid., draft, Hansi Pollak, UNRRA Combined Displaced Persons Executive, 22 Aug. 1945.

46 Ibid., Alspach to J.A. Edmison, 20 July 1945; Flügge-Oeri to Alspach, 25 July 1945.

47 Ibid., Alspach to DP Division, ERO, 26 July 1945; Olgiati to Alspach, undated; PAG 4/3.0.11.0.1:3, 2 Child Welfare: "Displaced Children in Switzerland - Report on Visit. 25th Aug. - 6th Sept. 1945," by R.L. Coigny and G.M. [Grace] Aves, 13 Sept. 1945.

48 Ibid., "Memorandum on the first children transport from Buchenwald," Don Suisse, 6 July 1945; A.R. Lindt, Special Delegate of the Don Suisse, to Pollak, 22 Sept. 1945.

49 Ibid., C.I. Schottland, Assistant Director, Relief Services, to Bernhard M.V. Baldegg, Don Suisse Representative, 7 Nov. 1945; Schottland to Director, US Zone, att: Cornelia Heise, 8 Nov. 1945; Schottland to Baldegg, 15 Nov. 1945.

50 Ibid., Schottland to Lt. Gen. Sir Frederick Morgan, Chief of Operations, Germany, att: Mary Gibbons, Relief Services, ERO, 13 Nov. 1945.

51 Ibid., report, "To the Wellfare [sic] Division UNRRA, European Office," att: Aves; "Trip to Switzerland with Kloster-Indersdorf Group, Nov. 14–18," by P. Bakeman; Lillian D. Robbins, Director, DP Children's Center, UNRRA Team 182, Kloster Indersdorf, to Eileen Davidson, Child Welfare Officer, EMD HQ, 21 Nov. 1945.

52 PAG 4/1.0.1.0.0:5, Children Unaccompanied and Displaced, 1947: Benjamin E. Youngdahl, Processing Center Section, SHAEF, DP Branch, to Sir George Reid, Tom Scott, and Fletcher Kettle, 7 May 1945; PAG 4/3.0.11.2.0.1:10, Policy - Planning UNRRA - BAOR Direcs 08/45–07/46: Sir Raphael Cilento, UNRRA, Zone Director, BAOR, initiated by Dorothy

T. Pearse, UNRRA Child Welfare Specialists, Zone HQ, BAOR, to UNRRA District Directors, 1st, 8, and 30 Corps Hqs, 24 Sept. 1945.

53 PAG 4/1.3.1.1.0:11, P.300.4a "Problem of Displaced Children in Germany," draft by Zimmerman, 12 July 1945.

54 PAG 4/3.0.11.2.0.1:10 Policy - Planning UNRRA - BAOR Direcs 08/45–07/46: Sir Raphael Cilento, UNRRA, Zone Director, BAOR, to UNRRA District Directors, 1st, 8, 30 Corps Hqs, 24 Sept. 1945.

55 PAG 4/3.0.11.2.0.2:12, Correspondence on Jewish Unaccompanied Children Land Niedersachsen Reg Aug. 11 '45 – Oct. 3 '46: "Report on the First Movement of Children from Belsen to England - 30th Oct. 1945," Dorothy Pearse, Child Welfare Consultant, UNRRA Zone HQ, BAOR, undated; Pearse to Betty Barton, UNRRA District Welfare Officer, 30 Corps (Wunstorf), BAOR, 16 Nov. 1945; PAG 4/3.0.11.3.3:13, Jewish Children (General): Simon H. Rifkind, Advisor to the Theater Commander on Jewish Affairs, USFET OMG - US Zone to Guyler, UNRRA US Zone, 14 Nov. 1945; PAG 4/3.0.11.3.0:60, Welfare – 3 Aug –11 Dec. 45: J.H. [Jack] Whiting, District Director, UNRRA EMD HQ, to Guyler, Zone Director UNRRA, att: Heise, Child Welfare Consultant, 15 Nov. 1945; G.K. [Gertrude] Richman, District Welfare Officer, UNRRA EMD HQ, to R.S. Winslow, Deputy Director and Whiting, District Director, UNRRA EMD HQ, 12 Nov. 1945.

56 PAG 4/3.0.11.0.1.3:8, Switzerland: Pollak for Sir Frederick Morgan, Chief of Operations, UNRRA Germany to Lyndt, Representative, Don Suisse, 15 Oct. 1945.

57 Ibid., "To the Wellfare [sic] Division, UNRRA, European Office," att: Aves; "Trip to Switzerland with Kloster-Indersdorf Group, Nov. 14–18," P. Bakeman; Unaccompanied Children - Switzerland: Lillian D. Robbins, Director, DP Children's Center, UNRRA Team 182, Kloster Indersdorf, to Eileen Davidson, Child Welfare Officer, EMD HQ, 21 Nov. 1945; Switzerland: "Report No. 1 from Miss Gwen Chesters (Child Welfare Specialist). Children in Switzerland. Notes for Week Oct. 12th–18th, 1945"; Susan Pettiss, Child Welfare Officer, X Corps Regional Office, UNRRA, to Eileen Davidson, 20 Oct. 1945.

58 S-0425–0005, Administrative – UNRRA Instructions: Vernon R. Kennedy, Director, US Zone UNRRA, to Acting District Director, UNRRA, EMD, att: District Welfare Officer, 31 Aug. 1945; Appendix, "Policy Regarding Movement of Children on Temporary Asylum," Combined Displaced Persons Executive, G-5 USFET.

59 PAG 4/3.0.11.0.1.3:7, 21 Polish Unaccompanied Children and Polish Red Cross: Schottland for Sir Frederick Morgan to Director, UNRRA, 19 Oct. 1945.

60 PAG 4/3.0.11.0.0:7, 014.6/A Unaccompanied Children – General
    Correspondence: C.I. Schottland for Morgan to Director, UNRRA US Zone,
    att: Heise, 28 Nov. 1945.
61 PAG 4/1.3.1.1.0:11, P.300.4a Problem of Displaced Children in Germany:
    draft report (untitled) by Zimmerman, 12 July 1945.
62 Ibid.
63 PAG 4/3.0.11.3.3:18, 168-L18 UNRRA: Bradford to Edmison, 22 June 1945.
64 PAG 4/3.0.11.0.1.1:4, B53 Child Search Repatriation Reports Welfare: cable
    S-15031 Eisenhower to 21st Army Group, 3rd US Army, 7th US Army, 1st
    French Army, 2 Aug. 1945.
65 PAG 4/3.0.11.3.3:14, C4 Child Search Procedures: "Proposed Plan for
    Locating and Registering DPs Outside of Assembly Centers," 10 Aug.
    1945.
66 PAG 4/1.3.1.1.2.1:1, Guide - Welfare: *Welfare Guide: Services to United
    Nations Nationals Displaced in Germany*, UNRRA-ERO-Welfare Division,
    15 March 1945.
67 PAG 4/3.0.11.3.3:13, F2 Field Representative Reports: "Field Report - Child
    Welfare, EMD, Aug. 12 to Aug. 26, 1945."
68 PAG 4/3.0.11.3.3:18 168-L18 UNRRA: "Plan for Locating and Registering
    Unaccompanied Children of UN Nationality and Those Assimilated to Them
    in Status Who Are outside Assembly Centers, US Zone," 28 Aug. 1945.
69 PAG 4/3.0.11.3.3:13, F2 Field Representative Reports: "Field Report - Child
    Welfare: EMD, Aug. 12 to Aug. 26, 1945."
70 PAG 4/3.0.11.2.0.2:56, File 65 Child Search Monthly Narrative Reports 45,
    46, 47: "Report on the Status of Plans for Unaccompanied Children," 31
    Aug. 1945.
71 Case service or casework was a relatively new approach to social
    welfare, pioneered in the United States and professionalized in the 1920s
    in the United States with the publication of *Social Diagnosis* by Mary
    Richmond in 1917. A "caseworker" is a person designated to assume
    primary responsibility for assessing the needs of a client, arranging and
    coordinating the delivery of a variety of essential goods and services, and
    working directly with the client to ensure that those goods and services
    are provided in a timely and effective manner. The nature of that care,
    goods, and services is determined only after careful diagnosis and research
    into the specific challenges, problems, and needs of the individual being
    assessed. It is a very time-consuming and individual client-focused
    approach to social welfare. Charles Zastrow, *Introduction to Social Work
    and Social Welfare: Empowering People* (Belmont, CA: Brooks/Cole Cengage
    Learning, 2010), 45.

72 PAG 4/3.0.11.3.3:15, Plans for Unaccompanied Children, Aug. 45–Oct.
45: Olive Biggar, District Welfare Officer, UNRRA Administrative Unit,
Seventh Army, to Eileen Blackey, Staff Welfare Officer, UNRRA, 28 Aug.
1945; Maria Liebeskind, Child Search Officer, to Biggar, 28 Aug. 1945.
73 Ibid., 1701(1) Plans for Unaccompanied Children, Aug. 45–Oct. 45: R.
O'Meara, Deputy Director, UNRRA HQ, US Zone, prepared by Heise,
Child Welfare Specialist, to Acting District Director, UNRRA WMD, att:
District Welfare Officer, 14 Sept. 1945.

3 Child Search Launched

1 PAG 4/3.0.11.3.1:10, Monthly Welfare Reports, Aug. 1945–21 Oct. 1946:
WMD Welfare Report, Aug. 1945, and WMD Welfare Report, Sept. 1945.
2 PAG 4/3.0.11.3.3:14, C86 Nationality Policy, Silesian: "Unaccompanied
Children–XII Corps, American Friends Report," attached to Whiting,
District Director, UNRRA EMD, to Guyler, Director UNRRA US Zone, att:
Heise, Zone Child Welfare Specialist, 29 Oct. 1945.
3 PAG 4/3.0.11.3.1:23, UNRRA District 5 Munich-Pasing: "About 22
Yougoslav [sic] Unaccompanied Children at the OKL DP Camp in
Berchtesgaden," Pettiss, Child Welfare Officer, XX Corps, Regional Office,
UNRRA, 19 Oct. 1945.
4 Ibid., "Landkreis Berchtesgaden," 9–29 Oct. 1945.
5 Ibid., "Czech. Children in Bad Reichenhall," 19 Nov. 1945, no author.
6 PAG 4/3.0.11.3.3:18, 168-L18 UNRRA: "Report about 200–300 Silesian
Children Coming from Klosterbruck near Oppeln," Pettiss, Child Search
Officer, 20 Oct. 1945 (copy in her private papers).
7 PAG 4/3.0.11.3.1:23, UNRRA District No. 5 Munich-Pasing: "Czech. children
in Bad Reichenhall."
8 PAG 4/1.3.1.1.0:11, P.300.4 Categories. Children: Conference
proceedings, "Inter-Zone Child Welfare Conference, Hochst, 3–4
Jan. 1946"; conference proceedings, "Conference on Location and
Documentation of UN Children in German Institutions and Families,
29 Jan. 1946"; PAG 4/3.0.11.0.1.1:14, Zone Director Report - US Zone
Oct. 1945–Mar. 1946: "UNRRA US Zone HQ, monthly child welfare
report, January 1946."
9 PAG 4/3.0.11.0.1.3:9, 35.19 Conference Minutes and Summaries: "Notes on
Location of UN Children in German Families," Welfare Section, UNRRA
CHQ Germany, 15 Dec. 1945; PAG 4/3.0.11.3.3:14, A3 Child Search and
Tracing Interest: Heise, Zone Child Welfare Specialist to District Office,
Regensburg, att: Child Welfare Officer, 9 Feb. 1946; "Procedures in

Handling Cases of Unaccompanied Children: A Statement of Current Practice in the U.S. Zone," Dec. 1945.

10 PAG 4/3.0.11.0.1.1:4, Child Search, Welfare Repatriation Reports: "Report on Child Welfare Services for November 1945."

11 See, e.g.: Larry Thompson, "*Lebensborn* and the Eugenics Policy of the *Reichsführer-SS*," *Central European History* 4/1 (1971): 54–77; Kjersti Ericsson and Eva Simonsen, *Children of World War II: The Hidden Enemy Legacy* (Oxford: Berg, 2005); Georg Lilienthal, *Der "Lebensborn e.V.": Ein Instrument nationalsozialisticher Rassenpolitik* (Stuttgart: G. Fischer, 1985); Thomas Bryant, *Himmlers Kinder: Zur Geschichte der SS-Organisation "Lebensborn" e.V. 1935–1945* (Wiesbaden: Marixverlag, 2011); Marc Hillel and Clarissa Henry, *Lebensborn e.V: Im Namen der Rasse* (Vienna: P. Zsolnay, 1975); and Catrine Clay and Michael Leapman, *Master Race: The Lebensborn Experiment in Nazi Germany* (London: Hodder and Stoughton, 1995).

12 PAG 4/3.0.11.0.1.3:7, 21 Polish Unaccompanied Children and Polish Red Cross, 1 Oct.–31 Dec. 1946: report, J. Makowiecka, Inspector for Maternal and Children Welfare and Repatriation, Polish Red Cross, Katowice, Silesia, 2 Jan. 1946.

13 Ibid., Hansi Pollak, Deputy Director, Relief Services Division, for Sir Frederick Morgan, Chief of Operations, Germany, 9 Jan. 1946; report, Makowiecka, 2 Jan. 1946; Morgan to Director, UNRRA, US Zone, att: Heise, 10 Jan. 1946; Makowiecka to Blackey, 7 Jan. 1946.

14 PAG 4/3.0.11.0.1.3:7, Polish Unaccompanied Children + Polish Red Cross - 1/10/1946–31/12/1946: "Notes on Meeting with Polish Red Cross Representatives in Connection with Repatriation of Polish Children," author unknown, 28 Dec. 1945.

15 PAG 4/3.0.11.3.3:14, C8.5 Nationality Policy, Russian: Heise to W.S. Boe, 26 April 1946.

16 PAG 4/3.0.11.3.3:14, I 3.1 Checking of Institutions: Child Registration Memo No. 13, Team 566, Regensdorf, 8 March 1946.

17 PAG 4/3.0.11.3.3:15, Rel. Series Child Welfare Jan. 1946–Dec. 1946 Search & Registration: Child Registration Memo Nos. 4, 5, 6 by Jean Troniak, Sarah L. Howells, Wm. B. Edgerton, UNRRA District HQ, Regensburg (US Zone), dated respectively 22, 24, 25 Jan. 1946; PAG 4/1.3.1.1.0:11, P.300.4a: Child Registration Memo Nos. 7, 8, and 9 by Troniak, Edgerton, W. Huysoon, Howells, dated respectively 28, 31 Jan., and 5 Feb. 1946; PAG 4/3.0.11.3.3:14 C4 Child Search Procedure: "UNRRA Registration Team for Unaccompanied Children," UNRRA Team 556, 26 Feb. 1946.

18 PAG 4/3.0.11.0.1.3:7, 21.Polish Unaccompanied Children and Polish Red Cross from 1st Oct. 1946–31st Dec. 1946: "Children's Homes in Silesia and Poland," UNRRA Team 566, 28 Feb. 1946.

19 PAG 4/3.0.11.0.1.1:3, Germany – Feb. reports: Attachment 4, Extracts from US Zone Child Welfare Report – February 1946.
20 PAG 4/3.0.11.3.3:14, C4 Child Search Procedure: "UNRRA Registration Team for Unaccompanied Children," UNRRA Team 556, 26 Feb. 1946.
21 PAG 4/3.0.11.3.3:14, A3 of Child Search/Tracing Interest: Heise, Zone Child Welfare Specialist to District Office, Regensburg, att: Child Welfare Officer, 9 Feb. 1946; "Procedures in Handling Cases of Unaccompanied Children: A Statement of Current Practice in the U.S. Zone," by Heise, Dec. 1945.
22 PAG 4/3.0.11.0.1.3:8, Unaccompanied Children - General: "Plan for Location and Documentation of UN Children in German Institutions and Families," Welfare Branch, UNRRA CHQ, 20 Feb. 1946.
23 PAG 4/3.0.11.3.0:60, Welfare-March 1946–Aug. 1946: Whiting, Director, US Zone to Commanding General, 3rd US Army, att: Deputy Chief of Staff, 8 Feb. 1946; Child Welfare, March 1946 to 31st July: Pearl Morris, UNRRA Liaison Officer, 3rd US Army to Commanding General, 3rd US Army, att: Col. Crittenberger, G-3, 20 Feb. 1946.
24 PAG 4/1.3.1.1.0:11, P.300.4 Categories: Children: UNRRA Weekly Bulletin, 30 March 1946, 23–4.
25 RG 260, OAG, General correspondence & other records, 1945–49, 390/40/21/2 Box 91, file AG 383.7 Displaced Persons (Refugees, Expellees, Internees), 1 of 2: OMGUS, Office of the Deputy Military Governor, APO 742, ref AG 091.4 (CO), subject: "Conduct of Searches by German Authorities in Connection with Living United Nations Orphaned Children," 25 March 1946; General correspondence & other records, 1945–49, 390/40/21/2 Box 92, file AG 383.7 Displaced Persons (Refugees, Expellees, Internees) OMGUS 1946: G.H. Garde Lt. Col. AGD, Adjutant General for Military Governor, OMGUS, 14 May 1946.
26 The second call had been issued in January 1946. OMGUS had ordered all German authorities in the US Zone to immediately compile and submit within 60 days a list of all UN military personnel and civilians who had entered the Zone after 2 September 1939 and were still there (with the exception of members of the occupation forces; those residing in DP centres under the control of the occupation forces, and those who had died), including all children up to and including 15 years of age. The results had been as inaccurate as the first attempt. RG 260, PW&DP Branch: Recs Relating to Displaced Persons and Their Movements, 1945–49: Legistic [sic] Support Thru Functional Programs of DP Selection, Box 119, unnamed file: directive, L.S. Ostrander, Brigadier General, USA, Adjutant General to Directors: OMG for Greater Hesse, Wuerttemberg-Baden, Bavaria; Commanding Generals: Berlin District, Bremen Port Command, 8 Jan. 1946.

27 PAG 4/3.0.11.3.3:14, A3 of Child Search/Tracing Interest: "Monthly Report sent to UNRRA CHQ US Zone and UNRRA HQ BAOR," 30 April 1946.

28 PAG 4/3.0.11.3.3:15, UNRRA US Zone HQ Dept of Field Operations, Rel Series Child Welfare, June 1946–Dec. 1946 Search & Registration: minutes, "Conference on Search and Registration of Unaccompanied Children, 6–7 May 1946."

29 PAG 4/3.0.11.3.3:18, 168-L18 UNRRA: Richman, Assistant Director, Relief Services Division, UNRRA to Director, US Zone Tracing Bureau, OMGUS, 22 May 1946.

30 PAG 4/3.0.11.3.3:14, I 3.1 Checking of Institutions: Child Registration Memo No. 12, Team 566, Regendorf, 8 March 1946.

31 PAG 4/3.0.11.3.0:60, Child Welfare, March 1946 to 31 July 1946: "Field Report - Frankfurt and British Zone - Investigation of Sources of Information on Children brought into Germany from surrounding Eastern countries, 2–13 March 1946."

32 Ibid., Whiting, Director US Zone UNRRA to War Crimes Branch, Judge Advocate General, US Army, 12 April 1946; Heise, "War crimes participation in locating United Nations' Children," 27 July 1946.

33 PAG 4/3.0.11.0.1.0:1, Child Research and Care C2: subject "Location and Documentation of United Nations Children in German Families and Institutions," Carl H. Martini, Assistant Director, Relief Services Department, UNRRA CHQ Germany, 29 April 1946; 4/3.0.11.3.3:14, C4 Child Search Procedure: Summary of interview with Fraulein Rampfell, NSV, by Heise and William Huyssoon, 16 June 1946.

34 PAG 4/3.0.11.3.3:18, UNRRA 169-L18 C8 Nationality Policy - General: Heise to Madeleine Ley, Child Welfare Consultant, UNRRA Mission to Poland, 28 May 1946.

35 PAG 4/3.0.11.3.1:19, District 5 Monthly Reports: "Work Report for April 1946," UNRRA Team 567.

36 PAG 4/3.0.11.3.3:18, C8 Nationality Policy - General: Madeleine Ley, Child Welfare Consultant, Mission to Poland, UNRRA to Heise, Chief Child Welfare Officer, American Zone, UNRRA, 29 April 1946; PAG 4/3.0.11.3.1:19, District 5 Monthly Reports: Report No. 5, (UNRRA Team 567), 27 April 1946.

37 PAG 4/3.0.11.3.1:19, District 5 Monthly Reports: (UNRRA Team 567), 30 April 1946.

38 After the French liaison officer verified Bernard Roby's nationality, he was returned to France by March 1946. It is unclear whether his mother was ever found. PAG 4/3.0.11.3.1:23, UNRRA District No. 5 Hqs Munich-Pasing. Child Care. July 1945–June 1947: Burghardt, Bavarian Red Cross - Munich,

to UNRRA Deutsches Museum, undated; attachment, Ilse Muller, Fleck Lenggries to Bavaria R.C.; E. Davidson, District Child Welfare Officer to Regional Director, Munich, att: Regional Child Welfare Officer, 21 Dec. 1945 (with handwritten notes dated 20/2/46 and 7/3/46).

39 PAG 4/3.0.11.0.1:3, 2.Child Welfare: H.G. Wilson, for Lt. Gen. Sir Frederick Morgan, Chief of Operations, Germany to Director, US Zone, att: Heise, 19 Feb. 1946.

40 PAG 4/3.0.11.0.1.1:13, Jewish Children - General: Heise, Zone Welfare Specialist to District Director, UNRRA, att: District Child Welfare Officer, 5 April 1946; RG 260, OMG Bavaria, CAD, Central Files, PW&DP Branch, Box 23, D-338 Weekly Summaries 1946–47: "Summary for Week Ending 2400 Hours 4 April 1946," L. Miniclier, Chief, Public Welfare Branch, OMGB, to Director, OMGB.

41 PAG 4.3.0.11.0.1.3:1, 2 Child Welfare: Martini, Assistant Director, Relief Services, UNRRA US Zone, to Biggar, District Welfare Officer, District 2, UNRRA att: Virginia Lloyd, 28 March 1946; W. Kornecki, Polish Liaison Officer, attached to 2nd Fbn. 15th Inf., to M.A. Honeyball, Principal Welfare Officer, UNRRA Team 105, 19 March 1946; Margarete Treviranus, Der Oberbürgermeister, Wohlfahrts- & Jugendamt, Amtsvormund, Marburg to Pschybyslawski, Officer of the Polish Troops, 11 Feb. 1946.

42 PAG 4/3.0.11.0.1.1:4, December Reports: "Monthly Statistical Report on Displaced Persons Operations, Germany, December 1946."

43 PAG 4/3.0.11.3.3:17, District Reports - Child Welfare - Search Reports - Dist. 1: "Monthly Report for month ending Oct. 23rd, 1946."

44 PAG 4/1.3.1.1.1:23, 230.23a: minutes, Interzonal Conference on Child Search and Repatriation – Oct. 16th, 17th & 18th, 1946.

45 PAG 4/3.0.11.3.3:2, Zone Director Child Search: Ralph [W.] Collins, Deputy Director, Department of Operations, US Zone UNRRA to Director, US Zone, UNRRA, 11 March 1947.

46 PAG 4/3.0.11.0.1.1:4, B53 Child Search Repatriation Reports, Welfare: "Monthly Report, March 1947: Child Search and Repatriation."

47 PAG 4/3.0.11.3.0:60, Child (Welfare) from Jan. 1, 1947: Paul B. Edwards, Director, US Zone UNRRA to Collins, Deputy Director, US Zone UNRRA, Department of Field Operations; Heise, Child Search Officer; and R.D. MacTavish, Director, Zone Bureau of Documents and Tracing, 1 April 1947.

48 PAG 4/3.0.11.3.3:2, Field Director. Reorganization Child Search: Heise, Child Search to Collins, Field Operations, 24 April 1947; Collins, Deputy Director, US Zone, UNRRA to Zone Director, att: Heise, Zone Tracing Bureau, 1 May 1947; Heise, 21 April 1947; Heise to Collins, 19 March 1947; Collins to Heise, 24 March 1947; PAG 4/3.0.11.3.3:13, C6 Child Search

Problems: Heise, for Zone Director, US Zone Bureau of Documents and Tracing to Directors, Child Search Teams 1006, 1048, 1071, 25 April 1947; F2 Field Representative Reports: "Report of Field Situation as of June 30th 1947," Lt. C. Beaurang, Field Representative, Bureau of Documents & Tracing, Field Office, Ansbach, 30 June 1947.

49 PAG 4/3.0.11.3.3:13, C6 Child Search (Problems): Heise, Chief, Child Search/Tracing Division to Melba Foltz, Deputy Director, 6 May 1947.

50 PAG 4/3.0.11.3.3:2, Zone Director Child Search: Collins, Deputy Zone Director, Department of Field Operations, US Zone, UNRRA to Edwards, Zone Director, US Zone, UNRRA, 15 May 1947.

51 PAG 4/3.0.11.0.1.3:8, Unacc. Ch. - Policy 26 (to 30.9.46); Unaccompanied Children - Policy: Blackey, Child Search Consultant to Palmowska, Polish Red Cross, 14 Feb. 1947.

52 PAG 4/3.0.11.3.3:13, F8.1 Reports Search Teams - 1071 (567): Mary Meylan, Child Welfare Consultant, District 5 to M.A. Steinmetz, Child Search & Repatriation Officer, District 5, 22 Feb. 1947.

53 RG 260, CAD, Prisoner of War & Displaced Persons Branch: Records of the Executive of the PW&DP Branch, 1945–49, box 134, Zonal Tracing Branch: C.M. Babinski, Assistant Welfare Officer, Area Team 1048 UNRRA to Troniak, Director, Area Team 1048, UNRRA, 21 Feb. 1947.

54 PAG 4/3.0.11.3.3:2, Field Director. Reorganization Child Search: Heise, Child Search Officer to Collins, 19 March 1947; Collins to Heise, 24 March 1947; PAG 4/3.0.11.3.3:13, C6 Child Search Problems: P. Debowski, Acting Transportation Officer, UNRRA Team 1048 to E. Davidson, Director, UNRRA Area Team 1048, 15 April 1947; PAG 4/3.0.11.3.3:16, Reports Child Care: PW to CDH, 1 April 1947 and attachments.

55 PAG 4/3.0.11.3.3:17, District Reports - Child Welfare - Search Reports Dist. 1: "Monthly Report of month ending Feb. 24th, '47."

56 PAG 4/3.0.11.3.3:15, Child Care - Reports 7 June 1945–30 June 1947: Thill, Immigration Office, UNRRA Special Team 1071 to Heise, Child Search and Repatriation Specialist, UNRRA US Zone Tracing Bureau, 15 May 1947.

57 43/AJ/941, Narrative Report - Child Care Zone Hqs: "Monthly Report for June 1947." Here and throughout these notes all archival documents beginning with 43/AJ/XXX are from the Archives Nationales de la France, International Refugee Organisation (IRO) Archives, Paris.

58 PAG 4/3.0.11.3.0:60, Child (Welfare) from Jan. 1, 1947: Edwards, Director, US Zone UNRRA to Fisher, Ministry of Social Welfare, Czechoslovakia, 13 Feb. 1947.

59 PAG 4/3.0.11.0.1.0:1, Child Search + Care C2: "Report on trip to Czechoslovakia for Conferences on Unaccompanied Children – 9–15 Jan.

1947," Blackey, Child Search and Repatriation Consultant, CHQ Germany, 24 Jan. 1947.

60 PAG 4/3.0.11.3.3:14, C81 Nationality policy - Czech: Edwards, Zone Director, UNRRA US Zone, to Commanding General, USFET HQ, att: Chief Czechoslovakian Liaison Officer, 17 Feb. 1947; Anna Lutack, Principal Welfare Officer, UNRRA Team 567, District 5 to Steinmetz, District Child Search and Repatriation Officer, 28 Jan. 1947 (in Aug. 1947, the children had still not been cleared by Czechoslovakia and remained in Germany); Troniak to Heise, 8 Aug. 1947; 4/3.0.11.3.1:19 District 5 Monthly Reports Jan.–Feb. 1947: 20 Feb. 1947; District 5 Monthly Reports Jan.–Feb. 1947, Steinmetz, Child Search & Repatriation Officer, District 5 to S.B. Zisman, Director, District 5, UNRRA, 22 Feb. 1947.

61 PAG 4/1.0.1.0.0:5, Children Unaccompanied & Displaced 1944–46: C.T. Lloyd, Assistant General Counsel to F.H. LaGuardia, 6 Jan. 1947.

62 PAG 4/3.0.11.0.1.3:8, Unaccompanied Children - Policy: Martini, Department of Field Operations to UNRRA Mission to Poland, Warsaw, att: Roland Berger, 21 Jan. 1947.

63 PAG 4/3.0.11.3.1:5, Unaccompanied Children: "Progress Report on Child Search Activities of Roman Hrabar and Wiktor Pietruszka, special representatives from Poland," Heise, Child Search Officer, to UNRRA DP HQ, att: Child Search and Repatriation Consultant, 31 March 1947; Heise to UNRRA DP HQ, att: Blackey, Child Search Consultant, 1 April 1947.

4 Legal Complications

1 PAG 4/3.0.11.0.1.3:1, 2.Child Welfare: cable EX-72609, 25 July 1945, HQ Com Zone to CG USFET Main; PAG 4/3.0.11.3.3:14, C1 Child Welfare General: E. Davidson to Whiting, 25 Oct. 1945; RG 260, OAG, General correspondence & other records, 1945–49, 390/40/21/2 Box 92, file AG 383.7 Displaced Persons, vol. 1, OMG 1945–46: cable S-14256, Eisenhower to US Group CC, 12th, 3rd, 7th, and15th Army Groups, VI Corps, USSTAF, EDATC, CFRC, ECAD, MIS, Berlin District, HQ COMDT, USFET, Com Z (USFET Rear), and MIS and GFRC, 28 July 1945.

2 PAG 4/3.0.11.3.1:23, UNRRA District No. 5 Hqs Munich-Pasing. Child Care, July 1945–June 1947: L.A. Schine, HPC Chief Proc & Supply Officer to Heise and Bakeman, undated; Heise, Zone Child Welfare Officer, Relief Services Division to District Dir - Munich (att: District Child Welfare Officer), 10 Jan. 1946.

3 Ibid., Heise to District Child Welfare Officer, 17 Jan. 1946.

4 PAG 4/3.0.11.3.3:14, C1 M. Hutton, Acting Director, UNRRA Team 182, Kloster Indersdorf to Heise, 21 Jan. 1946.
5 PAG 4/3.0.11.3.1:23, UNRRA District No. 5 Hqs Munich-Pasing. Child Care, July 1945–June 1947: Schine to Heise and Bakeman, undated; Heise to District Director - Munich (att: District Child Welfare Officer), 10 Jan. 1946.
6 PAG 4/3.0.11.3.3:14, C1: V. Lloyd, Child Welfare Specialist, UNRRA District 2, US Zone, to Heise, 5 Feb. 1946.
7 PAG 4/3.0.11.3.1:10, Monthly Welfare reports: Virginia L. Poste, Child Welfare Specialist, UNRRA District No. 2, to Biggar, Relief Services Officer, 21 June 1946; PAG 4/3.0.11.3.3:14, C1 Child Welfare General: C. Babinski, Assistant Welfare Officer, Team 566, Regensburg to Troniak, Director, Team 566, Regensburg, 16 Aug. 1946; PAG 4/3.0.11.3.0:60, II. Reports. a) Regular and Special Reports. Zone HQ - Welfare - Relief Services. March 1946 - Aug. 1946 (Section 2.): Biggar, Relief Services Officer, UNRRA District Office No. 2, Wiesbaden, to R.C. Raymond, District Director, 23 July 1946.
8 PAG 4/3.0.11.3.3:14, C1: Child Welfare General, CDH to MJM, 27 May 1946.
9 PAG 4/3.0.11.3.1:23, UNRRA District No. 5 Hqs Munich-Pasing. Child Care, July 1945–June 1947: Schine to Heise and Bakeman, undated; Heise to District Dir - Munich (att: District Child Welfare Officer), 10 Jan. 1946.
10 PAG 4/3.0.11.0.1.1:3, Germany - Feb. Reports: "Report for February 1946," Sir Frederick Morgan, Chief of Operations, Germany.
11 PAG 4/3.0.11.3.3:14, CI: Child Welfare General: Whiting, Zone Director, US Zone to Major Strauss, Displaced Persons Officer, USFET, 23 Feb. 1946.
12 Ibid., M. Hutton, Acting Director UNRRA Team 182, Kloster Indersdorf to Heise, 21 Jan. 1946.
13 Ibid., A.T. Berney-Ficklin, District Director to Zone Child Search Officer, UNRRA US Zone HQ, 3 March 1947; S.M. Davis, Child Search Officer, UNRRA Team 1006 to Ellen Trigg, District Child Search Officer, District 1, 27 Feb. 1947; PAG 4/3.0.11.3.1:4, District 1 Monthly Report Feb. 1947: "District Child Search Officer's Monthly Report, Feb. 1947"; Eileen M. Davidson, Director, UNRRA Child Search Team 1048 to Zone Child Search Officer, US Zone, UNRRA, 15 April 1947; S. Margaret Davis, Child Search Team 1006 to UNRRA US Zone HQ, att: Child Search Officer, 10 April 1947.
14 PAG 4/3.0.11.3.3:14, C1 Child Welfare General: "Conference Held on Army Mascots in Bremen 6.3.47," Jeanette Gevev, Principal Welfare Officer, Child Search Team 1028, UNRRA District 2, to Margaret J. Newton, Child Search Officer, District 2 Headquarters, 12 March 1947.
15 Ibid., Gevev, "Conference Held on Army Mascots in Bremen, 6.3.47."
16 PAG 4/3.0.11.3.3:14, C1 Child Welfare General: Heise, Chief, Child Search/ Tracing Division to Lt. Rapp, Field Representative, Zone Division of

Tracing and Child Search, 11 June 1947; 43/AJ/948, Army Mascots: N. Lange, Child Search Officer, Bremen to Gevev, 26 March 1947.

17 43/AJ/948, Army Mascots: Lange to Newton, Director, Child Search Team, Mannheim, 13 May 1947; PAG 4/3.0.11.3.3:14, C1 Child Welfare General: Heise to Rapp, 11 June 1947.

18 43/AJ/954, Yugoslavian Affairs: Circular No. 1, G.J. Skapski, A/C Administrator, IRO Area Team 1066 Munich, School Wartenberg, 15 Sept. 1947.

19 PAG 4/3.0.11.3.3:14, C35 Colored Children, "AG 158 GAP-AGO Paternity Claims by Non-Nationals": J.V. Sheldon, Lt. Col., Assistant Adjutant General, by command of General McNarney, USFET to all Commanding Generals and Directors of OMG Bavaria, Wuerttemberg-Baden and Greater Hesse, 5 March 1946.

20 PAG 4/3.0.11.3.3:14, C3.5 Colored Children: Heise, Child Welfare Branch, Relief Services Division to District Directors, Districts 1, 2, 3, 5 att: District Child Welfare Officer, 23 July 1946.

21 Ibid., Biggar, Relief Services Officer to Richmond, Relief Services Div, UNRRA US Zone, att: Heise, Child Welfare Officer, 5 Aug. 1946.

22 The US Committee for the Care of European Children was approved by the US government as the sole agency authorized to arrange the transfer to and adoption of unaccompanied children in the United States.

23 PAG 4/3.0.11.3.3:15, Child Welfare (Gen.) Jan. 1946–Jan. 1947: Heise, Child Search Officer, to UNRRA CHQ Germany, att: Child Search Officer, 5 Nov. 1946; PAG 4/3.0.11.0.0:7, 014.6 Unaccompanied Children - Reports on: Martini, Department of Field Operations to ERO, att: Deborah Pentz, 20 Dec. 1946.

24 PAG 4/3.0.11.3.1:12, District 3 Monthly Reports Jan.–Feb. 1947: E. Davidson, District Child Search Officer, UNRRA District 3 to Field Operations, US Zone UNRRA, 22 Jan. 1947; PAG 4/3.0.11.3.3:14, C1: Child Welfare General: Heise to Collins, Deputy Zone Director, Department of Field Operations, US Zone HQ, 27 Jan. 1947; Collins to Heise, 31 Jan. 1947.

25 PAG 4/3.0.11.3.1:23, UNRRA District No. 5 Hqs Munich-Pasing. Child Care, July 1945–June 1947:19: D. Ryan, Infantry Caserne, to Carpenter, 25 Feb. 1946; A. Lutack, Asst Child Welfare Officer to Bruce, Relief Services Officer, 11 March 1946; M. Bruce, Relief Services Officer, to J.H. Smith, Director, UNRRA Team 114 Augsburg, 11 March 1946.

26 PAG 4/3.0.11.3.1:4, Director's Monthly Report 30 June 1946: "Child Welfare Report - June."

27 PAG 4/3.0.11.3.3:14, Child Welfare General: "Notes taken at Meeting held at UNRRA US Zone HQ on Friday Feb. 21st 1947, to discuss infant mortality and medical care problems in DP Camps."

28 PAG 4/3.0.11.0.0:7, .014.6/B: Whiting, Zone Director, UNRRA, US Zone to UNRRA CHQ, att: Legal Advisor & Child Welfare Officer, 23 Feb. 1946.

29 PAG 4/3.0.11.3.3:17, District Reports - Child Welfare - Search Reports - District 1: "Child Welfare Report - February."

30 PAG 4/3.0.11.3.1:4, Director's Monthly Report 30 April 1946: "Monthly Report - April."

31 PAG 4/3.0.11.3.1:12, District 3 Monthly Reports Jan.–Feb. 1947: E. Davidson, District Child Search Officer, UNRRA District 3 to Field Operations, US Zone UNRRA, 22 Jan. 1947; PAG 4/3.0.11.3.3:14, C1: Child Welfare General: Heise, Child Search Officer to Collins, Deputy Zone Director, Department of Field Operations, US Zone HQ, 27 Jan. 1947; Collins to Heise, 31 Jan. 1947.

32 PAG 4/3.0.11.0.0:7, .014.6/B: Whiting, Zone Director, UNRRA, US Zone to UNRRA CHQ, att: Legal Advisor & Child Welfare Officer, 23 Feb. 1946.

33 PAG 4/3.0.11.3.3:13, C6 Child Search (Problems): John W. Rourk to Heise, 13 May 1946.

34 In April 1946, Eileen Davidson drew the US Zone's attention to a special home for pregnant girls that had been established in the British Zone: the Loccum Home. The idea appealed to many, as it would be a means of providing the young mothers with good medical care and protection from social censure while they worked out the best solution for themselves and their children in a supportive and sheltered environment. Unfortunately, it was never replicated in the US Zone. PAG 4/3.0.11.3.3:14, Displaced Persons - Children - Child Welfare Policy - Delinquency: E. Davidson, District Child Welfare Officer, UNRRA District No. 3, Regensburg to Assistant Director, Relief Services, UNRRA US Zone HQ, Pasing, att: Zone Child Welfare Specialist, 3 June 1946; PAG 4/3.0.11.0.1.1:14, Zone Director Report - US Zone July 1946: June 1946 report.

35 PAG 4/3.0.11.0.1.1:14, Zone Director Report - US Zone Oct/45-Mar/46: Extracts from "US Zone Child Welfare Report - Feb. 1946"; PAG 4/3.0.11.3.1:4, Director's Monthly Report, 30 April 1946: "Monthly Report - April"; PAG 4/3.0.11.0.1.3:8, Policy - Unacc Ch: Selene Gifford, Director, Welfare and Repatriation Division, ERO to Chief of Operations, UNRRA CHQ Germany, att: Relief Services, 1 June 1946, "Statement on Problems Relating to Unaccompanied Children and Recommended Action by Military Authorities" attached.

36 PAG 4/1.3.1.1.0:11, P.300.4 Categories: Children: "Recommendations Pertaining to the Report on 'Unaccompanied children' dated 20 July 1944, by Expert Commission III, Subcommittee on Welfare for Europe, UNRRA."

37 PAG 4/1.3.1.1.2.1:1, Guide, Welfare: *Welfare Guide: Services to UN Nationals Displaced in Germany*, UNRRA ERO Welfare Division, 15 March 1945.

38 PAG 4/3.0.11.0.1.3:9: note to file, "for discussion with Schottland," Heise, 4 Sept. 1945; PAG 4/1.3.1.1.0:11, P.300.4 Categories: Children: minutes, "Inter-Zone Child Welfare Conference, Hochst, 3-4 Jan. 1946"; 4/1.0.1.0.0:32 Displaced Persons chron file (ERO Legal Advisor) 1946: C.T. Lloyd, Legal Advisor to Aves, Child Care Consultant, Welfare and Repatriation Division, 12 April 1946; PAG 4/1.0.1.0.0:32, Displaced Persons Directives - DPs 1945–1947: European Region Order No. 40K, 14 Aug. 1946; PAG 4/3.0.11.3.3:15, C2 Child Welfare legal matters: Whiting, Zone Director, UNRRA US Zone to Commanding General, USFET, att: Assistant Chief of Staff G-5, 14 Nov. 1946.

39 PAG 4/3.0.11.0.0:7, 0.14.6/A Unaccompanied Children - General Correspondence: M.L. Barble, Asst Legal Adviser to Legal Adviser, UNRRA, US Zone HQ, 28 May 1946; PAG 4/3.0.11.0.1.3:8, Policy - Unacc Ch: Gifford, Director, Welfare and Repatriation Division, ERO to Chief of Operations, UNRRA CHQ Germany, att: Relief Services, 1 June 1946, "Statement on Problems Relating to Unaccompanied Children and Recommended Action by Military Authorities"; S-0412-0013, United States Zone - Administrative Orders, No. 1-85: Administrative Order No. 47, "Immigration to United States, unaccompanied children," 11 April 1946.

40 RG 260, POW&DP Branch: Recs Relating to Displaced Persons and Their Movements, 1945–49: Legistic [*sic*] Support Thru Functional Programs of DP Selection, Box 119, file unnamed: directive, subject: "Unaccompanied Children," HQ USFET, July 1946; CAD, POW&DP Branch, Records Relating to DPs in Germany and Other Countries, 1945-49, Box 141, Title 20: MGR Title 20, "Displaced Persons, Refugees and Expellees," 1 June 1947; PAG 4/3.0.11.3.3:14, A3 of Child Search/Tracing Interest: L.S. Ostrander, Brigadier General, for General McNarney, HQ USFET to Commanding Generals, OMGUS; Third US Army Area; Berlin District; Continental, Base Section, 11 May 1946.

41 PAG 4/3.0.11.0.0:7, .014.6 Unaccompanied Children - Reports on: "Proposed statement to ACC on problems relating to UN Unaccompanied Children in Germany," 27 April 1946, issued by UNRRA CHQ Germany, Arolsen.

42 PAG 4/1.3.1.1.1:23, 230.23a Germany:DP Unaccompanied Children: UNRRA CHQ, guide, 15 May 1946, ref: General Bulletin 78, "Decisions Affecting Status and Repatriation of Unaccompanied Children."

43 PAG 4/3.0.1.0.1.3:8, Unaccompanied Children-General: "Planning for Unaccompanied D.P. Children (Under 18)," District Bulletin, UNRRA

US Zone, 3 Sept. 1945; RG 260, Office of the Adjutant General, General Correspondence & other records, 1945–49, 390/40/21/2, Box 91, AG 383.7 Displaced Persons (Refugees, Expellees, Internees), 1 of 2: OMGUS, "Conduct of Searches by German Authorities in Connection with Living United Nations Orphaned Children," Office of the Deputy of Military Governor, OMGUS, 25 March 1946; Prisoner of War & Displaced Persons Branch: Recs Relating to Displaced Persons and Their Movements, 1945–49: Legistic [sic] Support Thru Functional Programs of DP Selection, Box 119, unnamed file: L.S. Ostrander, Brigadier General, USA, Adjutant General to Directors: OMG for Greater Hesse, Wuerttemberg-Baden, Bavaria; Commanding Generals: Berlin District, Bremen Port Command, 8 Jan. 1946.

44 See chapter 7 for an extensive discussion of the Allied Control Authority directive.

45 PAG 4/1.3.1.1.1:23, 230.23a Germany: DP Unaccompanied Children: "Proposed A.C.A. Directive on Determination of Nationality of Unaccompanied Children" and "ACA Revised Draft Directive on Unaccompanied Children," UNRRA, Central Committee of the Council (CC(46)129), 2 Dec. 1946; PAG 4/3.0.11.0.1.1:4, Child Search Repatriation Reports - Welfare, Minutes: "Child Welfare Conference - Schloss Muhlenberg Thursday and Friday, June 13th and 14th 1946."

46 PAG 4/3.0.11.3.3:15, C 5 2 Child Search Policy EUCOM. OMGUS: Martini, Department of Field Ops, to Zone Director, UNRRA, US Zone, att: Director of Field Ops, 2 Nov. 1946.

47 PAG 4/3.0.11.0.1.4:4, Reports - Special: "Summary Report on Child Welfare & Child Search for Preparatory Commission of IRO," 24 May 1947; 43/ AJ/597, Unaccompanied Children 39/1 General Policies and General Reports 1947: "UNRRA Closure Report of United Nations Unaccompanied Children in Germany, June 1947," Blackey, Child Search Consultant, UNRRA DPHQ.

48 PAG 4/1.3.1.1.1:23, 230.23a Germany: DP Unaccompanied Children: minutes, inter-zonal conference on Child Search and Repatriation, 16–18 Oct. 1946.

49 PAG 4/3.0.11.0.0:7, .014.6 Unaccompanied Children - Reports on: "Proposed Statement to ACC on problems related to UN Unaccompanied Children in Germany," 27 April 1946; PAG 4/3.0.11.0.1.3:8, Policy-Unacc Ch: Gifford, Director, Welfare and Repatriation Division, ERO to Chief of Operations, UNRRA CHQ, att: Relief Services, 1 June 1946; "Proposed Statement to ACC on Problems Relating to UN Unaccompanied Children in Germany," Blackey, 1 May 1946; PAG 4/3.0.11.0.1.4:4, Reports-Special

38: "Report on Unaccompanied United Nations' Children in Germany," Blackey, Child Welfare Consultant, 24 June 1946; RG 260, PW&DP Branch: Recs relating to Displaced Persons and Their Movements, 1945-49: Legistic [sic] Support Thru Functional Programs of DP Selection, Box 119, unnamed file: Martini, Assistant Director, Relief Services, UNRRA CHQ Germany to UNRRA HQs: British Zone, US Zone, French Zone, 16 May 1946; "Decisions Affecting Status and Repatriation of Unaccompanied Children," 15 May 1946; PAG 4/3.0.11.0.0:7, 014.6/A Unaccompanied Children - General Correspondence: M.L. Barble, Assistant Legal Adviser, UNRRA CHQ Germany to Legal Adviser, US Zone HQ, 28 May 1946..

50 PAG 4/3.0.11.0.1.0:1, Child Research + Care C.2: "Problems in Relation to Repatriation of Unaccompanied Children," Agenda Item, DPHQ Conference, 13–15 March 1947.

51 PAG 4/3.0.11.0.1.4:4, Reports to Repatriation Missions: "Summary Statement on Unaccompanied Children in Germany," Child Search Consultant for Germany, 24 March 1947.

52 PAG 4/3.0.11.0.0:7, .014.6/B: M. [Manfred] Simon to Lt. Col. B.H. Brown, Legal Branch, G-5 USFET, 19 Jan. 1946.

53 PAG 4/3.0.11.0.1.3:1, Adoptions - Unaccompanied Children: E. Davidson, District Child Welfare Officer, UNRRA District HQ No. 3, Regensburg to Richman, Assistant Director Relief Services, US Zone HQ, 11 April 1946, att: Heise, Zone Welfare Specialist.

54 PAG 4/3.0.11.0.0:7, .014.6/B: Simon to Gen. Counsel, ERO, 19 Jan. 1946; PAG 3.0.11.3.3:15 Child Care - Reports 7 June 1945–30 June 1947: A.T. Berney-Ficklin, Director, District 1, to Assistant Director Relief Services, att: Child Welfare Specialist, 11 Feb. 1946.

55 PAG 4/3.0.11.0.1.3:8, Policy - Unacc Ch: Gifford to Chief of Operations, UNRRA CHQ Germany, att: Relief Services, 1 June 1946, "Statement on Problems Relating to Unaccompanied Children and Recommended Action by Military Authorities."

56 PAG 4/3.0.11.0.1.3:1, Adoptions-Unaccompanied Children: Blackey to Mrs Robert A Boyd, Tracy, California, 25 April 1946.

57 PAG 4/3.0.11.0.1.3:7, 21. Polish Unaccompanied Children + Polish Red Cross 1/10/46–31/12/46: Blackey, Child Welfare Consultant to W. Wolski, Repatriation Mission, Warsaw, 23 Sept. 1946.

58 PAG 4/3.0.11.0.0:7, .014.6/B: Simon to General Counsel, ERO, 19 Jan. 1946; PAG 4/3.0.11.3.3:15, Child Care - Reports: 7 June 1945–30 June 1947, Berney-Ficklin to Assistant Director Relief Services, att: Child Welfare Specialist, 11 Feb. 1946.

59 RG 260, Legal Division, Records of Legal Advice Branch, Legal Files, 1945–50, Box 52, LA 30.1 Adoptions: cable SC-22431 McNarney to OMGUS for Keating, 17 Nov. 1946; PAG 4/3.0.11.0.1.3:1, Adoptions - Unaccompanied Children: Martini, Department of Field Operations to ERO, att: Deborah Pentz, 23 Dec. 1946.

60 PAG 4/3.0.11.0.1.3:8, Policy - Unacc Ch: Gifford to Chief of Operations, UNRRA CHQ Germany, att: Relief Services, 1 June 1946, "Statement on Problems Relating to Unaccompanied Children and Recommended Action by Military Authorities."

61 RG 260, Legal Division, Records of Legal Advice Branch, Box 52, LA-30.1 Adoptions: C. Fahy, Legal Div to G-5 USFET, 26 April 1946.

62 Ibid., Blackey, Child Welfare Consultant, UNRRA CHQ Germany, to Dickman, Legal Division, OMGUS, 6 May 1946.

63 43/AJ/597, Unaccompanied Children 39/1 General Policies and General Reports 1947: "UNRRA Closure Report of United Nations Unaccompanied Children in Germany," Blackey, Child Search Consultant, UNRRA DPHQ, June 1947.

64 Ibid.

65 RG 260, Legal Div/Legal Advice Branch, Box 52, LA 30.1 Adoptions: Blackey, Child Welfare Consultant, UNRRA CHQ Germany, to Dickman, Legal Division, OMGUS, 6 May 1946.

66 Ibid., cable CC-9677 Keating, OMGUS, to WDSCA GO, 26 June 1947; Legal Division, Records of Legal Advice Branch, Box 52, LA-30.1 Adoptions: Fahy to G-5 USFET, 26 April 1946; OMGB, Records of the Legal Division/ Records re: Adoption Policy and US State Adoption Laws, 1947–50, Box 108, Adoption Policy: excerpt, Daily Bulletin, OMGB, 8 Oct. 1947; PAG 4/3.0.11.3.0: 60 II. Reports. a) Regular and Special Reports. Zone HQ-Welfare-Relief Services, March 1946–Aug. 1946: "Consolidated Report for July, 1946, District Relief Services Department, District No. 5, UNRRA"; 43/AJ/597, Unaccompanied Children 39/1 General Policies and General Reports 1947: "UNRRA Closure Report of United Nations Unaccompanied Children in Germany."

67 PAG 4/3.0.11.0.1.3:1, Adoptions - Unaccompanied Children: Blackey to Mrs Robert A. Boyd, Tracy CA, 25 April 1946, as an example (the file is full of similar letters); PAG 4/3.0.11.0.1.0:1, Child Search + Care C2: "Report on Joint Conference with Austrian Mission on Unaccompanied Children, Bad Wiessee, Germany, 7–8 Jan. 1947."

68 PAG 4/3.0.11.3.0:60, Adoption. Child Care: Heise, Chief, Child Search/ Tracing Division to Trigg, Child Care Division, UNRRA US Zone HQ, 12 June 1947; Rhea Radin, Chief, Repatriation and Care Division, for Myer Cohen, Acting Chief, DP Operations to Edwards, Director, UNRRA

US Zone HQ, 22 May 1947; E.A. Reich, Director, Division of DP Care,
for Cohen, Acting Chief, DP Operations to Heise, 16 April 1947; cable
(unnumbered), Reich to UNRRA HQ Washington, 10 April 1947.

69 Martha Branscombe began her employment in 1931 as an assistant to
the Speaker of the Alabama House of Representatives. During the 1930s,
she served as county director of the Department of Social Welfare for the
Alabama Relief Administration, and then as consultant on family relations
to the Land Management Division for the Tennessee Valley Authority.
In 1942, she worked as a consultant on international planning for the US
Children's Bureau of the Department of Labor, charged with preliminary
planning for postwar relief for children. When the Department of
State became involved in planning for international relief, she was
loaned to them as an assistant to the director. She ultimately joined the
newly formed UNRRA headquarters in Washington, DC, as part of the
team organizing and staffing its Social Welfare Section. In early 1944,
Branscombe was assigned to assist in the creation of the Social Service
Division of the European Office of UNRRA. See www.naswfoundation
.org/pioneers/b/branscombe.htm (consulted 5 July 2010).

70 "Ad litem" means, literally, "for the purposes of the suit." A guardian is
appointed by the court to appear before the court on behalf of a minor
child or an incompetent person. Unless appointed in some additional
capacity such as a "special guardian," the guardian does not have power
over the child's estate or person and their decision-making power is
limited to what is necessary for carriage of the action or defence.

71 PAG 4/1.0.1.0.1:15, Ger-DP1: Branscombe to Sir George Reid, 26 Oct. 1944.

72 Ibid., A.H. Robertson to Dudley Ward, 13 Nov. 1944.

73 PAG 4/1.3.1.1.0:11, P.300.4B Unaccompanied and/or Stateless Children:
Branscombe to Reid, 6 Dec. 1944.

74 PAG 4/1.0.1.0.1:15, Ger-DP1: Carter to Scott, 15 Nov. 1944; Carter to Reid,
27 Dec. 1944.

75 PAG 4/1.3.1.1.0:11, P300.4a Categories - Unaccompanied Children:
Branscombe to Capt. [J.S.] Paterson, 30 March 1945.

76 PAG 4/1.0.1.0.1:15, Ger-DP1: Branscombe to Reid, 5 Jan. 1945.

77 PAG 4/1.3.1.1.0:11, P.300.4a Categories – Unaccompanied Children: Bradford
to Paterson, 21 March 1945; PAG 4/1.3.1.1.0:11, P.300.4B: Branscombe to Reid,
15 Jan. 1945.

78 PAG 4/1.3.1.1.0:11, P.300.4a Categories – Unaccompanied Children: Paterson
to Reid, 21 March 1945.

79 Ibid., Roger Carter to Berger, 7 March 1945.

80 Ibid., Paterson to Reid, 21 March 1945.

81 Ibid., Branscombe to Paterson, 30 March 1945.

82 RG 260, PW&DP Branch: Recs Relating to Displaced Persons and Their
    Movements, 1945–49: Correspondence July 1949 Thru Correspondence
    Misc, Box 121, "Correspondence - Misc": "Care and Protection of Displaced
    Children Uncovered in Germany", H.H. Newman, Col., AGD, Assistant
    Adjutant General, for Supreme Commander, SHAEF, 6 March 1945; RG
    331, OCS, Secretary, General Staff, Decimal File May 1943–Aug. 1945,
    Entry 1, Box 88, 383.7 vol. 2 (Refugees and Displaced Persons of European
    nationality): A.E. Grasett, Lt. General, Assistant Chief of Staff, G-5 SHAEF
    to Chief of Staff, 28 Feb. 1945; T.J. Davis, Brigadier General, USA, Adjutant
    General, SHAEF to HQ 21st Army Group; Commanding General of 12
    Army Group, 6 Army Group and Communications Zone, 22 Feb. 1945.
83 PAG 4/3.0.11.3.3:15, C2 Welfare Legal Matters: Heise, Zone Welfare
    Specialist, to C. Bern, Deputy Director, UNRRA Team 533, 12 Aug. 1946; PAG
    4/3.0.11.0.1.3:1, Adoptions - Unaccompanied Children: Richman, Assistant
    Director, Relief Services Division for US Zone Director, UNRRA to J.H. Roe,
    Relief Services Officer, UNRRA/USFET Liaison Office, 5 Aug. 1946; PAG
    4/3.0.11.0.0:7, .014.6 Unaccompanied Children - Reports on: Legal Division
    OMGUS to PW&DP, 23 Aug. 1946; RG 260, CAD, PW&DP Branch, Records
    Relating to DPs in Germany and Other Countries, 1945–49, Box 146, 014.33
    Repatriation (Unclassif): telegram (unnumbered), Messec, POW&DP OMGUS,
    to Director, OMG Greater Hesse, for Public Welfare and DP, 29 Aug. 1946.
84 PAG 4/3.0.11.0.1.3:8, Policy - Unaccompanied Children: Gifford to Chief of
    Operations, UNRRA CHQ, att: Relief Services, 1 June 1946, "Statement on
    Problems Relating to Unaccompanied Children and Recommended Action
    by Military Authorities"; PAG 4/1.0.1.0.0:32, Displaced Persons chron
    file (ERO Legal Advisor) 1946: Charlotte T. Lloyd, Legal Advisor to Aves,
    Child Care Consultant, Welfare and Repatriation Division, 12 April 1946.
85 PAG 4/1.0.0.0:21, Displaced Persons (thru 31 March 1947): Ian M. Hudson,
    Foreign Office, London to Lt. General Sir Humfrey Gale, ERO, UNRRA, 14
    Oct. 1946; Gale to Major General Lowell Rooks, Director General, UNRRA
    HQ, 16 Jan. 1947; PAG 4/3.0.11.0.1.0:1, Child Search + Care C2: "Report
    on Joint Conference with Austrian Mission on Unaccompanied Children,"
    Bad Wiessee, Germany, 7–8 Jan. 1947.
86 Ibid (both documents).

5 The Infiltrees

1 PAG 4/1.3.1.1.0:12, P.300.10 Categories, Jews, Bulgaria and Roumania:
   Aickin to Lehman, 13 Feb. 45 (draft). The Hungarian situation at the end
   of the Second World War was disastrous. The war had ended militarily

for Hungary when its army was defeated in Jan.–Feb. 1943. Even before then, the Hungarian government had attempted to surrender to the Western allies. By late March 1944, the presence of Soviet troops near the country's borders had given added emphasis to this drive. In response, the German forces occupied Hungary, installed a fascist regime, and looted the country, with the new, pro-Nazi regime's assistance. With the Soviet invasion of Hungary in late 1944, Hungary became a battleground, and the devastation, especially in Budapest, was extensive. In the aftermath of the Soviet occupation, the Hungarian economy (which was denied Marshall Plan aid) was racked with hyperinflation (reaching more than 50% per month by July 1945), "merciless" Soviet economic exploitation and looting, steep reparations payments, stiff occupation costs (Hungary had to feed and house the Soviet occupation forces), desperate food shortages, and the imposition of a ruthless Communist occupation regime. There were, in addition, a series of small-scale pogroms directed against those Hungarian Jews who had survived the Holocaust and returned home, part of a wave of postwar pogroms against Jews that swept Eastern Europe, fed by the newly established Communist regime in an effort to consolidate its power. The worst of these pogroms erupted in July 1946. By March 1946, 108,500 Jews intended to leave Hungary for Palestine or elsewhere, according to a joint memorandum of the Hungarian Jewish organizations issued at the time. In this environment, the Zionist movement flourished. See: Pierre L. Siklos, *War Finance, Reconstruction, Hyperinflation and Stabilization in Hungary, 1938–48* (Basingstoke, UK: Macmillan, 1991), 97; Peter Kenez, *Hungary from the Nazis to the Soviets: The Establishment of the Communist Regime in Hungary, 1944–1948* (Cambridge: Cambridge University Press, 2006), chapter 3, passim, 149–62; Vera Ranki, *The Politics of Inclusion and Exclusion: Jews and Nationalism in Hungary* (New York: Holmes and Meier, 1999), chapter 7, passim; *European Jewry Ten Years after The War: An Account of the Development and Present Status of the Decimated Jewish Communities of Europe* (New York: Institute of Jewish Affairs of the World Jewish Congress, 1956), 67.

2 PAG 4/3.0.11.3.0:1, 15.07 Team 501, Berlin, 24 Aug.–7 Nov. 1945: G.J. Taylor, Director UNRRA Team 501, to Vernon H. Kennedy, Zone Director UNRRA HQ Germany, 27 Aug. 1945.

3 PAG 4/3.0.11.3.3:13, F2 Field Representative reports: "Field Report - Child Welfare EMD, 17–19 September 1945."

4 PAG 4/3.0.11.3.0:60, Child Welfare 1 Aug. 1946–1 Dec. 1946: Heise, Zone Child Welfare Specialist to Whiting, Director, US Zone UNRRA, 23 Jan. 1946; PAG 4/3.0.11.0.1.1:13, Central HQ Child Welfare Material Jewish

Children - General: D. de Traz, International Red Cross, Czechoslovakia to Headquarters, 3rd Army, 5 Jan. 1946; PAG 4/3.0.11.3.0:60, Welfare Jan. 1946–Aug. 1946: Heiset to US Zone Director, 8 Feb. 1946.

5 PAG 4/3.0.11.0.1.1:5, B8 Reports on Jewish DPs: "Observations on the Problem of Jewish Infiltrees," J.B. Krane, Chief, Reports and Analysis Branch, UNRRA CHQ Germany, 18 Jan. 1946; PAG 4/3.0.11.3.3:13, F2 Field Representative reports: "Field Report - Child Welfare EMD, 17–19 September 1945."

6 PAG 4/3.0.11.3.0:1, 15.07 Team 501 – Berlin, 24 Aug. 1945–7 Nov. 1945: John A. Sabo, Captain, Camp Commandant to Major Harold Mercer, Chief of DP and Welfare Section, 29 Aug. 1945; PAG 4/3.0.11.3.1:2, Various Reports, Field Supervisors etc. EMD. July 1945–Dec. 1945: Taft to Winslow, 6 Nov. 1945; PAG 4/3.0.11.3.0:20, Westerman Field Supervisor: J. Westerman, Field Supervisor to District Director, WMD, 5 Nov. 1945.

7 PAG 4/3.0.11.0.0:5, 013.0 Displaced Persons - General Correspondence on Eligibility for UNRRA Assistance: Krane, Reports and Analysis Branch to Sir Frederick Morgan, Brigadier Stawell, Pollak, Simon, de Maerel, Magolin, 6 Dec. 1945; paraphrase of USFET cable, from OMG Bavaria, cc'd OMGUS from USFET signed Eisenhower, 23 Oct. 1945.

8 PAG 4/3.0.11.3.0:1, 15.07 Team 501 – Berlin, 24 Aug. 1945–7 Nov. 1945: Sabo to Mercer, 29 Aug. 1945.

9 PAG 4/3.0.11.3.0:20, Westerman Field Supervisor, June 1945–Dec. 1945: Westerman to District Director, WMD, 12 Nov. 1945.

10 Ibid., Westerman to District Director, WMD, 1 Dec. 1945.

11 PAG 4/3.0.11.3.1:2, Reports EMD HQ, 27 July–15 Nov. 1945: R.S. Winslow, Deputy District Director to Whiting, District Director, EMD, 17 Nov. 1945.

12 PAG 4/1.3.1.1.1:25, R&W Divison - Missions Germany 1946-400.1: Harold K. Baron, Counselor at Law, New York to F.H. LaGuardia, New York City, 9 April 1946; Sidney Flatow to Lou and Bobby, 4 Dec. 1945.

13 S-0425–0002, Administrative - Correspondence - Divisions in Zone Headquarters: Director, US Zone, UNRRA, to Deputy Director i/c German Operations, UNRRA, 12 Oct. 1945.

14 It had proven impossible to get quadripartite agreement on what to do with these infiltrees, so the matter was turned over to the individual sectors' Kommandantura in Berlin for resolution. PAG 4/3.0.11.0.1.1:5, B8 Reports on Jewish DPs: "Observations on the Problem of Jewish Infiltrees," Krane, Chief, Reports and Analysis Branch, UNRRA CHQ Germany, 18 Jan. 1946.

15 S-0412–0001, Allied Control Authority, Directorate of Prisoners of War and Displaced Persons - DPOW/P 1946–47: "Treatment of Non-Germans entering

Germany," PW and DP Directorate, Appendix A to DPOW/P(46)8, undated;
"Treatment of Non-Germans entering Germany," memorandum to the Allied
Secretariat, A.W. Ward, Lt. Col. Duty Secretary, PW&DP Directorate, Allied
Control Authority (ACA), 22 Jan. 1946 DPOW/P(46)8(Final); Appendix A,
"Treatment of Non-Germans Entering Germany," to DPOW/P(46)8(Final),
22 Jan. 1946.

16 Ibid., A.W. Ward, Lt.Col. Duty Secretary, PW&DP Directorate, ACA, 12 Jan.
1946 to unknown recipient; T.N. Grazebrook, Brigadier, Chief Secretary,
Allied Secretariat, ACA to PW& DP Directorate, 7 Jan. 1946; R.G. Raw,
Lt. Col., Chief of Staff, Allied Kommandantura Berlin, to Chief Secretary,
Allied Secretariat, ACA, 5 Jan. 1946.

17 PAG 4/3.0.11.0.1.1:13, Central HQ Child Welfare Material Jewish Children -
General: Traz to Headquarters, 3rd Army, 5 Jan. 1946; PAG 4/3.0.11.0.1.1:5 B8
Reports on Jewish DPs: "Observations on the Problem of Jewish Infiltrees."

18 PAG 4/1.0.1.0.0:32, Displaced Persons - files No. 3 1945–46: cable
8855, A.E. Davidson, General Counsel to London, 27 Dec. 1945; PAG
4/3.0.11.3.0:20, Westerman Mr, Field Supervisor: Squadrilli, District
Director, WMD to all Team Directors and all Field Supervisors, 11 Dec.
1945; Guyler, Zone Director, to Director, WMD, 14 Nov. 1945.

19 PAG 4/1.0.1.0.0:33, Displaced persons - Legal and Policy Decisions 1946:
cable 7382, London to Washington, 12 Dec. 1945; PAG 4/3.0.11.0.0:5, 013.0
Displaced Persons - General Correspondence on Eligibility for UNRRA
Assistance: Sir Frederick Morgan, Chief of Operations, CHQ Germany to
General Sir H. Gale, ERO, London, 14 Dec. 1945.

20 PAG 4/3.0.11.0.0:5, 013.0 Displaced Persons - General Correspondence on
Eligibility for UNRRA Assistance: cable 41815, UNRRA London to UNRRA
Frankfurt (46), 3 Jan. 1946.

21 PAG 4/1.0.1.0.0:33, Displaced persons - Legal and Policy Decisions
1946: cable 7382, personal Presiding No. 182, London, to Washington,
12 Dec. 1945; cable 49, D. Ward, Office of the General Counsel, London,
to Washington, 2 Jan. 1946; M. Franklin, UNRRA Italian Mission to
Robertson, 8 Jan. 1946; cable 1675, Ward to Washington, 9 Feb. 1946;
cable 799, Davidson to Ward, 14 Feb. 1946; cable 2277, Ward to Davidson,
21 Feb. 1946; PAG 4/1.0.1.0.0:32, Displaced Persons - files No 3 1945–46:
cable 8855, Davidson, to London, 27 Dec. 1945; PAG 4/3.0.11.0.0:5, 013.0
Displaced Persons - General Correspondence on Eligibility for UNRRA
Assistance: Simon, Legal Advisor to G.W. Rabinoff, ERO, 8 Jan. 1946; PAG
4/1.3.1.1.0:12, P.300.11 Post-Hostility Refugees: cable 10688, O. Schachter,
General Counsel, to London, 23 Jan. 1946; cable 2278, Ward to Davidson,
Washington, 22 Feb. 1946.

22 PAG 4/1.3.1.1.0:12, P.300.11 Post-Hostility Refugees: cable 2347, Davidson to London, 12 March 1946; cable 4195, Schachter to London, 12 April 1946.

23 PAG 4/3.0.11.0.1.4:1, Conferences - US Zone: "Notes Taken at District Directors' Meeting Held at US Zone Headquarters, Munich, on 27 and 28 May 1946."

24 PAG 4/1.0.1.0.0:23, Displaced Persons - Legal and Policy Decisions 1946: Gifford, Director, Welfare & Repatriation Division, UNRRA to Sir Frederick Morgan, Chief of German Operations, UNRRA, 25 June 1946; RG 260, OAG correspondence & other records, 1945–49, 390/40/21/2, Box 91, AG 383.7 Displaced Persons (Refugees, Expellees, Internees), 2 of 2: cable S-5239, McNarney, USFET to Commanding Generals of US Army, Berlin District, cc'd to OMGUS and UNRRA Zone Director, 7 June 1946.

25 PAG 4/3.0.11.0.1.1:5, B8 Reports on Jewish DPs: "Observations on the Problem of Jewish Infiltrees."

26 PAG 4/3.0.11.0.1.4:2, Infiltrees: Krane, Chief, Reports and Analysis Branch to Sir Frederick Morgan, 18 Feb. 1946.

27 PAG 4/3.0.11.3.1:19, District 5 Monthly Reports: "Monthly Report for May [1946]."

28 PAG 4/3.0.11.0.1.4:1, Conferences - US Zone, "Notes taken at District Directors' Meeting Held at US Zone Headquarters, Munich on 27 and 28 May 1946."

29 RG 260, OAG, General correspondence & other records, 1945–49, 390/21/2 Box 91 AG 383.7 Displaced Persons (Refugees, Expellees, Internees), 1 of 2: "Weekly intelligence report for week ending 1 June 1946," DET E-291 Landkreis Wolfratshausen (Y-73).

30 PAG 4/3.0.11.3.0:60, Welfare Jan. 1946–Aug. 1946: Whiting, Director US Zone, UNRRA to Assistant Director, Relief Services Division, CHQ Germany att: Hansi Pollak, 9 Jan. 1946; "Jewish Infiltree Children," Eileen Davidson, Zone Child Welfare Worker, US Zone, UNRRA, undated.

31 PAG 4/3.0.11.0.1.1:13, Central HQ Child Welfare Material Jewish Children - General: Traz to Headquarters, 3rd Army, 5 Jan. 1946; 4/3.0.11.3.3:14 A3 of Child Search/Tracing Interest: Heise, Zone Child Welfare Specialist to District Office, Regensburg, att: Child Welfare Officer, 9 Feb. 1946; "Procedures in Handling Cases of Unaccompanied Children: A Statement of Current Practice in the U.S. Zone," Dec. 1945.

32 S-0412-0008, Central Headquarters - Monthly Narrative Reports - April 1/8/1946: "Narrative Report for April 1946"; PAG 4/3.0.11.3.1:19 District 5 Monthly Reports: "Monthly Report for May [1946]."

33 PAG 4/3.0.11.0.1.1:14, Zone Director: "Report - US Zone July 1946."

34 PAG 4/3.0.11.3.1:12, District 3 Monthly Reports July–Dec. 1946: "Monthly Report, 31 August 1946."

35 S-0425-0050, Statistics - Special Surveys - Statistical Reports Prepared by Statistics and Reports Branch - US Zone HQ: "Fluctuation of Population in US Zone, 1st July–15th Sept," Statistics and Reports Branch, US Zone UNRRA HQ, 12 Sept. 1946.

36 PAG 4/3.0.11.0.1.1:13, Jewish Children - General: Richman, Assistant Director, Relief Services, UNRRA US Zone HQ to Relief Services: Child Welfare, Education, Employment, Voluntary Agencies, Recreation, Repatriation & Immigration; District Directors, Districts 1, 2, 3, 5, extract, "Intelligence Summary" (ICIS No. 32, 23 Feb. 1946), "the Jewish Problem," 16 April 1946.

37 PAG 4/3.0.11.3.1:9, District 5 Monthly Reports: "District Director's Monthly Report for May 1946 - District 5"; RG 260 OAG, General correspondence & other records, 1945–49, 390/21/2 Box 91, AG 383.7 Displaced Persons (Refugees, Expellees, Internees), 1 of 2: "Report on Displaced Persons for June 1946, 19 July 1946."

38 Ibid., "District Director's Monthly Report for May 1946 - District 5"; District 2 Monthly Reports, July–Dec. 1946: report dated 27 July 1946; RG 260 OAG, General correspondence & other records, 1945–49, 390/21/2 Box 91 AG 383.7 Displaced Persons (Refugees, Expellees, Internees) 1 of 2: weekly intelligence report for week ending 1 June 1946.

39 PAG 4/3.0.11.0.1.4:2, Infiltrees: "Report on Infiltrees in the U.S. Zone," Krane, 10 July 1946; L.A. Dawson, Director Team 547, Funk Caserne, Munich to Director District 5, US Zone UNRRA, 5 June 1946; 4/3.0.11.3.0:60 II. Reports. a) Regular and Special Reports. Zone HQ - Welfare - Relief Services. March 1946–Aug. 1946: "District Director's Monthly Report for June 1946."

40 PAG 4/3.0.11.0.1.4:2, Infiltrees: "Report on Infiltrees in the U.S. Zone"; RG 260, OAG, General correspondence & other records, 1945–49, 390/21/2 Box 91, AG 383.7 Displaced Persons (Refugees, Expellees, Internees), 2 of 2: cable S-5239 McNarney to CG, US Army; CG Berlin District, cc'd OMGUS, UNRRA Zone Director, 7 June 1946; AG 383.7 Displaced Persons (Refugees, Expellees, Internees), 1 of 2: Division Director, POW&DP Division to Civ. Affairs Policy Enforcement Branch, 14 June 1946.

41 S-0412-0013, United States Zone - Administration Orders, No. 86-146: Administrative Order No. 108 (US Zone), 19 July 1946.

42 PAG 4/1.0.1.0.0:33, Displaced Persons - Legal and Policy Decisions #5 1946: Gifford, Director, Welfare & Repatriation Division to Sir Frederick Morgan, Chief of German Operations, UNRRA, 25 June 1946; S-0412-0013,

United States Zone - Administration Orders, No. 86-146: Administrative Order No. 108 (US Zone), 19 July 1946.

43 PAG 4/3.0.11.3.1:10, Infiltrees 30 Aug. 1946–26 Sept. 1946: James L. Smiley, Capt, DP Officer, Ninth Division Artillery DP Section, Kassel Sub-Area to Commanding General, Ninth Division Artillery, US Army, att: S-5, 16 Sept. 1946; E.H. Norby, Acting Director, District No. 2 UNRRA to G.E. Pratt, 17 Sept. 1946; Norby to Pratt, 18 Sept. 1946.

44 Michal Palgi and Shulamit Reinharz, eds., *One Hundred Years of Kibbutz Life: A Century of Crises and Reinvention* (New Brunswick, NJ: Transaction, 2011), 3–5.

45 Sarah E. Karesh and Mitchell M. Hurvitz, eds., *Encyclopedia of Judaism* (New York: Facts on File, 2006), 271–2.

46 PAG 4/3.0.11.0.1.4:2, Infiltrees: "Report on Infiltrees in the U.S. Zone"; L.A. Dawson, Director Team 547, Funk Caserne, Munich to Director District 5, US Zone UNRRA, 5 June 1946.

47 Ibid. (both documents); RG 260, OAG, General correspondence & other records, 1945–49, 390/21/2 Box 91, AG 383.7 Displaced Persons (Refugees, Expellees, Internees) 1 of 2: "Report on Displaced Persons for June 1946."

48 PAG 4/3.0.11.3.1:12, District 3 Monthly Reports March, April, May, June 1946: report dated 25 June 1946.

49 PAG 4/3.0.11.2.0.1:10, Policy - Planning UNRRA - BAOR Direcs 08/45-07/46: G.W. Erskine, Major General, Deputy Chief of Staff (Policy), Office of the Deputy Military Governor, HQ BAOR to UNRRA CHQ, Germany, 29 July 1946; PAG 4/1.3.1.1.0:12 P.300.11 Post-Hostility Refugees: cable 11402, Robertson GC to London, 25 July 1946.

50 S-0412-0008, Central Headquarters - Monthly Narrative Reports - July 7, 1946–4/9/1946: "Monthly Narrative Report of Chief of Operations, July 1946"; PAG 4/3.0.11.2.0.2:32, 469, Children's Homes and Holidays, Chronological,Area Team 903, July 27, 1946–June 17, 1947: Technical Instruction No. 6, UNRRA BAOR.

51 S-0412-0008, Central Headquarters - Monthly Narrative Reports - July 7, 1946–4/9/1946: "Monthly Narrative Report of Chief of Operations, July 1946"; PAG 4/3.0.11.3.0:20, Field Ops. File 8. Feb. 1946-Nov.1946: cable F-1954, Keyes, G-5 Third US Army to Director UNRRA US Zone, 15 July 1946; 4/3.0.11.3.1:4 Director's Monthly Report 31 Aug. 1946: "District Monthly Report. District Office No. 1," 30 Aug. 1946; 4/3.0.11.3.1:9 District 2 Monthly Reports July-Dec 1946: "Monthly Report for Aug. 1946 - District No. 2"; PAG 4/3.0.11.3.1:12, Monthly Report: A.C. Dunn, Director, UNRRA District No. 3 to Whiting, Director, US Zone UNRRA, 31 Aug. 1946.

52 PAG 4/3.0.11.3.0:20, Field OPS file 8 Feb 46-Nov 46: Whiting, Director, US Zone UNRRA to the Commanding General, Third US Army, 9 Aug. 1946; Whiting to the Commanding General, Third US Army, 16 Aug. 1946; PAG 4/3.0.11.3.1:12, District 3 Monthly Reports July–Dec. 1946: "District Director's Monthly Report," 30 Sept. 1946.

53 PAG 4/3.0.11.3.1:23, UNRRA District No. 5 Munich-Pasing: "Child Welfare Statistics, UNRRA District No. 5," 20 Jan. 1946; PAG 4/3.0.11.3.3:14, C3.4 Jewish Infiltree Children: "Infiltration of Jewish Children," Pettiss, UNRRA Child Welfare & Care Division, 25 June 1947.

54 PAG 3.0.11.0.1.4:31, Jewish Infiltree Children: "Report on Jewish Infiltree Children," Pettiss, Child Welfare Officer for Jewish Children, 5 Dec. 1946.

55 PAG 4/3.0.11.3.3:15, UNRRA US Zone HQ Dept of Field Operations Rel Sers Child Welfare, June 1946–Dec. 1946, Search & Repatriation: Biggar, District Welfare Officer, UNRRA District 2, to Heise, Child Welfare Specialist, UNRRA Zone HQ, 1 March 1946.

56 PAG 4/3.0.11.3.1:19, District 5 Monthly Reports July–Dec. 1946: "District Director's Monthly Report for July 1946"; PAG 4/3.0.11.3.3:14, C3.4 Jewish Infiltree Children: "Infiltration of Jewish Children."

57 PAG 4/3.0.11.3.3:14, C3.4 Jewish Infiltree Children: Martini, Assistant Chief of Operations (Relief Services) to UNRRA Mission to Czechoslovakia, att: G. Gates, 10 Aug. 1946; Blackey to B.R. Alpert, 10 Aug. 1946.

58 PAG 4/3.0.11.3.3:13, Jewish Children: E.Davidson, District Child Search Officer to Lowenthal, JAFP, 14 Oct. 1946; M.J. Newton, District Child Search Officer, for G.R. Pratt, Field Operations Officer to Pettiss, Zone Child Welfare, Third Army HQ, 10 Oct. 1946; H Conferences, minutes, "Meeting on Plans for Jewish Infiltree Children," 10 Oct. 1946.

59 In mid-Aug., the US Zone had four small camps for Jewish children, with a total capacity of 1,800, but with a total population of 1,330 before the infiltrees. There were four other possible camps available, with an additional total capacity of 971, but with 800 children already in them. In addition, there were 2,500 "free-living" unaccompanied children already in the Zone in urgent need of accommodations in a children's centre. The shortage of space was a very real one. PAG 4/3.0.11.3.3:15, Rel Ser: Child Welfare (Gen) Jan. 1946–Jan. 1947: Whiting, Zone Director, US Zone UNRRA to Commanding General, Third US Army, att: Engineer Real Estate, 14 Aug. 1946.

60 PAG 4/3.0.11.3.3:14, C3.4 Jewish Infiltree Children: "Infiltration of Jewish Children."

61 PAG 4/3.0.11.0.1.1:13, Central Headquarters - Child Welfare Material, Jewish Children - General: "Proposed Information Bulletin on Planning

for Jewish Unaccompanied Children and Youth," Heise, Zone Child
Welfare Specialist, 26 Feb. 1946; PAG 4/3.0.11.0.1.1:5, CHQ Child Welfare
Material: "Notes on Conference with Heise, US Zone," Blackey, 12 March
1946; 4/3.0.11.3.1:12 District 3 Monthly Reports March, April, May, June
1946: "Report of Relief Services Section for the Month ending 21 June
1946"; RG 260, OAG, General correspondence & other records, 1945–49,
390/40/21/2, Box 92, AG 383.7 Displaced Persons Reports. OMGUS 1945–46:
"Displaced Persons Monthly Report No. 8, 31 March 1946," UNRRA CHQ;
RG 260, CAD, Combined Repatriation Executive, US Elements, Box 211,
CRX UNRRA Monthly and Bi-Monthly Reports (vol. 1), 3.13: "Displaced
Persons Monthly Report No. 10," UNRRA CHQ, 31 May 1946; "Displaced
Persons Monthly Report No. 12," UNRRA CHQ, 31 July 1946.
62 PAG 4/3.0.11.3.3:13, Jewish Children - General: BKR to J. Mathers, Child
Welfare, 28 Aug. 1946, and attachments.
63 PAG 4/3.0.11.0.0:1, 0.11.3/D British Agreement - Interpretation 11/4/46-
5/5/47: Simon, Legal Advisor, UNRRA to Dudley Ward, UNRRA General
Council, ERO, 8 Aug. 1946; cable (unnumbered), UNRRA Main LEMGO to
430 UNRRA Wunstorf, 460 UNRRA Iserlohn, Schleswig-Holstein Region;
Simon to Chief of Operations, UNRRA CHQ Germany, 26 Aug. 1946;
PAG 4/1.0.1.0.0:33, Displaced Persons - Legal and Policy Decisions 1946:
cable 1996, Arolsen to Washington, repeated London, Sept. 1946; PAG
4/3.0.11.0.0:1, 0.11.3/D British Agreement - Interpretation 11/4/46-5/5/47:
K. Aicken, Assistant General Counsel to Cohen, Chief of DP Operations,
Germany, 16 Sept. 1946; PAG 4/2.0.0.0:6, UNRRA Policy re DP Assistance:
Hector McNeil, Minister of State, Foreign Office, London to F. LaGuardia,
Director General, UNRRA, 20 Nov. 1946.
64 RG 260, OAG, General correspondence & other records, 1945–49,
390/40/25/, Box 282, AG 383.7 United Nations Displaced Persons: Leo
W. Schwarz, US Zone Director, American Joint Distribution Committee
to Joseph Schwartz, Chairman, European Executive Council, 13 Jan.
1947; PAG 4/3.0.11.3.0:20, Field Ops. File 8. Feb. 1946 - Nov. 1946: cable
(unnumbered), Keyes G-5 to Director, UNRRA US Zone, 15 July 1946.
65 PAG 4/3.0.11.3.3:13, General (Jewish Infiltree Children) - Jewish children:
Heise to Field Ops, 20 June 1946; Virginia L. Poste, Child Welfare
Specialist, UNRRA District No. 2, Wiesbaden, for Biggar, Relief Services
Officer to Heise, Child Welfare Officer, UNRRA US Zone HQ, Pasing, 20
June 1946.
66 PAG 4/3.0.11.3.3:14, C 3.4 Jewish Infiltree Children: Heise, Zone Child
Welfare Specialist to Director, UNRRA District No. 5, att: child welfare
officer, 22 Feb. 1946.

67 Ibid., Martini, Assistant Chief of Operations (Relief Services), UNRRA CHQ to UNRRA Mission in Hungary, 15 Aug. 1946.

68 PAG 4/3.0.11.3.3:14, C3.4 Jewish Infiltree Children: "Infiltration of Jewish Children."

69 PAG 4/3.0.11.3.1:9, District 2 Monthly Reports March–June 1946: "Monthly Report for June - District No. 2."

70 PAG 4/3.0.11.3.1:19, District 5 Monthly Reports Jan.–Feb. 1947: Steinmetz, District Child Welfare Officer to Marnie Bruce, Relief Services Officer, 24 July 1946.

71 PAG 4/3.0.11.3.3:14, C 3.4 Jewish Infiltree Children, "Infiltration of Jewish Children."

72 PAG 4/3.0.11.0.1.1:14, 038.1 Zone Director report US Zone Oct. 1945 to March 1946: "Field Operations Report for March 1946," Whiting, US Zone Director, UNRRA.

73 PAG 4/3.0.11.3.3:14, C3.4 Jewish Infiltree Children, "Infiltration of Jewish Children."

74 PAG 4/3.0.11.0.1.1:14, Zone Director Report - US Zone Aug.–Dec. 1946: "Report for November 1946"; 4/3.0.11.3.1:4, District No. 1 - Directors Monthly Report – Dec. 31, 1946: "Child Search Officer's Report - December 1946"; RG 260, OAG, General correspondence & other records, 1945–49, 390/40/25/, Box 282, AG 383.7 United Nations Displaced Persons: Leo W. Schwarz, US Zone Director, American Joint Distribution Committee to Joseph Schwartz, Chairman, European Executive Council, 13 Jan. 1947.

75 PAG 4/3.0.11.3.3:17, Minutes of Jewish Child Care Committee Meetings: "Minutes of Meeting of Jewish Child Care Committee held at UNRRA US Zone Headquarters, Heidelberg on 16 Jan. 1947," Pettiss, 21 Jan. 1947.

76 PAG 4/3.0.11.3.0:60, Training: Jewish Children: Heise, Zone Child Search Officer to Director, UNRRA District No. 5, 28 Nov. 1946; memo to file, Pettiss, Child Infiltree Officer, 25 Nov. 1946; PAG 4/3.0.11.3.3:14, C3:4 Jewish Infiltree Children: "Meeting held in Munich, Oct. 22nd, 1946," Pettiss, Child Infiltree Officer, 2 Nov. 1946; PAG 4/3.0.11.3.0:20, Field Trips: "Report on Field Trip May 13th through May 18th - Munich Area," Pettiss, Child Welfare Officer for Jewish Children; PAG 4/3.0.11.3.3:14, C3.4 Jewish Infiltree Children: "Infiltration of Jewish Children."

77 PAG 4/3.0.11.3.0:20, Field Trips: "Report on Field Trip May 13th through May 18th - Munich Area"; "Report on Field Trip - May 24th to May 31st - Munich Area"; "Field Trip - June 12–18, 1947," Pettiss, 19 June 1947.

78 PAG 4/3.0.11.3.0:60, II. Reports. a) Regular and Special Reports. Zone HQ - Welfare - Relief Services. March 1946–Aug. 1946: Biggar, Relief Services

Officer, UNRRA District 2 to R.C. Raymond, Director, District 2, 23 July 1946.
79 PAG 4/3.0.11.3.3:14, C3.4 Jewish Infiltree Children: Blackey to Alpert, 10 Aug. 1946.
80 PAG 4/3/0/11/3/3/:17, District Reports - Child Welfare - Search Reports - District 1: "Child Welfare Report-September 1946."
81 PAG 4/3.0.11.3.1:12, District 3 Monthly Reports March, April, May, June 1946: report dated 22 June 1946; PAG 4/3.0.11.3.1:11, Jewish Affairs. Dist 2. 26 Nov. 1945–14 March 1947: M.J. Newton, Child Search Officer, District 2 UNRRA to G. Pratt, Field Operations Officer, 23 Sept. 1946; PAG 4/3.0.11.3.3:17, District Reports - Child Welfare - Search Reports - Dist 1: "Child Search Report - October 1946."
82 PAG 4/3.0.11.3.3:13, C6 Child Search (Problems): Harry Liebster, UNRRA Child Search Team 567 to Jean L. Bailly, Director, Team 567, 30 March 1946.
83 PAG 4/3.0.11.3.1:9, District 2 Monthly Reports March–June 1946: "Monthly Report for June [1946] - District No. 2."
84 PAG 4/3.0.11.0.1.4:4, Jewish Infiltree Children: Heise, Zone Child Welfare Specialist, US Zone UNRRA to Assistant Chief of Operations, Germany (Relief Services), 27 July 1946, att: Child Welfare Officer.
85 PAG 4/3.0.11.3.3:15, unnamed file: Heise, US Zone Child Search Officer, UNRRA to Ralph B. Price, Division of Repatriation, 1 Oct. 1946; 4/1.3.1.1.1:23 230.23a: minutes, "Interzonal Conference on Child Search and Repatriation - Oct. 16th, 17th & 18th, 1946"; PAG 4/3.0.11.3.3:17, District Reports - Child Welfare - Search Reports - Dist 1: "Child Search Report - October 1946"; PAG 4/3.0.11.3.3:14, C3.4 Jewish Infiltree Children: minutes, "Conference at Rosenheim Children's Center: Reuniting Jewish Infiltree Children with Relatives," Pettiss, Zone Infiltree Officer, 12 Nov. 1946; RG 260, OAG, General correspondence & other records, 1945–49, 390/40/25/, Box 282, AG 383.7 United Nations Displaced Persons: Leo W. Schwarz, US Zone Director, American Joint Distribution Committee to Joseph Schwartz, Chairman, European Executive Council, 13 Jan. 1947; PAG 4/3.0.11.0.1.4:4, Jewish Infiltree Children: "Report on Jewish Infiltree Children."
86 PAG 4/3.0.11.3.3:15, C2 Child Welfare legal matters: Susan Pettiss, Child Infiltree Officer, US Zone HQ, to Directors, UNRRA Districts 1, 2, 3, 5, att: District Child Welfare Officers, 4 Nov. 1946.
87 PAG 4/3.0.11.0.1.1:4, Child Search Repatriation Reports - Welfare: "Report on Field Trip to US and British Zones. 17th April–4th May 1947," Blackey, Child Search Consultant, Displaced Persons Operations, UNRRA CHQ, 6 May 1947.

88 43/AJ/597, Unaccompanied Children 39/1 General Policies and General Reports 1947: "Conference with Ellen Trigg, Child Care and Repatriation Officer, US Zone – 25–26 July 1947," D. Pentz, Division of Family and Individual Services; "Conference with Amelia Igel, AJDC, in regard to Mutual Problems on Unaccompanied Children," Pentz, 18 July 1947; 43/AJ/598, Unaccompanied Children 39/1 General Policies and General Reports 1948: Heise, Chief Child Search Section to M. Thudichum, Chief, ITS, 24 May 1948.

89 43/AJ/941, Cumulative Narrative Report: " Cumulative Narrative Report - Child Care, 1 July 1947–30 June 1949," Ellis, US Zone Child Care Officer, IRO; 43/AJ/598, Unaccompanied Children 39/1 General Policies and General Reports 1948: Heise to Thudichum, Chief, ITS, IRO, 24 May 1948; 43/AJ/939, Area No. 1-1948: Troniak, Area Child Care Officer, Area 1 to Ellis, 20 Sept. 1948; 43/AJ/940, Area #7/1948: G.H.A. Frank, Area Child Care Officer, Area 7 to Ellis, 2 Nov. 1948.

90 43/AJ/941, Cumulative Narrative Report: "Cumulative Narrative Report - Child Care, 1 July 1947–30 June 1949," Ellis, US Zone Child Care Officer, IRO; 43/AJ/598, Unaccompanied Children 39/1 General Policies and General Reports 1948: Heise to Thudichum, 24 May 1948; 43/AJ/939, Area No. 1-1948: Troniak, Area Child Care Officer, Area 1 to Ellis, 20 Sept. 1948; 43/AJ/940, Area #7/1948, Frank to Ellis, 2 Nov. 1948.

6 Obstacle: The Landesjugendamt

1 S-0412-0007, Central Headquarters - Field Orders - Displaced Persons Headquarters 8/3/1947–26/6/1947: UNRRA Resolution No. 92, 26 March 1946 (issued 29 April 1946).

2 PAG 4/3.0.11.3.1:12, District 3 Monthly Reports March, April, May, June 1946: "Report of Relief Services Section for the Month ending 25 April 1946."

3 PAG 4/3.0.11.0.1.3:8, Unaccompanied Children - General: "Plan for Location and Documentation of United Nations' Children in German Institutions and Families," Welfare Branch, UNRRA CHQ, 20 Feb. 1946.

4 PAG 4/1.3.1.1.0:11, P.300.4 Categories: Children: Van Hyning, Director, Welfare and Repatriation Division ERO to Alspach, Acting Director, Welfare Division, UNRRA HQ Washington DC, 28 Feb. 1946; "Conference on Location and Documentation of UN Children in German Institutions and Families," held 29 Jan. 1946 (in Hochst Germany).

5 PAG 4/3.0.11.3.3:13, F2 Field Representative Reports: "Field Report - Child Welfare, EMD, August 12 to August 26, 1945."

6 PAG 4/3.0.11.3.3:17, District Reports - Child Welfare - Search Reports - Dist. 1: "Report of Child Welfare Division for month of November 1946."

7 MInn 81115, Elternlose Kinder, die von der Unra reklamiert wurden - 1946: E. Davidson, District Child Welfare Officer, UNRRA District 3, US Zone to Senior Public Welfare Officer, OMG Bavaria, 16 Aug. 1946; Whiting, Zone Director to Commanding General, OMG Bavaria, att: Senior Public Welfare Officer, 26 June 1946; R.A. Reese, Chief, Internal Affairs and Comm. Division, OMG Bavaria to Minister President for Bavaria, att: Ministry of Interior, Director, Dept II, Public Welfare, 6 July 1946; Flüchtlingskommissar der Stadt München to Referat 6, Stadtjugendamt, München, 17 Aug. 1946; Bayer Staatskommissar für das Flüchtlingswesen to Regierungskommissare für das Flüchtlingswesen und Lagerleiter der Regierungs-Durchgangslager, 26 July 1946. Here and throughout these notes all archival documents beginning with MInn (Bayerisches Staatsministeriums des Innern) are from the Staatlichen Archive Bayerns, Munich, Germany.

8 In this case, the Military Government chose to support UNRRA's action. By this time, five of the children had been reunited with their grandparents. Ultimately (by Sept. 1946), eleven returned to Poland and four were moved to the children's centre in Aglasterhausen. RG 466, Records of the US High Commissioner for Germany, Bavaria Land Commissioner (BLC), Pol. Affairs Div (PAD), Displaced Populations Br., 1946-52, Correspondence concerning Displaced Children, Box 1, Children's Home Kallmunz #537: Chief, Department Care, Bavarian Red Cross to UNRRA, Central Office for Bavaria, att: Schreiber, 24 May 1946; memo to file, re: Placzek, Gaudenski, Born, Pobaretski, Rascke, Spialek, Galiorz, Baborski, Klisch children, undated; PAG 4/3.0.11.3.1:12, District 3 Monthly Reports March, April, May, June 1946: "Report of Relief Services Section for the Month ending 21 May 1946."

9 PAG 4/3.0.11.3.3:14, C8. Nationality Policy - General: Whiting, Zone Director, US Zone UNRRA to Commanding Officer, Displaced Persons Division, G-5 USFET, 6 May 1946; 4/3.0.11.3.3:13 C6 Child Search (Problems): "German protests on removal of children," CDH to Richman, 11 May 1946.

10 PAG 4/3.0.11.3.3:15, Rel Ser: Child Welfare (Gen) Jan. 1946–Jan. 1947: Heise, Child Search Officer, UNRRA US Zone HQ to Directors, UNRRA Districts 1, 2, 3, 5, att: Child Search Officers, 5 Nov. 1946.

11 RG 466, BLC, PAD, DP Branch, Correspondence re DP Children, Box 1, Waldschule Neustift: Bamberger to OMG Bavaria, Public Welfare Branch, 16 July 1946.

12 MInn 81115, Elternlose Kinder, die von de Unra reklamiert wurden - 1946: Bamberger, Bayer, Landesjugendamt to Militärregierung, Wohlfahrtsabteilung, München, 26 Aug. 1946; Bamberger, städt Direktorin, Stadtrat to Militärregierung von Bayern, Wohlfahrtsoffizier, München, 31 Aug. 1946.

13 PAG 4/3.0.11.3.3:15, Rel. Ser: Child Welfare (Gen) Jan. 1946–Jan. 1947: Whiting, Director, US Zone UNRRA to Commanding Officer, G-5, Third US Army, att: Capt. M.H. Sill, G-5 Intelligence, 14 Oct. 1946; RG 466, BLC, Pol. Affairs Div, Displaced Persons Br., 1946–52, Correspondence concerning Displaced Children, Box 1, Yugoslav. #532.

14 PAG 4/3.0.11.0.1.1:14, Zone Director Report: "Zone Director Report - US Zone July 1946."

15 RG 260, OAG, General correspondence & other records, 1945–49, 390/40/21/2 Box 92, file AG 383.7 Displaced Persons, vol. 1, OMG 1945–46, HQ US Group Control Council (Germany): F.M. Albrecht, Col, GSC, Deputy, Army (Ground) Div. to Deputy Mil Governor, 29 Sept. 1945.

16 Ibid., Box 91, file AG 383.7 Displaced Persons (Refugees, Expellees, Internees), 2 of 2: "Determination and Reporting of Nationalities," C.L. Adcock, Maj. Gen., GSC, Dir., USFET, to Directors OMG: Western District and Bavaria, 16 Nov. 1945.

17 Ibid.

18 Ibid.

19 PAG 4/2.0.6.2:13, Eligibility of Displaced Persons, vol. 2, from Jan 1st 1946: cable 2192, Van Hyning, UNRRA London, to UNRRA Washington, 18 Feb. 1946.

20 PAG 4/1.0.1.0.0:33, Displaced Persons - Legal and Policy Decisions 1946: cable 1861, London to Washington, 14 Feb. 1946; cable 9638, Oscar Schachter, General Counsel, to London, 12 Jan. 1946.

21 PAG 4/3.0.11.3.1:12, District 3 Monthly Reports March, April, May, June 1946: "District Director's Monthly Report," 25 April 1946.

22 PAG 4/2.0.6.2:13, Eligibility of Displaced Persons, Screening of Displaced Persons: AG 383.7 GNMCA-26, issued by Headquarters, Third United States Army, 6 April 1946; S-0412-0010, Central Headquarters - Screening of Displaced Persons - Problems: Whiting, Director, US Zone UNRRA, to P. Morris, UNRRA Liaison Officer, Third US Army Headquarters, 3 May 1946; Whiting, to Sir Frederick Morgan, Chief of Operations in Germany, UNRRA CHQ, 7 May 1946; 4/3.0.11.3.1:4 District No. 1 - Director's Monthly Reports May 31, 1946: "Monthly Report Relief Services April 23rd to May 23rd Incl."; PAG 4/3.0.11.3.1:12, District 3 Monthly Reports March, April, May, June 1946: "Preliminary Report on Screening, Districts

I and III," Rebekah L. Taft, Chief, Reports and Statistics, 30 May 1946; PAG 4/3.0.11.3.1:19, District 5 Monthly Reports: "District Director's Monthly Report for May 1946 - District 5."

23 S-0412-0010, Central Headquarters - Screening of Displaced Persons - Problems: "Screening Operations in the US Zone," Krane, Chief, Reports & Analysis Division, 10 July 1946; 4/3.0.11.3.1:9 District 2 Monthly Reports July–Dec. 1946: report dated 27 July 1946; PAG 4/3.0.11.3.1:12, District 3 Monthly Reports July–Dec. 1946: "District Director's Monthly Report, July 1946."

24 S-0412-0013, United States Zone - Administration Orders, No. 86-146: Administrative Order No. 113 (US Zone), 22 July 1946.

25 PAG 4/1.0.1.0.0:34, Displaced Persons - screening & eligibility 1945–47: R.F. Shearer, Major, AGD, Assistant Adjutant General, USFET by command of General McNarney to Commanding General, 3rd US Army Area, att: G-5 DPBr, 3 Aug. 1946.

26 PAG 4/2.0.6.2:13, Eligibility of Displaced Persons: UNRRA US Zone, Administrative Order No. 146, 31 Aug. 1946.

27 Ibid., ERO Order No. 40G, 11 Aug. 1946.

28 RG 466, BLC, PAD, Displaced Populations Br., 1946–52, Correspondence concerning Displaced Children, Box 1, Neuhaus - Englisches Institut #535: Eileen Davidson, District Child Welfare Officer, UNRRA to Director, Team 143, Passau, att: Principal Welfare Officer, 28 July 1946.

29 RG 466, BLC, PAD, Displaced Populations Br., 1946–52, Correspondence concerning Displaced Children, Box 1, Neuhaus - Englisches Institut #535; MInn 81115, Elternlose Kinder, die von de Unra reklamiert wurden - 1946: Miniclier, Chief, PWBr, OMG Bavaria to Bayer. Staatsministerium des Innern, Abt. Landesjugendamt, 9 Aug. 1946.

30 PAG 4/3.0.11.3.3:15, Rel. Ser: Child Welfare (Gen) Jan. 1946–Jan. 1947: Whiting, Director, US Zone UNRRA to Commanding Officer, G-5, Third US Army, att: Capt. M.H. Sill, G-5 Intelligence, 14 Oct. 1946.

31 RG 466, BLC, PAD, Displaced Persons Br., 1946–52, Correspondence concerning Displaced Persons, Box 1, Klosterbruck Kaufbeuren #538: Bamberger, Bayer. Staatsministerium des Innern, Abt. Wohlfahrtswesen, Land Youth Welfare Bureau to OMG Bavaria, Public Welfare Branch, 4 Dec. 1946; Box 1, "Children's Home Kallmunz #537: Bamberger to OMG Bavaria, Public Welfare Branch, 12 Dec. 1946.

32 MInn 8115, Elternlose Kinder, die von der Unra reklamiert wurden - 1946: "List of children claimed by UNRRA," Land Youth Welfare Bureau (Landesjugendamt), Munich, 2 Oct. 1946; memo to file, Munich, 16 Nov. 1946.

33 RG 466, BLC, PAD, DP Branch, Correspondence re DP Children, Box 1, "Waldschule Neustift." All of the material for the following section has been drawn from this voluminous file.
34 MInn 81115, Elternlose Kinder, die von der Unra [sic] reklamiert wurden - 1946: Bamberger, Bayer. Landesjugendamt to Militärregierung, Wohlfahrtsabteilung, Munich, 26 Aug. 1946; Eileen Davidson, District Child Welfare Officer, UNRRA District 3 HQ, to Senior Public Welfare Officer, OMG Bavaria, 16 Aug. 1946; Bamberger to Militärregierung, Wohlfahrtsabteilung, Munich, 6 Sept. 1946.
35 RG 260, CAD, PW&DP Branch, Records Relating to DPs in Germany and Other Countries, 1945–49, Box 147, 014.33 - Repat of DP Children: Bamberger, Ministry of the Interior, Department of Welfare, Land Youth Office, Munich to Military Government, Munich, 19 Feb. 1947.
36 MInn 81114, Elternlose Kinder, die von der Unra reklamiert wurden - 1946: A.D. Sims, Lt. Col., Exec. Officer Internal Affairs and Communications Division (IA&CD), OMG Bavaria to Minister President for Bavaria, att: Ministry of Interior, Dept II, Director, Land Jugendamt, 12 Nov. 1946; PAG 4/3.0.11.3.3:15, Rel Ser: Child Welfare (Gen) Jan. 1946–Jan. 1947: "Conference on Investigation of a newly reported group of Silesian Children in German Care," Heise, 6 Nov. 1946; PAG 4/3.0.11.0.1.3:7, 21 Polish Unaccompanied Children and Polish Red Cross: Heise, Child Search Officer to UNRRA CHQ, att: Blackey, Child Search Consultant, 25 Nov. 1946; Martini, Department of Field Operations, UNRRA Germany to Polish Red Cross, Warsaw, att: Palmowska, 9 Dec. 1946.
37 MInn 81114, Elternlose Kinder, die von der Unra reklamiert wurden - 1946: Suchdienst, Deutscher Caritas-Verband, Bayerisches Rotes Kreuz, Meldekopf Bamberg to Bayer. Staatsministerium des Innern, Abtl. Wohlfahrtswesen-Landesjugendamt-München, 6 Dec. 1946; Bamberger, Landesjugendamt to Caritasverband, Regensburg, 26 Nov. 1946; Fritz, Landesdirektor, Deutscher Caritasverband e.V., Hauptvertretung München, Landesverband Bayern to Diözesan-Caritasverbände Bayerns, 12 Dec. 1946.
38 Ibid.: Fritz, Landesdirektor, Deutscher Caritasverband e.V., Hauptvertretung München, Landesverband Bayern to Diözesan-Caritasverbände Bayerns, 12 Dec. 1946; Stelvertr. Leiterin der bischöflin Suchstelle, Caritasverband, Regensburg to Bayer. Staatsministerium des Innern, Abt. Wohlfahrtswesen, Landesjugendamt, München, 13 Dec. 1946; Stelvertr. Leiterin der bischöflin Suchstelle to Landesjugendamt, 8 Jan. 1947; Bamberger, Landesjugendamt to Militärregierung von Bayern, Wohlfahrtsabteilung, att: Groves, 14 Jan. 1947.

39 PAG 4/3.0.11.0.0:7, .014.6: "Report on Trip to US Zone, 24-26 Oct 46," M. Buché; PAG 4/1.3.1.1.1:23, 230.23a: "Interzonal Conference on Child Search and Repatriation - Oct. 16th, 17th & 18th, 1946"; PAG 4/3.0.11.3.3:18, C4. Child Search Procedure: report, Knut Okkenhaug, UNRRA Child Search and Registration Team 1071, 15 Nov. 1946.

40 PAG 4/3.0.11.3.3:13, H Conferences: Heise, Child Search Officer, UNRRA US Zone HQ to Directors, UNRRA Districts No. 1, 2, 3, 5, att: District Child Welfare Officers, 21 Oct. 1946.

41 PAG 4/3.0.11.0.0:7, 014.6 Unaccompanied Children - Reports on: Martini, Department of Field Operations to UNRRA HQ British Zone, att: D. Pearse, 15 Nov. 1946; PAG 4/3.0.11.3.3:15, Rel Ser: Child Welfare (Gen) Jan. 1946–Jan. 1947: Heise, Child Search Officer to Directors, UNRRA Districts 1, 2, 3, 5, att: District Child Search Officers, 14 Nov. 1946. For the Belgian children uncovered, UNRRA CHQ decided to compile a complete dossier on each child rejected by the liaison officers and submit them to the Belgian government for an "official answer." If it still failed to accept the children, it would be pressed for the decision in writing, in effect releasing UNRRA to make other plans for the children.

42 PAG 4/3.0.11.3.1:12, District 3 Monthly Reports Jan.–Feb. 1947: E. Davidson, District Child Search Officer, UNRRA District 3 to Field Operations, US Zone UNRRA, 22 Jan. 1947; PAG 4/3.0.11.3.1:14, Child Search Section 11.5.46–17.2.47: Davidson to Heise, Zone Child Search Officer, 23 Jan. 1947.

43 PAG 4/3.0.11.3.1:14, Child Search Section 11.5.46–17.2.47: Davidson to Heise, 23 Jan. 1947.

44 PAG 4/3.0.11.3.1:19, District 5 Monthly Reports Jan.–Feb. 47: Jean L. Bailly, Child Search & Repatriation Consultant, District 5 UNRRA to Steinmetz, Child Search & Repatriation Officer, District 5 HQ, UNRRA, 20 Feb. 1947.

45 PAG 4/3.0.11.3.3:14, A3 of Child Search/Tracing Interest: L.S. Ostrander, Brigadier General, for General McNarney, HQ USFET to Commanding Generals, OMGUS; Third US Army Area; Berlin District; Continental, Base Section, 11 May 1946.

46 PAG 4/3.0.11.0.1.3:1, Adoptions - Unaccompanied Children: Paul B. Edwards, Director, US Zone, UNRRA to Commanding General EUCOM, att: Theater Director of Civil Affairs, 3 March 1947; Heise, Child Search Officer to Directors, UNRRA Districts 1, 2, 3, 5, att: Child Search Officers, 10 March 1947.

47 PAG 4/3.0.11.0.1.3:1, Adoptions - Unaccompanied Children: Edwards to Theater Director of Civil Affairs, 22 March 1947.

48 PAG 4/3.0.11.3.3:14, C5.1 Child Search Policy - OMGUS: M.G. Karsner, Capt Inf A/ Asst Adj Gen, OMG Bavaria to Director, US Zone, UNRRA, att: Heise, Director, Child Search and Repatriation Service, 28 April 1947.

49 PAG 4/3.0.11.3.3:15, Child Care - Correspondence 28 Jan. 1946–21 Aug. 1947: Heise, Chief, Child Search/Tracing Division, US Zone, UNRRA to Trigg, Child Care Division, US Zone HQ, UNRRA, 19 June 1947.

50 RG 260, OMG Bavaria, CAD, Central Files, PW&DP Branch, Box 23, Statistical Reports: 1947 Statistical and Analytical Reports for the Weeks Ending 12, 19, and 26 Feb.; 7, 13, and 27 March; 3, 10, 17, and 24 April; 1, 7, 15, 22, and 29 May; 5, 12, and 19 June; and 10 July.

51 PAG 4/3.0.11.3.2:17, Area Team 1048 (Team 566) Regensburg: E. Davidson, UNRRA Team 1048, Child Search Team, Regensburg to Heise, Chief, Child Search Division, US Zone Bureau of Documents and Tracing, 6 June 1947; 43/AJ/597, Unaccompanied Children 39/1 General Policies and General Reports 1947: "UNRRA Closure Report of United Nations Unaccompanied Children in Germany, June 1947."

7 Obstacle: The ACA Directive

1 RG 260, CAD, PW&DP Branch, Records Relating to DPs in Germany and Other Countries, 1945–49, Box 167, 383.7 Administration of DPs: Charles Fahy, Director, to Director, PW and DP Division, 8 Jan. 1946; US Element of Allied Control Authority, Directorate of Prisoners of War and Displaced Persons (DPOW); General Records, Box 374, DPOW/P(46) 31–64: DPOW/P(46)11, 15 Jan. 1946.

2 RG 260, US Element of Allied Control Authority; Directorate of Prisoners of War and Displaced Persons; General Records, Box 374, DPOW/P(46) 31-64: PDOW/P(46)11, 15 Jan. 1946; DPOW/P(46) 11 (Final), 1 Feb. 1946; S-0412-0001, Allied Control Authority, Directorate of Prisoners of War and Displaced Persons - DPOW/P 1946–47 1/1/1946–30/4/1946: "Need for a uniform Legislation in cases of doubtful nationality amongst Displaced Persons' Children in Germany," A.W. Ward, Lt. Col. Duty Secretary, PW&DP Directorate, Allied Control Authority, 1 Feb. 1946. DPOW/P(46)11(Final); Allied Control Authority, Directorate of Prisoners of War and Displaced Persons to Legal Division, 1 Feb. 1946, DPOW/P(46)11(Final).

3 PAG 4/3.0.11.3.3:14, A3 of Child Search/Tracing Interest: "Principles for the Determination of the Citizenship of Displaced Persons in Germany - Note by the Duty Secretary," Y. Lekoan, Duty Secretary, Legal Directorate, Allied Control Authority, DLEG/P(46)12, 15 Feb. 46; draft proclamation, "Principles for the Determination of the Citizenship of Displaced Persons within Germany," 15 Feb. 1946.

4 RG 260, US Element of Allied Control Authority; Directorate of Prisoners of War and Displaced Persons (DPOW); General Records, Box 374,

DPOW/P(46) 65-85, DPOW/P(46)71: "Principles for Determining the true nationality of people of doubtful nationality in Germany," 7 June 1946; PAG 4/3.0.11.0.1.1:4, B53 Child Search Repatriation Reports - Welfare: "Child Welfare Conference - Schloss Muhlenberg Thursday and Friday, June 13th and 14th 1946."

5 PAG 4/3.0.11.0.1.3:8, Unaccompanied Children - Policy: draft, Office of Deputy Military Governor, OMGUS, to both Military and Military Government, re: "principles for the determination of the citizenship of United Nations Displaced Persons," April 1946; attached: P.E. Barringer, Major GSC Duty Secretary, Allied Control Authority Legal Directorate, 27 April 1946 (DLEG/P(46)12 (draft); Allied Control Authority Control Council Directive No. ..., 27 April 1946 (draft).

6 PAG 4/3.0.11.0.1.1:3, Germany March Reports: "Narrative Report for March 1946," UNRRA CHQ.

7 Pertti Ahonen, *After the Expulsion: West Germany and Eastern Europe, 1945–1990* (Oxford: Oxford University Press, 2003), 1–2; Philipp Ther, "The Integration of Expellees in Germany and Poland after World War II: A Historical Reassessment," *Slavic Review* 55/4 (1996): 779–800; 785–9.

8 Jeffrey M. Diefendorf, *In the Wake of War: The Reconstruction of German Cities after World War II* (Oxford: Oxford University Press, 1993), 125–6.

9 Ibid., 130.

10 See Adam Seipp, *Strangers in the Wild Place: Refugees, Americans, and a German Town, 1945–1952* (Bloomington: Indiana University Press, 2013), for an excellent exploration of this dynamic.

11 PAG 4/3.0.11.0.1.1:14, 038.1 Zone Director Report UNRRA US Zone April to July: "Monthly Report of Director, US Zone of Occupation, May 1946."

12 PAG 4/3.0.11.3.1:4, District No. 1 - Director's Monthly Reports May 31, 1946: "Monthly Report Relief Services, April 23rd to May 23rd Incl."

13 RG 260, CAD, Combined Repatriation Executive, US Elements, Box 211, CRX UNRRA Monthly and Bi-Monthly Reports (vol. 1), 3.13: "Displaced Persons Monthly Report No. 10," UNRRA CHQ Germany, 31 May 1946.

14 PAG 4/3.0.11.3.3:17, District Reports - Child Welfare - Search Reports Dist. 1: "Monthly Report for Month ending 20th April 1946"; 4/3.0.11.3.1:12 District 3 Monthly Reports March, April, May, June 1946: "Report of Relief Services Section for the Month ending 25 April 1946"; PAG 4/3.0.11.3.1:19, District 5 Monthly Reports: "Work Report for April 1946"; PAG 4/3.0.11.0.1.4:4, Reports - Special: "Summary Statement on United Nations' Unaccompanied Children in Germany," Martini, Assistant Chief of Operations (Relief Services), UNRRA CHQ Germany, 26 June 1946; PAG 4/3.0.11.0.1.1:3, Germany May Reports: "Monthly Narrative Report of Chief of Operations, Germany, May 1946."

15 PAG 4/3.0.11.0.1.1:4, B53 Child Search Repatriation Reports, Welfare: H.G. Wilson, Chief Welfare Officer, UNRRA CHQ to Martini, Assistant Director, Relief Services, 8 April 1946.

16 PAG 4/3.0.11.3.1:9, District 2 - Monthly Reports March–June 1946: "Comments from Director, District No. 2, on Welfare," 8 April 1946.

17 Ibid., District Director's Report, April 1946.

18 Ibid., District Director's Report, 30 April 1946.

19 PAG 4/3.0.11.3.0:60, II Reports. a) Regular and Special Reports. Zone HQ - Welfare - Relief Services. March 1946–Aug. 1946: "District Director's Monthly Report for April 1946 - District 5."

20 PAG 4/3.0.11.0.0:7, .014.6 Unaccompanied Children - Reports on: "Proposed statement to ACC on problems relating to UN Unaccompanied Children in Germany," UNRRA CHQ Germany, 27 April 1946.

21 PAG 4/3.0.11.0.1.3:8, Unaccompanied Children - Policy: "Statement Submitted by UNRRA Representative on the Care of Unaccompanied Displaced Children," 15 May 1946.

22 PAG 4/3.0.11.0.0:7, 014.6 Unaccompanied Children - Reports on: "Report on Field Trip to Berlin May 1–10, 1946," Blackey, Child Care Consultant, UNRRA CHQ, 14 May 1946.

23 PAG 4/3.0.11.0.1.3:8, Unaccompanied Children - Policy 26: letter to Col. S.R. Mickelson, Displaced Persons Division, USFET, 21 May 1946; PAG 4/3.0.11.3.3:14, C4, Child Search Procedure: Heise, Child Welfare Branch, Relief Services Division to District Directors, UNRRA Districts 1, 2, 3 and 5, 13 May 1946.

24 PAG 4/3.0.11.0.1.3:8, Policy - Unacc Ch: Gifford, Director, Welfare and Repatriation Division, ERO to Chief of Operations, UNRRA CHQ, att: Relief Services, 1 June 1946.

25 Ibid., "Report on Unaccompanied UN Children in Germany," by Blackey, 24 June 1946.

26 RG 260, CAD, PW&DP Branch, Records Relating to DPs in Germany and Other Countries, 1945–49, Box 146, 014.33 Repatriation (Unclassif): L.S. Ostrander, Brigadier General, Office of the Adjutant General to Commanding Generals: OMGUS, 3rd US Army Area, Berlin District, Continental Base Section, 11 May 1946.

27 Ibid., Harry S Messec, Lt. Col. GSC, PW&DP Division to DP G-5 USFET, 12 June 46.

28 PAG 4/3.0.11.0.1.1:14, Zone Director Report - US Zone July 1946: June 1946 report; 4/3.0.11.3.0:60 II Reports a) Regular and Special Reports. Zone HQ - Welfare - Relief Services. March 1946–Aug. 1946: "District Director's Monthly Report for June 1946 (District 5)."

29 PAG 4/3.0.11.0.1.4:4, Field Trips (33), "Report on Field Trip to the US Zone July 12ᵗʰ–19th, 1946," Blackey, Child Welfare Consultant, CHQ Germany, 29 July 1946.
30 PAG 4/3.0.11.0.1.4.:4 Field Trips (33): "Report on Field Trip to the US Zone July 12ᵗʰ-19ᵗʰ, 1946," Blackey, Child Welfare Consultant, CHQ Germany, 29 July 1946; 4/3.0.11.0.1.1.:14 Zone Director Report - US Zone July 1946; RG 260 OAG, General correspondence & other records, 1945-49, 390/40/21/2 box 92, AG 383.7 DPs. OMGUS 1945-46 Vol II: "Record of Conference on the Co-ordination of Activities of US Forces, Military Government and UNRRA with Particular Regard to Searching for and Identifying United Nations Children in Germany Held in Frankfurt, 18 July 1946," Abbott, Lt. Col. GSC, Acting Chairman, for DP Branch, PW&DP Division, OMGUS, 22 July 1946.
31 RG 260, OMG Bavaria, CAD, Central Files, PW&DP Branch, Box 23, D-336 Weekly Summaries 1946–47: "Summary for Week Ending 2400 Hours 25 July 1946," Miniclier, Chief, Public Welfare Branch OMGB to Director, OMGB.
32 PAG 4/3.0.11.0.0:7, .014.6 Unaccompanied Children - Reports on: "Proposed statement to ACC on problems relating to UN Unaccompanied Children in Germany," UNRRA CHQ, 27 April 1946.
33 PAG 4/1.3.1.2.1.0:1, Children - Unaccompanied: "Proposed US Zone Directive on Unaccompanied Children prepared by UNRRA at the request of USFET, July 1946," Headquarters USFET; PAG 4/3.0.11.0.1.3:8, Unaccompanied Children - Policy: directive "Unaccompanied Children," Headquarters, US Forces, European Theatre, July 1946.
34 PAG 4/3.0.11.3.3:15, Rel Ser: Child Welfare (Gen) Jan. 1946–Jan. 1947: Heise, Child Welfare Branch, Relief Services Division, UNRRA CHQ Germany to District Director, UNRRA District No. 1, att: District Child Welfare Officer, 22 July 1946.
35 PAG 4/3.0.11.3.0:60, Child Welfare Mar. 1946 to 31st July: Martini, Assistant Chief of Operations (Relief Services) to UNRRA HQ, US Zone, att: Zone Director, 24 July 1946.
36 RG 260, OAG, General correspondence & other records, 1945–49, 390/40/21/2 Box 91, AG 383.7 Displaced Persons (Refugees, Expellees, Internees), 1 of 2: cable S-1115, McNarney, USFET, to OMGUS, Third US Army, Berlin District, Director UNRRA US Zone HQ, Director, UNRRA CHQ Germany, 3 Aug. 1946.
37 RG 260, CAD, PW&DP Branch, Records Relating to DPs in Germany and Other Countries, 1945–49, Box 147, 014.33 - Repat of DP Children: Abbott to Col. Messec, 5 Aug. 1946.

38 RG 260, OAG, General correspondence & other records, 1945–49, 390/40/21/2 Box 92, AG 383.7 DPs. OMGUS 1945–46, vol. 2: Sewall, Director, IA&CD to PW&DP, 6 Aug. 1946.

39 RG 260, CAD, PW&DP Branch, Records Relating to DPs in Germany and Other Countries, 1945–49, Box 147, 014.33 - Repat of DP Children: General McNarney, USFET, to OMGUS, Third Army, Berlin District, and Director UNRRA US Zone HQ, 3 Aug. 1946; PAG 4/3.0.11.3.3:14, A13. Proposed USFET Directives: cable CC-1430, Clay, OMGUS to USFET, 10 Aug. 1946.

40 PAG 4/3.0.11.3.3:13, C6 Child Search Problems: Heise, Child Search Officer, UNRRA US Zone HQ to C.J. Taylor, Field Operations, 1 Oct. 1946; RG 260, OAG, General Correspondence & other records, 1945–49, Box 20, AG 014.33 Repatriation - Enemy and Ex-Enemy Nationals OMGUS, 1945–46, vol. 2 (Germans, Refugees, Volksdeutsche): Sewall, Director, PW Sec PH&W Branch, IA&CD, Alden Bevier, Chief, Public Welfare Section, H.T. Marshall, Colonel, MC Deputy Chief, PH&W Branch, 4 Oct. 1946.

41 RG 260, OMG Bavaria, CAD, Central Files, PW&DP Branch, Box 23, D-338 Weekly Summaries 1946–47: "Summary for Week Ending 2400 Hours 3 October 1946," Miniclier, Chief, Public Welfare Branch, OMGB; RG 260, OAG, General Correspondence & other records, 1945–49, Box 20, AG 014.33 Repatriation - Enemy and Ex-Enemy Nationals OMGUS, 1945–46, vol. 2 (Germans, Refugees, Volksdeutsche): cable 030850, Muller, OMG Bavaria, for Public Welfare Sec PH&W, IA&CD, to Deputy Military Governor, OMGUS, 3 Oct. 1946.

42 PAG 4/3.0.11.3.3:13, C6 Child Search Problems, Heise to Taylor, 1 Oct. 1946; RG 260, OAG, General Correspondence & other records, 1945–49, Box 20, AG 014.33 Repatriation - Enemy and Ex-Enemy Nationals OMGUS, 1945–46, vol. 2 (Germans, Refugees, Volksdeutsche): Sewall, Director, PW Sec PH&W Branch, IA&CD; Alden Bevier, Chief, Public Welfare Section; H.T. Marshall, Colonel, MC Deputy Chief, PH&W Branch, 4 Oct. 1946.

43 Ibid., Sewall, Bevier, Marshall, 4 Oct. 1946.

44 RG 260, CAD, PW&DP Branch, Records Relating to DPs in Germany and Other Countries, 1945–49, Box 146, 014.33 Repatriation (Unclassif): draft memo to "Radio Officer," 10 Oct. 1946.

45 PAG 4/3.0.11.0.0:7, .014.6 Unaccompanied Children - Reports on: "Report on Field Trip to Berlin. 1st and 2nd Oct. 1946," Blackey, Child Welfare Consultant, UNRRA CHQ, 8 Oct. 1946; 4/1.3.1.1.1:23 230.23a: "Interzonal Conference on Child Search and Repatriation - Oct. 16th, 17th & 18th, 1946."

46 RG 260, OAG, General correspondence & other records, 1945–49, 390/40/21/2 Box 92, AG 383.7 Displaced Persons Reports, OMGUS, 1945–46, vol. 2: "Identification, protection and USFET," 11 Oct. 1946.

47 Ibid., Lt. Col. Harry S. Messec, for Director, PW&DP Division, OMGUS, to DP Branch, Office of Acting Chief of Staff, G-5 USFET, 12 Oct. 1946.

48 PAG 4/1.0.1.0.0:5, Children Unaccompanied & Displaced, 1944–46: Rhea Radin, Chief, Repatriation Division for Cohen, Acting Chief, DP Operations to Major General L. Rooks, Director General, UNRRA HQ, Washington, att: General Counsel, 11 April 1947; PAG 4/3.0.11.0.0:7, HG 014.6/C Unaccompanied Children - General Correspondence: Blackey, Child Search Consultant, UNRRA HQ DP Ops to L.C. Stephens, Office of General Counsel, 23 May 1947.

49 PAG 4/1.3.1.2.1.0:1, Children - Unaccompanied: Cohen, Acting Chief of Operations, Germany UNRRA to PW&DP Division, Allied Control Authority, 9 Oct. 1946.

50 PAG 4/1.3.1.2.1.0:1, Children - Unaccompanied: Cohen to PW&DP Division, Allied Control Authority, 9 Oct. 1946; 4/3.0.11.0.0:7 .014.6 Unaccompanied Children - Reports on: "Report on Field Trip to Berlin. 1st and 2nd October 1946," Blackey, 8 Oct. 1946.

51 PAG 4/3.0.11.3.0:60, Child Welfare Aug. 1946–Dec. 1946: cable MISC-34, Whiting, UNRRA US Zone, to UNRRA CHQ, 29 Oct. 1946; PAG 4/3.0.11.0.1.3:8, Policy - Unacc. Ch. 26: cable 2224, C. Greenslade, ACOG, UNRRA CHQ to UNRRA London, 29 Oct. 1946; PAG 4/3.0.11.3.3:15, C2 Child Welfare legal matters: unnumbered cable, M.O. Talent, Legal Advisor, UNRRA CHQ to USFET ACS G-5, 29 Oct. 1946; PAG 4/3.0.11.0.1.0:1, Child Search + Care C2: "Minutes of Field Trip to Berlin 4th and 5th November 1946," Blackey, Child Search Consultant; PAG 4/3.0.11.0.0:7, 014.6 Unaccompanied Children - Reports on: Martini, Department of Field Operations to UNRRA HQs British, French, US Zones, 4 Nov. 1946.

52 PAG 4/3.0.11.3.3:16, Special Reports + District No. 2: George Pratt, Deputy District Supply Officer, District 2, UNRRA to H.K. Charles, District Supply Officer, District 2, UNRRA, 31 July 1946; PAG 4/3.0.11.3.3:15, C2 Child Welfare Legal Matters: Whiting, Zone Director, US Zone UNRRA to Commanding General, USFET HQ, att: Assistant Chief of Staff G-5, 14 Nov. 1945 (two versions).

53 PAG 4/1.3.1.1.1:23, 230.23a Germany, DP Unaccompanied Children: Alspach, Deputy Director, Federal-State Relations to Ellen Woodward, Welfare Consultant, US Delegation, UNRRA, 21 Nov. 1946; Alspach to Aleta Brownlee, Child Welfare Specialist, Welfare and Repatriation Division, UNRRA, NY, 3 Dec. 1946.

54 PAG 4/1.0.1.0.0:5, Children Unaccompanied & Displaced, 1947: C.T. Lloyd to Commander R.G.A. Jackson, Senior Deputy Director General, UNRRA,

27 Nov. 1946; PAG 4/3.0.11.3.3:15, C2 Child Welfare Legal Matters: Martini, Department of Field Operations to Zone Director, US Zone, UNRRA, att: Heise, 26 Nov. 1946; cable GR117, KHYD to UNRRA Arolsen, 23 Nov. 1946.

55 PAG 4/3.0.11.0.1.4:4, Reports to Repatriation Missions: "Report on the Location & Repatriation of ____ Children in Germany," Cyrus Greenslade, Acting Chief of Operations, Germany, 22 Nov. 1946.

56 PAG 4/3.0.11.3.3:15, C2 Child Welfare Legal Matters: Cyrus Greenslade, Acting Chief of Operations, UNRRA Germany to Allied Secretariat, ACA, Berlin, 20 Dec. 1946.

57 PAG 4/3.0.11.0.1.1:4, Germany Jan. 1947 Reports: "Monthly Narrative Report of Chief of Operations, Germany, UNRRA, January 1947"; PAG 4/3.0.11.2.0.1:14, UN/BZ/HQ/419 ACA Paper, file 419: cable 1255, Washington to Arolsen, 31 Jan. 1947.

58 PAG 4/3.0.11.3.3:15, Child Care - Reports. 7 June 1945–30 June 1947: Martini, Department of Field Operations, UNRRA Germany to UNRRA HQ, US Zone, att: Heise, 4 Feb. 1947; S-0412-0009, Central Headquarters - Monthly Narrative Reports - Nov.: "Monthly Narrative Report of Chief of Operations, Germany, Feb. 1947."

59 PAG 4.3.0.11.0.1.0:1, Child Search + Care C2: "Report on Joint Conference with Austrian Mission on Unaccompanied Children, Bad Wiessee, Germany, 7–8 January 1947"; PAG 4/1.3.1.1.1:23, F230.23: "Germany: DP, Children, Notes, Cross-References, etc.," Blackey, UNRRA HQ, DP Ops to Molly Flynn, UNRRA, Washington, 24 June 1947.

60 PAG 4/3.0.11.0.1.1:4, Child Search Repatriation Reports - Welfare: "Report on Field Trip to US Zone, 3–11 March 1947."

61 Ibid., "Present Status of ACA Directive on Unaccompanied Children in Germany," no author, 14 March 1947.

62 Ibid., "Report on Field Trip to US and British Zones. 17th April–4th May 1947."

63 RG 260, CAD, PW&DP Division, PW&DP Branch, Records Relating to DPs in Germany and Other Countries, 1945–49, Box 162, 393.7: Staff Study, A.D. Sims, Acting Chief, Internal Affairs Division, OMG Bavaria to Director, PW&DP Division, OMGUS, 18 Feb. 1947; RG 260, CAD, PW&DP Branch, Records Relating to DPs in Germany and Other Countries, 1945–49, Box 150, 092.2 International Tracing Scale: Harry S. Messec, Executive for Division Director, Prisoners of War and Displaced Persons Division, OMGUS to Chief of Staff, 25 Feb. 1947.

64 PAG 4/3.0.11.0.1.1:4, Child Search Repatriation Reports - Welfare: "Report on Field Trip to US and British Zones. 17th April–4th May 1947."

65 Ibid.

66 The US Committee for the Care of European Children (CCEC) was approved by the American government as the sole agency authorized to admit orphaned children to the United States. These children were restricted to those whose sole surviving relatives were in the United States; those who have been "disclaimed" by the national liaison officer of the only country in which they could claim nationality; those of unknown nationality or of a nation without a liaison officer in Germany (such as the Baltic countries); and Jewish children who had expressed a "decided preference" for going to the United States. It was emphasized in the Administrative Order authorizing its operation in Germany that any child referred to the CCEC had to be clearly a candidate for one of these categories, with no ambiguities. S-0412-0013, United States Zone - Administrative Orders: Administrative Order No. 47, "Immigration to the United States, unaccompanied children," UNRRA US Zone Headquarters, 11 April 1946; RG 260, CAD, Combined Repatriation Executive, US Elements, Box 211, CRX UNRRA Monthly and Bi-Monthly Reports (vol. 1) 3.13: "Displaced Persons Monthly Report No. 11," UNRRA CHQ, 30 June 1946.

67 PAG 4/3.0.11.3.1:19, District 5 Monthly Reports, Jan.–Feb. 1947: Thill, Child Welfare Consultant, District 5 UNRRA to Zisman, Director, District 5, att: Steinmetz, Child Search & Repatriation Officer, District 5, UNRRA, 21 Feb. 1947.

68 PAG 4/3.0.11.3.1:4, District 1 Monthly Report Feb. 1947: "District Child Search Officer's Monthly Report February 1947."

69 PAG 4/3.0.11.0.1.1:4, Child Search Repatriation Reports - Welfare: "Report on Field Trip to US and British Zones. 17th April–4th May 1947."

70 PAG 4/3.0.11.3.3:15, Child Care - Reports 7 June 1945–30 June 1947: Thill, Immigration Division, UNRRA Special Team 1071, Child Search and Repatriation Section to Heise, Child Search and Repatriation Specialist, UNRRA US Zone Tracing Bureau, 15 May 1947.

71 PAG 4/3.0.11.0.1.3:9, 35.19 Conference Minutes & Summaries: "Outline of Services and Problems in Child Welfare Program for Germany," Blackey, Child Search Consultant, UNRRA CHQ, 3 March 1947; S-0412-0009, Central Headquarters - Monthly Narrative Reports - Nov.: "Monthly Narrative Report of Chief of Operations, Germany, Feb. 1947"; PAG 4/3.0.11.0.1.1:4, B53 Child Search Repatriation Reports, Welfare: "Monthly Report - February 1947: Child Search and Repatriation."

72 For example, if the foster family had natural children (biological children of the foster parents), the family was not permitted under German law to adopt. This left the legal status of the foster child in doubt, as the child

had no claim to German citizenship nor on his country of origin. PAG
4/3.0.11.0.1.4:4, Reports - Special: "Summary Report on Child Welfare &
Child Search for Preparatory Commission of IRO," 24 May 1947; 43/
AJ/597, Unaccompanied Children 39/1 General Policies and General
Reports 1947: "UNRRA Closure Report of United Nations Unaccompanied
Children in Germany, June 1947," Blackey, Child Search Consultant,
UNRRA DPHQ.

73 RG 260, CAD, PW&DP Branch: Records of the Executive of the PW&DP
Branch, 1945–49: Box 127, Constitutions: draft, "MG Title 20 - Displaced
Persons, Refugees, and Expellees," 1 June 1947; Harry S. Messec,
Executive, OMGUS, 15 June 1947.

74 Ibid., Box 137, Child Tracing Records: "General Principles for Determining the
Eligibility for Certain Measures of Protection, Care and Treatment of Children
Brought into Germany or Born of Displaced Persons with Germany," Central
Tracing Policy Board, Directorate of PW&DP, ACA, 8 July 1947.

8 Child Search under the IRO

1 PAG 4/3.0.11.3.0:20, Operations Information: "Operation Information,"
Office of Field Operations, US Zone UNRRA, 16 April 1947.

2 RG 59, General Records of the Department of State, Records Relating
to the International Refugee Organization and the Displaced Persons
Commission (DPC), IRO Subject File, 1946–52, Box 1, unnamed file:
"Agreement between the International Refugee Organization (IRO) and
the Commander-in-Chief, European Command as to IRO's Operation in
the US Area of Control in Germany, 9 July 1947."

3 RG 260, CAD, PW&DP Branch, Records Relating to DPs in Germany and
Other Countries, 1945–49, Box 178, 319.1 Reports CFM: "Report No. 8 on
Displaced Persons," PW&DP Div, OMGUS, 28 Sept. 1947.

4 43/AJ/950, ITS Quarterly Reports: "IRO-ITS-Child Search Branch Yearly
Report 1948."

5 RG 466, Bavaria Land Commissioner (BLC), Pol. Affairs Div. (PAD), DPBr,
1946–52, Children's Case Files, Box 1, A-Bo, Atlas, Peter: Bamberger, Bayer.
Staatsministerium des Innern, Abtlg Wohlfahrtswesen to OMGB, Welfare
Branch, 24 Sept. 1947; RG 260, OMG Bavaria, CAD, Central Files, PW&DP
Branch, Box 22, Semi-Monthly Reports Pub Welfare Br D-335: Semi-
monthly Reports on Public Welfare Activities for the period ending 10 July;
31 July; 14 Aug. 1947.

6 MInn 81115, Elternlose Kinder, die von der Unra [sic] reklamiert
wurden, 1946: Bamberger, Bayer, Landesjugendamt to Militärregierung,

Wohlfahrtsabteilung, Munich, 16 May 1947; Kreisjugendamt Vohenstrauss to Regierung von Niederbayern und der Oberpfalz, 21 May 1947; Rachner, Landesjugendamt to Kreisjugendamt Schongau, 31 May 1947; Wein, Regierungspräsidenten von Niederbayern und der Oberpfalz to Bayer. Staatsministerium des Innern, Landesjugendamt, 12 June 1947; Mantler, Oberregierungsrat, Regierung von Niederbayern und der Oberpfalz, Regensburg to Bayer. Staatsministerium des Innern, Abt. Wohlfahrtswesen, 24 June 1947; Wein to Bayer. Staatsministerium des Innern, Landesjugendamt, 5 July 1947; Bamberger to OMG Bavaria, Welfare Bureau, 1 Aug. 1947.

7 RG 260, OMGB, Records of the Land Director, Records of the Deputy Director Land Commissioner, 1947–49, Box 292, Public Welfare: Al D. Sims, Acting Chief, Internal Affairs Division OMGB to Minister President for Bavaria, 21 Aug. 1947.

8 43/AJ/929, Allied Children in German Homes: Heise, Chief, Child Search/Tracing Section, US Zone to Director, PCIRO Team 1049, att: Area Welfare Officer, 9 Sept. 1947; Heise to Trigg, Chief, Child Care Division, PCIRO US Zone HQ, 10 July 1947.

9 43/AJ/597, Unaccompanied Children 39/1 General Policies and General Reports 1947, D.B. Pentz to Cohen, 12 Sept. 1947.

10 43/AJ/950, ITS Quarterly Reports: "IRO-ITS-Child Search Branch Yearly Report 1948"; 43/AJ/919 55/3/Act GUZ Mission, vol. 31: Conference of IRO and Voluntary Organizations, Geneva, 19–21 Jan. 1949.

11 43/AJ/941, Cumulative Narrative Report: "Cumulative Narrative Report-Child care. 1 July 1947–30 June 1949."

12 Ibid.

13 43/AJ/958, 1947/1948//Geneva: "Report on Field Trip to US Zone, Germany, 20th–26th June, 1948," Y. de Jong; 43/AJ/856, unnamed file: 39/1 GUZ Secondary Material, vol. 4, Child Care Dept.: Ellis, US Zone Child Care Officer, IRO to Dunn, Chief, Care and Maintenance, PCIRO, US Zone HQ, 11 June 1948; 43/AJ/940, Area #8: Frank Jurkovic, Assistant Child Care Officer to Troniak, Child Care Officer, Area 8, 2 Oct. 1948.

14 43/AJ/598, Unaccompanied Children 39/1 General Policies and General Reports, 1948: Provisional Order No. 33, "Unaccompanied Children," PCIRO, 18 Nov. 1947.

15 43/AJ/926, 1949//Policy/1950: "Statement of General Principles and Procedures Established by IRO in the Child Recovery Program," 19 March 1949.

16 Ibid.; 43/AJ/926, Recovery Program, 1949: Provisional Order No. 75, PCIRO, 26 July 1948.

17 43/AJ/926, Recovery Program, 1949: Provisional Order No. 75.

18 43/AJ/958, 1947–48//Geneva: "Report on Field Trip to US Zone, Germany, 20th–26th June, 1948."

19 43/AJ/926, Recovery Program, 1949: Provisional Order No. 75.

20 RG 260, OMGUS CAD PW&DP Branch, Box 118, PCIRO Administration and Related Matters: "IRO International Tracing Service. Monthly Report for October and November, 1948."

21 43/AJ/927, Child Care Field Representative - Area III, IV, V, VI, VII - Munich: M.M. [Marjorie] Farley, Child Care Field Representative, Munich to Ellis, Zone Child Care Officer, IRO HQ, 25 Jan. 1949.

22 Ibid., "Report on Conference on 20 Dec. 48 of Child Care Field Representative for Bavaria with Area Child Care Officers regarding the 'Recovery Program.'"

23 43/AJ/941, Cumulative Narrative Report: "Cumulative Narrative Report-Child care. 1 July 1947–30 June 1949."

24 MInn 81112, IRO, Lager A–Z: A. Schweizer, Director, CAD, OMG Bavaria to Minister of the Interior (Bavaria), att: Dept II, Land Youth Welfare Bureau, 19 May 1948.

25 RG 466, BLC, PAD, Displaced Populations Br., 1946–52, Children's Case Files, Box 1, A–Bo, Atlas, Peter: OMGB to Director ITS, Area 7, US Zone, att: M.A. [Martha] Vondracek, Field Representative, 8 June 1948.

26 RG 466, BLC, PAD, Displaced Populations Br., 1946–52, Correspondence concerning Displaced Persons, Box 1, Hungarian Children #542: Heise, Chief, Child Search Section, PCIRO, ITS HQ to Director, PCIRO Area 4, att: Senior Tracing Officer, 18 May 1948.

27 Ibid., Yugoslav. #532: Vondracek, Field Representative, ITS to Ellis, Chief, US Zone Child Care Department, IRO US Zone HQ, 15 Oct. 1948.

28 43/AJ/958, 1947–48//Geneva: Dunn, Chief, Department of Care and Maintenance to Executive Secretary, IRO HQ Geneva, att: Cohen, Assistant Director General, Health, Care and Maintenance Department, 29 Nov. 1948.

29 RG 260, OMG Bavaria, CAD, Central Files, PW&DP Branch, Box 41, Welfare Reports: "Welfare Report for the Month of March 1948," Ritter, Ministerialrat, Bayerisches Staatsministerium des Innern, 15 April 1948.

30 43/AJ/956, 1948–49//Military Govt: S.L. Hatch, Chief PW&DP Branch, OMG Hesse to Director, PCIRO, US Zone, att: Ellis, 10 Nov. 1948.

31 43/AJ/926, Recovery Program. 1949: Zone Child Care Section to Legal Advisor, IRO US Zone HQ, undated.

32 43/AJ/958, 1947/1948//Geneva: Ellis, Zone Child Care Officer, IRO US Zone to M.D. Lane, Chief, Welfare Division, Health, Care and Maintenance Department, IRO Geneva, 15 July 1948.

33 RG 260, OMG Bavaria, CAD, Central Files, PW&DP Branch, Box 41, Welfare Reports: "Welfare Report for the Month of Oct. 1948," Ritter, Ministerialrat, Bayerisches Staatsministerium des Innern, 15 Nov. 1948.

34 43/AJ/949, Polish Red Cross: Ellis, US Zone Child Care Officer for Chief of Operations, US Zone, to W.S. Boe, Chief, Voluntary Societies Division, 22 Nov. 1948; Ellis to Boe, 30 Nov. 1948.

35 RG 466, BLC, PAD, Displaced Populations Br., 1946–52, Correspondence concerning Displaced Children, Box 1, Ukrainian Babies #533: Theodora Allen, European Representative, US Committee for [the Care of] European Children to Vondracek, Field Representative, ITS Area 7, 21 Sept. 1948; Land Director, OMGB to Vondracek, 11 Oct. 1948.

36 RG 260, OMG Bavaria, CAD, Central Files, PW&DP Branch, Box 40, Reports on Important Meetings in the Various Laender: "Bi-monthly Zonal Welfare Conference, 4–5 Jan. 1949"; Box 24, Youth Welfare (4th folder): Josephine Groves, Chief, Youth Welfare Section to Miniclier, undated.

37 Ibid., Box 24, Youth Welfare (4th folder): Groves to Grosser, 11 June 1948.

38 43/AJ/956, 1948–49//Military Government, Franz Miller [sic], Caritasrektor, Deutscher Caritasverband, Munich to the Militärregierung für Bayern, Abtlg. Public Welfare, att: Groves, 20 Nov. 1948.

39 RG 466, BLC, PAD, Displaced Populations Br., 1946–52, Correspondence concerning Displaced Children, Box 1, Waldschule Neustift #536: A.C. Schweizer, Director, CAD, OMGB to Caritasrektor, Franz Mueller, Munich, 13 Dec. 1948.

40 43/AJ/598, Unaccompanied Children 39/1 General Policies and General Reports, 1948: "Removal from German families of Allied Children. Reasons why this is to the best interest of the child," E. Davidson, Deputy Chief, Child Search Section, Tracing/Child Search Division, IRO, 21 Jan. 1948.

41 Ibid.

42 RG 260, OMG Bavaria, CAD, Central Files, PW&DP Branch, Box 42, Welfare Reports: "Welfare Report for the Month of Aug. 1947," Bayer. Staatsministerium des Innern; MInn 81115, Elternlose Kinder, die von der Unra [sic] reklamiert wurden, 1946: Bamberger, Landesjugendamt to OMG Bavaria, att: Public Welfare Office, 2 Sept. 1947.

43 RG 260, CAD, PW&DP Branch: Records of the Executive of the PW&DP Branch, 1945–49, Box 134, Zonal Tracing Bureau: Thudichum, Director, International Tracing Service, IRO to Chief, DP Branch, CAD Headquarters, European Command, 12 April 1948.

44 43/AJ/598, Unaccompanied Children 39/1 General Policies and General Reports, 1948: Heise, Chief Child Search Section, IRO to Thudichum, Chief, ITS, IRO, 24 May 1948.

45 IRO 43/AJ/926, 1948//Policy: Draft Directive, revised by Child Care, "Location, Recovery, Care, Repatriation and Resettlement of Unaccompanied Children coming under the Mandate of PCIRO," 28 Aug. 1948.

46 RG 260, Prisoner of War & Displaced Persons Branch: Recs Relating to Displaced Persons and Their Movements, 1945–49: Correspondence Jan. 1949 Thru Claims Against PCIRO, Box 118, Correspondence, Jan. 1949: Legal Division, OMGUS to Commander-in-Chief, EUCOM, 20 Jan. 1949.

47 43/AJ/956, EUCOM - Directions for unaccompanied children: Ellis, US Zone Child Care Officer IRO, for Chief of Operations, US Zone IRO to E.M. Hughes, HQ EUCOM, Civil Affairs Division, 10 Feb. 1949.

48 RG 260, CAD, PW&DP Branch, Records of the Executive of the PW&DP Branch, 1945–49, Box 134, Zonal Tracing Bureau: Thudichum, Director, International Tracing Service, IRO to Chief, DP Branch, CAD Headquarters, European Command, 12 April 1948; 43/AJ/598 Unaccompanied Children 39/1 General Policies and General Reports, 1948: Heise, Chief Child Search Section, IRO to Thudichum, 24 May 1948.

49 43/AJ/194, 80/1/G.US.Z. Legal (Monthly Narrative Reports) Germany - US Zone: "Narrative Report for Oct. 1948," IRO US Zone Headquarters.

50 This had, according to IRO's legal counsel, basis in international law. According to its analysis of the law, each government of residence was the guardian of unaccompanied children, including all foundlings and orphans and children who had been separated from their families, provided they lived in the territory of that government. These governments had an obligation to care for these children when within their boundaries, whether they were citizens of that state, foreigners, or stateless. Thus, the new state of Germany would be responsible for all unaccompanied children within its boundaries, German or not, once it was established as a sovereign state. 43/AJ/926, 1948//Policy: L.E. Levitan, Chief, US Zone Division, ITS to Chief, Care and Maintenance Department, PCIRO HQ, Geneva, att: Child Welfare Consultant, 5 March 1948; attached: comments by Jevginis Migla.

51 RG 260, OMG Bavaria, CAD, Central Files, PW&DP Branch, Box 33, Individual Adoption Cases: A.C. Schweitzer, Director, CAD, OMGB to Director, CAD, OMGUS, att: Chief, Public Welfare Branch, 15 Dec. 1948.

52 43/AJ/958, 1947/1948//Geneva: "Report on Field Trip to US Zone, Germany, 20th–26th June, 1948," Y. de Jong.

53 43/AJ/950, ITS Quarterly Reports: "IRO-ITS-Child Search Branch Yearly Report 1948."

54 Ibid.

55 43/AJ/919, 55/3/Act GUZ Mission, vol. 31: "Conference of IRO and Voluntary Organizations, Geneva, 19–21 Jan. 1949"; 43/AJ/941, Narrative Report - Child Care zone Hqs: "Narrative Report for Jan. 1949 (e) Department of Field Operations (III) Unaccompanied Children," US Zone HQ, Germany; RG 260, OMGB, Records of the Field Operations Division, HQ Records - General Corresp and Other Records, Box 311, Civil Matters: G.H. Garde, Lt Col, AGD Adjutant General, OMGUS to Directors, OMG: Hesse, Wuerttemberg-Baden, Bavaria, Bremen, Berlin Sector, 21 Feb. 1949; attached: "Basic Outline of a Plan for the Registration of All Children," 2nd revision, 1 Nov. 1948.

56 RG 260, Prisoner of War & Displaced Persons Branch, Box 118, Correspondence, Jan. 1949: memo, subject: US Military Government Directive issued 16 Feb. 1949, "Tracing of United Nations Children Believed to be Missing in Germany," undated, no author; RG 260 Legal Division, Records of Legal Advice Branch, Legal Files, 1945–50, Box 51, File LA-24 Displaced Persons, Refugees, Internees: "Tracing of United Nations Children Believed to be Missing in the United States Zone of Germany," 16 Feb. 1949.

57 RG 260, OMG Bavaria, CAD, PW&DP Division, Box 117, Correspondence, April 1949: "Procedures for Tracing United Nations Children," M.D. Van Wagoner, Land Director, OMG Bavaria to Ehard, Minister President for Bavaria, 18 March 1949.

58 IRO 43/AJ/949, Polish Red Cross: Rudzinski, Senior Representative for Germany, Polish Red Cross to Thudichum, Director, ITS, 28 March 1949.

59 RG 260, Prisoner of War & Displaced Persons Branch: Recs Relating to Displaced Persons and Their Movements, 1945–49: Liaison Mission Thru Correspondence June 1949, Box 120, Correspondence, July 1949: Major General R. Pehacek, Head, Yugoslavian Military Mission, Berlin to Deputy Military Governor, Major General G.P. Hays, OMGUS, 30 June 1949.

60 43/AJ/941, Cumulative Narrative Report: "Cumulative Narrative Report-Child care. 1 July 1947–30 June 1949."

61 RG 260, OMGUS CAD, PW&DP Branch, Box 118, PCIRO Administration and Related Matters; IRO 43/AJ/941 Narrative Report-Child Care Zone Hqs: "Narrative Report for Dec. 1948 (d) Care and Maintenance (iv) Unaccompanied Children," US Zone HQ Germany, 4 Jan. 1949.

62 43/AJ/941, Area 3 - Child Care Monthly Narrative Reports: "Monthly Narrative Report. Child Care Department for the period 15th March–15th April 1949."

63 43/AJ/950, Child Search Policy: "Cases which should not be Registered," IRO, ITS, Child Search Branch, June 1949.

64 MInn 81143, Such nach Kindern der Vereinten Nationen 1949: Strauss, Oberregierungsrat, Bayer. Landesjugendamt, München to Stadt- und Kreisjugendämter, 5 April 1949; Strauss to Regierung von Oberfranken, 16 May 1949; Strauss to all Jugendämter, 18 May 1949.

65 See, e.g., Ibid., Such nach Kindern der Vereinten Nationen (Nr. 6737/112 IRO-Schriftverhehr) (Oberbayern): Luxnburger [sic], Direktor, Stadtrat der Landeshauptstadt München, Stadtjugendamt, Abteilung Anstaltsfürsorge, München to Bayerische Landesjugendamt, 26 April 1949; Kinderheilstätte Haus Datzellehen, Bayerisch Gmain to Bayer. Landesjugendamt, 28 April 1949; Kinderheilstätte der Innern Mission, Kinderkurheim, Garmisch-Partenkirchen to Bayer. Landesjugendamt, 29 April 1949; Ibid., Such nach Kindern der Vereinten Nationen (Nr. 6737/112 IRO-Schriftverhehr) (Oberpfalz). The files contain numerous similar letters of protest.

66 Ibid., Such nach Kindern der Vereinten Nationen 1949; Such nach Kindern der Vereinten Nationen (Nr. 6737/112 IRO-Schriftverhehr) (Oberbayern).

67 Ibid., Such nach Kindern der Vereinten Nationen (Nr. 6737/112 IRO-Schriftverhehr) (Oberbayern): Luxnburger [sic], Direktor, Stadtrat der Landeshauptstadt München, Stadtjugendamt, Abteilung Anstaltsfürsorge, München to Bayerische Landesjugendamt, 2 May 1949; Liphart, Kreisjugendamt, Landratsamt Starnberg to Bayer. Landesjugendamt, 8 April 1949.

68 Ibid., Such nach Kindern der Vereinten Nationen 1949: H.H. Meyer, Chief, Child Search Branch, ITS US Zone to Landesjugendamt Bayern, 13 Oct. 1949; Lades, Regierungsrat, Bayer. Landesjugendamt to the Internationalen Suchdienst, Esslingen/Neckar, 30 Oct. 1949; Such nach Kindern der Vereinten Nationen (Nr. 6737/112 IRO-Schriftverhehr) (Oberbayern): Lades to Landratsamt-Kreisjugendamt-Laufen, 31 Oct. 1949; H.H. Meyer, Chief, Child Search Branch, ITS to Landesjugendamt, Bayern, 13 Oct. 1949; Lades to Landratsamt-Kreisjugendamt-München Am Lilienberg, 25 Oct. 1949.

69 43/AJ/941, Area 3-Child Care Monthly Narrative Reports: Department of Care and Maintenance to Child Care Officer, 19 Aug. 1949.

70 Ibid., Narrative Report - Child Care Zone Hqs: "Narrative Report for August 1949 (v) Department of Field Operations (c) Unaccompanied Children," US Zone HQ, Germany; Area 5- Child Care Monthly Narrative Reports: Dept of Care and Maint to IRO US Zone Child Care Officer, 29 Aug. 1949; Narrative Report-Child Care Zone Hqs: "Narrative Report for October 1949 (v) Department of Field Operations (c) Unaccompanied Children," US Zone Hq, Germany, 7 Nov. 1949; 43/AJ/927 Child Care Field Representative - Area III, IV, V, VI, VII-Munich: Vinita V. Lewis,

Deputy Zone Child Care Officer to Grigg, Chief, Care and Elig., 14 Sept. 1949.

71 43/AJ/927, Child Care Field Representative - Area III, IV, V, VI, VII-Munich: Farley, Child Care Field Representative for Land Bavaria, IRO US Zone to Ellis, Zone Child Care Officer, IRO US Zone HQ, 9 Sept. 1949; 43/AJ/941, Area 5-Child Care Monthly Narrative Reports: "Narrative Report - Child Care Section, period 15 Dec. 1949–15 January 1950."

72 43/AJ/941, Area 3-Child Care Monthly Narrative Reports: report dated 15 Sept. 1949.

73 Ibid., "Child Care Narrative Report for period ending 15 November 1949."

74 Ibid., Area 5 - Child Care Monthly Narrative Reports: "Narrative Report - Child Care Section period 15 December 1949–15 January 1950."

75 Ibid., Narrative Report - Child Care Zone Hqs: "Narrative Report for August 1949 (v) Department of Field Operations (c) Unaccompanied Children."

76 43/AJ/927, 1949//General: "Field Trip to the Munich Area, US Zone, Germany 1st–5th October 1949," Yvonne de Jong, Child Welfare Consultant, Geneva HQ, 16 Nov. 1949.

77 RG 59, Records Relating to the International Refugee Organization (IRO) and the Displaced Persons Commission (DPC), IRO Subject File, 1946–52, Box 12, Office of Specialized Agency Affairs - Roseman (Geneva) 1950: Alvin Roseman, Representative for Specialized Agency Affairs, Geneva to G. Warren, Adviser on Refugees, Department of State, Washington, 7 June 1950; "Unaccompanied Refugee Children - Paper for International Union of Child Welfare," 1 June 1950.

78 43/AJ/926, 1949//Policy/1950: "Report of the Director-General on the Child Search and Child Welfare Programs and the General Problem of Unaccompanied Children," Executive Committee, IRO, 18 Feb. 1950; 43/AJ/927, 1949//General: unnumbered cable, Geneva to Child Care, 14 July 1949.

79 43/AJ/941, Narrative Report - Child Care Zone Hqs: "Narrative Report for July 1949 (v) Department of Field Operations (c) Unaccompanied Children."

80 43/AJ/926, 1949//Policy/1950: B.G. Ferris, Col GSC, Director, EUCOM-CAD to W.H. Tuck, Director General, IRO Geneva, 10 June 1949; Recovery Program. 1949: "Appendix I. 1. Adminstrative Order #109. 2. Provisional Order #75. 3. General Comment on Policies of IRO, EUCOM, OMGUS with respect to resettlement and repatriation of unaccompanied children," Ellis, Zone Child Care Officer, US Zone HQ to Hughes, HQs: EUCOM, CAD, undated; Recovery Program. 1950: draft memo, "Basic Statement

regarding the Child Recovery Program," marked 3.34; 43/AJ/939 Area #4: L. Lefson, Child Care Officer, Area 4 to E.L. Deiglmayer, Area Child Care Officer, Area 4, 4 March 1949; RG 260, CAD, PW&DP Branch, Records Relating to DPs in Germany and Other Countries, 1945–49, Box 147, 014.33 - Repat of DP Children: H.S. Messec, Executive Officer, for Director, PW&DP Division to Legal Division, 26 Aug. 1947; W.W. Schott, Chief, US Elm Allied L&P (Liaison and Protocol) to PW, 4 Sept. 1947.

81 RG 260, Prisoner of War & Displaced Persons Branch, Recs Relating to Displaced Persons and Their Movements, 1945–49, Liaison Mission Thru Correspondence June 1949, Box 120, Correspondence - July 1949: E.K. Neumann, Chief, Legal Division to PWBr, 27 July 1949; 43/AJ/956, 1948/49//Military Govt: S.L. Hatch, Chief, Social Affairs Branch to P.E. Ryan, Chief of Operations, IRO US Zone, att: V.V. Lewis, Child Care Officer, 2 Aug. 1949.

82 RG 260, Prisoner of War & Displaced Persons Branch, Recs Relating to Displaced Persons and Their Movements, 1945-49, Liaison Mission Thru Correspondence June 1949, Box 120, Correspondence, July 1949: James Campbell, Social Affairs Adviser to Commanding General, OMGUS, att: PWBr, 29 July 1949.

83 Ibid.

84 43/AJ/940, Area No.7/1949: E. Laursen, Subarea Child Care Officer, Rosenheim to Area Child Care Officer, G. Frank, Munich, 7 July 1949.

85 43/AJ/926, Recovery Program. 1949: Ellis, Zone Child Care Officer to Director, Area 7, att: G. Frank, Child Care Officer, 19 July 1949 and 20 July 1949.

86 RG 59, Records Relating to the International Refugee Organization (IRO) and the Displaced Persons Commission (DPC), IRO Subject File, 1946–52, Box 8, IRO General April–June 1949: Dunn, Chief of Department of Care and Maintenance, IRO US Zone to R.S. Winslow, 31 May 1949.

87 Text of the Occupation Statute of Germany (Bonn, 12 May 1949), http://www.cvce.eu/obj/en-6750efd3-4b34-4fec-9a4a-df0ff125d302 (consulted on 16 Feb. 2016).

88 43/AJ/410, Germany-Occupation Statute: "Memorandum of the Director-General on Questions Connected with the Proposed Occupation Statute for the Three Western Zones of Germany, 25 January 1949."

89 43/AJ/197, 102/1/GWZ(1) Legal Status: J.D.R. Kelly, Legal Adviser for Director, British Zone to IRO HQ Geneva, att: Protection Division, 25 May 1949; "Legal Status of Hardcore."

90 Ibid., Legal (Status) Germany Western Zones Jacket 1: B.G. Alexander to G.G. Kullmann, 29 June 1949.

91 Ibid., Legal Status: J.D.R. Kelly, Legal Adviser for Director, British Zone to IRO HQ Geneva, att: Protection Division, 25 May 1949; "Legal Status of Hardcore"; "Notes on Conference Held at Schloss Spenge, 22 June 1949"; G.G. Kullmann to W.H. Tuck and Sir Arthur Ruck, 4 July 1949; "Memorandum on the Status of Refugees in Germany," 7 Sept. 1949.
92 Ibid., "Notes on Conference Held at Schloss Spenge, 22 June 1949."
93 Ibid., Kullmann to Tuck and Ruck, 4 July 1949; "Memorandum on the Status of Refugees in Germany."

9 The Residual

1 RG 466, US High Commissioner for Germany, US High Commissioner John McCloy, Classified General Records, 1949–52, Box 7:1950 #123-263, Jan 50 D(50)113 thru D(5)145: Swope, HICOG to John McCloy, High Commissioner, HICOG, 19 Jan. 1950.
2 Ibid., cable 120, Secretary of State, Washington, DC, to Geneva, 20 Jan. 1950.
3 Ibid., memo to file, H.A. Gerhardt, 30 Jan. 1950; RG 59, Records Relating to the International Refugee Organization (IRO) and the Displaced Persons Commission (DPC), DP Subject File, 1944–52, Box 7, DP Germany March 1950: telegram 2036, Hays, HICOG, to Secretary of State, 10 March 1950.
4 43/AJ/410, Germany - US zone (1950): cable 677, 30 June 1950.
5 Ibid., Germany - Occupation Statute: J.R. Kelly, Liaison Officer to Allied High Commission, IRO, to Cohen, Assistant Director General, IRO, Geneva, 24 Oct. 1950; Kelly to Cohen, 28 Oct. 1950.
6 43/AJ/198, 102/2/GWZ (III) Legal (Status) Future Legal Status (Hard Core) Germany Western Zones Jacket III: "Relinquishment of the Reserved Powers under Paragraph 2(d) of the Occupation Statute," 20 March 1951.
7 43/AJ/197, 102/1/GWZ(1)Legal Status: L.M. Nacking, Acting Director, Department of Protection, Mandate and Reparation to J.D. Kingsley, Director General, IRO Geneva, 25 Aug. 1949; 43/AJ/926, Legal. 1949/1950: Ellis, Zone Child Care Officer to Legal Advisor, att: Kinnare, 7 Oct. 1949; RG 466, Office of the Executive Secretary, General Records, 1947–52, Box 39, 796 (2 of 2): E.C. Goodwin and O.T.L. Steger, Secretariat to Allied High Commission for Germany, Political Affairs Committee, 15 Oct. 1949, attached: Cohen, Acting Director General, IRO Geneva, to Sir Brian Robertson, UK High Commissioner, 14 Sept. 1949; L. Handley-Derry, G.P. Glain, J.E. Slater, Allied General Secretariat to IRO Geneva (draft reply), 31 Oct. 1949; RG 466, US High Commissioner for Germany, US High Commissioner, John McCloy, Classified General Records, 1949–52, Box 6:1950 #1-122, Jan 50 D(50)97 to D(50)112: Swope, HICOG to McCloy, High

Commissioner, HICOG, 16 Jan. 1950; Lt. Col. H.A. Gerhardt, HICOG to McCloy, 18 Jan. 1950.

8 S-0412-0013, United States Zone - Administrative Orders: Administrative Order No. 47, "Immigration to the United States, unaccompanied children," UNRRA US Zone Headquarters, 11 April 1946; RG 260, CAD, Combined Repatriation Executive, US Elements, Box 211, CRX UNRRA Monthly and Bi-Monthly Reports (vol. 1), 3.13: "Displaced Persons Monthly Report No. 11," UNRRA CHQ, 30 June 1946.

9 S-0412-0014, United States Zone-General Bulletins, No. 127-201: General Bulletin No. 168, "UNRRA's responsibility with regard to resettlement of Displaced Persons," 1 March 1947 (originally UNRRA policy directive UNa 7981, 4 Dec. 1946).

10 4/3.0.1.3.3.:15, C5 2 Child Search Policy EUCOM OMGUS: "Resume of Child Search Program and Problems," Heise, for Arthur Altmeyer, Executive Secretary, IRO Preparatory Commission, 31 March 1947.

11 RG 260, CAD, PW&DP Branch, Records Relating to DPs in Germany and Other Countries, 1945–49, Box 173, Cables and Correspondence on DP Immigration Act of 48: E.H. Litchfield, Director to Chief of Staff, 30 July 1948.

12 43/AJ/958, 1947–48//Geneva: Dunn, Chief, Care and Maintenance Department, IRO US Zone to Cohen, Assistant Executive Secretary, Care and Maintenance Department, IRO Geneva, att: Evelyn Rauch, Chief, Welfare Division, 2 Feb. 1948.

13 RG 260, CAD, PW&DP Branch, Records Relating to DPs in Germany and Other Countries, 1945–49, Box 173, Cables and Correspondence on DP Immigration Act of 48: "Fact Sheet on the Displaced Persons Act of 1948," Office of Public Affairs, Department of State, 12 Nov. 1948; The Displaced Persons Act of 1948: cable WX-84420, Dept of the Army, CAD to OMGUS, EUCOM, USFA Vienna, 10 Dec. 1948.

14 RG 59, Records Relating to the International Refugee Organization (IRO) and the Displaced Persons Commission (DPC), DP Subject File, 1944–52, Box 15, Displaced Persons Commission, June–Oct. 1948: unnumbered cable, Squadrilli, DP Commission Coordinator to US Embassy Rome for Wm. H. Tuck, Director General IRO Rome, undated; unnumbered cable, IRO Bad Kissingen to IRO Rome, Geneva and US DP Commission Frankfurt, 10 Dec. 1948; Pettiss, Voluntary Agency Liaison Officer, IRO US Office, to G. Warren, Adviser on Refugees and Displaced Persons, State Department, Washington, 17 Jan. 1949; Robert [J.] Corkery, Chief of Dept of Repat and Resettlement, IRO US Zone Germany to Squadrilli, 31 Dec. 1948.

Notes to pages 245–9

15 RG 260, OMGB, Records of the Legal Division, General Records of the
Legislative Branch, 1946–50, Box 77, 75 DP's. (LA): excerpt, "US Displaced
Persons Act of 1948," as amended 16 June 1950.
16 43/AJ/926, 1947/48//Adoption-General: L.J. Ganse, Acting Director,
Legal Division, OMG Bavaria to Chief Legal Officer, IRO Area 7, Munich,
10 Nov. 1948.
17 RG 260, Legal Division, Records of the Office of the Director, Central Files,
1945–50, Box 7, 37D Staff Studies: G.H. Garde. Lt. Colonel AGD, Adjutant
General for Military Governor, OMG to Directors OMG: Bavaria, Hesse,
Wuerttemberg-Baden, Bremen, Berlin Sector, 3 March 1948.
18 RG 59, Records Relating to the International Refugee Organization (IRO)
and the Displaced Persons Commission (DPC), DP Subject File, 1949–52,
Box 15, Displaced Persons Commission, May–Aug. 1950: Foreign Service
despatch 235, Dwight J. Porter, Chief, Organization and Management
Division, HICOG to Department of State, 24 July 1950.
19 RG 278, Records of the Resettlement Division, Records of the Orphan
Section, Subject File, Entry 27, Box 132, Frankfurt and General: Mildred
Arnold, Director, Division of Social Services to Administrators of State
Public Welfare Agencies and Directors of Child Welfare, 15 June 1951;
"Placement of European Children in the United States," Federal Security
Agency, Social Security Administration, Children's Bureau, June 1951;
Elmer Falk, Assistant Coordinator for Europe, DP Commission to John
W. Gibson, Chairman, USDPC, Washington DC, att: Evelyn Rauch,
10 March 1951.
20 Ironically, Alex Squadrilli had worked for UNRRA as deputy director of
the Western Military District just a few years earlier.
21 RG 59, Records Relating to the International Refugee Organization (IRO)
and the Displaced Persons Commission (DPC), DP Subject File, 1944–52,
Box 15, Displaced Persons Commission Sept.–Dec. 1950: Squadrilli to J.D.
Kingsley, Director General, IRO Geneva, 8 Sept. 1950.
22 Ibid., telegram 496, Rosenfield, DPC (through Acheson), Department of
State to Kingsley IRO, 29 Nov. 1950.
23 Ibid., Foreign Service despatch 24 (OLC Bremen), C.P. Oakes, Chief, PAD,
OLC Bremen to Office of Political Adviser, Frankfurt, 11 Oct. 1950.
24 Ibid., UNA, Sandifer and GER, Byroade to the Acting Secretary, 29 Sept.
1950; Advisory Committee to the Displaced Persons Commission to
Commissioners U. Carusi, Edward O'Connor and H. Rosenfield, 21 Aug.
1950; cable 954, Kingsley IRO Geneva to Rosenfield, DPC, 15 Sept. 1950;
W.A. Wood Jr, US Office, IRO to G.L. Warren, Adviser on Refugees and
DPs, Department of State, 14 Sept. 1950.

25 Robert Corkery has served as chief of the Department of Repatriation and Resettlement for IRO CHQ (Washington D.C.) and chief of Field Services (IRO Geneva) before assuming this role.

26 Ibid., Corkery, Coordinator of Europe, DPC to George Warren, Department of State, 9 March 1951; H.C. Madison, UNA/R to UNA/R (Warren, Dawson, Col. Frost), 23 March 1951.

27 Ibid., Box 12, Office of Specialized Agency Affairs - Roseman (Geneva), 1950: G.L. Warren, Adviser on Refugees and Displaced Persons to Alvin Roseman, US Representative for Specialized Agency Affairs, Geneva, 24 July 1950.

28 43/AJ/941, Narrative Report - Child Care Zone Hqs: "Narrative Report for March 1949 (e) Department of Field Operations (III) Unaccompanied Children," US Zone HQ, Germany, 4 April 1949; 43/AJ/927, 1949// General: M.D. Lane, Chief Welfare Division, Health, Care & Maintenance Department, IRO Geneva to Ryan, Chief of Operations, US Zone IRO, 3 Aug. 1949; RG 260, PW&DP Branch, Recs Relating to Displaced Persons and Their Movements, 1945–49, Correspondence Jan. 1949 Thru Claims Against PCIRO, Box 118, file PCIRO Administration and Related Matters: Administrative Order No. 140, IRO US Zone HQ, 26 April 1949; Administrative Order No. 139, 26 April 1948.

29 43/AJ/958, 1947–48//Geneva: "Report on Field Trip to US Zone, Germany, 20th–26th June, 1948," Y. de Jong; 43/AJ/927 1949//General: Ellis, Zone Child Care Officer to M.D. Lane, Chief, Welfare Division, IRO Geneva, 6 May 1949; 43/AJ/919, 55/3/Act GUZ Mission, vol. 31: "Conference of IRO and Voluntary Organizations, Geneva, 19–21 January 1949."

30 43/AJ/941, Cumulative Narrative Report: "Cumulative Narrative Report-Child care. 1 July 1947–30 June 1949," Ellis, US Zone Child Care Officer, US Zone HQ.

31 Ibid., "Narrative Report for March 1949 (e) Department of Field Operations (III) Unaccompanied Children, US Zone HQ, Germany."

32 43/AJ/927, 1949//General: Ryan, Chief of Operations, US Zone to M.D. Lane, Chief, Welfare Division, Health, Care and Maintenance Department, IRO Geneva, 22 Aug. 1949.

33 43/AJ/941, Cumulative Narrative Report: "Cumulative Narrative Report - Child Care. 1 July 1949–30 September 1950," Ellis, US Zone Child Care Officer, IRO US Zone HQ.

34 43/AJ/941, Narrative Report-Child Care Zone Hqs: "Narrative Report for March 1950 (v) Department of Field Operations (c) Unaccompanied Children," US Zone Hq, Germany.

35 Ibid., "Narrative Report for December 1948 (d) Care and Maintenance (iv) Unaccompanied Children, US Zone HQ Germany."

36 43/AJ/927, 1949//General: P.E. Ryan, Chief of Operations, US Zone to M.D. Lane, Chief, Welfare Division, Health, Care and Maintenance Department, IRO Geneva, 22 Aug. 1949.

37 43/AJ/941, Cumulative Narrative Report: "Cumulative Narrative Report - Child Care. 1 July 1949–30 September 1950 (US Zone)."

38 43/AJ/928, Instructions to All Areas - on Child Care Program: Ellis, Zone Child Care Officer to all Areas, Field Offices, Children's Village, 14 July 1950.

39 43/AJ/927 1949//General: M.D. Lane, Chief Welfare Division, Health, Care & Maintenance Department, Geneva to Ryan, Chief of Operations, IRO US Zone, 13 Sept. 1949.

40 Ibid., M.D. Lane, Chief, Welfare Division, Health, Care & Maintenance Department, IRO Geneva to Ryan, Chief of Operations, US Zone IRO, 3 Aug. 1949; Ryan to IRO Geneva, att: M.D. Lane, Chief, Welfare Division, Health, Care and Maintenance Department, 12 July 1949.

41 43/AJ/927, 1950. Field Representative Munich: Ellis, Zone Child Care Officer, IRO US Zone to M.D. Lane, Chief, Welfare Division, Department of Health, Care & Maintenance Department, IRO Geneva, 21 March 1950.

42 RG 59, Records Relating to the International Refugee Organization (IRO) and the Displaced Persons Commission (DPC), IRO Subject File, 1946–52, Box 8, IRO General Jan.–March 1949: Georgia S. Allen, Procedure Officer to Gertrude Gates, Chief Division of Budget and Administrative Management, 24 Feb. 1949.

43 43/AJ/930, New Zealand - Unaccompanied Youth: R.J. McPherson, Australian, Canadian & NZ Branch to Zone Child Care, att: Ellis, 29 Jan. 1951; Ellis, Zone Child Care Officer, US Zone to Directors, all IRO Offices, 30 Jan. 1951, att: Child Care Officer; unnumbered cable, McPherson, 12 April 1951; cable 635, incoming, from Geneva, 30 April 1951 for inforefug Munich; unnumbered cable, McPherson to Resettlement Centers of Zone (Munich, Ludwigsburg, Augsburg, Bremen, Frankfurt), 1 May 1951; 43/AJ/957, 485/71 Child Care Conference, T. Jamieson, Director of Field Services, IRO Geneva to Ryan, Chief of Mission, IRO US Zone, 20 Jan. 1951.

44 43/AJ/948, NCWC - Nat. Cath. Welf. Comm.: Ellis, US Zone Child Care Officer to Director of Areas, att: Child Care Officers, 29 March 1951.

45 Ibid.; 43/AJ/856, 39/1 GUZ Secondary Material Vol. 4: Ellis to E. Brown, Chief, Zone Welfare, 15 Jan. 1951.

46 43/AJ/929, German Economy: Ryan, Chief of Mission, IRO US Zone to Corkery, Chief of Field Services, IRO Geneva, 13 Oct. 1950; 43/AJ/955, Immigration Projects/General: Law No. 11, "Repatriation and

Resettlement of Unaccompanied Displaced Children," Office of the United
States High Commissioner for Germany (HICOG), 5 Oct. 1950.

47 43/AJ/956, EUCOM-Directions for unaccompanied children: Ellis, US
Zone Child Care Officer, for Chief of Operations, IRO US Zone to E.M.
Hughes, HQ EUCOM, Civil Affairs Division, 10 Feb. 1949; 43/AJ/926,
1949//Adoption-General: V.V. Lewis, Deputy Zone Child Care Officer to
Acting Chief Legal Division, 18 Jan. 1949; 43/AJ/194, 80/1/G.US.Z Legal
(Monthly Narrative Reports) Germany - US Zone: "Narrative Report for
May 1949 (ix) Legal and Political Protection," IRO US Zone HQ.

48 43/AJ/926, Recovery Program. 1950: draft memo with cover note, Welfare
to Child Care, 21 Feb. 1950.

49 43/AJ/406, Mr. Blanchard's Office - Unaccompanied Children - 41:
B.G. Alexander, Acting Director, Office of Protection IRO to Cohen and
G. Rickford, 6 Dec. 1950.

50 43/AJ/926, Childrens Review Board: H.H. Ruthrauff, Chief, Division
of Employment and Vocational Training to Division of Administrative
Services, att: Civil Labour Office, 27 Sept. 1949; Ellis, Zone Child Care
Officer to Dunn, Chief, C&M Department, 23 Nov. 1949; Child Care Daily
Report: daily reports from Child Care to C&M, 15 Dec. 1949 and 10 Feb.
1950; RG 59, 1950–54, Decimal File 862A.441/2-450 to 862A.411/6-3050, Box
5243: telegram 3486, Department of State to HICOG Frankfurt, 8 May 1950.

51 43/AJ/941 Cumulative Narrative Report: "Cumulative Narrative Report -
Child Care. 1 July 1949–30 September 1950."

52 Ibid., Narrative Report - Child Care Zone Hqs: "Narrative Report for
October 1950 (v) Department of Field Operations (c) Unaccompanied
Children," US Zone HQ Germany.

53 43/AJ/931, Children's Court: Ellis, Zone Child Care to Zone Welfare, att:
H.A. Washington, 13 Feb. 1951.

54 43/AJ/927, Children's Court - Policy: "Concerning Law No. 11 of
the United High Commissioner for Germany on the repatriation and
resettlement of unaccompanied displaced children," O. Bayer, Legal
Advisor, IRO US Zone, 11 Dec. 1950; 43/AJ/941 Area 1 Child Care
Monthly Narrative Report: "Narrative Report (15 Dec 50-15 Jan 51)."

55 43/AJ/941, Narrative Report - Child Care Zone Hqs: "Narrative Report
for December 1950 (v) Department of Field Operations (c) Unaccompanied
Children," US Zone HQ Germany.

56 43/AJ/956, HICOG 1950 and 1951: Ryan, Chief of Mission, IRO US Zone
to Swope, draft, 6 March 1951.

57 43/AJ/941, Narr. Rep. Area 5: "Narrative Report - Child Care Section
period 15 February 51-15 Mar 51"; 43/AJ/931, Children's Court: Allen,

European Representative, US Committee for Care of European Children to J. Collins, Chief, US Desk, IRO Geneva, 19 March 1951.

58 RG 278, DP Commission - Resettlement Division - Orphan Section, Entry 27, Box 131, Children's Courts: Allen, Committee for the Care of European Children, European HQ to Ingeborg Olsen, 16 April 1951; RG 278, Records of the Resettlement Division, Records of the Orphan Section, Subject File, Entry 27, Box 131, Children's Courts: Roland Elliott, Director, Resettlement Program, National Council of the Churches of Christ, Church World Service, NY, NY, to John W. Gibson, Chairman, DP Commission, 4 April 1951; 43/AJ/302, 488/22 Children - General Questions - Children's Courts (HICOG Law No.11): C.W. Bell, Centre Quaker International de Geneve to D.J. Kingsley, IRO Geneva, 16 April 1951.

59 43/AJ/931, Children's Court: Ellis, Zone Child Care Officer to Legal Office, att: O. Bayer, 11 April 1951.

60 43/AJ/941, Narr. Rep. Area 5: "Narrative Report - Child Care Section period 15 February 51-15 Mar 51"; 43/AJ/931, Children's Court: Allen to Collins, 19 March 1951.

61 RG 278, DP Commission - Resettlement Division - Orphan Section, Entry 27, Box 131, Children's Courts: Allen to Olsen, 16 April 1951.

62 43/AJ/927, Childrens' Court - General: O. Bayer, Legal Advisor, IRO US Zone to M. Braude, 2 Feb. 1951; Farley, Child Care Field Representative to Zone Legal Division, att: J. Toliszus, 14 Feb. 1951; 43/AJ/931, Children's Court: Ellis, Zone Child Care to Zone Welfare, att: H.A. Washington, 13 Feb. 1951.

63 RG 278, DP Commission - Resettlement Division - Orphan Section, Entry 27, Box 131, Children's Courts: Allen to Olsen, 16 April 1951; RG 278, Records of the Resettlement Division, Records of the Orphan Section, Subject File, Entry 27, Box 131, Children's Courts: Elliott to Gibson, 4 April 1951; 43/AJ/302, 488/22 Children-General Questions-Children's Courts (HICOG Law No.11): Bell to Kingsley,16 April 1951.

64 43/AJ/927, Children's Court - Policy: Farley, Child Care Field Representative to Wm. Gosser, DP Branch, OLC Bavaria, 19 March 1951; 43/AJ/931, Children's Court: Farley to unknown addressee, 4 April 1951; 43/AJ/856, 39/1: Ellis, Zone Child Care Officer, IRO US Zone to E. Brown, Chief, Zone Welfare Division, IRO US Zone, 5 April 1951.

65 RG 59, 1950–54, Decimal File 862A.441/2-450 to 862A.411/6-3050, Box 5243: telegram 3486, Department of State to HICOG Frankfurt, 8 May 1950; 43/AJ/931, Children's Court - General: Bikart, PRC Senior Representative for Germany and US Zone to Ellis, Zone Child Care Officer, IRO US Zone, 30 Jan. 1951; Decimal File 862A.411/6/451 to

862A.411/12-1151, Box 5245: Foreign Service despatch 243, Swope to Department of State, 27 July 1951.

66 RG 278, DP Commission - Resettlement Division - Orphan Section, Entry 27, Box 131, Children's Courts: Allen to Olsen, 16 April 1951; RG 278, Records of the Resettlement Division, Records of the Orphan Section, Subject File, Entry 27, Box 131, Children's Courts: Elliott to Gibson, 4 April 1951; 43/AJ/302, 488/22 Children-General Questions-Children's Courts (HICOG Law No.11): Bell to Kingsley, 16 April 1951.

67 43/AJ/857, 1023-FULDA PRIVATE-575: T. Sherrard, Operations Officer, IRO US Zone to T. Jamieson, Chief, Department of Field Operations, IRO US Zone, 23 April 1951.

68 RG 278, DP Commission - Resettlement Division - Orphan Section, Entry 27, Box 131, Children's Courts: Allen to Olsen, 16 April 1951.

69 43/AJ/927, Children's Court - Policy: E. Starner, Area Child Care Officer, IRO Area 5 to Ellis, Zone Child Care Officer, IRO US Zone HQ, 13 April 1951.

70 Ibid.

71 43/AJ/931, Children's Court - General: J. Toliszus, Legal Officer to Farley, 26 Jan. 1951.

72 43/AJ/941, Narrative Report - Child Care Zone Hqs: "Narrative Report for January 1951 (v) Department of Field Operations (c) Unaccompanied Children," US Zone HQ Germany.

73 43/AJ/856, 39/1: Ellis to Brown, 5 April 1951; 43/AJ/927 Children's Courts - Policy: Farley to Ellis, 10 April 1951; RG 278, Records of the Resettlement Division, Records of the Orphan Section, Subject File, Entry 27, Box 131, Children's Courts: Pettiss, Resettlement Officer, IRO Washington DC to Ingeborg Olsen, US Committee for the Care of European Children; Betty Barton, Office of German Public Affairs, State Department; Evelyn Smith, Children's Bureau; Evelyn Rauch, DP Commission, 12 April 1951.

74 43/AJ/931, Children's Court: E. Brown, Zone Welfare Officer to Jamieson, Chief, Department of Field Operations, 30 March 1951; G.J. Swope, Chief, DP Division to Ryan, Chief of Mission, IRO US Zone HQ, 2 April 1951; 43/AJ/302, 488/22 Children-General Questions-Children's Courts (HICOG No. 11): H. Hinchcliffe, Chief Legal Adviser, IRO US Zone to L.C. Stephens, General Counsel, IRO Geneva, 19 Sept. 1951.

75 43/AJ/856, 39/1: Ellis to Brown, 5 April 1951; 43/AJ/927 Children's Courts - Policy: Farley to Ellis, 10 April 1951; RG 278, Records of the Resettlement Division, Records of the Orphan Section, Subject File, Entry 27, Box 131, Children's Courts: Pettiss to Olsen, Barton, Smith, and Rauch, 12 April 1951.

76 43/AJ/927, Children's Courts - Policy: Farley, Child Care Field Representative, Land Bavaria to Ellis, Zone Child Care, 16 March 1951;

Farley to Zone Legal Division, att: Toliszus, 16 March 1951; Farley to Ellis, 10 April 1951; Farley to Ellis, 28 March 1951.

77 43/AJ/410, Legal Protection, Children Germany: Bergman to Grigg, May 51.

78 43/AJ/931, Children's Court: Allen to Collins, 19 March 1951; RG 278 DP Commission - Resettlement Division - Orphan Section, Entry 27, Box 131, Children's Courts: Allen to Olsen, 16 April 1951.

79 43/AJ/931, Children's Court: Farley to unknown addressee, 4 April 1951; 43/AJ/856 39/1 GUZ Secondary Material, vol. 4: Child Care Department, IRO Children's Village Bad Aibling to Ellis, Zone Child Welfare Officer, IRO US Zone, 10 April 1951.

80 43/AJ/302, 488/22 Children - General Questions - Children's Courts (HICOG Law No. 11): Allen to Kingsley, 23 April 1951.

81 43/AJ/857, 1023-FULDA PRIVATE-575: Sherrard to Jamieson, 23 April 1951.

82 Thirty-five were sent from Child Care to Legal and 14 filed with the court in Jan.; 65 sent to Legal and 39 filed with the court in Feb.; 50 and 34, respectively, in March; and 20 and 52 in April. The first 9 cases were heard in March, of which 7 received "final decrees" (the cases were settled); and another 25 heard in April, of which 13 were closed. 43/AJ/410, Legal Protection - Children Germany: Bergman to Grigg, May 1951.

83 43/AJ/856, 39/1: Ellis to Brown, 5 April 1951; 43/AJ/927 Children's Courts - Policy: Farley to Ellis, 10 April 1951; RG 278, Records of the Resettlement Division, Records of the Orphan Section, Subject File, Entry 27, Box 131, Children's Courts: Pettiss to Olsen, Barton, Smith, and Rauch, 12 April 1951.

84 43/AJ/931, Children's Court: Farley to unknown addressee, 4 April 1951; 43/AJ/941 Area 1 Frankf. Narrative Report: "Narrative Report (15 Mar 51-15 Apr 51)."

85 RG 59, Records Relating to the International Refugee Organization (IRO) and the Displaced Persons Commission (DPC), DP Subject File, 1944–52, Box 6, DP Germany March–April 1951: telegram 8137, Frankfurt to Secretary of State, 9 April 1951.

86 43/AJ/410, Legal Protection - Children Germany: Grigg, Director of Field Services to C.W. Bell, Centre Quaker International de Geneve, 27 April 1951; P. Jacobsen, Assistant Director General, Operations, IRO Geneva to Ryan, Chief, IRO US Zone, 4 May 1951; RG 278, Records of the Resettlement Division, Records of the Orphan Section, Subject File, Entry 27, Box 131, Children's Courts: Corkery, Coordinator for Europe, DP Commission to J.W. Gibson, Chairman, 24 May 1951; Katharine Lenroot, Chief, Children's Bureau, DP Commission to Henry A. Byroade, Director, Bureau of German Affairs, Department of State, Washington, DC, 9 May

1951; Martha H. Biehle, IRO Washington DC to Evelyn Rauch, DP Commission, Washington DC, 23 May 1951.

87 43/AJ/410, Legal Protection - Children Germany: Cohen, Acting Director General, IRO Geneva to P. Jacobsen, Assistant Director General, in Charge of Operations, 26 April 1951.

88 RG 278, DP Commission - Resettlement Division - Orphan Section, Entry 27, Box 131, Children's Courts: Allen to Olsen, 16 April 1951.

89 43/AJ/928, Child Care Committee: minutes, Child Care Meeting, US Zone HQ, 17 May 1951; "Closure Plans - 1951," Ellis, Zone Child Care Officer to Zone Welfare Division, 24 May 1951; 43/AJ/410, Legal Protection - Children Germany: Bergman to Grigg, May 51; T. Jamieson, Chief, Department of Field Operations to all Areas, Children's Village, draft, undated; 43/AJ/496, Children ¼ 1951-: Grigg, Director of Field Services, IRO to Ryan, Chief, IRO US Zone, 26 July 1951, att: Chief, Department of Operations.

90 43/AJ/857, GUZ Secondary material - Vol. 1 - Unaccompanied Children - Legal Status: unnumbered cable, Ryan, Chief of Mission, IRO US Zone to Geneva, Washington, Frankfurt/HICOG, US Committee for Care of European Children, 5 June 1951; Allen, US Committee for the Care of European Children to M.A. Brauda, Special Assistant to the Chief of Mission, IRO Germany, 19 June 1951.

91 43/AJ/302, 488/22 Children - General Questions - Children's Courts (HICOG Law No. 11): memo to file, Pettiss, Resettlement Officer, IRO Geneva, 30 March 1951.

92 43/AJ/941, Area 1 Frankfurt: "Narrative Report (15 May 51-15 June 51), Area 1"; "Narrative Report (15 June 51-15 July 51), Area 1"; Area 2 - 1951: "Monthly Narrative Report, report dated 18 July 1951."

93 43/AJ/496, Children ¼ 1951-: Grigg to Ryan, 26 July 1951.

94 43/AJ/302, 488/14 Vol. 2 Care of Children after IRO's Termination: T. Jamieson, Chief, Department of Field Operations to IRO Geneva, att: Grigg, Director of Field Services, Aug. 1951; 488/22 Children-General Questions-Children's Courts (HICOG No. 11): Susan Pettis, Resettlement Officer, IRO Washington DC to Grigg, Director of Field Services, IRO Geneva, 13 Sept. 1951.

95 RG 59, 1950–54, Decimal File 862A.411/6/451 to 862A.411/12-1151, Box 5245: Foreign Service despatch 694, American Embassy Warsaw to Department of State, 25 June 1951; 43/AJ/410 Legal Protection - Children Germany: Louis C. Stephens, General Counsel to Herbert W. Besser, Office of the General Counsel, Federal Security Agency, Washington DC, 27 Aug. 1951.

96 43/AJ/302, 488/22 Children - General Questions - Children's Courts (HICOG No. 11): W. Rothhole, Legal Adviser, IRO US Zone to L.C. Stephens, General Counsel, IRO Geneva, 6 Aug. 1951.

97 43/AJ/857, 39/3 GUZ 2ndary: Pettiss, Resettlement Officer, IRO Geneva
to Grigg, Director of Field Services, IRO Geneva, 8 Aug. 1951; RG 278,
Records of the Resettlement Division, Records of the Orphan Section,
Subject File, Entry 27, Box 131, Federal Security Agency 1: Katharine F.
Lenroot, Chief, Children's Bureau to Henry A. Byroade, Director, Bureau
of German Affairs, Department of State, 21 Aug. 1951.

98 43/AJ/931, Children's Court - Statistics: "Unaccompanied Children's
Cases Under Law No. 11," 9 Nov. 1951.

99 43/AJ/496, Children 1/4 1951-: W.G. Fuller, Deputy Chief, Migration
Services, Provisional Intergovernmental Committee for the Movement
of Migrants from Europe to Col. O.E. Cound, IRO Liquidator, Geneva,
1 April 1952; J.R. Pollock, Special Advisor to E.S. Broughton, Mission
Liquidator, 18 March 1952; 43/AJ/603 Unaccompanied Children 39/1
General Policies and General Reports 1950: Ellis, Zone Child Welfare
Officer to T.D. Sherrard, Field Operations, IRO Zone HQ, 31 Jan. 1952.

100 43/AJ/929, German Economy: Corkery, Director of Field Services, IRO
Geneva to Ryan, Chief of Mission, IRO US Zone, 21 Sept. 1950; Ellis, Zone
Child Care Officer to All Areas and Bad Aibling, 2 Oct. 1950.

101 Ibid., Corkery, Director of Field Services, IRO Geneva to Ryan, Chief
of Mission, IRO US Zone, 30 June 1950; Ryan to Corkery, 11 Aug.
1950; "Report on Field Trip to Germany, 22 Aug. 1950 to 8 September
1950," Youdin; 43/AJ/941, Cumulative Narrative Report: "Cumulative
Narrative Report - Child Care. 1 July 1949–30 September 1950."

102 RG 59, Records Relating to the International Refugee Organization (IRO)
and the Displaced Persons Commission (DPC), IRO Subject File, 1946–52,
Box 8, IRO General April–June 1949: Dunn, Chief of Department of Care
and Maintenance, IRO US Zone to R.S. Winslow, 31 May 1949.

103 43/AJ/941, Narrative Report - Child Care zone Hqs: "Narrative Report
for January 1949 (e) Department of Field Operations (III) Unaccompanied
Children," US Zone HQ, Germany; Area 5 - Child Care Monthly Narrative
Reports: "Narrative Report - Child Care Section, 15 Jan. 1949 to 15 Feb.
1949"; 43/AJ/955, US Immigration (Bill): E.M. Falk, Deputy Chief, R&R to
Thomas, 12 Aug. 1949.

104 43/AJ/958, 1947/1948//Geneva: Dunn, Chief, Department of Care and
Maintenance to Executive Secretary, IRO HQ Geneva, att: Cohen, Assistant
Director General, Health, Care and Maintenance Department, 29 Nov. 1948.

105 43/AJ/927, 1949//General: M.D. Lane, Chief Welfare Division, IRO
Geneva to Ryan, Chief of Operations, IRO US Zone, 6 April 1949.

106 43/AJ/938, Medical Centers: Ellis, Zone Child Care Officer, US Zone to
Chief, Medical Department, att: Hennessy, 7 March 1949; 43/AJ/941 Area

3-Child Care Monthly Narrative Reports: "Monthly Narrative Report-Child Care Dept for period 15th Feb–15th March 1949."

107 43/AJ/930, Temporary Care for Accomp. Children: Ellis, Zone Child Care Officer, US Zone IRO to M.D. Lane, Chief, Welfare Division, Health, Care and Maintenance Department, IRO Geneva, 20 April 1949.

108 43/AJ/927, 1949//General: Ellis, Zone Child Care Officer for Chief of Operations, IRO Germany to M.D. Lane, Chief of Welfare Division, IRO Geneva, 20 May 1949.

109 43/AJ/930, Temporary Care for Accomp. Children: Ellis, Zone Child Welfare Officer, US Zone to Medical Department, att: F. Hennessey, 3 and 29 Aug. 1949.

110 Ibid., G.H.A. Frank, Area Child Care Officer to V. Lewis, Deputy Zone Child Care Officer, 31 Oct. 1949.

111 Ibid., M.D. Lane, Chief, Welfare Division, IRO Geneva to Ryan, IRO US Zone, 11 April 1950.

112 Ibid., Ellis, Zone Child Care Officer, US Zone to Dr. S. Ernst, Pediatric Consultant, Health Department, AJDC, Munich, 27 June 1950.

113 43/AJ/941, Narrative Report - Child Care Zone Hqs: "Narrative Report for October 1950 (v) Department of Field Operations (c) Unaccompanied Children," US Zone HQ, Germany.

114 43/AJ/930, Temporary Care for Accomp. Children: Dr. A. Belinfante, Chief, Health Department for Area Director, Area 1 to Health Division, US Zone HQ, att: Dr. S. Flache, Assistant Deputy Chief Medical Officer, 2 Dec. 1949; 43/J/927, 1950. Field Representative Munich: "Anticipated Residual Child Care Case Load and Proposed Closure Plans," Ellis, undated.

115 43/AJ/930, Temporary Care for Accomp. Children: "Special note re: Goddelau and mentally deficient children"; Dr. L. Findlay, Chief, Department of Health and Ellis, Zone Child Care Officer to Areas' Medical and Child Care Officers, 6 Jan. 1950; 43/AJ/941, Narrative Report - Child Care Zone Hqs: "Narrative Report for March 1950 (v) Department of Field Operations (c) Unaccompanied Children," US Zone HQ, Germany; "Narrative Report for February 1950 (v) Department of Field Operations (c) Unaccompanied Children, US Zone Germany"; 43/AJ/940, 1950 Area #5: "Narrative Report, Area 5, for period 15 May-15 June 1950."

116 RG 466, Bavaria Land Commissioner (BLC); Officer of the Land Commissioner Central Files, Box 27, 570.1 Refugees & DPs: conference notes, Robert I. Hood, MD, Public Health Advisor, Public Affairs Division, OLCB, HICOG, 22 May 1950.

117 MArb 1988/1, Vermerkung: memo to file, Wokatsch, Abt III, Munich, 14 Aug. 1951; T.D. Sherrard, Operations Officer, IRO US Zone to Oberlander, Ministry of Refugees, Bavaria, 17 Aug. 1951; P.E. Ryan, Chief of Mission, IRO US Zone to G.J. Swope, Chief, Displaced Persons Division, Office of Political Affairs, HICOG, Aug. 1951, minutes of meeting at IRO HQ, to discuss Dorfen transfer, 28 Aug. 1951; Arbeiterwohlfahrt, Landesverband Bayern E.V. Munich, 29 Aug. 1951; W. Högner, Staatsminister und Stellv. des Ministerpräsidenten, Bayer. Staatsministerium des Innern to Hans Ehard, Ministerpräsidenten, Munich, 29 Aug. 1951.

118 RG 466, BLC, Office of the Land Commissioner Central Files, Box 27, 570.1 Refugees & DPs: minutes of meeting held at OLCB, 31 Jan. 1951.

119 Ibid., minutes, meeting held at OLCB, 3 April 1951.

120 43/AJ/929, German Economy: Ellis, Zone Child Care Officer to Health Department, att: Dr. Flache, 26 June 1950; MInn 81113, IRO - Lager A-Z: Laubenthal, Bayerisches Landesjugendamt to Herrn Min. Rat Ritter, Frl. von Drygalski, 12 June 1950.

121 43/AJ/941, Area 5 - Child Care Monthly Narrative Reports: "Narrative Report - Child Care Section period 15 Oct 50-15 Nov 50."

122 RG 278, Records of the Resettlement Division, Records of the Orphan Section, Subject File, Entry 27, Box 132, Frankfurt and General: Corkery, Coordinator for Europe, US DP Commission to John W. Gibson, Chairman, USDPC, Washington, DC, 26 July 1951.

123 Ibid., Harry N. Rosenfield to John W. Gibson, Chairman and Edward M. O'Connor, 12 July 1951.

124 Heide Fehrenbach, *Race after Hitler* (Princeton, NJ: Princeton University Press, 2005), chapter 5, ad passim.

125 RG 466, BLC, Office of the Land Commissioner Central Files, Box 27, 570.1 Refugees & DPs: minutes of meeting held at OLCB, 31 Jan. 1951.

126 Ibid., minutes, meeting held at OLCB, 19 Feb. 1951.

127 43/AJ/948, NCWC - Nat. Cath. Welf. Comm.: F. Hoppe, NCWC Child Welfare Officer, War Relief Services, National Catholic Welfare Conference to Ellis, US Zone Child Welfare Officer, 27 Aug. 1951; Hoppe to Ellis, 19 Nov. 1951; Ellis to Hoppe, 29 Nov. 1951.

128 MInn 81113, IRO - Lager A-Z: Laubenthal to Ritter, Frl. von Drygalski, 12 June 1950.

129 43/AJ/941, Cumulative Narrative Report: "Cumulative Narrative Report - Child Care. 1 July 1949–30 September 1950 (IRO US Zone Hq)"; 43/AJ/927, 1950. Field Representative Munich: Farley, Child Care Field Representative for Land Bavaria to W.R. Gosser, Chief, DP Populations Branch, Office of the Land Commissioner, Munich, 19 April 1950.

130 43/AJ/929, German Economy: "Report on Field Trip to Germany, 22 August 1950 to 8 September 1950."
131 Ibid., Corkery, Director of Field Services, IRO Geneva to Ryan, Chief of Mission, IRO US Zone, 21 Sept. 1950.
132 43/AJ/920, 55/3/ACT GUZ Secondary Material - 2.G1. Reports on Residual Programs: "Report from the NCWC Legal Office, Munich-Pasing for May, June 1951"; "Service to the Residual DPs in the US Zone - May, June, July 1951/Report from NCWC Child Care Officer."
133 Ibid. (both documents).
134 43/AJ/857, 1023-FULDA Private - 575: T. Jamieson, Chief, Department of Field Operations to N. Moore, Chief, Department of Field Operations, IRO British Zone HQ, 15 Oct. 1951.
135 43/AJ/928, Closure Plans - 1951: J. Aland, Zone Resettlement Placement Officer to J. Thomas, Chief, R&R Division, Zone HQ, 1 Aug. 1951.
136 43/AJ/496, Children 1/4 1951–: G. Rickford, Deputy Chief, Department of Operations, IRO to IRO Washington, att: M.H. Biehle, 3 Oct. 1951; 43/AJ/928 Closure Plans - 1951: E. Brown, Zone Welfare Officer to T. Jamieson, Chief, Department of Field Operations, 18 July 1951.
137 RG 278, Records of the Resettlement Division, Records of the Orphan Section, Subject File, Entry 27, Box 132, Frankfurt and General: IRO, US Zone to IRO HQ Geneva, 5 Oct. 1951.
138 43/AJ/928, Closure Plans - 1951: H.A. Washington, Deputy Chief, Zone Welfare Division to Ellis, Zone Child Care Officer, 19 Nov. 1951.
139 43/AJ/496, Children 1/4 1951-: G. Rickford, Deputy Chief, Department of Operations, IRO to IRO Washington, att: M.H. Biehle, 3 Oct. 1951.
140 RG 59, Records Relating to the International Refugee Organization (IRO) and the Displaced Persons Commission (DPC), DP Subject File, 1944–52, Box 15, Displaced Persons Commission 1951: E. O'Connor, Acting Chairman, Displaced Persons Commission, Washington, DC to Dean Acheson, Secretary of State, Washington, DC, 5 Oct. 1951.
141 Ibid., airgram A-1407, Webb, Acting, Department of State to HICOG, att: Wolfe, 1 Nov. 1951.
142 RG 59, 1950-54, Decimal File 82A.411/6-451 to 862A.411/12-1151, Box 5245: telegram 3476, Paris to Secretary of State, 11 Dec. 1951.
143 Ibid., telegram 749, Department of State, G.L. Warren for Acheson to HICOG, 21 Dec. 1951.
144 MInn 81113, IRO - Lager A-Z: Laubenthal to von Drygalski, 12 June 1950.
145 The International Social Service (ISS) was an international NGO that had been established in 1924 to provide a new type of social service that had become necessary as a result of the new kinds of intercountry relationships

that had emerged as a result of mass migrations in Europe after the First World War. Families that had been ripped apart by the war, and found themselves scattered across two or more countries, faced special challenges in trying to reunite, and the ISS was created to assist in that process. By the end of the Second World War, the ISS was operating in a number of countries and was recognized for its expertise in navigating the shoals of intercountry social work and conflicts in law. Its focus was on the reunification of families, and especially on children – either reuniting them with their kin or finding socially sound plans and tracing services for those whose family's location or fate was unknown. "ISS History," International Social Service website, see http://www.iss-ssi.org/index.php/en/home/history#1-iss-history-in-more-details (consulted 17 Feb. 2016).

146 RG 59, 1950–54, Decimal File 862A.411/1.352 to 862A.411/12-3152, Box 5425: Foreign Service Despatch 629, HICOG to Department of State, 4 Sept. 1952; Foreign Service Despatch 1868, HICOG to Department of State, 31 Dec. 1952.

147 RG 278, Records of the Resettlement Division, Records of the Orphan Section, Subject File, entry 27, Box 132, Frankfurt and General: Lois S. McVey, Child Welfare Officer, US DP Commission HQ to Corkery, Coordinator for Europe, DP Commission, 23 May 1952.

10 Nationality

1 RG 260, CAD, PW&DP Branch, Records Relating to DPs in Germany and Other Countries, 1945–49, Box 140, Headquarters US Group CC - Policy Book - PoW&DP Division: cable S-87880, SCAEF, to C-in-C 21st, 12th, 6th Army Groups, CG Com Zone, 22 May 1945.

2 RG 331, OGS, G-1 Division, Administrative Section, Decimal Correspondence File, 1944–45, Entry 6, Box 28, 383.6/8 Russian Prisoners of War, General: cable WX-63626, Joint Chiefs of Staff, to Eisenhower, 5 April 1945.

3 Ibid., cable S-86755 SCAEF to CG Com Zone (cc'd to the Army Groups), 1 May 1945.

4 RG 260, CAD, PW&DP Branch, Records Relating to DPs in Germany and Other Countries, 1945–49, Box 140, Headquarters US Group CC - Policy Book - PoW&DP Division: cable S-87880, 22 May 1945.

5 RG 331, OGS, G-5, Secretariat, Numeric File Aug. 1943–July 1945, Entry 47, Box 49, Displaced Persons Branch. SHAEF/G-5/2719. Baltic States: H Price-Williams, Brigadier, Executive, G-5 SHAEF to AG Div SHAEF, 4 July 1945, plus attached memorandum, Latvian Minister of France and Councillor of the Lithuanian Legation in Paris, 13 June 1945.

6 They were Albania, Argentina, Australia, Belgium, Bolivia, Brazil, Canada, Chile, China, Colombia, Costa Rica, Cuba, Czechoslovakia, Denmark, Dominican Republic, Ecuador, Egypt, El Salvador, Ethiopia, France, Greece, Guatemala, Haiti, Honduras, Iceland, India, Iraq, Iran, Lebanon, Liberia, Luxembourg, Mexico, Netherlands, New Zealand, Nicaragua, Norway, Panama, Paraguay, Peru, Philippine Islands, Poland, Saudi Arabia, Syria, Turkey, Union of South Africa, United Kingdom and Northern Ireland, USA, USSR, Uruguay, Venezuela, and Yugoslavia.

7 RG 260, OAG, General correspondence & other records, 1945–49, 390/40/21/2 Box 91, file AG 383.7 Displaced Persons (Refugees, Expellees, Internees), 2 of 2: "Determination and Reporting of Nationalities," C.L. Adcock, Major General, GSC, Director, USFET to Directors OMG: Western District and Bavaria, 16 Nov. 1945.

8 S-0425-0004, Administrative-Reporting Procedures (15): E.S. Seldon, Reports Officer, for District Director to Chief, Reports and Statistics Branch, UNRRA, US Zone HQ, 8 June 1946.

9 As cited in Leonard Dinnerstein, *America and the Survivors of the Holocaust* (New York: Columbia University Press, 1982), 13.

10 RG 331, OGS, G-5 Division, Secretariat, Numeric File Aug. 1943–July 1945, Entry 47, Box 54, Displaced Persons Branch. SHAEF/G-5/2814. DPs Welfare - Children: P.M. Malin, Vice-Director, Intergovernmental Committee on Refugees (IGCR), SHAEF to Chief, DP Branch, and Executive, DP Branch, 12 June 1945.

11 RG 331, OCS, Secretary, General Staff, Decimal File, May 1943–Aug. 1945, Entry 1, Box 89, 383.7 vol III (Refugees and Displaced Persons of European nationality): cable FWD 23780, SCAEF to CG 12th and 6th Army Groups (G-5), C-in-C 21st Army Group (Mil Govt), 6 June 1945; RG 260, CAD, PW&DP Branch, Records Relating to DPs in Germany and Other Countries, 1945–49, Box 165 383.7 Stateless Persons: Schottland, Lt. Col., CMP Chief, Processing Center Section, CDPX, G-5 USFET to Executive, CDPX, 5 Aug. 1945.

12 Angelika Königseder and Juliane Wetzel, *Waiting for Hope: Jewish Displaced Persons in Post-World War II Germany* (Evanston, IL: Northwestern University Press, 2001), 18; Yosef Grodzinsky, *In the Shadow of the Holocaust: The Struggle between Jews and Zionists in the Aftermath of World War II* (Monroe, ME: Common Courage Press, 2004), 67–9.

13 Atina Grossman, *Jews, Germans, and Allies: Close Encounters in Occupied Germany* (Princeton, NJ: Princeton University Press, 2007), 138; Königseder and Wetzel, *Waiting for Hope*, 18–19; Arieh J. Kochavi, *Post-Holocaust Politics: Britain, the United States, and Jewish Refugees, 1945–1948* (Chapel Hill, NC: University of North Carolina Press, 2001), 90.

14 Report submitted by Earl G. Harrison to President Truman, 22 Aug. 1945 (it can be found online at https://www.ushmm.org/exhibition/displaced -persons/resourc1.html (consulted 20 Feb. 2017).

15 RG 260, CAD, PW&DP Branch, Records Relating to DPs in Germany and Other Countries, 1945–49, Box 140, Headquarters US Group CC - Policy Book - PoW&DP Division: minutes of second meeting of the Deputy Military Governor with Army Commanders, held 25–26 July 1945.

16 Ibid., Box 165, 383.7 Stateless Persons: H.H. Newman, Col AGD, Acting Adjutant General to Commanding Generals, EMD and WMD, 22 Aug. 1945.

17 Ibid.

18 RG 260, Legal Div/Legal Advice Branch, Box 52, LA 30.1 Adoptions: Blackey, Child Welfare Consultant, UNRRA CHQ Germany to Dickman, Legal Division, OMGUS, 6 May 1946; PAG 4/3.0.11.0.1.1:4, Child Search Repatriation Reports - Welfare: "Report on Field Trip to US Zone, 3–11 March 1947"; PAG 4/3.0.11.0.1.4:4, Reports - Special: "Summary Report on Child Welfare & Child Search for Preparatory Commission of IRO," 24 May 1947; 43/AJ/597, Unaccompanied Children, 39/1 General Policies and General Reports 1947: "UNRRA Closure Report of United Nations Unaccompanied Children in Germany, June 1947."

19 RG 331, OGS, G-5 Division, Secretariat, Numeric File, Aug. 1943–July 1945, Entry 47, Box 51, Displaced Persons Branch. SHAEF/G-5/2719. Baltic States: Donald R. Heath, Counselor to Ambassador Murphy, US Political Adviser to Col. A.H. Moffitt, Jr, Executive Officer, Displaced persons, Refugees, and Welfare Branch, G-5 SHAEF, 14 April 1945.

20 Foreign Relations of the United States: Diplomatic Papers, 1945. General: Political and Economic Matters (Washington, DC: US Government Printing Office, 1945), II: 1160.

21 RG 260, OAG, General correspondence and other records, 1945–49, 390/40/21/2, Box 91, AG 383.7 Displaced Persons (Refugees, Expellees, Internees), 2 of 2: unnumbered cable, unknown sender to USFET Main, OMGUS, 28 Nov. 1945.

22 Foreign Relations of the United States, Europe (1945), V: 1076–7, 1098, 1103.

23 The United States, among other nations, would never recognize the incorporation of Estonia, Latvia, and Lithuania into the USSR, but also did not recognize the three republics as independent states again until 1991.

24 RG 260, Legal Division/Legal Advice Branch, Box 51, LA-24 Displaced Persons, Refugees, Internees: Charles Fahy, Legal Advisor to UNRRA CHQ Germany, 29 April 1946.

25 PAG 4/3.0.11.0.1.1:6, Central Headquarters - Child Welfare Material: "Notes on Conference with Cornelia Heise, US Zone," Eileen Blacky, 12 March 1946.

26 PAG 4/1.0.1.0.0:33, DPs-Legal and Policy Decisions 1946 #3: cable 788, K.A. Aickin, Office of General Counsel, London to Washington, 20 Jan. 1946; DPs-Legal and Policy Decisions 1945-1946: cable 1118, Dudley Ward, Office of General Counsel, London to Washington, 28 Jan. 1946; DPs-Legal and Policy Decisions 1946 #2: cable 75, Washington to Ward, 2 Feb. 1946.

27 PAG 4/3.0.11.0.1.1:5, CHQ Child Welfare Material: "Notes on Conference with Miss Cornelia Heise, U.S. Zone."

28 PAG 4/1.0.0.0.0:21, Displaced Persons (thru 31 March 1947): Ian M. Hudson, Foreign Office, London to Lt. General Sir Humfrey Gale, ERO, UNRRA, 14 Oct. 1946; Gale to Major General Lowell Rooks, Director General, UNRRA HQ, 16 Jan. 1947; PAG 4/3.0.11.0.1.0:1, Child Search + Care C2: "Report on Joint Conference with Austrian Mission on Unaccompanied Children, Bad Wiessee, Germany, 7–8 January 1947," Blackey, Child Search and Repatriation Consultant, 24 Jan. 1947.

29 PAG 4/3.0.11.0.1.1:4, Child Search Repatriation Reports - Welfare: "Report on Field Trip to US and British Zones. 17th April–4th May 1947," Blackey, Child Search Consultant, Displaced Persons Operations, UNRRA CHQ, 6 May 1947.

30 43/AJ/953, Baltic Children: R. Radin, Chief, Repatriation and Care Division, for Cohen, Acting Chief, DP Operations to Edwards, Director, UNRRA HQ, US Zone, 29 May 1947, att: Repatriation Division.

31 PAG 4/3.0.11.0.1.1:4, Child Search Repatriation Reports - Welfare: "Report on Field Trip to US and British Zones. 17th April–4th May 1947"; RG 260, Legal Division, Records of Legal Advice Branch, Legal Files, 1945–50, Box 54, International Questions and Citizenship LA 31 vol. No. 1 Closed: J.M. Raymond, Col GSC Associate Director, Legal Division to Director, OMG Greater Hesse, att: Chief Legal Officer, 4 Jan. 1947.

32 43/AJ/953, Baltic Children: Edwards, US Zone Director to Commander-in-Chief, EUCOM, att: Department of Civil Affairs, Assistant Chief of Staff, G-5, 4 June 1947; 43/AJ/941, Narrative Report - Child Care Zone Hqs: "Monthly Report for June 1947"; 43/AJ/597, Unaccompanied Children 39/1 General Policies and General Reports 1947: P.M. Woods, Major Infantry, Asst Executive, HQ EUCOM, Civil Affairs Division to PCIRO, US Zone, Edwards, Director, 14 July 1947; PAG 4/1.0.1.0.0:5, Children Unaccompanied & Displaced 1944-46: C.T. Lloyd to Burinski, 2 July 1947; cable 2705, Lloyd to Paris, 7 July 1947; cable 197, PCIRO Geneva, 14 Aug. 1947; Keith Aikin to Fred Chait, 2 Sept. 1947; "Seventh Report on Displaced Persons Operations under Resolution 92," CC(47)93, 30 July 1947, in UNRRA, *The Central Committee of the Council: Reports of the Administration on Displaced Persons Operations as required by Resolution 92, 1946-47* (United Nations: New York, 1948).

33 RG 260, CAD, PW&DP Branch, Records Relating to DPs in Germany and Other Countries, 1945–49, Box 147, 014.33 - Repat of DP Children: cable WX-87795, HQ Civil Affairs Div. to EUCOM, 8 Oct. 1947; 43/AJ/597, Unaccompanied Children 39/1 General Policies and General Reports 1947: cable SX-3262, HQ EUCOM to HQ Dept of the Army for Civil Affairs Division, 11 Oct. 1947.

34 43/AJ/598, Unaccompanied Children 39/1 General Policies and General Reports 1948: Rev. E.J. Killion, Field Representative, Vatican Migration Bureau to G.G. Kullmann, Director, Legal Department, IRO, 11 Nov. 1947.

35 Ibid., Killion to Kullmann, 11 Nov. 1947; 43/AJ/958, 1947–48//Geneva: Rev. S.A. Bernas, Zone Director, WRS-NCWC, Germany and Austria to W.H. Tuck, Executive Secretary, PCIRO Geneva, 13 Nov. 1947.

36 RG 260, CAD, PW&DP Branch, Records Relating to DPs in Germany and Other Countries, 1945–49, Box 147, 014.33 - Repat of DP Children: cable WX-87795, HQ Civil Affairs Div. to EUCOM, 8 Oct. 1947; 43/AJ/597, Unaccompanied Children 39/1 General Policies and General Reports 1947: cable SX-3262, HQ EUCOM to HQ Dept of the Army for Civil Affairs Division, 11 Oct. 1947.

37 43/AJ/597, Unaccompanied Children 39/1 General Policies and General Reports 1947: Dunn, Chief, Department of Care and Maintenance, IRO US Zone to HQ EUCOM CAD, 21 Oct. 1947.

38 43/AJ/958, 1947/1948//Geneva: Cohen, Assistant Executive Secretary, Health, Care and Maintenance Department, IRO Geneva to Edwards, Chief, IRO US Zone, 26 May 1948; "Informal Meeting with Representatives of the United States, United Kingdom and French Governments to consider problems in connection with Unaccompanied Children and Child Search - held on May 10, 1948."

39 RG 331, OCS, Secretary, General Staff, Decimal File May 1943–Aug. 1945, Entry 1, Box 89, 383.7 vol. 3 (Refugees and Displaced Persons of European nationality): A.E. Grasett, Lt. General, Assistant Chief of Staff (AC of S), G-5 SHAEF to Chief of Staff, 25 June 1945.

40 RG 331, Special Staff, Adjutant General's Division, Executive Section, Decimal File 1945, entry 56, Box 189, 383.7-1 #6: cable FX-80915, SACMED to 15th Army Group, ALCOM Rome, 23 May 1945.

41 RG 331, HQ 6th Army Group, Special Staff, Adj Gen Section, Decimal File 1944, Entry 242A, Box 188, 383.7-II: cable S-94216, SCAEF to CG 21st, 12th, 6th Army Groups, and Com Zone, 30 June 1945.

42 RG 260, OAG, General correspondence & other records, 1945–49, Box 20, AG 014.33 Repatriation of Displaced Persons (Misc_OMGUS 1945–46): C.L. Adcock, Major General GSC, Director, USFET, to Directors OMG: EMD, WMD, Berlin District, 1 Nov. 1945.

43 Zoran Janjetovic, "The Disappearance of the Germans from Yugoslavia: Expulsion or Emigration?" *Gesellschaft für serbisch-deutsche Zusammenarbeit* (1991), 9–11, http://www.drustvosns.org (consulted 22 June 2011); Steffen Prauser and Arfon Rees, eds., "The Expulsion of the 'German' Communities from Eastern Europe at the End of the Second World War," *EUI Working Paper HEC 2004/1* (Dept. of History and Civilisation, European University Institute, Florence), 54–6; S-0412-0001, Allied Control Authority, Directorate of Prisoners of War and Displaced Persons - DPOW/P 1946–47: Lt. General Jaka Avsic, Chief, Yugoslav Military Mission to Allied Control Council for Germany, Berlin, 11 Feb. 1946.

44 PAG 4.3.0.11.3.3:15, Rel. Ser, Child Welfare. Search and Registration Teams. Jan. 1946– Dec. 1946: Heise, Child Search Officer to Boe, Voluntary Agencies Branch, 19 Dec. 1946.

45 Ibid., Rel Ser, Child Welfare (Gen) Jan. 1946–Jan. 1947: Robert A. Reese, Lt. Col., AC Chief, Internal Affairs & Communications Division, OMG Bavaria to Director OMGUS, att: Child Welfare Specialist, PH&W Branch, IA&CD, 4 Nov. 1946; Heise, Child Search Officer to District Director, UNRRA District 5, att: District Child Search Officer, 3 Dec. 1945; Whiting, Zone Director, US Zone to Commanding General, OMG Bavaria, att: Senior Public Welfare Officer, 6 July 1946; RG 260, CAD, PW&DP Branch, Records Relating to DPs in Germany and Other Countries, 1945–49, Box 147, 014.33 - Repat of DP Children: Bamberger, Ministry of the Interior, Department Welfare Office, Land Youth Office to Military Government, Bavaria, 19 Feb. 1947; PAG 4/3.0.11.3.3:14, C87 Nationality Policy - Yugoslav: minutes, "Conference on Planning for the 17 Yugoslav Children removed from the Weihersmühle Orphanage," 22 Oct. 1946; RG 260, OMG Bavaria, CAD, Central Files, PW&DP Branch, Box 23, Weekly Reports and Summaries: "Sectional Weekly Report on Public Welfare Activities for the week ending 23 Oct. 1946 (OMGB)"; RG 260, OAG, General Correspondence, 1945–49, Box 138 AG 014.33 Citizenship: G.H. Garde, Lieutenant Colonel, AGD Adjutant General, for the Military Governor OMGUS to Commander-in-Chief, European Command, US Army, 25 Jan. 1947.

46 43/AJ/954, Yugoslavian Affairs: Ellis, US Zone Child Care Officer for Chief of Operations, US Zone, to Grigg, Chief, Care and Eligibility, 26 July 1948; 43/AJ/939, Area #4: Grigg to Director, PCIRO Area 4, 5 Aug. 1948; RG 466, Bavaria Land Commissioner (BLC), Pol. Affairs Div. (PAD), Displaced Populations Br., 1946–52, Correspondence concerning Displaced Children, Box 1, Yugoslav #532: Vondracek, Field Representative, ITS Munich to Ellis, 15 Oct. 1948.

47 43/AJ/927 1949//General: Thudichum, Director ITS to Sir Arthur Rucker, Deputy Director General, IRO Geneva, 28 Jan. 1949.

48 RG 331, OCS, Secretary, General Staff, Decimal File May 1943–Aug. 1945, Entry 1, Box 89, 383.7 vol. 3 (Refugees and Displaced Persons of European nationality): cable S-96972, McClure signed Eisenhower to Jackson OWI, 12 July 1945; RG 59, Records Relating to the International Refugee Organization (IRO) and the Displaced Persons Commission (DPC), DP Subject File, 1944–52, Box 13, Displaced Persons - Poland File Copies April 1945–June 1946: Robert Murphy, to Secretary of State, Washington, 14 July 1945; plus Foreign Office Questionnaire and Answers.

49 US Department of State, *Foreign Relations of the United States: Diplomatic Papers, the Conference of Berlin (the Potsdam Conference), 1945*, 737; Keith Sword, *The Formation of the Polish Community in Great Britain 1939–1950* (London: School of Slavonic and East European Studies, University of London, 1989), 221.

50 RG 331, OCS, Secretary, General Staff, Decimal File May 1943–Aug. 1945, Entry 1, Box 89, 383.7 vol. 3 (Refugees and Displaced Persons of European nationality): cable S-96972, McClure signed Eisenhower to Jackson OWI, 12 July 1945.

51 RG 59, Records Relating to the International Refugee Organization (IRO) and the Displaced Persons Commission (DPC), DP Subject File, 1944–52, Box 13, Displaced Persons - Poland File Copies April 1945–June 1946: airgram A-116, Murphy, US Political Adviser for Germany to Department of State, 25 July 1945.

52 Ibid., Robert Murphy to Secretary of State, 24 Sept. 1945 (despatch 1009).

53 RG 260, OMGB, Records of the Field Operations Division - Dist III - Displaced Persons, Refugees and Former POWS, 1945-6, Box 1065, DP Directives: General Eisenhower to Commanding Generals, EMD, WMD, 25 Oct. 1945.

54 See, e.g., RG 59, Records Relating to the International Refugee Organization (IRO) and the Displaced Persons Commission (DPC), DP Subject File, 1944–52, Box 13, Displaced Persons - Poland File Copies April 1945–June 1946: Arthur B. Lane, American Embassy, Warsaw to Secretary of State, Washington, DC, 7 Nov. 1945; Antoni Czeslowski, Zagorze to American Embassy, Warsaw, 3 Oct. 1945.

55 RG 260, CAD, PW&DP Branch, Records Relating to DPs in Germany and Other Countries, 1945–49, Box 141, 005-Policy: cable WX-32562, Combined Chiefs of Staff AGWAR to AFHQ, for Alexander, July 1945.

56 PAG 4/3.0.11.3.3:15, Rel Ser, Child Welfare (Gen) Jan. 1946–Jan. 1947: Heise, Child Search Officer, UNRRA US Zone HQ to Directors, UNRRA Districts 1, 2, 3, 5, att: Child Search Officers, 5 Nov. 1946.

57 RG 466, BLC, PAD, DP Branch, Correspondence re DP Children, Box 1, Waldschule Neustift: Bamberger to OMG Bavaria, PWBr, 16 July 1946.

58 PAG 4/3.0.11.0.0:6, 013.1/C Displaced Persons - Ukrainians: Paul N. Carter, Office of Legal Advisor to Acting Chief of Operations, 10 Dec. 1946; PAG 4/1.0.1.0.0:35, Poland: memo to file, C.T. Lloyd, 2 Dec. 1946; RG 59, Records Relating to the International Refugee Organization (IRO) and the Displaced Persons Commission (DPC), DP Subject File, 1944–52, Box 12, DP-Poles-File Copies July 1946–Dec. 1946: telegram 1934, Lane, Warsaw to Secretary of State, 16 Dec. 1946.

59 43/AJ/954, 1947 - Polish Affairs: M. Zembruzski, Col. Chief, Polish Liaison Section, EUCOM to UNRRA US Zone HQ, 31 May 1947.

60 S-0425-0050, Statistics, Special Surveys, Statistical Reports Prepared by Statistics and Reports Branch, US Zone HQ: "Summary of DP Population, District No. 5, as of 28 December 1946."

61 RG 331, Special Staff, Adjutant General's Division, Executive Section, Decimal File 1945, entry 56, Box 189, 383.7-1 #6: cable S-97158, SCAEF to C-in-C EXFOR, 13 July 1945.

62 RG 260, CAD, PW&DP Branch, Records Relating to DPs in Germany and Other Countries, 1945–49, Box 141, 005 - Policy: cable S-16517, Eisenhower to CG, USFA: CG, 3rd US Army; 7th US Army, undated.

63 RG 59, Records Relating to the International Refugee Organization (IRO) and the Displaced Persons Commission (DPC), DP Subject File, 1944–52, Box 13, Displaced Persons - Poland File Copies April 1945–June 1946: Lane to Secretary of State, 7 Nov. 1945; Czeslowski to American Embassy, Warsaw, 3 Oct. 1945.

64 RG 260, OAG, General correspondence & other records, 1945–49, 390/40/21/2 Box 91, file AG 383.7 Displaced Persons (Refugees, Expellees, Internees), 2 of 2: "Determination and Reporting of Nationalities."

65 PAG 4/3.0.11.0.0:7, .014.5 Stateless Persons: Sir Frederick Morgan, Chief of Operations, Germany to Whiting, US Zone Director, 9 April 1946.

66 PAG 4/3.0.11.0.0:6, 013.1/C Displaced Persons - Ukrainians: Paul N. Carter, Office of Legal Advisor to Acting Chief of Operations, 10 Dec. 1946; PAG 4/1.0.1.0.0:35, Poland: memo to file, C.T. Lloyd, 2 Dec. 1946; RG 59, Records Relating to the International Refugee Organization (IRO) and the Displaced Persons Commission (DPC), DP Subject File, 1944–52, Box 12, DP-Poles-File Copies July 1946–Dec. 1946: telegram 1934, Lane, Warsaw to Secretary of State, 16 Dec. 1946.

67 RG 59, Records Relating to the International Refugee Organization (IRO) and the Displaced Persons Commission (DPC), DP Subject File, 1944–52, Box 12, DP-Poles: telegram 94, from Marshall, Department of State, to

Amembassy Warsaw, 31 Jan. 1947; memorandum of conversation between A-H/R Warren and Polish Ambassador Winiewicz, 26 Feb. 1947; telegram 168, Marshall, Department of State to Amembassy, Warsaw, 27 Feb. 1947.

68 PAG 4/1.0.1.0.0:33, DPs - Legal and Policy Decisions 1946 #2: cable 1989 London to Warsaw, originated by Repatriation Division, Linney, 20 Nov. 1946.

69 S-0425-0050, Statistics, Special Surveys, Statistical Reports Prepared by Statistics and Reports Branch, US Zone HQ: "Summary of DP Population, District No. 5, as of 28 December 1946."

70 RG 59, Records Relating to the International Refugee Organization (IRO) and the Displaced Persons Commission (DPC), DP Subject File, 1944–52, Box 12, DP - Poles: telegram 123, Acheson (Acting), Department of State to USPOLAD, Frankfurt, 27 March 1947.

71 43/AJ/958, 1947/1948//Geneva: Cohen, Assistant Executive Secretary, Health, Care and Maintenance Department, IRO Geneva to Edwards, Chief, IRO US Zone, 26 May, 1948; "Informal Meeting with Representatives of the United States, United Kingdom and French Governments to consider problems in connection with Unaccompanied Children and Child Search - held on May 10, 1948."

72 PAG 4/3.0.11.0.0:7, .014.5 Stateless Persons: Whiting, Director, US Zone to Sir Frederick Morgan, Chief of Operations, UNRRA Germany, 20 March 1946.

73 S-0425-0004, Administrative - Reporting Procedures (15): "Summary of Proceedings - Inter-Zone Conference of Reports Officers," 5 April 1946.

74 PAG 4/3.0.11.0.1.1:14, 038.1 Zone Director report US Zone Oct 45 to Mar 46: "Summary Report: Displaced Persons Operation - US Zone, Germany, for period ending 31 October 1945"; PAG 4.3.0.11.0.0:5, 013.1 Displaced Persons General Correspondence on Eligibility for UNRRA Assistance, Simon, Legal Advisor to Sir Frederick Morgan, Chief, German Operation, UNRRA, 10 Dec. 1945.

75 PAG 4/3.11.0.0.7, 014.5 Stateless Persons: P.N. Carter, Legal Adviser, UNRRA CHQ Germany to E.A. Reich, Executive Assistant, CHQ, 5 July 1946.

76 PAG 4/3.0.11.0.0:7, 014.5: Krane, Chief, Reports and Analysis Branch, CHQ Germany, UNRRA to Whiting, 3 April 1946.

77 RG 260, CAD, PW&DP Branch, Records Relating to DPs in Germany and Other Countries, 1945–49, Box 175, 319.1 General Policy File 1946: Harry S. Messec, Lt. Col. OSC Executive to IA&CD, 23 Oct. 1946.

78 PAG 4/3.0.11.0.0:7, 014.5: Krane to Whiting, 3 April 1946.

79 PAG 4/1.3.1.1.0:12, P300.12: "A Study on 'Stateless Persons'," 21 Feb. 1945; 4/3.0.11.0.0:7 .014.5 Stateless Persons: Louis C. Stephens to A.H. Robertson, 1 Nov. 1945.

80 S-0425-0010, Displaced Persons - Relevant to Nationality Reporting:
M. Ettinger, Director Assembly Centre No. 690, Ettingen to Douglas
Dean, Field Representative, Stuttgart, 11 April 1947; PAG 4/1.0.1.0.0:33,
Displaced Persons - Legal and Policy Decisions 1946: cable 13052, London
to Washington, originated by Radin, 12 Nov. 1946; S-0412-0006, Central
Headquarters - Correspondence with Chief of Operations (Cohen)
16/1/1947-3/6/1947: Edwards, Zone Director, US Zone, UNRRA to
Acting Chief of Operations, UNRRA DP HQ, Paris, 7 Feb. 1947.
81 S-0425-0040, Reports Branch, Including Administrative Files, Monthly
Reports and Special Reports - US Zone Headquarters Inter-Office: E.S.
Seldon, Chief, Reports and Statistics Branch, UNRRA US HQ, Germany
to Deputy Zone Director, Department of Field Operations, 11 April 1947.
82 UNRRA - Central Committee of the Council: memo CC(46)113, Director
General to the Central Committee, 25 Oct. 1946; PAG 4/1.0.1.0.0:33,
Displaced Persons - Legal and Policy Decisions 1946: cable 16047,
Washington to London, 25 Oct. 1946; PAG 4/1.0.1.0.0:36, Displaced
Persons - undetermined nationality - DPs of: A.E. Davidson to C.T. Lloyd,
21 Oct. 1946.
83 PAG 4/3.0.11.0.0:7, .014.5 Stateless Persons: Whiting to Morgan, 20 March
1946.
84 Ibid., Morgan to Whiting, 9 April 1946.
85 PAG 4/1.0.1.0.0:33, Displaced Persons - Legal and Policy Decisions 1946:
cable 13052, London to Washington, 12 Nov. 1946.
86 RG 260, CAD, PW&DP Branch, Records Relating to DPs in Germany
and Other Countries, 1945–49, Box 147, 014.33 - Repat of DP Children:
J. Prawin, Major General, Minister Plenipotentiary and Chief, Polish
Military Mission to General L.D. Clay, Military Governor for Germany
and Commander-in-Chief, EUCOM, 7 Dec. 1948.

Conclusion

1 Tara Zahra: *Kidnapped Souls: National Indifference and the Battle for Children
in theBohemian Lands, 1900–1948* (Ithaca NY: Cornell University Press,
2008); "Lost Children: Displacement, Family, and Nation in Postwar
Europe," *Journal of Modern History* 81/1 (2009): 45–86; "'A Human
Treasure': Europe's Displaced Children between Nationalism and
Internationalism," *Past and Present* (2011), Suppl. 6: 332–50.
2 See, e.g.: Sylvia Schafer, *Children in Moral Danger and the Problem of
Government in Third Republic France* (Princeton, NJ: Princeton University
Press, 1997); Harry Hendrick, *Images of Youth: Age, Class, and the Male Youth
Problem, 1880–1920* (Oxford: Clarendon Press, 1990); Robert Talmy, *Histoire*

du mouvement familial en France (1896–1939), vol. 2 (Aubenas: Union nationale des caisses d'allocations familiales, 1962); Stephen Humphries, *Hooligans or Rebels? An Oral History of Working-Class Childhood and Youth, 1889–1939* (Oxford: Basil Blackwell, 1981); Sarah Fishman, *The Battle for Children: World War II, Youth Crime, and Juvenile Justice in Twentieth-Century France* (Cambridge, MA: Harvard University Press, 2002); Robert O. Paxton, *The Anatomy of Fascism* (New York: Knopf, 2004); Laura Lee Downs, *Childhood in the Promised Land: Working-Class Movements and the Colonies de Vacances in France, 1880–1960* (Durham, NC: Duke University Press, 2002).

3 See, for example, Lynne Taylor, *The Polish Orphans of Tengeru* (Toronto: Dundurn Press, 2009).

4 John Torpey, *The Invention of the Passport: Surveillance, Citizenship, and the State* (Cambridge: Cambridge University Press, 2000). For other works dealing with the history of identification documents, see Mark B. Salter, *Rights of Passage: The Passport in International Relations* (Boulder, CO: Lynne Rienner, 2003); Derek Heater, *A Brief History of Citizenship* (New York: New York University Press, 2004); Jane Caplan and John Torpey, eds., *Documenting Individual Identity: The Development of State Practices in the Modern World* (Princeton, NJ: Princeton University Press, 2001); Gérard Noiriel, *The French Melting Pot: Immigration, Citizenship, and National Identity* (Minneapolis, MN: University of Minnesota Press, 1996); Mae Ngai, *Impossible Subjects: Illegal Aliens and the Making of modern America* (Princeton, NJ: Princeton University Press, 2014).

5 Torpey, *Invention of the Passport*, 7.

6 Ibid., 1.

7 Ibid., 7.

8 Ibid., 8.

9 Gérard Noiriel, *The French Melting Pot: Immigration, Citizenship, and National Identity*, translated by Geoffroy de Laforcade (Minneapolis, MN: University of Minnesota Press, 1996), chapter 2.

10 Ibid., 45.

11 Torpey, *Invention of the Passport*, 13.

12 Hannah Arendt, *The Origins of Totalitarianism* (New York: Harcourt, 1994 [1948]), 295.

Bibliography

Archives and Record Groups Consulted

United Nations Archives, New York City

United Nations Relief and Rehabilitation Administration – PAG 4 (renumbered as S-0XXX-XXXX)

Archives Nationales de la France, Paris

International Refugee Organisation – 43/AJ/XXX

*National Archives and Records Administration,
United States, College Park, MD*

RG 59 General Records of the Department of State
RG 260 Records of the Occupation Headquarters WWII (OMGUS)
RG 278 Records of the Displaced Persons Commission, 1948–1952
RG 331 Supreme Headquarters Allied Expeditionary Forces (SHAEF)
RG 466 Records of the US High Commissioner for Germany

Staatlichen Archive Bayerns, Munich, Germany

MInn Bayerisches Staatsministeriums des Innern

Secondary Sources

Arendt, Hannah. *The Origins of Totalitarianism.* New York: Harcourt, 1994 (1948).
Ahonen, Pertti. *After the Expulsion: West Germany and Eastern Europe, 1945–1990.*
   Oxford: Oxford University Press, 2003.

Armstrong-Reid, Susan, and David Murray. *Armies of Peace: Canada and the UNRRA Years.* Toronto: University of Toronto Press, 2008.

Bach, Julian. *America's Germany: An Account of the Occupation.* New York: Random House, 1946.

Balfour, Michael. *Four-Power Control in Germany and Austria, 1945–1946.* London: Oxford University Press, 1956.

Ballinger, Pamela. *History in Exile: Memory and Identity at the Borders of the Balkans.* Princeton, NJ: Princeton University Press, 2003.

Bankier, David, ed. *The Jews Are Coming Back: The Return of the Jews to Their Countries of Origin after WWII.* New York: Berghahn, 2005.

Bar-On, Dan. *Legacy of Silence: Encounters with Children of the Third Reich.* Cambridge, MA: Harvard University Press, 1991.Bodemann, Y. Michal, ed. *Jews, Germans, Memory: Reconstructions of Jew.*

Caplan, Jane and John Torpey, eds. *Documenting Individual Identity: The Development of State Practices in the Modern World.* Princeton, NJ: Princeton University Press, 2001.

Cohen, Gerard Daniel. "The Politics of Recognition: Jewish Refugees in Relief Policies and Human Rights Debates, 1945–1950." *Immigrants and Minorities* 24/2 (2006): 125–43.

–. *In War's Wake: Europe's Displaced Persons in the Postwar Order.* Oxford: Oxford University Press, 2012.

Coudry, Georges. "La rapatriement des ressortissants soviétiques de 1945 à 1947: Avatars de la réciprocité." *Guerres mondiales et conflits contemporains* 45/178 (1995): 119–40.

Danys, Milda. *DP: Lithuanian Immigration to Canada after the Second World War.* Toronto: Multicultural History Society of Ontario, 1986.

deGraffenreid, Julie K. *Sacrificing Childhood: Children and the Soviet State in the Great Patriotic War.* Lawrence, KS: University Press of Kansas, 2014.

Diefendorf, Jeffry M., Axel Frohn, and Hermann-Josef Rupieper, eds. *American Policy and the Reconstruction of West Germany, 1945–1955.* Washington, DC: German Historical Institute, 1993.

Diefendorf, Jeffrey M. *In the Wake of War: The Reconstruction of German Cities after World War II.* Oxford: Oxford University Press, 1993.

Diner, Dan. "Jewish DPs in Historical Context." *Birth of a Refugee Nation: Displaced Persons in Postwar Europe, 1945–1951.* Workshop Draft Papers, 20–1 April 2001.

Dinnerstein, Leonard. *America and the Survivors of the Holocaust.* New York: Columbia University Press, 1982.

Downs, Laura Lee. *Childhood in the Promised Land: Working-Class Movements and the Colonies de Vacances in France, 1880–1960.* Durham, NC: Duke University Press, 2002.

Elliott, Mark R. *Pawns of Yalta: Soviet Refugees and America's Role in Their Repatriation*. Urbana, IL: University of Illinois Press, 1982.

Fast, Vera K. *Children's Exodus: A History of the Kindertransport*. London: I.B. Tauris, 2011.

Fehrenbach, Heide. *Race after Hitler*. Princeton, NJ: Princeton University Press, 2005.

Feinstein, Margarete Myers. *Holocaust Survivors in Postwar Germany, 1945–1957*. Cambridge: Cambridge University Press, 2010.

Fishman, Sarah. *The Battle for Children: World War II, Youth Crime, and Juvenile Justice in Twentieth-Century France*. Cambridge, MA: Harvard University Press, 2002.

Frederiksen, O.J. *The American Occupation of Germany 1945–1953*. Historical Division, Headquarters, United States Army, Europe, 1953.

Friedmann, W. *The Allied Military Government of Germany*. London: Stevens & Sons, 1947.

Gaida, Pranas, et al. *Lithuanians in Canada*. Toronto: Lights Printing and Publishing, 1967.

Geller, Jay Howard. *Jews in Post-Holocaust Germany, 1945–1953*. Cambridge: Cambridge University Press, 2005.

Gemie, Sharif, Fiona Reid, and Laure Humbert, with Louise Ingram. *Outcast Europe: Refugees and Relief Workers in an Era of Total War, 1936–48*. New York: Continuum International, 2012.

Gigliotti, Simone. *The Young Victims of the Nazi Regime: Migration, the Holocaust, and Postwar Displacement*. London: Bloomsbury Academic, 2016.

Gilbert, Martin. *The Boys: The Story of 732 Young Concentration Camp Survivors*. New York: Henry Holt, 1998.

Gimbel, John. *The American Occupation of Germany: Politics and the Military, 1945–1949*. Stanford, CA: Stanford University Press, 1968.

Greenfeld, Liah. *Nationalism: Five Roads to Modernity*. Cambridge, MA: Harvard University Press, 1992.

Greenfield, Howard. *The Hidden Children*. New York: Ticknor and Fields, 1993.

Grodzinsky, Yosef. *In the Shadow of the Holocaust: The struggle between Jews and Zionists in the Aftermath of World War II*. Monroe, ME: Common Courage Press, 2004.

Grodzinsky, Yosef. *In the Shadow of the Holocaust: The Struggle between Jews and Zionists in the Aftermath of World War II*. Monroe, ME: Common Courage Press, 2004.

Grossmann, Atina. *Jews, Germans, and Allies: Close Encounters in Occupied Germany*. Princeton, NJ: Princeton University Press, 2007.

Gulgowski, Paul W. *The American Military Government of United States Occupied Zones of Post World War II Germany in Relation to Policies Expressed by Its*

Civilian Governmental Authorities at Home, during the Course of 1944/45 through 1949. Frankfurt am Main: HAAG + HERCHEN Verlag, 1983.

Heater, Derek. *A Brief History of Citizenship*. New York: New York University Press, 2004.

Heberer, Patricia. *Children during the Holocaust*. Lanham, MA: AltaMira Press, 2011.

Hendrick, Henry. *Images of Youth: Age, Class, and the Male Youth Problem, 1880–1920*. Oxford: Clarendon Press, 1990.

Holborn, Louise W. *The International Refugee Organization: A Specialized Agency of the United Nations – Its History and Work, 1946–1952*. London: Oxford University Press, 1956.

Holian, Anna. *Between National Socialism and Soviet Communism: Displaced Persons in Postwar Germany*. Ann Arbor, MI: University of Michigan Press, 2011.

– "The Ambivalent Exception: American Occupation Policy in Postwar Germany and the Formation of Jewish Refugee Spaces.

Humphries, Stephen. *Hooligans or Rebels? An Oral History of Working-Class Childhood and Youth, 1889–1939*. Oxford: Basil Blackwell, 1981.

Isajiw, W.W., Y. Boshyk, and R. Senkus, eds. *The Refugee Experience: Ukrainian Displaced Persons after World War II*. Edmonton: Canadian Institute of Ukrainian Studies Press, 1992.

Jacobmeyer, Wolfgang. *Heimatlosen Ausländer: Die Displaced Persons in Westdeutschland, 1945–1951*. Göttingen: Vandenhoeck & Ruprecht, 1985.

Janjetovic, Zoran. "The Disappearance of the Germans from Yugoslavia: Expulsion or Emigration?" *Gesellschaft für serbisch-deutsche Zusammenarbeit*, 1991, http://www.drustvosns.org (consulted 22 June 2011).

Jaroszynska-Kirchmann, Anna D. *The Exile Mission: The Polish Political Diaspora and Polish Americans, 1939–1956*. Athens, OH: Ohio University Press, 2004.

Junker, Detlef, ed. *The United States and Germany in the Era of the Cold War, 1945–1990*, vol. 1, *1945–1968*. Cambridge: Cambridge University Press, 2004.

Kaslas, Bronis. *La Lituanie et la Seconde Guerre mondiale*. Paris: Maisonneuve and Larose, 1981.

Kenez, Peter. *Hungary from the Nazis to the Soviets: The Establishment of the Communist Regime in Hungary, 1944–1948*. Cambridge: Cambridge University Press, 2006.

Kochavi, Arieh J. *Post-Holocaust Politics: Britain, the United States, and Jewish Refugees, 1945–1948*. Chapel Hill, NC: University of North Carolina Press, 2001.

Königseder, Angelika, and Juliane Wetzel. *Waiting for Hope: Jewish Displaced Persons in Post-World War II Germany*. Evanston, IL: Northwestern University Press, 2001.

Kucas, Antanas. *Lithuanians in America*. Boston: Encyclopedia Lithuanica Press, 1975.

Kulischer, E.M. *Europe on the Move: War and Population Changes 1914–47*. New York: Columbia University Press, 1948.

Lavsky, Hagit. *New Beginnings: Holocaust Survivors in Bergen-Belsen and the British Zone in Germany, 1945–1950*. Detroit, MI: Wayne State University Press, 2002.

Luciuk, Lubomyr Y. *Searching for Place: Ukrainian Displaced Persons, Canada, and the Migration of Memory*. Toronto: University of Toronto Press, 2000.

Mackenzie, David. *A World beyond Borders: An Introduction to the History of International Organizations*. Toronto: University of Toronto Press, 2010.

Mankowitz, Zeev W. *Life between Memory and Hope: The Survivors of the Holocaust in Occupied Germany*. Cambridge: Cambridge University Press, 2002.

Marrus, Michael. *The Unwanted: European Refugees in the Twentieth Century*. New York: Oxford University Press, 1985.

Merritt, Richard L. *Democracy Imposed: U.S. Occupation Policy and the German Public, 1945–1949*. New Haven, CT: Yale University Press, 1995.

Miller, Sarah Lew, and Joyce Block Lazarus, *Hiding in Plain Sight: Eluding the Nazis in Occupied France*. Chicago, IL: Academy Chicago, 2012.

Morgan, Roger. *The United States and West Germany, 1945–1973: A Study in Alliance Politics*. London: Oxford University Press, 1974.

Nadich, Judah. *Eisenhower and the Jews*. New York: Twayne, 1953.

Ngai, Mae. *Impossible Subjects: Illegal Aliens and the Making of modern America*. Princeton, NJ: Princeton University Press, 2014.

Nicholas, Lynn H. *Cruel World: The Children of Europe in the Nazi Web*. New York: Knopf, 2005.

Noiriel, Gérard. *The French Melting Pot: Immigration, Citizenship, and National Identity*. Minneapolis, MN: University of Minnesota Press, 1996.

Pack, Janet, and Margaret Weis. *Lost Childhood: Children of World War II*. New York: J. Messner, 1986.

Paxton, Robert O. *The Anatomy of Fascism*. New York: Knopf, 2004.

Peterson, Edward N. *The American Occupation of Germany: Retreat to Victory*. Detroit, MI: Wayne State University Press, 1977.

Pogue, Forrest C. *United States Army in World War II: The European Theater of Operations – The Supreme Command*. Washington, DC: Office of the Chief of Military History, Department of History, 1954.

Prauser, Steffen and Arfon Rees, eds. "The Expulsion of the 'German' Communities from Eastern Europe at the End of the Second World War," *EUI Working Paper HEC 2004/1*. Dept. of History and Civilisation, European University Institute, Florence.

Proudfoot, Malcolm J. *European Refugees, 1939–1952: A Study in Forced Population Movement.* London: Faber and Faber, 1957.

Ranki, Vera. *The Politics of Inclusion and Exclusion: Jews and Nationalism in Hungary.* New York: Holmes and Meier, 1999.

Reinisch, Jessica, and Elizabeth White, eds. *The Disentanglement of Populations: Migration, Expulsion and Displacement in Post-War Europe, 1944–9.* Basingstoke: Palgrave Macmillan, 2011.

Saffle, Sue. *To the Bomb and Back: Finnish World War II Children Tell Their Stories.* New York: Berghahn, 2015.

Salter, Mark B. *Rights of Passage: The Passport in International Relations.* Boulder, CO: Lynne Rienner, 2003.

Schafer, Sylvia. *Children in Moral Danger and the Problem of Government in Third Republic France.* Princeton. NJ: Princeton University Press, 1997.

Schechtman, J.B. *European Population Transfers, 1939–1945.* New York: Oxford University Press, 1946.

Schwartz, Thomas Alan. *America's Germany: John J. McCloy and the Federal Republic of Germany,* Cambridge, MA: Harvard University Press, 1991.

Seipp, Adam. *Strangers in the Wild Place: Refugees, Americans, and a German Town, 1945–1952.* Bloomington: Indiana University Press, 2013.

Siklos, Pierre L. *War Finance, Reconstruction, Hyperinflation and Stabilization in Hungary, 1938–48.* Basingstoke, UK: Macmillan, 1991.

Sjöberg, Tommie. *The Powers and the Persecuted: The Refugee Problem and the Intergovernmental Committee on Refugees (IGCR), 1938–1947.* Lund: Lund University Press, 1991.

Stargardt, Nicholas. *Witnesses of War: Children's Lives under the Nazis.* London: Pimlico, 2006.

Steinert, Johannes-Dieter. *Deportation und Zwangsarbeit: Polnische und sowjetische Kinder im nationalsozialistischen Deutschland und im besetzten Osteuropa 1939–1945.* Essen: Klartext Verlag, 2013.

Sword, Keith. *The Formation of the Polish Community in Great Britain 1939–1950.* London: School of Slavonic and East European Studies, University of London, 1989.

Talmy, Robert. *Histoire du mouvement familial en France (1896–1939),* vol. 2. Aubenas: Union nationale des caisses d'allocations familiales, 1962.

Taylor, Lynne. *The Polish Orphans of Tengeru.* Toronto: Dundurn Press, 2009.

Ther, Philipp, and Ana Siljak. *Redrawing Nations: Ethnic Cleansing in East-Central Europe, 1944–48.* Lanham, MD: Rowman and Littlefield, 2001.

Ther, Philipp. "The Integration of Expellees in Germany and Poland after World War II: A Historical Reassessment." *Slavic Review* 55/4 (1996): 779-805.

Torpey, John. *The Invention of the Passport: Surveillance, Citizenship, and the State.* Cambridge: Cambridge University Press, 2000.

Völkl, Ekkehard. "Ukrainische Emigration in Bayern 1945–1949," in Hermann
  Beyer-Thoma, ed., *Bayern und Osteuropa: Aus der Geschichte der Beziehungen
  Bayerns, Frankens und Schwabens mit Russland, der Ukraine und Weissrussland.*
  Wiesbaden: Harassowitz, 2000.
Warhaftig, Zorach. *Uprooted: Jewish Refugees and Displaced Persons after Liberation.*
  New York: Institute of Jewish Affairs of the American Jewish Congress and
  World Jewish Congress, Nov. 1946.
Willoughby, John. *Remaking the Conquering Heroes: The Social and Geopolitical
  Impact of the Post-War American Occupation of Germany.* London: Palgrave,
  2001.
Wolfe, Robert, ed. *Americans as Proconsuls: United States Military Government in
  Germany and Japan, 1944–1952.* Carbondale, IL: Southern Illinois University
  Press, 1984.
Woodbridge, George, ed. *UNRRA: The History of the United Nations Relief and
  Rehabilitation Administration.* 3 vols. New York: Columbia University Press,
  1950.
Wyman, Mark. *DP: Europe's Displaced Persons, 1945–1951.* Philadelphia: Balch
  Institute, 1989.
Zahra, Tara. *Kidnapped Souls: National Indifference and the Battle for Children in
  the Bohemian Lands, 1900–1948.* Ithaca, NY: Cornell University Press, 2008.
– *The Lost Children: Reconstructing Europe's Families after World War II.*
  Cambridge, MA: Harvard University Press, 2011.
– "Lost Children: Displacement, Family, and Nation in Postwar Europe,"
  Journal of Modern History 81/1 (2009): 45–86.
– "'A Human Treasure': Europe's Displaced Children between Nationalism
  and Internationalism," *Past and Present* (2011), Suppl. 6: 332–50.
Zertal, Idith. *From Catastrophe to Power: Holocaust Survivors and the Emergence of
  Israel.* Berkeley, CA: University of California Press, 1998.
Ziemke, Earl F. *The U.S. Army in the Occupation in Germany, 1944–1946.*
  Washington, DC: Center of Military History, United States Army, 1975.
Zink, Harold. *The United States in Germany, 1944–1955.* Westport, Conn.:
  Greenwood Press, 1957.

Index

18, 20, 28–9, 42, 47; IRO mandate, 4, 194, 199–200, 204, 220; SHAEF's mandate, 19–20, 42; United Nations, 11; UNRRA's mandate, 4–5, 17, 20, 38, 42–4, 161–2, 167, 179, 195, 327
unaccompanied children (disposition). *See also* adoption; repatriation; resettlement; famility reunification, 11, 161–2, 167, 179, 220, 322, 327, 420–1n145; long-term temporary care, 273–5; temporary care abroad programs, 47–59; transfer to West Germany, 278–9
unaccompanied children (issues). *See also* citizenship; legal security of child; nationality (ethnicity); guardianship, 88, 104–10, 164–5, 325–6, 342; lack of documentation, 44, 142, 155, 195, 310–1
unaccompanied children (residual). *See also* Children's Court; disabled children; illegitimate children; Children's Village, 275, 276–7; defining, 240; delays in handling, 248–50, 252, 255–6, 265; IRO extension, 241–2; in long-term temporary care, 273–5; resettlement option, 242–8, 250–2, 253
unaccompanied infiltree children, British attitude to, 117, 123, 128; caring for, 130–2; first wave, 124–6; in kibbutzim, 121–2, 126, 127–8, 129, 130, 133; legal issues, 132–5; overview, 118–9; registering challenges, 128–30; second wave, 126–7; ultimate destination, 118
United Nations children, 61, 70, 76, 79–80, 123. *See also* unaccompanied children

United Nations displaced persons. *See also* United Nations children; Baltic situation, 289, 290; defining, 28, 30, 283, 284; Jewish situation, 285–6; Yugoslavian situation, 294
United Nations nationality, 60–1, 63–4
United Nations Organization, origins, 13–4; United Nations Declaration, 14; UNRRA and IRO as responsible to, 323–4
United States. *See also* US Committee for the Care of European Children; US Department of State (State Department); adoptions to, 101–4, 241–5, 247; on the Baltic states, 108, 288–9, 290, 291; Combined Chiefs of Staff, 17; on Control Council, 19; as emigration destination, 81, 84, 89–92, 129, 194–5, 245, 253; on Poland, 301; racial prejudice in, 93
UNRRA (United Nations Relief and Rehabilitation Administration). *See also* Central Headquarters (UNRRA); child search; Child Welfare Division (UNRRA); Displaced Persons Division (UNRRA); unaccompanied children; adoption issues, 99–100; advisory role, 20–1, 23; age of majority, 62, 96–7; casework, 366n71; in command structure, 18–23, 27–30, 32–3, 39–40; commitment to child search, 76; conflict with OMGUS, 64, 120, 137–8, 170, 172, 179, 324, 328; creation, 4, 13–4, 16; handling stateless classification, 314–5; Harris's critique, 35–6; issue of organization's dependency,

German and European Studies

9 781487 521943